MATHEMATICS OF INVESTMENT AND CREDIT

Third Edition

Samuel A. Broverman, ASA, Ph.D.
University of Toronto

ACTEX Publications, Inc.
Winsted, Connecticut

Requests for permission should be addressed to
ACTEX Publications
PO Box 974
Winsted, CT 06098

Manufactured in the United States of America

10 9 8 7 6 5 4

Cover design by Kathleen H. Borkowski

Library of Congress Cataloging-in-Publication Data

Broverman, Samuel A., 1951-
  Mathematics of investment and credit / Samuel A. Broverman.-- 3rd ed.
     p. cm.
  Includes bibliographical references and index.
  ISBN 1-56698-475-0
  1. Interest--Mathematical models. 2. Interest--Problems, exercises, etc.
  I. Title.

HG4515.3.B76 2004
332.8--dc22

                                                    2004021397

ISBN: 1-56698-475-0

CONTENTS

CHAPTER 3

LOAN REPAYMENT   171

CHAPTER 4

BOND VALUATION   223

CHAPTER 5

CHAPTER 6

CHAPTER 7

CHAPTER 8

ADDITIONAL TOPICS IN FINANCE AND INVESTMENT   389

PREFACE

While teaching an intermediate level university course in mathematics of investment over a number of years, I found an increasing need for a textbook that provided a thorough and modern treatment of the subject, while incorporating theory and applications. This book is an attempt (as a 3rd edition, it must be a third attempt) to satisfy that need. It is based, to a large extent, on notes that I developed while teaching and my use of a number of textbooks for the course. The university course for which this book was written has also been intended to help students prepare for the mathematics of investment topic that is covered on one of the professional examinations of the Society of Actuaries and the Casualty Actuarial Society. A number of the examples and exercises in this book are taken from questions on past SOA/CAS examinations.

As in many areas of mathematics, the subject of mathematics of investment has aspects that do not become outdated over time, but rather become the foundation upon which new developments are based. The traditional topics of compound interest and date cashflow valuations, and their applications, are developed in the first five chapters of the book. In addition, in Chapters 6 to 8, a number of topics are introduced which have become of increasing importance in modern financial mathematics over the past several years. The past decade or so has seen a great increase in the use of derivative securities, particularly financial options. The subjects covered in Chapters 6 and 8 such as the term structure of interest rates and forward contracts form the foundation for the mathematical models used to describe and value derivative securities.

The purpose of the methods developed in this book is to do financial valuations. This book emphasizes a direct calculation approach, assuming that the reader has access to a financial calculator with standard financial function. An enhancement in this edition over previous editions of the book is that the ACTEX website, www.actexmadriver.com, has a link to a collection of EXCEL routines that illustrate many of the methods covered in this book.

The mathematical background required for the book is a course in calculus at the Freshman level. Chapter 8 introduces a couple of topics that involve the notion of probability, but only at an elementary level. A very basic understanding of probability concepts should be sufficient background for those topics.

The topics in the first five Chapters of this book are arranged in an order that is similar to traditional approaches to the subject, with Chapter 1 introducing the various measures of interest rates, Chapter 2 developing methods for valuing a series of payments, Chapter 3 considering amortization of loans, Chapter 4 covering bond valuation, and Chapter 5 introducing the various methods of measuring the rate of return earned by an investment.

The content of this book is probably more than can reasonably be covered in a one-semester course at an introductory or even intermediate level. At the University of Toronto, the course on this subject is taught in a one semester course at the Sophomore level. We generally try to cover all of Chapter 1, Chapter 2 up to the end of Section 2.3, Chapter 3 up to the end of Section 3.3, all of Chapters 4 and 5, and sections 6.1 and 6.1 of Chapter 6.

I would like to acknowledge the support of the Actuarial Education and Research Foundation, which provided support for the early stages of development of this book. I would also like to thank those who provided so much help and insight in the earlier editions of this book: John Mereu, Michael Gabon, Steve Linney, Walter Lowrie, Srinivasa Ramanujam, Peter Ryall, David Promislow, Robert Marcus, Sandi-Lynn Scherer, Marlene Lundbeck and Richard London.

I have had the benefit of many insightful comments and suggestions for this edition of the book from Louis Florence, Rob Brown, Matt Hassett, David Scollnick, David Promislow, Dick London and Robert Alps. I want to give a special mention of my sincere appreciation to Warren Luckner of the University of Nebraska and his students Toby Adams, Dan Becker, Nyi Htoon, Wing Yew Koh, Xiaofang Liu, Luis Gutierrez, and Lingfeng Zhang, whose extremely careful reading of both the text and exercises caught a number of errors in the early drafts of this edition.

Marilyn Baleshiski is the format and layout editor, and Gail Hall is the mathematics editor at ACTEX. It has been a great pleasure for me to have worked with them on the book.

Finally, I am grateful to have had the continuous support of my wife, Sue Foster, throughout the development of each edition of this book.

Samuel A. Broverman, ASA, Ph.D.
University of Toronto
September 2004

MATHEMATICS OF INVESTMENT AND CREDIT

Third Edition

To Sue, Alison, Amelia and Andrea

"Neither a borrower nor lender be …, "
Polonius advises his son Laertes,
Act I, Scene III, Hamlet, by W. Shakespeare

CHAPTER 1

INTEREST RATE MEASUREMENT

Almost everyone, at one time or another, will be a saver, borrower, or investor, and will have access to insurance, pension plans, or other financial benefits. There is a wide variety of financial transactions in which individuals, corporations, or governments can become involved. The range of available investments continues to broaden all the time, accompanied by an increase in the complexity of many of these investments.

Financial transactions invariably involve numerical calculations, and, depending on their complexity, may require detailed mathematical formulations. It is therefore important to establish fundamental principles upon which these calculations and formulations are based. The objective of this book is to systematically develop insights and mathematical techniques which lead to these fundamental principles upon which financial transactions can be modeled and analyzed.

The initial step in the analysis of a financial transaction is to translate a verbal description of the transaction into a mathematical model. Unfortunately, in practice a transaction may be described in language that is vague and which may result in disagreements regarding its interpretation. The need for precision in the mathematical model of a financial transaction requires that there be a correspondingly precise and unambiguous understanding of the verbal description before the translation to the model is made. To this end, terminology and notation, much of which is in standard use in financial and actuarial practice, will be introduced.

A component that is common to virtually all financial transactions is **interest**, the "time value of money." Most people are aware that interest rates play a central role in their own personal financial situations as well as in the economy as a whole. Many governments and private enterprises employ economists and analysts who make forecasts regarding the level of interest rates. It is not unusual to see immediate and significant effects

1

on the various financial markets, particularly stock and bond markets, when, for example, the U.S. Federal Reserve Board announces a change in the "federal funds discount rate," or even when new forecasts of interest rate levels are released by prominent economists.

The variety of interest rates and the investments and transactions to which they relate is extensive. Figure 1.1 was taken from the website of Bloomberg L.P. on September 7, 2003, and is an illustration of just a few of the types of interest rates that arise in practice.

KEY RATES					
	Current	**1 Month Prior**	**3 Month Prior**	**6 Month Prior**	**1 Year Prior**
Fed Funds Effective Rate	1	0.5	1.25	1.19	1.75
3-Month Libor	1.14	1.14	1.24	1.32	1.78
Prime Rate	4	4	4.25	4.25	4.75
5-Year AAA Banking and Finance	4.07	4.18	3.06	3.53	3.96
10-Year AAA Banking and Finance	5.31	5.47	4.24	4.63	5.1
MORTGAGE RATES provided by Bankrate.com					
	Current	**1 Month Prior**	**3 Month Prior**	**6 Month Prior**	**1 Year Prior**
15-Year Mortgage	5.38	5.41	4.45	4.82	5.35
30-Year Mortgage	6.03	6.1	4.99	5.44	5.88
1-Year ARM	3.81	3.71	3.56	3.84	4.21

U.S. TREASURIES					
Bills					
	Coupon	**Maturity Date**	**Current Price/Yield**	**Price/Yield Change**	**Time**
3-Month	N.A.	12/04/2003	0.92/0.94	−0.02/−0.015	09/05
6-Month	N.A.	03/04/2004	1/1.02	−0.02/−0.019	09/05

http://www.bloomberg.com/markets/rates/index.html   Used with Permission from Bloomberg L.P.

FIGURE 1.1

To analyze financial transactions, a clear understanding of the concept of interest is required. Interest can be defined in a variety of contexts, and most people have at least a vague notion of what it is. In the most common context, interest refers to the consideration or rent paid by a borrower of money to a lender for the use of the money over a period of time. Other definitions may be found in dictionaries and legal statutes, and, in essence, they agree with this definition.

This chapter provides a detailed development of the mechanics of interest rates: how they are measured and applied to amounts of principal over time to calculate amounts of interest. In the next section of the chapter a standard measure of interest rates is defined and two commonly used growth patterns for investments, simple and compound interest, are discussed. Later in the chapter various alternative standard measures of interest, such as nominal annual rate of interest, rate of discount, and force of interest, are discussed. Also developed in this chapter is the general way in which a financial transaction is modeled in mathematical form, using the notions of accumulated value, present value and equation of value.

1.1   INTEREST ACCUMULATION AND EFFECTIVE RATES OF INTEREST

An interest rate is most typically quoted as an annual percentage. If interest is credited or charged annually, the quoted annual rate, in decimal fraction form, is multiplied by the amount invested or loaned to calculate the amount of interest that accrues over a one-year period. It is generally understood that as interest is credited or paid, it is reinvested. This reinvesting of interest leads to the process of compounding interest. The following example illustrates this process.

EXAMPLE 1.1   (*Compound interest calculation*)

The current rate of interest quoted by a bank on its savings account is 9% per annum, with interest credited annually. Smith opens an account with a deposit of 1000. Assuming that there are no transactions on the account other than the annual crediting of interest, determine the account balance just after interest is credited at the end of 3 years.

SOLUTION

After one year the interest credited will be $1000 \times .09 = 90$, resulting in a balance (with interest) of $1000 + 1000 \times .09 = 1000(1.09) = 1090$. It is generally understood in common practice that this balance is reinvested and earns interest in the second year, producing a balance of

$$1090 + 1090 \times .09 = 1090(1.09) = 1000(1.09)^2 = 1188.10$$

at the end of the second year. The balance at the end of the third year will be

$$1188.10 + 1188.10 \times .09 = (1188.10)(1.09) = 1000(1.09)^3 = 1295.03.$$

The following time diagram illustrates this process.

0	1	2	3
↑	↑	↑	↑
1000	$1000 \times .09 = 90$	$1090 \times .09 = 98.10$	$1188.10 \times .09 = 106.93$
Deposit	Interest	Interest	Interest
Total	$1000 + 90$	$1090 + 98.10$	$1188.10 + 106.93$
	$= 1090$	$= 1188.10$	$= 1295.03$
	$= 1000 \times 1.09$	$= 1090 \times 1.09$	$= 1188.10 \times 1.09$
		$= 1000(1.09)^2$	$= 1000(1.09)^3$

FIGURE 1.2   □

It can be seen from Example 1.1 that with an interest rate of i per annum and interest credited annually, an initial deposit of C will earn interest of Ci for the following year. The accumulated value at the end of the year will be $C + Ci = C(1+i)$. If this amount is reinvested and left on deposit for another year, the interest earned in the second year will be $C(1+i)i$, so that the accumulated balance is $C(1+i) + C(1+i)i = C(1+i)^2$ at the end of the second year. The account will continue to grow by a factor of $1+i$ per year, resulting in a balance of $C(1+i)^n$ at the end of n years. This is the pattern of accumulation that results from compounding, or reinvesting, the interest as it is credited.

0	1	2	$n-1$	n
↑	↑	↑	↑	↑
C ⟶	Ci	$C(1+i)i$	$C(1+i)^{n-2}i$	$C(1+i)^{n-1}i$
Deposit	Interest	Interest	Interest	Interest
	↑	↑	↑	↑
	$C + Ci$	$C(1+i)$	$= C(1+i)^{n-1}$	$C(1+i)^{n-1}$
Total	$= C(1+i)$	$+ C(1+i)i$		$+ C(1+i)^{n-1}i$
		$= C(1+i)^2$		$= C(1+i)^n$

FIGURE 1.3

In Example 1.1, if Smith were to observe the accumulating balance in the account by looking at regular bank statements, he would see only one entry of interest credited each year. For instance, if Smith made the initial deposit on January 1, 2004 then he would have interest added to his account at the close of business on December 31 of 2004 and every December 31 after that as long as the account remained open. It would be generally understood, however, that interest is accruing on the account throughout the year, so that if Smith were to close the account between interest credit dates, say on August 1, 2004, a fraction of that year's interest would be paid. It is useful to regard the underlying accumulation of interest as a continuous process for which the annual (or quarterly or monthly) crediting of interest reflects the practical aspect of administering the accumulation. This is discussed more fully just after Example 1.3.

It is possible that the rate of interest will change from one year to the next. If the interest rate is i_1 in the first year, i_2 in the second year, and so on, then after n years an initial amount C will accumulate to $C(1+i_1)(1+i_2)\cdots(1+i_n)$, where the growth factor for year t is $1+i_t$ and the interest rate for year t is i_t. Note that "year t" starts at time $t-1$ and ends at time t. This is illustrated in the following example.

Example 1.2 (*Average annual rate of return*)

The excerpts below are taken from the 2002 year-end report of Altamira Corp., a Canadian mutual fund investment company. The excerpts below focus on the performance of the Altamira Income Fund during the five year period ending December 31, 2002.

	CANADIAN INCOME FUNDS				
	Altamira Income Fund				
Data per Unit	2002	2001	2000	1999	1998
Ratios/Supplemental Data					
Total net assets, end of year ($millions)	$410.0	$386.1	$376.4	$422.8	$519.5
Average net assets ($millions)	$398.6	$377.1	$382.5	$478.1	$538.9
Management expense ratio	1.07%	1.07%	1.07%	1.07%	1.07%
Portfolio turnover rate	188.8%	417.7%	374.7%	184.5%	726.5%
Annual rate of return	6.9%	6.4%	9.4%	(3.0%)	7.8%

	Average Annual Return			
	for the periods ended December 31, 2002			
	Inception Date	1 yr %	2 yrs %	3 yrs %	5 yrs %
Canadian Money Market Fund					
Altimira T-Bill Fund	05/05/97	2.2	3.2	3.9	4.1
Canadian Income Funds					
Altamira Income Fund	02/19/70	6.9	6.7	7.6	5.4
Altamira Bond Fund	07/21/87	10.0	6.8	8.8	6.0
Altamira High Yield Bond Fund	08/03/95	(6.6)	(4.7)	(5.4)	(1.4)

http://www.altamira.com **FIGURE 1.4**

The highlighted line "Annual rate of return" gives the annual return for the Altamira Income Fund for each of the five calendar years 1998 through 2002. The highlighted line "Altamira Income Fund" gives the average annual return for various lengths of time ending December 31, 2002. For the five year period, the total compound growth in the fund can be found by compounding the annual rates of return of 7.8% in 1998, −3.0% in 1999, 9.4% in 2000, 6.4% in 2001 and 6.9% in 2002:

$$(1+.078)(1-.03)(1+.094)(1+.064)(1+.069) = 1.3011.$$

This would be the value on December 31, 2002 of an investment of 1 made into the fund on January 1, 1998. The five year growth can be described by means of an average annual return per year for the five year period. It is understood in financial practice that the phrase "average annual return" refers to annual compound rate of interest for the period of years being considered. The average annual return would be i, where $(1+i)^5 = 1.3011$. Solving this equation for i results in a value of $i = .054$. This is the interest rate listed as the average annual return for the fund for the five year period ending December 31, 2002. Other average annual rates can be found in a similar way. □

1.1.1 EFFECTIVE RATES OF INTEREST AND COMPOUNDING

In practice interest may be credited or charged more frequently than once per year. For example many bank accounts pay interest monthly and credit cards generally charge interest monthly on previous unpaid balances. If an initial deposit is allowed to accumulate in an account over time, the algebraic form of the accumulation will be similar to the one given earlier for annual interest. At interest rate j per compounding period, an initial deposit of amount C will accumulate to $C(1+j)^n$ after n compounding periods. (It is typical to use i to denote an annual rate of interest, and in this text j will often be used to denote an interest rate for a period of other than a year.)

For instance, at an interest rate of .75% per month on a bank account, with interest credited monthly, an initial deposit of C would accumulate to $C(1.0075)^n$ at the end of n months. The growth factor for a one-year period at this rate would be $(1.0075)^{12} = 1.0938$. The account earns 9.38% over the full year. This interest rate of 9.38% is called the **effective annual rate of interest** earned on the account. In general, the effective annual rate of interest earned by an investment during a one-year period is the percentage change in the value of the investment from the beginning to the end of the year, without regard to the investment behavior at intermediate points in the year. In Example 1.2, the effective annual rates of return for the Altamira Income Fund are given for years 1998 through 2002. Comparisons of the performance of two or more investments are often done by comparing the respective effective annual interest rates earned by the investments over a particular year.

If the monthly compounding at .75% described above were to continue for another year, the accumulated value after two years would be $C(1.0075)^{24} = C(1.0938)^2$. We see that over an integral number of years a month-by-month accumulation at a monthly rate of .75% is equivalent to annual compounding at an annual rate of 9.38%; the word "equivalent" is used in the sense that they result in the same accumulated value. Two rates of interest are said to be **equivalent** if they result in the same pattern of growth over the same time period. For some transactions, a standard way of comparing interest rates is to calculate and compare their equivalent effective annual rates. It is a common practice to have interest rates quoted on an annual basis, with compounding taking place more frequently than once per year. The monthly rate of .75% would be quoted as 9% *per year compounded monthly*; the 9% rate is not the effective annual rate of interest. This leads to the notion of *nominal annual rate of interest*, which is considered in detail in Section 1.3.

When compound interest is in effect, and deposits and withdrawals are occurring in an account, the resulting balance at some future point in time can be determined by accumulating all individual transactions to that future time point. The next example illustrates this.

EXAMPLE 1.3 (*Compound interest calculation*)

Smith deposits 1000 into an account on January 1, 2000. The account credits interest at an effective annual rate of interest of 5% every December 31. Smith withdraws 200 on January 1, 2002, deposits 100 on January 1, 2003, and withdraws 250 on January 1, 2005. What is the balance in the account just after interest is credited on December 31, 2006?

SOLUTION

One approach is to recalculate the balance after every transaction. On December 31, 2001 the balance is $1000(1.05)^2 = 1102.50$ (after two years of compound interest);

on January 1, 2002 the balance is $1102.50 - 200 = 902.50$;

on December 31, 2002 the balance is $902.50(1.05) = 947.63$;

on January 1, 2003 the balance is $947.63 + 100 = 1047.63$;

on December 31, 2004 the balance is $1047.63(1.05)^2 = 1155.01$;

on January 1, 2005 the balance is $1155.01 - 250 = 905.01$; and

on December 31, 2006 the balance is $905.01(1.05)^2 = 997.77$.

An alternative approach is to accumulate each transaction to the December 31, 2006 date of valuation and combine all accumulated values, adding deposits and subtracting withdrawals. Then we have

$$1000(1.05)^7 - 200(1.05)^5 + 100(1.05)^4 - 250(1.05)^2 \quad = \quad 997.77$$

for the balance on December 31, 2006. This is illustrated in the following time line:

1/1/00 $\cdots$	1/1/02	1/1/03 $\cdots$	1/1/05 $\cdots$	12/31/06
+1000 (initial Deposit)				$\longrightarrow$ $1000(1.05)^7$
	−200			$\longrightarrow$ $-200(1.05)^5$
		+100		$\longrightarrow$ $100(1.05)^4$
			−250	$\longrightarrow$ $-250(1.05)^2$

Total $= 1000(1.05)^7 - 200(1.05)^5 + 100(1.05)^4 - 250(1.05)^2 = 997.77$.

FIGURE 1.5   □

The pattern for compound interest accumulation at rate i per period described above results in an accumulation factor of $(1+i)^n$ over n periods. We will use the expression $a(t)$ to represent the accumulation factor, or growth factor for an investment from time 0 to time t; $a(t)$ is the accumulated value at time t of an investment of 1 made at time 0. The notation $A(t)$ will be used to denote the accumulated amount of an investment at time t, so that if the initial investment amount is $A(0)$, then the accumulated value at time t is $A(t) = A(0) \cdot a(t)$.

Examples 1.1 and 1.3 have interest credited every year, and the implication from those examples is that compound interest must be applied to an integer number of years or a completed number of interest credit periods. A more general definition of **compound interest accumulation at rate i per period** is

$$a(t) = (1+i)^t \qquad (1.1)$$

over t interest periods, where t is any positive real number. If, in Example 1.1, Smith closed his account in the middle of the fourth year (3.5 years after the account was opened), the accumulated value at time $t = 3.5$ would be $1000(1.09)^{3.5} = 1000(1.09)^3(1.09)^{.5} = 1352.05$, which is the balance at the end of the third year followed by accumulation for one-half more year to the middle of the fourth year.

It is an actuarial convention to denote an annual rate of interest by i. This is not a strict rule, and it is important to consider carefully the context in which interest rate notation is used. Throughout this book, it will usually be the case that i refers to an effective annual rate of interest, and an effective rate of interest for a shorter period of time (say one month, or one quarter) will usually be denoted j.

In practice, financial transactions can take place at any point in time, and it may be necessary to represent a period which is a fractional part of a year. A fraction of a year is generally described in terms of either an integral number of m months, or an exact number of d days. In the case that time is measured in months, it is common in practice to formulate the fraction of the year t in the form $t = \frac{m}{12}$, even though not all months are exactly $\frac{1}{12}$ of a year. In the case that time is measured in days, t is often formulated as $t = \frac{d}{365}$ (some investments use a denominator of 360 days instead of 365 days, in which case $t = \frac{d}{360}$).

1.1.2 SIMPLE INTEREST

In practice, when calculating interest accumulation over a fraction of a year, a variation on compound interest is often used. This variation is commonly known as **simple interest**. At an interest rate of i per year, an amount of 1 invested at the start of the year grows to $1+i$ at the end of the year. If t represents a fraction of a year, then under the application of simple interest, the accumulated value at time t of the initial invested amount of 1 is

$$a(t) \;=\; 1+it. \tag{1.2}$$

As in the case of compound interest, for a fraction of a year, t is usually either $\frac{m}{12}$ or $\frac{d}{365}$, depending on whether time is described in m months or d days. Short term transactions for periods of less than one year are often formulated on the basis of simple interest at a quoted annual rate. The following example refers to a **promissory note**, which is a short-term contract (generally less than one year) requiring the issuer of the note (the borrower) to pay the holder of the note (the lender) a principal amount plus interest on that principal at a specified annual interest rate for a specified length of time, at the end of which the payment is due. It is the convention in financial practice that promissory note interest is calculated on the basis of simple interest. The interest rate earned by the lender is sometimes referred to as the "*yield rate*" earned on the investment. As concepts are introduced throughout this text, we will see the expression "yield rate" used in a number of different investment contexts with differing meanings. In each case it will be important to relate the meaning of the yield rate to the context in which it is being used.

EXAMPLE 1.4   (*Promissory note and simple interest*)

On January 31 Smith borrows 5000 from Brown and gives Brown a promissory note. The note states that the loan will be repaid on April 30 of the same year, with interest at 12% per annum. On March 1 Brown sells the promissory note to Jones, who pays Brown a sum of money in return for the right to collect the payment from Smith on April 30. Jones pays Brown an amount such that Jones' yield (interest rate earned) from March 1 to the maturity date can be stated as an annual rate of interest of 15%.

(a) Determine the amount that Jones paid to Brown and the yield rate (interest rate) Brown earned quoted on an annual basis. Assume all calculations are based on simple interest and a 365 day year.

(b) Suppose instead that Jones pays Brown an amount such that Jones' yield is 12%. Determine the amount that Jones paid.

SOLUTION

(a) We first find the payment required on the maturity date April 30. This is $5000\left[1+(.12)\left(\frac{89}{365}\right)\right] = 5146.30$ (there are 89 days from January 31 to April 30 in a non-leap year; financial calculators often have a function that calculates the number of days between two dates). Let X denote the amount Jones pays Brown on March 1. We will denote by j_1 the annual yield rate earned by Brown based on simple interest for the period of $t_1 = \frac{29}{365}$ years from January 31 to March 1, and we will denote by j_2 the annual yield rate earned by Jones for the period of $t_2 = \frac{60}{365}$ years from March 1 to April 30. Then $X = 5000(1+t_1 j_1)$ and the amount paid on April 30 by Smith is $X(1+t_2 j_2) = 5146.30$. The following time-line diagram indicates the sequence of events.

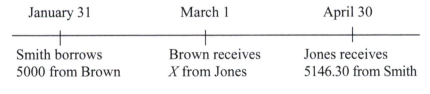

January 31	March 1	April 30
Smith borrows 5000 from Brown	Brown receives X from Jones	Jones receives 5146.30 from Smith

FIGURE 1.6

We are given $j_2 = .15$ (the annualized yield rate earned by Jones) and we can solve for X from $X = \frac{5146.30}{1+t_2 j_2} = \frac{5146.30}{1+\left(\frac{60}{365}\right)(.15)} = 5022.46$. Now that X is known, we can solve for j_1 from

$$X = 5022.46 = 5000(1+t_1 j_1) = 5000\left(1+\tfrac{29}{365}\cdot j_1\right)$$

to find that Brown's annualized yield is $j_1 = .0565$.

(b) If Jones' yield is 12%, then Jones paid

$$X \;=\; \frac{5146.30}{1+t_2 j_2} \;=\; \frac{5146.30}{1+\left(\frac{60}{365}\right)(.12)} \;=\; 5046.75. \qquad \square$$

In the previous example, we see that to achieve a yield rate of 15% Jones pays 5022.46 and to achieve a yield rate of 12% Jones pays 5046.75. This inverse relationship between yield and price is typical of a "**fixed-income**" investment. A fixed-income investment is one for which the future payments are predetermined (unlike an investment in, say, a stock, which involves some risk, and for which the return cannot be predetermined). Jones is investing in a 60-day investment which will pay him 5146.30 at the end of 60 days. If the interest (yield) rate desired by an investor increases for an investment with fixed future payments, the price that the investor (Jones) is willing to pay for the investment decreases (the less paid, the better the return on the investment). When Brown makes the loan to Smith, we can regard Brown as having made a fixed-income investment, since he is to receive a specified amount, 5146.30, on specified date, April 30. An alternative way of describing the inverse relationship between yield and price on fixed-income investments is to say that the holder of a fixed income investment (Brown) will see the market value of the investment decrease if the yield rate to maturity demanded by a buyer (Jones) increases. This can be explained by noting that a higher yield rate requires a smaller investment amount to achieve the same dollar level of interest payments. This will be seen again when the notion of *present value* is discussed later in this chapter.

From Equations 1.1 and 1.2 it is clear that accumulation under simple interest forms a linear function whereas compound interest accumulation forms an exponential function. This is illustrated in Figure 1.7 showing the graph of the accumulation of an initial investment of 1 at both simple and compound interest.

From Figure 1.7 it appears that simple interest accumulation at annual rate i is larger than compound interest accumulation at effective annual rate i for values of t between 0 and 1, but compound interest accumulation is greater than simple interest accumulation for values of t greater than 1. Using an annual interest rate of $i = .08$, we have, for example, at time $t = .25$,

$1 + it \;=\; 1 + (.08)(.25) \;=\; 1.02 > 1.0194 \;=\; (1.08)^{.25} \;=\; (1+i)^t$, and at $t = 2$

we have $1+it = 1+(.08)(2) = 1.16 < 1.1664 = (1.08)^2 = (1+i)^t$. The relationship between simple and compound interest is verified algebraically in Exercise 1.1.11 at the end of this chapter. Note that in practice the use of simple interest is generally restricted to periods of less than a year $(t<1)$.

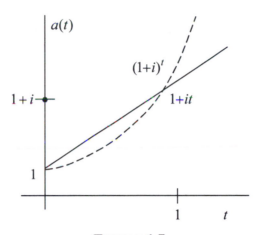

FIGURE 1.7

In practice, interest accumulation is often based on a combination of simple and compound interest. Compound interest would be applied over the completed (integer) number of interest compounding periods, and simple interest would be applied from then to the fractional point in the current interest period. For instance, under this approach, at annual rate 9%, over a period of length 4 years and 5 months, an investment would grow by a factor of $(1.09)^4\left[1+\frac{5}{12}(.09)\right]$.

1.1.3 ACCUMULATED AMOUNT FUNCTION

When analyzing the accumulation over time of a single invested amount, the value of the investment is generally regarded as a function of time. For example, $A(t)$ is the value of the investment at time t, with t usually measured in years. Time $t=0$ usually, although not necessarily, corresponds to the time at which the original investment was made. The amount by which the investment grows from time t_1 to time t_2 is often regarded as the amount of interest earned over that period, and this can be written as $A(t_2)-A(t_1)$. Also, with this notation, the effective annual interest rate for the one-year period from time u to time $u+1$ would be i_{u+1}, where $A(u+1) = A(u)(1+i_{u+1})$, or equivalently,

$$i_{u+1} = \frac{A(u+1) - A(u)}{A(u)}. \qquad (1.3)$$

The subscript "$u+1$" indicates that we are measuring the interest rate in year $u+1$.

For example, if $u = 0$, i_1 is the interest rate in year 1, which starts at time 0 and ends at time 1; if $u = 5$, i_6 is the interest rate in year 6, which starts at time 5 and ends at time 6. This relationship for i_{u+1} shows that the effective annual rate of interest for a particular one-year period is the amount of interest for the year as a proportion of the value of the investment at the start of the year, or equivalently, the rate of investment growth per dollar invested. In other words,

effective annual rate of interest for a specified one-year period

$$= \frac{amount\ of\ interest\ earned\ for\ the\ one\text{-}year\ period}{value\ (or\ amount\ invested)\ at\ the\ start\ of\ the\ year}.$$

The accumulated amount function can be used to find an effective interest rate for any time interval. For example, the effective three-month interest rate for the three months from time $3\frac{1}{4}$ to time $3\frac{1}{2}$ would be

$$\frac{A\left(3\frac{1}{2}\right) - A\left(3\frac{1}{4}\right)}{A\left(3\frac{1}{4}\right)}.$$

From a practical point of view, the accumulated amount function $A(t)$ would be a step function, changing by discrete increments at each interest credit time point, since interest is credited at discrete points of time, such as every year or month. For more theoretical analysis of investment behavior, it may be useful to assume that $A(t)$ is a continuous, or differentiable, function, such as in the case of compound interest growth on an initial investment of amount $A(0)$ at time $t = 0$, where $A(t) = A(0)(1+i)^t$ for any non-negative real number t.

1.2 PRESENT VALUE AND EQUATIONS OF VALUE

1.2.1 PRESENT VALUE

If we let X be the amount that must be invested at the start of a year to accumulate to 1 at the end of the year at effective annual interest rate i, then $X(1+i)=1$, or equivalently, $X = \frac{1}{1+i}$. The factor $\frac{1}{1+i}$ is the **present value of an amount of 1 due in one year**. The factor $\frac{1}{1+i}$ is often denoted v in actuarial notation and is called a **present value factor** or discount factor. When a situation involves more than one interest rate, the symbol v_i may be used to identify the interest rate i on which the present value factor is based.

The present value factor is particularly important in the context of compound interest. Accumulation under compound interest has the form $A(t) = A(0)(1+i)^t$. This expression can be rewritten as

$$A(0) \quad = \quad \frac{A(t)}{(1+i)^t} \quad = \quad A(t)(1+i)^{-t} \quad = \quad A(t)v^t.$$

Thus Kv^t is the present value at time 0 of an amount K due at time t when investment growth occurs according to compound interest. This means that Kv^t is the amount that must be invested at time 0 to grow to K at time t under compound interest growth, and the present value factor v acts as a "compound present value" factor in determining the present value. Accumulation and present value are inverse processes of one another.

When considering the equation $X(1+i)^t = Y$ (or equivalently, $X = Yv^t$), given any three of the four variables X, Y, i, t, it is possible to find the fourth. If the unknown variable is t, then solving for the time factor results in $t = \frac{\ln(Y/X)}{\ln(1+i)}$ (ln is the natural log function). If the unknown variable is the interest rate i, then solving for i results in $i = \left(\frac{Y}{X}\right)^{1/t} - 1$. Financial calculators have functions that allow you to enter three of the variables and calculate the fourth. Examples of these functions are given in the Appendix at the end of this book.

EXAMPLE 1.5   (*Present value calculation*)

Ted wants to invest a sufficient amount in a fund in order that the accumulated value will be one million dollars on his retirement date in 25 years. Ted considers two options. He can invest in Equity Mutual Fund, which invests in the stock market. E.M. Fund has averaged an annual compound rate of return of 19.5% since its inception 30 years ago, although its annual growth has been as low as 2% and as high as 38%. The E.M. Fund provides no guarantees as to its future performance. Ted's other option is to invest in a *zero-coupon bond or stripped bond* (this is a bond with no coupons, only a payment on the maturity date; see Chapter 6), with a guaranteed effective annual rate of interest of 11.5% until its maturity date in 25 years.

(a) What amount must Ted invest if he chooses E.M. Fund and assumes that the average annual growth rate will continue for another 25 years?

(b) What amount must he invest if he opts for the stripped bond investment?

(c) What minimum effective annual rate is needed over the 25 years in order for an investment of $25,000 to accumulate to Ted's target of one million?

(d) How many years are needed for Ted to reach $1,000,000 if he invests the amount found in part (a) in the stripped bond?

SOLUTION

(a) If Ted invests X at $t = 0$, then $X(1.195)^{25} = 1,000,000$, so that the present value of 1,000,000 due in 25 years at effective annual rate .195 is $1,000,000v^{25} = 1,000,000(1.195)^{-25} = 11,635.96$.

(b) The present value of 1,000,000 due in 25 years at $i = .115$ is $1,000,000v^{25} = 1,000,000(1.115)^{-25} = 65,785.22$.   Note   that   no subscript was used on v in part (a) or (b) since it was clear from the context as to the interest rate being used.

(c) We wish to solve for i in the equation $25,000(1+i)^{25} = 1,000,000$. The solution for i is $i = \left(\frac{1,000,000}{25,000}\right)^{1/25} - 1 = .1590$.

(d) In t years Ted will have $11,635.96(1.115)^t = 1,000,000$. Solving for t

results in $t = \dfrac{\ln\left(\frac{1,000,000}{11,635}\right)}{\ln(1.115)} = 40.9$ years. □

If simple interest is being applied for investment accumulation, then $A(t) = A(0)(1+it)$ and the present value at time 0 of amount $A(t)$ due at time t is $A(0) = \frac{A(t)}{1+it}$. It is important to note that implicit in this expression is the fact that simple interest accrual begins at the time specified as $t = 0$. The present value based on simple interest accumulation assumes that interest begins accruing at the time the present value is being found. There is no standard symbol representing present value under simple interest that corresponds to v under compound interest.

EXAMPLE 1.6

(Canadian Treasury bills – present value based on simple interest)

The figure below is an excerpt from the website of the Bank of Canada describing a sale of **Treasury Bills** by the Canadian federal government on Thursday, August 28, 2003 (www.bankofcanada.ca). A **T-Bill** is a debt obligation that requires the issuer of the T-Bill to pay the owner of the T-Bill a specified sum (the *face amount* or *amount*) on a specified date (the *maturity date*). The issuer of the T-Bill is the borrower, the Canadian government in this case. The purchaser of the T-Bill would be an investment company or an individual. Canadian T-Bills are issued to mature in a number of days that is a multiple of 7. Canadian T-Bills are generally issued on a Thursday, and mature on a Thursday, mostly for periods of (approximately) 3 months, 6 months or 1 year.

BANK OF CANADA		BANQUE DE CANADA

For Release: 10:40 E.T.	OTTAWA
Publication: 10 h 40 HE	2003.08.26

Treasury Bills – Regular	Bons du Trésor réguliers
Auction Results	Résultats de l'adjudication

On behalf of the Minister of Finance, it was announced today that tenders for Government of Canada treasury bills have been accepted as follows:

On vient d'annoncer aujourd'hui, au nom du ministre des Finances, que les soumissions suivantes ont été acceptées pour les bons du Trésor du gouvernement du Canada:

Auction Date	**2003.08.26**	Date d'adjudication
Bidding Deadline	**10:30:00**	Heure limite de soumission
Total Amount	**$9,500,00,000**	Montant total

Multiple Price / Prix multiple

Amount Montant	Issue Émission	Maturity Échéance	Outstanding After Auction Encours après l'adjudication	(%) Yield and Equivalent Price Taux de rendement et prix correspondant	(%) Allotment Ratio Ratio de répartition	Bank of Canada Purchase Achat de la Banque du Canada
5,300,000,000	2003.08.28	2003.12.04	$8,800,000,000	Avg/Moy: **2.700 99.28029**		$500,000,000
				Low/Bas: **2.697 99.28108**		
ISIN: **CA1350Z7DL50**				High/Haut: **2.704 99.27923**	53.45667	
2,100,000,000	2003.08.28	2004.02.12	4,200,000,000	Avg/Moy: **2.741 98.75411**		$250,000,000
				Low/Bas: **2.738 98.75545**		
ISIN: **CA1350Z7D765**				High/Haut: **2.744 98.75276**	84.58961	

FIGURE 1.8

Two T-Bills are described in Figure 1.8, both issued August 28, 2003. The first one is set to mature December 4, 2003, which is 98 days (14 weeks) after issue. The *yield* is quoted as 2.700% and the price (per face amount of 100) is 99.28029. The price is the present value on the issue date, of 100 due on the maturity date, and present value is calculated on the basis of simple interest and a 365-day year. The quoted price based on the quoted average yield rate of 2.700% can be calculated as follows:

$$Price = 100 \times \frac{1}{1+(.02700)\left(\frac{98}{365}\right)} = 99.28029.$$

The price of the second T-Bill can be found in a similar way. The second T-Bill matures February 12, 2004, which is 168 days (24 weeks) after the issue date. The quoted average yield for this T-Bill is 2.741%. The price is

$$Price \;=\; 100 \times \frac{1}{1+(.02741)\left(\frac{168}{365}\right)} \;=\; 98.75411.$$

Valuation of Canadian T-Bills is algebraically identical to valuation of promissory notes described in Example 1.4. □

Given an accumulated amount function $A(t)$, the investment grows from amount $A(t_1)$ at time t_1 to amount $A(t_2)$ at time $t_2 > t_1$. Therefore an amount of $\frac{A(t_1)}{A(t_2)}$ invested at time t_1 will grow to amount 1 at time t_2. In other words, $\frac{A(t_1)}{A(t_2)}$ is a generalized present value factor from time t_2 back to time t_1.

1.2.2 EQUATION OF VALUE

From a general point of view, when a financial transaction is represented algebraically it is usually formulated by means of one or more equations that represent the values of the various components of the transaction and their interrelationships. Along with the interest rate, the other components of the transaction are amounts already disbursed or yet to be disbursed and amounts already received or yet to be received. These amounts are called *dated cash flows*. A mathematical representation of the transaction will be an equation that balances the dated cash outflows and inflows, according to the particulars of the transaction. A transaction will usually consist of a series of one or more payments disbursed in combination with a series of one or more payments received, all at various points in time. The equation balancing these payments must take into account the "time values" of these payments, the accumulated and present values of the payments made at the various time points. Such a balancing equation is called an **equation of value** for the transaction, and its formulation is a central element in the process of analyzing a financial transaction.

In order to formulate an equation of value for a transaction, it is first necessary to choose a reference time point or valuation date. At the reference time point the equation of value balances, or equates, the following two factors:

(1)   the accumulated value of all payments already disbursed plus the
       present value of all payments yet to be disbursed, and

(2)   the accumulated value of all payments already received plus the
       present value of all payments yet to be received.

EXAMPLE 1.7   (*Choice of valuation point for an equation of value*)

Every Friday in February (the 7, 14, 21, and 28) Walt places a $1000 bet,
on credit, with his off-track bookmaking service, which charges an
effective weekly interest rate of 8% on all credit extended. Unfortunately
for Walt, he loses each bet and agrees to repay his debt to the
bookmaking service in four installments, to be made on March 7, 14, 21,
and 28. Walt pays $1100 on each of March 7, 14, and 21. How much
must Walt pay on March 28 to completely repay his debt?

SOLUTION

The payments in the transaction are represented in Figure 1.9. We must
choose a reference time point at which to formulate the equation of
value. If we choose February 7 ($t = 0$ in Figure 1.9) as the reference
point, then Walt receives 1000 right "now" and all other amounts
received and paid are in the future, so we find their present values. The
value at time 0 of what Walt has already received and is yet to receive
(on credit) is $1000(1 + v + v^2 + v^3)$, representing the four weekly credit
amounts received in February, where $v = \frac{1}{1.08}$ is the weekly present
value factor and t is measured in weeks. The value at $t = 0$ of what Walt
must pay is $1100(v^4 + v^5 + v^6) + Xv^7$, representing the three payments of
1100 and the fourth payment of X.

Received				Paid			
1000	1000	1000	1000	1100	1100	1100	X
2/7	2/14	2/21	2/28	3/7	3/14	3/21	3/28
t 0	1	2	3	4	5	6	7

FIGURE 1.9

Equating the value at time 0 of what Walt will receive with the value of what he will pay results in the equation

$$1000\left(1+v+v^2+v^3\right) \;=\; 1100\left(v^4+v^5+v^6\right)+Xv^7. \tag{A}$$

Solving for X results in

$$X \;=\; \frac{1000\left(1+v+v^2+v^3\right)-1100\left(v^4+v^5+v^6\right)}{v^7} \;=\; 2273.79. \tag{B}$$

If we choose March 28 $(t=7)$ as the reference time point for valuation, then we accumulate all amounts received and paid to time 7. The value of what Walt has received is $1000\left[(1+j)^7+(1+j)^6+(1+j)^5+(1+j)^4\right]$, and the value of what he has repaid is $1100\left[(1+j)^3+(1+j)^2+(1+j)\right]+X$, where again $j=.08$ is the effective rate of interest per week.

The equation of value formulated at $t=7$ can be written as

$$1000\left[(1+j)^7+(1+j)^6+(1+j)^5+(1+j)^4\right]$$
$$= \;1100\left[(1+j)^3+(1+j)^2+(1+j)\right]+X. \tag{C}$$

Solving for X results in

$$1000\left[(1+j)^7+(1+j)^6+(1+j)^5+(1+j)^4\right]$$
$$-1100\left[(1+j)^3+(1+j)^2+(1+j)\right] \;=\; 2273.79. \tag{D}$$

Note that most financial transactions will have interest rates quoted as annual rates, but in the weekly context of this example it was unnecessary to indicate an annual rate of interest. □

We see from Example 1.7 that an equation of value for a transaction involving compound interest may be formulated at more than one reference time point with the same ultimate solution. Notice that Equation C can be obtained from Equation A by multiplying Equation A by $(1+j)^7$. This corresponds to a change in the reference point upon which the equations are based, Equation A being based on $t = 0$ and Equation C being based on $t = 7$. In general, when a transaction involves only compound interest, an equation of value formulated at time t_1 can be translated into an equation of value formulated at time t_2 simply by multiplying the first equation by $(1+i)^{t_2 - t_1}$. In Example 1.7, when $t = 7$ was chosen as the reference point, the solution was slightly simpler than that required for the equation of value at $t = 0$, in that no division was necessary. For most transactions there will often be one reference time point that allows a more efficient solution of the equation of value than any other reference time point.

1.3   NOMINAL RATES OF INTEREST

Quoted annual rates of interest frequently do not refer to the effective annual rate. Consider the following example.

EXAMPLE 1.8   (*Monthly compounding of interest*)

Sam has just received a credit card with a credit limit of $1000. The card issuer quotes an annual charge on unpaid balances of 24%, payable monthly. Sam immediately uses his card to its limit. The first statement Sam receives indicates that his balance is 1000 but no interest has yet been charged. Each subsequent statement includes interest on the unpaid part of his previous month's statement. He ignores the statements for a year, and makes no payments toward the balance owed. What amount does Sam owe according to his thirteenth statement?

SOLUTION

Sam's first statement will have a balance of 1000 outstanding, with no interest charge. Subsequent monthly statements will apply a monthly interest charge of $\left(\frac{1}{12}\right)(24\%) = 2\%$ on the unpaid balance from the previous month. Thus Sam's unpaid balance is compounding monthly at a rate of 2% per month; the interpretation of the phrase "payable monthly" is that the quoted annual interest rate is to be divided by 12 to get the one-month interest rate. The balance on statement 13 (12 months after statement 1) will have compounded for 12 months to $1000(1.02)^{12} = 1268.23$ (this value is based on rounding to the nearest penny each month; the exact value is 1268.24). The effective annual interest rate charged on the account in the 12 months following the first statement is 26.82%. The quoted rate of 24% is a **nominal annual rate of interest, not an effective annual rate of interest**. This example shows that a *nominal annual interest rate of 24% compounded monthly* is equivalent to an effective annual rate of 26.82%.   □

The 24% rate quoted in Example 1.8 is sometimes called an *annual percentage rate*, and the rate of 2% per month is the *periodic rate*. In practice, a credit card issuer will usually quote an "APR" (annual percentage rate), and may also quote a daily percentage rate which is $\frac{APR}{365}$. When a monthly billing cycle ends, an "average daily balance" is calculated (typically this is calculated by taking the average of the account balances at the start of each day during the billing cycle). This average daily balance is multiplied by the daily percentage rate, and this is multiplied by the number of days in the billing cycle. Under this approach, the monthly interest rates compounded in Example 1.8 would not be exactly 2% per month, but would be $\frac{.24}{365} \times 31 = .02038356$ for a 31 day billing cycle, $\frac{.24}{365} \times 30 = .01972603$ for a 30 day billing cycle, etc.

Nominal rates of interest occur frequently in practice. They correspond to situations in which interest is credited or compounded more often than once per year. Example 1.8 illustrates a case in which the quoted nominal annual rate was based on monthly compounding. A nominal annual rate can be associated with any interest compounding period, such as six months, one month, or one week. In order to apply a quoted nominal annual rate, it is necessary to know the associated interest compounding period, or, equivalently, the number of interest conversion periods in a year. In Example 1.8 the associated interest compounding period is indicated by the phrase "payable monthly," and this tells us that the interest compounding period is one month. This could also be stated in any of the following ways:

(i) annual interest rate of 24%, compounded monthly,

(ii) annual interest rate of 24%, convertible monthly, or

(iii) annual interest rate of 24%, convertible 12 times per year.

All of these phrases mean that the 24% quoted annual rate is to be transformed to an effective one-month rate that is one-twelfth of the quoted annual rate, $\left(\frac{1}{12}\right)(.24) = .02$. The effective interest rate per interest compounding period is a fraction of the quoted annual rate corresponding to the fraction of a year represented by the interest compounding period.

In Example 1.8 the quoted nominal annual rate of 24% compounded monthly was seen to be equivalent to an effective annual rate of 26.82%. The notion of equivalence of two rates was introduced in Section 1.1, where it was stated that rates are equivalent if they result in the same pattern of compound accumulation over any equal periods of time. This can be seen in the case of the nominal annual 24% compounded monthly and effective annual 26.82%. The nominal annual 24% refers to a compound monthly rate of 2%. Then in t years ($12t$ months) the growth of an initial investment of amount 1 will be

$$(1.02)^{12t} = \left[(1.02)^{12}\right]^{t} = (1.2682)^{t}.$$

Since $(1.2682)^{t}$ is the growth in t years at effective annual rate 26.82%, this verifies the equivalence of the two rates. The typical way to verify equivalence of rates is to convert one rate to the compounding period of the other rate, using compound interest. In the case just considered, the compound monthly rate of 2% can be converted to an equivalent effective annual growth factor of $(1.02)^{12} = 1.2682$. Alternatively, an effective annual rate of 26.82% can be converted to a compound monthly growth factor of $(1.2682)^{1/12} = 1.02$.

Once the nominal annual interest rate and compounding interest period are known, the corresponding compound interest rate for the interest conversion period can be found. Then the accumulation function follows a compound interest pattern, with time usually measured in units of effective interest conversion periods. When comparing nominal annual interest rates with differing interest compounding periods, it is necessary to convert the rates to equivalent rates with a common effective interest period. The following example illustrates this.

| EXAMPLE 1.9 | (*Comparison of nominal annual rates of interest*)

Tom is trying to decide between two banks in which to open an account. Bank A offers an annual rate of 15.25% with interest compounded semiannually, and Bank B offers an annual rate of 15% with interest compounded monthly. Which bank will give Tom a higher effective annual growth?

| SOLUTION |

Bank A pays an effective 6-month interest rate of $\frac{1}{2}(15.25\%) = 7.625\%$. In one year (two effective interest periods) a deposit of amount 1 will grow to $(1.07625)^2 = 1.158314$ in Bank A.

Bank B pays an effective monthly interest rate of $\frac{1}{12}(15\%) = 1.25\%$. In one year (12 effective interest periods) a deposit of amount 1 in Bank B will grow to $(1.0125)^{12} = 1.160755$. Bank B has an equivalent annual effective rate that is almost .25% higher than that of Bank A.   □

In order to make a fair comparison of quoted nominal annual rates with differing interest conversion periods, it is necessary to transform them to a common interest conversion period, such as an effective annual period as in Example 1.9.

There is *standard actuarial notation* for denoting nominal annual rates of interest, although this notation is not generally seen outside of actuarial practice. In actuarial notation, the symbol i is generally reserved for denoting an effective annual rate, and the symbol $i^{(m)}$ is reserved for denoting a nominal annual rate with interest compounded (or convertible) m times per year. Note that the superscript is for identification purposes and is <u>not an exponent</u>. $i^{(m)}$ refers to an interest compounding period of $\frac{1}{m}$ years and compound rate per period of $\frac{1}{m} \cdot i^{(m)} = \frac{i^{(m)}}{m}$. In Example 1.8, $m = 12$, so the nominal annual rate would be denoted as $i^{(12)} = .24$. The information indicated by the superscript "(12)" in this notation is that there are 12 interest conversion periods per year, and that the effective rate of 2% per month is $\frac{1}{12}$ of the quoted rate of 24%. Similarly, in Example 1.9 the nominal annual rates would be $i_A^{(2)} = .1525$ and $i_B^{(12)} = .15$ for Banks A and B, respectively.

In Example 1.8 the equivalent effective annual growth factor is $1+i = \left(1+\frac{.24}{12}\right)^{12} = 1.2682$. In Example 1.9 the equivalent effective annual growth factors for Banks A and B, respectively, are

$$1+i_A = \left(1+\frac{.1525}{2}\right)^2 = 1.158314$$

and

$$1+i_B = \left(1+\frac{.15}{12}\right)^{12} = 1.160755.$$

The general relationship linking equivalent nominal annual interest rate $i^{(m)}$ and effective annual interest rate i is

$$1+i = \left[1+\frac{i^{(m)}}{m}\right]^m. \qquad (1.4)$$

The relationships linking the effective annual interest rate i and the equivalent nominal annual interest rate $i^{(m)}$ can be summarized in the following two equations

$$i = \left[1+\frac{i^{(m)}}{m}\right]^m -1 \text{ and } i^{(m)} = m\left[(1+i)^{1/m} -1\right]. \qquad (1.5)$$

Note that $(1+i)^{1/m}$ is the $\frac{1}{m}$-year growth factor, and $(1+i)^{1/m} -1$ is the equivalent effective $\frac{1}{m}$-year compound interest rate.

It should be emphasized that $i^{(m)}$ is a notational convenience for describing a nominal annual rate. Once the compounding period and rate are known, accumulation follows the pattern of compound interest. It should be clear from general reasoning that with a given nominal annual rate of interest, the more often compounding takes place during the year, the larger the year-end accumulated value will be, so the larger the equivalent effective annual rate will be as well. This is verified algebraically in Exercise 1.3.9 at the end of the chapter. The following example considers the relationship between equivalent i and $i^{(m)}$ as m changes.

> **EXAMPLE 1.10**

(*Equivalent effective and nominal annual rates of interest*)
Suppose the effective annual rate of interest is 12%. Find the equivalent nominal annual rates for $m = 1, 2, 3, 4, 6, 8, 12, 52, 365, \infty$.

> **SOLUTION**

$m = 1$ implies interest is convertible annually ($m = 1$ time per year), which implies the effective annual interest rate is $i^{(1)} = i = .12$. We use Equation (1.5) to solve for $i^{(m)}$ for the other values of m. The results are given in Table 1.1.

TABLE 1.1

m	$(1+i)^{1/m} - 1$	$i^{(m)} = m\left[(1+i)^{1/m} - 1\right]$
1	.12	.12
2	.0583	.1166
3	.0385	.1155
4	.0287	.1149
6	.0191	.1144
8	.0143	.1141
12	.0095	.1139
52	.00218	.1135
365	.000311	.113346
∞	$\displaystyle\lim_{m\to\infty} m\left[(1+i)^{1/m} - 1\right]$	$= \ln(1+i) = .113329$

☐

Note that $(1.12)^{1/2} - 1 = .0583$ is the effective 6-month rate of interest that is equivalent to an effective annual rate of interest of 12% (two 6-month periods of compounding at effective 6-month rate 5.83% results in one year growth of $(1.0583)^2 = 1.12$). The limit in the final line of Table

1.1 is a consequence of l'Hospital's Rule (see Exercise 1.3.9). It can also be seen from Table 1.1 that the more frequently compounding takes place (i.e., as m increases), the smaller is the equivalent nominal annual rate. As compounding goes from annual $(m = 1)$ to semiannual $(m = 2)$ to monthly $(m = 12)$, there are significant decreases in the equivalent nominal annual rate $(i^{(12)} < i^{(2)} < i)$. The decreases are less significant, however, in going from monthly to weekly or even daily compounding, so we see that there is a limit to the benefit of compounding. With an effective annual rate of 12%, the minimum equivalent nominal annual rate needed is 11.333%. No matter how often compounding takes place, the nominal annual rate needed will not be less than 11.333%. The limiting case $(m \to \infty)$ in Example 1.10 is called *continuous compounding* and is related to the notions of *force of interest* and instantaneous growth rate of an investment. This is discussed in detail in Section 1.5.

A nominal rate, although quoted on an annual basis, might refer to only the immediately following fraction of a year. For instance, in Example 1.9 Bank B's quoted nominal annual rate of 15% with interest credited monthly might apply only to the coming month, after which the quoted rate (still credited monthly) might change to something else, say 13.5%. Thus when interest is quoted on a nominal annual basis, the actual rate may change during the course of the year, from one interest period to the next.

In the past few sections of this chapter we have characterized investment growth by means of interest accumulating into the future based on amounts invested at the present time. It is sometimes convenient to measure investment growth in terms of present or "discounted" values of specified amounts due at specified points in the future; we have already seen this concept in the discussion of present value in the previous section. The next section considers an alternative way of describing present value.

1.4 EFFECTIVE AND NOMINAL RATES OF DISCOUNT

1.4.1 EFFECTIVE ANNUAL RATE OF DISCOUNT

In previous sections of this chapter, interest amounts have been regarded as paid or charged at the end of an interest compounding period, and the corresponding interest rate is the ratio of the amount of interest paid at the end of the period to the amount of principal invested or loaned at the start of the period. Interest rates and amounts viewed in this way are sometimes referred to as *interest payable in arrears* (payable at the end of an interest period). This is the standard way in which interest rates are quoted, and it is the standard way by which interest amounts are calculated. In many situations it is the method required by law.

Occasionally a transaction calls for *interest payable in advance*. In this case the quoted interest rate is applied to obtain an amount of interest which is payable at the start of the interest period. For example, if Smith borrows 1000 for one year at a quoted rate of 10% with interest payable in advance, the 10% is applied to the loan amount of 1000, resulting in an amount of interest of 100 for the year. However, the interest is payable in advance, at the time the loan is made. Smith receives the loan amount of 1000 and must immediately pay the lender 100, the amount of interest on the loan. One year later he must repay the loan amount of 1000. The net effect is that Smith receives 900 and repays 1000 one year later. The effective annual rate of interest on this transaction is $\frac{100}{900} = .1111$, or 11.11%. It is also possible to describe this transaction by saying that the 10% rate is applied as interest payable in advance. This rate of 10% payable in advance is called the **rate of discount** for the transaction. The rate of discount is the rate used to calculate the amount by which the year end value is reduced to determine the present value.

The effective annual rate of discount is another way of describing investment growth in a financial transaction. In the example just considered we see that an effective annual interest rate of 11.11% is equivalent to an effective annual discount rate of 10%, since both describe the same transaction, growth from 900 to 1000.

In terms of an accumulated amount function $A(t)$, the general definition of the effective annual rate of discount from time $t = 0$ to time $t = 1$ is

$$d = \frac{A(1) - A(0)}{A(1)}. \tag{1.6}$$

This definition is in contrast with the definition for the effective annual rate of interest, given earlier in this chapter, which has the same numerator but has a denominator of $A(0)$. Effective annual interest measures growth on the basis of the initially invested amount, whereas effective annual discount measures growth on the basis of the year-end accumulated amount. Either measure can be used in the analysis of a financial transaction.

Equation (1.6) can be rewritten as $A(0) = A(1) \cdot (1-d)$, so we see that $1 - d$ acts as a present value factor. The value at the start of the year is the principal amount of $A(1)$ minus the interest payable in advance, which is $d \cdot A(1)$. On the other hand, on the basis of effective annual interest we have $A(0) = A(1) \cdot v$. We see that for d and i to be equivalent rates, present values under both representations must be the same, so we must have $\frac{1}{1+i} = v = 1 - d$, or equivalently, $d = \frac{i}{1+i}$, or $i = \frac{d}{1-d}$. With $d = .10$ in the situation outlined above, we have $i = \frac{.1}{1-.1} = .1111$, or 11.11%. The relationships between equivalent interest and discount rates for periods of other than a year are similar. Suppose that j is the effective rate of interest for a period of other than one year. Then $d_j = \frac{j}{1+j}$ where d_j is the equivalent effective rate of discount for that period.

From a practical point of view, $A(0)$ in Equation (1.6) will not be less than 0. Then assuming $A(1) > A(0)$, an effective rate of discount can be no larger than 1 (100%). Note that an effective discount rate of $d = 1$ (100%), implies a present value factor of $1 - d = 1 - 1 = 0$ at the start of the period. In the equivalence between i and d we see that $\lim_{i \to \infty} d = 1$, so that very large effective interest rates correspond to equivalent effective discount rates near 100%.

One of the main applications in practice of discount rates occurs in the context of United States Treasury Bills. In Section 1.2 it was seen that Canadian T-Bills are quoted with prices and annual yield rates, where an annual yield rate is applied using simple interest for the period to the maturity of the T-Bill. The pricing of U.S. T-Bills is based on **simple discount**. With a quoted annual discount rate of d, based on simple discount the present value of 1 payable t years from now is $1 - dt$. Simple discount is generally only applied for periods of less than one year.

EXAMPLE 1.11   (*U.S. Treasury Bill*)

Treasury Bills issued by the Treasury Department of the U.S. government are similar to Canadian T-Bills. A T-Bill represents an obligation by the issuing government to pay a specified maturity amount on a specified maturity date. Quotations are based on a maturity amount of $100. The table below was excerpted from the website of the United States Bureau of the Public Debt in June, 2004. The website provides a brief description of how the various quoted values are related to one another.

Recent Treasury Bill Auction Results

Term	Issue Date	Maturity Date	Discount Rate%	Investment Rate%	Price Per $100	CUSIP
12-day	06/3/2004	06/15/2004	0.965	0.974	99.968	912795QP9
28-day	06/3/2004	07/01/2004	0.940	0.952	99.927	912795QR5
91-day	06/3/2004	09/02/2004	1.130	1.150	99.714	912795RA1
182-day	06/3/2004	12/02/2004	1.400	1.430	99.292	912795RP8

(www.publicdebt.treas.gov/sec/secpry.htm)

The "Price Per $100" is the present value of $100 due in the specified number of days. The relationship between the quoted price and the discount rate is based on simple discount in which a fraction of a year is calculated on the basis of a 360-day year. The quoted discount and investment rates are annual rates.

For instance, for the 182-day bill issued June 3, 2004 and maturing December 2, 2004, the price is found from the relationship $P = 100(1-dt)$. With discount rate $d = .01400$, and fraction of a year $t = \frac{182}{360}$, we have $P = 100\left[1 - (.01400)\left(\frac{182}{360}\right)\right] = 99.292$ (rounded to the 3rd decimal place, which is the practice for quoting T-Bill prices).

The "Investment Rate" is an annual rate of simple interest that is equivalent to the return over the 182-day period. The investment growth for the 182-day period is $\frac{100}{99.292} = 1.0071305$. If this is converted to an annual return based on simple interest for a 365-day year, the corresponding return for 365 days is $.00713 \times \frac{365}{182} = .01430$ which can be quoted as a rate of 1.430% (rounded to the nearest .001%). Calculations for the other T-Bills quoted above are done in the same way.   □

The U.S. government's Truth in Lending legislation requires that financial institutions making loans based on discount rates make clear to borrowers the equivalent interest rate being charged. Thus an annual discount rate of 8% cannot be presented as a loan rate of 8%, but must rather be presented as the equivalent interest rate, $i = \frac{d}{1-d} = \frac{.08}{1-.08} = .0870$ (8.70%).

Corresponding to an effective annual discount rate d is the present value factor $1-d = v$. The present value of 1 due in n years can then be represented in the form $v^n = (1-d)^n$, so that present values can be represented in the form of *compound discount*. This underlines the fact that the concepts of discount rate and compound discount form an alternative to the concepts of interest rate and compound interest in characterizing the behavior of an investment.

1.4.2 NOMINAL ANNUAL RATE OF DISCOUNT

Discount rates may be quoted on a nominal annual basis in the same way as interest rates. The relationship between equivalent nominal and effective annual discount rates parallels the relationship between nominal and effective annual interest rates. The actuarial symbol $d^{(m)}$ refers to a quoted annual rate which is applied as an effective discount rate of $\frac{d^{(m)}}{m}$ for a period of $\frac{1}{m}$ years. The $\frac{1}{m}$-year present value factor would be $1 - \frac{d^{(m)}}{m}$. For instance, the notation $d^{(4)} = .08$ refers to a 3-month $\left(\frac{1}{4}\text{-year}\right)$ discount rate of $\frac{.08}{4} = .02$, and a 3-month present value factor of $1-.02 = .98$. This would be compounded 4 times during the year to an effective annual present value factor of $(.98)^4 = .9224$. This annual present value factor could then be described as being equivalent to an effective annual discount rate of .0776.

In general, given a nominal annual discount rate $d^{(m)}$, there would be m compounding periods during the year, so the equivalent effective annual present value factor would be $\left(1 - \frac{d^{(m)}}{m}\right)^m$. If d is the equivalent effective annual rate of discount, then we have the relationship

$$1 - d = \left(1 - \frac{d^{(m)}}{m} \right)^m . \tag{1.7}$$

EXAMPLE 1.12

(*Equivalent effective and nominal annual rates of discount*)

Suppose that the effective annual rate of discount is $d = .107143$. Find the equivalent nominal annual discount rates $d^{(m)}$ for

$$m = 1, 2, 3, 4, 6, 8, 12, 52, 365, \infty.$$

SOLUTION

Using Equation (1.7) we solve for $d^{(m)} = m\left[1 - (1-d)^{1/m} \right]$. The numerical results are tabulated below in Table 1.2.

TABLE 1.2

m	$1 - (1-d)^{1/m}$	$d^{(m)} = m\left[1 - (1-d)^{1/m} \right]$
1	.107143	.107143
2	.0551	.1102
3	.0371	.1112
4	.0279	.1117
6	.0187	.1123
8	.0141	.1125
12	.0094	.1128
52	.0022	.1132
365	.0003	.11331
∞	$\lim_{m \to \infty} m\left[1 - (1-d)^{1/m} \right] = -\ln(1-d) = .113329$	

Note that in Example 1.12, $1 - (1 - .107143)^{1/2} = .055089$ is the effective 6-month rate of discount that is equivalent to an effective annual rate of discount of 10.7143% (two 6-month periods of compounding at effective 6-month discount rate 5.5089% results in one year present value of $(1 - .055089)^2 = 1 - .107143$).

Note also in Table 1.2 that as m increases, $d^{(m)}$ increases with upper limit $d^{(\infty)}$. Thus if $m > n$ then $d^{(m)} > d^{(n)}$ for equivalent rates. This is the opposite of what happens for equivalent nominal interest rates (see Example 1.10). This can be explained by noting that interest compounds on amounts increasing in size whereas discount compounds on amounts decreasing in size.

The effective annual discount rate used in Example 1.12 is $d = .107143$, which is equivalent to an effective annual interest rate of $i = .12$. It was chosen to facilitate comparison with the table in Example 1.10. The exercises at the end of the chapter examine in more detail the numerical relationship between equivalent nominal annual interest and discount rates, and refer to the equivalent rates in the tables from Examples 1.10 and 1.12. We see that the nominal annual interest rate convertible continuously from Example 1.10 is $i^{(\infty)} = .1133$, which is equal to $d^{(\infty)}$ in Example 1.12. In general, for equivalent rates i and d it is always the case that $d^{(\infty)} = i^{(\infty)}$, referred to earlier as the force of interest.

It is not practical to have interest compounding continuously in the sense of actually updating accumulated values instantaneously. In practice, the continuous function $(1+i)^t$ would be approximated by a step function, where interest is credited at certain points of time, such as daily, monthly, or semiannually. Nevertheless, the notions of force of interest and continuous compounding are useful and important in the creation of mathematical models of financial transactions and for other theoretical purposes. The next section presents a more general discussion of the force of interest.

1.5   THE FORCE OF INTEREST

In the earlier discussion of nominal rates of interest it was pointed out that a quoted nominal annual rate may refer only to a fraction of a year. For example, if a bank credits interest at a 3-month compound rate of 2% for the three-month period of January-February-March, the nominal annual rate convertible quarterly quoted by the bank would be 8% for that period (2% per quarter, scaled up for the four quarters in a year). It is possible that for April-May-June the 3-month compound interest rate credited by the bank (and therefore the quoted nominal rate) may be adjusted. The point being made here is that although quoted on an annual basis, a specified nominal annual interest rate might only be valid for a particular fraction of a year.

Suppose that the accumulated value of an investment at time t is represented by the function $A(t)$, where time is measured in years. The amount of interest earned by the investment in the $\frac{1}{4}$-year period from time t to time $t+\frac{1}{4}$ is $A\left(t+\frac{1}{4}\right)-A(t)$, and the $\frac{1}{4}$-year interest rate for that period is $\frac{A\left(t+\frac{1}{4}\right)-A(t)}{A(t)}$. The $\frac{1}{4}$-year interest rate can be described in terms of a nominal annual interest rate by multiplying the $\frac{1}{4}$-year interest rate by 4. The nominal annual interest rate compounded quarterly that describes the interest rate for the $\frac{1}{4}$-year period from time t to time $t+\frac{1}{4}$ is $4\times\frac{A\left(t+\frac{1}{4}\right)-A(t)}{A(t)}$ (we could use the notation $i^{(4)}$ to denote this nominal annual rate). Again it is emphasized that we are using a (nominal) annual interest rate measure to describe what occurs in the $\frac{1}{4}$-year period from time t to time $t+\frac{1}{4}$ with the understanding that the rate may change from one quarter to the next.

The $\frac{1}{4}$-year period just considered can be generalized to any fraction of a year. The interest rate earned by the investment for the $\frac{1}{m}$-year period from time t to time $t+\frac{1}{m}$ is $\frac{A\left(t+\frac{1}{m}\right)-A(t)}{A(t)}$. This rate can be described in terms of a nominal annual rate of interest compounded m times per year. The nominal annual rate would be found by scaling up the $\frac{1}{m}$-year rate by a factor of m so that $i^{(m)} = m\times\frac{A\left(t+\frac{1}{m}\right)-A(t)}{A(t)}$. Again, although described as an annual rate, $i^{(m)}$ is the quoted nominal annual rate of interest based on the investment performance from time t to time $t+\frac{1}{m}$, and it is understood that the interest rate may be different in subsequent periods of time.

If m is increased, the time interval $\left[t, t+\frac{1}{m}\right]$ decreases, and we are focusing more and more closely on the investment performance during an interval of time immediately following time t. Taking the limit of $i^{(m)}$ as $m \to \infty$ results in

$$i^{(\infty)} \quad = \quad \lim_{m \to \infty} i^{(m)} \quad = \quad \lim_{m \to \infty} m \times \frac{A\left(t+\frac{1}{m}\right) - A(t)}{A(t)}.$$

This limit can be reformulated by making the following variable substitution. Define the variable h to be $h = \frac{1}{m}$, so that $h \to 0$ as $m \to \infty$. The limit can then be written in the form

$$i^{(\infty)} \quad = \quad \frac{1}{A(t)} \cdot \lim_{h \to 0} \frac{A(t+h) - A(t)}{h} \quad = \quad \frac{1}{A(t)} \cdot \frac{d}{dt} A(t) \quad = \quad \frac{A'(t)}{A(t)}. \qquad (1.8)$$

$i^{(\infty)}$ is a nominal annual interest rate compounded infinitely often or **compounded continuously**. $i^{(\infty)}$ is also interpreted as the instantaneous rate of growth of the investment per dollar invested at time point t and it is called the **force of interest at time t.** Note that $A'(t) dt$ represents the instantaneous amount of growth of the invested amount at time point t (just as $A(t+1) - A(t)$ is the *amount* of growth in the investment from t to $t+1$), whereas $\frac{A'(t)}{A(t)}$ is the relative instantaneous rate of growth per unit amount invested at time t (just as $\frac{A(t+1) - A(t)}{A(t)}$ is the relative rate of growth from t to $t+1$ per unit invested at time t).

The force of interest may change as t changes. The actuarial notation that is used for the force of interest at time t is usually δ_t instead of $i^{(\infty)}$. In order for the force of interest to be defined, the accumulated amount function $A(t)$ must be differentiable (and thus continuous, because any differentiable function is continuous). In practice, the most frequently interest would be calculated is on a daily basis, so continuous accumulation of interest would be used for theoretical models of investment behavior. Continuous investment growth models have been central to the analysis and development of financial models with important practical applications, most notably for models of investment derivative security valuation such as stock options. Some basic investment derivatives will be described in Chapter 8.

In the following example the force of interest is derived for both simple and compound interest accumulation.

EXAMPLE 1.13   (*Force of interest*)

Derive an expression for δ_t if accumulation is based on

(a) simple interest at annual rate i, and

(b) compound interest at annual rate i.

SOLUTION

(a) $A(t) = A(0) \cdot [1+i \cdot t]$, so $A'(t) = A(0) \cdot i$. Then $\delta_t = \dfrac{A'(t)}{A(t)} = \dfrac{i}{1+i \cdot t}$.

(b) $A(t) = A(0) \cdot (1+i)^t$, so that $A'(t) = A(0) \cdot (1+i)^t \cdot \ln(1+i)$, and then

$\delta_t = \dfrac{A'(t)}{A(t)} = \ln(1+i)$. This was the form of force of interest denoted

earlier as $i^{(\infty)}$. In the case of compound interest growth, the force of interest is constant as long as the effective annual interest rate is constant. In the case of simple interest, δ_t decreases as t increases.   □

The force of interest can be used to describe investment growth. Using Equation (1.8) we have $\delta_t = \dfrac{A'(t)}{A(t)} = \dfrac{d}{dt}\ln[A(t)]$. Integrating this equation from time $t = 0$ to time $t = n$, we get

$$\int_0^n \delta_t\, dt = \int_0^n \frac{d}{dt}\ln[A(t)]dt = \ln[A(n)] - \ln[A(0)] = \ln\left[\frac{A(n)}{A(0)}\right].$$

This can be rewritten in the form

$$\exp\left[\int_0^n \delta_t\, dt\right] = \frac{A(n)}{A(0)} \tag{1.9a}$$

or

$$A(n) = A(0) \cdot \exp\left[\int_0^n \delta_t\, dt\right] \tag{1.9b}$$

or

$$A(0) = A(n) \cdot \exp\left[-\int_0^n \delta_t\, dt\right] \tag{1.9c}$$

The *n*-year accumulation factor from time 0 to time *n* is $e^{\int_0^n \delta_t \, dt}$ and the *n*-year present value factor for that period is $e^{-\int_0^n \delta_t \, dt}$. The general form of the accumulation factor from time $t = n_1$ to time $t = n_2$ (where $n_1 \leq n_2$) is $e^{\int_{n_1}^{n_2} \delta_t \, dt}$ and the general form of the present value factor for the same period of time is $e^{-\int_{n_1}^{n_2} \delta_t \, dt}$. In the case in which δ_t is constant with value δ from time n_1 to time n_2, the accumulation factor for that period simplifies to $e^{(n_2 - n_1)\delta}$ and the present value factor is $e^{-(n_2 - n_1)\delta}$.

Another identity involving the force of interest is based on the relationship $\frac{d}{dt} A(t) = A(t) \cdot \delta_t$. $A(t) \cdot \delta_t$ is the instantaneous amount of interest earned by the investment at time *t*. Integrating both from time 0 to time *n* results in

$$\int_0^n A(t) \cdot \delta_t \, dt = \int_0^n \frac{d}{dt} A(t) \, dt = A(n) - A(0). \qquad (1.10)$$

This is the amount of interest earned from time 0 to time *n*.

EXAMPLE 1.14   (*Force of interest*)

Given $\delta_t = .08 + .005t$, calculate the accumulated value over five years of an investment of 1000 made at each of the following times:

(a) Time 0, and

(b) Time 2.

SOLUTION

(a) In this case, $A(0) = 1000$ and $A(5) = A(0) \cdot \exp\left[\int_0^5 \delta_t \, dt\right]$, so that the accumulated value is

$$1000 \cdot \exp\left[\int_0^5 (.08 + .005t) \, dt\right],$$

which is

$$1000 \cdot \exp\left[(.08)(5) + (.0025)(25)\right] = 1000 \cdot e^{.4625} = 1588.04.$$

(b) This time we have $A(2) = 1000$ and $A(7) = A(2) \cdot \exp\left[\int_2^7 \delta_t \, dt\right]$, so that the accumulated value at time 7 is

$$1000 \cdot \exp\left[\int_2^7 (.08 + .005t) \, dt\right],$$

leading to

$$1000 \cdot \exp[(.08)(7-2) + (.0025)(49-4)] \quad = \quad 1669.46.$$

Note that both (a) and (b) involve 5 year periods, but the accumulations are different as a result of the non-constant force of interest. □

It was shown in Example 1.13 that if the effective annual interest rate i is constant then $\delta_t = \ln(1+i)$. Let us now suppose the force of interest δ_t is constant with value δ from time 0 to time n. Then

$$A(n) \quad = \quad A(0) \cdot e^{\int_0^n \delta_t \, dt} \quad = \quad A(0) \cdot e^{n\delta} \quad = \quad A(0) \cdot (e^\delta)^n.$$

This form of accumulation is algebraically identical to compound interest accumulation, which is of the form $A(n) = A(0) \cdot (1+i)^n$, where $e^\delta = 1+i$, or equivalently, where $\delta = \ln(1+i)$. In other words, a constant force of interest δ is equivalent to a constant effective annual interest rate i if they satisfy the relationship $e^\delta = 1+i$, or, equivalently, $\delta = \ln(1+i)$. Example 1.13 illustrates the relationship that δ and i must satisfy in order to be equivalent rates. This relationship was already seen in Example 1.10, where an effective annual rate of $i = .12$ was used to find equivalent nominal annual rates $i^{(m)}$ for various values of m. For $m = \infty$ in Example 1.10, the rate $i^{(\infty)}$ was found to be $i^{(\infty)} = \ln(1+i) = \ln(1.12) = .1133$, the constant force of interest that is equivalent to $i = .12$.

In Example 1.12, the nominal annual discount rates $d^{(m)}$ equivalent to $d = .107143$ (which is equivalent to $i = .12$) were found for various values of m. In particular it was seen that $d^{(\infty)} = .1133$, which is the same numerical value as the $i^{(\infty)}$ equivalent to $i = .12$. When investment accumulation is based on compound interest at a constant rate, it will always be the case that $i^{(\infty)} = d^{(\infty)}$.

The explicit use of the force of interest does not often arise in a practical setting. For transactions of very short duration (a few days or only one day), a nominal annual interest rate convertible daily, $i^{(365)}$, might be used. This rate is approximately equal to the equivalent force of interest, as illustrated in Table 1.1. Major financial institutions routinely borrow and lend money among themselves overnight, in order to cover their transactions during the day. The interest rate used to settle these one day loans is called the *overnight* rate. The interest rate quoted will be a nominal annual rate of interest compounded every day ($m = 365$).

| EXAMPLE 1.15 | (*Overnight Rate*)

Bank A requires an overnight (one-day) loan of 10,000,000 and is quoted a nominal annual rate of interest convertible daily of 12% by Bank B. Calculate the amount of interest Bank A must pay for the one-day loan. Suppose the loan was quoted at an annual force of interest of 12%. Calculate the interest Bank A must pay in this case.

| SOLUTION |

With $i^{(365)} = .12$, the one-day rate of interest is $\frac{.12}{365} = .000328767$, so that interest on 10,000,000 for one day will be 3,287.67 (to the nearest cent). Note that if $\delta = .12$, then interest for one day will be

$$10,000,000(e^{.12/365} - 1) \;\; = \;\; 3,288.21.$$

The difference between these amounts of interest is 0.54 (a very small fraction of the principal amount of 10,000,000). $\qquad\qquad\square$

Measuring investment growth by using the force of interest is important in developing models of financial transactions. This is due to the continuous-differential nature of many theoretical financial models and the relative ease with which exponential factors can be combined algebraically.

1.6 INFLATION AND THE "REAL" RATE OF INTEREST

Along with the level of interest rates, one of the most closely watched indicators of a country's economic performance and health is the rate of inflation. A widely used measure of inflation is the change in the *Consumer Price Index* (CPI), generally quoted on an annual basis. The change in the CPI measures the (effective) annual rate of change in the cost of a specified "basket" of consumer items. Alternative measures of inflation might be based on more specialized sectors in the economy. Inflation rates vary from country to country. They may be extremely high in some economies and almost insignificant in others. It is sometimes the case that an economy experiences deflation for a period of time (negative inflation), characterized by a decreasing CPI. Politicians and economists have been involved in numerous debates on the causes and effects of inflation, its relationship to the country's economic health, and how best to reduce or prevent inflation.

Investors are also concerned with the level of inflation. It is clear that a high rate of inflation has the effect of rapidly reducing the value (purchasing power) of currency as time goes on. It is not surprising then that periods of high inflation are usually accompanied by high interest rates, since the rate of interest must be high enough to provide a "real" return on investment. The study of the cause and effect relationship between interest and inflation is the concern of economists. We are concerned here with analyzing the relationship between interest and inflation in terms of the measurement of return on investments.

We have used the phrase *real return* a few times already without being very specific as to its meaning. The **real rate of interest** refers to the *inflation-adjusted* return on an investment. The simple and commonly used measure of the real rate of interest is $i - r$, where i is the annual rate of interest and r is the annual rate of inflation. This measure is often seen in financial newspapers or journals. As a precise measure of the real growth of an investment, or real growth in purchasing power, $i - r$ is not quite correct. This is made clear in the following example.

> **EXAMPLE 1.16**   (*The "real" rate of interest*)

Smith invests 1000 for one year at effective annual rate 15.5%. At the time Smith makes the investment, the cost of a certain consumer item is 1. One year later, when interest is paid and principal returned to Smith, the cost of the item has become 1.10. The price of the item has experienced annual inflation of 10%. What is the annual growth rate in Smith's purchasing power with respect to the consumer item?

| SOLUTION |

At the start of the year, Smith can buy 1000 items. At year end he receives $1000(1.155) = 1155$, and is able to buy $\frac{1155}{1.10} = 1050$ items. Thus Smith's purchasing power has grown by 5% (i.e., $\frac{50}{1000}$). Regarding the 10% increase in the cost of the item as a measure of inflation, we have $i - r = .155 - .10 = .055$, so, in this case, $i - r$ is not a correct representation of the "real" return earned by Smith.   □

In Example 1.16 Smith would have to receive 1100 at the end of the year just to stay even with the 10% inflation rate. He actually receives interest plus principal for a total of 1155. Thus Smith receives

$$1000(1+i) - 1000(1+r) \quad = \quad 1000(i-r) \quad = \quad 55$$

more than necessary to stay even with inflation, and this 55 is his "real" return on his investment. To measure this as a percentage, it seems natural to divide by 1000, the amount Smith initially invested. This results in a rate of $\frac{55}{1000} = .055 = i - r$, the simplistic measure of real growth mentioned prior to Example 1.16. A closer look, however, shows that the 55 in real return earned by Smith is paid in end-of-year dollars, whereas the 1000 was invested in beginning-of-year dollars. The dollar value at year end is not the same as that at year beginning, so that to regard the 55 as a percentage of the amount invested, we must measure the real return of 55 and the amount invested in equivalent dollars (dollars of equal value). The 1000 invested at the beginning of the year is equal in value to 1100 after adjusting for inflation at year end. Thus, based on end-of-year dollar value, Smith's real return of 55 should be measured as a percentage of 1100, the inflation-adjusted equivalent of the 1000 invested at the start of the year. On this basis the real rate earned by Smith is $\frac{55}{1100} = .05$, the actual growth in purchasing power.

In general, with annual interest rate i and annual inflation rate r, an investment of 1 at the start of a year will grow to $1+i$ at year end. Of this $1+i$, an amount of $1+r$ is needed to maintain dollar value against inflation, i.e., to maintain purchasing power of the original investment of 1. The remainder of $(1+i) - (1+r) = i - r$ is the "real" amount of growth in the investment, and this real return is paid at year end. The investment of 1 at the start of the year has an inflation-adjusted value of $1+r$ at year end in end-of-year dollars. Thus the percentage growth in the investment, based in terms of end-of-year dollars, is

$$i_{real} = \frac{value\ of\ amount\ of\ real\ return\ (yr\text{-}end\ dollars)}{value\ of\ invested\ amount\ (yr\text{-}end\ dollars)} = \frac{i-r}{1+r}, (1.11)$$

which is a more accurate measure of the real rate of interest. Then the real growth factor is given by $1+i_{real} = 1+\frac{i-r}{1+r} = \frac{1+i}{1+r}$, so that $(1+i_{real})(1+r) = 1+i$.

Notice that the lower the inflation rate r, the closer $1+r$ is to 1, and so the closer $i-r$ is to $\frac{i-r}{1+r}$. On the other hand, if inflation is high, and it has been known to reach levels of a few hundred percent in some countries, then the denominator $1+r$ becomes an important factor in $\frac{i-r}{1+r}$. For instance, if inflation is at a rate of 100% $(r=1)$ and interest is at a rate of 120% $(i=1.2)$, then $i-r = .20$ but $i_{real} = \frac{i-r}{1+r} = .10$. It is usually the case that the rate of interest is greater than inflation.

One more point to note when considering the combination of interest and inflation to determine a real rate of interest is that inflation rates are generally quoted as the rate that has been experienced in the year just completed, whereas interest rates are usually quoted as those to be earned in the coming year. In order to make a meaningful comparison of interest and inflation, both rates should refer to the same one-year period. Thus it may be more appropriate to use a projected rate of inflation for the coming year when inflation is considered in conjunction with the interest rate for the coming year.

1.7 NOTES AND REFERENCES

Standard International Actuarial Notation was first adopted in 1898 at the 2nd International Actuarial Congress, and has been updated periodically since then. The current version of the notation is found in the article "International Actuarial Notation," on pages 166-176 of Volume 48 (1947) of the Transactions of the Actuarial Society of America.

Governments at all levels (federal, state, provincial, and even municipal) have statutes regulating interest rates. These include usury laws limiting the level of interest rates and statutes specifying interest rate disclosure and interest calculation. For example, Section 347 of Part IX of the Canadian Criminal Code contains a law limiting interest to an effective annual rate of 60%, and the US Government's Truth in Lending legislation of 1968 requires nominal interest disclosure for most consumer borrowing.

Vaguely worded statutes regulating interest rates can result in legal disputes as to their interpretation. Section 4 of Canada's century-old *Interest Act* states that "Except as to mortgages on real estate, whenever interest is... made payable at a rate or percentage per day, week, month, or... for any period less than a year, no interest exceeding... five per cent per annum shall be chargeable unless the contract contains an express statement of the yearly rate or percentage to which such other rate... is equivalent." This legislation has resulted in numerous civil suits over which of nominal and effective annual rates are to be interpreted as satisfying the requirement of being equivalent to an interest rate quoted per week or month. The Canadian courts have mostly ruled that either nominal or effective annual rates satisfy the requirements of Section 4.

The book *Standard Securities Calculation Methods* published by the Securities Industry Association in 1973 was written as a reference for "the entire fixed-income investment community" to provide a "readily available source of the formulas, standards and procedures for performing calculations." Included in that book are detailed descriptions of the various methods applied in practice in finding t for simple interest calculations.

A great deal of information on financial theory and practice can be found on the internet. The ACTEX website, www.actexmadriver.com, has resource links for this book that include internet links for government and industry financial information along with a collection of EXCEL spreadsheets that illustrate modern approaches to investment calculations.

1.8 EXERCISES

The exercises without asterisks are intended to comprehensively cover the material presented in the chapter. Exercises with a asterisk can be regarded as supplementary exercises which cover topics in more depth, either theoretically or computationally, than those without a asterisk.

SECTION 1.1

1.1.1   Carl puts 10,000 into a bank account that pays an effective annual interest rate of 4% for ten years, with interest credited at the end of each year. If a withdrawal is made during the first five and one-half years, a penalty of 5% of the withdrawal is made. Carl withdraws K at the end of each of years 4, 5, 6 and 7. The balance in the account at the end of year 10 is 10,000. Calculate K.

1.1.2   (a) Unit values in a mutual fund have experienced annual growth rates of 10%, 16%, –7%, 4%, and 32% in the past five years. The fund manager suggests the fund can advertise an average annual growth of 11% over the past five years. What is the actual average annual compound growth rate over the past five years?

   (b) A mutual fund advertises that average annual compound rate of returns for various periods ending December 31, 2005 are as follows:

   10 years - 13%; 5 years - 17%; 2 years - 15%; 1 year - 22%.

   Find the 5-year average annual compound rates of return for the period January 1, 1996 to December 31, 2000, and find the annual rate of return for calendar year 2004.

   (c) Using the fact that the geometric mean of a collection of positive numbers is less than or equal to the arithmetic mean, show that if annual compound interest rates over an n-year period are i_1 in the first year, i_2 in the second year ,...,i_n in the nth year, then the average annual compound rate of interest for the n-year period is less than or equal to $\frac{1}{n} \cdot \sum_{k=1}^{n} i_k$.

1.1.3   2500 is invested. Find the accumulated value of the investment 10 years after it is made for each of the following rates:

(a) 4% annual simple interest

(b) 4% effective annual compound interest

(c) 6-month interest rate of 2% compounded every 6 months

(d) 3-month interest rate of 1% compounded every 3 months

1.1.4   Joe deposits 10 today and another 30 in five years into a fund paying simple interest of 11% per year. Tina will make the same two deposits, but the 10 will be deposited n years from today and the 30 will be deposited $2n$ years from today. Tina's deposits earn an effective annual rate of 9.15%. At the end of 10 years, the accumulated amount of Tina's deposits equals the accumulated amount of Joe's deposits. Calculate n.

1.1.5   Smith has just filed his income tax return and is expecting to receive, in 60 days, a refund check of 1000. The tax service that helped Smith fill out his return offers to buy Smith's refund check from him. Their policy is to pay 85% of the face value of the check. What annual simple interest rate is implied? Smith negotiates with the tax service and sells his refund check for 900. To what annual simple interest rate does this correspond? Smith decides to deposit the 900 in an account which earns simple interest at annual rate 9%. What is the accumulated value of the account on the day he would have received his tax refund check? How many days would it take from the time of his initial deposit of 900 for the account to reach 1000?

1.1.6   (a)   Smith's business receives an invoice from a supplier for 1000 with payment due within 30 days. The terms of payment allow for a discount of 2.5% if the bill is paid within 7 days. Smith does not have the cash on hand 7 days later, but decides to borrow the 975 to take advantage of the discount. What is the largest simple interest rate, as an annual rate, that Smith would be willing to pay on the loan?

        (b)   Repeat part (a) with 30 replaced by n, .025 replaced by j, and 7 replaced by $m(<n)$.

1.1.7   (a)   Jones invests 100,000 in a 180-day short term guaranteed investment certificate at a bank, based on simple interest at annual rate 7.5%. After 120 days, interest rates have risen to

9% and Jones would like to redeem the certificate early and reinvest in a 60-day certificate at the higher rate. In order for there to be no advantage in redeeming early and reinvesting at the higher rate, what early redemption penalty (from the accumulated book value of the investment certificate to time 120 days) should the bank charge at the time of early redemption?

(b) Jones wishes to invest funds for a one-year period. Jones can invest in a one-year guaranteed investment certificate at a rate of 8%. Jones can also invest in a 6-month GIC at annual rate 7.5%, and then reinvest the proceeds at the end of 6 months for another 6-month period. Find the minimum annual rate needed for a 6-month deposit at the end of the first 6-month period so that Jones accumulates at least the same amount with two successive 6-month deposits as she would with the one-year deposit.

1.1.8 (a) At an effective annual interest rate of 12%, calculate the number of years (including fractions) it will take for an investment of 1000 to accumulate to 3000.

(b) Repeat part (a) using the assumption that for fractions of a year, simple interest is applied.

(c) Repeat part (a) using an effective monthly interest rate of 1%.

(d) Suppose that an investment of 1000 accumulated to 3000 in exactly 10 years at effective annual rate of interest i. Calculate i.

(e) Repeat part (d) using an effective monthly rate of interest j. Calculate j.

1.1.9   For each of the following pairs of rates, determine which one
         results in more rapid investment growth.

    (a) 17-day rate of $\frac{3}{4}\%$ or 67-day rate of 3%

    (b) 17-day rate of $\frac{3}{2}\%$ or 67-day rate of 6%

1.1.10   Smith has 1000 with which she wishes to purchase units in a
         mutual fund. The investment dealer takes a 9% "front-end load"
         from the gross payment. The remainder (910 in this case) is used
         to purchase units in the fund, which are valued at 4.00 per unit at
         the time of purchase. Six months later the units have a value of
         5.00 and the fund managers claim that "the fund's unit value has
         experienced 25% growth in the past 6 months." When units of
         the fund are sold, there is a redemption fee of 1.5% of the value
         of the units redeemed. If Smith sells after 6 months, what is her
         6-month return for the period? Suppose instead of having grown
         to 5.00 after 6 months, the unit values had dropped to 3.50. What
         is Smith's 6-month return in this case?

1.1.11   Suppose that $i > 0$. Show that
    (i) if $0 < t < 1$ then $(1+i)^t < 1+i \cdot t$, and
    (ii) if $t > 1$ then $(1+i)^t > 1+i \cdot t$.

*1.1.12 If 1 is invested at periodic interest rate j, show that the amount of
         interest earned in the second period exceeds the amount of interest
         earned in the first period by j^2. Give a verbal explanation for this.

*1.1.13 (a) Show that at an effective annual compound interest rate of i,
         the amount of interest earned in successive years on an
         investment of 1 grows by a factor of $1+i$ and these amounts
         are i, $(1+i) \cdot i$, $(1+i)^2 \cdot i, \ldots, (1+i)^{n-1} \cdot i$ for the first, second,
         third$,\ldots,$ n^{th} year, respectively.

    (b) Using the fact that the amount of interest earned from time 0
         to time n is $(1+i)^n - 1$, derive a formula for the sum

$$1 + (1+i) + (1+i)^2 + \cdots + (1+i)^{n-1}.$$

*1.1.14 At time 0, Al borrows 1 from Bob and issues Bob a promissory note for the loan, with payment due at time $t < 1$ (years) at interest rate i per annum. At time $t_1 < t$, Bob sells the promissory note to Carl. Carl pays Bob an amount X so that Bob's yield during the time he held the promissory note (from time 0 to time t_1) can be quoted as j_1 per annum and Carl's yield can be quoted as j_2 per annum. Recall that interest on promissory notes is calculated using simple interest.

(a) Derive an expression for X in terms of j_1.

(b) Derive an expression for X in terms of j_2, and i.

(c) Show that if $j_1 = j_2$ then they are less than i.

(d) Show that if j_2 increases then j_1 decreases, so that as prevailing interest rates rise and Carl's yield increases, the value of Bob's promissory note decreases.

(e) Suppose that time 0 is March 15, time t is November 30, and time t_1 is June 12. Suppose also that $i = .13$. Find X and j_2 for each of the following values of j_1: .03, .08, .13, .18, .23. Note the pattern in the behavior of j_2 as it relates to j_1.

*1.1.15 (a) For an investment whose accumulation is based on simple interest, show that doubling the interest rate has the same effect on the accumulated amount as doubling the time for accumulation.

(b) For compound interest accumulation, show that the result in part (a) does not hold, and determine which has a greater effect on the accumulated amount.

*1.1.16 Suppose compound interest is in effect on an account at effective annual rate i. The account is opened at time 0 with deposit X_0, and a series of transactions (deposits or withdrawals) takes place in the account. The transactions are $X_1, X_2, \ldots, X_n$ (positive for deposit and negative for withdrawal), taking place at times $0 < t_1 < t_2 < \cdots < t_n$. Use mathematical induction to show that the two approaches in the solution of Example 1.3 result in the same balance in the account at time t_n, immediately after the transaction at that time (Hint: Assume that the two methods give the same balance after the transaction at time t_k and show it then follows that the two methods give the same balance at time t_{k+1}.)

*1.1.17 Suppose that $i > 0$. Prove each of the following inequalities:

(a) $(1+i) + (1+i)^3 > 2(1+i)^2$

(b) $(1+i)^{10} + (1+i)^{30} > 2(1+i)^{20}$

(c) $(1+i)^n + (1+i)^m > 2(1+i)^{(n+m)/2}$, if $m > n \geq 0$

*1.1.18 At an effective annual compound interest rate of $i > 0$, it is found that an investment doubles in a years, triples in b years, and 1 grows to 5 in c years.

(a) Is c greater than, equal to, or less than $\frac{3a+b}{2}$?

(b) To what amount does 10 grow in $3a + 2b$ years?

(c) In how many years will 1000 grow to 1200?

*1.1.19 Investment growth is sometimes plotted over time with the vertical axis transformed to an exponential scale, so that the numerical value of y is replaced by e^y or 10^y at the same position on the vertical axis. Show that the graph of compound interest growth over time with the vertical axis transformed in this way is linear.

*1.1.20 Smith deposits 1000 in Bank A on January 1. Bank A credits interest at annual rate $i = .15$. If Smith closes his account, he receives simple interest up to the time of withdrawal. Smith visits Bank B across the street and is told that he can open an account anytime that year and receive simple interest at annual rate $i = .145$, paid from the date of deposit to December 31. Smith consults his math of finance text and realizes that if he chooses the right day to close his account at Bank A and immediately redeposits the proceeds in a new account in Bank B he will maximize the return on his 1000 over that year. What is that day?

SECTION 1.2

1.2.1   A person has debts of 200 due July 1, 2004 and 300 due July 1, 2006. A payment of 100 was made on July 1, 2001 to reduce those debts. What additional amount payable on July 1, 2005 would cancel the remaining debts, assuming effective annual interest at rate 4%?

1.2.2   Ed buys a TV from Al for 480 by paying 50 in cash, 100 every three months for one year (four payments of 100), and a final payment in 15 months (three months after the final quarterly payment). Find the amount of the final payment if Al earns a 3-month compound interest rate of 3%. What is the final payment if Al earns a one-month rate of 1%?

1.2.3   A magazine offers a one-year subscription at a cost of 15 with renewal the following year at 16.50. Also offered is a two-year subscription at a cost of 28. What is the effective annual interest rate that makes the two-year subscription equivalent to two successive one-year subscriptions?

1.2.4   What is the present value of 1000 due in 10 years if the effective annual interest rate is 6% for each of the first 3 years, 7% for the next 4 years, and 9% for the final 3 years?

1.2.5   A manufacturer can automate a certain process by replacing 20 employees with a machine. The employees each earn 24,000 per year, payable on the last day of each month, with no salary increases scheduled for the next 4 years. If the machine has a lifetime of 4 years and interest is at a monthly rate of .75%, what is the most the manufacturer would pay for the machine (on the first day of a month) in each of the following cases?

(a) The machine has no scrap value at the end of 4 years.

(b) The machine has scrap value of 200,000 after 4 years.

(c) The machine has scrap value of 15% of its purchase price at the end of 4 years.

1.2.6   A contract calls for payments of 750 every 4 months for several years. Each payment is to be replaced by two payments of 367.85 each, one to be made 2 months before, and one to be made at the time of, the original payment. Find the 2-month rate of interest implied by this proposal if the new payment scheme is financially equivalent to the old one.

1.2.7   The parents of three children aged 1, 3, and 6 wish to set up a trust fund that will pay 25,000 to each child upon attainment of age 18, and 100,000 to each child upon attainment of age 21. If the trust fund will earn effective annual interest at 10%, what amount must the parents now invest in the trust fund?

1.2.8   Fisheries officials are stocking a barren lake with pike, whose number will increase annually at the rate of 40%. The plan is to prohibit fishing for two years on the lake, and then allow the removal of 5000 pike in each of the third and fourth years, so that the number remaining after the fourth year is the same as the original number stocked in the lake. Find the original number, assuming that stocking takes place at the start of the year and removal takes place at midyear.

1.2.9   Smith lends Jones 1000 on January 1, 2007 on the condition that Jones repay 100 on January 1, 2008, 100 on January 1, 2009, and 1000 on January 1, 2010. On July 1, 2008, Smith sells to Brown the rights to the remaining payments for 1000, so Jones makes all future payments to Brown. Let j be the 6-month rate earned on Smith's net transaction, and let k be the 6-month rate earned on Brown's net transaction. Are j and k equal? If not, which is larger?

1.2.10 Smith has debts of 1000 due now and 1092 due two years from now. He proposes to repay them with a single payment of 2000 one year from now. What is the implied effective annual interest rate if the replacement payment is accepted as equivalent to the original debts?

1.2.11 Calculate each of the following derivatives.

(a) $\frac{d}{di}(1+i)^n$ (b) $\frac{d}{di}v^n$ (c) $\frac{d}{dn}(1+i)^n$ (d) $\frac{d}{dn}v^n$

1.2.12 At time 0 a balance of amount B_0 is in an account earning simple interest at rate i per period, paid at the end of the period. Various deposits and withdrawals are made during the period, with a transaction of amount a_k made at time t_k for $k = 1, 2, \ldots, n$ where $0 < t_k < 1$. ($a_k > 0$ indicates a deposit to the account, and $a_k < 0$ indicates a withdrawal). Assume that $t = 1$ is the reference point (focal date) for the account and interest on deposits and withdrawals begins accruing at the time of the deposit or withdrawal.

(a) Find an expression for B_1, the account balance at $t = 1$.

(b) Find an expression for B, the average balance in the account during the period from time 0 to time 1.

(c) Show that $B_1 = B_0 + \sum\limits_{k=1}^{n} a_k + \overline{B} \cdot i$.

1.2.13 A 182-day Canadian T-bill for 100 has a quoted price of 94.771 and a quoted yield rate of 11.07%. Show that any price from 94.767 to 94.771 inclusive has a corresponding yield rate of 11.07%. This shows that the yield rate quote to .01% is not as accurate a measure for the T-bill as is the price to 10^{ths} of a cent.

1.2.14 Smith just bought a 100,000 182-day Canadian T-bill at a quoted yield rate of 10%.

(a) Find the price, P, that Smith paid for the T-bill.

(b) What is the volatility of the bill's value with respect to the nominal annual yield rate (i.e., what is $\frac{dP}{di}$)? Use the differential to approximate the change in the price of the T-bill if the yield rate changes to 10.1% immediately after Smith purchases it.

(c) Suppose the T-bill matures in 91-days instead of 182 days. Find the price and volatility with respect to the yield rate at a quoted nominal yield of 10%. What happens to the volatility with respect to the yield rate as a T-bill approaches its due date?

*1.2.15 Smith wishes to buy a TV set and is offered a time payment plan whereby he makes 24 monthly payments of 30 each starting now. Smith wants the payments to start in 2 months rather than now. If interest is at a one-month interest rate of 1%, what is the present value now of the saving to Smith if the seller agrees to Smith's terms?

*1.2.16 Starting in 2005, Smith receives a dividend check on the 15th of each January, April, July, and October. He immediately deposits it into an account earning a monthly interest rate of .75%, crediting interest on the last day of each calendar month, and paying simple interest for amounts on deposit for less than a month. The dividend checks are 100 each in 2005, and increase to 105 each in 2006. What is the account balance just after interest is credited on December 31, 2006?

*1.2.17 Smith receives a paycheck of 3500 on the last day of each month, and immediately deposits all but 1000 of it in a bank account. The first deposit is on December 31, 2004. Smith deposits an additional 1000 on the 15th of every month. The account pays an annual interest rate of 10%. Find the balance in the account on March 31, 2005, after the deposit is made and interest is credited, in each of the following cases.

(a) Simple interest based on minimum monthly balance and credited on the last day of March (no interest in January or February)

(b) Simple interest based on minimum daily balance and credited on the last day of March (no interest in January or February)

(c) Same as (a) but with interest credited on the last day of every month

(d) Same as (b) but with interest credited on the last day of every month

It follows from Exercise 1.2.12 that use of minimum daily balances for simple interest calculations is equivalent to using average balances. That is, minimum daily balances with interest credited at the end of each quarter is equivalent to basing interest for the quarter on the average balance, and minimum daily balances with interest credited at the end of each month is equivalent to basing interest for the month on the average balance for the month.

*1.2.18 David can receive one of the following two payment streams:

(i) 100 at time 0, 200 at time n, and 300 at time $2n$.

(ii) 600 at time 10

At an effective annual interest rate of i, the present values of the two streams are equal. Given $v^n = 0.75941$, determine i.

SECTION 1.3

1.3.1   Suppose the nominal annual rate is 12%. Find the equivalent effective annual rates for $m = 1, 2, 3, 4, 6, 8, 12, 52, 365, \infty$.

1.3.2   Find the present value of 1000 due at the end of 10 years if
(a) $i^{(2)} = .09$,   (b) $i^{(6)} = .09$, and   (c) $i^{(12)} = .09$.

1.3.3   Mountain Bank pays interest at rate $i^{(2)} = .15$. River Bank pays interest compounded daily. What minimum nominal annual rate must River Bank pay in order to be as attractive as Mountain Bank?

1.3.4   Eric deposits X into a savings account at time 0, which pays interest at a nominal rate of i, compounded semiannually. Mike deposits $2X$ into a different savings account at time 0, which pays simple interest at an annual rate of i. Eric and Mike earn the same amount of interest during the last 6 months of the 8th year. Calculate i.

1.3.5   Smith receives income from his investments in Japanese currency (yen). Smith does not convert the yen to dollars, but invests the yen in a term deposit that pays interest in yen. He finds a bank that will issue such a term deposit, but it charges a 1% commission on each initial placement and on each rollover. The current interest rate on the yen deposits is a nominal annual rate of 3.25% convertible quarterly for a 3-month deposit. To keep his yen available, Smith decides to roll over the deposit every 3 months. What is the effective annual after-commission rate that Smith earns?

1.3.6 The nominal interest rate $i^{(m)}$ can be defined for values of $m < 1$. Algebraically the definition follows the relationship in Equation (1.4).

(a) If $i = .10$, find the equivalent $i^{(.5)}$, $i^{(.25)}$, $i^{(.1)}$, and $i^{(.01)}$. Rank the values in increasing size, and compare with the relationship $i^{(m)} < i$ for $m > 1$.

(b) Find the equivalent effective annual i if (i) $i^{(.5)} = .10$, (ii) $i^{(.25)} = .10$, (iii) $i^{(.1)} = .10$, and (iv) $i^{(.01)} = .10$.

1.3.7 Smith buys a 1000 Canada savings bond, with an issue date of November 1, paying interest at 11.25% per year. The bond can be cashed in anytime after January 1 of the following year, and it will pay simple interest during the first year of $\frac{1}{12}$ of the annual interest for every completed month since November 1. The government allows purchasers to pay for their bonds as late as November 9, with full interest still paid for November. Smith pays 1000 on November 9 and cashes in the bond on the following January 1. What is his equivalent effective annual rate of interest for his transaction?

*1.3.8 (a) Smith buys a one-year guaranteed investment certificate with principal of X. (A Canadian GIC has an interest rate guaranteed for the term of the certificate, a significant penalty for redemption prior to the specified maturity date, and principal and interest usually secured by a government deposit insurance program.) The annual interest rate quoted on the certificate is 9%, with interest payable monthly, on the monthly anniversary date of the certificate. Immediately upon receiving an interest payment. Smith reinvests it in an account earning a nominal annual rate of 9% convertible monthly, with interest compounded from a deposit date. Show that after one year Smith has the same total that she would have had if she had deposited the full X in the account and left it on deposit for the year.

(b) Smith is considering two one-year guaranteed investment certificates. The first pays 9.75% on the maturity date and the second has an annual rate of 9.5% with interest paid semiannually. Suppose in the case of the second GIC Smith is able to reinvest the first interest payment for the rest of the year. What equivalent effective annual rate does Smith require for the reinvested interest payment in order that the two GIC's be equivalent?

*1.3.9 (a) Show that if $j > 0$ then the function $f(m) = \left(1 + \frac{j}{m}\right)^m$ is an increasing function of m.

(b) Show that if $j > 0$ then $g(m) = m\left[(1+j)^{1/m} - 1\right]$ is a decreasing function of m.

(c) Use l'Hospital's Rule to show that $\lim_{m \to \infty} f(m) = e^j$ for the function $f(m)$ defined in part (a).

(d) Show that $\lim_{m \to \infty} g(m) = \ln(1+j)$ for the function $g(m)$ defined in part (b).

*1.3.10 Bank A has an effective annual rate of 18%. Bank B has a nominal annual rate of 17%. What is the smallest whole number of times per year that Bank B must compound its interest in order that the rate at Bank B be at least as attractive as that at Bank A on an effective annual basis? Repeat the exercise with a nominal rate of 16% at Bank B.

*1.3.11 The nominal interest rate $i^{(m)}$ can be defined for values of $m < 1$. Algebraically the definition follows the relationship in Equation (1.4) . For the functions $f(m)$ and $g(m)$ defined in Exercise 1.3.9, find the limits as m approaches 0.

*1.3.12 Nominal interest can be defined even if m is not an integer. The algebraic definition is still valid. Suppose a bank advertises an annual rate of 10% on short-term deposits. An investor chooses a term of 45 days with interest calculated on the basis of simple interest. This nominal rate of 10% can be expressed as $i^{(m)}$ for an appropriate m. Find m and the equivalent effective annual rate of interest.

SECTION 1.4

1.4.1   Let j be the compound interest rate for the T-year period from time r to time $r+T$, and let d_j be the corresponding rate of discount for that time period. Show that (a) $d_j = \frac{j}{1+j}$ and (b) $j = \frac{d_j}{1-d_j}$.

1.4.2   A store has a normal markup of 30% on the purchase price of goods bought at wholesale. During a promotion the markup is only 15%. What percent reduction in the retail price will result?

1.4.3   A discounted note of face amount X, due in one-half year, is valued today at 4992. Find X under each of the following interest calculation methods.

(a) Compound interest at effective annual rate 8%

(b) Simple interest at annual rate 8%

(c) Compound discount at effective annual rate 8%

(d) Simple discount at annual rate 8%

1.4.4   Bruce and Robbie each open up new bank accounts at time 0. Bruce deposits 100 into his bank account, and Robbie deposits 50 into his. Each account earns an effective annual discount rate of d. The amount of interest earned in Bruce's account during the 11th year is equal to X. The amount of interest earned in Robbie's account during the 17th year is also equal to X. Calculate X.

1.4.5   Given an effective annual discount rate of d, show that, with compounding, the accumulated value after n years of an initial investment of amount 1 is $(1-d)^{-n}$. In other words, if an amount X due in n years has present value 1, then $X = (1-d)^{-n}$.

1.4.6   (a) Smith has a promissory note due in n days. A bank will buy the note from Smith using a simple discount rate d. What is the equivalent simple interest rate i earned by the bank over the period? What happens to i as n increases?

(b) A lender wishes to earn interest at an annual simple rate of 11%. What annual simple discount rate should be charged on a loan for 1 year? for 6 months? for 1 month?

1.4.7 For the 91-day U.S. Treasury Bill in Example 1.11, check the consistency of the numerical values of the discount rate, investment rate, and price per 100.

1.4.8 Smith buys a 182-day US T-Bill at a price which corresponds to a quoted annual discount rate for 182-day T-bills of 10%. 91 days later Smith sells the T-Bill, at which time the prevailing quoted annual discount rate of 91-day T-Bills is also 10%. Find the actual rate of return (91-day interest rate) that Smith earned during the time he held the T-Bill.

1.4.9 If the 3-month compound interest rate is 3%, find the equivalent 1-month, 2-month, 3-month, 4-month, 6-month, and 1-year compound interest and discount rates.

1.4.10 Show that equivalent nominal interest and discount rates $i^{(m)}$ and $d^{(m)}$ satisfy the relationships

(a) $d^{(m)} = \dfrac{i^{(m)}}{1+\frac{i^{(m)}}{m}}$ and

(b) $i^{(m)} = \dfrac{d^{(m)}}{1-\frac{d^{(m)}}{m}}$,

and show that these relationships are consistent with the results of Exercise 1.4.1 and Examples 1.10 and 1.12.

1.4.11 Jeff deposits 10 into a fund today and 20 fifteen years later. Interest is credited at a nominal discount rate of d compounded quarterly for the first 10 years, and at a nominal interest rate of 6% compounded semiannually thereafter. The accumulated balance in the fund at the end of 30 years is 100. Calculate d.

*1.4.12 Bob borrows 1000 from Ed at effective annual interest rate i, agreeing to repay in full at the end of one year. When the year is up, Bob has no money, but they agree that he can repay one year later in such a way that the effective annual discount rate d in the second year is numerically equal to the interest rate i in the first year. At the end of the second year Bob pays 1200. What is i in the first year?

*1.4.13 Smith has 960 to invest on January 1. He has the following two investment options.

(a) He can buy a 6-month 1000 T-bill for a purchase price of 960, and reinvest the proceeds on July 1 at a 6-month interest rate j.

(b) He can buy a one-year 1000 T-bill for a purchase price of 920 and invest the remaining 40 in an account earning interest at the same effective 6-month interest rate j as in option (a).

If options (a) and (b) result in the same accumulated amount on December 31, including interest and T-bill maturity, find the value of j (assuming $j < 10\%$). The period from January 1 to July 1 is regarded as exactly ½-year and the time from January 1 to December 31 is regarded as exactly 1 year for time measurement.

*1.4.14 (a) Suppose the nominal rate of discount compounded semi-annually is 100%, so that the 6-month discount rate is 50%. What is the present value at time 0 of an amount of 1 due in 1 year? What is the amount of discount from time $t = 1$ back to time $t = ½$? What is the amount of discount from time $t = ½$ back to time $t = 0$? Note that the further back in time discounting is applied, the smaller the actual amount of discount for the corresponding period, so that although the effective 6-month discount rate is 50% for both halves of the year, the amount of discount in the second half is .50 but the amount in the first half is only .25, for a total of .75 (and an equivalent effective annual discount rate of .75). This is the opposite of what occurs when compounding interest forward, and it accounts for the fact that an equivalent effective rate of discount is smaller than the corresponding nominal rate of discount.

(b) What is the largest that $d^{(m)}$ could be?

(c) Show that the function $f(m) = \left(1 - \frac{d}{m}\right)^m$ is increasing (i.e., $f'(m) > 0$).

(d) Show that $g(m) = m\left[1 - (1-d)^{1/m}\right]$ is increasing.

(e) Show that $\lim_{m \to \infty} f(m) = e^{-d}$.

(f) Show that $\lim\limits_{m\to\infty} g(m) = d^{(\infty)} = -\ln(1-d)$. Suppose d and i are equivalent discount and interest rates. Recall from part (d) of Exercise 1.3.9 that $i^{(\infty)} = \ln(1+i)$. Show that $d^{(\infty)} = i^{(\infty)}$.

*1.4.15 Given any set of equivalent positive rates $d^{(6)}$, $d^{(12)}$, $i^{(6)}$, and $i^{(12)}$, show that $\dfrac{d^{(12)}}{d^{(6)}} > \dfrac{i^{(12)}}{i^{(6)}}$.

SECTION 1.5

1.5.1 At time $t = 0$, 1 is deposited into each of Fund X and Fund Y. Fund X accumulates at a force of interest $\delta_t = \frac{t^2}{k}$. Fund Y accumulates at a nominal rate of discount of 8% per annum convertible semiannually. At time $t = 5$, the accumulated value of Fund X equals the accumulated value of Fund Y. Determine k.

1.5.2 Tawny makes a deposit into a bank account which credits interest at a nominal interest rate of 10% per annum, convertible semiannually. At the same time, Fabio deposits 1000 into a different bank account, which is credited with simple interest. At the end of 5 years, the forces of interest on the two accounts are equal, and Fabio's account has accumulated to Z. Determine Z.

1.5.3 Ernie makes deposits of 100 at time 0, and X at time 3. The fund grows at a force of interest $\delta_t = \frac{t^2}{100}$, $t > 0$. The amount of interest earned from time 3 to time 6 is X. Calculate X.

1.5.4 Bruce deposits 100 into a bank account. His account is credited interest at a nominal rate of interest convertible semiannually. At the same time, Peter deposits 100 into a separate account. Peter's account is credited interest at a force of interest of δ. After 7¼ years, the value of each account is 200. Calculate $i - \delta$.

1.5.5 An investment of 1000 accumulates to 1360.86 at the end of 5 years. If the force of interest is δ during the first year and 1.5δ in each subsequent year, find the equivalent effective annual interest rate in the first year.

1.5.6   Smith forecasts that interest rates will rise over a 5-year period
         according to a force of interest function given by $\delta_t = .08 + \frac{.025t}{t+1}$
         for $0 \le t \le 5$.

(a) According to this scheme, what is the average annual
    compound effective rate for the 5-year period?

(b) What are the equivalent effective annual rates for each of
    years 1, 2, 3, 4, and 5?

(c) What is the present value at $t = 2$ of 1000 due at $t = 4$?

1.5.7   The present value of K payable after 2 years is 960. If the force of
         interest is cut in half, the present value becomes 1200. What is the
         present value if the effective annual discount rate is cut in half?

1.5.8   If the force of interest is doubled, are the corresponding
         equivalent effective annual interest and discount rates more or
         less than doubled?

1.5.9   A customer is offered an investment where interest is calculated
         according to the following force of interest:

$$\delta_t = \begin{cases} .02t & 0 \le t \le 3 \\ .045 & t > 3 \end{cases}$$

The customer invests 1000 at time $t = 0$. What nominal rate of
interest, compounded quarterly, is earned over the first four-year
period?

1.5.10 $A_1(t)$ is an accumulation function at force of interest $\delta_t^{(1)}$, and $A_2(t)$
         is an accumulation function at force $\delta_t^{(2)}$. Let $A_1(0) = A_2(0) = 1$.
         What is $A(t)$ for $\delta_t = \delta_t^{(1)} + \delta_t^{(2)}$, in terms of $A_1(t)$ and $A_2(t)$?

*1.5.11 At time 0, K is deposited into Fund X, which accumulates at a
         force of interest $\delta_t = 0.006t^2$. At time m, $2K$ is deposited into
         Fund Y, which accumulates at an effective annual interest rate of
         10%. At time n, where $n > m$, the accumulated value of each
         fund is $4K$. Determine m.

*1.5.12 On January 1 Smith deposits 1000 into an account earning $i^{(4)} = .08$ with interest credited on the last day of March, June, September, and December. If Smith closes the account during the year, simple interest is paid on the balance from the most recent interest credit date.

(a) What is Smith's close-out balance on July 19?

(b) Suppose all four quarters in the year are considered equal, and time is measured in years. Derive expressions for Smith's accumulated amount function $A(t)$, the close-out balance at time t. Consider separately the four intervals $0 \leq t \leq .25$, $.25 \leq t \leq .50$, $.50 \leq t \leq .75$ and $.75 \leq t \leq 1$.

(c) Using part (b), show that if $0 \leq t \leq .25$, then it follows that $\delta_t = \delta_{t+.25} = \delta_{t+.50} = \delta_{t+.75}$.

*1.5.13 (a) Find an expression for the $\frac{1}{m}$-year discount rate from time t to time $t + \frac{1}{m}$ in terms of an accumulated amount function A.

(b) If $d^{(m)}$ is the nominal annual discount rate corresponding to the rate in part (a), find an expression for $d^{(m)}$ in terms of A.

(c) Take the limit as $m \to \infty$ of the expression for $d^{(m)}$ in part (b) to show that $d^{(\infty)} = \dfrac{A'(t)}{A(t)} = \delta_t$.

*1.5.14 Find the derivatives with respect to δ of i, d, $i^{(m)}$, and $d^{(m)}$.

*1.5.15 Express $\frac{d}{dt}\delta_t$ in terms of $A(t)$ and its derivatives.

*1.5.16 (a) It was shown in Exercise 1.1.11 that over t years, $0 < t < 1$, accumulation to time t at simple interest exceeded accumulation at compound interest. Show that for a given rate of interest i, the maximum of $(1+it) - (1+i)^t$ occurs at $t_i = \frac{1}{\delta}[\ln i - \ln \delta]$.

(b) Show that $\lim_{i \to 0} t_i = \frac{1}{2}$ and $\lim_{i \to \infty} t_1 = 1$.

*1.5.17 Show that $\lim_{i\to\infty} = \frac{i}{\delta} = \infty$, $\lim_{i\to\infty} \frac{\delta}{d} = \infty$, and $\lim_{i\to\infty} \frac{i/\delta}{\delta/d} = \infty$.

*1.5.18 (a) Suppose an accumulated amount function is a polynomial of the form $A(t) = a_0 + a_1 \cdot t + \cdots + a_n \cdot t^n$, where $a_n > 0$ and $n > 0$. Show that $\lim_{t\to\infty} \delta_t = 0$.

(b) Let $\delta_t = \frac{k}{\sqrt{t}}$, $K > 0$. Find an expression for the accumulation function $A(t)$, where $A(0) = 1$. Show $\lim_{t\to\infty} \frac{A(t)}{1+it} = \infty$ for any $i > 0$, and $\lim_{t\to\infty} \frac{A(t)}{(1+i)^t} = 0$.

SECTION 1.6

1.6.1 (a) Suppose that for the coming year inflation is forecast at an effective annual rate of $r = .15$ and interest is forecast at effective annual rate $i = .10$. What will be the corresponding real, or inflation-adjusted rate of interest for the coming year?

(b) Using the values of r and i in part (a), suppose Smith borrows 100,000 for a year at $i = .10$, and buys 100,000 units of a certain item that has a current cost of 1 per unit. Suppose the price of this item is tied to the rate of inflation $(r = .15)$. One year from now Smith sells the items at the inflated price. What is his net gain on this transaction? (This illustrates that during times when inflation rates exceed interest rates, there is great incentive to borrow at the negative real rate of interest. This demand by borrowers is a factor in the inevitable correction that leads to the interest rate becoming larger than the inflation rate.)

1.6.2 A person's savings earn an effective rate of $i = .12$ on which 45% income tax is paid. If the inflation rate is 10% per year, what is the annual after-tax real rate of return?

1.6.3   Smith earned gross income of 40,000 last year. According to the income tax structure, taxes are 25% of the first 20,000 of gross income plus 50% of the excess over 20,000. Thus Smith paid 15,000 in taxes and had after-tax income (ATI) of 25,000. Inflation is forecast at 5% this year, and Smith's gross income will rise by 5% to 42,000. The government is considering a new tax structure of 25% of the first 21,000 plus 50% of the excess over 21,000 (full indexing).

(a) Show that if the government adopts the new tax structure then the real annual rate of growth in both Smith's ATI and in his paid taxes is 0%.

(b) Find the real annual rate of growth in Smith's ATI and his taxes paid if the government continues with the old scheme (no indexing).

1.6.4   If the force of interest for the coming year will be δ and the force of inflation will be δ_r, show that the inflation-adjusted force of interest is $\delta - \delta_r$.

1.6.5   The newly independent nation of Falkvinas has a unit of currency called the Britarg. In the coming year inflation in Falkvinas will be 100%, whereas Canada's inflation rate will be 14%. A Canadian investor can earn interest in Canada on Canadian dollars at an annual rate of 18%. What effective annual rate must an investor earn on Britargs in Falkvinas in order that his real rate of interest match the real rate earned by an investor in Canadian dollars?

1.6.6   Smith will need 1000 US dollars one year from now. He can invest funds in a US dollar account for the next year at 9%. Alternatively Smith can now buy Canadian dollars at the exchange rate of 0.73 US = 1 CDN, and invest in a Canadian dollar account for the next year at 10%. If both of these alternatives require the same amount of currency today, what is the implied exchange rate between the two currencies one year from now?

1.6.7   Show that the present value of $(1+r)^n$ due in n years at effective annual rate i is equal to the present value of 1 due in n years at effective annual rate $\frac{i-r}{1+r}$.

*1.6.8 (a) In an attempt to reduce interest rates during times of high inflation, a government allows banks to issue "indexed term deposits" upon which only the "real" interest earned is taxed. If inflation is at rate r, and the bank pays interest at real rate i', then on a one-year deposit of initial amount 1 an investor receives inflation-adjusted principal of $1+r$, plus "real interest" on the inflation-adjusted principal of $i'(1+r)$, for a total amount paid at year end of $(1+r)(1+i')$. The investor pays tax only on the real interest paid [i.e., on $i'(1+r)$.] This is compared to the usual term-deposit situation in which interest at rate i is paid at the end of the year. Derive expressions in terms of i, i', r and t_x, (where $0 < t_x < 1$ is the investor's tax rate) for the real after-tax rates of return on the indexed term deposit and on the standard term deposit .

       (b) Suppose $r = 12\%$ and a bank offers inflation-adjusted term deposits at a real rate of 2%. What rate of interest would an investor have to earn on a standard term deposit in order to have the same after-inflation, after-tax return as on the indexed term deposit if the investor has a tax rate of

           (i) 0%,   (ii) 25%,   (iii) 40%,   (iv) 60%?

CHAPTER 2

VALUATION OF ANNUITIES

Many financial transactions involve a series of payments, such as periodic dividend payments on a holding of common stock, monthly payments on a loan, or annual interest payments on a coupon bond. It is often the case (as in the loan and bond examples) that the payments are made at regularly scheduled intervals of time. In the examples in Chapter 1 that dealt with transactions involving more than one payment, each payment was treated and valued separately. When a transaction involves a number of payments made in a systematic way, it is often possible to apply algebraic methods to simplify the valuation of the series. In this chapter we will develop methods for valuing a series of payments.

Prior to the availability of sophisticated calculators and computer spreadsheet programs, it was important to have algebraic representations for series of payments that required as little calculation by hand as possible. Many of the algebraic methods developed in the past for representing series of payments are no longer important for calculation purposes, but some remain important for the insight that they may provide in analyzing and valuing a series of payments.

The generic term used to describe a series of periodic payments is **annuity**. In a life insurance context, an annuity is a "life-contingent" series of payments, and the payments are contingent on the survival of a specific individual or group of individuals. The more precise term for a series of payments that are not contingent on the occurrence of any specified events is **annuity-certain** (an annuity whose payments will definitely be made). Since this book deals almost entirely with annuities-certain, we shall use the term annuity to refer to an annuity-certain, unless otherwise specified.

The calculations in many of the examples presented here can be done in an efficient way using a financial calculator or computer spreadsheet program. Calculator methods are considered in a comprehensive way in the Appendix at the end of the book and may be referred to only occasionally in this

Chapter. There is a collection of computer spreadsheet illustrations, including illustrations of annuity calculations available at the website of the publisher of this book, www.actexmadriver.com. The presentation here emphasizes understanding the algebraic relationships involved in annuity valuation.

A key algebraic relationship used in valuing a series of payments is the familiar geometric series summation formula

$$1+x+x^2+\cdots+x^k \; = \; \frac{1-x^{k+1}}{1-x} \; = \; \frac{x^{k+1}-1}{x-1}. \qquad (2.1)$$

This is illustrated in the following example.

EXAMPLE 2.1   (*Accumulation of a level payment annuity*)

The federal government sends Smith a family allowance payment of $30 every month for Smith's child. Smith deposits the payments in a bank account on the last day of each month. The account earns interest at the annual rate of 9% compounded monthly and payable on the last day of each month, on the minimum monthly balance. If the first payment is deposited on May 31, 1998, what is the account balance on December 31, 2009, including the payment just made?

SOLUTION

The one-month compound interest rate is $j = .0075$. The balance in the account on June 30, 1998, including the payment just deposited and the accumulated value of the May 31 deposit is

$$C_2 \; = \; 30(1+j)+30 \; = \; 30[(1+j)+1].$$

The balance on July 31, 1998 is

$$C_3 \; = \; C_2(1+j)+30 \; = \; 30\big[(1+j)+1\big](1+j)+30 \; = \; 30\big[(1+j)^2+(1+j)+1\big].$$

Continuing in this way we see that the balance just after the mth deposit is $C_m \; = \; 30\big[(1+j)^{m-1}+\cdots+(1+j)^2+(1+j)+1\big]$, the accumulation of those first m deposits. The balance on December 31, 2009, just after the 140th deposit is

$$30\left[(1+j)^{139}+(1+j)^{138}+\cdots+(1+j)+1\right]$$

$$=\ 30\left[\frac{(1+j)^{140}-1}{(1+j)-1}\right]\ =\ 30\left[\frac{(1.0075)^{140}-1}{.0075}\right]\ =\ 7385.91.$$

We have applied the geometric series formula in the equation above. The following line diagram illustrates the accumulation in the account from one deposit to the next.

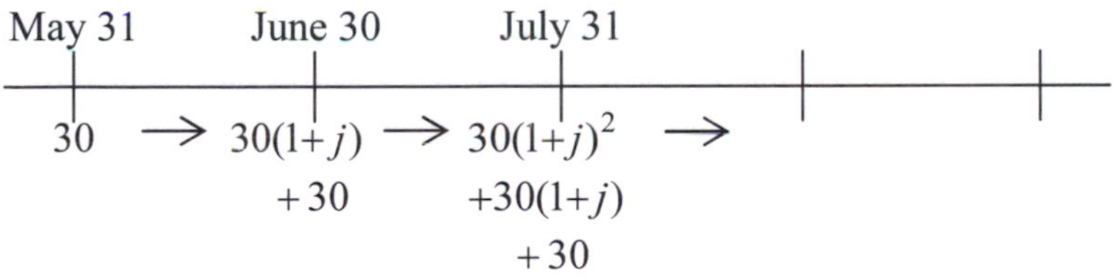

FIGURE 2.1

2.1 LEVEL PAYMENT ANNUITIES

2.1.1 ACCUMULATED VALUE OF AN ANNUITY

In Example 2.1, the expression for the aggregate accumulated value on December 31, 2009 is

$$30\left[(1+j)^{139}+(1+j)^{138}+\cdots+(1+j)+1\right]$$

$$=\ 30(1+j)^{139}+30(1+j)^{138}+\cdots+30(1+j)+30.$$

The right hand side of the equation is the sum of the accumulated values of the individual deposits. $30(1+j)^{139}$ is the accumulated value on December 31, 2009 of the deposit made on May 31, 1998, $30(1+j)^{138}$ is the accumulated value on December 31, 2009 of the deposit made on June 30, 1998, and so on.

In general, when valuing a series of payments, it is often efficient to consider the corresponding series of values of the individual payments, rather than updating the accumulated total from one payment point to the next. Let us consider a series of n payments (or deposits) of amount 1 each, made at equally spaced intervals of time, and for which interest is at compound rate i per payment period, with interest credited on payment dates. The accumulated value of the series of payments, valued at the time of (and including) the final payment, can be represented as the sum of the accumulated values of the individual payments. This is

$$(1+i)^{n-1}+(1+i)^{n-2}+\cdots+(1+i)+1 \; = \; \frac{(1+i)^{n}-1}{(1+i)-1} \; = \; \frac{(1+i)^{n}-1}{i} \quad (2.2)$$

This is illustrated in the following diagram. We can see from the diagram that since the valuation point is the time that the nth deposit is made, this is actually $n-1$ periods after the first deposit. Therefore the first deposit has grown with compound interest for $n-1$ periods.

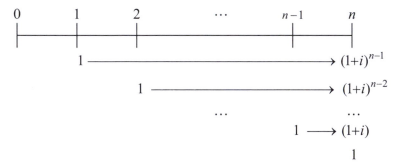

FIGURE 2.2

The accumulated value of the general annuity with level payments of 1 each per period for n periods considered above has standard actuarial notation and terminology associated with it. The symbol $s_{\overline{n}|\,i}$ denotes the accumulated value, at the time of (and including) the final payment of a series of n payments of 1 each made at equally spaced intervals of time, where the rate of interest per payment period is i.

$$s_{\overline{n}|\,i} \; = \; (1+i)^{n-1}+(1+i)^{n-2}+\cdots+(1+i)+1 \; = \; \sum_{t=0}^{n-1}(1+i)^{t} \; = \; \frac{(1+i)^{n}-1}{i}. \quad (2.3)$$

This and other related annuity symbols can be used to efficiently represent transactions that involve one or more series of level payments. If there is no possibility of confusion with other interest rates in a particular situation, the subscript i is omitted from $s_{\overline{n}|i}$ and the accumulated value is denoted $s_{\overline{n}|}$, without the subscript i. The number of payments in the series is called the term of the annuity, and the time between successive payments is called the payment period, or **frequency**. Note that for any interest rate i, $s_{\overline{1}|i} = 1$, but if $i > 0$ and $n > 1$, then $s_{\overline{n}|i} > n$ because of interest on earlier deposits.

It should be emphasized that the $s_{\overline{n}|i}$ notation can be used to express the accumulated value of an annuity provided the following conditions are met:

(1) the payments are of equal amount;

(2) the payments are made at equal intervals of time, with the same frequency as the interest rate is compounded;

(3) the accumulated value is found at the time of and including the final payment.

A series of payments whose value is found at the time of the final payment is referred to in actuarial terminology as an accumulated **annuity-immediate**. We often see a series of payments described with the phrase "payments occur at the end of each year (or month)," with a valuation made at the end of n years. The conventional interpretation of this phrase is to regard the valuation as an accumulated annuity-immediate.

Equation 2.3 can be rewritten as

$$(1+i)^n \;=\; i \cdot s_{\overline{n}|i} + 1 \;=\; i \cdot \left[(1+i)^{n-1} + (1+i)^{n-2} + \cdots + (1+i) + 1 \right] + 1.$$

We can interpret this expression in the following way. Suppose that a single amount of 1 is invested at time 0 at periodic interest rate i, so that an interest payment of i is generated at the end of each period. Suppose further that each interest payment is reinvested and continues to earn interest at rate i. This is allowed to continue for n periods. Then the accumulation of the reinvested interest, along with the return of the initial amount 1 invested (the right hand side of the equation above), must be equal to the compound accumulation of 1 at rate i per period invested for n periods.

EXAMPLE 2.2

(*Accumulated value of an annuity at the time of final payment*)
What level amount must be deposited on May 1 and November 1 each year
from 1998 to 2005, inclusive, to accumulate to 7000 on November 1, 2005
if the nominal annual rate of interest compounded semi-annually is 9%?

SOLUTION

A first step in translating the verbal description of this annuity into an
algebraic form is to determine the number of deposits being made. There
are a total of 16 deposits (2 per year for each of the 8 years from 1998 to
2005 inclusive) and they occur every $\frac{1}{2}$-year. As a second step, we note
that the $\frac{1}{2}$-year interest rate is 4.5%, and the $\frac{1}{2}$-year payment period
corresponds to the $\frac{1}{2}$-year interest compounding period. If the level
amount deposited every $\frac{1}{2}$-year is denoted by X, the accumulated value
of the deposits at the time of the 16th deposit is

$$X \cdot \left[(1.045)^{15} + (1.045)^{14} + \cdots + 1.045 + 1 \right]$$

$$= \quad X \cdot \frac{(1.045)^{16} - 1}{.045} \quad = \quad X \cdot s_{\overline{16}|.045} \quad = \quad 22.719337X$$

(note that the factor $(1.045)^{15}$ arises as a result of there being 15 half-
year periods from the time of the first deposit on May 1, 1998 to the time
of the 16th deposit on November 1, 2005). Then

$$X \quad = \quad \frac{7000}{s_{\overline{16}|.045}} \quad = \quad \frac{7000}{22.719337} \quad = \quad 308.11. \qquad \square$$

All financial calculators have functions that calculate the accumulated
value of an annuity at the time of the final payment if the payment amount,
number of payments, and interest rate are known. The calculator
comments in the Appendix provide a number of examples of this for two
popular financial calculators, the Texas Instruments BA II PLUS and the
Hewlett-Packard HP-12C.

Accumulated Value of an Annuity Some Time After the Final Payment

Occasionally after a series of deposits is completed, the accumulated balance continues to accumulate with interest only. The following example illustrates this.

EXAMPLE 2.3

(*Accumulated value of an annuity some time after the final payment*)
Suppose that in Example 2.1, Smith's child is born in April, 1998 and the first payment is received in May (and deposited at the end of May). The payments continue and the deposits are made at the end of each month until (and including the month of) the child's 16th birthday. The payments cease after the 16th birthday, but the balance in the account continues to accumulate with interest until the end of the month of the child's 21st birthday. What is the balance in the account at that time?

SOLUTION

At the end of the month of the child's 16th birthday, Smith makes the 192nd deposit at the end of April, 2014 (there are 12 deposits per year for 16 years for a total of 192 deposits) into the account. The accumulated value at the end of the month of the child's 16th birthday is

$$30\left[(1.0075)^{191} + (1.0075)^{190} + \cdots + (1.0075) + 1\right]$$

$$= \ 30 \cdot s_{\overline{192}|.0075} \ = \ 30 \cdot \frac{(1.0075)^{192} - 1}{.0075} \ = \ 12,792.31.$$

Five years (60 months) later, at the end of the month of the child's 21st birthday, the account will have grown, with interest only, to

$$12,792.31(1.0075)^{60} = 20,028.68. \qquad \Box$$

We have seen that the value at the time of the nth deposit of a series of n deposits of amount 1 each is $\frac{(1+i)^n - 1}{i} = s_{\overline{n}|}$. If there are no further deposits but the balance continues to grow with compound interest, then the accumulated value k periods after the nth deposit is

$$\frac{(1+i)^n - 1}{i} \times (1+i)^k \quad = \quad s_{\overline{n}|} \times (1+i)^k$$

$$= \quad \textit{Value at time } n \times \textit{growth factor from time } n \textit{ to time } n+k.$$

This can be also be represented in the following way.

$$s_{\overline{n}|} \times (1+i)^k \quad = \quad \frac{(1+i)^n - 1}{i} \times (1+i)^k$$

$$= \quad \frac{(1+i)^{n+k} - (1+i)^k}{i}$$

$$= \quad \frac{(1+i)^{n+k} - 1}{i} - \frac{(1+i)^k - 1}{i}$$

$$= \quad s_{\overline{n+k}|} - s_{\overline{k}|}. \tag{2.4}$$

Using Equation (2.4), the accumulated value of the account on April 30, 2019 (the end of the month of the child's 21st birthday) in Example 2.3 can be written as $30\left[s_{\overline{252}|} - s_{\overline{60}|}\right]$.

Figures 2.3a and 2.3b below illustrate the formulations given in Equation 2.4. If the annuity payments had continued to time $n+k$, which is the time of valuation, the accumulated value would be $s_{\overline{n+k}|}$. Since there are not any payments actually made for the final k payment periods, $s_{\overline{n+k}|}$ must be reduced by $s_{\overline{k}|}$, the accumulated value of k payments of 1 each ending at time $n+k$.

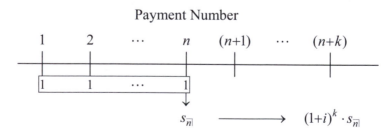

Payment Number

FIGURE 2.3a

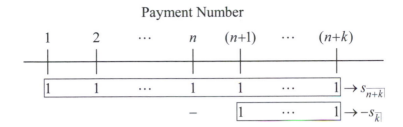

FIGURE 2.3b

Equation (2.4) can be reformulated as

$$s_{\overline{n+k}|} \quad = \quad s_{\overline{n}|}(1+i)^k + s_{\overline{k}|} \quad = \quad s_{\overline{k}|}(1+i)^n + s_{\overline{n}|}. \tag{2.5}$$

Equation 2.5 shows that a series of payments can be separated into components, and the accumulated value of the entire series at a valuation point can be represented as the sum of the accumulated values (at that valuation point) of the separate component series.

Accumulated Value of an Annuity With Non-Level Interest Rates

This concept of dividing a series of payments into subgroups and valuing each subgroup separately can be applied to find the accumulated value of an annuity when the periodic interest rate changes during the term of the annuity. This is illustrated in the following modification of Example 2.1.

EXAMPLE 2.4

(*Annuity accumulation with non-level interest rates*)
Suppose that in Example 2.1 the nominal annual interest rate earned on the account changes to 7.5% (still compounded monthly) as of January 1, 2004. What is the accumulated value of the account on December 31, 2009?

SOLUTION

In a situation in which the interest rate is at one level for a period of time and changes to another level for a subsequent period of time, it is necessary to separate the full term into separate time intervals over which the interest rate is constant. We first calculate the accumulated value in the account on December 31, 2003, since the nominal interest rate is level at 9% up until this point. This accumulated value is

$$30 \cdot \frac{(1.0075)^{68} - 1}{.0075} = 30 \cdot s_{\overline{68}|.0075} = 2{,}648.50.$$

From January 1, 2004 onward, the accumulation in the account can be separated into two components: the accumulation of the 2648.50 that was on balance as of January 1, 2004, and the accumulation of the continuing deposits from January 31, 2004 onward. The 2648.50 accumulates to

$$2{,}648.50 \times (1.00625)^{72} = 4{,}147.86$$

as of December 31, 2009, and the remaining deposits continuing from January 31, 2004 accumulate to

$$30 \cdot \frac{(1.00625)^{72} - 1}{.00625} = 30 \cdot s_{\overline{72}|.00625} = 2{,}717.36,$$

for a total of 6865.22. The accumulated value on December 31, 2009 can be written as

$$30 \cdot \left[s_{\overline{68}|.0075} \times (1.00625)^{72} + s_{\overline{72}|.00625} \right].$$

Keep in mind that the actual calculations of these annuity values would typically be done on a calculator, but the algebraic representations help with the understanding of the relationships underlying the calculations. □

We can generalize the concept presented in the Example 2.4. Suppose that we consider an $n+k$-payment annuity with equally spaced payments of 1 per period and with an interest rate of i_1 per payment period up to the time of the nth payment, followed by an interest rate of i_2 per payment period from the time of the nth payment onward. The accumulated value of the annuity at the time of the final payment can be found in the following way.

(a)   The accumulated value of the first n payments valued at the time of
the nth payment is $s_{\overline{n}|\,i_1}$.

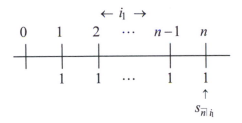

(b)   The accumulated value found in part (a) grows with compound
interest for an additional k periods at compound periodic interest
rate i_2, to a value of $s_{\overline{n}|\,i_1} \cdot (1+i_2)^k$ as of time $n+k$.

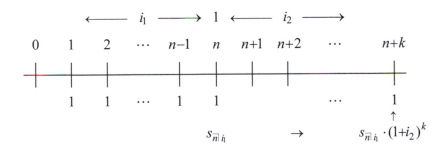

(c)   The accumulated value of the final k payments is $s_{\overline{k}|\,i_2}$.

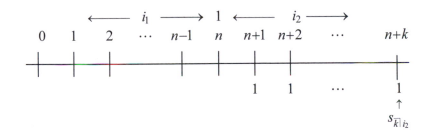

(d)   The total accumulated value at time $n+k$ is the sum of (b) and
(c), and equals $s_{\overline{n}|\,i_1} \cdot (1+i_2)^k + s_{\overline{k}|\,i_2}$.

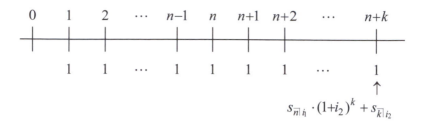

Note that if the interest rate is level over the $n+k$ periods, so that $i_2 = i_1$, then Equation 2.5 is the same as the expression in (d). This method can be extended to situations in which the interest rate changes more than once during the term of the annuity.

The relationship in Equation 2.5 can also be used to find the accumulated value of an annuity for which the payment amount changes during the course of the annuity. The following example illustrates this point.

EXAMPLE 2.5

(*Annuity whose payment amount changes during annuity term*)
Suppose that 10 monthly payments of 50 each are followed by 14 monthly payments of 75 each. If interest is at an effective monthly rate of 1%, what is the accumulated value of the series at the time of the final payment?

SOLUTION

Using the same technique as in Example 2.3 for finding the accumulated value of an annuity some time after the final payment, at the time 24 (months), the accumulated value of the first 10 payments is

$$50 s_{\overline{10}|.01} \cdot (1.01)^{14} = 601.30.$$

The value of the final 14 payments, also valued at time 24 is

$$75 s_{\overline{14}|.01} = 1{,}121.06.$$

The total accumulated value at time 24 is 1722.36. There is an alternative way of approaching this situation. Note in Figure 2.4 below that the original (non-level) sequence of payments can be decomposed into two separate level sequences of payments, both of which end at time 24.

Time	0	1	2	$\cdots$	10	11	12	$\cdots$	24
Original Series		50	50	$\cdots$	50	75	75	$\cdots$	75
New Series 1		50	50	$\cdots$	50	50	50	$\cdots$	50
New Series 2						25	25	$\cdots$	25

FIGURE 2.4

The associated EXCEL files found at the ACTEX website include a general recursive procedure for finding the accumulated value of an annuity which has payments and interest rates that change from one year to the next.

The accumulated value (at time 24) of the alternate form of the series is
$50s_{\overline{24}|.01} + 25s_{\overline{14}|.01} = 1,348.67 + 373.69 = 1,722.36.$ ☐

2.1.2 PRESENT VALUE OF AN ANNUITY

The discussion above has been concerned with formulating and calculating the accumulated value of a series of payments at the time the payments end or some time after the payments end. We now consider the present value of an annuity.

EXAMPLE 2.6 (*Present value of a series of payments*)

Smith's grandchild will begin a four year college program in one year. Smith wishes to open a bank account with a single deposit today so that her grandchild can withdraw $1000 per year for four years from the account, starting one year from now. The account has an effective annual interest rate of 6% and the deposit is calculated so that the account balance will be reduced to 0 when the fourth withdrawal is made four years from now. Determine the amount of the deposit Smith makes today.

SOLUTION

Suppose that the amount of the initial deposit is X. If we track the account balance after each withdrawal, we see the following:

Balance after 1st withdrawal:

$$X(1.06) - 1000$$

Balance after 2nd withdrawal:

$$[X(1.06)-1000](1.06)-1000 \quad = \quad X(1.06)^2 -1000(1.06)-1000$$

Balance after 3rd withdrawal:

$$[X(1.06)^2 -1000(1.06)-1000](1.06)-1000$$
$$= X(1.06)^3 -1000(1.06)^2 -1000(1.06)-1000$$

Balance after 4th withdrawal:

$$X(1.06)^4 -1000(1.06)^3 -1000(1.06)^2 -1000(1.06)-1000.$$

In order for the balance to be 0 just after the 4th withdrawal, we must have

$$X(1.06)^4 \quad = \quad 1000(1.06)^3 +1000(1.06)^2 +1000(1.06)+1000,$$

or equivalently,

$$X \quad = \quad \frac{1000}{1.06}+\frac{1000}{(1.06)^2}+\frac{1000}{(1.06)^3}+\frac{1000}{(1.06)^4}$$
$$= \quad 1000\left[v+v^2+v^3+v^4\right] \quad = \quad 3,465.11.$$

$\square$

It can be seen from Example 2.6 that the deposit amount needed is the combined present value of the four payments (withdrawals) that will be made. The present value of an annuity of payments is the value of the payments at the time, or some time before, the payments begin. Consider again a series of n payments of amount 1 each, made at equally spaced intervals for which interest is at effective interest rate i per payment period. The present value of the series of payments, valued one period before the first payment, can be represented as the sum of the present values of the individual payments:

$$v+v^2 +\cdots+v^{n-1} +v^n \quad = \quad v\left[1+v+\cdots+v^{n-1}\right]$$
$$= \quad v\cdot\frac{1-v^n}{1-v} \quad = \quad \frac{1-v^n}{i}. \tag{2.6}$$

Applying Equation 2.6 to Example 2.6 we see that the present value of the four payment annuity received by Smith's grandchild is:

$$1000\left[v+v^2+v^3+v^4\right] \;=\; 1000\left[\frac{1-v^4_{.06}}{.06}\right] \;=\; 3,465.11.$$

It is often the case that a valuation of a series of payments is done one period before the first payment. This is the case in Example 2.6, in which the payments are annual and the valuation is done one year before the first payment (a "payment" in this example is a withdrawal from the account). There is a specific actuarial symbol that represents the present value of a series of equally spaced payments of amount 1 each when the valuation point is one payment period before the payments begin. The symbol $a_{\overline{n}|i}$ is specifically used to denote this present value, so that

$$a_{\overline{n}|i} \;=\; v+v^2+\cdots+v^n \;=\; \sum_{t=1}^{n}v^t \;=\; \frac{1-v^n}{i}. \qquad (2.7)$$

This valuation is illustrated in the line diagram below.

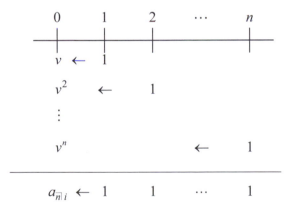

Similar to the use of the notation $s_{\overline{n}|}$, the symbol $a_{\overline{n}|}$, can be used to express the present value of an annuity provided the following conditions are met.

(1)   There are n payments of equal amount.

(2)   The payments are made at equal intervals of time, with the same frequency as the frequency of interest compounding.

(3)   The valuation point is one payment period before the first payment is made.

The value of an annuity one payment period before the first payment is made is referred to as the present value of an **annuity-immediate**. A typical situation in which the present value of an annuity-immediate arises is the repayment of a loan. It is generally understood in financial practice that for a loan being repaid with a series of payments, the loan is structured so that the original loan amount advanced to the borrower is equal to the present value of the loan payments to be made by the borrower, and the first loan payment is made one period after the loan is made. The present value is calculated using the loan interest rate.

EXAMPLE 2.7 (*Loan repayment*)

Brown has bought a new car and requires a loan of 12,000 to pay for it. The car dealer offers Brown two alternatives on the loan:

(a)   monthly payments for 3 years, starting one month after purchase, with an annual interest rate of 12% compounded monthly, or

(b)   monthly payments for 4 years, also starting one month after purchase, with annual interest rate 15%, compounded monthly.

Find Brown's monthly payment and the total amount paid over the course of the repayment period under each of the two options.

SOLUTION

We denote the monthly payment under option (a) by P_1 and under option (b) by P_2. "12% compounded monthly" refers to a one month interest rate of 1%, and alternative (b) refers to a one-month interest rate of 1.25%. Since payments begin one month (one payment period) after the loan, the equations of value for the two options are

(a) $12,000 = P_1 \cdot a_{\overline{36}|.01}$ and

(b) $12,000 = P_2 \cdot a_{\overline{48}|.0125}$.

Then $P_1 = \dfrac{12,000}{a_{\overline{36}|.01}} = \dfrac{12,000(.01)}{1-(1.01)^{-36}} = \dfrac{12,000}{30.107505} = 398.57$, and

$$P_2 = \frac{12,000}{a_{\overline{48}|.0125}} = \frac{12,000}{35.931363} = 333.97.$$

The total paid under option (a) would be $36 \cdot P_1 = 14,348.52$, and under option (b) it would be $48 \cdot P_2 = 16,030.56$.   □

Present Value of an Annuity Some Time Before Payments Begin

As in the case of an accumulated annuity in which the value was found some time after the final payment, it may be necessary to find the present value of a series of payments some time before the first payment is made. This is illustrated in the following modification of Example 2.7.

EXAMPLE 2.8

(*Valuation of an annuity some time before payments begin*)
Suppose that in Example 2.7 Brown can repay the loan, still with 36 payments under option (a) or 48 payments under option (b), with the first payment made 9 months after the car is purchased in either case. Assuming interest accrues from the time of the car purchase, find the payments required under options (a) and (b).

SOLUTION

We denote the new payments under options (a) and (b) by P_1' and P_2', respectively. Then the equation of value for option (a) is

$$12,000 = P_1' \cdot \left[v^9 + v^{10} + \cdots + v^{44} \right] = P_1' \cdot v^8 \cdot a_{\overline{36}|.01},$$

which leads to

$$P_1' = \frac{12,000}{v^8 \cdot a_{\overline{36}|.01}} = (1.01)^8 \cdot \frac{12,000}{a_{\overline{36}|.01}} = (1.01)^8 \cdot P_1 = 431.60.$$

In a similar manner,

$$P_2' = (1.0125)^8 \cdot \frac{12,000}{a_{\overline{48}|.0125}} = (1.0125)^8 \cdot P_2 = 368.86.$$

Since the payments are deferred for 8 months as compared to the situation in Example 2.7, it should not be surprising that in each of cases (a) and (b) the new payment is equal to the old payment multiplied by an 8-month accumulation factor. □

Suppose an n-payment annuity of 1 per period is to be valued $k+1$ payment periods before the first payment is made. The present value can be expressed as $v^{k+1} + v^{k+2} + \cdots + v^{k+n}$, which can be reformulated as

$$v^k \cdot [v + v^2 + \cdots + v^n] \;=\; v^k \cdot a_{\overline{n}|}.$$

Since $a_{\overline{n}|}$ represents the present value of the annuity one period before the first payment, the value k periods before that (for a total of $k+1$ periods before the first payment) should be $v^k \cdot a_{\overline{n}|}$. With a derivation similar to that for Equation (2.4), we have

$$v^k \cdot a_{\overline{n}|} \;=\; a_{\overline{n+k}|} - a_{\overline{k}|}. \tag{2.8}$$

Such an annuity is called a **deferred annuity**. The annuity considered in Equation (2.8) is an n-payment annuity-immediate deferred for k payment periods, usually called a k-period deferred, n-payment annuity of 1 per period. This annuity present value is denoted by $_{k|}a_{\overline{n}|}$. Note that for a k-period deferred annuity, the first payment comes $k+1$ periods after the valuation date, not k periods after. Equation (2.8) can be rewritten in the form

$$a_{\overline{n+k}|} \;=\; a_{\overline{k}|} + v^k \cdot a_{\overline{n}|} \;=\; a_{\overline{n}|} + v^n \cdot a_{\overline{k}|}. \tag{2.9}$$

Just as Equation (2.5) can be used for accumulated annuities, Equation (2.9) can be applied to find the present value of an annuity for which the interest rate changes during the term of the annuity. If we consider an $n+k$-payment annuity with equally spaced payments, with an interest rate of i_1 per period up to the time of the nth payment followed by a rate of i_2 per period from the nth payment onward, the present value of the annuity one period before the first payment can be found in the following manner.

(a)   The present value of the first n payments valued one period before the first payment is $a_{\overline{n}|\, i_1}$.

(b)   The present value of the final k payments valued at time n (one period before the first of the final k payments) at rate i_2 is $a_{\overline{k}|\, i_2}$.

(c)   The value of (b) at time 0 (one period before the first payment of the entire series) at interest rate i_1 per period over the first n periods is $v_{i_1}^n \cdot a_{\overline{k}|i_2}$.

(d)   The total present value at time 0 is the sum of (a) and (c), which is

$$a_{\overline{n}|i_1} + v_{i_1}^n \cdot a_{\overline{k}|i_2}.$$

This is illustrated in the following line diagram.

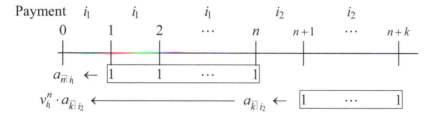

FIGURE 2.5

We now return to annuities with a level interest rate. The valuation point for an n-payment accumulated annuity-immediate is the time of the nth payment and the accumulated value at that time is $s_{\overline{n}|i}$. The valuation point for the present value of an n-payment annuity-immediate is one period before the first payment, and the present value is $a_{\overline{n}|i}$. We see that the valuation point for the present value of the annuity is n periods earlier than the valuation point for the accumulated value. Then it follows that

$$s_{\overline{n}|i} \quad = \quad (1+i)^n \cdot a_{\overline{n}|i} \tag{2.10}$$

and

$$a_{\overline{n}|i} \quad = \quad v^n \cdot s_{\overline{n}|i}. \tag{2.11}$$

This can be easily verified algebraically by observing that

$$v^n \cdot s_{\overline{n}|i} \quad = \quad v^n \left[\frac{(1+i)^n - 1}{i} \right] \quad = \quad \frac{1 - v^n}{i} \quad = \quad a_{\overline{n}|i}.$$

For a particular value of i, both $s_{\overline{n}|i}$ and $a_{\overline{n}|i}$ increase as n increases. Furthermore $s_{\overline{n}|i} = 1 + (1+i) + \cdots + (1+i)^{n-1}$ increases as i increases (a higher interest rate results in greater accumulated values of the payments). However, since $v = \frac{1}{1+i}$ decreases as i increases, we can see that $a_{\overline{n}|i} = v + \cdots + v^n$ decreases as i increases. This again illustrates the inverse relationship between the present value of an income stream and the interest rate (yield rate) used for valuation.

Valuation of Perpetuities

It was pointed out in Chapter 1 that if $i > 0$, then v^n decreases as n increases, and, in fact, $v^n \to 0$ as $n \to \infty$. Furthermore it was noted earlier in this section that $a_{\overline{n}|i}$ increases as n increases. As $n \to \infty$ it is easy to see that

$$\lim_{n \to \infty} a_{\overline{n}|i} = \lim_{n \to \infty} \frac{1-v^n}{i} = \frac{1}{i}.$$

This expression can also be derived by summing the infinite series of present values of payments $v + v^2 + v^3 + \cdots$. The infinite series becomes $v + v^2 + v^3 + \cdots = v \cdot \frac{1}{1-v} = \frac{1}{i}$. The infinite period annuity that results as $n \to \infty$ is called a **perpetuity**, and a notation that may be used to represent the present value of this perpetuity is $a_{\overline{\infty}|i} = \frac{1}{i}$. Since the valuation of the perpetuity occurs one period before the first payment, it would be referred to as a perpetuity-immediate.

This notion of perpetuity can be considered from another point of view. Suppose that X is the amount that must be invested at interest rate i per period in order to generate a perpetuity of 1 per period (starting one period from now). In order to generate a payment of 1 without taking anything away from the existing principal amount X, the payment of 1 must be generated by interest alone. Therefore $X \cdot i = 1$, or equivalently, $X = \frac{1}{i}$. It is not possible to formulate the accumulated value of perpetuity.

| **EXAMPLE 2.9** | (*Valuation of a perpetuity*) |

A perpetuity-immediate pays X per year. Brian receives the first n payments, Colleen receives the next n payments, and Jeff receives the remaining payments. Brian's share of the present value of the original perpetuity is 40%, and Jeff's share is K. Calculate K.

| **SOLUTION** |

The present value of the perpetuity is $Xa_{\overline{\infty}|i} = \frac{X}{i}$. The present value of Brian's portion of the perpetuity is $Xa_{\overline{n}|i} = X\left(\frac{1-v^n}{i}\right)$, which we are told is 40% of $\frac{X}{i}$. Therefore, $1-v^n = .4$, so that $v^n = .6$. The present value of Colleen's portion of the perpetuity is $Xv^n a_{\overline{n}|i} = .6Xa_{\overline{n}|i} = (.6)(.4)\frac{X}{i}$, which is 24% of the value of the original perpetuity. Therefore, Jeff's share of the perpetuity is $(100-40-24)\% = 36\%$. Alternatively, note that Jeff's share can be formulated as

$$Xv^{2n}a_{\overline{\infty}|i} = (.6)^2 Xa_{\overline{\infty}|i} = (.36)\frac{X}{i}. \qquad \square$$

It is possible to interpret a level n-payment annuity as the "difference" between two perpetuities. The present value of a perpetuity-immediate of 1 per year is $a_{\overline{\infty}|i} = \frac{1}{i}$. An "$n$-year deferred" perpetuity-immediate of 1 per year would have payments starting in $n+1$ years, and would have present value $v^n \cdot a_{\overline{\infty}|i} = \frac{v^n}{i}$. Subtracting the second present value from the first, we get $a_{\overline{\infty}|i} - v^n \cdot a_{\overline{\infty}|i} = \frac{1-v^n}{i} = a_{\overline{n}|i}$. Subtracting the deferred perpetuity cancels all payments after the nth payment, leaving an n-payment annuity-immediate.

2.1.3 ANNUITY-IMMEDIATE AND ANNUITY-DUE

To make a valuation of a level series of equally spaced payments, the information needed is

(1)   the number of the payments,
(2)   the valuation point, and
(3)   the interest rate per payment period.

There are a few particular valuation points that arise frequently in practice, and there are actuarial notation and terminology to represent those valuations. For a level series of payments of 1 each, we have already seen $s_{\overline{n}|}$, the accumulated value at the time of the final payment, and $a_{\overline{n}|}$, the present value one period before the first payment. As noted earlier, these valuation points are referred to as **annuity-immediate** valuations. Annuity-immediate refers to a valuation that is at the time of the final payment for an accumulated annuity valuation, and it refers to a valuation one payment period before the first payment for a present value. Annuity-immediate is often identified by the phrase "payments are made at the end of each period." For instance, a loan may be described as having payments at the end of each month. The implication is that the first payment is one month after the loan is actually made, making the valuation an annuity-immediate. Also, when deposits are made into a bank account, say at the end of each year, it is usually the case that an accumulated value is calculated at the time of a deposit, so the valuation is an accumulated annuity-immediate. In general, if we are told that an annuity has n payments made at the end of each period, this is interpreted as regarding the payments being made at times 1 (end of 1st period), 2 (end of 2nd period),...,n (end of nth period). It would also be understood that the present value of the annuity is found at the <u>beginning</u> of the 1st period, which is time 0 (one period before the first payment), and the accumulated value would be found at the end of the nth period, which is time n. Most financial calculators have a setting denoted "END" which will set the calculator for annuity-immediate calculations.

Another standard annuity form is that of the **annuity-due**. This form occurs most frequently in the context of life annuities, but can also be defined in the case of annuities-certain. In the case of present value, an annuity-due refers to the valuation of the annuity at the time of (and including) the first payment. In the case of accumulated value, annuity-due refers to the valuation of the annuity one payment period after the final payment. If an annuity is described as having payments occurring at the beginning of each period, the implication is that annuity-due valuation is intended. There would be payments at time 0 (beginning of the 1st period), time 1 (beginning of 2nd period),..., time $n-1$ (beginning of nth period). The present value of the annuity would be found at time 0 (the time of the first payment) and the accumulated value would be found at time n (one period after the final payment). The calculator setting "BEGIN" or "BGN" sets annuity valuation in the form of annuity-due. For n-payment annuities with payments of amount 1 each, the annuity-due present value is given by

$$\ddot{a}_{\overline{n}|i} = 1+v+v^2+\cdots+v^{n-1} = \frac{1-v^n}{1-v} = \frac{1-v^n}{d}, \qquad (2.12)$$

and the accumulated value is given by

$$\begin{aligned} \ddot{s}_{\overline{n}|i} &= (1+i)+(1+i)^2+\cdots+(1+i)^n \\ &= (1+i)\left[\frac{(1+i)^n-1}{i}\right] = \frac{(1+i)^n-1}{d}, \qquad (2.13) \end{aligned}$$

where d is the discount rate equivalent to interest rate i. Figure 2.6 summarizes the annuity-immediate and annuity-due valuation points.

FIGURE 2.6

Note that for both the present value and accumulated value of the annuity-due, the valuation point is one period after the valuation point for the corresponding annuity-immediate. This leads to the relationships

$$\ddot{a}_{\overline{n}|i} = (1+i)\,a_{\overline{n}|i}$$

and

$$\ddot{s}_{\overline{n}|i} = (1+i)\,s_{\overline{n}|i}.$$

A perpetuity-due of 1 per year has present value

$$\ddot{a}_{\overline{\infty}|i} = 1+v+v^2+\cdots = \frac{1}{1-v} = \frac{1}{d} = \frac{1+i}{i} = (1+i)a_{\overline{\infty}|i} = 1+a_{\overline{\infty}|i}$$

| **EXAMPLE 2.10** | (*Annuity due*)

Jim began saving money for his retirement by making monthly deposits of 200 into a fund earning 6% interest compounded monthly. The first deposit occurred on January 1, 1995. Jim became unemployed and missed making deposits 60 through 72. He then continued making monthly deposits of 200. How much did Jim accumulate in his fund on December 31, 2009, assuming payments continued through to December 1, 2009?

| **SOLUTION** |

The savings plan originally called for a total of 180 deposits (15 years of monthly deposits). We note that 13 deposits will be missed, the 60th to the 72nd, inclusive. The 60th deposit would have occurred on December 1, 1999, and the 72nd deposit would have occurred on December 1, 2000. The valuation point is December 31, 2009, which is one month after the final deposit on December 1, 2009. If none of the deposits had been missed, then there would have been 180 deposits and the accumulated value one month after the 180th monthly deposit can be expressed as an annuity-due. The interest rate is .5% per month, so the accumulated value on December 31, 2009 would be

$$200 \cdot \left[(1.005)^{180} + (1.005)^{179} + \cdots + (1.005) \right]$$

$$= \ 200 \cdot \ddot{s}_{\overline{180}|.005} \ = \ 200 \cdot \frac{(1.005)^{180} - 1}{.005} \cdot (1.005) \ = \ 58,454.56.$$

The actual accumulated value is 58,454.56 minus the accumulated value of the missed payments. The first missed payment was December 1, 1999, and the valuation date of December 31, 2009 is 121 months later. The value on December 31, 2009 of the missed payments is

$$200 \cdot \left[(1.005)^{121} + (1.005)^{120} + \cdots + (1.005)^{109} \right]$$

$$= \ 200 \cdot (1.005)^{109} \cdot \left[(1.005)^{12} + (1.005)^{11} + \cdots + 1 \right]$$

$$= \ 200 \cdot (1.005)^{109} \cdot \frac{(1.005)^{13} - 1}{.005}$$

$$= \ 200 \cdot (1.005)^{109} \cdot s_{\overline{13}|.005} \ = \ 4,614.73.$$

Note that the accumulated value of the missed payments was formulated as $200 \cdot (1.005)^{109} \cdot s_{\overline{13}|.005}$. It could also be formulated as $200 \cdot (1.005)^{108} \cdot \ddot{s}_{\overline{13}|.005}$ (this follows from the relationship $(1.005) \cdot s_{\overline{13}|.005} = \ddot{s}_{\overline{13}|.005}$), which can be interpreted as the accumulated value of the 13 missed payments valued on December 31, 2000 (one month after the 13th missed payment) and then accumulating this amount for another 9 years (108 months).

The value of the deposits made is $58,454.56 - 4,614.73 = 53,839.83$.   □

2.2. LEVEL PAYMENT ANNUITIES – SOME GENERALIZATIONS

2.2.1 DIFFERING INTEREST AND PAYMENT PERIOD

In the annuities considered in Section 2.1 it had been assumed that the quoted compounding interest period is the same as the annuity payment period. In practice it may often be the case that the quoted interest rate has a compounding period that does not coincide with the annuity payment period. For the purpose of a numerical evaluation of the annuity, we focus on the annuity payment period and find and use the interest rate per payment period that is equivalent to the quoted interest rate. What is meant by equivalence here is "compound equivalence" as defined in Chapter 1. The following example illustrates this.

EXAMPLE 2.11 (*Differing interest and payment period*)

On the last day of every March, June, September, and December, Smith makes a deposit of 1000 into a savings account. The first deposit is March 31, 1995 and the final one is December 31, 2010. Find the balance in Smith's account on January 1, 2011 in each of the following two cases. A calendar quarter is regarded as exactly $\frac{1}{4}$-year.

(a)   Interest is quoted at a 9% nominal annual interest rate compounded monthly.

(b)   Interest is quoted at an effective annual rate of 10%, with compound interest paid for amounts on deposit for a fraction of a year.

| SOLUTION |

Smith makes a total of 64 deposits (4 per year for 16 years). If the effective 3-month rate of interest j were known, then the accumulated value just after the final deposit would be $1000\frac{(1+j)^{64}-1}{j} = 1000s_{\overline{64}|j}$. In case (a), from the quoted nominal annual rate of interest we see that the effective 1-month rate of interest is .0075, so j satisfies the relationship $1+j = (1.0075)^3$; this is the "compound equivalence" relationship relating the effective 3-month interest rate j to the effective 1-month interest rate .0075. Solving for j results in $j = .02266917$. The accumulated value of the annuity is then

$$1000\frac{(1.02266917)^{64}-1}{.02266917} = 1000s_{\overline{64}|.02266917} = 141,076.$$

In case (b), j satisfies the relationship $1+j = (1.10)^{1/4} = 1.02411369$; the effective 3-month rate is found by compounding the effective annual rate for a $\frac{1}{4}$-year period. The accumulated value of the annuity is

$$1000\frac{(1.02411369)^{64}-1}{.02411369} = 1000s_{\overline{64}|.02411369} = 149,084. \qquad \square$$

The payment period for the annuity in Example 2.11 is 3 months, so for each of the two parts of the example, the quoted interest rate was converted to an equivalent 3-month interest rate. This is the way in which such a situation is dealt with in practice. For example, most mortgage loans are set up to have monthly payments. In Canada, the Canada Interest Act (originally enacted in the late 19th century) requires that the interest rate on a mortgage on real property be quoted as either an effective annual rate of interest or as a nominal annual rate of interest compounded semi-annually. Canadian financial institutions generally quote mortgage rates as nominal annual rates compounded twice per year, but use an equivalent one month rate of interest for calculating the monthly mortgage payment.

Round-off error can occur if an approximate interest rate is used. Note that in Example 2.11 if we had used approximate values of j rounded to the nearest .01%, for (a) $j = .0227$ and for (b) $j = .0241$, then the accumulated values would be 141,242 in case (a) and 149,006 in case (b). Calculators generally have at least 8 digits of accuracy, which is sufficient for all practical purposes.

When the quoted interest rate is an effective annual rate of interest and the payments are made more frequently than once per year, the actuarial concept of an m^{thly} *payable annuity* can be applied. Part (b) of Example 2.11 can be used as an illustration. There are $m = 4$ payments per year of 1,000 each, and the interest rate is quoted as an effective annual interest rate of 10%. The total paid per year is 4,000 for 16 years. The actuarial notation $4000 s_{\overline{16}|.10}^{(4)}$ can be used to represent the accumulated value at the time of the final quarterly payment of 1,000. The coefficient 4000 is total paid per year, and the superscript "(4)" indicates that this total of 4,000 is split into 4 payments of 1,000 each to be made at the end of each quarter. In the exercises it is shown that $s_{\overline{16}|.10}^{(4)} = \dfrac{(1.10)^{16}-1}{i^{(4)}} = s_{\overline{16}|.10} \cdot \dfrac{i}{i^{(4)}}$, where $i^{(4)}$ is the nominal annual rate of interest compounded 4 times per year that is equivalent to the effective annual interest rate of $i = .10$.

The general form of an accumulated m^{thly} payable annuity-immediate is $Ks_{\overline{n}|i}^{(m)}$, which is interpreted as follows. The effective annual interest rate is i and payments of amount $\dfrac{K}{m}$ each occur at the end of every $\dfrac{1}{m}$-year period (total amount paid per year is K). $Ks_{\overline{n}|i}^{(m)}$ denotes the accumulated value of this series of payments at the end of n years of payments; there would be a total of $m \times n$ payments, and the valuation point is the time of the final payment. There is a similar notation for the present value of an m^{thly} payable annuity. For the same set of payments just described, $Ka_{\overline{n}|i}^{(m)}$ denotes the present value of the series one *payment period* before the first payment; the valuation point would be $\dfrac{1}{m}$-year before the first payment. In the exercises at the end of this chapter it is shown that $a_{\overline{n}|i}^{(m)} = \dfrac{1-v_i^n}{i^{(m)}} = a_{\overline{n}|i} \cdot \dfrac{i}{i^{(m)}}$. This m^{thly} payable annuity notation arises in a life-annuity context, where it is more likely to be used.

2.2.2 Continuous Annuities

The annuities considered up to now all have specified individual payments at specified points in time. They are *discrete annuities* and would actually occur in practical situations, such as annuities with annual, monthly, weekly, or even daily payments. For theoretical purposes and for modeling complex situations, it is sometimes useful to consider *continuous annuities,* those which have payments made continuously over a period of time.

In part (b) of Example 2.11 a situation is considered in which an annuity has quarterly payments and interest is quoted on an effective annual basis. The exercises at the end of the chapter consider a generalization of this situation in which payments are made every $\frac{1}{m}^{th}$ of a year. As m becomes larger the time between successive payments becomes smaller. Although it would not be physically possible to reach the limit of this payment pattern as $m \to \infty$, the interpretation of that limit would be an annuity *payable continuously.*

Suppose an annuity has a level rate of continuous payment of 1 per period, and an effective rate of interest of i per period. Then the amount paid during the interval from time t_1 to time t_2 (measured using the period as the unit of time) is equal to $t_2 - t_1$. Suppose the payment continues for n periods, measured from time 0 to time n. In order to find the accumulated value at time n of the n periods of payment, it is not possible to add up the accumulated values of individual payments as was done for the discrete annuities considered earlier. Because of the continuous nature of the payment, for each time t between 0 and n we can focus on the accumulated value at time n of the infinitesimal amount paid between time t and time $t+dt$. With $t_1 = t$ and $t_2 = t+dt$, the amount paid during the infinitesimal interval from time t_1 to time t_2 is $t_2 - t_1 = dt$. The accumulated value as of time n of this amount is $(1+i)^{n-t} dt$. These accumulated amounts are "added up" by means of an integral, so that the accumulated value of the continuous annuity, paid at rate 1 per period for n periods, denoted by $\overline{s}_{\overline{n}|i}$, is given by

$$\overline{s}_{\overline{n}|i} = \int_0^n (1+i)^{n-t}\, dt. \qquad (2.14a)$$

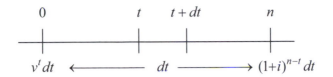

FIGURE 2.7

Integrating the right side of (2.14a) we obtain

$$\bar{s}_{\overline{n}|i} = \left.\frac{-(1+i)^{n-t}}{\ln(1+i)}\right|_0^n = \frac{(1+i)^n - 1}{\delta}$$

$$= \frac{e^{n\delta} - 1}{\delta} = \frac{(1+i)^n - 1}{i} \cdot \frac{i}{\delta} = \frac{i}{\delta} \cdot s_{\overline{n}|i}, \qquad (2.14b)$$

Note also that $\bar{s}_{\overline{n}|i} = \frac{(1+i)^n - 1}{\delta} = \lim_{m \to \infty} \frac{(1+i)^n - 1}{i^{(m)}} = \lim_{m \to \infty} s_{\overline{n}|i}^{(m)}$. The interpretation

of this relationship is that as m gets larger, the annuity payment is paid more frequently during the year and is spread more evenly throughout the year, with the limit being a continuous distribution of payment throughout the year.

EXAMPLE 2.12 (*Continuous annuity*)

In 2004 and 2005 Smith deposits 12 every day into an account and in 2006 he deposits 15 every day into the account. The account earns interest from the exact time of the deposit, with interest quoted as an effective annual rate, with compound interest credited every December 31. The rates are 9% in 2004 and 2005, and 12% in 2006. Find the amount in the account after interest is credited on December 31 2006 (a) exactly based on the daily deposits, and (b) using the approximation that deposits are made continuously.

SOLUTION

(a) j_1 denotes the equivalent daily compound interest rates in 2004 and 2005, and j_2 denotes the equivalent daily compound interest rate in 2006. It then follows that $j_1 = (1.09)^{1/365} - 1 = .00023631$, and $j_2 = (1.12)^{1/365} - 1$. Using the approach illustrated in part (b) of Example 2.11, the accumulated value on December 31, 2006 is

$$12 \cdot s_{\overline{730}|j_1}(1.12) + 15 \cdot s_{\overline{365}|j_2}$$

$$= 12(1.12)\left[\frac{(1.09)^2 - 1}{j_1}\right] + 15\left[\frac{(1.12) - 1}{j_2}\right]$$

$$= 10,706.19 + 5,796.40$$

$$= 16,502.59.$$

(b)   If deposits are made continuously, then the total paid per year in 2004-2005 is $12 \times 365 = 4380$, and in 2006 it is $15 \times 365 = 5475$.

The accumulated value would be

$$4380(1.12) \cdot \bar{s}_{\overline{2}|.09} + 5475 \cdot \bar{s}_{\overline{1}|.12}$$

$$= 4380(1.12)\left[\frac{(1.09)^2 - 1}{\ln(1.09)}\right] + 5475\left[\frac{(1.12) - 1}{\ln(1.12)}\right]$$

$$= 10,707.45 + 5,797.30 \quad = \quad 16,504.75. \qquad \square$$

The present value, at the time payment begins, of a continuous annuity paying a total of 1 per period at effective periodic interest rate i is

$$\bar{a}_{\overline{n}|i} \quad = \quad \int_0^n v^t \, dt \qquad\qquad\qquad (2.15a)$$

$$= \quad \frac{1 - v^n}{\ln(1+i)} \quad = \quad \frac{1 - v^n}{\delta} \quad = \quad \frac{1 - e^{-n\delta}}{\delta}$$

$$= \quad \frac{i}{\delta} \cdot a_{\overline{n}|i} \quad = \quad \lim_{m \to \infty} a_{\overline{n}|i}^{(m)}. \qquad\qquad (2.15b)$$

Many of the identities valid for discrete annuities also hold for continuous annuities. The relationships in Equations (2.4), (2.5), (2.6), (2.8), (2.9), (2.10), and (2.11) are valid if the discrete annuity is replaced by the corresponding continuous annuity.

Suppose a general accumulation function is in effect, where $a(t_1, t_2)$ is the accumulated value at time t_2 of an amount 1 invested at time t_1.

Then $\int_{t_0}^{t_e} a(t,t_e)dt$ and $\int_{t_0}^{t_e} \frac{1}{a(t_0,t)} dt$ represent the accumulated value at time t_e and the present value at time t_0, respectively, of a continuous annuity of 1 per unit time, payable from time t_0 to time t_e. If accumulation is based on force of interest δ_r, then

$$a(t_1,t_2) = \exp\left[\int_{t_1}^{t_2} \delta_r \, dr,\right] \qquad (2.16)$$

and we have present and accumulated annuity values at time 0 and time n, respectively, given by

$$\bar{a}_{\overline{n}|\delta_r} = \int_0^n e^{-\int_0^t \delta_r dr} \, dt \qquad (2.17a)$$

and

$$\bar{s}_{\overline{n}|\delta_r} = \int_0^n e^{\int_t^n \delta_r dr} \, dt, \qquad (2.17b)$$

along with the relationship

$$\bar{s}_{\overline{n}|\delta_r} = \bar{a}_{\overline{n}|\delta_r} \cdot e^{\int_0^n \delta_r \, dr}. \qquad (2.17c)$$

2.2.3 SOLVING FOR THE NUMBER OF PAYMENTS IN AN ANNUITY (UNKNOWN TIME)

When considering a transaction involving a series of payments, there are a number of considerations that can arise. We have looked at formulations for the accumulated and present values of a series of level payments. For instance, suppose we consider the basic relationship for the accumulated value, M, of an annuity-immediate with n level payments of amount J each with an interest rate of i per payment period. The relationship is

$$M = J\left[(1+i)^{n-1} + (1+i)^{n-2} + \cdots + (1+i) + 1\right] = J\left[\frac{(1+i)^n - 1}{i}\right] = Js_{\overline{n}|i}.$$

We can regard M, J, i, and n as "variables" in this equation, and given any three of these variables it is possible to solve for the fourth variable.

In examples considered so far we have been given either J, i, and n, and solved for M, or we have been given M, i, and n, and solved for J. If we are given M, J, and i, then we can solve for the "unknown time" n, and if we are given M, J, and n, then we can solve for the "unknown interest" i. We can solve for the unknown time factor n algebraically as follows:

$$M = J \cdot \frac{(1+i)^n - 1}{i} \quad \rightarrow \quad (1+i)^n = 1 + \frac{Mi}{J} \quad \rightarrow \quad n = \frac{\ln\left[1 + \frac{Mi}{J}\right]}{\ln(1+i)}.$$

In general, it will not be possible to solve algebraically for the unknown interest rate factor i. In either case, the solution would be done using appropriate functions on a financial calculator – see the Appendix (the calculator function would likely use a numerical approximation method). Most financial calculators have functions that solve for the fourth variable if any three of M, J, i, and n are known. The same comments apply to the present value of a level payment annuity-immediate,

$$L \quad = \quad K\left[v + v^2 + \cdots + v^n\right] \quad = \quad K\left[\frac{1 - v^n}{i}\right]$$

where the four variables are the present value L, the payment amount K, the number of payments n, and the interest rate i. Solving for n results in $n = \frac{\ln\left[1 - \frac{Li}{K}\right]}{\ln[v]}$. Calculator functions also allow the distinction between annuity-immediate and annuity-due.

Solving for the unknown time will usually result in a value for n that is not an integer. The integer part will be the number of full periodic payments required, and there will be an additional fractional part of a payment required to complete the annuity. This additional fractional payment may be made at the time of the final full payment (called a "balloon payment") or may be made one period after the final full payment. The following examples illustrate these ideas.

EXAMPLE 2.13 (*Finding the unknown number of payments*)

Smith wishes to accumulate 1000 by means of semiannual deposits earning interest at nominal annual rate $i^{(2)} = .08$, with interest credited semiannually.

(a) The regular deposits will be 50 each. Find the number of regular deposits required and the additional fractional deposit in each of the following two cases:

(i) the additional fractional deposit is made at the time of the last regular deposit, and

(ii) the additional fractional deposit is made six months after the last regular deposit.

(b) Repeat the problem with a regular deposit amount of 25.

SOLUTION

(a) Solving the relationship $1000 = 50 \cdot s_{\overline{n}|.04}$ results in a value of $n = \dfrac{\ln(1.8)}{\ln(1.04)} = 14.9866$. Thus 14 deposits of the full amount of 50 are required. The accumulated amount on deposit at the time of, and including, the 14th deposit is $50 \cdot s_{\overline{14}|.04} = 914.60$. If the additional fractional deposit is made at the time of the 14th regular deposit, then it must be $1000 - 914.60 = 85.40$, which is actually larger than the regular semiannual deposit. If the account is allowed to accumulate another half-year, then the accumulated amount in the account six months after the 14th deposit, but not including a 15th deposit, is $50 \cdot \ddot{s}_{\overline{14}|.04} = 50(1.04) \cdot s_{\overline{14}|.04} = 951.18$. In this case an additional fractional deposit of amount $1000 - 951.18 = 48.82$ is required to bring the amount on deposit to a total of 1000.

(b) With the problem repeated at a deposit amount of 25, solving $1000 = 25 \cdot s_{\overline{n}|.04}$ results in $n = 24.3624$. The accumulated amount at the time of the 24th deposit is $25 \cdot s_{\overline{24}|.04} = 977.07$, so that the additional fractional deposit required would be 22.93, if it were made at the time of the 24th deposit. The accumulated amount six months after the 24th deposit is $25 \cdot \ddot{s}_{\overline{24}|.04} = 1016.15$. No additional fractional payment would be required since the accumulated value is already 16.15 larger than the target value of 1000. □

In situations not so elementary as those in Example 2.13, an unknown time problem may not have an analytic solution for n. In that case some sort of approximation technique must be applied. The following example illustrates this.

EXAMPLE 2.14 *(Unknown Time)*

Smith makes a gross contribution of 100 per month to a retirement fund earning $i^{(12)} = .09$, with interest credited on the last day of each month. At the time each deposit is made, the fund administrators deduct 10 from the deposit for expenses and administration fees. The first deposit is made on the last day of January 2000. In which month does the accumulated value of the fund become greater than the total gross contribution to that point?

SOLUTION

We wish to solve for the smallest integer n for which the inequality $90 \cdot s_{\overline{n}|.0075} \geq 100n$ is true. The net deposit is 90 and the monthly rate is $j = \frac{.09}{12} = .0075$. The relationship $90 \left[\frac{(1.0075)^n - 1}{.0075} \right] \geq 100n$ is equivalent to $(1.0075)^n \geq 1 + .008333n$, which we cannot solve analytically. An elementary approach to a solution is by "trial-and-error," where we try various values of n until the inequality is satisfied. From an inspection of the inequality, since the exponential factor $(1.0075)^n$ ultimately increases faster than the linear factor $1 + .008333n$, we see that the inequality will eventually be satisfied (for a large enough n). With the arbitrary choice of $n = 10$, we have $(1.0075)^{10} = 1.077583$ and $1 + .008333(10) = 1.08333$, so the inequality is not satisfied. We try a larger n, say $n = 20$, in which case $(1.0075)^{20} = 1.161184$ and $1 + .008333(20) = 1.1666$, so the inequality is still not satisfied. Continuing in this way we obtain the results shown in Table 2.1.

TABLE 2.1

n	$(1.0075)^n$	$1 + .008333n$	Satisfied
10	1.0775825	1.08333	No
20	1.1611841	1.16666	No
30	1.2512720	1.24999	Yes
25	1.2053870	1.20833	No
28	1.2327120	1.23332	No
29	1.2419570	1.24166	Yes

Therefore $n = 29$ is the smallest n for which the inequality is satisfied The 29th deposit occurs at the end of May 2002. Note that Table 2.1 could be generated in a computer spreadsheet program. The "Solver" function in an EXCEL spreadsheet could be also used to solve for n. $\quad\square$

EXAMPLE 2.15 (*Unknown Time*)

A loan of 5000 is being repaid by monthly payments of 100 each, starting one month after the loan is made, for as long as necessary plus an additional fractional payment. At interest rate $i^{(12)} = .09,$ find the number of full payments required to repay the loan, and the amount of the additional fractional payment required if (a) the additional fractional payment is made at the time of the final regular payment, and (b) the additional fractional payment is made one month after the final regular payment.

SOLUTION

The monthly compound interest rate is $j = \frac{i^{(12)}}{12} = .0075.$ We solve the equation

$$5000 = 100 \cdot a_{\overline{n}|.0075} = 100\left[\frac{1 - v_{.0075}^n}{.0075}\right],$$

so that we find

$$v^n = 1 - .375 = .625,$$

or, equivalently, $n = \frac{\ln(.625)}{\ln(1/1.0075)} = 62.9.$ Thus the repayment will require 62 regular payments of 100 each plus an additional fractional payment. In order to find the amount of the additional fractional payment X, an equation of value must now be set up for each case.

(a) $\quad 5000 = 100 \cdot a_{\overline{62}|.0075} + X \cdot v_{.0075}^{62},$ so $X = \dfrac{5000 - 100 \cdot a_{\overline{62}|.0075}}{v_{.0075}^{62}},$

$\quad$ or $X = 5000(1.0075)^{62} - 100 \cdot s_{\overline{62}|.0075} = 89.55.$

(b) $5000 = 100 \cdot a_{\overline{62}|.0075} + X \cdot v^{63}_{.0075}$, so $X = \dfrac{5000 - 100 \cdot a_{\overline{62}|.0075}}{v^{63}_{.0075}}$.

Note that the value of X in this case is simply 1.0075 times the value of X in case (a), so that $X = 90.22$. It will generally be true that if the additional fractional payment Y is made one payment period after the final full payment, then $Y = X(1+j)$, where X is the additional fractional payment amount if made at the time of the final full payment, and j is the effective periodic interest rate.   □

The calculator function summary in the Appendix illustrates examples similar to 2.13 and 2.15.

The solution for n in the equation $L = Ka_{\overline{n}|i}$ was seen to be $n = \dfrac{\ln\left[1 - \frac{Li}{K}\right]}{\ln[v]}$.

It is implicitly assumed that $1 - \frac{Li}{K} > 0$, since otherwise it would be impossible to find the natural logarithm. Upon closer inspection, if $1 - \frac{Li}{K} \leq 0$, then $K \leq L \cdot i$, so the loan payment will at most cover the periodic interest due on the loan and will never repay any principal. Therefore, if the loan payment isn't sufficient to cover the periodic interest due, the loan will never be repaid and $n = \infty$.

2.2.4 SOLVING FOR THE INTEREST RATE IN AN ANNUITY (UNKNOWN INTEREST)

In the previous section it was seen that it is often possible to solve algebraically for the number of payments in an annuity if the other annuity parameters are known. This is not the case when solving for the interest rate. It is generally necessary to use a calculator function or computer routine to solve for an unknown interest rate.

The following example is based on an example of an Individual Retirement Account (IRA) found on the website of the Western & Southern Financial Group (Cincinnati, OH). An IRA is a deposit account in which funds accumulate tax-free until withdrawn at the time of retirement. There is also some income tax reduction at the time of each deposit. An excerpt from the website is below.

IRA Advantage: Tax-Favored Compounding

This chart assumes a $3,000 annual contribution at the beginning of each year, a hypothetical 6% average rate of return, and a 30% combined federal and state income tax bracket.

This example assumes deductible contributions. Earnings grow tax-deferred until withdrawn at the end of the period.

Should the IRA be withdrawn as a lump sum at the end of the period, its value would be $359,941 after 30% taxes.

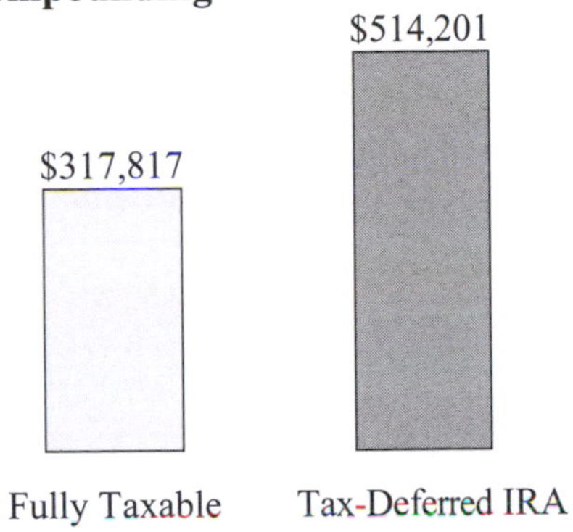

www.westernsouthernlife.com

$514,201

$317,817

Fully Taxable   Tax-Deferred IRA

Tax-deferred IRA versus fully taxable growth of $3,000 annual contributions over 40 years assuming 6% growth.

FIGURE 2.8

| EXAMPLE 2.16 |

(*Individual Retirement Account – Unknown Interest*)
Verify the numerical values shown in Figure 2.8 above.

| SOLUTION |

For the tax-deferred accumulation in the IRA, with deposits of $3,000 at the start of each year for 40 years, at a 6% effective annual rate of interest, the deposits should accumulate to

$$3000\ddot{s}_{\overline{40}|.06} = 3000(1.06)\frac{(1.06)^{40}-1}{.06} = 492,143$$

at the end of the 40th year. This is not the stated amount of $514,201 in Figure 2.8 above. We can find the effective annual interest rate i which results in the stated accumulated value: $3000\ddot{s}_{\overline{40}|i} = 514,201$.

Using a financial calculator, we get the value $i = 6.17\%$. This is the effective annual rate of interest that is equivalent to a nominal annual rate of interest of 6% compounded monthly (.5% per month). It is not explicitly stated on the webpage that the quoted rate of 6% is a nominal annual rate compounded monthly. Note that withdrawals from the $514,201 balance become taxable. For additional information on solving for i using the BA II Plus calculator, see Appendix A.

Figure 2.8 has an example of fully taxable accumulation with an indicated tax rate of 30%. This means that any interest earned on the deposits will be taxed at that rate. The before-tax .5% monthly rate of interest becomes an after-tax rate of $.5\% \times .7 = .35\%$.

The equivalent effective annual after-tax rate of interest is

$$(1.0035)^{12} - 1 = .042818 \,(4.28\%).$$

The fully taxable accumulated value at the end of 40 years is

$$3000\ddot{s}_{\overline{40}|.042818} = 3000(1.042818)\frac{(1.042818)^{40} - 1}{.042818} = 317,817,$$

as indicated in Figure 2.8.   □

Part of the solution to Example 2.16 involved finding an interest rate in a transaction involving level deposits. Solving for the interest rate in a more general financial transaction whose deposits or payments are not level can lead to significant complications. For many standard financial transactions, such as loans, there is often only one non-negative interest rate solution to the unknown interest rate. Occasionally a complicated situation may arise in which it is not clear whether there is even a solution for i, and if so whether it is unique. The considerations of existence and uniqueness of solutions for i in a more general equation of value will be addressed in Chapter 5.

There are a few points to keep in mind when considering a situation involving an unknown rate of interest. Except in unusual circumstances, it can be assumed that interest rates are greater than or equal to -100%, since at a rate of -100% the accumulated value of 1 would be 0 at any future point. One circumstance in which i could be less than -100% would be where an investor has at risk more than the amount invested, such as with "leveraged" investments or when investing on "margin" (see Chapter 8). Another situation would be where the investment consists of a series of varying cashflows, each one of which can be either positive and negative (i.e., disbursements and receipts). We will consider the determination of the unknown interest rate, also called the *internal rate of return* in a more general context in Chapter 5.

2.3 ANNUITIES WITH NON-CONSTANT PAYMENTS

Many loans call for level payments during the life of the loan, however there are a number of situations which involve a non-level series of payments. We have already considered some situations in which annuity payments were not level over the course of the annuity (see Example 2.5). In order to value the annuity (either present value or accumulated value) if the payment amounts do not follow any uniform pattern, it would be necessary to value the payments individually and then add the values of the individual payments. This can be done in a straightforward way. Suppose we consider a series of n payments that are separated by equal intervals of time and suppose that the payment amounts are $K_1, K_2, \ldots, K_n$. If the valuation rate of interest is i per payment period, then the accumulated value of the series valued at the time of the final payment is $K_1(1+i)^{n-1} + K_2(1+i)^{n-2} + \cdots + K_{n-1}(1+i) + K_n$. The present value of the series of payments valued one payment period before the first payment would be $K_1 v + K_2 v^2 + \cdots + K_{n-1} v^{n-1} + K_n v^n$. In the EXCEL worksheets on the ACTEX website is a worksheet that allows for valuation of a general series of payments. Both the TI BA II PLUS and the HP-12C calculators have cashflow worksheet functions which compute accumulated and present values of a series of up to 20 different payment amounts. An example is given in the Appendix.

2.3.1 ANNUITIES WHOSE PAYMENTS FORM A GEOMETRIC PROGRESSION

Some financial calculators have the capability of valuing a series of non-level payments. It is not difficult to create valuation routines in a computer spreadsheet program that allow for any number of payments of any amounts as well as varying rates of interest. Examples of these sorts of routines are included in the collection of EXCEL routines available at the ACTEX website.

When there is some systematic way in which the payments of an annuity vary, it may be possible to algebraically simplify the present or accumulated value. Retirement annuities often have a "cost-of-living" increase or inflation-adjustment provision. This means that the annuity payment is adjusted periodically (usually annually) at a rate related to some measure of the change in the inflation rate. Often the payment adjustment is related to a "consumer price index," or some other standard measure of price inflation. Algebraically, an annuity whose payments are adjusted according to inflation would have payments that tend to increase geometrically. Inflation is unlikely to be constant from year to year, but if we consider a simplified situation where there is a level rate of inflation every year, say r, then an inflation adjusted annuity would have payments which grow by a factor of $1+r$ each year. Many insurance companies sell indexed annuities with a fixed index rate r. The following example illustrates this idea.

EXAMPLE 2.17

(*Annuity whose payments form a geometric progression*)
Smith wishes to purchase a 20-year annuity with annual payments beginning one year from now. The annuity will be valued at an effective annual rate of 11%. Smith anticipates an effective annual inflation rate over the next 20 years of 4% per year, so he wants to index his annuity at a 4% rate. In other words he would like each payment after the first to be 4% larger than the previous one. If Smith's first payment is to be 26,000, what is the present value of the annuity?

SOLUTION

The series of payments is

$$26,000;\ 26,000(1.04);\ 26,000(1.04)^2;\ldots;\ 26,000(1.04)^{19},$$

and has present value

$$26,000 \cdot v_{.11} + 26,000(1.04) \cdot v_{.11}^2 + 26,000(1.04)^2 \cdot v_{.11}^3 + \cdots$$
$$+26,000(1.04)^{19} \cdot v_{.11}^{20}.$$

This can be written as $26,000 \cdot v \left[1 + 1.04v + (1.04v)^2 + \cdots + (1.04v)^{19} \right]$,

which then simplifies to $26,000 \cdot v \left[\frac{1-(1.04v)^{20}}{1-1.04v} \right] = 270,484$. □

The important point to note in Example 2.17 is that when payments form a geometric progression, the ratio in the geometric progression combines with the present value factor so that the present value of the annuity reduces to another geometric progression. Another way of viewing an annuity whose payments form a geometric progression is illustrated in the next example.

EXAMPLE 2.18 (*Geometric progression*)

A series of n periodic payments has first payment of amount 1, and all subsequent payments are $(1+r)$ times the size of the previous payment. At a rate of interest i per payment period, show that the present value of the series at the time of the first payment can be written as $\ddot{a}_{\overline{n}|j}$ for an appropriately defined interest rate j.

SOLUTION

The present value of the series at the time of the first payment is

$$1 + (1+r)v_i + \left[(1+r)v_i \right]^2 + \cdots + \left[(1+r)v_i \right]^{n-1}$$

$$= \frac{1 - \left[(1+r)v_i \right]^n}{1 - (1+r)v_i} = \frac{1 - \left(\frac{1+r}{1+i} \right)^n}{1 - \frac{1+r}{1+i}}.$$

We want this to be $\ddot{a}_{\overline{n}|j} = \frac{1-v_j^n}{1-v_j}$. If we let $v_j = \frac{1+r}{1+i}$, then the present value will be of the proper form. But if $\frac{1}{1+j} = v_j = \frac{1+r}{1+i}$, then $1+j = \frac{1+i}{1+r}$, so that

$j = \frac{i-r}{1+r}$. □

We see from Example 2.18 that the present value of an annuity whose payments form a geometric progression can be formulated as an annuity with level payments valued at a modified rate of interest (an *inflation-adjusted* rate of interest), as described in Section 1.6. In most practical situations i would be larger than r as in Example 2.18, so that j would be positive. Algebraically the method of Example 2.18 is valid whenever $i \neq r$. In particular, note that for the series of payments in Example 2.18, the present value one period before the first payment can be expressed as

$$v + (1+r)v^2 + (1+r)^2 v^3 + \cdots + (1+r)^{n-1} v^n \;\; = \;\; \frac{1 - \left(\frac{1+r}{1+i}\right)^n}{i - r},$$

and the accumulated value at the time of the final payment can be expressed as

$$\frac{1 - \left(\frac{1+r}{1+i}\right)^n}{i - r} \cdot (1+i)^n \;\; = \;\; \frac{(1+i)^n - (1+r)^n}{i - r}.$$

If $i = r$ then the present value one period before the first payment is

$$v + (1+r)v^2 + (1+r)^2 v^3 + \cdots + (1+r)^{n-1} v^n \;=\; v + v + \cdots v \;=\; nv,$$

and the accumulated value at the time of the final payment is

$$nv(1+i)^n \;=\; n(1+i)^{n-1}.$$

It is possible that the geometric increase period (or frequency) and the payment period do not coincide. In such a situation it is usually necessary to modify the payment period to coincide with the geometric increase period; in other words we find an equivalent payment per geometric increase period. We can then apply one of the expressions just given for present and accumulated values. The following example illustrates this.

EXAMPLE 2.19   *(Differing payment period and increase period)*

Smith's child was born January 1, 2001. Smith receives monthly family allowance payments on the last day of each month, beginning January 31, 2001. The payments are increased by 12% each calendar year to meet cost-of-living increases. Monthly payments are constant during each calendar year, being 25 each month in 2001, rising to 28 each month in 2002, 31.36 each month in 2003, and so on. Immediately upon receipt of a payment, Smith deposits it in an account earning $i^{(12)} = .12$ with interest credited on the last day of each month. Find the accumulated amount in the account on the child's 18th birthday.

SOLUTION

The change in payment amount occurs once each year, but the payments are made monthly. The accumulated value on January 1, 2019, the 18th birthday, can be written as the sum of the accumulated values of each of the deposits as

$$25(1.01)^{215} + 25(1.01)^{214} + \cdots + 25(1.01)^{204}$$
$$+25(1.12)(1.01)^{203} + 25(1.12)(1.01)^{202} + \cdots + 25(1.12)(1.01)^{192}$$
$$+25(1.12)^2(1.01)^{191} + 25(1.12)^2(1.01)^{190} + \cdots + 25(1.12)^2(1.01)^{180}$$
$$+\cdots + 25(1.12)^{17}(1.01)^{11} + 25(1.12)^{17}(1.01)^{10} + \cdots + 25(1.12)^{17}.$$

A way of simplifying this sum is to first group the deposits on an annual basis, and for each year find the accumulated value of that year's deposits at the end of that year, as shown in Table 2.2.

TABLE 2.2

Year	Accumulated Value of Deposits on December 31
2001	$25 \cdot s_{\overline{12}|.01} = X$
2002	$28 \cdot s_{\overline{12}|.01} = 25(1.12) \cdot s_{\overline{12}|.01} = (1.12)X$
2003	$31.36 \cdot s_{\overline{12}|.01} = 25(1.12)^2 \cdot s_{\overline{12}|.01} = (1.12)^2 X$
$\vdots$	
2018	$25(1.12)^{17} \cdot s_{\overline{12}|.01} = (1.12)^{17} X$

The monthly deposits are equivalent to 18 geometrically increasing annual deposits of $X, (1.12)X, (1.12)^2 X, \ldots, (1.12)^{17} X$. The accumulated value at the time of the final deposit is

$$(1+i)^{17} X + (1+i)^{16}(1.12)X + (1+i)^{15}(1.12)^2 X + \cdots + (1+i)^0 (1.12)^{17} X.$$

This is the accumulated value of a geometric payment annuity with $n = 18$ payments, geometric growth rate $1+r = 1.12$, effective annual interest rate $i = (1.01)^{12} - 1$, and initial payment $25 \cdot s_{\overline{12}|.01} = X$. The accumulated value at the end of 18 years (time of the final payment) is

$$X\left[\frac{(1+i)^{18} - (1+r)^{18}}{i-r}\right] = 25 \cdot s_{\overline{12}|.01} \cdot \frac{(1.01)^{216} - (1.12)^{18}}{(1.01)^{12} - 1 - .12}.$$

Since $X = 25 \cdot s_{\overline{12}|.01} = 317.06$ and $i = (1.01)^{12} - 1 = .1268$, the accumu-
lated value is 41,282.55.   □

An elementary model for the value of a share of stock is the *dividend
discount model*. According to this model, the value of a share of stock is
the present value of the future dividends that will be paid by the stock. A
basic form of this model assumes a constant rate of increase in the
amount of the dividend paid, so that the future stream of dividends forms
a geometric payment perpetuity. We make the following assumptions:

(i)   the next dividend payable one year from now is of amount K,

(ii)   the annual compound growth rate of the dividend is r, and

(iii)   the interest rate used for calculating present values is i.

The present value one payment period before the first dividend payment is

$$K\left[\frac{1}{1+i} + \frac{1+r}{(1+i)^2} + \frac{(1+r)^2}{(1+i)^3} + \cdots\right].$$

This present value can be formulated as

$$\frac{K}{1+i}\left[1 + \left(\frac{1+r}{1+i}\right) + \left(\frac{1+r}{1+i}\right)^2 + \cdots\right] = \frac{K}{1+i} \cdot \frac{1}{1 - \frac{1+r}{1+i}} = \frac{K}{i-r}.$$

This would be the value of the stock based on the dividend discount model.
This value is sometimes referred to as the *theoretical price* of the stock. Note
that this is just the limit as $n \to \infty$ of the finite geometric payment annuity-
immediate considered earlier. In this derivation, there is an implicit
assumption that $i > r$ in order for the infinite geometric series to converge
(sum to a finite number). It would be prudent for an investor to assume that
there is some risk as to whether or not the anticipated future dividends will
actually be paid. This would be accounted for by using a "risk-adjusted"
interest rate i for finding the present value of the future dividends. The risk-
adjusted rate i would be larger than interest rates on (essentially) riskless
government securities.

EXAMPLE 2.20 (*The theoretical price of a stock*)

Common stock X pays a dividend of 50 at the end of the first year, with each subsequent annual dividend being 5% greater than the preceding one. John purchases the stock at a theoretical price to earn an expected effective annual yield of 10%. Immediately after receiving the 10th dividend, John sells the stock for a price of P. His effective annual yield over the 10-year period was 8%. Calculate P.

SOLUTION

The initial price paid by John to buy the stock is the theoretical price based on a first dividend of amount 50 to be paid in one year, with subsequent dividends growing by $r = 5\%$ per year, and with valuation based on a yield rate of $i = 10\%$ per year. The theoretical price of the stock is $\frac{50}{.10-.05} = 1,000$. John sells the stock for amount P at the end of 10 years. To say that John's yield over the 10 year period is 8% per year is to say that his investment of 1,000 is equal to the present value of what he receives, using a valuation rate of 8%. What he receives is the 10 years of dividends and the sale price P at the end of 10 years. The dividends form a 10 year geometrically increasing annuity-immediate, with first payment $K = 50$ and geometric growth rate $r = 5\%$. The present value at $j = 8\%$ of the 10 years of dividends is $K\left[\frac{1-\left(\frac{1+r}{1+j}\right)^{10}}{j-r}\right] = 50\left[\frac{1-\left(\frac{1.05}{1.08}\right)^{10}}{.08-.05}\right] = 409.18$. The present value at time 0 of the sale price P (received when the stock is sold at the end of 10 years) is $Pv_{.08}^{10} = .46319P$. Then,

$$1,000 = 409.18 + .46319P,$$

so that

$$P = 1,275.54. \qquad \square$$

2.3.2 ANNUITIES WHOSE PAYMENTS FORM AN ARITHMETIC PROGRESSION

Another systematic pattern of payment that can arise is one in which the payments follow an arithmetic progression. We consider two basic forms of annuity with arithmetic payments and then show that any annuity with arithmetic payments can be valued by combining a level payment annuity with one of these basic types.

Increasing Annuities

We first consider an *n*-payment annuity whose first payment is 1 and with each subsequent payment being 1 more than the previous payment. With an interest rate of *i* per period and equally spaced payments, the present value of the series of payments valued one period before the first payment can be expressed as

$$v + 2v^2 + 3v^3 + \cdots + (n-1)v^{n-1} + nv^n.$$

The typical algebraic method of simplifying a series that involves a arithmetic component is as follows. We let X denote the series above. Then

$$(1+i)X \quad = \quad 1 + 2v + 3v^2 + \cdots + nv^{n-1}.$$

Subtracting the first series from the second results in

$$iX \quad = \quad 1 + v + v^2 + \cdots + v^{n-1} - nv^n.$$

The first part of the right hand side of this expression happens to be the present value of an *n*-payment annuity-due. Therefore

$$X \quad = \quad \frac{1 + v + v^2 + \cdots + v^{n-1} - nv^n}{i} \quad = \quad \frac{\ddot{a}_{\overline{n}|} - nv^n}{i}.$$

In a similar way, the accumulated value of the series of payments valued at the time of the final payment can be shown to be equal to $\frac{\ddot{s}_{\overline{n}|} - n}{i}$ (which is $(1+i)^n$ times the present value). The present and accumulated values just calculated have standard actuarial notation and terminology to denote them. The term **n-payment increasing annuity immediate** is used to refer to an annuity whose payments are the sequence of integers from 1 to *n*. The present value, X, of the increasing series is denoted $(Ia)_{\overline{n}|i}$. The accumulated value is denoted $(Is)_{\overline{n}|i}$.

EXAMPLE 2.21   (*Reinvested interest and increasing annuity*)

Mary invests 1000 at the end of each year for 5 years at an effective annual rate of 9% and reinvests the interest at an effective annual rate of 9%. At the end of 5 years, her investment has a value of X. John invests 1000 at the beginning of each year for 5 years at an effective annual rate of 10% and reinvests the interest at an effective annual rate of 8%. At the end of 5 years, his investment has a value of Y. Calculate $Y - X$.

SOLUTION

At the end of 5 years, the value of Mary's investment is the sum of the 5 deposits of 1000 each and the accumulated reinvested interest. Since Mary's first deposit of 1000 into her primary account is at the end of the first year, the first interest payment from the primary account is at the end of the second year for amount 90; this is deposited into the secondary account (but the original deposit of 1000 stays in the primary account). At the end of the second year she adds 1000 to the primary account to bring the balance to 2000, and the interest generated from the primary account at the end of the third year is 180.

Each year she adds 1000 to the primary account, so each year the interest generated by that account is 90 more than the previous year. The interest generated by the primary account is 90, 180, 270, and 360 at the end of the $2^{nd}, 3^{rd}$, and 4th and 5th years. These interest payments are deposited into the secondary account (which also earns interest at a rate of 9%). The time diagram representation of Mary's investment is as follows:

Mary's Time Diagram

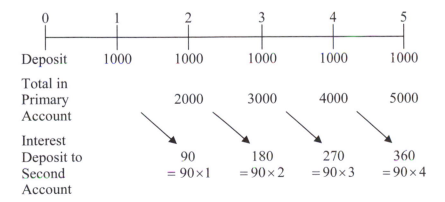

Mary's total investment at the end of 5 years is

$$X = 5000 + 90(Is)_{\overline{4}|.09} = 5,984.71.$$

Notice that since the reinvestment rate for the interest payments is 9%, which is the same as the interest rate on the initial deposits, Mary's accumulation at the end of 5 years can also be formulated as $1000s_{\overline{5}|.09} = 5,984.71$; it is the same as if she had left the interest payments in the primary account to accumulate at the 9% rate.

John's deposits are made at the beginning of each year, so the first interest payment from John's primary account occurs at the end of the first year, and the amount of that interest payment is 100; it is deposited into the secondary account earning 8%. John's subsequent interest payments are then 200, 300, 400 and 500 at the ends of years 2, 3, 4 and 5. The time diagram for John's investment is as follows.

John's Time Diagram

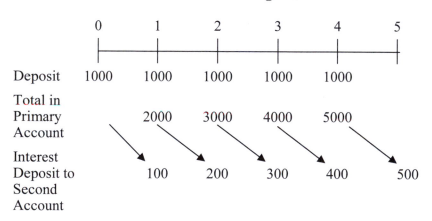

John's accumulated investment at the end of year 5 is

$$Y = 5000 + 100(Is)_{\overline{5}|.08} = 6,669.91,$$

Then, $Y - X = 685.20$.   ☐

If the payments in an increasing annuity immediate are allowed to continue forever, the result is an *increasing perpetuity immediate*, whose present value is

$$(Ia)_{\overline{\infty}|i} = v + 2v^2 + 3v^3 + \cdots = \lim_{n\to\infty} (Ia)_{\overline{n}|i} = \lim_{n\to\infty} \frac{\ddot{a}_{\overline{n}|} - nv^n}{i}.$$

From l'Hospital's rule of limits it follows that

$$\lim_{n\to\infty} nv^n = \lim_{n\to\infty} \frac{n}{(1+i)^n} = \lim_{n\to\infty} \frac{1}{(1+i)^n \ln(1+i)} = 0.$$

Also, since $\ddot{a}_{\overline{\infty}|i} = \frac{1}{d}$, it follows that $(Ia)_{\overline{\infty}|i} = \frac{1}{id} = \frac{1+i}{i^2} = \frac{1}{i^2} + \frac{1}{i}$.

EXAMPLE 2.22 (*Increasing Perpetuity*)

Perpetuity X has annual payments of $1,2,3,\ldots$ at the end of each year. Perpetuity Y has annual payments of $q,q,2q,2q,3q,3q,\ldots$ at the end of each year. The present value of X is equal to the present value of Y at an effective annual interest rate of 10%. Calculate q.

SOLUTION

Perpetuity X has present value

$$v + 2v^2 + 3v^3 + \cdots = (Ia)_{\overline{\infty}|.1} = \frac{1}{.1} + \frac{1}{(.1)^2} = 110.$$

Perpetuity Y can be separated into two groups of payments, those at the ends of years $1,3,5,7,9,\ldots$ of amounts $q,2q,3q,\ldots$, and those at the ends of years $2,4,6,8,10,\ldots$ also of amounts $q,2q,3q,\ldots$. The second set of payments forms an increasing perpetuity-immediate payable every second year. The effective 2-year rate of interest equivalent to the effective annual rate of 10% is $j = (1.1)^2 - 1 = .21 (21\%)$. The present value of the second set of payments is

$$q(v_{.21} + 2v_{.21}^2 + 3v_{.21}^3 + \cdots) = q(Ia)_{\overline{\infty}|.21} = q\left(\frac{1}{.21} + \frac{1}{(.21)^2}\right) = 27.44q.$$

Since the first set of payments is identical to the second, except that it starts one year earlier, its present value will be 1.1 times larger (one less year of present value factor), so that the present value of the first series of payments is $27.44q(1.1) = 30.18q$. The total present value of perpetuity Y is $27.44q + 30.18q = 57.62q$. We are told that this is the same present value as the value of perpetuity X of 110, so that $q = 1.91$. $\square$

Decreasing Annuities

Another basic annuity with payments that follow an arithmetic progression is the **n-payment decreasing annuity immediate**. This annuity has first payment of amount n and each subsequent payment is of amount 1 less than the previous payment. The standard actuarial notation used for this annuity is $(Da)_{\overline{n}|i}$, and this represents the present value of the sequence of payments of amounts $n, n-1, n-2, \ldots, 2, 1$, with payment starting one period from now. In Exercise 2.3.25 at the end of this chapter you are asked to show that $(Da)_{\overline{n}|} = nv + (n-1)v^2 + (n-2)v^3 + \cdots + 2v^{n-1} + v^n = \frac{n - a_{\overline{n}|}}{i}$.

If this same decreasing series of payments is valued at the time of the final payment, then we get the accumulated value of the n-payment decreasing annuity immediate, $(Ds)_{\overline{n}|} = \frac{n(1+i)^n - s_{\overline{n}|}}{i} = (Da)_{\overline{n}|} \cdot (1+i)^n$. There are a number of algebraic relationships involving the increasing and decreasing annuities that are considered in the exercises at the end of the chapter. The following example illustrates how the basic increasing and decreasing annuities can be used to formulate valuations of more general annuities with payments that follow an arithmetic progression.

EXAMPLE 2.23 (*Increasing annuity*)

Jeff bought an increasing perpetuity-due with annual payments starting at amount 5 and increasing by 5 each year until the payment amount reaches 100. The payments remain at 100 thereafter. The effective annual interest rate is 7.5%. Determine the present value of this perpetuity.

SOLUTION

There are at least two ways in which this perpetuity present value can be formulated.

(i) We can separate the first 20 payments (increasing from 5 to 100) from the 21st payment and beyond (level at 100). The present value as a perpetuity-due (valued at the time of the first payment) is

$$5(I\ddot{a})_{\overline{20}|.075} + v^{20} \cdot 100\,\ddot{a}_{\overline{\infty}|.075} \;=\; 5(1.075)(Ia)_{\overline{20}|.075} + v^{20} \cdot 100\,\ddot{a}_{\overline{\infty}|.075}$$

$$= \; 5(1.075)\left(\frac{\ddot{a}_{\overline{20}|} - 20v^{20}}{.075}\right) + v^{20} \cdot \frac{100}{d}$$

$$= \; 447.975 + 337.426 \;=\; 785.40.$$

Note that the 20-payment increasing annuity-due can be formulated as

$$(I\ddot{a})_{\overline{20}|} = \frac{\ddot{a}_{\overline{20}|} - 20v^{20}}{d} = \frac{\ddot{a}_{\overline{20}|} - 20v^{20}}{i/(1+i)} = (1+i) \cdot \frac{\ddot{a}_{\overline{20}|} - 20v^{20}}{i} = (1+i)(Ia)_{\overline{20}|}.$$

The time-diagram below illustrates the overall valuation.

0	1	2	$\cdots$	18	19	20	21	$\cdots$
[5	10	15	$\ldots$	95	100]	[100	100	$\ldots$
$\uparrow$					$\leftarrow$	$\uparrow$		
$5(I\ddot{a})_{\overline{20}|}$						$100\ddot{a}_{\overline{\infty}|}$		

(ii) We can separate the series into a combination of a level perpetuity-due minus a 19 year decreasing annuity-due.

Original series   5   10   15 $\cdots$ 95   100   100   100 $\cdots$

is equivalent to

Level perp-due 100   100   100 $\cdots$ 100   100   100   100 $\cdots$
combined with

Decreasing -95 -90 -85 $\cdots$ -5
annuity-due

Note the negative payments on the decreasing annuity-due. The present value of the two combined series is

$$100\ddot{a}_{\overline{\infty}|} - 5(D\ddot{a})_{\overline{19}|}$$

$$= 100\left(\frac{1}{d}\right) - 5\left[\frac{19 - a_{\overline{19}|}}{d}\right] = 1{,}433.333 - 647.933 = 785.40. \quad \square$$

Continuous Annuities With Varying Payments

The general form of a varying annuity defined at the start of this section had a payment of amount K_t payable at time t. The value of a continuous annuity with varying payments can also be formulated in a general context. In this case the payment pattern is described by a continuous function $h(t)$, which represents the *instantaneous rate* or *density of payment* being made at time t. Then $h(t)\,dt$ would be the instantaneous payment at time t, all of whose present or accumulated values would be "added," in the form of an integral, from time 0 to time n, producing

$$\int_0^n h(t) \cdot v^t \, dt \qquad\qquad (2.18a)$$

for the present value at time 0, and

$$\int_0^n h(t) \cdot (1+i)^{n-t} \, dt \qquad\qquad (2.18b)$$

for the accumulated value at time n. Corresponding to the standard increasing annuity in the discrete case is the continuously increasing annuity, for which $h(t) = t$. The notation used for the present value of this annuity is

$$(\overline{I}\,\overline{a})_{\overline{n}|\,i} \;=\; \int_0^n t \cdot v^t \, dt \qquad\qquad (2.\,19a)$$

and for the accumulated value is

$$(\overline{I}\,\overline{s})_{\overline{n}|\,i} \;=\; \int_0^n t \cdot (1+i)^{n-t} \, dt. \qquad\qquad (2.19b)$$

These can be simplified by applying integration by parts, producing

$$(\overline{Ia})_{\overline{n}|\,i} \;=\; \frac{\overline{a}_{\overline{n}|} - nv^n}{\delta} \tag{2.20a}$$

and

$$(\overline{I}\,\overline{s})_{\overline{n}|\,i} \;=\; \frac{\overline{s}_{\overline{n}|} - n}{\delta}, \tag{2.20b}$$

where $\delta = \ln(1+i)$. If the force of interest is varying as well, say δ_t at time t, then the more general expressions for the present and accumulated values of the annuities at times 0 and n, respectively, are

$$\int_0^n h(t) \cdot e^{-\int_0^t \delta_r\, dr}\, dt \tag{2.21a}$$

and

$$\int_0^n h(t) \cdot e^{\int_t^n \delta_r\, dr}\, dt. \tag{2.21b}$$

Unknown Interest Rate for Annuities With Varying Payments

In Section 2.2 we considered methods of determining the interest rate on an annuity when it is not given. For the cases considered there, and for varying annuities as well, it is generally true that there is a unique solution for i. The following example shows this.

EXAMPLE 2.24

Suppose that an annuity consists of payments $K_1, K_2, \ldots, K_n$ made at times $0 < t_1 < t_2 < \cdots < t_n$, where each $K_r > 0$. Suppose also that $L > 0$. Show that there is a unique i $(i > -1)$ for which L is the present value at time 0 of the given series of payments, where i is the interest rate per time unit measured by t.

SOLUTION

With $v = \frac{1}{1+i}$, the present value at time 0 of the series of payments is $f(i) = K_1 \cdot v^{t_1} + K_2 \cdot v^{t_2} + \cdots + K_n \cdot v^{t_n}$. Since the K_r's and t_r's are all > 0, it follows that $f(i)$ is a decreasing function of i, since v^{t_k} decreases as i increases. But $\lim\limits_{i \to \infty} f(i) = 0$, since each $v^{t_k} \to 0$ as $i \to \infty$, and $\lim\limits_{i \to -1} f(i) = +\infty$, since $v^{t_k} \to +\infty$ as $i \to -1$. Then since $0 < L < +\infty$ and $f(i)$ decreases from $+\infty$ to 0 as i goes from -1 to $+\infty$, it follows that there is a unique $i > -1$ for which $L = f(i)$. Note that $i > 0$ if $L < \sum\limits_{r=1}^{n} K_r$ and $i < 0$ if $L > \sum\limits_{r=1}^{n} K_r$. $\qquad\qquad\qquad\qquad\qquad\qquad$ $\square$

In a more general setting, a financial transaction may involve a series of disbursements (payments made out) and payments received. A computer routine such as "Solver" in EXCEL would be needed to solve for the unknown interest rate in a general setting. Financial calculators are usually limited to finding the unknown interest rate when payments are level (or with a balloon payment) or have a limited number of varying payments. Solving for an unknown interest rate, yield rate, or internal rate of return in a general setting is considered in Chapter 5.

2.4   APPLICATIONS AND ILLUSTRATIONS

2.4.1 YIELD RATES AND REINVESTMENT RATES

Suppose that a single amount L is invested for an n year period and the value of the investment at the end of n years is M. A reasonable definition of the annual yield rate earned by the investment over the n year period is the rate i that satisfies the equation $L(1+i)^n = M$. In other words, the yield rate is the annual compound interest rate earned by the investment over the n year period.

Now suppose that a loan of amount L is made at effective annual interest rate i and is repaid by n level annual payments of amount K each. The equation of value for the loan is $L = K \cdot a_{\overline{n}|i}$. Suppose that we regard the loan as an investment from the point of view of the lender. We would like to have a measure of the annual rate of return or interest rate or yield rate earned by the lender over the n year period. In order to use the yield rate definition given in the previous paragraph, we would need a value of the investment at the end of n years. This implicitly suggests that the lender is reinvesting the loan payments as they are being received, and has accumulated an amount M at the end of n years. In order for the lender to realize an annual yield rate of i (the original loan rate) over the n year period, the lender should have accumulated $L(1+i)^n$ as of time n. In order for this to occur, it can be seen from the equation of value for the loan that the amount the lender must have accumulated as of time n is $L(1+i)^n = Ka_{\overline{n}|i}(1+i)^n = Ks_{\overline{n}|i}$. We see that in order for the lender to realize an annual yield rate of i (the loan rate), the annual rate of interest earned by the reinvested payments must also be i. If reinvestment is at a rate other than i, then the lender's annual yield will be different from i.

A more general principle can be stated regarding the concept of yield rate described in the previous two paragraphs. Suppose that a loan of amount L at effective annual interest rate i is to be repaid over an n year period and the loan payments are reinvested as they are received. In order for the investor to realize an annual yield of i (same as the loan rate) over the n year period (so that the lender has accumulated $L(1+i)^n$ as of time n), the payments must be reinvested at rate i, the same as the loan rate.

Consider the case of a 10-year loan of 10,000 at $i = .05$. We look at three ways in which the loan can be repaid.

(1) Ten level annual payments of $\dfrac{10,000}{a_{\overline{10}|.05}} = 1295.05$. If these payments are reinvested at 5% as they are received, the accumulated value at the time of the tenth payment is $1295.05 s_{\overline{10}|.05} = 16,288.95$. Since $10,000(1.05)^{10} = 16,288.95$, the lender realizes an annual compound rate of return (or yield) of 5%.

(2) Ten level annual interest payments of 500, plus a return of the entire 10,000 principal at the end of ten years. If the payments of 500 are reinvested at 5%, the accumulated value after ten years is $500 s_{\overline{10}|.05} = 6,288.95$. Along with the payment of 10,000 at time 10, the accumulated value is again 16,288.95 (this also follows from the relationship $1 + i \cdot s_{\overline{n}|i} = (1+i)^n$), which indicates an annual compound rate of return of 5%.

(3) A single payment of $10,000(1.05)^{10} = 16,288.95$. In this case it is clear that the lender receives an annual compound rate of return of 5%.

As long as the reinvestment rate is 5% (or, in general, the interest rate i on the loan), then for any repayment schedule for which the present value of the payments is 10,000 at $i = .05$, the accumulated value of the reinvested payments will be 16,288.95.

Now let us assume instead that the interest rate earned on reinvested payments is 3%. A reinvestment rate is irrelevant in Case (3), since no reinvestment takes place. In Case (1) the accumulated value of the reinvested payments is $1295.05 \cdot s_{\overline{10}|.03} = 14,846.30$. In Case (2) the accumulated value is $500 \cdot s_{\overline{10}|.03} + 10,000 = 15,731.94$. In Cases (1) and (2) the accumulated value does not give an annual rate of 5% compounded for 10 years on an initial investment of 10,000. For Case (1), the average annual compound rate of return j is found from $10,000(1+j)^{10} = 14,846.30$, which results in $j = .0403$, and for Case (2) the average annual compound rate of return is found from $10,000(1+j)^{10} = 15,731.94$, which results in $j = .0464$. The reason the average annual compound interest rate is less than 5% is that the reinvestment rate is less than 5%. Furthermore, the less reinvestment that takes place, the less of a reduction there is below 5%. In other words Case (3) has no reinvestment and results in an annual compound rate of 5%, and Case (2) has more reinvestment than Case (3), but less reinvestment than Case (1) which has the lowest average compound return.

An important measure of rate of return on an investment is the **internal rate of return (IRR) on a transaction.** In the context of a loan regarded as an investment, the internal rate of return is the rate of interest for which the loan amount is equal to present value of the loan payments. In other words, the internal rate of return on a loan transaction is simply the interest rate at which the loan is made. The internal rate of return can be applied to more general financial transactions, and will be considered in some detail in Chapter 5. In each of Cases (1), (2) and (3) above, the internal rate of return is 5%, since in each case, the present value, at 5%, of the loan payments is 10,000. The reinvestment rate is relevant to the determination of the yield rate on a transaction as defined above, but the reinvestment rate is irrelevant in determining the internal rate of return.

When interest compounds at rate i per period it is generally assumed that as periodic interest is credited it is reinvested at the same rate i. It may be the case, however, that as interest is credited at rate i, it is reinvested at a rate other than i for future compounding. In other words only the initial amount invested earns i per period, and the interest generated by that initial amount is reinvested at rate j.

EXAMPLE 2.25   (*Yield rates*)

Smith owns a 10,000 savings bond that pays interest monthly at $i^{(12)} = .06$. Upon receipt of an interest payment, he immediately deposits it into an account earning interest, payable monthly, at a rate of $i^{(12)} = .12$. Find the accumulated value of this account just after the 12th, 24th, and 36th deposit. In each case find Smith's average annual yield $i^{(12)}$ based on his initial investment of 10,000. Assume that the savings bond may be cashed in at any time for 10,000.

SOLUTION

The savings bond pays interest of 50 per month, so the accumulated values in the account are $50 \cdot s_{\overline{12}|.01} = 634.13$, $50 \cdot s_{\overline{24}|.01} = 1348.67$, and $50 \cdot s_{\overline{36}|.01} = 2153.84$ after 12, 24 and 36 months, respectively. If j is the average monthly yield rate earned on the initial 10,000 investment, then if Smith was to cash in his bond at the end of 12 months, j would be the solution to the equation

$$10,000(1+j)^{12} = 10,634.13,$$

resulting in $j = .00514$ and $i^{(12)} = 12j = .0616$. For the 24-month period $10,000(1+j)^{24} = 11,348.67$, so that $j = .00529$ and $i^{(12)} = .0634$; for the 36-month period we find $j = .00543$ and $i^{(12)} = .0652$.   □

In general if an amount L is invested and generates interest at rate i per period which is then reinvested at rate j, the accumulated value of the reinvested interest at time n will be $L \cdot i \cdot s_{\overline{n}|j}$, and the total value of the investment will be $L + L \cdot i \cdot s_{\overline{n}|j} = L\left[1 + i \cdot s_{\overline{n}|j}\right]$ (initial principal plus reinvested interest).

EXAMPLE 2.26   (*Yield rates*)

Suppose that Smith, on a payroll savings plan, buys a savings bond for 100 at the end of every month, with the bond paying monthly interest at $i^{(12)} = .06$. The interest payments generated are reinvested in an account earning $i^{(12)} = .12$. Find the accumulated value in the deposit account at the end of 12 months, 24 months and 36 months. Find the yield rate in the form $i^{(12)}$ that Smith realizes over each of these time periods on his investment.

SOLUTION

At the end of 12 months Smith will have bought 1200 in bonds. The first 100 bond was bought at the end of the first month, so Smith received interest of 0.50 at the end of the second month, at which time he bought the second 100 bond, bringing his total in bonds to 200. At the end of the third month Smith receives 1.00 (monthly interest on the 200 in bonds), and buys a third 100 bond. At the end of the fourth month he receives 1.50 in interest and buys a fourth 100 bond. Therefore the interest Smith receives from the bonds is $0.50, 1.00, 1.50, 2.00, \ldots, 5.50$ at the ends of months $2, 3, 4, 5, \ldots, 12$. The accumulated value in the deposit account after 12 months is $(.50) \cdot (Is)_{\overline{11}|.01} = 34.13$, after 24 months it is

$$(.50) \cdot (Is)_{\overline{23}|.01} = 148.67,$$

and after 36 months the accumulated value is

$$(.50) \cdot (Is)_{\overline{35}|.01} = 353.84.$$

What is meant by the monthly yield rate j is the rate at which the original payments must be invested to accumulate to the actual amount that Smith has at the later point in time. Smith's monthly yield j on the 1200 (100 per month) invested over 12 months is the solution of $100 \cdot s_{\overline{12}|j} = 1234.13$, for which the solution is $j = .00508$, or $i^{(12)} = .061$. Over 24 months j is found from $100 \cdot s_{\overline{24}|j} = 2548.67$, which gives $j = .00518$, or $i^{(12)} = .0622$. Over 36 months we have $100 \cdot s_{\overline{36}|j} = 3953.84$, which gives $j = .00529$, or $i^{(12)} = .06348$.   □

As a general approach to the situation in Example 2.26, suppose that a series of n deposits of amount 1 each generate interest at rate i per payment period, and that the interest is reinvested as it is received at rate j per period. The first interest payment is i, which comes one period after the first of the original deposits. The second interest payment is $2i$ and is paid one period after the second of the original deposits. The following table illustrates the original deposits and the interest generated by them.

TABLE 2.3

Time	0	1	2	3	4	$\cdots$	$n-2$	$n-1$	n		Total
Payment	1	1	1	1	$\cdots$		1	1	1	$\rightarrow$	n
Interest			i	$2i$	$3i$	$\cdots$	$(n-3)i$	$(n-2)i$	$(n-1)i$	$\rightarrow$	$i \cdot (Is)_{\overline{n-1}|j}$

The interest is reinvested at rate j per period, with the interest payments forming an increasing annuity since interest at rate i is being earned on an increasing principal amount. The total accumulated value of the reinvested interest is $i \cdot (Is)_{\overline{n-1}|j}$, which, along with the original n deposits of 1 each, results in a total of $n + i \cdot (Is)_{\overline{n-1}|j}$ at time n.

2.4.2 DEPRECIATION

Among the various assets owned by a business may be an automobile. As time goes on, the resale value of the automobile decreases, and eventually the automobile may be worth nothing. Tax and accounting rules generally allow the business to take as an expense the annual reduction in value of the asset. Each year the business would make an accounting for the amount of depreciation (reduction in value) of the asset, and the depreciated value (reduced value) after the depreciation has been applied. Eventually, the asset will be sold for some amount (the "salvage value") or may have no value at some point.

To set up a schedule of depreciation for an asset, we would need to have the following information:

(i) the initial value or purchase price of the asset, say P_0,

(ii) the number of years over which the asset will be depreciated, say n, and

(iii) the salvage value of the asset at the end of the asset's useful lifetime, say P_n.

A depreciation schedule would provide the year-by-year sequence of depreciated values, $P_0, P_1, P_2, \ldots, P_{n-1}, P_n$, where P_t denotes the depreciated value at time t, the end of the tth year. The amounts of depreciation year-by-year would be $D_1, D_2, \ldots, D_{n-1}, D_n$, where D_t denotes the amount of depreciation for the tth year. D_t is the amount of reduction in asset value from the end of the $t-1^{st}$ year to the end of the tth year, so that $D_t = P_{t-1} - P_t$, and $P_t = P_{t-1} - D_t$. We see that over the course of the n years we have the following relationships:

$$P_0 - D_1 - D_2 - \cdots - D_{n-1} - D_n$$

$$= P_0 - (P_0 - P_1) - (P_1 - P_2) - \cdots - (P_{n-2} - P_{n-1}) - (P_{n-1} - P_n) = P_n$$

and

$$P_t - P_{t+k} = D_{t+1} + D_{t+2} + \cdots + D_{t+k}$$

(the reduction in asset value from one point in time to another is the sum of the yearly depreciation charges during that time interval).

There are several conventional methods for constructing the schedule of annual depreciation amounts and depreciated values. We consider four depreciation methods.

In each case, the formulations for P_t and D_t are given.

Depreciation Method 1 – The Declining Balance Method

The declining balance method (also known as the constant percentage method, or the compound discount method) requires the assumption of an annual discount factor d.

The factor is applied each year to the previous year-end's depreciated value to calculate this year's amount of depreciation, so that

$D_t = P_{t-1} \cdot d$. We get the following sequence of depreciation amounts and depreciated values.

Starting asset value $\qquad$ P_0

Amount of depreciation in 1st year $\quad D_1 = P_0 \cdot d$

1st year-end depreciated value $\qquad P_1 = P_0 - D_1 = P_0 \cdot (1-d)$

Amount of depreciation in 2nd year $\quad D_2 = P_1 \cdot d = P_0 \cdot (1-d) \cdot d$

2nd year-end depreciated value $\qquad P_2 = P_1 - D_2 = P_1 \cdot (1-d) = P_0 \cdot (1-d)^2$

The pattern continues in this way, so that the depreciated value at the end of t years is $P_t = P_0 \cdot (1-d)^t$, and the amount of depreciation for the tth year is $D_t = P_0 \cdot (1-d)^{t-1} \cdot d$. Note that the salvage value is $P_n = P_0 \cdot (1-d)^n$.

Depreciation Method 2 – The Straight-Line Method

The straight-line method is quite simple. The total amount of depreciation that occurs over the n-year period is $P_0 - P_n$. In the straight-line method, the amount of depreciation each year for n years is $\frac{1}{n}^{th}$ of the n year total depreciation charge, so that $D_t = \frac{1}{n} \cdot (P_0 - P_n)$ for each year, $t = 1, 2, ..., n$. The depreciated value at the end of t years will be the initial value minus the t years of depreciation charges, so that

$$P_t \;=\; P_0 - (D_1 + D_2 + \cdots + D_t) \;=\; P_0 - t \cdot \frac{1}{n} \cdot (P_0 - P_n).$$

Notice that this can be rewritten in the form $P_t = \frac{n-t}{n} \cdot P_0 + \frac{t}{n} \cdot P_n$; this shows that the depreciated value is just the linearly interpolated value $\frac{t}{n}$ of the way from the asset value at time 0 to the asset value at time n (not surprising, since there is a constant annual reduction in asset value).

Depreciation Method 3 – The Sum of Years Digits Method

In this method, the amount of depreciation for a particular year is a fraction of the total n-year depreciation charge, $P_0 - P_n$. We define the following factor, $S_k = 1 + 2 + \cdots + k = \frac{k(k+1)}{2}$; this is the sum of the integers from 1 to k.

In the first year, the amount of depreciation taken is $\frac{n}{S_n} \cdot (P_0 - P_n)$, and in the second year, the amount of depreciation taken is $\frac{n-1}{S_n} \cdot (P_0 - P_n)$. In the tth year, the amount of depreciation taken is $\frac{n-t+1}{S_n} \cdot (P_0 - P_n)$. In the exercises, you are asked to show that the depreciated value at the end of the tth year is $P_t = P_n + \frac{S_{n-t}}{S_n} \cdot (P_0 - P_n)$. For instance, with a 20-year depreciation period, the depreciated value at the end of 8 years would be $P_8 = P_{20} + \frac{S_{12}}{S_{20}} \cdot (P_0 - P_{20}) = P_{20} + \frac{78}{210} \cdot (P_0 - P_{20})$, since

$$S_{12} = 1 + 2 + \cdots + 12 = \frac{12 \times 13}{2} = 78$$

and

$$S_{20} = 1 + 2 + \cdots + 20 = \frac{20 \times 21}{2} = 210.$$

Depreciation Method 4 – The Compound Interest Method

This method may also be referred to as the sinking fund method of depreciation. This method requires the assumption of an interest rate i. The amount of depreciation in the tth year is $D_t = \frac{(1+i)^{t-1}}{s_{\overline{n}|i}} \cdot (P_0 - P_n)$ and the depreciated value at the end of t years is $P_t = P_0 - \frac{s_{\overline{t}|i}}{s_{\overline{n}|i}} \cdot (P_0 - P_n)$. Note that in this method, the annual depreciation charges are getting larger as time goes on. For the compound discount method and the sum of years digits method, the depreciation charge is largest in the first year and decreases as time goes on; that would be what is usually seen in practice.

EXAMPLE 2.27 *(Depreciation)*

An asset has a purchase price of 1,000 and a salvage value of 100 at the end of 10 years. For each of the depreciation methods presented above, set up tables for the depreciated value and amount of depreciation for each of the 10 years of the life of the asset. For the declining balance method use a discount factor of 20.56% and for the compound interest method use an interest rate of 10%.

SOLUTION

Depreciated Values

t	DB(1) $1000(.7944)^t$	SL(2) $1000 - 90t$	SY(3) $100 + \dfrac{900S_{\overline{10-t}}}{55}$	CI(4) $1000 - \dfrac{900s_{\overline{t}.1}}{15.937}$
1	794.40	910	836.36	943.53
2	631.07	820	689.09	881.41
3	501.32	730	558.18	813.08
⋮	⋮	⋮	⋮	⋮
9	125.99	190	116.36	233.13
10	100	100	100	100

Yearly Amounts of Depreciation

t	DB(1) $205.60(.7944)^{t-1}$	SL(2) 90	SY(3) $\dfrac{900(10-t+1)}{55}$	CI(4) $\dfrac{900(1.1)^{t-1}}{15.937}$
1	205.60	90	163.64	56.47
2	163.32	90	147.27	62.12
3	129.75	90	130.91	68.33
⋮	⋮	⋮	⋮	⋮
9	32.61	90	32.73	121.05
10	25.90	90	16.36	133.16

2.4.3 CAPITALIZED COST

An asset (such as a machine used in a production process) that is purchased may have a finite lifetime, after which it will need to be replaced. The asset may have some salvage value at the end of its lifetime. Even if it is not necessary to borrow in order to obtain the asset, there will be an interest cost or interest loss because funds have to be used to purchase (or borrow) the asset. Also, the asset may have periodic maintenance costs (assumed to occur at the end of each period, unless otherwise specified). It may be necessary to replace the asset at the end of its lifetime. We define the asset's capitalized cost to be the original cost of the asset, plus the present value of an infinite number of replacements, plus the present value of maintenance costs in perpetuity. In other words, it is the present value of the costs involved in having use of the asset forever.

The components of the asset purchase and maintenance can be summarized as follows:

- initial asset value is P
- lifetime of the asset is n years
- salvage value at the end of n years is S
- interest rate for cost of capital (borrowing) is i (sometimes called the required annual yield rate)
- periodic (end of each year, usually) maintenance cost is M

The cashflows required to maintain the asset indefinitely are:

(i) a payment of amount P at time 0,

(ii) payments of amount $P - S$ at times $n, 2n,\ldots$, forever,

(iii) payments of amount M each year forever starting one year from now.

The capitalized cost of the asset is then

$$C \;=\; P + (P-S)\left(v^n + v^{2n} + \cdots\right) + M\left(v + v^2 + \cdots\right).$$

This can be reformulated as $C \;=\; P + \dfrac{P-S}{i \cdot s_{\overline{n}|i}} + \dfrac{M}{i}$, since

$$v^n + v^{2n} + \cdots \;=\; \frac{v^n}{1 - v^n} \;=\; \frac{1}{(1+i)^n - 1} \;=\; \frac{1}{i \cdot s_{\overline{n}|i}}.$$

| **EXAMPLE 2.28** | (*Capitalized Cost*)

Machines X and Y each sell for 100,000 and each has a life of 17 years. Machine X produces 1000 units per year, has an annual maintenance expense of 1000 and a salvage value of 33,750. Machine Y produces U units per year, has an annual maintenance expense of 1100 and no salvage value. At an effective annual rate of interest of 8%, a buyer is indifferent between the two machines. Determine U.

| **SOLUTION** |

To say that the buyer is indifferent means that the capitalized cost per unit produced (annual) is the same for both machines. The capitalized cost of Machine X is

$$100,000 + \frac{100,000 - 33,750}{(1.08)^{17} - 1} + \frac{1,000}{.08} = 137,037.$$

The capitalized cost of Machine Y is

$$100,000 + \frac{100,000}{(1.08)^{17} - 1} + \frac{1,100}{.08} = 150,787.$$

The capitalized cost per unit produced annually is $\frac{137,037}{1000} = 137$ for Machine X, and is $\frac{150,787}{U}$ for Machine Y. In order for the buyer to be indifferent between the two machines, the unit costs must be the same, so that $\frac{150,787}{U} = 137$, from which we get $U = 1100$. □

Related to the capitalized cost is the *periodic charge* to maintain the asset. The periodic charge is equal to the capitalized cost multiplied by the interest rate, so that

$$\text{Periodic Charge} = \left(P + \frac{P - S}{i \cdot s_{\overline{n}|i}} + \frac{M}{i} \right) \times i = Pi + \frac{P - S}{s_{\overline{n}|i}} + M.$$

We can interpret this periodic charge as being made up of the annualized interest on the initial purchase price ($P \cdot i$), plus the annual cost to make up the shortfall between purchase price and salvage value that will occur when the asset has to be repurchased in n years $\left(\frac{P-S}{s_{\overline{n}|i}}\right)$, plus the annual maintenance cost (M).

2.4.4 BOOK VALUE AND MARKET VALUE

An investor considering the purchase of an annuity (or series of cashflows) at time t_0 will typically calculate the present value of the series of cashflows at some interest rate, say i_0. This rate would be related to rates in effect for similar investments at the time of valuation. The investor's *yield-to-maturity* on the series of cashflows is i_0 if the series is received for its full term. At any intermediate point during the term of the series of cashflows, the present value of the remaining payments in the series based on the original rate i_0 is called the **book value** of the cashflow at that time. Such a valuation might be needed for accounting purposes. If the investor decides at time $t_1 > t_0$ to sell to another investor, the remainder of the series of cashflows that he is entitled to receive an appropriate interest rate, called the market rate, say i_1, would be used at t_1 for the valuation. The present value of the remaining series at t_1 based on the market rate is called the market value of the series of cashflows. These notions of book value and **market value** arise in the context of loan amortization (Chapter 3) and in the valuation of bonds (Chapter 4).

| EXAMPLE 2.29 | (*Book value and market value*)

Smith borrows 10,000 at effective annual interest rate $i_0 = .10$. The loan will be repaid by 10 annual payments of amounts $2000, 1900, 1800, \ldots,$ 1100, with the first payment made one year after the loan. Determine the book value and the market value of the loan payments just after the 5th payment if the market rate of interest then is $.12$.

| SOLUTION |

Note that the present value at $t = 0$ of the loan payments at $i_0 = .10$ is $1000 \cdot a_{\overline{10}|.10} + 100 \cdot (Da)_{\overline{10}|.10} = 10,000$. The book value just after the 5th

payment is $BV_5 = 1000 \cdot a_{\overline{5}|.10} + 100 \cdot (Da)_{\overline{5}|.10} = 5000$, and the market value is $MV_5 = 1000 \cdot a_{\overline{5}|.12} + 100 \cdot (Da)_{\overline{5}|.12} = 4767.46$. □

2.4.5 THE SINKING FUND METHOD OF VALUATION

A situation may arise in which a lender is considering the purchase of an annuity (a specified series of payments). In previous sections of this chapter we have considered the valuation of the series of payments in the form of the present value of the series at some interest rate i per payment period. However, as noted above, in order to actually realize a return of i per period to the end of the term, we must have a reinvestment rate of i as well. It may be the case that the reinvestment rate j is not equal to i. In practice, the rate i on a loan would tend to be larger than the rate j earned on reinvestment, such as in a deposit account. The **sinking fund method** is a way for an investor to value the annuity when $j \neq i$. The sinking fund method of valuing (finding the purchase price for) a level annuity of K per period for n periods allows an investor to receive a periodic return of i per period while recovering his initial investment amount (the principal) in a sinking fund (deposit account). The idea is that the investor pays an amount P for the series of payments, and receives a periodic return at rate i on the initial outlay, which would be $P \cdot i$ per period. The actual payment being received from the annuity is K per period, so the amount of the payment in excess of the periodic return is $K - P \cdot i$. This excess is the amount that is deposited into the sinking fund at rate j. At the end of the n-period term, the sinking fund has accumulated to $(K - P \cdot i) \cdot s_{\overline{n}|j}$. This accumulated amount should be just enough to repay the investor's initial outlay, allowing him to recover the principal. This scenario is illustrated in Table 2.4.

TABLE 2.4

Time	0	1	2	$\cdots$	n
Initial outlay	P				
Interest per period		$P \cdot i$	$P \cdot i$	$\cdots$	$P \cdot i$
Actual payment		K	K	$\cdots$	K
Sinking fund deposit		$K - P \cdot i$	$K - P \cdot i$	$\cdots$	$K - P \cdot i \rightarrow (K - P \cdot i) \cdot s_{\overline{n}|j} = P$

Then we see that

$$(K - P \cdot i) \cdot s_{\overline{n}|j} \;\; = \;\; P \tag{2.22a}$$

or, equivalently,

$$P \;\; = \;\; \frac{K \cdot s_{\overline{n}|j}}{1 + i \cdot s_{\overline{n}|j}}. \tag{2.22b}$$

This situation is similar to Case (2) considered at the start of this section, where the 10,000 loan is repaid by interest alone and the principal is returned at the end of the term. In this case the initial investment of P earns interest of $P \cdot i$ per period, and the principal amount is returned at the end of the term by means of the accumulated sinking fund.

EXAMPLE 2.30   (*Sinking fund*)

A manufacturer is considering the purchase of some equipment to increase production that will generate income of 15,000 per year, payable at the end of the year. The equipment has a lifetime of 8 years and no salvage value. What price should be paid for this equipment in order to realize an annual return of 10% while recovering the principal in a sinking fund earning 7 % per annum?

SOLUTION

We can apply Equation (2.22b) with $K = 15,000$, $n = 8$, $i = .10$, and $j = .07$, obtaining $P = \frac{15,000 \cdot s_{\overline{8}|.07}}{1 + (.10) \cdot s_{\overline{8}|.07}} = 75,961.77$ as the solution of the equation $(15,000 - .10P)s_{\overline{8}|.07} = P$. Note that the income of 15,000 per year can be split into 7596.18 plus 7403.82, and the 8 deposits of 7403.82 accumulate to 75,961.73 at 7%. The present value of the income at $i = .10$ is $15,000 \cdot a_{\overline{8}|.10} = 80,023.89$. ☐

Exercises at the end of this chapter relate to various aspects of the sinking fund approach to valuing a series of payments. The relationship between the usual present value method (or amortization method) of valuing an annuity and the sinking fund method is considered in the following example.

| **EXAMPLE 2.31** | (*Valuation methods*) |

Let P_1 be the present value of an n-payment level annuity-immediate valued in the usual way at a periodic interest rate of i per period. Let P_2 be the "present" value of the annuity based on the sinking fund method with annual return of $i > 0$ (the same interest rate as in the calculation of P_1) to the investor along with recapture of principal in a sinking fund at rate $j > 0$. (The quotation marks around "present" indicate that present value is not being found in the usual sense with a present value factor v at some specified rate of interest.) Derive each of the relationships (a) $i = j \to P_1 = P_2$, (b) $i > j \to P_1 > P_2$, and (c) $i < j \to P_1 < P_2$.

| **SOLUTION** |

Let the periodic payment be 1. Then $P_1 = a_{\overline{n}|i}$ and $P_2 = \dfrac{s_{\overline{n}|j}}{1 + i \cdot s_{\overline{n}|j}}$. If $i = j$, then $P_2 = \dfrac{s_{\overline{n}|i}}{1 + i \cdot s_{\overline{n}|i}} = \dfrac{s_{\overline{n}|i}}{(1+i)^n} = a_{\overline{n}|i} = P_1$, establishing relationship (a). Note that P_2 can be written (after some simple algebraic manipulation) in the form $P_2 = \dfrac{1}{i} \cdot \left[1 - \dfrac{1}{1 + i \cdot s_{\overline{n}|j}} \right]$. Then we have the following sequence of implications:

$$i > j \to s_{\overline{n}|i} > s_{\overline{n}|j} \to 1 + i \cdot s_{\overline{n}|i} > 1 + i \cdot s_{\overline{n}|j} \to \frac{1}{1 + i \cdot s_{\overline{n}|i}} < \frac{1}{1 + i \cdot s_{\overline{n}|j}}$$

$$\to P_1 = a_{\overline{n}|i} = \frac{1}{i}\left[1 - \frac{1}{1 + i \cdot s_{\overline{n}|i}} \right] > \frac{1}{i}\left[1 - \frac{1}{1 + i \cdot s_{\overline{n}|j}} \right] = P_2,$$

which establishes relationship (b). Relationship (c) is established in the same way as (b), except that all inequalities are reversed. □

The sinking fund method of valuation can be applied to a varying series of payments $K_1, K_2, \ldots, K_n$ made at times $1, 2, \ldots, n$. Suppose L is the purchase price of this varying annuity-immediate to provide the purchaser with a return of i per payment period while allowing the recapture of principal in a sinking fund at rate j. Then L must be the accumulated value at time n of the series of sinking fund deposits, where the sinking fund deposit at time t is $K_t - L \cdot i$. Then

$$L = (K_1 - L \cdot i)(1+j)^{n-1} + (K_2 - L \cdot i)(1+j)^{n-2}$$
$$+ \cdots + (K_{n-1} - L \cdot i)(1+j)^1 + (K_n - L \cdot i)(1+j)^0$$
$$= \sum_{t=1}^{n} K_t (1+j)^{n-t} - L \cdot i \cdot s_{\overline{n}|j}.$$

Solving for L results in

$$L = \frac{\sum_{t=1}^{n} K_t (1+j)^{n-t}}{1 + i \cdot s_{\overline{n}|j}}. \tag{2.23}$$

The most general case would also allow for varying rates of return $i_1, i_2, \ldots, i_n$ and sinking fund rates $j_1, j_2, \ldots, j_n$.

2.5 NOTES AND REFERENCES

A finite difference approach to simplifying the present value of a varying annuity is discussed in the *Theory of Interest*, by S. Kellison. Chapter 2 of *Compound Interest* by M. Butcher and C. Nesbitt contains an extensive collection of numerical and algebraic problems on annuities.

2.6   EXERCISES

The exercises without asterisks are intended to comprehensively cover the material presented in the chapter. Exercises with a asterisk can be regarded as supplementary exercises which cover topics in more depth, either theoretically or computationally, than those without a asterisk.

SECTION 2.1

2.1.1   Write the annuity $s_{\overline{n+k}|i}$ in series form (assume n and k are integers). Group separately the accumulated values (as of the time of the final payment) of the first n payments and final k payments. Use this formulation to derive Equation (2.4).

2.1.2   Since June 30, 2002 Smith has been making deposits of 100 each into a bank account on the last day of each month. For all of 2002 and 2003 Smith's account earned nominal interest compounded monthly at an annual rate of 9%. For the first 9 months of 2004 the account earned $i^{(12)} = .105$, and since then the account has been earning $i^{(12)} = .12$. Find the balance in the account on February 1, 2005. Find the amount of interest credited on February 28, 2005.

2.1.3   To accumulate 8000 at the end of $3n$ years, deposits of 98 are made at the end of each of the first n years and 196 at the end of each of the next $2n$ years. The effective annual rate of interest is i. You are given $(1+i)^n = 2.0$. Determine i.

2.1.4 (a) In a series of 40 payments the first 10 payments are 10 each, the second 10 payments are 20 each, the third ten payments are 30 each, and the final 10 payments are 40 each. The payments are equally spaced and the interest rate is 5% per payment period. Find the accumulated value at the time of the final payment.

(b) Show that the accumulated value of the series is equal to
$$10\left[s_{\overline{10}|.05} + s_{\overline{20}|.05} + s_{\overline{30}|.05} + s_{\overline{40}|.05} \right].$$

2.1.5   Given $s_{\overline{10}|.10} = S$, find the value of $\sum\limits_{t=1}^{10} s_{\overline{t}|.10}$ in terms of S.

2.1.6   A deposit of 1 is made at each of times $t = 1, 2, \ldots, n$ to an account earning interest at rate i per payment period. Let I_t denote the interest payable at time t. Find an expression for I_t, and show that $\sum\limits_{t=1}^{n} I_t = s_{\overline{n}|i} - n$. What is the interpretation of this relationship?

2.1.7   Smith buys 100 shares of stock ABC at the same time Brown
        buys 100 shares of stock XYZ. Both stocks are bought for 10 per
        share. Smith receives a dividend of .80 per share, payable at the
        end of each year, for 10 years, at which time (just after receiving
        the 10th dividend) he sells his stock for 2 per share. Smith
        invests his dividends at annual rate 6%, and invests the proceeds
        of the sale of his stock at the same rate. Brown receives no
        dividends for the first 10 years, but starts receiving annual
        dividends of .40 per share at the end of 11 years. Brown also
        invests his dividends in an account earning 6%. If Brown sells
        his shares n years after purchase, what should be the sale price
        per share in order that his accumulated investment matches that
        of Smith, for each of $n = 15, 20$ and 25?

2.1.8   (a) If $s_{\overline{n}|} = 70$ and $s_{\overline{2n}|} = 210$, find the values of $(1+i)^n, i$, and
            $s_{\overline{3n}|}$.

        (b) If $s_{\overline{3n}|} = X$ and $s_{\overline{n}|} = Y$, express v^n in terms of X, Y and
            constants.

        (c) If $s_{\overline{n}|} = 48.99$, $s_{\overline{n-2}|} = 36.34$, and $i > 0$, find i.

2.1.9   An $m+n$ year annuity of 1 per year has $i = 7\%$ during the first
        m years and has $i = 11\%$ during the remaining n years. If
        $s_{\overline{m}|.07} = 34$ and $s_{\overline{n}|.11} = 128$, what is the accumulated value of the
        annuity just after the final payment?

2.1.10 Chuck needs to purchase an item in 10 years. The item costs 200
        today, but its price inflates 4% per year. To finance the purchase,
        Chuck deposits 20 into an account at the beginning of each year
        for 6 years. He deposits an additional X at the beginning of years
        4, 5, and 6 to meet his goal. The effective annual interest rate is
        10%. Calculate X.

2.1.11 Show that Equation (2.7) can be written as $1 = v^n + i \cdot a_{\overline{n}|i}$, and
        give an interpretation of this relationship.

2.1.12 For the situation described in Exercise 2.1.2, find the present
        value of the series on June 1, 2002. The final payment is made
        on January 31, 2005.

2.1.13 Smith makes deposits of 1000 on the last day of each month in an account earning interest at rate $i^{(12)} = .12$. The first deposit is January 31, 2005 and the final deposit is December 31, 2029. The accumulated account is used to make monthly payments of Y starting January 31, 2030 with the final one on December 31, 2054. Find Y.

2.1.14 A scholarship fund is started on January 1, 2000 with an initial deposit of 100,000 in an account earning $i^{(2)} = .08$, with interest credited every June 30 and December 31. Every January 1 from 2001 on, the fund will receive a deposit of 5000. The scholarship fund makes payments to recipients totaling 12,000 every July 1 starting in 2000. What amount is in the scholarship account just after the 5000 deposit is made on January 1, 2010?

2.1.15 At an effective annual interest rate of $i, i > 0$, both of the following annuities have a present value of X:

  (a) a 20-year annuity-immediate with annual payments of 55

  (b) a 30-year annuity-immediate with annual payments that pays 30 per year for the first 10 years, 60 per year for the second 10 years, and 90 per year for the final 10 years.

  Calculate X.

2.1.16 10,000 can be invested under two options:

  Option 1. Deposit the 10,000 into a fund earning an effective annual rate of i; or

  Option 2. Purchase an annuity-immediate with 24 level annual payments at an effective annual rate of 10%. The payments are deposited into a fund earning an effective annual rate of 5%.

  Both options produce the same accumulated value at the end of 24 years. Calculate i.

2.1.17 Dottie receives payments of X at the end of each year for n years. The present value of her annuity is 493. Sam receives payments of $3X$ at the end of each year for $2n$ years. The present value of his annuity is 2748. Both present values are calculated at the same effective annual interest rate. Determine v^n.

2.1.18   The situation in Example 2.2 is modified so that payments begin on November 1, 1997 and end May 1, 2005, but the accumulated value is still 7000 on November 1, 2005. What is the payment amount in this case? What is the ratio of the payment found in Example 2.2 to this payment ?

2.1.19   A loan of 10,000 is being repaid by 10 semiannual payments, with the first payment made one-half year after the loan. The first 5 payments are K each, and the final 5 are $K + 200$ each. What is K if $i^{(2)} = .06$?

2.1.20   Show that $a_{\overline{n}|}$ can be written as the difference between a perpetuity-immediate and an n-year deferred perpetuity-immediate.

*2.1.21 In a series of $n \cdot m$ payments the first m payments are K each, the second m payments are $2K$ each, and so on, with the final m payments of amount nK each. The payments are equally spaced and interest is at rate i per payment period. Show that the accumulated value of the series at the time of the final payment is

$$K \cdot \sum_{t=1}^{n} s_{\overline{m \cdot t}|\, i}.$$

*2.1.22 Smith opens a bank account, paying interest at rate i, with a deposit of R. The bank credits interest annually, but will pay simple interest up to the day the account is closed if this occurs less than a year after it is opened. Smith gets a bright idea and decides that if he closes the account after 6 months and immediately opens a new account for six months, his annual return will be based on $i^{(2)}$ numerically equal to i. Later Smith realizes that if he closes his account and immediately reopens a new account n times per year, his annual return will be $i^{(n)}$ numerically equal to i. The bank, anticipating such behavior, has in place a mechanism that discourages closing and immediately reopening accounts. The bank has a service charge of k at the time an account is closed if this occurs within one year of the date it was opened.

(a) If Smith's initial deposit is R and he closes and reopens his account n times per year equally spaced, derive an expression in terms of $R, n, k,$ and i for the effective annual rate of return that Smith realizes on his account.

(b) If $i = .12$ and $k = 1$, find the value of n that optimizes his effective annual return if R is (i) 10,000, (ii) 1000 and (iii) 100.

*2.1.23 Explain the relationship in terms of the amounts deposited, interest, and interest on interest: $s_{\overline{3}|i} = 3 + 3i + i^2$.

*2.1.24 Derive Equation (2.8): (a) by means of a line diagram similar to the derivation of Equation (2.4), (b) by considering the series forms of the annuities in Equation (2.8), and

(c) show that $v^m + v^{m+1} + \cdots + v^n = \dfrac{v^{m-1} - v^n}{i}$.

*2.1.25 For the series of part (a) of Exercise 2.1.4, find the present value one payment period before the first payment. Show that this present value can be written as

$$10\left[4 \cdot a_{\overline{40}|.05} - a_{\overline{10}|.05} - a_{\overline{20}|.05} - a_{\overline{30}|.05}\right].$$

*2.1.26 Suppose an annuity of $n + k$ equally-spaced payments (where n and k are integers) of amount 1 each is subject to interest at rate i per payment period until the nth payment, and at rate j per payment period starting just after the nth payment. If Y is the accumulated value of the series at the time of the final payment and X is the present value of the series one period before the first payment, show that $Y = (1+i)^n(1+j)^k \cdot X$.

*2.1.27 Derive the relationship $\dfrac{1}{a_{\overline{n}|i}} = \dfrac{1}{s_{\overline{n}|i}} + i.$

*2.1.28 For an annuity of $3n$ payments of equal amount at periodic interest rate i, it is found that one period before the first payment the present value of the first n payments is equal to the present value of the final $2n$ payments. What is the value of v^n?

*2.1.29 Derive the following identities:

(a) $\ddot{a}_{\overline{n}|i} = (1+i)a_{\overline{n}|i} = a_{\overline{n}|i} + 1 - v^n = 1 + a_{\overline{n-1}|i}$

(b) $\ddot{s}_{\overline{n}|i} = (1+i)s_{\overline{n}|i} = s_{\overline{n}|i} - 1 + (1+i)^n = s_{\overline{n+1}|i} - 1$

(c) $\dfrac{1}{\ddot{a}_{\overline{n}|i}} = \dfrac{1}{\ddot{s}_{\overline{n}|i}} + d$

*2.1.30 A loan of 5000 can be repaid by payments of 117.38 at the end of each month for n years ($12n$ payments), starting one month after the loan is made. At the same rate of interest, $12n$ monthly payments of 113.40 each accumulate to 10,000 one month after the final payment. Find the equivalent effective annual rate of interest.

*2.1.31 (a) A perpetuity pays 1 every January 1 starting in 2015. The effective annual rate of interest will be i in odd-numbered years and j in even-numbered years. Find an expression for the present value of the perpetuity on January 1, 2014.

   (b) A perpetuity starting January 1, 2015 pays 1 every January 1 in odd years and 2 every January 1 in even years. Find an expression for the present value at rate i per year of the perpetuity on (i) January 1, 2014, and (ii) January 1, 2015.

*2.1.32 (a) Three schemes are considered for the repayment of a loan of amount L which is to be repaid with 10 annual payments. Scheme (i) has 5 payments of X each followed by 5 payments of $2X$ each, scheme (ii) has 10 payments of Y each, and scheme (iii) has 5 payments of $2Z$ each followed by 5 payments of Z each. For each scheme the first payment is made one year after the loan. Assuming that $i > 0$, show that $X > \frac{2Y}{3} > Z$.

   (b) A loan of amount L is to be repaid by $n > 1$ equal annual payments, starting one year after the loan. If interest is at effective annual rate i the annual payment is P_1, and if interest is at effective annual rate $2i$ the annual payment is P_2. Show that $P_2 < 2P_1$.

*2.1.33 Smith borrows 5000 on January 1, 2005. She repays the loan with 20 annual payments starting January 1, 2006. The payments in even-numbered years are Y each and the payments in odd-numbered years are X each. If $i = .08$ and the total of all 20 loan payments is 10,233, find X and Y.

*2.1.34 A loan of 11,000 is made with interest at a nominal annual rate of 12% compounded monthly. The loan is to be repaid by 36 monthly payments of 367.21 over 37 months, starting one month after the loan is made, there being a payment at the end of every month but one. At the end of which month is the missing payment?

*2.1.35 Suppose that the effective interest rates in successive periods are $i_1, i_2, i_3, \ldots$.

(a) For an n-payment annuity-immediate of 1 per period starting at the end of the first period, show that

$$s_{\overline{n}|} = 1 + (1+i_n) + (1+i_n)(1+i_{n-1}) + \cdots + (1+i_n)(1+i_{n-1})\cdots(1+i_2).$$

(b) For an n-payment annuity-due of 1 per period starting at the beginning of the first period, show that

$$\ddot{s}_{\overline{n}|} = (1+i_n) + (1+i_n)(1+i_{n-1}) + \cdots + (1+i_n)(1+i_{n-1})\cdots$$
$$(1+i_2) + (1+i_n)(1+i_{n-1})\cdots(1+i_2)(1+i_1).$$

*2.1.36 Give algebraic proofs for each of the following relationships:

(a) $s_{\overline{90}|} = s_{\overline{30}|}\left(1 + (1+i)^{30} + (1+i)^{60}\right)$

(b) $a_{\overline{2n}|} = a_{\overline{n}|}(1+v^n)$

(c) $s_{\overline{n}|} + s_{\overline{2n}|} < s_{\overline{3n}|}$ if both n and i are > 0.

(d) $a_{\overline{n}|} + a_{\overline{2n}|} > a_{\overline{3n}|}$ if both n and i are > 0.

(e) If $0 = t_0 \le t_1 \le t_2 \le \cdots \le t_{k-1} \le t_k = n$, then

(i) $s_{\overline{n}|} = \sum_{j=1}^{k} (1+i)^{n-t_j} \cdot s_{\overline{t_j - t_{j-1}}|}$, and

(ii) $a_{\overline{n}|} = \sum_{j=1}^{k} v^{t_{j-1}} \cdot a_{\overline{t_j - t_{j-1}}|}$.

*2.1.37 An accumulated amount function is defined as $A(t) = (1.12)^{\sqrt{t}}$ for $t \ge 0$. Find $s_{\overline{10}|}$ and $a_{\overline{10}|}$, the values at times 10 and 0, respectively, of a series of 10 payments of 1 starting at time 1, and calculate $\dfrac{s_{\overline{10}|}}{a_{\overline{10}|}}$ (strictly speaking the notations $s_{\overline{10}|}$ and $a_{\overline{10}|}$ should not be used since they apply to a situation in which the interest rate is constant in successive periods).

*2.1.38 The force of interest has the form $\delta_t = \dfrac{.10}{\sqrt{1+.10t}}$. An annuity has payments of amount 1 each at integral times 3 through 7 inclusive. Find the accumulated value of the annuity at time 10.

*2.1.39 Derive the following identities assuming $t < n$.

(a) $v^t \cdot s_{\overline{n}|} = a_{\overline{t}|} + s_{\overline{n-t}|} = \ddot{a}_{\overline{t+1}|} + \ddot{s}_{\overline{n-t-1}|}$

(b) $(1+i)^t \cdot a_{\overline{n}|} = s_{\overline{t}|} + a_{\overline{n-t}|} = \ddot{s}_{\overline{t-1}|} + \ddot{a}_{\overline{n-t+1}|}$

(c) $v^t \cdot \ddot{s}_{\overline{n}|} = \ddot{a}_{\overline{t}|} + \ddot{s}_{\overline{n-t}|} = a_{\overline{t-1}|} + s_{\overline{n-t+1}|}$

(d) $(1+i)^t \cdot \ddot{a}_{\overline{n}|} = \ddot{s}_{\overline{t}|} + \ddot{a}_{\overline{n-t}|} = s_{\overline{t+1}|} + a_{\overline{n-t-1}|}$

Formulate corresponding expressions for the case $t > n$.

*2.1.40 Verify the identities $s_{\overline{n+1}|} \cdot a_{\overline{n}|} = s_{\overline{n}|} \cdot \ddot{a}_{\overline{n+1}|} = \dfrac{s_{\overline{n+1}|} - \ddot{a}_{\overline{n+1}|}}{i} = \dfrac{\ddot{s}_{\overline{n}|} - a_{\overline{n}|}}{i}$.

SECTION 2.2

2.2.1   Jerry will make deposits of 450 at the end of each quarter for 10 years. At the end of 15 years, Jerry will use the fund to make annual payments of Y at the beginning of each year for 4 years, after which the fund is exhausted. The effective annual rate of interest is 7%. Determine Y.

2.2.2   Kathryn deposits 100 into an account at the beginning of each 4-year period for 40 years. The account credits interest at an effective annual interest rate of i. The accumulated amount in the account at the end of 40 years is X, which is 5 times the accumulated amount in the account at the end of 20 years. Calculate X.

2.2.3   A perpetuity paying 1 at the beginning of each 6-month period has a present value of 20. A second perpetuity pays X at the beginning of every 2 years. Assuming the same effective annual interest rate, the two present values are equal. Determine X.

2.2.4   Sally lends 10,000 to Tim. Tim agrees to pay back the loan over 5 years with monthly payments payable at the end of each month. Sally can reinvest the monthly payments from Tim in a savings account paying interest at 6%, compounded monthly. The yield rate earned on Sally's investment over the five-year period turned out to be 7.45%, compounded semi-annually. What nominal rate of interest, compounded monthly, did Sally charge Tim on the loan?

2.2.5   The following is an excerpt from the website of the Bank of Montreal (http://www4.bmo.com), and gives some examples of accumulation in a Registered Retirement Savings Plan (the Canadian version of an IRA).

Derek, Ira, and Anne each contribute $1,200 annually to their RRSPs earning a 6% average annual compounded return.

- Derek contributes $1,200 at the beginning of each calendar year.
- Ira contributes $100 at the start of each month throughout the year.
- Anne contributes $1,200 each year on the very last day for RRSP contributions deductible in the tax year (assume that this is the last day of the calendar year).

Verify the accumulated values in the three numerical examples given.

	Derek	Ira	Anne
total value	$69,788	$67,958	$65,837
investment	$30,000 total over 25 years	$30,000 total over 25 years	$30,000 total over 25 years

2.2.6   A 50,000 loan made on January 1, 2000 is to be repaid over 25 years with payments on the last day of each month, beginning January 31, 2000.

(a) If $i^{(2)} = .10$, find the amount of the monthly payment X.

(b) Starting with the first payment, the borrower decides to pay an additional 100 per month, on top of the regular payment of X, until the loan is repaid. An additional fractional payment might be necessary one month after the last regular payment of $X + 100$. On what date will the final payment of $X + 100$ be made, and what will be the amount of the additional fractional payment?

2.2.7   A sum of 10,000 was invested on September 1, 1970 at an effective annual interest rate of 5% in order to provide an annual scholarship of 2000 every September 1 forever, starting as soon as possible. In what year will the first payment of 2000 be made? What smaller payment could be made one year earlier while still permitting the annual scholarships of 2000 thereafter? Assume that interest is credited every August 31.

2.2.8   On the first day of each month, starting January 1, 1995, Smith deposits 100 in an account earning $i^{(12)} = .09$, with interest credited the last day of each month. In addition, Smith deposits 1000 in the account every December 31. On what day does the account first exceed 100,000?

2.2.9   On the first day of every January, April, July and October Smith deposits 100 in an account earning $i^{(4)} = .16$. He continues the deposits until he accumulates a sufficient balance to begin withdrawals of 200 every 3 months, starting 3 months after the final deposit, such that he can make twice as many withdrawals as he made deposits. How many deposits are needed?

2.2.10 Ten annual deposits of 1000 each are made to Account A, starting on January 1, 1986. Annual deposits of 500 each are made to Account B indefinitely, also starting on January 1, 1986. Interest on both accounts is at rate $i = .05$, with interest credited every December 31. On what date will the balance for Account B first exceed the balance for Account A? Assume that the only transactions to the accounts are deposits and interest credited every December 31.

2.2.11 A loan of 1000 is repaid with 12 annual payments of 100 each starting one year after the loan is made. The effective annual interest rate is 3.5% for the first 4 years. Find the effective annual interest rate i for the final 8 years.

2.2.12 (a) Let $A = a_{\overline{n}|i}$ and $B = s_{\overline{n}|i}$; express i in terms of A and B.

   (b) Let $A = a_{\overline{n}|i}$ and $B = a_{\overline{2n}|i}$; express i in terms of A and B.

   (c) Let $A = a_{\overline{n}|i}$ and $B = s_{\overline{2n}|i}$; express i in terms of A and B.

2.2.13 An insurance company offers a "capital redemption policy" whereby the policyholder pays annual premiums (in advance) of 3368.72 for 25 years, and, in return, receives a maturity (or redemption) amount of 250,000 one year after the 25th premium is paid. The insurer has determined that administrative expenses are 20% of the first premium and 10% of all remaining premiums, and these expenses are incurred at the time the premium is paid. The insurer anticipates investing the net (after expenses) premiums received at an effective annual interest rate of 12.5%. What is the insurer's accumulated profit just after the policy matures and the redemption amount of 250,000 is paid? Find the effective annual rate of return earned by the policyholder for the 25-year period.

2.2.14 Smith is negotiating to purchase a car, and he determines that he must borrow 12,000 to complete the purchase. He is offered financing at a nominal interest rate of $i^{(12)}$ with monthly payments beginning one month after the loan is made. He can repay the loan over a 2-year period (24 payments) at 592.15 per month, or over a 3-year period (36 payments) at 426.64 per month (the same interest rate in both cases). Find $i^{(12)}$ and the monthly amount payable if he were able to repay the loan over a 4-year period (still at the same interest rate).

2.2.15 A loan of 10,000 is made on January 1, 2005 at an interest rate $i^{(12)} = .12$. The loan calls for payments of 500 on the first day of April, July and October each year, with an additional fractional payment on the next scheduled payment date after the final regular payment of 500. Find the date and amount of the additional fractional payment.

*2.2.16 At an effective annual interest rate of $i, i > 0$, the present value of a perpetuity paying 10 at the end of each 3-year period, with the first payment at the end of year 6, is 32 . At the same effective annual rate of i, the present value of a perpetuity-immediate paying 1 at the end of each 4-month period is X. Calculate X.

*2.2.17 Payments of 25 each are made every 2 months from June 1, 2003 to April 1, 2009, inclusive. Find the value of the series (a) 2 months before the first payment at effective annual interest rate $i = .06$, (b) 10 months before the first payment at nominal annual rate $i^{(3)} = .06$, (c) 8 months before the first payment at nominal annual rate $i^{(4)} = .06$, (d) 2 months after the final payment at nominal annual rate $d^{(2)} = .06$, and (e) 1 year after the final payment at annual force of interest $\delta = .06$. Express the values in terms of the notation defined in Exercise 2.2.29 wherever possible.

*2.2.18 12 payments of 2000 each are made at 2-year intervals. Find the value of the series (a) 2 years before the first payment at effective annual interest rate $i = .08$, (b) 8 years before the first payment at nominal annual interest rate $i^{(2)} = .08$, (c) at the time of the final payment at nominal annual discount rate $d^{(4)} = .08$, (d) 18 months after the final payment at nominal annual interest rate $i^{(8)} = .08$, and (e) at the time of the first payment at nominal annual interest rate $i^{(4/3)} = .08$.

*2.2.19 A perpetuity consists of monthly payments. The payment pattern follows a repeating 12-month cycle of eleven payments of 1 each followed by a payment of 2. The effective monthly interest rate is j. Show that the present value of the perpetuity valued one month before the first payment is $\frac{1}{j}\left[1 + \frac{1}{s_{\overline{12}|j}}\right]$.

*2.2.20 Find the present value at time 0 of an n-year continuous annuity based on force of interest $\delta_t = p + \frac{s}{1 + re^{st}}$.

*2.2.21 (a) A loan of amount L is to be repaid with n periodic payments of amount K each at periodic interest rate $i > 0$, where n is even. The same loan can be repaid by $\frac{n}{2}$ payments if the periodic payment is increased to an amount larger than K. Determine whether the new payment is exactly double, more than double, or less than double the value of K.

(b) A loan of amount L at interest rate $i > 0$ is being repaid by n payments of K each. Show that if the payment is doubled to $2K$, and m is the number of doubled payments required to repay the loan, then $m < \frac{n}{2}$.

*2.2.22 Deposits of 500 each are made into an account on the first day of every January and July beginning on January 1,1999.

    (a) If $i^{(6)} = .06$ and interest is credited on the last day of every February, April, June, August, October and December, on what date does the account balance first exceed (i) 10,000, and (ii) 11,000?

    (b) Suppose instead that $i = .04$ and interest is credited only on December 31 each year, with simple interest credited for fractions of a year. On what date should the account be closed in order that the closing balance be nearest (i) 10,000, and (ii) 11,000?

*2.2.23 Find the smallest integer n for which deposits of 1 per period accumulate to at least 100 in each of the following cases.

    (a) 20 deposits at 3% followed by n deposits at 4%

    (b) n deposits at 3% followed by n deposits at 4%

*2.2.24 Apply the following approximation method to find n in Example 2.14. Take natural logarithms of both sides of the equation

$$(1.0075)^n = 1 + .008333n,$$

and use the Taylor expansion of $\ln(1+.008333n)$ to: (i) 2 terms and (ii) 3 terms.

*2.2.25 Solve for i and n in terms of A and B, where $A = s_{\overline{n}|i}$ and $B = s_{\overline{n+1}|i}$.

*2.2.26 (a) For the equation $L = K \cdot a_{\overline{n}|i}, L, K, n > 0$, note that $L = n \cdot K$ if $i = 0$. Use the following principles:

    (i) $\lim\limits_{i \to \infty} a_{\overline{n}|i} = 0$,

    (ii) $\lim\limits_{i \to -1} a_{\overline{n}|i} = \infty$, and

    (iii) $a_{\overline{n}|i}$ is a decreasing function of i

    to show that the equation has a unique solution for i between -1 and ∞ if L, K and n are given. Also show that $i > 0$ if $L < n \cdot K$ and $i < 0$ if $L > n \cdot K$.

(b) Derive a result similar to that in part (a) for the accumulated annuity relationship $M = J \cdot s_{\overline{n}|\,i}$.

(c) Derive similar results in the case of an annuity-due.

(d) Use the fact that $\delta \to -\infty$ as $i \to -1$ to derive similar results for continuous annuities.

*2.2.27 A fund has value A at the start of a year, B at the end of the year, and interest of I earned for the year. Assuming that both interest and non-interest income accrues continuously on the fund, use the approximate relationship $\frac{i}{\delta} \approx 1 + \frac{i}{2}$ to show that the annual interest rate earned by the fund is approximately $\frac{2I}{B+A-I}$.

*2.2.28 An annuity has n annual payments of amount 1 each. Interest is quoted at a nominal annual rate of $i^{(m)}$.

(a) Let $j = \frac{i^{(m)}}{m}$. Express the equivalent effective annual rate of interest i in terms of j.

(b) Show that (i) $s_{\overline{n}|\,i} = \frac{(1+j)^{m \cdot n} - 1}{(1+j)^m - 1}$,   (ii) $a_{\overline{n}|\,i} = \frac{1 - v_j^{m \cdot n}}{(1+j)^m - 1}$,

(iii) $\ddot{s}_{\overline{n}|\,i} = \frac{(1+j)^{m \cdot n} - 1}{1 - v_j^m}$, and (iv) $\ddot{a}_{\overline{n}|\,i} = \frac{1 - v_j^{m \cdot n}}{1 - v_j^m}$.

(c) Let $P = \frac{1}{s_{\overline{m}|\,j}}$ be the payment required every $\frac{1}{m}^{th}$ of a year for one year to accumulate to 1 at the end of the year (i.e., at the time of the mth payment of P) at interest rate j per $\frac{1}{m}^{th}$ of a year. Show that $s_{\overline{n}|\,i}$ from part (b) is equal to $P \cdot s_{\overline{m \cdot n}|\,j} = s_{\overline{m}|\,j}$.

(d) Find appropriate m^{thly} replacement payments for the other three annuities in part (b) and verify the following relationships:

(i) $a_{\overline{n}|\,i} = \frac{a_{\overline{m \cdot n}|\,j}}{s_{\overline{m}|\,j}}$,   (ii) $\ddot{s}_{\overline{n}|\,i} = \frac{s_{\overline{m \cdot n}|\,j}}{a_{\overline{m}|\,j}}$,   (iii) $a_{\overline{n}|\,i} = \frac{a_{\overline{m \cdot n}|\,j}}{a_{\overline{m}|\,j}}$.

(Note that $\ddot{s}_{\overline{n}|i} \neq \frac{\ddot{s}_{\overline{m \cdot n}|j}}{s_{\overline{m}|j}}$, but $\ddot{s}_{\overline{n}|i} = (1+j)^m \cdot s_{\overline{n}|i}$ and $\ddot{a}_{\overline{n}|i} \neq \frac{\ddot{a}_{\overline{m \cdot n}|j}}{s_{\overline{m}|j}}$,

but $\ddot{a}_{\overline{n}|i} = (1+j)^m \cdot a_{\overline{n}|i}$.) Note that these formulations apply whenever the payment period is an integral multiple of the interest period. They are algebraically valid even if m is not an integer, in which case a meaning must be assigned to $s_{\overline{m}|j}$ for nonintegral m.

(e) If the quoted rate is $i^{(\infty)} = \delta$, the annual force of interest, show that $s_{\overline{n}|i} = \frac{e^{n\delta}-1}{e^{\delta}-1}$.

(f) Repeat parts (b) and (d) for the present value of perpetuities, both immediate and due.

*2.2.29 An annuity has level payments of $\frac{1}{m}$ every $\frac{1}{m}^{th}$ of a year for n years (a total of $n \cdot m$ payments). Interest is at effective annual rate i. Let j denote the interest rate for $\frac{1}{m}^{th}$ of a year that is equivalent to i.

(a) Show that the accumulated value of the annuity at the time of the final payment is

$$\frac{1}{m} \cdot s_{\overline{n \cdot m}|j} = \frac{1}{m} \cdot \frac{(1+i)^n - 1}{(1+i)^{1/m} - 1}.$$

(b) If the series is valued one payment period (i.e., $\frac{1}{m}^{th}$ of a year) before the first payment, show that this present value is

$$\frac{1}{m} \cdot a_{\overline{n \cdot m}|j} = \frac{1}{m} \cdot \frac{1 - v^n}{(1+i)^{1/m} - 1}.$$

(c) Show that the accumulated value one payment period after the final payment is

$$\frac{1}{m} \cdot \ddot{s}_{\overline{n \cdot m}|j} = \frac{1}{m} \cdot \frac{(1+i)^n - 1}{1 - v_i^{1/m}},$$

and the present value at the time of the first payment is

$$\frac{1}{m} \cdot \ddot{a}_{\overline{n \cdot m}|j} = \frac{1}{m} \cdot \frac{1 - v_i^n}{1 - v_i^{1/m}},$$

(d) Show each of the following:

(i) $\quad \dfrac{1}{m} \cdot s_{\overline{n \cdot m}\,j} = \dfrac{(1+i)^n - 1}{i^{(m)}} = s_{\overline{n}|i} \cdot \dfrac{i}{i^{(m)}}$

(ii) $\quad \dfrac{1}{m} \cdot a_{\overline{n \cdot m}\,j} = \dfrac{1 - v_i^n}{i^{(m)}} = a_{\overline{n}|i} \cdot \dfrac{i}{i^{(m)}}$

(iii) $\quad \dfrac{1}{m} \cdot \ddot{s}_{\overline{n \cdot m}\,j} = \dfrac{(1+i)^n - 1}{d^{(m)}} = s_{\overline{n}|i} \cdot \dfrac{i}{d^{(m)}}$

(iv) $\quad \dfrac{1}{m} \cdot \ddot{a}_{\overline{n \cdot m}\,j} = \dfrac{1 - v_i^n}{d^{(m)}} = a_{\overline{n}|i} \cdot \dfrac{i}{d^{(m)}}$

(e) The standard actuarial notation used for the annuity forms in (a) through (d) is

$$\frac{1}{m} \cdot s_{\overline{n \cdot m}\,j} = \frac{(1+i)^n - 1}{i^{(m)}} = s_{\overline{n}|i} \cdot \frac{i}{i^{(m)}} = s_{\overline{n}|i}^{(m)},$$

$$\frac{1}{m} \cdot a_{\overline{n \cdot m}\,j} = \frac{1 - v_i^n}{i^{(m)}} = a_{\overline{n}|i} \cdot \frac{i}{i^{(m)}} = a_{\overline{n}|i}^{(m)},$$

$$\frac{1}{m} \cdot \ddot{s}_{\overline{n \cdot m}\,j} = \frac{(1+i)^n - 1}{d^{(m)}} = s_{\overline{n}|i} \cdot \frac{i}{d^{(m)}} = \ddot{s}_{\overline{n}|i}^{(m)}, \text{ and}$$

$$\frac{1}{m} \cdot \ddot{a}_{\overline{n \cdot m}\,j} = \frac{1 - v_i^n}{d^{(m)}} = a_{\overline{n}|i} \cdot \frac{i}{d^{(m)}} = \ddot{a}_{\overline{n}|i}^{(m)}.$$

Derive the following identities:

(i) $\quad \ddot{s}_{\overline{n}|i}^{(m)} = \left(1 + \dfrac{i^{(m)}}{m}\right) \cdot s_{\overline{n}|i}^{(m)} = \left(\dfrac{i}{i^{(m)}} + \dfrac{i}{m}\right) \cdot s_{\overline{n}|i} = s_{\overline{n}|i}^{(m)} + \dfrac{(1+i)^n - 1}{m}$

(ii) $\quad \ddot{a}_{\overline{n}|i}^{(m)} = \left(1 + \dfrac{i^{(m)}}{m}\right) \cdot a_{\overline{n}|i}^{(m)} = a_{\overline{n}|i} \cdot \left(\dfrac{i}{i^{(m)}} + \dfrac{i}{m}\right)$

$$= a_{\overline{n}|i}^{(m)} + \frac{1}{m}\left(1 - v_i^n\right).$$

(f) Show $\ddot{s}_{\overline{n}|i}^{(m)} = s_{\overline{n+1/m}|i}^{(m)} - \dfrac{1}{m}$ and $\ddot{a}_{\overline{n}|i}^{(m)} = a_{\overline{n-1/m}|i}^{(m)} + \dfrac{1}{m}$. It is possible to use the "upper m" notation to represent $s_{\overline{k/m}|i}^{(m)}$.

Show that this is equal to $\dfrac{1}{m} \cdot s_{\overline{k}|j}$.

(g) Prove the identities $\dfrac{1}{a_{\overline{n}|i}^{(m)}} = \dfrac{1}{s_{\overline{n}|i}^{(m)}} + i^{(m)}$ and $\dfrac{1}{\ddot{a}_{\overline{n}|i}^{(m)}} = \dfrac{1}{\ddot{s}_{\overline{n}|i}^{(m)}} + d^{(m)}$.

(h) Use the binomial expansion for $(1+i)^{1/m}$ to show that $a_{\overline{n}|i}^{(m)}$ is approximately equal to

$$a_{\overline{n}|i} + \frac{m-1}{2m}(1-v^n) = \frac{1}{2m}\left[(m+1)a_{\overline{n}|i} + (m-1)\ddot{a}_{\overline{n}|i}\right].$$

Calculate the exact values and the approximate values for $i = 0, .01, .025, .05, .10, .20,$ and $.50,$ and for $n = 10$ and $m = 12$.

*2.2.30 (a) Show that $\lim\limits_{m\to\infty} s_{\overline{n}|i}^{(m)} = \lim\limits_{m\to\infty} \ddot{s}_{\overline{n}|i}^{(m)} = \ddot{s}_{\overline{n}|i}^{(\infty)} = s_{\overline{n}|i}^{(\infty)} = \overline{s}_{\overline{n}|i}$.

(b) Show that $\lim\limits_{m\to\infty} a_{\overline{n}|i}^{(m)} = \lim\limits_{m\to\infty} \ddot{a}_{\overline{n}|i}^{(m)} = \ddot{a}_{\overline{n}|i}^{(\infty)} = a_{\overline{n}|i}^{(\infty)} = \overline{a}_{\overline{n}|i}$.

(c) If $i > 0$ and $m > 1$, rank the following values in increasing order: $a_{\overline{n}|i}, \ddot{a}_{\overline{n}|i}, a_{\overline{n}|i}^{(m)}, \ddot{a}_{\overline{n}|i}^{(m)}, \overline{a}_{\overline{n}|i}$.

(d) Assuming simple interest at rate i, find $\overline{s}_{\overline{1}|i}$.

*2.2.31 (a) In the solution for n in the equation $L = K \cdot a_{\overline{n}|i}$, find

$$\frac{dn}{di}, \frac{dn}{dK}, \text{ and } \frac{dn}{dL}.$$

(b) In the solution for n in the equation $M = J \cdot s_{\overline{n}|i}$, find

$$\frac{dn}{di}, \frac{dn}{dJ}, \text{ and } \frac{dn}{dM}.$$

SECTION 2.3

2.3.1 Stan elects to receive his retirement benefit over 20 years at the rate of 2000 per month beginning one month from now. The monthly benefit increases by 5% each year. At a nominal interest rate of 6% convertible monthly, calculate the present value of the retirement benefit.

2.3.2   Jeff and Jason spend X dollars each to purchase annuities. Jeff buys a perpetuity-immediate, which makes annual payments of 30. Jason buys a 10-year annuity-immediate, also with annual payments. The first payment is 53, with each subsequent payment $k\%$ larger than the previous year's payment. Both annuities use an effective annual interest rate of $k\%$. Calculate k.

2.3.3   Mike buys a perpetuity-immediate with varying annual payments. During the first 5 years, the payment is constant and equal to 10. Beginning in year 6, the payments start to increase. For year 6 and all future years, the current year's payment is $K\%$ larger than the previous year's payment. At an effective annual interest rate of 9.2%, the perpetuity has a present value of 167.50. Calculate K, given $K < 9.2$.

2.3.4   A senior executive is offered a buyout package by his company that will pay him a monthly benefit for the next 20 years. Monthly benefits will remain constant within each of the 20 years. At the end of each 12-month period, the monthly benefits will be adjusted upwards to reflect the percentage increase in the CPI . You are given:

(i) The first monthly benefit is R and will be paid one month from today.

(ii) The CPI increases 3.2% per year forever.

At an effective annual interest rate of 6%, the buyout package has a value of 100,000. Calculate R.

2.3.5   (a) Show that the accumulated value one period after the final payment of the annuity in Example 2.18 is $(1+r)^n \cdot \ddot{s}_{\overline{n}|j}$.

(b) Show that the present value one period before the first payment of the annuity in Example 2.18 is $\frac{1}{1+r} \cdot a_{\overline{n}|j}$.

2.3.6   Smith has 100,000 with which she buys a perpetuity on January 1, 2005. Suppose that $i = .045$ and the perpetuity has annual payments beginning January 1, 2006. The first three payments are 2000 each, the next three payments are $2000(1+r)$ each,..., increasing forever by a factor of $1+r$ every three years. What is r?

2.3.7   An employee serves 37 years before retiring on a pension. His initial salary was 18,000 per year and increased by 4% each year. Assume that the whole year's salary is paid at the middle of each year.

(a) If his pension is 70% of his average annual salary over his entire career, what is his ultimate pension?

(b) If the pension is 2.5% of career average salary multiplied by years of service, what is his ultimate pension?

(c) If his pension is 2.5% of his average salary over the final 10 years he worked, multiplied by his total years of service, then what is his ultimate pension?

(d) If he contributes 3% of his salary (at the time it is paid), matched by an equal contribution from his employer, to an account earning annual interest at rate $i = .06$, and the accumulated value (at the end of his 37th year of employment) is used to purchase a 20-year annuity-due with annual payments, valued at $i = .06$, find the annual payment from the annuity.

2.3.8   The first of a series of 30 annual payments is 1000 and each subsequent payment is 1% smaller than the previous one. What is the accumulated value of this series at the time of the final payment if (i) $i = .01$, (ii) $i = .05$, and (iii) $i = .10$?

2.3.9   The following is an excerpt from The Hartford Insurance Company website (http://institutional.hartfordlife.com/). It describes a "structured settlement" in which an income stream is to be paid out over time. Verify that the total payout over the 20 years is $644,889.

Installment Payment Example

Situation: A young man, 25 years old, is injured in an automobile accident.

Needs: Financial Security to provide young man with funds to satisfy **current obligations** and guaranteed payments to provide for **future needs** such as:
- **Replacement of Lost Income** ($2,000 per month with 3% annual cost of living increase)

Claim Summary

Future Needs	Structured Settlement		
	Guaranteed Payout	Life Expectancy Payout	Annuity Cost
Replace Loss Income Age 25-45 monthly payment range $2,000 to $3,507	**$644,889**	**$644,889**	**$346,851**

Find the effective annual rate of interest that was used to get the present value of $346,851 (this will require a numerical approximation routine such as the EXCEL Solver program).

2.3.10 Susan invests Z at the end of each year for seven years at an effective annual interest rate of 5%. The interest credited at the end of each year is reinvested at an effective annual rate of 6%. The accumulated value at the end of seven years is X. Lori invests Z at the end of each year for 14 years at an effective annual interest rate of 2.5%. The interest credited at the end of each year is reinvested at an effective annual rate of 3%. The accumulated value at the end of 14 years is Y. Calculate Y/X.

2.3.11 Sandy purchases a perpetuity-immediate that makes annual payments. The first payment is 100, and each payment thereafter increases by 10. Danny purchases a perpetuity-due which makes annual payments of 180. Using the same effective annual interest rate, $i > 0$, the present value of both perpetuities are equal. Calculate i.

2.3.12 Olga buys a 5-year increasing annuity for X. Olga will receive 2 at the end of the first month, 4 at the end of the second month, and for each month thereafter the payment increases by 2. The nominal interest rate is 9% convertible quarterly. Calculate X.

2.3.13 1000 is deposited into Fund X, which earns an effective annual rate of 6%. At the end of each year, the interest earned plus an additional 100 is withdrawn from the fund. At the end of the tenth year, the fund is depleted. The annual withdrawals of interest and principal are deposited into Fund Y, which earns an effective annual rate of 9%. Determine the accumulated value of Fund Y at the end of year 10.

2.3.14   A perpetuity costs 77.1 and makes annual payments at the end of
          the year. The perpetuity pays 1 at the end of year 2, 2 at the end
          of year 3,..., n at the end of year $(n+1)$. After year $(n+1)$, the
          payments remain constant at n. The effective annual interest rate
          is 10.5%. Calculate n.

2.3.15   A loan of 12,000 is repaid by 36 monthly payments starting one
          month after the loan. The first 12 payments are $395 + X$ each,
          the next 12 payments are 395 each, and the final 12 payments are
          $395 - X$ each. If $i^{(12)} = .12$, find X.

2.3.16   What series of payments is represented by the present value
          $A \cdot a_{\overline{n}|} + B \cdot (Da)_{\overline{n}|}$? Formulate the present value of a 25-year
          decreasing annuity-immediate with first payment of 100 and
          subsequent payments decreasing by 3 per period.

2.3.17   Victor invests 300 into a bank account at the beginning of each
          year for 20 years. The account pays out interest at the end of
          every year at an effective annual interest rate of i%. The interest
          is reinvested at an effective annual rate of $\frac{i}{2}$%. The yield rate
          on the entire investment over the 20 year period is 8% effective
          annual. Determine i.

*2.3.18 Find the present value, as of January 1, 2001, of the payments in
          Example 2.19. Find the present value (on January 1, 2001) and
          the accumulated value (on the 18th birthday) of the payments in
          Example 2.19 at the following nominal interest $\left(i^{(12)} \right)$ rates and
          annual rate of increase in the payments.

          (i)   12% interest, 9% increase in payments

          (ii) 9% interest, 6% increase in payments

          (iii) 6% interest, 3% increase in payments

          (iv) 3% interest, 0% increase in payments

*2.3.19 A government provides each citizen over the age of 65 with a monthly pension payable for life. The current monthly payment is 400. The payment is indexed to inflation so that every year there is an adjustment to reflect the rate of inflation for the year (but payments within a year are level). The government proposes a cost-cutting measure whereby the payments will be "partially de-indexed," so that the payment increase will be the excess of the inflation rate over 3%. The increase is 0 if the inflation is less than 3%. As a simplified model the government regards the lifetime payments as a perpetuity. What are the pension present values both before an after de-indexing under each of the following annual interest/inflation scenarios?

(i) $i = .12, r = .09$ (ii) $i = .12, r = .06$,   (iii) $i = .12, r = .03$
(iv) $i = .09, r = .06$ (v) $i = .09, r = .03$ (vi) $i = .06, r = .03$

*2.3.20 On January 1, 2005 Smith deposits 500,000 in an account earning an effective monthly rate of 1%, with interest credited on the last day of each month. Withdrawals are made on the first day of each month starting February 1, 2005, with an initial withdrawal of 1000. Each subsequent withdrawal is 1% larger than the previous one, continuing in this pattern for as long as possible.

(a) When does the account finally become exhausted, and what is the amount of the last regular withdrawal?

(b) What is the maximum amount the account balance reaches during this process?

*2.3.21 For 100,000, Smith purchases a 20-payment annuity-immediate with annual payments. For each of the following cases find the unknown interest rate i.

(a) The first payment is 7000 and each subsequent payment is 750 more than the previous one.

(b) The first payment is 7000 and each subsequent payment is 10% larger than the previous one.

This problem requires a numerical approximation routine such as the EXCEL Solver program.

*2.3.22 A perpetuity pays 1 on January 1, 2006, $1+r$ on January 1, 2007, with subsequent payments increasing by a factor of $1+r$ each until January 1, 2016, when the payment is $(1+r)^{10}$. From then on the annual payment remains level at $(1+r)^{10}$. If the effective annual interest rate is $i = .10$ and $r = .12$, find the present value of the perpetuity on its starting date, January 1, 2006. Repeat the problem with r and $i = r + .02$.

*2.3.23 Joe can purchase one of two annuities:

Annuity 1: A 10-year decreasing annuity-immediate, with annual payments of $10, 9, 8, \ldots, 1$.

Annuity 2: A perpetuity-immediate with annual payments. The perpetuity pays 1 in year 1, 2 in year 2, 3 in year 3,..., and 11 in year 11. After year 11, the payments remain constant at 11.

At an effective annual interest rate of i, the present value of Annuity 2 is twice the present value of Annuity 1. Calculate the value of Annuity 1.

*2.3.24 (a) Write out the terms of the series for $(Is)_{\overline{n}|i}$.

Show $(Is)_{\overline{n}|i} = \dfrac{\ddot{s}_{\overline{n}|i} - n}{i}$.

(b) Draw a line diagram and explain verbally why $s_{\overline{n+1}|i}$ must equal $(n+1) + i \cdot (Is)_{\overline{n}|i}$.

*2.3.25 Write out the terms of the series for $(Ds)_{\overline{n}|i}$ and $(Da)_{\overline{n}|i}$.

*2.3.26 Show that the following relationships are valid, and illustrate them using line diagrams:

(a) $(Ia)_{\overline{n}|} + (Da)_{\overline{n}|} = (n+1) \cdot a_{\overline{n}|}$

(b) $(Is)_{\overline{n}|} + (Ds)_{\overline{n}|} = (n+1) \cdot s_{\overline{n}|}$

(c) $(Ia)_{\overline{n}|} = \displaystyle\sum_{k=0}^{n-1} k \cdot a_{\overline{n-k}|}$ and $(Is)_{\overline{n}|} = \displaystyle\sum_{k=1}^{n} s_{\overline{k}|}$

(d) $\quad (I\ddot{a})_{\overline{n}|} = (Ia)_{\overline{n}|} + \ddot{a}_{\overline{n}|} - nv^n$

(e) $\quad (I\ddot{s})_{\overline{n}|} = (Is)_{\overline{n}|} + \ddot{s}_{\overline{n}|} - n$

(f) $\quad (D\ddot{a})_{\overline{n}|} = (Da)_{\overline{n}|} + n - a_{\overline{n}|}$

(g) $\quad (D\ddot{s})_{\overline{n}|} = (Ds)_{\overline{n}|} + n(1+i)^n - s_{\overline{n}|}$

(h) $\quad (Is)_{\overline{n}|} + (Da)_{\overline{n}|} = a_{\overline{n}|} \cdot s_{\overline{n+1}|} = \ddot{a}_{\overline{n+1}|} \cdot s_{\overline{n}|}$

(i) $\quad (Ia)_{\overline{n+1}|} = (Ia)_{\overline{n}|} + (n+1)v^{n+1} = a_{\overline{n+1}|} + v \cdot (Ia)_{\overline{n}|}$

(j) $\quad (Da)_{\overline{n+1}|} = (n+1)v + v \cdot (Da)_{\overline{n}|} = a_{\overline{n+1}|} + (Da)_{\overline{n}|}$

(k) $\quad (Is)_{\overline{n+1}|} = (1+i) \cdot (Is)_{\overline{n}|} + (n+1) = s_{\overline{n+1}|} + (Is)_{\overline{n}|}$

(l) $\quad (Ds)_{\overline{n+1}|} = (n+1)(1+i)^n + (Ds)_{\overline{n}|} = s_{\overline{n+1}|} + (1+i) \cdot (Ds)_{\overline{n}|}$

(m) $\quad (Da)_{\overline{n}|} = \sum_{k=1}^{n} a_{\overline{k}|}$

*2.3.27 Show that if $i > 0$ then $(Ia)_{\overline{\infty}|} = \dfrac{1}{i} + \dfrac{1}{i^2} = \dfrac{1}{i \cdot d} = a_{\overline{\infty}|} \cdot \ddot{a}_{\overline{\infty}|}$.
Give a verbal interpretation for the final expression.

*2.3.28 (a) Show that

(i) $\dfrac{d}{di} a_{\overline{n}|i} = -v \cdot (Ia)_{\overline{n}|}$,

(ii) $\dfrac{d}{di} s_{\overline{n}|i} = (Ds)_{\overline{n-1}|}$, and

(iii) $\dfrac{d}{d\delta} \bar{a}_{\overline{n}|i} = -(\bar{I}\bar{a})_{\overline{n}|}$.

(b) Find expressions for $\dfrac{d}{dn} \bar{a}_{\overline{n}|}$ and $\dfrac{d}{dn} \bar{s}_{\overline{n}|}$.

*2.3.29 Smith is arranging a mortgage loan of 100,000 to be repaid with monthly payments over 25 years, with the first payment due one month after the loan is made. Interest is quoted at a nominal annual rate compounded semiannually of $i^{(2)}$. The loan will not be issued for several months, and the interest rate will be set at the time of the loan. Smith, in determining the sensitivity of his monthly payment to the interest rate, calculates $\frac{d}{di^{(2)}} K$, where K is the monthly payment. Find the value of this derivative for the following values of $i^{(2)}$: 21%, 13%, 10%, 5%.

*2.3.30 Smith retires on January 1, 2004. She deposits 500,000 in an account earning effective annual interest at $i = .10$, with interest credited every December 31. Smith withdrawals $\frac{1}{19}$ of the balance in the account on January 1, 2005, $\frac{1}{18}$ of the balance on January 1, 2006,..., $\frac{1}{2}$ of the balance on January 1, 2022, and the entire balance on January 1, 2023. Find an expression for the amount of the withdrawal on January 1, $2004 + t$, for $t = 1, 2, ..., 19$.

*2.3.31 A loan of 10,000 made on January 1, 2005 is to be repaid by monthly payments on the last date of each month starting January 31, 2005. The first payment is 1000, the second is 900, the third is 800, the fourth 700, the fifth 600, and the sixth and subsequent payments are 500 each for as long as necessary with a final smaller payment one month after the final regular payment. Find the date and the amount of the final smaller payment if $i^{(12)} = .12$.

*2.3.32 On January 1 Smith deposits 100,000 in an account earning interest at rate $i^{(12)} = .09$, credited on the final day of each month.

(a) Suppose Smith withdraws 1000 on the first day of each month starting on February 1. Smith continues the withdrawals as long as possible with a smaller withdrawal one month after the final regular withdrawal of 1000. Find the number of regular withdrawals and the date and amount of the final smaller withdrawal.

(b) Instead of level withdrawals of 1000 each, let Smith's monthly withdrawals start at 1000 on February 1, and increase by 10 each month (March 1 is 1010, April 1 is 1020, and so on). Withdrawals continue in this pattern for as long as possible with a final smaller withdrawal one month after the last regular increasing withdrawal. Find the number of regular withdrawals and the date and amount of the final smaller withdrawal.

(c) Repeat part (b) assuming that the withdrawals grow by 1% per month, so that March 1 is 1010, April 1 is 1020.10, and so on.

(d) For each of parts (a), (b), and (c) find the total amount withdrawn, and explain the relationship among the three totals.

*2.3.33 Each year on Smith's child's birthday, Smith makes a deposit of 100 multiplied by the child's age (100 on the 1st birthday, 200 on the 2nd, and so on) to an account earning effective annual interest rate i. The final deposit is on the child's 12th birthday The account continues to accumulate, and on the child's 18th birthday the balance is 17,177.70. Find i. The solution requires the use of a program such as EXCEL Solver or the cashflow worksheet of the BA II PLUS calculator.

*2.3.34 For $i > 0$ and $n > 1$, show that $(Ia)_{\overline{n}|} < \left(\frac{n+1}{2}\right) a_{\overline{n}|} < (Da)_{\overline{n}|}$.

*2.3.35 (a) An increasing perpetuity at effective annual interest rate i has a payment once every k years, with payment amounts $1, 2, 3, \ldots$. Show that the present value of the perpetuity at the time of the first payment is $\dfrac{1}{\left(i \cdot a_{\overline{k}|}\right)^2}$.

(b) Find an expression for the present value of an increasing perpetuity-due with annual payments whose first k payments are 1 each, next k payments are 2 each, and so on, increasing in this way forever. Assume effective annual interest rate i.

*2.3.36 Show in Example 2.24 that $i > 0$ if $L < \sum\limits_{s=1}^{n} K_s$, and $i < 0$ if $L > \sum\limits_{s=1}^{n} K_s$.

*2.3.37 Suppose that $K_1, K_2, \ldots, K_n$ are payments made to an account at times $0 < t_1 < t_2 < \cdots < t_n$. Show that if $L > 0$, then there is a unique interest rate $i > -1$ for which L is the accumulated value of the series of payments at time t_n.

*2.3.38 A perpetuity-due with annual payments pays 1 now, $1 + 2 = 3$ in one year, $1 + 2 + 3 = 6$ in two years,..., $1 + 2 + \cdots + n$ in $n - 1$ years, and so on. Show that the present value of this perpetuity-due is $\ddot{a}_{\overline{\infty}|} \cdot (I\ddot{a})_{\overline{\infty}|}$.

*2.3.39 A $(2n - 1)$-payment annuity has payments in the pattern $1, 2, \ldots,$ $n - 1, n, \ n - 1, \ n - 2, \ldots, 2, 1$. Show that the present value of this annuity one payment period before the first payment is $\ddot{a}_{\overline{n}|} \cdot a_{\overline{n}|}$.

*2.3.40 Show that $\dfrac{\ddot{a}_{\overline{n}|}}{i}$ is the present value of a perpetuity-immediate whose payments increase by 1 per period for n periods, from 1 to n, and then remain level at n forever.

*2.3.41 (a) If K_t is a polynomial of degree m in the variable t, show that $K_{t+1} - K_t$ is a polynomial of degree at most $m - 1$.

(b) A 15-payment annuity has annual payments of 225, 224, 221, 216, 209, 200,..., $225 - t^2$ for $t = 0, 1, 2, \ldots, 14$. What is the present value of this series valued one period before the first payment at $i = .08$?

(c) Show that $\sum\limits_{t=1}^{n} t^2 v^t = \ddot{a}_{\overline{n}|} + 2(Ia)_{\overline{n-1}|} - n^2 v^n$.

*2.3.42 Consider an increasing annuity with payments made every $\frac{1}{m}^{th}$ of a year for a total of n years ($n \cdot m$ payments).

(a) $(Ia)_{\overline{n}|}^{(m)}$ denotes the present value $\frac{1}{m}^{th}$ of a year before the first payment of the series in which the payments in the first year are level at amount $\frac{1}{m}$, in the second year are level at amount $\frac{2}{m}$, and so on. In each subsequent year the payments are $\frac{1}{m}$ larger than the year before, but stay level for the year. Show that this present value is equal to $\frac{\ddot{a}_{\overline{n}|} - nv^n}{i^{(m)}} = (Ia)_{\overline{n}|} \cdot \frac{i}{i^{(m)}}$.

(b) $(I^{(m)}a)_{\overline{n}|}^{(m)}$ denotes the present value $\frac{1}{m}^{th}$ of a year before the first payment of a series with first payment $\frac{1}{m^2}$, and subsequent payments $\frac{1}{m^2}$ larger than the previous one. Show that this present value is equal to $\frac{\ddot{a}_{\overline{n}|}^{(m)} - nv^n}{i^{(m)}}$.

*2.3.43 (a) Show that $\lim_{m \to \infty} (I^{(m)}a)_{\overline{n}|}^{(m)} = (\overline{I}\,\overline{a})_{\overline{n}|}$.

(b) $\lim_{m \to \infty} (Ia)_{\overline{n}|}^{(m)}$ is denoted $(I\overline{a})_{\overline{n}|}$. Give a verbal description of this expression.

(c) Repeat part (b) of Exercise 2.3.24 in the continuous context; i.e., explain why $\overline{s}_{\overline{n}|}$ is equal to $n + \delta \cdot (\overline{I}\,\overline{s})_{\overline{n}|}$.

*2.3.44 A general continuous annuity has rate of payment $h(t)$ at time t, $t > 0$, and had an initial discrete payment of F_0 at time 0. If the force of interest is δ and F_t denotes the accumulated value in the fund at time t, show that $\frac{d}{dt}F_t = \delta \cdot F_t + h(t)$.

*2.3.45 (a) If $h(t) = n - t, 0 \le t \le n$, in the general continuously varying annuity, the present value is denoted $(\overline{Da})_{\overline{n}|}$. Using integration by parts, derive an expression for $(\overline{Da})_{\overline{n}|}$. Show that $(\overline{Ia})_{\overline{n}|} + (\overline{Da})_{\overline{n}|} = n \cdot \overline{a}_{\overline{n}|}$.

(b) Show that $(\overline{Ia})_{\overline{n}|} = \int_0^n {}_t|\overline{a}_{\overline{n-t}|} \, dt$ and $(\overline{Da})_{\overline{n}|} = \int_0^n \overline{a}_{\overline{t}|} \, dt$.

(c) If $h(t) = e^{\alpha t}$ and the force of interest is $\delta > \alpha$, what is the present value at $t = 0$ of (i) an n-year continuous annuity, and (ii) a continuous perpetuity.

(d) Show that for the general forms of the present and accumulated value of a continuous annuity paying at rate $h(t)$ and with force of interest δ_t at time t, the accumulated value at time n is equal to the present value at time 0 multiplied by $\exp\left[\int_0^n \delta_r \, dr \right]$.

*2.3.46 An n-payment annuity has the following series of payments:

$$A, A + B, A + 2B, \ldots, A + (n-1)B$$

Formulate expressions in terms of level and increasing annuity notation for the present value of the series of payments one period before the first payment, and the accumulated value of the series at the time of the final payment.

SECTION 2.4

2.4.1 A loan is set up at periodic interest rate i, to be repaid by n periodic payments of amount K each. As the lender receives the payments, he reinvests them at interest rate j. Show that the average compound periodic rate of interest earned by the lender based on his initial outlay and his accumulated amount at time n is i', where i' is the solution of the equation $(1+i')^n = \frac{s_{\overline{n}|\, j}}{a_{\overline{n}|\, i}}$. Show also that i' is between i and j (i.e., if $j < i$ then $j < i' < i$; if $i < j$ then $i < i' < j$; if $i = j$ then $i = i' = j$).

2.4.2   Jones buys from Smith the right to receive 20 annual payments
of 1000 each beginning 1 year hence.

(a) In their discussion regarding this transaction, Smith and
Jones consider three ways of determining the amount Jones
must pay to Smith. Find this amount according to each of the
following approaches:

(i) The present value at $i = .12$.

(ii) A price to yield Jones an annual return of .12 while
recovering his principal in a sinking fund earning an
annual rate of 6%.

(iii) Accumulate the payments at 6% and then find the
present value at 12% of that accumulated value.

(b) Jones calculates his annual rate of return a number of
different ways. In case (iii) of part (a) Jones earns an annual
rate of return of 12% for the 20 years. Find his annual
"yield" according to each of the following approaches.

(i) In part (a)(i) above, assume that Jones can reinvest the
payments at 6% per year; find Jones' average annual
compound rate of return based on the accumulated
amount after 20 years compared to his initial investment.

(ii) Using the amount invested based on the approach in
(a)(ii) as the present value of the annuity, find the
unknown interest rate (internal rate of return).

(iii) Assuming that the full 1000 is deposited in the sinking
fund at 6%, find the average annual compound rate of
return over the 20 years based on the accumulated value of
the sinking fund and the initial amount invested in (a)(ii).

2.4.3   An investor is considering the purchase of an annuity of K per
year for n years, starting one year from the purchase date. He
calculates a purchase price on each of two bases: (i) the present
value of the annuity at rate i per year, resulting in price P_1, and
(ii) the sinking fund method with annual return of i per year
(same i as in (i)), recovering the principal in a sinking fund with
an accumulation rate of j per year, resulting in price P_2.

(a) Derive the following relationships by comparing $\frac{1}{P_1}$ and $\frac{1}{P_2}$ and using the identity $\frac{1}{s_{\overline{n}|k}} + k = \frac{1}{a_{\overline{n}|k}}$.

    (i) $P_1 = P_2$ if $i = j$

    (ii) $P_1 > P_2$ if $i > j$

    (iii) $P_1 < P_2$ if $i < j$

(b) Let i' be the unknown interest rate in the solution of $P_2 = K \cdot \frac{1}{a_{\overline{n}|i'}}$. Show each of the following results.

    (i) $i' = i$ if $i = j$

    (ii) $i' > i$ if $i > j$

    (iii) $i' < i$ if $i < j$

(c) Let i'' be the solution of $P_2(1+i'')^n = K \cdot s_{\overline{n}|j}$. Show that i'' lies between i and j. How does i'' compare with the i' found in Exercise 2.4.1?

2.4.4   Repeat part (a)(ii) of Exercise 2.4.2 for each of the following situations.

(a) Jones wishes to receive a return of 12% per year for the first 10 years and 8% per year for the final 10 years, while recovering the principal in a sinking fund earning 6% per year.

(b) Jones wishes to receive a return of 12% per year, while recovering the principal in a sinking fund earning 6% per year for the first 10 years and 4% per year for the final 10 years.

(c) Jones wishes to receive a return of 12% per year for the first 10 years and 8% for the final 10 years, while recovering the principal in a sinking fund earning 6% per year for the first 10 years and 4% per year for the final 10 years.

2.4.5   Repeat Exercises 2.4.2 and 2.4.4 if the first 10 payments are 500 each and the final 10 payments are 1500 each.

2.4.6   Repeat Example 2.30 in each of the following cases

(a) If the equipment has a salvage value after 8 years of 10,000, find the purchase price based on the sinking fund method using the same i and j as before.

(b) Find the salvage value for which the purchase price would be 85,000 based on the sinking fund method using the same i and j as before.

2.4.7   Repeat Example 2.31 by showing that $\frac{d}{dj} P_2 > 0$.

2.4.8   (a) Show that P_2 in Example 2.31 can be written as
$$P_2 = \frac{a_{\overline{n}|j}}{1+(i-j)\cdot a_{\overline{n}|j}}.$$

(b) Show that L in Equation (2.23) can be written as
$$L = \frac{\sum\limits_{t=1}^{n} K_t \cdot v_j^t}{1+(i-j)\cdot a_{\overline{n}\,j}}.$$

(c) Construct a numerical example for L in Equation (2.23) (i.e., K_t's and i), such that $\frac{dL}{dj} > 0$.

2.4.9   Repeat Example 2.25 with the bond earning monthly interest at a nominal annual rate of 12%, and the deposit account earning monthly interest at a nominal annual rate of 6%.

2.4.10 (a) The average periodic compound yield rate earned over an n-period term on an investment of initial amount 1 that generates interest at periodic rate $i > 0$ which is reinvested at rate $j > 0$ is i', where $(1+i')^n = 1+i\cdot s_{\overline{n}|j}$. Show that i' lies between i and j, and that if $i = j$ then $i' = i = j$.

(b) The average periodic compound yield rate earned over an n-period term on an annuity of 1 per period whose payments earn initial interest of i per period which is then reinvested at rate j is i', where $s_{\overline{n}|i'} = n+i\cdot(Is)_{\overline{n-1}|j}$. Show that i' lies between i and j, and that if $i = j$ then $i' = i = j$.

(c) For each of parts (a) and (b), show that $\lim\limits_{n\to\infty} i' = j$.

2.4.11 A purchaser pays 245,000 for a mine which will be exhausted at the end of 18 years. What level annual revenue (received at the end of each year) is required in order for the purchaser to receive a 5% annual return on his investment if he can recover his principal in a sinking fund earning 3.5% per year?

2.4.12 Smith wishes to purchase an increasing annuity with 20 annual payments of 1000, 2000, 3000, ..., 20,000. Smith considers the following three methods of valuing the annuity one period before the first payment Find the purchase price in each case.

(a) Present value method at $i = .10$.

(b) Sinking fund method, earning annual interest of 10% on the initial investment and recovering the initial investment in a sinking fund earning 6% per year. (Note that this involves negative sinking fund deposits for several years, which is algebraically feasible but unrealistic from a practical point of view.)

(c) Capitalizing unpaid interest each year at rate 10%: with initial investment P_0 the outstanding balance at time 1 is $P_1 = P_0(1.10) - 1000$; at time 2 it is $P_2 = P_1(1.10) - 2000$, and so on. This continues until P_t is such that the payments are large enough to support the sinking fund method with a purchase price of P_t, and Smith earns 10% per year on P_t for the remaining years while accumulating P_t in a sinking fund earning interest at 6%.

2.4.13 Machine I costs X, has a salvage value of $\frac{X}{8}$, and is to be depreciated over 10 years using the declining balance method.

Machine II costs Y, has a salvage value of $\frac{X}{8}$, and is to be depreciated over 10 years using the sum-of-the-years digits method.

The total amount of depreciation in the first seven years for Machine I equals the total amount of depreciation in the first seven years for Machine II. Calculate $\frac{Y}{X}$.

2.4.14 A copier costs X and will have a salvage value of Y after n years.

(i) Using the straight line method, the annual depreciation expense is 1000.

(ii) Using the sum of the years digits method, the depreciation expense in year 3 is 800.

(iii) Using the declining balance method, the depreciation expense is 33.125% of the book value in the beginning of the year.

Calculate X.

2.4.15 A manufacturer buys a machine for 20,000. The manufacturer estimates that the machine will last 15 years. It will be depreciated using the constant percentage method with an annual depreciation rate of 20%. At the end of each year, the manufacturer deposits an amount into a fund that pays 6% annually. Each deposit is equal to the depreciation expense for that year. How much money will the manufacturer have accumulated in the fund at the end of 15 years?

2.4.16 A machine is purchased for 5000 and has a salvage value of S at the end of 10 years. The machine is depreciated using the sum-of-the-years-digits method.

At the end of year 4, the machine has a book value of 2218. At that time, the depreciation method is changed to the straight-line method for the remaining years. Determine the new depreciation charge for year 8.

CHAPTER 3

LOAN REPAYMENT

When a loan is being repaid by a series of payments, the total of all payments must repay the original amount of the loan (the principal) as well as pay interest on the loan. It is usually the case that each loan payment can be separated into two components, one component being the amount of interest being paid and the other being the amount of principal being paid. There are several ways in which a loan repayment scheme can be set up, each of which specifies the division of payments into interest paid and principal repaid. In this chapter we will consider various loan repayment schemes. The most common one is the *amortization method*, which we will consider first.

3.1 THE AMORTIZATION METHOD OF LOAN REPAYMENT

The definition and basic properties of an amortized loan can best be described by means of a simple illustration. We consider a loan of amount 1000 with an interest rate of 10% per year. Suppose that there is a payment of 200 at the end of 1 year, and a payment of 500 at the end of 2 years, and a final payment at the end of 3 years to completely repay the loan. At the end of the first year, before the first payment is made, the amount owing, including interest, is $1000(1.10) = 1100$. The payment of 200 reduces the amount owing to 900 just after the first payment; this is the outstanding balance on the loan just after the first payment is made. At the end of the second year, before the second payment is made, the amount owing is $900(1.10) = 990$. The payment of 500 reduces the amount owing to 490 just after the second payment; this is outstanding balance on the loan just after the second payment is made. At the end of the third year, before the third payment is made, the amount owing is $490(1.10) = 539$. This is the amount needed to completely repay the loan at the end of the third year.

This illustration captures a defining feature of an amortized loan. Each time a payment is made, the outstanding balance from the previous payment point is accumulated with interest to the current payment point, and the new payment is subtracted from that accumulated amount, resulting in the new outstanding balance at the current point.

Another important aspect of an amortized loan is the separation of each payment into interest paid and principal paid. Continuing the illustration, we see that at the end of the first year there will be interest of 100 owing on the loan, along with the previous original loan balance of 1000. The amortization method requires that whenever a payment is made, interest is paid first, and any amount remaining is applied toward reducing the loan balance. Therefore, for the payment of 200 made at the end of the first year, 100 is interest paid, and the remaining 100 is principal repaid. The outstanding loan balance is reduced by 100 from 1000 to 900. At the end of the second year there will be interest of 90 (10% of 900). According to the amortization method, the payment of 500 at the end of the second year is made up of an interest payment of 90, and the remaining 410 is principal repaid. The outstanding balance after the second payment is 490 (the previous balance of 900 minus the 410 in principal just paid). At the end of the third year there will be interest due of 49 (10% of 490). The total payment required to completely repay the loan at the end of the third year is the interest payment of 49 plus the principal amount of 490 still owing; the total payment required is 539.

Considering this illustration a little further we see that the outstanding loan balance can be updated from one point to the next as follows.

$$1000(1.10) - 200 = 900, \ 900(1.10) - 500 = 490, \ 490(1.10) - 539 = 0.$$

Combining these expressions, we get

$$1000(1.10)^3 - 200(1.10)^2 - 500(1.10) - 539 = 0.$$

This can also be written in the form $1000 = 200v + 500v^2 + 539v^3$. We have illustrated another important aspect of loan amortization, which is that the original loan amount is equal to the present value of the loan payments using the loan interest rate. In general, the amortization method of loan repayment at a specified rate of interest corresponds to setting the present value of all amounts loaned out equal to the present value of all loan payments, with present values based on the specified loan rate.

3.1.1 THE GENERAL AMORTIZATION METHOD

For a loan amortized at interest rate i per period, the loan amount is equal to the present value of the loan payments at rate i. Suppose a loan of amount L is made at time 0, to be repaid with payments of amounts $K_1, K_2, \ldots, K_n$ at times $1, 2, \ldots, n$ (where the payment period corresponds to the interest period). The equation of value at time 0 for this loan is

$$L = K_1 v + K_2 v^2 + \cdots + K_n v^n.$$

The simplest example of a loan repayment is one in which a loan made at a specified point in time is to be repaid by a single payment at some later point in time. If a loan of amount L, made at time 0 with interest at rate i per period, is to be repaid by a single payment one interest period later, the amount of that single payment is $L(1+i) = L + L \cdot i$. It is clear that in this payment L represents the repayment of the original principal on the loan, and $L \cdot i$ is a payment of interest due (the interest that accrued over the period). Just before the payment is made the accumulated amount owed is $L(1+i)$, and the payment of that amount reduces the amount owed to zero. Suppose that the payment made after one period, say K_1, is somewhat less than $L(1+i)$. In this case the loan is not fully repaid by the payment of K_1, and there remains a balance owing, called the **outstanding balance** or *outstanding principal*. The amount of the outstanding balance just after that first payment is the unpaid part of the loan, so that

$$OB_1 = L(1+i) - K_1. \tag{3.1}$$

The process involved in the amortization method of loan repayment can be described by reformulating Equation (3.1) as

$$OB_1 = L(1+i) - K_1 = L - (K_1 - L \cdot i). \tag{3.2}$$

$L \cdot i$ represents the accrued interest on the original principal amount for the period. The payment of K_1 is regarded as first paying the accrued interest, $L \cdot i$, and then the remainder of the payment, $K_1 - L \cdot i$, is applied to reduce the principal, or balance owing, so that the outstanding balance that remains is equal to the initial balance owing minus the amount of principal repaid. Thus $L - (K_1 - L \cdot i) = OB_1$.

The general description of the amortization method of loan repayment is as follows. A loan of amount L at interest rate i per period will be completely repaid by a series of n successive payments, starting one period after the loan is made, with the payments made at equally spaced intervals in amounts (in order) $K_1, K_2, \ldots, K_n$. It will be assumed that the interest period and payment period coincide, since if they do not it is easy to find the equivalent rate of interest for the payment period. We denote the initial loan amount L by OB_0, the outstanding balance at time 0. At the end of the first period the loan has accumulated, with interest, to $OB_0(1+i)$. The payment of amount K_1 is then applied, so that the resulting outstanding balance at time 1 (just after the first payment) is $OB_1 = OB_0(1+i) - K_1$. This relationship can also be written as $OB_1 = OB_0 - (K_1 - OB_0 \cdot i)$, where $OB_0 \cdot i = I_1$ represents the amount of **interest paid** at the end of the first period, and $K_1 - OB_0 \cdot i = K_1 - I_1 = PR_1$ represents the rest of the payment, the amount applied to reduce the outstanding balance. Thus PR_1 is the amount of **principal repaid** by the first payment. Then we have

$$OB_1 \;=\; OB_0 - (K_1 - OB_0 \cdot i) \;=\; OB_0 - (K_1 - I_1) \;=\; OB_0 - PR_1.$$

This process can now be extended to the end of the second payment period, where we have an accumulated balance of $OB_1(1+i)$ which is then reduced by the second payment K_2, resulting in an outstanding balance just after the second payment of $OB_2 = OB_1(1+i) - K_2$. This can be rewritten as

$$\begin{aligned}
OB_2 \;=\; OB_1(1+i) - K_2 \;&=\; OB_1 - (K_2 - OB_1 \cdot i) \\
&=\; OB_1 - (K_2 - I_2) \;=\; OB_1 - PR_2.
\end{aligned}$$

In this expression, $I_2 = OB_1 \cdot i$ is the interest due at the end of the second period, and $PR_2 = K_2 - I_2$ is the rest of the second payment which is applied to repay principal. This process continues from one payment period to the next. Just after the tth payment there will be an outstanding balance of OB_t. During the following period this outstanding balance will accumulate with interest to $OB_t(1+i)$, at which time the $t+1^{st}$ payment K_{t+1} is made so that the outstanding balance is $OB_{t+1} = OB_t(1+i) - K_{t+1}$. This can be rewritten as

$$OB_{t+1} \;=\; OB_t - (K_{t+1} - OB_t \cdot i) \;=\; OB_t - (K_{t+1} - I_{t+1}) \;=\; OB_t - PR_{t+1},$$

where $I_{t+1} = OB_t \cdot i$ is the interest due at the end of the $t+1^{st}$ period, and $PR_{t+1} = K_{t+1} - I_{t+1}$ is the rest of the $t+1^{st}$ payment which is applied to repay principal. This continues until the time of the nth, and final, payment, which reduces the outstanding balance to zero. That is, $OB_n = OB_{n-1}(1+i) - K_n = 0$. Therefore, we see that each payment can be decomposed into a part that pays the interest that has accrued since the last payment and a part that repays some of the principal outstanding. The following time diagram illustrates the successive outstanding balances as the amortization progresses.

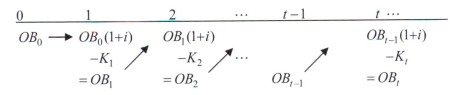

FIGURE 3.1

3.1.2 THE AMORTIZATION SCHEDULE

The amortization of a loan as described above can be summarized in an *amortization schedule*, which sets out at each point in time the outstanding balance just after the payment made at that time, the interest paid, and the principal repaid. Table 3.1 presents the amortization schedule symbolically.

TABLE 3.1

t	Payment	Interest Due	Principal Repaid	Outstanding Balance
0	—	—	—	$L = OB_0$
1	K_1	$I_1 = OB_0 \cdot i$	$PR_1 = K_1 - I_1$	$OB_1 = OB_0 - PR_1$
2	K_2	$I_2 = OB_1 \cdot i$	$PR_2 = K_2 - I_2$	$OB_2 = OB_1 - PR_2$
$\vdots$	$\vdots$	$\vdots$	$\vdots$	$\vdots$
t				OB_t
$t+1$	K_{t+1}	$I_{t+1} = OB_t \cdot i$	$PR_{t+1} = K_{t+1} - I_{t+1}$	$OB_{t+1} = OB_t - PR_{t+1}$
$\vdots$	$\vdots$	$\vdots$	$\vdots$	$\vdots$
n	K_n	$I_n = OB_{n-1} \cdot i$	$PR_n = K_n - I_n$	$OB_n = OB_{n-1} - PR_n$

From Table 3.1 we see that the total amount paid during the course of repaying the loan is $K_T = \sum_{t=1}^{n} K_t$, of which $I_T = \sum_{t=1}^{n} I_t$, is the total interest paid over the course of the loan, and the total principal repaid is $K_T - I_T = \sum_{t=1}^{n}(K_t - I_t)$. In Exercise 3.1.1 you are asked to show that $K_T - I_T$ is equal to $L = OB_0$. The total amount of principal repaid during the term of the loan is the original loan amount L. Note that total interest paid I_T can be written as

$$I_T = \sum I_t = \sum(OB_{t-1} \cdot i) = i \cdot \sum OB_{t-1} = i\left[OB_0 + OB_1 + \cdots + OB_{n-1}\right].$$

If the final loan payment occurs at time n to completely repay the loan, then $OB_n = 0$.

EXAMPLE 3.1   (*Amortization table*)

A loan of amount 1000 at rate $i^{(12)} = .12$ is repaid by 6 monthly payments, starting one month after the loan is made. The first three payments are amount X each and the final three payments are amount $2X$ each. Construct the amortization schedule for this loan.

SOLUTION

To solve for X we have $1000 = X \cdot a_{\overline{3}|.01} + 2X \cdot v^3 \cdot a_{\overline{3}|.01}$ as the equation of value, so that $X = 115.61$ to the nearest cent and $2X = 231.21$ to the nearest cent. The amortization schedule, with t measured in months, is given in Table 3.2. The exact value of OB_6 is 0, and the value of $-.01$ in the schedule is due to roundoff error which accumulates in the calculation of all quantities to the nearest cent. In practice the final payment would have been increased by 1 cent to 231.22 in order to reduce OB_6 to zero. If X and the various quantities in the schedule had been calculated with a few additional digits of accuracy, the value of OB_6 would be closer to its exact value of zero. The total amount paid on the loan is 1040.46, of which 40.47 is interest and 1000 (999.99 because of roundoff) is principal repayment.

TABLE 3.2

t	Payment	Interest Due	Principal Repaid	Outstanding Balance
0	–	–	–	$L = OB_0 = 1000$
1	$K_1 = 115.61$	$I_1 = OB_0 \cdot i$ $= 10$	$PR_1 = K_1 - I_1$ $= 105.61$	$OB_1 = OB_0 - PR_1 = 894.39$
2	$K_2 = 115.61$	$I_2 = OB_1 \cdot i$ $= 8.94$	$PR_2 = K_2 - I_2$ $= 106.67$	$OB_2 = OB_1 - PR_2 = 787.72$
3	$K_3 = 115.61$	$I_3 = OB_2 \cdot i$ $= 7.88$	$PR_3 = K_3 - I_3$ $= 107.73$	$OB_3 = OB_2 - PR_3 = 679.99$
4	$K_4 = 231.21$	$I_4 = OB_3 \cdot i$ $= 6.80$	$PR_4 = K_4 - I_4$ $= 224.41$	$OB_4 = OB_3 - PR_4 = 455.58$
5	$K_5 = 231.21$	$I_5 = OB_4 \cdot i$ $= 4.56$	$PR_5 = K_5 - I_5$ $= 226.65$	$OB_5 = OB_4 - PR_5 = 228.93$
6	$K_6 = 231.21$	$I_6 = OB_5 \cdot i$ $= 2.29$	$PR_6 = K_6 - I_6$ $= 228.92$	$OB_6 = OB_5 - PR_6 = .01$
Totals	1040.46	40.47	999.99	

3.1.3 RETROSPECTIVE FORM OF THE OUTSTANDING BALANCE

If we follow the amortization process from one period to the next for the general n-payment loan we see that the successive outstanding balance amounts can be formulated as

$$OB_1 = OB_0(1+i) - K_1$$
$$OB_2 = OB_1(1+i) - K_2 = OB_0(1+i)^2 - K_1(1+i) - K_2$$
$$OB_3 = OB_2(1+i) - K_3 = OB_0(1+i)^3 - K_1(1+i)^2 - K_2(1+i) - K_3$$
$$\vdots$$
$$OB_t = OB_0(1+i)^t - K_1(1+i)^{t-1} - K_2(1+i)^{t-2} - \cdots - K_{t-1}(1+i) - K_t$$
$$\vdots$$
$$OB_n = OB_0(1+i)^n - K_1(1+i)^{n-1} - K_2(1+i)^{n-2} - \cdots - K_{n-1}(1+i) - K_n = 0.$$

The general relationship given by

$$OB_t = OB_0(1+i)^t - K_1(1+i)^{t-1} - K_2(1+i)^{t-2} - \cdots - K_{t-1}(1+i) - K_t \quad (3.3)$$

is the **retrospective method** of formulating the outstanding balance of the loan just after the tth payment. The retrospective method formulates OB_t as the amount of the original loan accumulated to time t (which is $L(1+i)^t = OB_0(1+i)^t$), minus the accumulated value of all payments to time t, including K_t, the payment made at time t.

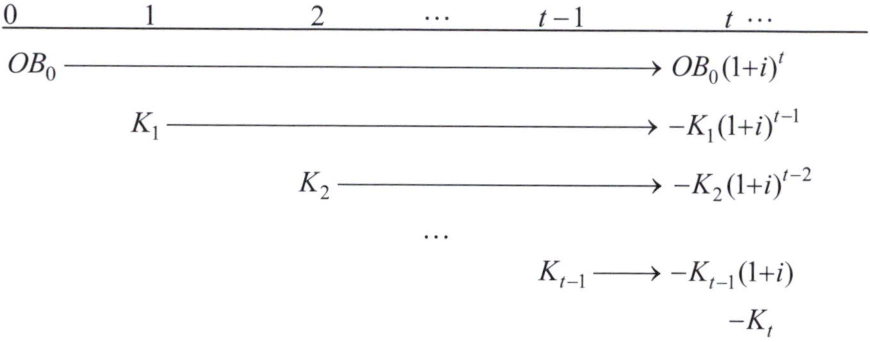

| 0 | 1 | 2 | $\cdots$ | $t-1$ | t $\cdots$ |

$OB_0 \longrightarrow OB_0(1+i)^t$

$\qquad K_1 \longrightarrow -K_1(1+i)^{t-1}$

$\qquad\qquad K_2 \longrightarrow -K_2(1+i)^{t-2}$

$\cdots$

$K_{t-1} \longrightarrow -K_{t-1}(1+i)$

$-K_t$

FIGURE 3.2

Applying the retrospective form of the outstanding balance to Example 3.1, we see that the outstanding balance of the loan just after the third payment is

$$OB_3 = 1000(1.01)^3 - 115.61(1.01)^2 - 115.61(1.01) - 115.61$$
$$= 1000(1.01)^3 - 115.61 \cdot s_{\overline{3}|.01} = 679.99.$$

In a general amortization, the loan is completely repaid by the nth payment, so

$$OB_n = OB_0(1+i)^n - K_1(1+i)^{n-1} - K_2(1+i)^{n-2} - \cdots - K_{n-1}(1+i) - K_n = 0.$$

Multiplying both sides of this equation by v^n and rearranging the terms we have

$$L = OB_0 = K_1 \cdot v + K_2 \cdot v^2 + \cdots + K_n \cdot v^n. \quad (3.4)$$

Thus it follows that under the amortization method of repaying a loan, the original loan amount is equal to the present value of the series of loan payments.

3.1.4 PROSPECTIVE FORM OF THE OUTSTANDING BALANCE

The general retrospective form of the outstanding balance at time t is given by Equation (3.3). If we replace OB_0 in that equation by

$$OB_0 \;=\; K_1 \cdot v + K_2 \cdot v^2 + \cdots + K_n \cdot v^n,$$

from Equation (3.4), then Equation (3.3) is transformed into

$$
\begin{aligned}
OB_t &= \Big[K_1 \cdot v + K_2 \cdot v^2 + \cdots + K_t \cdot v^t + K_{t+1} \cdot v^{t+1} + \cdots + K_n \cdot v^n \Big](1+i)^t \\
&\quad - K_1(1+i)^{t-1} - K_2(1+i)^{t-2} - \cdots - K_{t-1}(1+i) - K_t \\
&= K_{t+1} \cdot v + K_{t+2} \cdot v^2 + \cdots + K_n \cdot v^{n-t}. \tag{3.5}
\end{aligned}
$$

Thus we see that OB_t is equal to the present value, *at time t*, of all remaining payments from time $t+1$ onward, but not including the payment just made at time t. This is the **prospective form** of the outstanding balance, and it is algebraically equivalent to the retrospective form. Just as the original loan amount is the present value of the loan payments, the amount owing at any point in time is the present value of the remaining payments.

0	1	2	$\cdots$	t	$t+1$	$t+2$	$\cdots$	n
				$\uparrow$				
				OB_t	K_{t+1}	K_{t+2}	$\cdots$	K_n

FIGURE 3.3

In Example 3.1 we can apply the prospective form to find OB_3 as

$$OB_3 \;=\; 231.21 \cdot v + 231.21 \cdot v^2 + 231.21 \cdot v^3 \;=\; 231.21 \cdot a_{\overline{3}|.01} \;=\; 679.98,$$

where the difference from the retrospective OB_3 value of 679.99 is due to roundoff error.

3.1.5 ADDITIONAL PROPERTIES OF AMORTIZATION

Non-Level Interest Rate

In the discussion of the amortization method given above, it was assumed that the interest rate on the loan remained unchanged from one period to the next. The amortization method can also be applied when the interest rate changes over time. Let i_1 denote the interest rate for the first period, which runs from time 0 to time 1, i_2 denotes the interest rate for the second period, and so on, with the interest rate for the $t+1^{st}$ period denoted by i_{t+1}. Then the amortization relationships become

$$OB_1 = OB_0 - (K_1 - OB_0 \cdot i_1) = OB_0 - (K_1 - I_1) = OB_0 - PR_1, \quad (3.6)$$

and, in general,

$$OB_{t+1} = OB_t - (K_{t+1} - OB_t \cdot i_{t+1}) = OB_t - (K_{t+1} - I_{t+1})$$
$$= OB_t - PR_{t+1}. \quad (3.7)$$

Capitalization of Interest

In Example 3.1 the interest due amounts are relatively small compared to the actual loan payments, and the excess of the payment amount over the interest due in that payment, $K_t - I_t$, is equal to the principal repaid in that payment, PR_t. It is possible that during the repayment of a loan by the amortization method, a particular payment is not large enough to cover the interest due $(K_t < I_t)$, so there is a shortfall of $I_t - K_t$ in the payment of interest. In this case PR_t, the amount of principal repaid, is negative $(PR_t < 0)$. Algebraically the new outstanding balance just after the tth payment is $OB_t = OB_{t-1} - PR_t$, and since $PR_t < 0$ we find that $OB_t = OB_{t-1} - (K_t - I_t) = OB_{t-1} + (I_t - K_t) > OB_{t-1}$. In other words the outstanding *balance increases by the amount of unpaid interest*. The unpaid interest is *capitalized* and added to the balance still owing. For the purpose of dividing payments into interest and principal, the unpaid interest, which will accumulate as time goes on, should still be regarded as interest when payments are made at a later time. If, in Example 3.1, the loan were being repaid with monthly payments for 12 years (144 payments), with the first payment made one month after the loan is made, and for the first 6 years the 72 payments are amount Z each and for the final 6 years the 72 payments are amount $2Z$ each, then solving for Z we obtain $Z = 9.89$ (the calculation in Exercise 3.1.11 at the end of the chapter). At the time of the first payment the interest due is $I_1 = 1000(.01) = 10$, but the payment made is only $K_1 = Z = 9.89$, so the principal repaid is $PR_1 = K_1 - I_t = -.11$. There is a shortfall in the first payment of .11 in the interest due, and this .11 is *added* to the outstanding balance, resulting in $OB_1 = 1000.11$. Algebraically the calculation of OB_1 is still done in the usual way:

$$OB_1 = OB_0(1+j) - K_1 = 1000(1.01) - 9.89 = 1000.11,$$

or

$$OB_1 = OB_0 - PR_1 = 1000 - (-.11) = 1000.11.$$

Level Payments of Principal

Repayment by means of level payments is the most common form of repaying a loan. In such a case, as shown in Table 3.4 in the next section of this chapter, the amounts of principal repaid increase from one payment to the next in a systematic way and the amounts of interest due decrease. Occasionally a loan repayment is structured to have specified amounts of principal repaid with each payment, along with payment of interest due on the previous period's outstanding balance. This is illustrated in the following example.

EXAMPLE 3.2   (*Loan with level payments of principal*)

A loan of 3000 at an effective quarterly interest rate of $j = .02$ is amortized by means of 12 quarterly payments, beginning one quarter after the loan is made. Each payment consists of a principal repayment of 250 plus interest due on the previous quarter's outstanding balance. Construct the amortization schedule.

SOLUTION

With an initial outstanding balance of $L = OB_0 = 3000$, we have interest due at the end of the first quarter of amount $I_1 = 3000(.02) = 60$. Since the principal paid in the first payment is $PR_1 = 250$, the total amount of the first payment is $K_1 = I_1 + PR_1 = 310$. Then

$$OB_1 \quad = \quad OB_0 - PR_1 \quad = \quad 3000 - 250 \quad = \quad 2750.$$

Table 3.3 gives the full amortization schedule, where t counts quarters.

TABLE 3.3

t	Payment	Interest Due	Principal Repaid	Outstanding Balance
0	–	–	–	$L = OB_0 = 3000$
1	$K_1 = 310$	$I_t = OB_0 \cdot i = 60$	$PR_1 = 250$	$OB_1 = OB_0 - PR_1 = 2750$
2	305	55	250	2500
3	300	50	250	2250
4	295	45	250	2000
5	290	40	250	1750
6	285	35	250	1500
7	280	30	250	1250
8	275	25	250	1000
9	270	20	250	750
10	265	15	250	500
11	260	10	250	250
12	255	5	250	0

The total interest paid during the course of the loan is $60+55+\cdots+5 = 390$, and the present value, at quarterly rate .02, of the payments is equal to 3000 (see Exercise 3.1.4). □

Interest Only With Lump Sum Principal Payment at the End

Occasionally a loan will call for periodic payments of interest only, and a single payment of the full principal amount at the end of a specified term. Such a loan of amount L at rate i per period for n periods has interest payments of $I_1 = I_2 = \cdots = I_n = L \cdot i$, and principal payments of

$$PR_1 = PR_2 = \cdots = PR_{n-1} = 0 \quad \text{and} \quad PR_n = L.$$

The outstanding balances are

$$OB_0 = L,$$

$$OB_1 = OB_0 - PR_1 = L,$$

$$OB_1 = L, \ldots, OB_{n-1} = L,$$

$$OB_n = OB_{n-1} - PR_n = L - L = 0.$$

The borrower is required to make payments of interest only to the lender during the term of the loan, but then he must pay the full amount of principal at the end of the term. In this situation the borrower might accumulate the principal amount L by means of deposits into an account during the term of the loan. The deposit account is called a **sinking fund**, and this method of loan repayment is called the **sinking fund method**, and it is similar to the theory described in Chapter 2. The sinking fund method of loan repayment is considered in detail in Section 3.3.

3.2 AMORTIZATION OF A LOAN WITH LEVEL PAYMENTS

A loan is typically repaid with level payments, and if this is the case the amortization schedule has a systematic form. Suppose a loan is repaid by n payments of amount 1 each, starting one payment period after the loan was made, and suppose that interest on the loan is at rate i per period. Then the original loan amount, based on the amortization method, is the present value of the payments, so that $L = OB_0 = a_{\overline{n}|i}$, and $K_1 = K_2 = \cdots = K_n = 1$.

The prospective form of the outstanding balance just after the tth payment is $OB_t = a_{\overline{n-t}|i}$, the present value of the remaining $n - t$ payments of amount 1 each. The retrospective form of the outstanding balance just after the tth payment is

$$OB_t = L(1+i)^t - Ks_{\overline{t}|i}.$$

This is algebraically equivalent to the prospective form:

$$OB_t = L(1+i)^t - Ks_{\overline{t}|i} = a_{\overline{n}|i}(1+i)^t - s_{\overline{t}|i} = s_{\overline{t}|} + a_{\overline{n-t}|} - s_{\overline{t}|} = a_{\overline{n-t}|}.$$

The full amortization schedule is shown in Table 3.4.

TABLE 3.4

t	Payment	Interest Due	Principal Repaid	Outstanding Balance
0	–	–	–	$L = OB_0 = a_{\overline{n}\rvert}$
1	$K_1 = 1$	$I_1 = OB_0 \cdot i$ $= i \cdot a_{\overline{n}\rvert}$ $= 1 - v^n$	$PR_1 = K_1 - I_1$ $= v^n$	$OB_1 = OB_0 - PR_1$ $= a_{\overline{n}\rvert} - v^n$ $= a_{\overline{n-1}\rvert}$
2	$K_2 = 1$	$I_2 = OB_1 \cdot i$ $= i \cdot a_{\overline{n-1}\rvert}$ $= 1 - v^{n-1}$	$PR_2 = K_2 - I_2$ $= v^{n-1}$	$OB_2 = OB_1 - PR_2$ $= a_{\overline{n-1}\rvert} - v^{n-1}$ $= a_{\overline{n-2}\rvert}$
$\vdots$		$\vdots$	$\vdots$	$\vdots$
$t-1$				$OB_{t-1} = a_{\overline{n-t+1}\rvert}$
t	$K_t = 1$	$I_t = OB_{t-1} \cdot i$ $= i \cdot a_{\overline{n-t+1}\rvert}$ $= 1 - v^{n-t+1}$	$PR_t = K_t - I_t$ $= v^{n-t+1}$	$OB_t = OB_{t-1} - PR_t$ $= a_{\overline{n-t+1}\rvert} - v^{n-t+1}$ $= a_{\overline{n-t}\rvert}$
$\vdots$		$\vdots$	$\vdots$	$\vdots$
n	$K_n = 1$	$I_n = OB_{n-1} \cdot i$ $= i \cdot a_{\overline{1}\rvert}$ $= 1 - v$	$PR_n = K_n - I_n$ $= v$	$OB_n = OB_{n-1} - PR_n$ $= a_{\overline{1}\rvert} - v$ $= 0$

The total amount paid during the term of the loan is $K_T = n$ (n payments of 1). The total amount of interest paid is

$$I_T \;=\; (1 - v^n) + (1 - v^{n-1}) + \cdots + (1 - v) \;=\; n - a_{\overline{n}\rvert},$$

and the total principal repaid is

$$K_T - I_T \;=\; n - (n - a_{\overline{n}\rvert}) \;=\; a_{\overline{n}\rvert} \;=\; L,$$

the original amount of the loan.

Another point to note about the amortization schedule for a loan with level payments concerns the principal repaid column. Moving down this column from time 1 to time 2 and onward, we see that

$$PR_2 = v^{n-1} = v^n(1+i) = PR_1(1+i),$$

and, in general,

$$PR_t = v^{n-t+1} = v^n(1+i)^{t-1} = PR_1(1+i)^{t-1}.$$

This relationship involving the principal repaid amounts is valid provided the payments and the interest rate remain level. In Exercise 3.1.2 it is shown that if two successive payments on an amortized loan are equal $(K_t = K_{t+1})$ and the corresponding periodic interest rates are also equal $(i_t = i_{t+1} = i)$, then $PR_{t+1} = PR_t(1+i)$. In Example 3.1 where $K_1 = K_2 = K_3$, according to this rule, we expect that $PR_2 = PR_1(1+j)$ and $PR_3 = PR_2(1+j)$. This is easily verified since

$$PR_2 = 105.61(1.01) = 106.67$$

and

$$PR_3 = 106.67(1.01) = 107.74.$$

Furthermore, since $K_4 = K_5 = K_6$, we have $PR_4(1+j) = PR_5$ and $PR_5(1+j) = PR_6$. Note that $\frac{PR_4}{PR_3} = \frac{224.41}{107.74} = 2.083 \neq 1+j$, since $K_3 \neq K_4$.

| **EXAMPLE 3.3** | *(A 30-year mortgage)* |

A homebuyer borrows \$250,000 to be repaid over a 30-year period with level monthly payments beginning one month after the loan is made. The interest rate on the loan is a nominal annual rate of 9% compounded monthly. Find each of the following:

(i) the amount of interest and the amount of principal paid in the first year,

(ii) the amount of interest and the amount of principal paid in the 30th year.

SOLUTION

The monthly interest rate is .75%, and the monthly payment is K, where $Ka_{\overline{360}|.0075} = 250,000$. Then $K = 2,011.556542$. In practice, the actual payment by the borrower would be rounded to the nearest .01 (cent). For the purpose of consistency in the algebraic relationships being illustrated, calculations will be based on full calculator accuracy without rounding.

(i) The outstanding balance at the end of the first year (12 months) is (prospectively) $2,011.556542\,a_{\overline{348}|.0075} = 248,292.0073$. The amount of principal paid in the first year is the amount by which the outstanding balance was reduced; this amount is

$$250,000 - 248,292.0073 \ = \ 1,707.9927.$$

The total amount paid in the first year is the 12 payments of 2,011.556542 for a total of 24,138.6785. Of that total, 1,707.9927 was principal repaid, so the remaining

$$24,138.6785 - 1,707.9927 \ = \ 22,430.6858$$

was interest paid in the first year.

(ii) The outstanding balance at the end of the 29th year is (prospectively) $2,011.556542\,a_{\overline{12}|.0075} = 23,001.9734$. Since the loan is completely repaid at the end of the 30th year, the amount of principal repaid during the 30th year must be the total amount of 23,001.9734 still outstanding when the 30th year begins. The total amount paid in the 30th year is still 12 payments of 2011.556542 for a total of 24,138.6785. Therefore, the total amount of interest paid in the 30th year is

$$24,138.6785 - 23,001.9734 \ = \ 1,136.7051.$$

Notice that since this is a level payment amortization, the amount of principal repaid grows by a factor of 1.0075 from one month to the next. Therefore, for each payment in the 30th year, the amount of principal repaid is $(1.0075)^{348}$ times as large as the principal paid in the corresponding payment in the first year (29 years or 348 months earlier). Therefore, the total principal paid in the 30th year should be $1,707.9927 \times (1.0075)^{348} = 23,001.9728$. The amount of principal paid in the 30th year calculated above is 23,001.9734. The difference from the value of 23,001.9728 is due to roundoff error within the calculator.

In practice, the payment made by the borrower would be rounded to the nearest one cent (.01) and any discrepancies that arise due to roundoff error would be corrected when the loan is finally settled. For instance, if the payment is 2,011.56, the retrospective outstanding balance calculation at the end of the first year would be

$$250,000(1.0075)^{12} - 2,011.56s_{\overline{12}|.0075} \quad = \quad 248,291.96.$$

There is a difference of .05 between this value and the value found in part (a) based on more accuracy in the payment amount.

Some entries in the amortization table for this loan are in the following table.

TABLE 3.5

t	Payment	Interest Due	Principal Repaid	Outstanding Balance
0	2011.56	–	–	250,000.00
1	2011.56	1875.00	136.56	249,863.44
2	2011.56	1873.98	137.58	249,725.86
3	2011.56	1872.94	138.62	249,587.25
4	2011.56	1871.90	139.65	249,447.60
5	2011.56	1870.86	140.70	249,306.90
6	2011.56	1869.80	141.75	249,165.14
⋮		⋮	⋮	⋮
240	2011.56	1197.08	814.48	158,795.68
⋮		⋮	⋮	⋮
300	2011.56	736.34	1275.22	96,903.46
⋮		⋮	⋮	⋮
348	2011.56	186.20	1825.35	23,001.97
⋮		⋮	⋮	⋮
358	2011.56	44.59	1966.97	3978.30
359	2011.56	29.84	1981.72	1996.58
360	2011.56	14.97	1996.58	0

Figure 3.4 below shows two graphs of the outstanding balance over the lifetime of the loan in Example 3.3. The first graph was generated by a

computer routine, and the second graph was taken from the financial calculation website www.dinkytown.net/java/SimpleLoan.html.

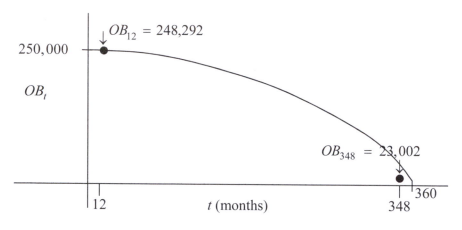

Loan payment is $2,011.56 for 360 payments.

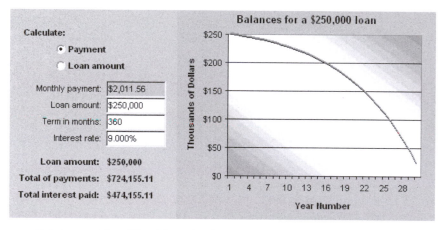

www.dinkytown.net/java/SimpleLoan.html

FIGURE 3.4

Mortgage Loans in Canada

The law regarding mortgage loans in Canada requires that the mortgage interest rate be quoted as either an effective annual rate of interest or as a nominal annual rate of interest compounded semi-annually, even though mortgage loans have monthly payments. If the loan in Example 3.3 referred to a Canadian mortgage, and if the interest rate of 9% was a nominal annual rate compounded semi-annually, then the equivalent monthly rate of interest would be $j = (1.045)^{1/6} - 1 = .00736312$. The monthly payment would be 1,982.08.

Mortgage Loans in the U.S.

The loan interest rate quoted for a mortgage in the United States is, by law, a nominal annual rate of interest compounded monthly. This is the rate that is used to calculate the monthly payment on the loan. When a mortgage loan is arranged, there may be some fees and other costs associated with the loan. The *Annual Percentage Rate* (APR) is a measure of the cost of the loan in terms an interest rate that takes into account the fees that must be paid.

Suppose that a loan is to be repaid with monthly payments for 30 years. With a quoted annual **loan rate** of i compounded monthly (so $j = \frac{i}{12}$ is the monthly loan rate) on a loan of amount L, the monthly payment is K, where $L = K a_{\overline{360}|j}$ (the loan amount is equal to the present value of the monthly payments at the quoted monthly loan rate). Suppose that the loan has associated fees of amount F, that are payable at the time the loan is made. The result of the payment of these fees at the time that the loan is advanced is that the borrower receives a net amount of $L - F$. The APR for the loan is a nominal annual rate of interest compounded monthly, say i', with a corresponding monthly rate of $j' = \frac{i'}{12}$, and which satisfies the relationship $L - F = K a_{\overline{360}|j'}$. Note that the payment amount originally calculated based on the loan rate is used in the APR calculation. The APR will be larger than the loan rate when there are fees on the loan, because a larger interest rate is needed to make the present value smaller than the loan amount L.

EXAMPLE 3.3 continued	*(APR for a 30 year mortgage)*

Suppose that the loan has fees of $5,000 that are paid at the time of the loan. Find the APR on the loan.

| SOLUTION |

The APR will be i', with corresponding monthly rate $j' = \frac{i'}{12}$, satisfying the relationship $250,000 - 5,000 = 2,011.56\, a_{\overline{360}|\,j'}$. Using a calculator unknown interest function, we get $j' = .007689577$, so that the APR is $i' = 12\,j' = .0922749$ (nominal annual rate of interest compounded monthly).

$\square$

3.3   THE SINKING-FUND METHOD OF LOAN REPAYMENT

The final comments in Section 3.1 considered the case of a loan which called for periodic payments of interest only during the term of the loan, along with repayment of the full principal amount at the end of the term. For such a loan of amount L at periodic rate of interest i for n periods, the borrower would have to make a series of n interest payments to the lender, each of amount $L \cdot i$, along with a payment of L at time n. The borrower might offset the obligation to pay the single lump sum of amount L at time n by accumulating that amount during the term of the loan by means of n periodic deposits into an interest-bearing savings account called a *sinking fund*. This method of loan repayment is called the **sinking-fund method**.

There is no guarantee that the rate earned in the sinking fund, say j, is the same as the periodic interest rate on the loan, i. In a practical situation it would usually be the case that the interest rate charged by the lender is larger than the rate that can be earned in a deposit account, so that $i > j$.

A standard way of accumulating the principal amount in the sinking fund is by using level deposits. If this is the case, then for the loan situation just described the borrower's payment would be $L \cdot i$, which is the interest payment to the lender, plus $\frac{L}{s_{\overline{n}|\,j}}$, which is the level sinking fund deposit, producing a total periodic outlay of $L\left[i + \frac{1}{s_{\overline{n}|\,j}} \right]$.

| EXAMPLE 3.4 | *(Sinking fund)*

A loan of 100,000 is to be repaid by ten annual payments beginning one year after the loan is made. The lender wants annual payments of only interest at a rate of 10% and repayment of the principal in a single lump sum at the end of 10 years. The borrower can accumulate the principal in a sinking fund earning an annual interest rate of 8%, and decides to do this by means of 10 level deposits starting one year after the loan is made.

(a) Find the borrowers' total annual outlay and compare this to the level annual payment required by the amortization method at 10%. Find the annual rate of interest i' for which the amortization method at rate i results in the same total annual outlay as the borrower pays in the sinking fund method in this example.

(b) Suppose that the lender's rate is 8% and the sinking fund rate is 10%. Repeat part (a), comparing this to the amortization method at 8%.

| SOLUTION |

(a) The total annual outlay under the sinking fund method is $100,000\left[.1+\dfrac{1}{s_{\overline{10}|.08}}\right] = 16,902.95$, and the annual payment under amortization at 10% is $\dfrac{100,000}{a_{\overline{10}|.10}} = 16,274.54$. To find i' we have $100,000 = 16,902.95 \cdot a_{\overline{10}|i'}$, which results in $i' = .1089$.

(b) The total annual outlay under the sinking fund method is $100,000\left[.08+\dfrac{1}{s_{\overline{10}|.10}}\right] = 14,274.54$, and the annual payment under amortization at 8% is $\dfrac{100,000}{a_{\overline{10}|.08}} = 14,902.95$. To find i' we have $100,000 = 14,274.54 \cdot a_{\overline{10}|i'}$, which results in $i' = .0706$. □

As deposits are made to the sinking fund, the fund balance grows toward the target value of L. For instance, in part (a) of Example 3.4, just after the fifth deposit into the sinking fund, the fund balance is $6902.95 \cdot s_{\overline{5}|.08} = 40,496.85$. This is the accumulated value after five years in the fund that will eventually pay back the principal amount. The value of the net debt outstanding after 5 years can be regarded as the initial loan amount minus the amount for repayment of principal that has already been accumulated to that point. This is

$$100,000 - 40,496.85 \ = \ 59,503.15.$$

This can be regarded as OB_5. Similarly OB_6 would be 100,000 minus the accumulated value of the sinking fund just after the sixth deposit, so $OB_6 = 100,000 - 6902.95 \cdot s_{\overline{6}|.08} = 49,360.45$. The principal repaid in the sixth year is the amount by which the value of the debt decreases, which is $PR_6 = OB_5 - OB_6 = 10,142.70$. Also in Example 3.4 we see that the amount of interest paid to the lender is $100,000(.1) = 10,000$ each year. This amount is offset by the interest earned in the sinking fund for the year. For the sixth year the amount of interest earned by the sinking fund is equal to .08 multiplied by the balance in the account at the end of the fifth year, producing $(.08)(40,496.85) = 3239.75$. Then the net interest paid for the sixth year is the amount paid to the lender minus the amount earned in the sinking fund, which is $I_6 = 10,000 - 3239.75 = 6760.25$. It then follows that $I_6 + PR_6 = 6760.25 + 10,142.70 = 16,902.95$, which is the total annual payment made by the borrower. It is possible to construct a schedule showing the principal repaid for each period (growth in the sinking fund for that period) and the net interest paid for each period (interest paid to lender for the period minus interest earned in the sinking fund that period). This is the equivalent of an amortization schedule in the context of loan repayment by the sinking fund method. This idea is outlined in the next paragraph.

Sinking Fund Schedule

Suppose we consider a loan of amount L, repaid by the sinking fund method over n periods, with the lender receiving interest at rate i per period from the borrower and the borrower making n level deposits into a sinking fund earning interest at rate j per period. The last deposit occurs at the end of the nth period giving an accumulated amount in the sinking fund of L. The periodic sinking fund deposits are amount $\frac{L}{s_{\overline{n}|j}}$, each.

Then the net amount of the debt at the end of the tth period, just after the tth deposit, is

$$OB_t \ = \ L - \frac{L}{s_{\overline{n}|j}} \cdot s_{\overline{t}|j} \ = \ L\left[1 - \frac{s_{\overline{t}|j}}{s_{\overline{n}|j}}\right], \tag{3.8}$$

and, similarly, $OB_{t-1} = L\left[1 - \frac{s_{\overline{t-1}|j}}{s_{\overline{n}|j}}\right]$.

The principal repaid in the tth period is

$$PR_t \;=\; OB_{t-1} - OB_t \;=\; L\left[\frac{s_{\overline{t}|j} - s_{\overline{t-1}|j}}{s_{\overline{n}|j}}\right] \;=\; \frac{L(1+j)^{t-1}}{s_{\overline{n}|j}}. \qquad (3.9)$$

Note that if the sinking fund deposits are level, then the amount of principal repaid grows by a factor of $1+j$ per period, which is similar to the growth of PR_t in the amortization method when payments are level.

The net interest paid in the tth payment is

$$I_t \;=\; L\cdot i - \frac{L\cdot s_{\overline{t-1}|j}}{s_{\overline{n}|j}}\cdot j \;=\; L\left[i - \frac{(1+j)^{t-1}-1}{s_{\overline{n}|j}}\right]. \qquad (3.10)$$

Note that $I_t + PR_t = L\left[i + \frac{1}{s_{\overline{n}|j}}\right]$, the borrower's total periodic outlay.

3.4 APPLICATIONS AND ILLUSTRATIONS

3.4.1 MAKEHAM'S FORMULA

We have seen examples of loans in which the lender receives payments of only interest each period, and then receives the full amount of principal after several periods. For a loan of this type of amount L at periodic interest rate i, with principal repaid after n periods, the sequence of payments received by the lender is $L\cdot i, L\cdot i,..., L\cdot i, L\cdot i + L$, where there are n terms in this sequence. Suppose the lender sells the loan to an investor, and the investor values the sequence of payments at the time the loan is made by finding the present value at periodic interest rate j. The investor will pay the original lender an amount equal to the present value of the payments, with the valuation based on interest rate j; the investor has purchased the right to receive the payments. This present value is $A = L\cdot v_j^n + L\cdot i\cdot a_{\overline{n}|j}$, where the first term is the present value of the principal amount repaid at time n, and the second term is the present value of the interest payments. This present value can be written as

$$
\begin{aligned}
A &= L \cdot v_j^n + L \cdot i \cdot a_{\overline{n}|j} \\
&= L \cdot v_j^n + L \cdot i \left(\frac{1 - v_j^n}{j} \right) \\
&= L \cdot v_j^n + \frac{i}{j} \left(L - L \cdot v_j^n \right) = K + \frac{i}{j} (L - K).
\end{aligned}
\tag{3.11}
$$

where $K = L \cdot v_j^n$ is the present value of the repayment of principal. Equation (3.11) is called **Makeham's formula** for valuing the original series of cashflows at rate j. Note that if $j = i$, then the total present value of principal and interest payments reduces to L, the original loan.

Makeham's formula provides a useful method for valuing a loan for which there is a schedule of repayments of principal at various points in time, along with payments of interest every period on the outstanding balance. The example considered above involves a single repayment of principal, with interest payable up to and including the time of that payment of principal. Suppose that a loan of amount L is to be repaid by m payments of principal of amounts $L_1, L_2, \ldots, L_m$ to be made at times $t_1, t_2, \ldots, t_m$ so that $L_1 + L_2 + \cdots + L_m = L$, with payments of interest at rate i on the outstanding balance at the end of every period. This situation can be regarded as m separate loans, all issued at the same time and each of the type described in the previous paragraph, and is illustrated in the following figure.

0	1	2	$\cdots$	t_1	$\cdots$	t_2	$\cdots$	t_m
$L_1 \rightarrow L_1 i$	$L_1 i$	$\cdots$		$L_1 i + L_1$				
$L_2 \rightarrow L_2 i$	$L_2 i$	$\cdots$		$L_2 i$	$\cdots$	$L_2 i + L_2$		
$\vdots \qquad \vdots$	$\vdots$			$\vdots$		$\vdots$		
$L_m \rightarrow L_m i$	$L_m i$	$\cdots$		$L_m i$	$\cdots$	$L_m i$	$\cdots$	$L_m i + L_m$

FIGURE 3.5

Note again that the interest payments on the original loan are at rate i but the valuation rate is j for the series of principal and interest payments. The present value of the sth loan at rate of interest j per period is found from Makeham's formula to be

$$A_s = L_s \cdot v_j^{t_s} + L_s \cdot i \cdot a_{\overline{t_s}|j} = K_s + \frac{i}{j}(L_s - K_s.)$$

The present value of the entire loan is then the sum of the present values of the m parts of the loan. This total present value is

$$A = \sum_{s=1}^{m} A_s = \sum_{s=1}^{m} \left[L_s \cdot v_j^{t_s} + L_s \cdot i \cdot a_{\overline{t_s}|j} \right]$$

$$= \sum_{s=1}^{m} \left[K_s + \frac{i}{j}(L_s - K_s) \right] = K + \frac{i}{j}(L - K), \quad (3.12)$$

where $K = \sum_{s=1}^{m} K_s$ and $L = \sum_{s=1}^{m} L_s$. We see that the form of the present value (at rate j) in Equation (3.12) for the series of cashflows represented by a loan repaid by a single principal repayment, with periodic interest at rate i, is also valid if the principal is repaid in a series of payments. However K now represents the total present value of all principal payments, $\frac{i}{j}(L-K)$ represents the present value of all interest payments, and L represents the total amount of principal. Note that Makeham's formula applies if the interest rate i on the original loan remains constant throughout the course of the loan (if not, the loan would have to be broken into separate loans each at the associated interest rate), and the investor's valuation rate j also remains constant for the term of the payments. The investor's valuation rate must be based on the same compounding period as are the payments of interest.

EXAMPLE 3.5 (*Makeham's formula*)

A loan of 100,000 is to be repaid with 10 annual payments of principal of 10,000 each, starting one year after the loan is made, plus monthly interest payments on the outstanding balance. The interest rate is $i^{(12)} = .12$. Two years after the loan is made (just after the second principal payment and monthly interest payment) the lender sells the loan to an investor. Find the price paid by the investor if he values the remaining payments at a nominal annual rate of interest convertible monthly of (a) .06, (b) .12, and (c) .18.

SOLUTION

(a) At the time the loan is sold, the outstanding balance is $L = 80,000$ with $m = 8$ annual principal payments of $L_1 = L_2 = \cdots = L_8 = 10,000$ and monthly interest payments at 1% per month on the outstanding balance. The present value of the principal payments is

$$
\begin{aligned}
K &= K_1 + K_2 + \cdots + K_8 = 10,000\left(v^{12} + v^{24} + \cdots + v^{96}\right) \\
&= 10,000\left(\frac{v^{12} - v^{108}}{1 - v^{12}}\right) = 61,687.68,
\end{aligned}
$$

where v is at $\frac{1}{2}\%$. The price paid by the investor is then

$$61,687.68 + \tfrac{.01}{.005}(80,000 - 61,687.68) = 98,312.33.$$

(b) In this case the monthly interest rate is $j = .01$, so $K = 48,513.85$ and the investor pays $48,513.85 + \tfrac{.01}{.01}(80,000 - 48,513.85) = 80,000$.

(c) In this case $j = .015$, so $K = 38,878.04$ and the investor pays $66,292.68$.

3.4.2 THE MERCHANT'S RULE AND THE U.S. RULE

According to the **Merchant's Rule** of loan repayment, all amounts advanced and all loan repayments made are accumulated with simple interest until the settlement date, at which time the aggregate accumulated values of the amounts advanced must be equal to the aggregate accumulated values of the repayments made. Example 3.6 illustrates the Merchant's Rule.

EXAMPLE 3.6	*(Merchant's Rule)*

Smith borrows 2000 on January 17 and makes payments of 800 each on the last day of each month, starting January 31. On March 15, he borrows an additional 2000. He continues the payments of 800 through May 31, and then pays the remainder of the obligation on June 30. What payment must be made on June 30 if the annual interest rate is 13% and the loan is based on the Merchant's Rule? (Assume a non-leap year.)

SOLUTION

All loan amounts and payments are accumulated with simple interest to the settlement date of June 30. Let X denote the payment required at that time. Then the equation of value is

$$2000\left[2+(.13)\cdot\frac{164+107}{365}\right] = 800\left[5+(.13)\cdot\frac{150+122+91+61+30}{365}\right]+X,$$

which has the solution $X = 63.68$.   □

As with most transactions involving simple interest, the Merchant's Rule would not normally be used in transactions whose duration is more than one year. Another method for calculating the loan repayment is the **United States Rule**, also known as the **actuarial method**. According to this method, interest is computed each time a payment is made or an additional loan amount is disbursed. The interest calculation is based on simple interest from the time the previous payment or additional loan disbursement was made. The balance on the loan after the current payment is the previous balance, plus interest accrued, minus the current payment (or plus the current addition to the loan). The following example repeats Example 3.6, solving according to the U.S. Rule.

EXAMPLE 3.7   (*U.S. Rule*)

Solve for X in Example 3.6 assuming the loan calculations are based on the U.S. method.

SOLUTION

The interest and outstanding balance calculations are summarized in the Table 3.6 below.

The payment required on June 30 is 65.76. A typical calculation made in Table 3.6 is the one for January 31. The amount of accrued interest is $2000(.13)\left(\frac{14}{365}\right)=9.97$, so the outstanding balance is

$$2000 + 9.97 - 800 = 1209.97.$$

TABLE 3.6

Date	Accrued Interest	Payment	Outstanding Balance
Jan 17	–	(2000)	2000.00
Jan 31	9.97	800	1209.97
Feb 28	12.07	800	422.04
Mar 15	2.25	(2000)	2424.29
Mar 31	13.82	800	1638.11
Apr 30	17.50	800	855.61
May 31	9.45	800	65.06
Jun 30	.70	65.76	0

The U.S. Rule is essentially amortization in which the interest rate for the fraction of a year from one transaction point to the next is the corresponding fraction of the annually quoted interest rate.   ☐

3.5 NOTES AND REFERENCES

The "double-up option" for loan repayment of Exercise 3.2.20 and the weekly repayment scheme in Exercise 3.2.26 are based on actual loan repayment options of financial institutions. These have been promoted in times of high interest rates because of the significant reduction in repayment time and interest paid. The situation in Exercise 3.2.42 in which a loan is amortized at a rate of interest higher than the lender's rate, with the difference used for an insurance premium or sales commission, is considered in detail in *Mathematics of Compound Interest*, by Butcher and Nesbitt.

There are a number of websites with information on loan amortization. An online mortgage and APR calculator with accelerated payment options can be found at www.dinkytown.net. A search of the internet for loan amortization examples can return some interesting results and examples, some of which may have incorrect calculations.

3.6 EXERCISES

The exercises without asterisks are intended to comprehensively cover the material presented in the chapter. Exercises with a asterisk can be regarded as supplementary exercises which cover topics in more depth, either theoretically or computationally, than those without a asterisk.

SECTION 3.1

3.1.1 For the general loan of amount L that is amortized over n periods by payments $K_1, K_2, \ldots, K_n$ at interest rate i per payment period (see Table 3.1), show that $K_T - I_T = L$.

3.1.2 Suppose that during the course of a loan, two successive periods have the same interest rate $(i_t = i_{t+1} = i)$. Show that $PR_{t+1} = PR_t(1+i) + K_{t+1} - K_t$. It then follows that if $K_{t+1} = K_t$ and $i_t = i_{t+1} = i$, then $PR_{t+1} = PR_t(1+i)$.

3.1.3 A loan at rate $i^{(12)} = .12$ is repaid with 120 monthly payments starting one month after the loan. The amount of the first payment is 600 and each subsequent payment is 5 larger than the previous payment. Find the original amount of the loan. Find PR_1 and use the result of Exercise 3.1.2 to show that $PR_t = PR_1(1.01)^{t-1} + 5 \cdot s_{\overline{t-1}|i}$. Find OB_{60} prospectively, retrospectively, and by verifying that $OB_{60} = L - \sum_{k=1}^{60} PR_k$, using the form of PR_k found earlier in this exercise. Find I_{61}. Find PR_{61} using the formula above and also from $PR_{61} = K_{61} - I_{61}$, and verify that they are equal.

3.1.4 Show that at quarterly interest rate $j = .02$, the total payments in Example 3.2 (i.e., $310, 305, \ldots, 255$) have present value 3000.

3.1.5   Betty borrows 19,800 from Bank X. Betty repays the loan by making 36 equal payments of principal at the end of each month. She also pays interest on the unpaid balance each month at a nominal rate of 12%, compounded monthly. Immediately after the 16*th* payment is made, Bank X sells the rights to future payments to Bank Y. Bank Y wishes to yield a nominal rate of 14%, compounded semi-annually, on its investment. What price does Bank X receive?

3.1.6   A loan is amortized over five years with monthly payments at a nominal interest rate of 9% compounded monthly. The first payment is 1000 and is to be paid one month from the date of the loan. Each succeeding monthly payment will be 2% lower than the prior payment. Calculate the outstanding loan balance immediately after the 40th payment is made.

3.1.7   A 30-year loan of 1000 is repaid with payments at the end of each year. Each of the first ten payments equals the amount of interest due. Each of the next ten payments equals 150% of the amount of interest due. Each of the last ten payments is X. The lender charges interest at an effective annual rate of 10%. Calculate X.

3.1.8   A loan of amount L at rate i per period calls for payments of interest only (at the end of each period) for n periods, plus a single repayment of principal of amount L at the end of n periods. Show that the present value at periodic rate i of the interest and principal payments is equal to L.

3.1.9   Smith borrows 20,000 to purchase a car. The car dealer finances the purchase and offers Smith two alternative financing plans, both of which require monthly payments at the end of each month for 4 years, starting at the end of the month in which the car is purchased (assume that the car is purchased at the start of the month).

          (i)   0% interest rate for the first year followed by 6% nominal annual interest rate compounded monthly for the following three years.

(ii) 3% nominal annual interest rate compounded monthly for the first year followed by 5% nominal annual interest compounded monthly for the following three years.

For each of (i) and (ii) find the monthly payment, and the outstanding balance on the loan at the end of the first year.

*3.1.10 Suppose that during the course of a loan, two successive periods have the same interest rate $(i_t = i_{t+1} = i)$. Show that

$$OB_t = L - PR_1 - PR_2 - \cdots - PR_t.$$

Suppose that $K_1 = K_2 = \cdots = K_t = K$ and $i_1 = i_2 = \cdots = i_t = i$. Use Exercise 3.1.2 to show that $OB_t = L - PR_1 \cdot s_{\overline{t}|i}$.

*3.1.11 Example 3.1 is modified so that monthly payments are made for 12 years starting one month after the loan. The monthly payment is K for the first 6 years (72 payments) and $2K$ for the last 6 years (72 payments).

(a) Find K and construct the amortization table for the first year.

(b) Verify that the result in Exercise 3.1.2 applies here, although the PR amounts are negative during this period.

(c) Using monthly payment amounts rounded to the nearest penny, find the amount of the final payment required at $t = 144$ to retire the debt.

(d) Use the retrospective and prospective forms of the OB to find the outstanding balance just after 3 years $(t = 36)$, 6 years $(t = 72)$, and 9 years $(t = 108)$.

(e) Find the total interest paid over the course of the loan, and in each of the twelve years of the loan separately. Find the amount of principal repaid in each of the twelve years of the loan. Check that the total principal repaid equals the original loan amount.

*3.1.12 Plot the OB_t functions for Example 3.1 and Example 3.2.

*3.1.13 A loan of amount L is repaid by 15 annual payments starting one year after the loan. The first 6 payments are 500 each and the final 9 payments are 1000 each. Interest is at effective annual rate i. Show that each of the following is a correct expression for PR_6.

(a) $500\left(2v^{10}-v\right)$

(b) $500\left(\left[1-i\left(2a_{\overline{10}|}-v\right)\right]\right)$

(c) $(500-L\cdot i)(1+i)^5$

SECTION 3.2

3.2.1   A loan of L is amortized by n level payments of amount K at rate i per period. The retrospective and prospective forms of the outstanding balance just after the tth payment are $L(1+i)^t - K\cdot s_{\overline{t}|i}$, and $K\cdot a_{\overline{n-t}|i}$, respectively. Show that these two expressions are equal. Note that $PR_1 = K - L\cdot i$. Show that $OB_t = L(1+i)^t - K\cdot s_{\overline{t}|i}$ $= L - PR_1\cdot s_{\overline{t}|i}$ (see Exercise 3.1.10).

3.2.2   Suppose the loan in Example 3.2 is repaid by 12 level quarterly payments at rate $j = .02$. Find the total amount of interest paid over the course of the loan. This total is larger than the total in Example 3.2. Provide a non-algebraic justification for this by general reasoning.

3.2.3   Fill in the blanks of the following amortization schedule for a loan with level 5 level payments.

t	OB_t	I_t	PR_t
0	—		
1	706.00	43.10	156.00
2	—	—	—
3	—	—	—
4	—	—	—
5	0	—	—

3.2.4   A 5-year loan made on July 1, 2004 is amortized with 60 level
        monthly payments starting August 1, 2004. If interest is at
        $i^{(12)} = .12$, find the date on which the outstanding balance first
        falls below one-half of the original loan amount.

3.2.5   (a) A 5-year loan is amortized with semiannual payments of 200
            each, starting 6 months after the loan is made. If $PR_1 = 156.24$,
            find $i^{(12)}$.

        (b) A loan is repaid by 48 monthly payments of 200 each. The
            interest paid in the first 12 payments is 983.16 and the
            principal repaid in the final 12 payments is 2215.86. Find
            $i^{(12)}$.

3.2.6   A loan is amortized by level payments every February 1, plus a
        smaller final payment. The borrower notices that the interest paid
        in the February 1, 2004 payment was 103.00, and the interest in
        the February 1, 2005 payment will be 98.00. The rate of interest
        on the loan is $i = .08$.

        (a) Find the principal repaid in the 2005 payment.

        (b) Find the date and amount of the smaller final payment made
            one year after the last regular payment.

3.2.7   Iggy borrows X for 10 years at an effective annual rate of 6%. If
        he pays the principal and accumulated interest in one lump sum
        at the end of 10 years, he would pay 356.54 more in interest than
        if he repaid the loan with 10 level payments at the end of each
        year. Calculate X.

3.2.8   A 10-year loan of 2000 is to be repaid with payments at the end
        of each year. It can be repaid under the following two options:

        (i) Equal annual payments at an effective annual rate of 8.07%.

        (ii) Installments of 200 each year plus interest on the unpaid
             balance at an effective annual rate of i.

        The sum of the payments under option (i) equals the sum of the
        payments under option (ii). Determine i.

3.2.9   A person borrows money at $i^{(12)} = .12$ from Bank A, requiring level payments starting one month later and continuing for a total of 15 years (180 payments). She is allowed to repay the entire balance outstanding at any time provided she also pays a penalty of k% of the outstanding balance at the time of repayment. At the end of 5 years (just after the 60th payment) the borrower decides to repay the remaining balance, and finances the repayment plus penalty with a loan at $i^{(12)} = .09$ from Bank B. The loan from Bank B requires 10 years of level monthly payments beginning one month later. Find the largest value of k that makes her decision to refinance correct.

3.2.10 (a) For each of Examples 3.1 and 3.2 find the total present value (at the time of the loan) of the interest payments and principal payments separately.

       (b) For a loan of amount L repaid by n level payments, find the total present value of the interest payments and principal payments separately.

3.2.11 A loan is being repaid with level payments of K every 6 months. The outstanding balances on three consecutive payment dates are 5190.72, 5084.68, and 4973.66. Find K.

3.2.12 Smith wishes to sell his house for 200,000. Jones has 100,000 available for a down payment, and can take a bank loan with monthly payments at $i^{(12)} = .15$. Smith offers to "take back" the mortgage for 100,000 with monthly payments at $i^{(12)} = .12$, based on a 25-year amortization period, with a provision that Jones will refinance the outstanding balance of the loan elsewhere after 3 years. Jones accepts Smith's offer. Immediately after the transaction Smith sells the loan to a broker for a price that yields the broker $i^{(12)} = .15$ over the 3-year period. (The broker becomes entitled to the 3 years of monthly payments as well as the outstanding balance.) What is the net amount that Smith receives for the house?

3.2.13 A loan of amount L is to be repaid by n payments, starting one period after the loan is made, with interest at rate i per period. Two repayment schemes are considered:

(i) level payments for the lifetime of the loan;

(ii) each payment consists of principal repaid of $\frac{L}{n}$ plus interest on the previous outstanding balance.

Find the total interest repaid under each scheme and show algebraically that the interest paid under scheme (i) is larger than that paid under scheme (ii). Show that for each $t = 1, 2, \ldots,$ $n-1$, OB_t is larger under scheme (i) than under scheme (ii). Verify algebraically that L is the present value at the time of the loan, at rate of interest i per payment period, of all payments made under scheme (ii).

3.2.14 An estate of 1,000,000, invested at an annual interest rate of 5%, is being shared by A, B, and C. Starting 1 year after the estate is established, A receives 125,000 of principal each year for 5 years, B receives 75,000 of principal each year for 5 years, and C receives the interest each year. Find the present values of the shares of A, B, and C at 5%, and verify that their sum is 1,000,000.

*3.2.15 (a) A loan of 1000 at interest of $i = .01$ per period is amortized by payments of 100 per period, starting one period after the loan, for as long as necessary, plus a final smaller payment one period after the last regular payment. Solve for the number of regular payments and the final smaller payment by constructing the amortization table (i.e., do calculations from one period to the next until the OB is reduced to zero).

(b) A deposit of 1000 is made to an account earning interest at rate $i^{(12)} = .12$, with interest credited monthly from the date of the initial deposit. Each month, just after interest is credited, a withdrawal of 100 is made. Find the number of withdrawals that will be made from the account. Set up a schedule showing the amount of interest credited to the account each period, and the balance remaining in the account.

*3.2.16 A loan of 15,000 at effective annual rate $i = .025$ is repaid by annual payments of 1000 for as long as necessary plus a smaller final payment one year after the last regular payment. The first payment is made one year after the loan. Find the t for which PR_t is most nearly equal to $4I_t$.

*3.2.17 Smith has two options to repay a loan at effective annual interest rate $i > 0$ over an n-year period: (i) n level annual payments starting one year after the loan, or (ii) $12n$ level monthly payments starting one month after the loan.

(a) Show that on each annual anniversary of the loan, the outstanding balance just after payment is made is the same under both options.

(b) Show that the total interest paid under scheme (i) is greater than under scheme (ii).

*3.2.18 A loan is being repaid by $2n$ level payments, starting one year after the loan. Just after the nth payment the borrower finds that she still owes ¾ of the original amount. What proportion of the next payment is interest?

*3.2.19 An amortized loan of 1000 is to be repaid with 24 monthly payments starting one month after the loan. The nominal interest rate convertible monthly is .09 for the first 18 months and .12 for the final 6 months. Construct the amortization table for this loan, and find the amount of principal repaid in the first year (first 12 payments).

*3.2.20 On July 1, 2005 Smith will borrow 75,000 at rate $i^{(12)} = .12$. He has three amortization options for repayment with monthly payments starting August 1, 2005.

(i)   A standard 25-year loan with monthly payment K.

(ii)   A "double up" option, with the same monthly payment K as in (i), except that every 6th payment is $2K$. Payments continue in this pattern for as long as necessary plus a final smaller payment one month after the last regular payment.

(iii) Constant principal of 250 per month for 25 years plus a monthly payment of interest on the previous month's outstanding balance.

For each option find the total amount of interest paid during the lifetime of the loan, and for part (ii) find when the loan is repaid and the final smaller payment required.

*3.2.21 On June 30, 2005 Smith deposits 1,000,000 in an account earning $i^{(12)} = .12$, with interest credited on the last day of each month. She makes withdrawals from the account on the last day of each month (just after interest is credited) starting July 31, 2005. The first withdrawal is 2500 and each subsequent withdrawal is 2% larger than the previous one. The increasing withdrawals continue for as long as possible, with a smaller final withdrawal which exhausts the account one month after the last regular increasing withdrawal.

(a) Find the date and amount of the final smaller withdrawal.

(b) Find the total of all amounts withdrawn.

(c) Find the amount of interest credited to the account from the time of the initial deposit until the account is exhausted, and also find the amount of interest credited in specific years:

(i) 2005, (ii) 2006, and (iii) 2015.

*3.2.22 A loan at $i = .05$ is to be repaid by n level annual payments of p each starting one year after the loan. The borrower misses the 5th and 6th payments. He is told that if he pays $1.16p$ for each of the remaining payments, the loan will be repaid at the originally scheduled time. Find the number of payments on the original loan. Give a verbal explanation of the equation $s_{\overline{2}|} = .16 \cdot a_{\overline{n-6|}}$ which arises in this situation.

*3.2.23 A loan of amount L is repaid by n level periodic payments at rate of interest i per period. Let $I(n)$ denote the amount of interest paid over the course of the loan. Show that $I(n)$ is an increasing function of n.

*3.2.24 A loan of amount L is being repaid by n level payments of amount K each at interest rate i per period. If $t + u \le n$, show that $OB_{t+u} = OB_t \cdot (1+i)^u - K \cdot s_{\overline{u}|}$. Formulate a general version of this relationship for a loan repayment scheme with payment amounts $K_1, K_2, \ldots, K_n$.

*3.2.25 A loan of 10,000 at effective annual rate $i = .08$ is to be repaid with 20 level annual payments of amount K each. The borrower is unable to make the 6th, 7th, and 8th payments. The lender allows the payments to be missed on the condition that the loan will still be repaid on time by increasing the 9th through 20th payments to $K + X$. Show that $X = \dfrac{K \cdot s_{\overline{3}|}}{a_{\overline{12}|}}$. Find the difference in the total interest paid between this repayment scheme and the repayment scheme in which no payments are missed.

*3.2.26 (a) In times of high interest rates, lending institutions may offer some variations in repayment schemes. Suppose a loan of amount L is to be amortized with level monthly payments of K each for 25 years. The lender offers an alternate repayment plan with weekly payments, starting one week after the loan is made. The borrower is offered two choices for the payment: (i) $B_1 = \frac{K}{4}$ and (ii) $B_2 = \frac{12K}{52}$. The weekly payments continue for as long as necessary with an additional final smaller payment. Suppose that $L = 100,000$. The one-week rate j_w is $j_w = (1+i)^{7/365} - 1$, where i is the equivalent effective annual rate. For each of cases (i) and (ii) find the term of repayment and the reduction in interest paid over the course of the loan as compared to the monthly repayment scheme for each of the interest rates $i^{(12)} = .06, .12, .18,$ and $.24$.

(b) In practice, the 52nd week each year is lengthened to end on the anniversary date of the loan, with a one-day (two-day in a leap year) adjustment for interest at the end of the year. Find the addition to the outstanding balance of the loan after one year if a one-day interest adjustment is added after 52 weeks, using a one-day interest rate of $(1+i)^{1/365} - 1$.

*3.2.27 Repeat Exercise 3.2.26 using $j_w = (1+i)^{1/52} - 1$.

*3.2.28 A loan of amount L is amortized according to scheme (ii) in Exercise 3.2.13.

(a) Show that $K_t = \frac{L}{n} + L \cdot i \cdot \left(\frac{n-t+1}{n}\right)$.

Use the result of Exercise 3.1.2 to show that $PR_k = \frac{L}{n}$.

(b) Use part (a) to show that $\sum_{t=1}^{n}\left[1 + (n-t+1) \cdot i\right] \cdot v^t = n$.

Give a verbal interpretation of this identity.

(c) Show that $\sum_{t=1}^{n}\left[1 + (n-t) \cdot d\right] \cdot v^{t-1} = n$, and give a verbal interpretation.

*3.2.29 A loan of amount L is being amortized by level continuous payments over n interest periods, with interest rate of i per period. The amount of payment per period is $\frac{L}{a_{\overline{n}|i}}$. Find the rate at which principal is being repaid at time t, the rate at which interest is being paid at time t, and OB_t. Find the amount of principal and interest paid in the interval from time t to time $t+1$. Show that $\frac{d^2}{dt^2}OB_t < 0$, so that the OB_t curve is concave downward.

*3.2.30 A bank customer borrows X at an effective annual rate of 12.5% and makes level payments at the end of each year for n years.

(i) The interest portion of the final payment is 153.86 .

(ii) The total principal repaid as of time $(n-1)$ is 6009.12.

(iii) The principal repaid in the first payment is Y. Calculate Y.

*3.2.31 (a) A loan of amount L at interest rate i per period is repaid by $n-1$ level periodic payments of K each, starting one period after the loan is made, followed by a single payment of amount B at time n to completely repay the loan. Show that the principal repaid in the tth payment $(t < n)$ is $K \cdot v^{n-t+1} + (K-B) \cdot v^{n-t} \cdot d$.

(b) Apply the result in part (a) to part (a) of Exercise 3.2.15, after finding the final payment B, to show that $PR_1 = 90$.

*3.2.32 Find the form of OB_t, I_t, and PR_t for each of the following loans.

    (a) $L = (Ia)_{\overline{n}|i}$, with n payments $K_1 = 1$, $K_2 = 2, \ldots, K_n = n$.

    (b) $L = (Da)_{\overline{n}|i}$, with n payments $K_1 = n$, $K_2 = n-1, \ldots, K_n = 1$.

*3.2.33 A loan of amount L at interest rate i per period has level payments of amount K per period, starting one period after the loan, for as long as necessary plus a final smaller payment one period after the last regular payment. Show that $OB_t = \frac{K}{i} - \left(\frac{K}{i} - L\right)(1+i)^t$.

*3.2.34 (a) Show that a loan of amount n at interest rate i per period can be repaid by the series of n geometrically increasing payments $K_1 = (1+i)$, $K_2 = (1+i)^2, \ldots, K_n = (1+i)^n$, with the first payment made one period after the loan.

    (b) Show that $OB_t = (n-1)(1+i)^t$.

*3.2.35 One of the basic relationships in the n-payment amortization of a loan at rate i is $OB_{t+1} = OB_t(1+i) - K_{t+1}$. This can be rewritten as $OB_t(1+i) - OB_{t+1} = K_{t+1}$. Multiply both sides of the second relationship by v^{t+1}, and then sum both sides from $t = 0$ to $t = n-1$ to show that the original loan amount L is equal to the present value of the n payments, $K_1, \ldots, K_n$. Show that the retrospective form of the outstanding balance at time h can be obtained by summing from $t = 0$ to $t = h-1$ and then solving for OB_h, and the prospective form can be found by summing from $t = h$ to $t = n-1$ and solving for OB_h.

*3.2.36 (a) A loan of amount L at interest rate i per period, with equivalent force of interest δ is repaid by means of continuous payment for n periods, at rate of payment K_t at time t, so that $L = \int_0^n K_s \cdot v^s \, ds$. Formulate the prospective and retrospective outstanding balance at time t and show that $\frac{d}{dt} OB_t = \delta \cdot OB_t - K_t$.

(b) A loan being repaid continuously satisfies the differential equation $\frac{d}{dt}OB_t = \delta \cdot OB_t - X_t$. Multiply both sides by $v^t = e^{-\delta t}$.

Use $\frac{d}{dt}v^t \cdot OB_t = v^t \cdot \frac{d}{dt}OB_t - \delta \cdot v^t \cdot OB_t$ to solve the differential equation using the boundary conditions $OB_0 = L$ and $OB_n = 0$.

(c) Find an expression for the amount of principal repaid and the amount of interest paid between times t_0 and t_1 on the loan in part (a).

*3.2.37 A loan of 100,000 is to be repaid by monthly payments starting one month after the loan. The borrower can choose a repayment term of 15 or 30 years. For each of these terms find the total interest paid during the loan at interest rate $i^{(12)}$ of (a) .06 and (b) .12. For a loan of amount L repaid with n periodic payments at interest rate i per period, sketch the graph of I_T as a function of n and then sketch the graph as a function of i.

*3.2.38 (a) A loan of 10,000 at effective annual rate $i = .08$ is to be repaid with 20 level annual payments of amount K each. At the time of the 5th payment, the borrower makes an additional payment of amount $PR_6 + PR_7 + PR_8$. The regular payments of amount K continue as usual from time 6 onward, for as long as necessary. Show that the loan will be repaid with the 17th payment, as measured from the date of the loan, and show that the amount of interest paid is $I_6 + I_7 + I_8$ less than would have been paid under the original scheme.

(b) Generalize part (a) for a loan of amount L at interest rate i to be repaid by n level payments, where, at the time of the t_0^{th} payment, the borrower makes an additional payment of $PR_{t_0+1} + PR_{t_0+2} + \cdots + PR_{t_0+m}$. Show that the loan is repaid with the $(n-m)^{th}$ payment, and the interest is $I_{t_0+1} + I_{t_0+2} + \cdots + I_{t_0+m}$ less than would have been paid under the original scheme.

*3.2.39 A loan of 10,000 is to be repaid by 10 annual payments of 1000 of principal, starting one year after the loan, plus periodic payments of interest on the outstanding balance. Find the total amount of interest paid in each of the following cases.

(a) Annual interest payments at effective annual rate of interest .12550881.

(b) Semiannual interest payments at effective 6-month rate of .0609.

(c) Quarterly interest payments at effective 3-month rate of .03.

Show that at rate $i^{(4)} = .12$ the present values on the loan issue date of the interest payments in each of cases (a), (b) and (c) are equal. Explain why this is so.

*3.2.40 A loan of amount L is made at interest rate i per period to be repaid by n periodic payments of amounts $K_1, K_2, \ldots, K_n$. When a payment is made, there is income tax payable at rate $r < 1$ on the interest portion of the payment; thus at the time of the tth payment the lender receives a net payment of $K_t - r \cdot I_t$. Show that the present value of the net after-tax payments received by the lender are equal to L at interest rate $i(1-r)$.

*3.2.41 (a) An amortized loan for 10,000 has interest at 8% per year on the first 5000 of outstanding balance, and 10% per year on the OB in excess of 5000. Suppose that annual payments are 1500 for as long as necessary. Construct the amortization table for the loan.

(b) Consider a more general amortization of a loan of amount L. The interest rate is i per period on the first L_0 of OB and j per period on the OB in excess of L_0. Suppose that $L > L_0$ and the periodic payment is level at amount K. Show by mathematical induction on the positive integers that as long as $OB_t > L_0$, the next year's outstanding balance will be

$$\begin{aligned} OB_{t+1} &= L_0(1+i) \cdot s_{\overline{t+1}|j} + L(1+j)^{t+1} - L_0 \cdot \ddot{s}_{\overline{t+1}|j} - K \cdot s_{\overline{t+1}|j} \\ &= L_0(1+i \cdot s_{\overline{t+1}|j}) + (L-L_0)(1+j)^{t+1} - K \cdot s_{\overline{t+1}|j}. \end{aligned}$$

(c) Verify the expression in part (b) by using it in part (a) for $t = 1, 2, \ldots, 7$.

(d) Once OB falls below L_0, the remaining amortization is at level interest rate i. If the loan is repaid exactly at time n with level payments of amount K each, and if $t+1$ is the first time that the OB falls below L_0, then $OB_{t+1} = K \cdot a_{\overline{n-(t+1)}|i}$. Using part (b) for OB_{t+1} when OB first falls below L_0, solve for an expression for K.

(e) The expression for K in part (d) cannot be solved in its present form because the value of t is not known. In other words, it is not known for which t the inequality $OB_t > L_0 > OB_{t+1}$ is satisfied. Use the expression for OB_t and OB_{t+1} in part (b) to translate the inequality $OB_t > L_0 > OB_{t+1}$ into the inequality

$$L_0 \cdot i + \frac{L - L_0}{a_{\overline{t+1}|j}} < K < L_0 \cdot i + \frac{L - L_0}{a_{\overline{t}|j}}.$$

(f) Substitute the expression for K from part (d) into the inequality for K in part (e). In order for the level payment K to repay this loan in exactly n payments, the time $t+1$ at which OB_{t+1} first falls below L_0 must satisfy this inequality.

(g) Using the example of part (a), with $L_0 = 5000$, $L = 5000$, $i = .08$, $j = .10$, and $n = 10$, substitute values of $t = 1$, then $t = 2$, then $t = 3$, etc., until the inequality in (f) is satisfied. (For $t = 1$, the values are $3280.95 < 1504.09 < 5500$ which is false.) When the inequality is satisfied, the corresponding values of t and $t+1$ (which are $t = 6$ and $t+1 = 7$) are the ones for which $OB_t > L_0 > OB_{t+1}$. Now that $t+1$ is known, it can be substituted into the expression for K in part (d) to solve for $K = 1536.64$.

(h) Using the value of K obtained in part (g) construct the amortization table for the loan.

*3.2.42 A loan of 100,000 at effective annual rate 12% is to be repaid by level annual payments for 10 years. Part of each payment is an insurance premium to insure the loan against default due to the death of the borrower. In each payment the amount of the insurance premium is 2% of the previous year's outstanding balance, so the net amount of interest paid to the lender is 10% of the previous year's outstanding balance. The principal repaid in each payment is the same as in an ordinary amortization at 12%. Construct a table showing the net amount of interest and principal received in each payment, and show that the present value at $i = .10$ of the principal plus net interest payments is 100,000.

SECTION 3.3

3.3.1   (a) The borrower's annual outlay in part (a) of Example 3.4 is 16,902.95. Suppose that an investor wishes to purchase a 10-payment annuity with payments of 16,902.95, starting one year after the purchase date, and is willing to pay a price that will yield 10% per year on his investment while allowing him to recover his principal (purchase price) in a sinking fund earning 8% per year. Find the purchase price the investor will pay.

(b) On a loan of amount L the lender receives interest only at rate i per period and a lump-sum principal repayment of amount L at the end of n periods. The borrower plans to accumulate the lump-sum payment by means of n level deposits into a sinking fund earning interest at rate j. An investor considers purchasing the right to receive the annuity formed by the series of total annual outlays (interest plus sinking fund deposit) by the borrower for the n periods. The investor will pay a price P so that he can receive a return of i per period (same as lender's rate) on his investment, while recovering his initial investment in a sinking fund earning interest at rate j (same rate as the borrower's sinking fund). Show that $P = L$. (In this situation the investor is the lender in the sense that he loans out an amount P, but the investor also plays the role of "borrower" accumulating the initial loan amount in a sinking fund.)

3.3.2   The lender of a loan of 100,000 receives annual interest payments at 12% per year for 10 years, and, in addition, will receive a lump-sum repayment of the principal along with the 10th interest payment. The borrower will pay the annual interest to the lender and accumulate the 100,000 by annual deposits to an 8% sinking fund. The borrower wishes to schedule the deposits so that his total annual outlay is X for each of the first 5 years, and $2X$ for each of the final 5 years. Find X. Construct a table listing "outstanding balance," "principal repaid" and "net interest paid" for each t from 1 to 10.

3.3.3   (a) With reference to part (a) of Example 3.4, suppose the loan amount of 100,000 was not given, but rather that the borrower's total annual outlay of 16,902.95 was given. Show that the loan amount is 100,000.

        (b) A borrower's total annual outlay is K per period for n periods, including interest at rate i to the lender on a loan of L, and accumulating the principal in a sinking fund at rate j with n level periodic deposits. Solve for L in terms of K, n, i and j.

3.3.4   (a) The lender of amount L receives annual interest payments at 12% per year for 10 years, and, in addition, will receive a lump-sum repayment of the principal L along with the 10th interest payment. The borrower will pay the annual interest to the lender and accumulate the principal amount L by means of annual deposits to an 8% sinking fund. The borrower has scheduled the deposits so that his total annual outlay is 10,000 for each of the first 5 years, and 20,000 for each of the final 5 years. Find L.

        (b) Repeat part (a) under the assumption that the sinking fund earns annual interest at 8% during the first 5 years, and 10% during the second 5 years.

3.3.5   The borrower of a loan of 10,000 makes monthly interest payments to the lender at rate $i^{(12)} = .15$, and monthly deposits of 100 to a sinking fund earning $i^{(12)} = .09$. When the sinking fund reaches 10,000 the borrower will repay the principal and discharge the loan. Find the total amount paid by the borrower over the course of the loan.

3.3.6   Smith can repay a loan of 250,000 in one of two ways:

(i) 30 annual payments based on amortization at $i = .12$;

(ii) 30 annual interest payments to the lender at rate $i = .10$, along with 30 level annual deposits to a sinking fund earning rate j.

Find the value of j to make the schemes equivalent.

3.3.7   A business currently produces 9000 units of its product each month, which sells for 85 per unit at the end of the month. The company considers an alternative process which has a startup cost of 1,500,000 and continuing monthly costs (on top of previous monthly costs) of 15,816 incurred at the end of each month. The alternative process will result in monthly production of 12,000 units. The company can borrow the 1,500,000 on an interest-only loan at monthly rate 1.5%, with the principal repayable after 40 months. The company can accumulate the principal in a sinking fund earning interest at 1% per month over the 40-month period. The company can reduce the selling price of the product to X per unit and still make a profit that is 30,000 more per month than it was before the new process was implemented. Find X.

*3.3.8   (a) For Example 3.4 construct a table showing, for each t from 1 to 10, the accumulated amount in the sinking fund, the "outstanding balance" just after the sinking fund deposit, the amount of "principal repaid," and the "net amount of interest" paid.

(b) Suppose that a loan is being repaid by the sinking fund method with n level periodic deposits into a sinking fund earning interest at rate j per period. Show that for each t from 1 to n the values of OB_t and PR_t are the same as the corresponding values in an n-period level payment amortization at rate j per period. Show that if the lender's interest rate i is equal to the sinking fund rate j, then for each t the values of I_t are the same as the corresponding values in an n-period level payment amortization at rate $i = j$.

*3.3.9 A loan is made so that the lender receives periodic payments of interest only at rate i per period for n periods plus the return of principal in a single lump-sum payment at the end of the n periods. The borrower will accumulate the principal by means of n level periodic deposits to a sinking fund earning periodic interest rate j, such that the accumulated value in the sinking fund is equal to the principal just after the nth level deposit is made. The borrower's total annual outlay is the same as if the loan were being amortized at periodic rate i'. Show that if $j < i$ then $i' > i$, and if $j = i$ then $i' = i$. An approximation to i' in terms of i and j is $i' \approx i + \frac{1}{2}(i-j)$. Compare the exact values for i' found in Example 3.4 to the approximate values found by this formula. Try various combinations of i, j and n, and compare the exact value of i' to that found by the formula.

*3.3.10 In repaying a loan of amount L, the total periodic outlay made by a borrower at time t is K_t for $t = 1, 2, \ldots, n$. The borrower pays interest on L at rate i, with the rest of the outlay going into a sinking fund earning rate j to accumulate to L at time n. Solve for L in terms of i, j, n, and the K_t's. Let X be the present value of the K_t's at rate j per period. Show that L can be written in the form $\frac{X}{Y}$, and solve for Y. Show that $Y = 1$ if $i = j$.

*3.3.11 (a) Redo part (a) of Example 3.4 if the agreement is that the lender receives annual interest payments of 5% of the loan, and a lump-sum payment of $100,000(1.05)^{10}$ at the end of 10 years.

(b) Repeat part (a) of this exercise if the lender receives no annual interest, but only a lump-sum payment of $100,000(1.10)^{10}$ at the end of 10 years.

*3.3.12 Show that the borrower's total outlay for a standard sinking-fund method repayment as described at the start of Section 3.3 can be written as $L\left[\frac{1}{a_{\overline{n}|i}} + \left(\frac{1}{s_{\overline{n}|j}} - \frac{1}{s_{\overline{n}|i}}\right)\right]$, and use this to compare to amortization at rate i.

*3.3.13 A loan of 100,000 is to be repaid by 20 level annual payments. The lender wishes to earn 12% per year on the full loan amount and will deposit the remainder of the annual payment to a sinking fund earning 8% annually.

(a) Find the amount of the level annual payment.

(b) Just after receiving the 10th payment, the lender sells the remaining 10 payments. The purchaser considers two ways of valuing the remaining payments:

(i) amortization at 10% per year, or

(ii) earning an annual return of 12% on his investment while recovering his principal in a sinking fund earning 8%.

Find the amount in the original lender's sinking fund at the time the remainder of the loan is sold, and in each of cases (i) and (ii) find the amount paid by the investor to the original lender.

(c) In each of cases (i) and (ii) of part (b), the original lender wants to calculate the average annual return (internal rate of return) on his investment for the 10 years. He uses two different approaches:

(α) Equating 100,000 to the present value (at rate i_α) of the 10 annual payments of 12,000 plus the present value of the accumulated amount in the sinking fund and the proceeds of the sale at time 10;

(β) Equating 100,000 to the present value (at rate i_β) of the 10 actual payments received plus the present value of the proceeds of the sale at time 10.

For each of cases (i) and (ii), find i_α and i_β.

*3.3.14 A loan of 100,000 is repaid on the amortization basis at $i' = .12$ with 25 level annual payments starting one year after the loan is made. The lender wishes to take interest only on the loan at rate i per year and deposit the rest of the annual payment in a sinking fund earning rate j to accumulate 100,000 at the end of 25 years.

(a) Solve for i if $j = .08; .12; .16$.

(b) Show for a general situation of the type in part (a) that i is between j and i'.

SECTION 3.4

3.4.1 Solve part (a) of Example 3.5 by setting up the full cashflow sequence and finding the present value. There would be 12 monthly payments of 800 each plus a payment of 10,000 with the 12th payment, followed by 12 monthly payments of 700 each plus a payment of 10,000 with the 12th payment, and so on.

3.4.2 A loan of 15,000 is repaid by annual payments of principal starting one year after the loan is made, plus quarterly payments of interest on the outstanding balance at a quarterly rate of 4%. Find the present value of the payments to yield an investor a quarterly rate of 3% if the principal payments are

(a) 1000 per year for 15 years; or

(b) 1000 in the 1st year, 2000 in the 2nd year,..., 5000 in the 5th year; or

(c) 5000 in the 1st year, 4000 in the 2nd year,..., 1000 in the 5th year.

3.4.3 An amortized loan of amount $a_{\overline{n}|i}$ at rate i per period has n periodic payments of 1 each. Show that if the payments on the loan are valued at rate j per period, then the present value of the interest payments on the original loan is

$$a_{\overline{n}|j} - \frac{v_i^n - v_j^n}{j - i} = \frac{i}{j}\left(a_{\overline{n}|i} - \frac{v_i^n - v_j^n}{j - i} \right).$$

3.4.4 A loan of amount L is being repaid by n annual payments of principal of $\frac{L}{n}$ each, along with annual interest payments on the outstanding balance at rate i per year. An investor wishes to purchase this loan at the time it is issued. The investor pays a price P which provides him a yield of j per year on his investment while accumulating his initial investment in a sinking fund earning annual rate h. Show that P can be expressed in the form $\frac{Y}{X}$, where Y is the present value on the issue date of all loan (principal and interest) payments valued at rate h.

3.4.5 A home builder offers homebuyers a financing scheme whereby the buyer makes a down payment of 10% of the price at the time of purchase. At the end of each year for 5 years the buyer makes principal payments of 2% of the original purchase price, as well as monthly payments of interest on the outstanding balance at a monthly rate of ½%. Just after the fifth annual principal payment, the full outstanding balance is due (the homebuyer will negotiate with a bank for a loan of this amount). The cost of the home to the builder is 200,000, and the builder will be selling the buyer's 5-year loan to an investor who values the loan at $i^{(12)} = .15$. What should the builder set as the purchase price of the house so as to realize a net profit of 40,000 after the sale of the loan to the investor?

3.4.6 (Alternative derivation of Makeham's Formula) A loan of amount L is repaid by a series of principal payments along with interest on the outstanding balance at the end of each period. If the rate of interest is i per period and the loan is valued on the issue date at a rate of j per period, denote the present value on the issue date by $A_j(i)$. Let K_j denote the present value at rate j of the principal payments. Then $A_j(i) - K_j$ is the present value (at rate j) of the interest payments. Show that (i) $\frac{A_j(i) - K_j}{A_j(i') - K_j} = \frac{i}{i'}$, and (ii) $A_j(j) = L$.
Use (i) and (ii) to show that $A_j(i) = K_j + \frac{i}{j}(L - K_j)$.

3.4.7 A loan of 500,000 is to be repaid by 25 annual principal payments of 20,000 each, starting one year after the loan, along with quarterly interest payments on the outstanding balance at a nominal annual rate of $i^{(4)} = .10$. An investor purchases the loan just after issue. Find the nominal annual yield convertible quarterly realized by the investor if the purchase price is (a) 450,000, (b) 500,000, or (c) 550,000. This will require the use of a computer routine such as Excel Solver.

3.4.8 Using Equation (3.11), show that $A < L$ is equivalent to $j > i$, $A = L$ is equivalent to $j = i$, and $A > L$ is equivalent to $j < i$.

3.4.9 Suppose the investor in Exercise 3.4.2 is subject to a tax on all interest payments at the time they are made. Find the net present value to the investor who is subject to a tax rate of (i) 25%, (ii) 40%, or (iii) 60%.

3.4.10 A loan amortized at effective monthly interest rate 1% calls for monthly payments of 1000 for 25 years. Five years after the loan is issued an investor wishes to purchase the remaining 20 years of payments. The investor wishes to earn a monthly after-tax interest rate of $1\frac{1}{4}\%$. Find the amount paid by the investor if (a) he is not subject to tax on the interest portion of the payments received, and (b) he is subject to 50% tax on the interest portion (in the original amortization) of payments received ((b) can be done by finding the present value of principal payments (of the original amortization) and subtracting this from $1000 \cdot a_{\overline{240}|.0125}$ to get the present value of the full interest payments; one-half of this is then the present value of the after-tax interest payments.)

3.4.11 Smith borrows 1000 on January 1 (of a non-leap year) at $i = .10$, and repays the loan with 5 equal payments of amount X each. The payments are made every 73 days, so that the final payment is made exactly one year after the loan was made. Calculate X based on the Merchant's Rule, and then based on the U.S. Method.

3.4.12 Suppose that a loan of amount L is made at time 0, and payments of $A_1, A_2, \ldots, A_{n-1}$ are made at times $0 < t_1 < t_2 < \cdots t_{n-1}$. Show that if $i > 0$, $A_k > 0$ for each k, and $\sum_{k=1}^{n-1} A_k < L$, then the amount A_n, required to repay the loan at time $t_n, t_n > t_{n-1}$, is larger under the U.S. Method than it is under the Merchant's Rule.

3.4.13 A corporation wishes to issue a zero-coupon bond due in 20 years with maturity value of 1,000,000 and compound annual yield rate of 9%. The corporation wants to charge the interest expense on an annualized basis and plans to use a straight-line approach (i.e., the difference between the proceeds of the bond and the maturity value is divided into 20 equal parts, one part to be charged as an expense in each of the 20 years). The tax authorities insist that the "actuarial method" is the appropriate way of determining the annual interest charge (i.e., the interest charge for year k is the amount of compound interest accrued on the debt in year k). For each of the first year and the 20th year, what is the interest charge under each of the two methods? In what year would the interest charges under the two methods be most nearly equal?

3.4.14 Smith has a *line of credit* with a bank, allowing loans up to a certain limit without requiring approval. Interest on the outstanding balance on the loan is based on an annual simple interest rate of 15%. Interest is charged to the account on the last day of each month, as well as the day on which the line of credit is completely repaid (the month-end balance is the accrued outstanding balance from the start of the month minus accrued payments). On January 15 Smith borrows 1000 from his line of credit, and borrows an additional 500 on March 1. Smith pays 250 on the 15th of March, April, May, June and July. What payment is required to repay the line of credit on August 15? Suppose that instead of charging interest on the last day of each month, the line of credit bases calculations on (a) the U.S. Rule, or (b) the Merchant's Rule. In each of cases (a) and (b) find the payment required on August 15.

3.4.15 Suppose Example 3.1 stated that the loan was to be repaid according to the U.S. Rule by monthly payments, starting one month after the loan, with $K_1 = K_2 = K_3 = 115.61$ and $K_4 = K_5 = 231.22$. Show that the payment K_6 required to retire the loan at time 6 is 231.20. (The U.S. Rule is the same as the amortization method in that at each time a payment is made the outstanding balance is accumulated with interest from the time of the previous payment and the current payment is then subtracted.)

CHAPTER 4

BOND VALUATION

It is often necessary for corporations and governments to raise funds. Corporations have two main ways of raising funds; one is to issue **equity** by means of common (or preferred) shares of ownership (stocks) which usually give the shareholder a vote in deciding the way in which the corporation is managed. The other is to issue **debt**, which is to take out a loan requiring interest payments and repayment of principal. For borrowing in the short term, the corporation might obtain a *demand loan* (a loan that must be repaid at the lender's request with no notice) or a *line of credit* (an account which allows the borrower to maintain outstanding balances up to a specified maximum amount, with periodic interest payable). For longer term borrowing it is possible to take out a loan that is amortized in the standard way, but this would usually be done only for loans of a relatively small amount. To borrow large amounts over a longer term a corporation can issue a **bond**, also called a *debenture*, which is a debt that calls for periodic interest payments called coupons (at a specified rate) for a stated term and the return of the principal at the end of the term. It will often be the case that the amount borrowed is too large for a single lender or investor, and the bond is divided into smaller units to allow a variety of investors to participate in the issue.

Governments generally have the option of raising funds via taxes. Governments also raise funds by borrowing, in the short term by issuing Treasury bills, and in the longer term by issuing coupon bonds. Government *savings bonds* pay periodic interest and might not have a fixed maturity date, and can usually be redeemed by the owner of the bond at any time for the return of principal and any accrued interest. Savings bonds would be purchased and held by individual investors, while government T-Bills and coupon bonds are held by individuals, financial institutions such as insurance companies and banks, and other investors.

The initial purchaser of a bond might not retain ownership for the full term to maturity, but might sell the bond to another party. Ownership of the bond refers to the right to receive the payments specified by the bond. There is a very active and liquid bond secondary market in which bonds are bought and sold. Bonds are crucial components in government and corporate financing. Through the bond market bonds also provide an important investment vehicle, and can make up large parts of pension funds and mutual funds. Bonds issued by corporations are usually backed by various corporate assets as collateral, although a type of corporate bonds called *junk bonds* has been used with little or no collateral, often to raise funds to finance the takeover of another company. Bonds issued by financially and politically stable governments are virtually risk-free and are a safe investment option. There are agencies that rate the risk of default on interest and principal payment associated with a bond issuer. The purchaser of a bond will take into account the level of risk associated with the bond when determining its value.

4.1 DETERMINATION OF BOND PRICES

A bond is a contract between the issuer and the purchaser that specifies a schedule of payments that will be made by the issuer to the bondholder (purchaser). The most common type of bond issue is the *straight-term bond*, for which the schedule of payments is similar to that of a loan with regular payments of interest plus a single payment of principal at the end of the term of the loan. A bond specifies a **face amount** and a *bond interest rate*, also called the **coupon rate**, which are analogous to the principal amount of a loan and rate at which interest is paid. The bond also specifies the *maturity date* or **term to maturity** during which the *coupons* (bond interest payments) are to be paid, and the **redemption amount** that is to be repaid on the maturity date. It is generally the case that the face amount and the redemption amount on a bond are the same, and this will be assumed to be the case throughout this chapter unless specified otherwise.

For bonds issued in Canada and the United States, the coupons are nearly always paid semiannually, with the coupon rate quoted on a nominal annual basis. (Some bonds issued in some European countries have coupons payable annually). Unless specified otherwise, when coupon rates are quoted in this chapter they will refer to annual rates payable semiannually, with the first coupon payable one period after the bond is issued, and with coupons payable up to and including the time at which the redemption amount is paid. Note that bonds may be issued on a non-coupon date, in which case the first coupon is paid less than one coupon period after issue.

The purchaser of a bond is purchasing the right to receive a specific series of payments. The payments will consist of a level series of *coupon payments* (usually paid semi-annually) along with a large lump sum payment (the redemption amount) at the time that the final coupon is paid.

The website of the U.S. Bureau of the Public Debt has a great deal of information about bonds issued by the U.S. Government. At that website, a historical record of all bonds (and T-Bills) issued by the U.S. Government is available.

TABLE 4.1

Historical Securities Search Results Treasury Notes							
Security Term	Auction Date	Issue Date	Maturity Date	Interest Rate %	Yield %	Price Per $100	CUSIP
2-year	02-25-2004	03-01-2004	02-28-2006	1.625	1.675	99.902	912828CB4
10-year	02-12-2004	02-17-2004	02-15-2014	4.000	4.060	99.511	912828CA6
5-year	02-11-2004	02-17-2004	02-15-2009	3.000	3.030	99.862	912828BZ2
3-year	02-10-2004	02-17-2004	02-15-2007	2.250	2.330	99.770	912828BY5
2-year	01-29-2004	02-02-2004	01-31-2006	1.875	1.930	99.893	912828BX7
10-year	01-08-2004	01-15-2004	01-15-2014	2.000	2.019	99.829	912828BW9
5-year	01-07-2004	01-15-2004	01-15-2009	3.250	3.260	99.954	912828BV1
2-year	12-23-2003	12-31-2003	12-31-2005	1.857	1.950	99.854	912828BU3
9-year, 11-month	12-11-2003	12-15-2003	11-15-2013	4.250	4.365	99.076	912828BR0
5-year	12-10-2003	12-15-2003	12-15-2008	3.375	3.375	100.000	912828BT6
2-year	11-26-2003	12-01-2003	11-30-2005	1.875	1.939	99.875	912828BS8
10-year	11-13-2003	11-17-2003	11-15-2013	4.250	4.360	99.116	912828BR0
5-year	11-12-2003	11-17-2003	11-15-2008	3.375	3.430	99.749	912828BO2
3-year	11-10-2003	11-17-2003	11-15-2006	2.265	2.625	100.000	912828BP4
2-year	10-29-2003	10-31-2003	10-31-2005	1.625	1.737	99.781	912828BN9
9-year, 9-month	10-09-2003	10-15-2003	07-15-2013	1.875	2.229	99.201	912828BD1
5-year	10-08-2003	10-15-2003	10-15-2008	3.125	3.139	99.936	912828BM1

www.publicdebt.treas.gov/sec/secpry.htm

The first bond in the website excerpt above has the following characteristics:

Issue Date:	March 1, 2004
Maturity Date:	February 28, 2006
Interest Rate:	1.625%
Yield Rate:	1.675%
Price per $100:	99.902

This describes a 2-year Treasury Note (U.S. government bonds are called "notes" if they mature in less than 10 years) with *face amount* of $100. The purchaser of this bond will receive payments of $\frac{1}{2} \times 1.625 = .8125$ every February 28 and August 31 (every 6 months), starting August 31, 2004 and ending February 28, 2006 (the maturity date of the bond). The purchaser will also receive $100 on February 28, 2006, the maturity date of the bond. This payment of $100 is the *redemption value* or *maturity value* of the bond.

This is an example of a series of cash flows that is being purchased. The "interest rate" referred to in the table is the coupon rate on the bond, quoted on an annual basis. It is understood in practice that coupons are paid semi-annually, so that the coupon rate is divided by 2 to calculate the actual coupon amount of .8125. The purchaser will pay a price that is equal to the present value of the series of payments based on a rate of return, or **yield rate,** that is indicated by current financial market conditions. For this example, at the time of purchase, it is indicated that the yield rate is 1.675%. This is the rate used by the purchaser to calculate the present value of the series of bond payments. It is the convention in practice that bond yield rates are quoted as nominal annual interest rates compounded twice per year. Therefore, the yield rate per half-year is .8375%. The purchase price of the bond is the present value on the purchase date of the series of bond cashflows. It should be emphasized again that the phrase "interest rate" in Table 4.1 is the rate used to determine the coupons that the bond will pay, and the phrase "yield rate" is the rate which is used to calculate the present value of the stream of coupons and redemption amount. During the lifetime of the bond, the coupon rate will not change; it is a part of the contract describing the stream of payments that the bond will make. The yield rate is set by market conditions, and will fluctuate as time goes on and market conditions change.

The following time diagram describes the payments made by the first bond in Table 4.1.

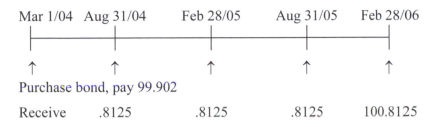

Mar 1/04   Aug 31/04   Feb 28/05   Aug 31/05   Feb 28/06

Purchase bond, pay 99.902

Receive   .8125   .8125   .8125   100.8125

If we regard the period from issue to the first coupon (March 1, 2004 to August 31, 2004) and the time from one coupon period to the next each as exactly one-half year, then the present value of the bond payments is

$$100\frac{1}{(1.008375)^4}$$
$$+.8125\left[\frac{1}{1.008375} + \frac{1}{(1.008375)^2} + \frac{1}{(1.008375)^3} + \frac{1}{(1.008375)^4}\right] = 99.902.$$

This is the listed purchase price of the bond. It is an anomaly of financial practice that if the details of this bond were to be quoted in the financial press, all quantities would be described as listed above, except for the price, which would be quoted as 99.29. This does not mean a price of 99 dollars and 29 cents. For U.S. government bond issues, the fractions of a dollar in price are quoted in multiples of $1/32^{nds}$ of a dollar, so that 99.29 refers to a price of $99\frac{29}{32}$ dollars, which is \$99.902.

The *Wall Street Journal* © generally publishes information daily on the previous day's activity in the bond market. In the "Money and Investing" section of the March 2, 2004 *Wall Street Journal* (reporting on trading for the previous day, March 1, 2004) the following quotation could be found relating to the treasury note mentioned above.

TABLE 4.2

Rate	Maturity Month/Year	Bid	Asked	Chg	Ask Yield
1.625	Feb 06	99.29	99.30	− 1	1.66

This is essentially the same information that was found on the Bureau of Public Debt website. There would have been trading in the bond on March

1, 2004, the issue date of the bond, and at the close of trading on March 1 there would be a record of the most recent "bid" and "asked" price on $100 face amount of the bond. The "bid" price is the most recent highest price that a buyer would be willing to pay for the bond and the "ask" price is the most recent lowest price that a seller would be willing to accept.

4.1.1 THE PRICE OF A BOND ON A COUPON DATE

The following notation will be used to represent the various parameters associated with a bond:

F - The face amount (also called the par value) of the bond
r - the coupon rate per coupon period (six months unless otherwise specified)
C - the redemption amount on the bond (equal to F unless otherwise noted)
n - the number of coupon periods until maturity

The coupons are each of amount Fr, and the sequence of payments associated with the bond is shown in the following time diagram

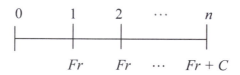

FIGURE 4.1

When an investor purchases a bond, he or she is purchasing the series of payments just described. The purchase price of the bond is determined as the present value, on the purchase date, of that series of payments. There will be a number of factors that influence the rate of interest used by the purchaser to find the price of the bond. We will not explore here the relationship between economic factors and interest rates on investments. We will simply accept that "market forces" determine the interest rate used to value the bond, or in other words, to determine the purchase price. As noted earlier, this valuation rate of interest is called the **yield rate** on the bond or the **yield to maturity**, since the rate is used to value all payments up to and including the redemption amount. Since coupons are payable semiannually, yield rates are quoted on a nominal annual basis convertible semiannually. We will use j to denote the six-month yield rate.

It is now a straightforward matter to formulate the price of the bond on a coupon date using the notation defined above. If the yield rate is j per coupon period, then the price is

$$P = C\frac{1}{(1+j)^n} + Fr\left[\frac{1}{1+j} + \frac{1}{(1+j)^2} + \cdots + \frac{1}{(1+j)^n}\right] = Cv_j^n + Fr\,a_{\overline{n}|j}.$$

The first term on the right hand side of the equation is the present value of the redemption amount to be received by the bondholder in n coupon periods. The second term on the right hand side of the equation is the present value of the annuity of coupons to be received until the bond matures. Note that it is being assumed that the next coupon is payable one full coupon period from the valuation point (hence the annuity-immediate symbol), and there are n coupon periods until the bond matures.

It is usually the case that the redemption amount and the face amount are the same $(C = F)$. If this is so, the bond price can be expressed as

$$P = Fv_j^n + Fr\,a_{\overline{n}|j}. \tag{4.1}$$

Using the identity $v_j^n = 1 - ja_{\overline{n}|j}$, Equation 4.1 becomes

$$P = F + F(r-j)a_{\overline{n}|j}. \tag{4.2}$$

Alternatively, writing $a_{\overline{n}|j}$ in Equation (4.1) as $a_{\overline{n}|j} = \dfrac{1-v_j^n}{j}$, and letting the present value of the redemption amount be denoted by $K = F \cdot v_j^n$, Equation (4.1) becomes

$$P = F \cdot v_j^n + \frac{r}{j}\left(F - F \cdot v_j^n\right) = K + \frac{r}{j}(F - K). \tag{4.3}$$

Equation (4.3) is known as *Makeham's Formula*, which is the same as Equation (3.11) with F replacing the loan amount L, and r replacing the interest rate i in Equation (3.11). Note that, as in Equation (3.11), Equation (4.3) requires r and j to be based on the same period (which for bonds is usually six months).

EXAMPLE 4.1   (*Price of a bond on a coupon date*)

A 10% bond with semiannual coupons has a face amount of 100,000,000 and was issued on June 18, 1990. The first coupon was paid on December 18, 1990, and the bond has a maturity date of June 18, 2010.

(a) Find the price of the bond on its issue date using a nominal annual yield rate $i^{(2)}$ of (i) 5%, (ii) 10%, and (iii) 15%.

(b) Find the price of the bond on June 18, 2000, just after the coupon is paid, using the yield rates of part (a).

SOLUTION

(a) We have $F = C = 100,000,000$, $r = .05$, and $n = 40$. Using Equation (4.1), we see that the price of the bond is

$$P = 100,000,000 \cdot v_j^{40} + (100,000,000)(.05)a_{\overline{40}|j}.$$

With (i) $j = .025$, (ii) $j = .05$, and (iii) $j = .075$, the bond prices are (i) $P = 162,756,938$, (ii) $P = 100,000,000$, and (iii) $P = 68,513,978$.

(b) We still have $F = C = 100,000,000$ and $r = .05$, but now $n = 20$ (since there are 10 years, or 20 coupons, remaining on the bond). Using Equation (4.2), we have

$$P \quad = \quad 100,000,000 + 100,000,000(.05 - j)a_{\overline{20}|j}.$$

This results in prices of (i) 138,972,906, (ii) 100,000,000, and (iii) 74,513,772.   □

Note that as the yield rate is increased in Example 4.1 the bond price decreases. This is due to the inverse relationship between interest rate and present value; the bond price is the present value of a stream of payments valued at the yield rate.

In the Canadian financial press bond prices are generally quoted as a value per 100 of face amount, to the nearest .001 and yield rates are quoted to the nearest .001% (one-thousandth of a percent). Thus the quoted prices in Example 4.1 would be (i) 162.757, (ii) 100.000, and (iii) 68.514 in part (a), and (i) 138.972, (ii) 100.000, and (iii) 74.514 in part (b).

In the U.S. there is a variety of quotation procedures. U.S. government bond prices are quoted to the nearest $\frac{1}{32}$ per 100 of face amount, and yields are quoted to the nearest .01%. For corporate bonds, price quotations are to the nearest $\frac{1}{8}$ per 100 of face amount and **current yields** are also quoted. The current yield is the coupon rate divided by the bond's price.

It is not surprising that the bond prices in (i), (ii) and (iii) decrease in both parts (a) and (b) of Example 4.1, since the present value of a series of payments decreases as the valuation rate increases. In looking at the bond price formulation of Equation (4.2) it is clear that the relative sizes of the bond price and face amount are directly related to the relative sizes of the coupon rate and yield rate. We have the relationships

$$P > F \quad \leftrightarrow \quad r > j, \tag{4.4a}$$

$$P = F \quad \leftrightarrow \quad r = j, \tag{4.4b}$$

and

$$P < F \quad \leftrightarrow \quad r < j, \tag{4.4c}$$

These relationships are similar to the ones between the loan amount L and the price paid for the loan based on Makeham's Formula in Section 3.4. The terminology associated with these relationships between P and F is as follows.

(a) If $P > F$, the bond is said to be bought **at a premium**.

(b) If $P = F$, the bond is said to be bought **at par**.

(c) If $P < F$, the bond is said to be bought **at a discount**.

Equation (4.2) can be rewritten as $P - F = F(r-j)a_{\overline{n}|j}$. Suppose that the bond is bought at a premium so that $P > F$. The rewritten version of Equation (4.2) indicates that the amount of premium in the purchase price $(P-F)$ is regarded as a loan (from the buyer to the seller) repaid at rate j by n payments of $F(r-j)$, the excess of coupon over yield.

We can also see from Equation (4.2) that if $r > j$ and the time n until maturity is increased, then the bond price P increases, but if $r < j$ then P decreases as n increases. This can be seen another way. If $r > j$ then $P > F$, so that the bondholder will realize a *capital loss* of $P - F$ at the time of redemption. Having the capital loss deferred would be of some value to the bondholder, so he would be willing to pay a larger P for such a bond with a later maturity date. The reverse of this argument applies if $r < j$. In any event, the level of bond yield rates would influence a bond issuer in setting the coupon rate and maturity date on a new issue, since both coupon rate and maturity date have an effect on the actual price received for the bond by the issuer.

It was pointed out earlier that it is generally the case that the face and redemption amounts of the bond are the same, so that $F = C$. In the case where they are not equal, an additional parameter can be defined, called the *modified coupon rate* and denoted by $g = \frac{F \cdot r}{C}$, so that $Cg = Fr$. Exercise 4.1.15 develops alternative formulations for bond prices when $C \neq F$ that are equivalent to Equations (4.1), (4.2) and (4.3). When $C = F$ the bond is said to be *redeemed at par*, when $C > F$ the bond is said to be *redeemed at a premium*, and when $C < F$ the bond is said to be *redeemed at a discount*.

4.1.2 BOND PRICES BETWEEN COUPON DATES

We have thus far considered only the determination of a bond's price on its issue date or at some later coupon date. In practice bonds are traded daily, and we now consider the valuation of a bond at a time between coupon dates. Let us regard the coupon period as the unit of time, and suppose that we wish to find the purchase price P_t of a bond at time t, where $0 \leq t \leq 1$, with t measured from the last coupon payment. The value of the bond is still found as the present value at the yield rate of all future payments (coupons plus redemption). Suppose that there are n coupons remaining on the bond, including the next coupon due. At yield rate j per coupon period, the value P_1 of the bond *just after* the next coupon could be found using one of Equations (4.1), (4.2) or (4.3). Then the value of the bond at time t is the present value of the amount $P_1 + Fr$ due at time 1 (the present value of both the coupon due then and the future coupons and redemption), so that

$$P_t = v_j^{1-t} [P_1 + Fr]. \qquad (4.5a)$$

0	t	1
↑	↑	↑
P_0	P_t	$Fr + P_1$

FIGURE 4.2

Alternatively, if we define P_0 to be the value of the bond just after the last coupon, then (see Exercise 4.1.26) we also have

$$P_t = P_0(1+j)^t. \qquad (4.5b)$$

The value P_t given by Equations (4.5a) and (4.5b) is the purchase price paid for the bond at time t, and it is called the **price-plus-accrued** of the bond.

In the calculation involved in Equations (4.5a) and (4.5b), the value of t is between 0 and 1 and measures the time since the last coupon was paid as a fraction of a coupon period. Given the coupon dates and the date of time t, the numerical value of t is

$$t = \frac{number\ of\ days\ since\ last\ coupon\ paid}{number\ of\ days\ in\ the\ coupon\ period}. \qquad (4.6)$$

The price given by Equations (4.5a) and (4.5b), with t defined by Equation (4.6), is not the price that would be quoted for the bond in a financial newspaper. The price quoted in the financial press is called simply the **price**, and is equal to the price-plus-accrued minus the fraction of the coupon accrued to time t (throughout this section, the terms *price* and *price-plus-accrued* will have the specific meanings given here). This fractional coupon is proportional to the fractional part of the coupon period that has elapsed since the last coupon was paid, so the fractional coupon is $t \cdot Fr$. The (quoted) price of the bond is then

$$Price_t = Price\text{-}plus\text{-}accrued_t - t \cdot Fr = P_0(1+j)^t - t \cdot Fr. \qquad (4.7)$$

EXAMPLE 4.2   *(Bond price between coupon dates)*

For each of the yield rates (i), (ii), and (iii) in Example 4.1, find both the price-plus-accrued and quoted price on August 1, 2000. Quote the prices (to the nearest .001) per 100 of face amount.

SOLUTION

Using the results in part (b) of Example 4.1, we see that on the last coupon date, June 18, 2000, the value of the bond was (i) 138,972,906, (ii) 100,000,000, and (iii) 74,513,772. The number of days from June 18 to August 1 is 44, and the number of days in the coupon period from June 18 to December 18 is 183. Using Equation (4.5b), with $t = \frac{44}{183}$, we have prices-plus-accrued of

(i) $138,972,906(1.025)^{44/183} = 139,800,445,$

(ii) $100,000,000(1.05)^{44/183} = 101,180,005,$ and

(iii) $74,513,772(1.075)^{44/183} = 75,820,791.$

Per 100 of face amount, the purchase prices, to the nearest .001, are (i) 139.800, (ii) 101.180, and (iii) 75.821.

The quoted prices are:

(i) $139,800,445 - \frac{44}{183}(.05)(100,000,000) = 138,598,259,$

(ii) $101,180,004 - \frac{44}{183}(.05)(100,000,000) = 99,977,818,$ and

(iii) $75,820,791 - \frac{44}{183}(.05)(100,000,000) = 74,618,605.$

Per 100 of face we have quoted prices of (i) 138.598, (ii) 99.978, and (iii) 74.619.   □

In reporting the value of assets at a particular time, a bondholder would have to assign a value to the bond at that time. This value is called the *book value* of the bond, and is usually taken as the current price of the bond valued at the original yield rate at which the bond was purchased. For accounting purposes the accrued interest since the last coupon would be considered as a separate item from the book value of the bond. The next section of this chapter looks at book value in more detail.

Figure 4.3 below displays the graph of the price-plus-accrued and the price of a bond over several consecutive coupon periods (all prices are calculated at the original yield rate of the bond). Nodes in the graph indicate the price just after a coupon is paid. The upper line in the graph is the price-plus-accrued, and the lower line is the price without the accrued coupon. This graph is for a bond bought at a premium. The graph for a bond bought at a discount would be rising, but otherwise would be similar. Note that the price (without the accrued coupon) is approximately the linear interpolation between two successive coupon dates (see Exercise 4.1.25), and the price-plus-accrued readjusts back to the price on the coupon dates.

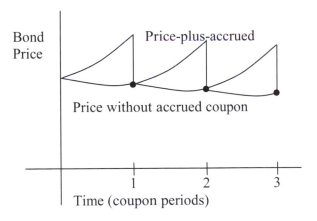

FIGURE 4.3

A bond trader would often be comparing the relative values of different bonds, and would want an equitable basis on which to compare, at a specific point in time, bonds with different calendar coupon dates. The price without accrued coupon (see Figure 4.3) provides a smooth progression of bond values from one coupon date to the next, and it is this price that is used by bond traders to compare relative bond values. This can easily be seen if we consider a bond for which $r = j$. We see from Equation (4.2) that if $r = j$ (the coupon and yield rates are equal), then on a coupon date the price of the bond would be F (the bond is bought at par). However the price-plus-accrued of the bond grows from $P_0 = F$ at $t = 0$ to $P_0(1+j)$ just before the coupon is paid at $t = 1$, and just after that coupon is paid the price drops to $P_1 = F$ (see Exercise 4.1.26). For a bond trader comparing two bonds with different coupon dates, but both with $r = j$, it would be convenient to regard both bonds as being at par at any time during the coupon period as they would be just after a coupon is paid. Note that in part (ii) of Example 4.2 with $r = j = .05$, the price is almost exactly the par value. Thus the price has eliminated a "distortion" caused by the accrued coupon included in the price-plus-accrued. With a more exact calculation the price would be exactly equal to the par value when $r = j$ (see Exercise 4.1.27).

The notion, introduced earlier, of a bond bought at a premium, at par, or at a discount just after a coupon is paid was based on comparing the bond price with the face amount. To describe a bond as being bought at a premium, par or discount when bought at a time between coupon dates, the comparison is made between the price and the face amount. It was pointed out that just after a coupon payment, a bond is priced at a premium, par or discount according to whether $r > j$, $r = j$, or $r < j$, respectively. This relationship remains valid when comparing the price with the face amount at a time between coupon dates.

When bonds are actually bought and sold on the bond market, the trading takes place with buyers and sellers offering "bid" and "ask" prices, respectively, with an intermediate settlement price eventually found. We have considered bond valuation mainly from the point of view of calculating the price of a bond when the coupon rate, time to maturity and yield rate are known. In practice, bond prices are settled first, and the corresponding yield rate is then determined and made part of the overall quotation describing the transaction. The determination of the yield rate from the price becomes an unknown interest rate problem which would be solved using an unknown interest function or bond yield function on a financial calculator.

For a bond with face amount F, coupon rate r, with n coupons remaining until maturity, and bought at a purchase price P one period before the next coupon is due, the yield rate j is the solution of the equation $P = Fv_j^n + Fr a_{\overline{n}|j}$. j is the *internal rate of return* for this transaction, and there is a unique positive solution, $j > 0$ (if the purchase price is positive, $P > 0$). If the bond is bought at time t, $0 < t < 1$, measured from the last coupon, and there are n coupons remaining, then j is the solution of the equation $P = [Fv_j^n + Fra_{\overline{n}|j}](1+j)^t$, where P is the price-plus-accrued of the bond. Again, there will be a unique positive solution, $j > 0$ (if $P > 0$).

EXAMPLE 4.3   (*Finding the yield rate from the price of a bond*)

A 20-year 8% bond has semi-annual coupons and a face amount of 100. It is quoted at a purchase price of 70.400 (in decimal form, not $\frac{1}{32}$ form).

(a) Find the yield rate.

(b) Suppose that the bond was issued January 15, 2000, and is bought by a new purchaser for a price of 112.225 on January 15, 2005 just after a coupon has been paid.

   (i) Find the yield rate for the new purchaser.

   (ii) Find the yield rate (internal rate of return) earned by the original bondholder.

   (iii) Suppose that the original bondholder was able to deposit coupons into an account earning an annual interest rate of 6% convertible semi-annually. Find the average effective annual rate of return earned by the original bond purchaser on his 5-year investment. Assume that interest on the deposit account is credited every January 15 and July 15.

(c) Suppose that the bond was issued January 15, 2000, and is bought by a new purchaser on April 1, 2005 for a *quoted* price of 112.225.

   (i) Find the yield rate for the new purchaser.

   (ii) Find the yield rate (internal rate of return) earned by the original bondholder.

SOLUTION

(a) We solve for j, the 6-month yield rate, in the equation

$$70.400 = 100v_j^{40} + 4a_{\overline{40}|j}$$

(40 coupon periods to maturity, each coupon amount is 4). Using a financial calculator returns a value of $j = .059565$. This would be a quoted yield rate of 11.913% (compounded semi-annually).

(b) (i) There are 30 coupons remaining when the new purchaser buys the bond. We solve for j, the 6-month yield rate, in the equation $112.225 = 100v_j^{30} + 4a_{\overline{30}|j}$ (30 coupon periods to maturity). Using a financial calculator returns a value of $j = .033479$. This would be a quoted yield rate of 6.696% (compounded semi-annually).

(ii) The original bondholder received 10 coupons plus the purchase price of 112.225 on January 15, 2005. The original bondholder's equation of value for that 5-year (10 half-years) period is $70.400 = 112.225v_j^{10} + 4a_{\overline{10}|j}$. A financial calculator returns a value of $j = .09500$ (6-month yield of 9.5%) or a quoted nominal annual yield compounded semiannually of 19.0%.

(iii) On January 15, 2005, just after the coupon is deposited, the balance in the deposit account is $4s_{\overline{10}|.03} = 45.86$. Along with the sale of the bond, the original bondholder has a total of $45.86 + 112.225 = 158.08$. For the five year period, the annualized return is i, the solution of the equation $158.08 = 70.40(1+i)^5$. Solving for i results in a value of $i = 17.6\%$.

(c) (i) There are 76 days from January 15, 2005 (the time of the most recent coupon) to April 1, 2005. The entire coupon period from January 15, 2005 to July 15, 2005 is 181 days. The price-plus-accrued of the bond on April 1, 2005 at yield rate j per coupon period is $\left[100v_j^{30} + 4a_{\overline{30}|j}\right](1+j)^{76/181}$. The quoted price is 112.225, so the price-plus-accrued is $112.225 + \frac{76}{181} \times 4 = 113.905$. The new purchaser's 6-month yield is j, the solution of the equation $113.905 = \left[100v_j^{30} + 4a_{\overline{30}|j}\right](1+j)^{76/181}$. This is an awkward equation to work with. Using a financial calculator with a function for calculating the yield rate on a bond, we get $j = .033421$ (annual yield rate of 6.684%, compounded semi-annually).

(ii) The original purchaser will receive 10 coupons of amount 4 each, plus a payment of 113.905 on April 1, 2005. The payment of 113.905 is made $10\frac{76}{181} = 10.420$ coupon periods after the bond was originally purchased. The original purchaser's 6-month yield j, is the solution of the equation $70.400 = 113.905v_j^{10.420} + 4a_{\overline{10}|j}$. Standard financial calculator functions will not be capable of solving for j, and some approximate computer routine such as EXCEL Solver would be needed. The resulting solution is $j = .093054$ (9.31% is the 6-month yield rate).   □

Several exercises at the end of the chapter look at various methods for approximating the yield rate. These methods may provide some insight into the price-yield relationship, but they would no longer be used in practice.

4.2 AMORTIZATION OF A BOND

For taxation and other accounting purposes, it may be necessary to determine the amount of interest received and principal returned in a bond coupon or redemption payment. This can be done by viewing the bond as a standard amortized loan.

The payments made during the term of a bond can be regarded as loan payments made by the bond issuer (the borrower) to the bondholder (the lender) to repay a loan whose original amount is equal to the purchase price of the bond. The bond price is calculated as the present value of those payments (coupons plus redemption amount) at a certain yield rate (the interest rate on the loan), so the transaction can be regarded as the amortization of a loan, assuming the bondholder continues to hold the bond to the end of the term. The loan amount is the purchase price P, of the bond, and the loan payments are the series of coupons and the redemption amount. (If the bond is sold before the end of the term, the new bondholder can regard the remaining payments on the bond as loan payments for a loan equal to the price that he paid at an interest rate equal to his yield rate). An amortization schedule for the bond would be constructed algebraically like the general amortization schedule in Table 3.1.

Assuming there are n coupons on the bond, the payment amounts in the schedule will be the coupon amounts Fr until the nth payment, which would be a coupon plus the redemption amount, $Fr + C$. The prospective form of the outstanding balance just after a coupon payment is the present value of all future coupons plus redemption amount, valued at the "loan interest rate" which is the yield rate on the bond when it was originally purchased. Thus the outstanding balance is equal to the price of the remainder of the bond payments valued at the original yield rate. In Section 4.1 the **book value** of the bond at a point in time was defined to be the price of the remainder of the bond, valued at the original yield rate at which the bond was purchased. Thus, just after a coupon payment, the outstanding balance is equal to the bond's book value.

For a bond of face amount F with n coupons at rate r per coupon period, bought to yield j per coupon period, the amortization schedule is given in the following table.

TABLE 4.3

k	Outstanding Balance (Book Value after Payment)	Payment	Interest Due	Principal Repaid
0	$P = F[1+(r-j)\cdot a_{\overline{n}|}]$	–	–	–
1	$F[1+(r-j)\cdot a_{\overline{n-1}|}]$	Fr	$F[j+(r-j)(1-v_j^n)]$	$F(r-j)\cdot v_j^n$
2	$F[1+(r-j)\cdot a_{\overline{n-2}|}]$	Fr	$F[j+(r-j)(1-v_j^{n-1})]$	$F(r-j)\cdot v_j^{n-1}$
$\vdots$	$\vdots$	$\vdots$	$\vdots$	$\vdots$
k	$F[1+(r-j)\cdot a_{\overline{n-k}|}]$	Fr	$F[j+(r-j)(1-v_j^{n-k+1})]$	$F(r-j)\cdot v_j^{n-k+1}$
$\vdots$	$\vdots$	$\vdots$	$\vdots$	$\vdots$
$n-1$	$F[1+(r-j)\cdot a_{\overline{1}|}]$	Fr	$F[j+(r-j)(1-v_j^2)]$	$F(r-j)\cdot v_j^2$
n	0	$Fr+F$	$F[j+(r-j)(1-v_j)]$	$F[1+(r-j)\cdot v_j]$

Notice that since the coupon payments are level throughout the term of the bond, except for the final payment, the principal repaid column forms a geometric progression with ratio $1+j$. The following example illustrates the form of a bond amortization.

EXAMPLE 4.4   (*Bond amortization*)

A 10% bond with face amount 10,000 matures 4 years after issue. Construct the amortization schedule for the bond over its term for nominal annual yield rates of (a) 8%, (b) 10%, and (c) 12%.

SOLUTION

(a) The entries in the amortization schedule are calculated as they were in Table 4.3, where k counts coupon periods. With a nominal yield rate of 8% the purchase price of the bond is 10,673.27. Then $I_1 = (10,673.27)(.04) = 426.93$, and so on. The complete schedule is shown in Table 4.4a.

TABLE 4.4a

k	Outstanding Balance	Payment	Interest Due	Principal Repaid
0	10,673.27	–	–	–
1	10,600.21	500	426.93	73.07
2	10,524.22	500	424.01	75.99
3	10,445.19	500	420.97	79.03
4	10,277.52	500	417.81	82.19
5	10,363.00	500	414.52	85.48
6	10,188.62	500	411.10	88.90
7	10,096.16	500	407.54	92.46
8	0	10,500	403.85	10,096.15

Note that since $OB_7 = 10,096.16$ and $PR_8 = 10.096.15$ we should have $OB_8 = .01$. Of course $OB_8 = 0$ and the one cent discrepancy is due to rounding. The values of OB_k decrease to the redemption value as k approaches the end of the term. The entry under Principal Repaid is called **the amount for amortization of premium** for that particular period. The amortization of a bond bought at a premium is also referred to as **writing down a bond**. If we sum the entries in the principal repaid column for k from 1 to 7 along with 96.15 at time 8 (the principal repaid before the redemption payment of 10,000), we get a total of

673.27 which is the total premium above redemption value at which the bond was originally purchased. The coupon payments are amortizing the premium, reducing the book value to 10,000 as of time 8 and then the redemption payment of 10,000 retires the bond debt.

(b) With a nominal yield rate of 10% the purchase price is 10,000. The schedule is shown in Table 4.4b.

TABLE 4.4b

k	Outstanding Balance	Payment	Interest Due	Principal Repaid
0	10,000.00	–	–	–
1	10,000.00	500	500.00	0
2	10,000.00	500	500.00	0
3	10,000.00	500	500.00	0
4	10,000.00	500	500.00	0
5	10,000.00	500	500.00	0
6	10,000.00	500	500.00	0
7	10,000.00	500	500.00	0
8	0	10,500	500.00	10,000

(c) With a nominal yield rate of 12% the purchase price is 9379.02; the schedule is shown in Table 4.4c.

TABLE 4.4c

k	Outstanding Balance	Payment	Interest Due	Principal Repaid
0	9379.02	–	–	–
1	9441.76	500	562.74	– 62.74
2	9508.27	500	566.51	– 66.51
3	9578.77	500	570.50	– 70.50
4	9653.50	500	574.73	– 74.73
5	9732.71	500	579.21	– 79.21
6	9816.67	500	583.96	– 83.96
7	9905.67	500	589.00	– 89.00
8	0	10,500	594.34	9905.66

Round-off error again gives a value of $OB_8 = .01,$ when it should be zero. Note that OB_k *increases* to the redemption amount as k approaches the end of the term. The negative of the principal repaid entry is called the **amount for accumulation of discount** when a bond is bought at a discount. This amortization is also referred to as **writing up a bond**. $\square$

It should be emphasized again that bond amortization relationships are algebraically identical to those of a loan amortization.

4.3 APPLICATIONS AND ILLUSTRATIONS

4.3.1 CALLABLE BONDS: OPTIONAL REDEMPTION DATES

A bond issuer may wish to add flexibility to a bond issue by specifying a range of dates during which redemption may occur, at the issuer's option. Such a bond is called a **callable bond**. From the point of view of an investor pricing the bond, a prudent approach is taken in which the investor assumes that the issuer will choose a redemption date that is to the issuer's greatest advantage, and the investor's least advantage. In order to earn a minimum yield of j, an investor will calculate the price of the bond at rate j for each of the redemption dates in the specified range, and choose the minimum of those as the purchase price. If the investor pays more than that minimum, and the issuer redeems at a point such that the price is the minimum, then the investor has "overpaid" and will earn a yield less then the minimum originally desired.

For a basic callable bond situation in which the redemption amount is constant for the range of possible redemption dates there is a straightforward way of determining the maximum price an investor should pay for the bond in order to achieve a specified minimum yield rate j. As noted above, that maximum price is the minimum bond price for the range of redemption dates. Suppose that the bond can be redeemed on any coupon date from the mth coupon to the kth coupon date. We use the bond price formula $P = C + (Fr - Cj)a_{\overline{n}|j},$ and we know that $m \le n \le k.$ If $Fr - Cj > 0$ (bond bought at a premium), then the minimum price occurs at the minimum possible value of n, which is the earliest possible redemption date, time m. Conversely, if $Fr - Cj < 0$ (bond bought at a discount), then the minimum price occurs at the maximum possible value of n, which is the latest possible redemption date, time k. It may be the case that the redemption amount may vary according to when redemption takes place. If so, then a more detailed analysis is necessary to determine the minimum price of the bond, as illustrated in the Example 4.6.

| EXAMPLE 4.5 | (*Callable bond*)

(a) A 10% bond with face amount 1,000,000 is issued with the condition that redemption can take place on any coupon date between 12 and 15 years from the issue date. Find the price paid by an investor wishing a minimum yield of (i) $i^{(2)} = .12$, and (ii) $i^{(2)} = .08$.

(b) Suppose the investor pays the maximum of all prices for the range of redemption dates. Find the yield rate if the issuer chooses a redemption date corresponding to the minimum price in each of cases (i) and (ii) of part (a).

(c) Suppose the investor pays the minimum of all prices for the range of redemption dates. Find the yield rate if the issuer chooses a redemption date corresponding to the maximum price in each of cases (i) and (ii) of part (a).

| SOLUTION |

(a) (i) From Equation (4.2) $P = 1,000,000\left[1 + (.05 - .06) \cdot a_{\overline{n}|.06}\right]$, where n is the number of coupons until redemption, $n = 24, 25, \ldots, 30$. The range of the price for this range of redemption dates is from 874,496 for redemption at $n = 24$ to 862,352 for redemption at $n = 30$. It is most prudent for the investor to offer a price of 862,352. As noted above, for a bond bought at a discount, the minimum price will occur at the latest possible redemption date.

(ii) The range of prices is from 1,152,470 if redemption occurs at 12 years, to 1,172,920 if redemption is at 15 years The prudent investor would pay 1,152,470.

(b) If the investor in (i) pays the maximum price of 874,496 (based on redemption at $n = 24$), and the bond is redeemed at the end of 15 years, the actual nominal yield is 11.80%. If the investor in (ii) pays 1,172,920 (based on redemption at $n = 30$), and the bond is redeemed at the end of 12 years, the actual nominal yield is 7.76%.

(c) If the investor in (i) pays 862,352 (based on 15 year redemption) and the bond is redeemed after 12 years, the actual nominal yield is 12.22%, and if the investor in (ii) pays 1,152,470 (based on 12 year redemption) and the bond is redeemed after 15 years, the actual nominal yield is 8.21%.   □

Equation (4.2) shows that for a bond bought at a discount, the longer the time to redemption, the lower will be the price, with the reverse being true for a bond bought at a premium. Thus for a callable bond for which the investor desires a minimum yield rate that is larger than the coupon rate (a bond bought at a discount), the price should be based on the latest optional redemption date, and for a callable bond for which the investor desires a yield rate that is smaller than the coupon rate (bought at a premium), the price should be based on the *earliest* optional redemption date. If something more than the minimum price is paid, the investor runs the risk of having redemption occur at a time which is to the investor's disadvantage (as in part (b) of Example 4.5), so that the actual yield to maturity is less than the desired minimum. On the other hand, if the investor pays the minimum price and the actual redemption date is other than the one on which that minimum price is based, then the investor will earn a yield rate greater than the minimum desired (as in part (c) of Example 4.5).

Suppose a bond is bought at a discount, so that $P < F$. The sooner the bond is redeemed, the sooner the investor will realize the gain of $F - P$, so it is to the investor's disadvantage to have a later redemption date. Since the investor prices the bond assuming the redemption will occur to his greatest disadvantage, the investor assumes the latest possible redemption date. Similar reasoning in the case of a bond bought at a premium results in an investor choosing the earliest possible redemption date for calculating the price, since if $P > F$ the investor takes a loss of $F - P$ when the bond is redeemed. It is to the investor's disadvantage to have this loss come early.

When the first optional call date arrives, the bond issuer, based on market conditions and its own financial situation, will make a decision on whether or not to call (redeem) the bond prior to the maximum term. If the issuer is not in a position to redeem at an early date, under appropriate market conditions, it still might be to the issuer's advantage to redeem the bond and issue a new bond for the remaining term. As a simple illustration of this point, suppose in Example 4.5(a) that 12 years after the issue date, the yield rate on a 3-year bond is 9%. If the issuer redeems the bond and immediately issues a new 3-year bond with the same coupon and face amount, the issuer must pay 1,000,000 to the bondholder, but then receives 1,025,789 for the new 3-year bond, which is bought at a yield rate of 9%.

A callable bond might have different redemption amounts at the various optional redemption dates. It might still be possible to use some of the reasoning described above to find the minimum price for all possible redemption dates. In general, however, it may be necessary to calculate the price at several (or all) of the optional dates to find the minimum price.

| Example 4.6 | *(Varying redemption amounts)*

A 15-year 8% bond with face amount 100 is callable (at the option of the issuer) on a coupon date in the 10th to 15th years. In the 10th year the bond is callable at par, in the 11th or 12th years at redemption amount 115, or in the 13th, 14th or 15th years at redemption amount 135.
(a) What price should an investor pay in order to ensure a minimum nominal annual yield to maturity of (i) 12%, and (ii) 6%?
(b) Find the investor's minimum yield if the purchase price is (i) 80, and (ii) 120.

| Solution |

(a) (i) Since the yield rate is larger than the coupon rate (or modified coupon rate for any of the redemption dates), the bond will be bought at a discount. Using Equation (4.2E) from Exercise 4.1.15, we see that during any interval for which the redemption amount is level, the lowest price will occur at the latest redemption date. Thus we must compute the price at the end of 10 years, 12 years and 15 years. The corresponding prices are 77.06, 78.60 and 78.56. The lowest price corresponds to a redemption date of 10 years, which is near the earliest possible redemption date. This example indicates that the principal of pricing a bond bought at a discount by using the latest redemption date may fail when the redemption amounts are not level.

(ii) For redemption in the 10th year and the 11th or 12th years, the yield rate of .03 every six months is smaller than the modified coupon rate of .04 (for redemption in year 10) or $\frac{100(.04)}{115} = .0348$ (for redemption in years 11 or 12). The modified coupon rate is

$.0296 < .03$ for redemption in the 13th to 15th years. Thus the minimum price for redemption in the 10th year occurs at the earliest redemption date, which is at $9\frac{1}{2}$ years, and the minimum price for redemption in the 11th or 12th years also occurs at the earliest date, which is at $10\frac{1}{2}$ years. Since $g < j$ in the 13th to 15th years, the minimum price occurs at the latest date, which is at 15 years. Thus we must calculate the price of the bond for redemption at $9\frac{1}{2}$ years, $10\frac{1}{2}$ years and 15 years. The prices are 114.32, 123.48, and 134.02. The price paid will be 114.32, which corresponds to the earliest possible redemption date.

(b) (i) Since the bond is bought at a discount (to the redemption value), it is to the investor's disadvantage to have the redemption at the latest date. Thus we find the yield based on redemption dates of 10 years, 12 years and 15 years. These nominal yield rates are 11.40%, 11.75% and 11.77% The minimum yield is 11.40%.

    (ii) Since the bond is bought at a premium to the redemption value in the 10th year and in the 11th and 12th years, the minimum yield to maturity occurs at the earliest redemption date for those periods, which is $9\frac{1}{2}$ years for the 10th year and $10\frac{1}{2}$ years for the 11th and 12th years The bond is bought at a discount to the redemption amount in the 13th to 15th years, so the minimum yield occurs at the latest redemption date, which is 15 years. We find the yield based on redemption at $9\frac{1}{2}$ years, $10\frac{1}{2}$ years and 15 years. These nominal yield rates are 5.29%, 6.38% and 7.15% The minimum is 5.29%.   □

Through the latter part of the 1980's, bonds callable at the option of the issuer became less common in the marketplace. The increased competition for funds by governments and corporations during that period produced various incentives that are occasionally added to a bond issue. One such incentive is a retractable-extendible feature, which gives the bondholder the option of having the bond redeemed (retracted) on a specified date, or having the redemption date extended to a specified later date. This is similar to a callable bond with the option in the hands of the bondholder rather than the bond issuer. Another incentive is to provide warrants with the bond. A warrant gives the bondholder the option to purchase additional amounts of the bond issue at a later date at a guaranteed price.

4.3.2 SERIAL BONDS AND MAKEHAM'S FORMULA

A bond issue may consist of a collection of bonds with a variety of redemption dates, or redemption in installments. This might be done so that the bond issuer can stagger the redemption payments instead of having a single redemption date with one large redemption amount. Such an issue can be treated as a series of separate bonds, each with its own redemption date, and it is possible that the coupon rate differs for the various redemption dates. It may also be the case that purchasers will want different yield rates for the different maturity dates. Such a bond is called a *serial bond* since redemption occurs with a series of redemption payments.

Suppose that a serial bond has redemption amounts $F_1, F_2, \ldots, F_m$, to be redeemed in $n_1, n_2, \ldots, n_m$ coupon periods, respectively, and pays coupons at rates $r_1, r_2, \ldots, r_m$, respectively, Suppose also that this serial bond is purchased to yield $j_1, j_2, \ldots, j_m$, respectively, on the m pieces. Then the price of the tth piece can be formulated using any one of Equation (4.1), (4.2) or (4.3). Using Makeham's bond price formula given by Equation (4.3), the price of the tth piece is

$$P_t \;=\; K_t + \frac{r_t}{j_t}(F_t - K_t), \qquad\qquad (4.8)$$

where $K_t = F_t \cdot v_{j_t}^{n_t}$. The price of the total serial issue would be $P = \sum_{t=1}^{m} P_t$. In the special case where the coupon rates on all pieces of the serial issue are the same ($r_1 = r_2 = \cdots = r_m = r$), and the yield rates on all pieces are also the same ($j_1 = j_2 = \cdots = j_m = j$), the total price of the issue can be written in a compact form using Makeham's Formula:

$$P \;=\; \sum_{t=1}^{m} P_t \;=\; \sum_{t=1}^{m}\left[K_t + \frac{r}{j}(F_t - K_t)\right] \;=\; K + \frac{r}{j}(F - K), \qquad (4.9)$$

where $K = \sum_{t=1}^{m} K_t$ is the present value of all redemption amounts for the

entire issue, and $F = \sum_{t=1}^{m} F_t$ is the total redemption amount for the issue.

If the series of redemptions has a systematic form, such as a level amount every period for a number of periods, then K can be conveniently formulated as the present value of the annuity formed by the series of redemption amounts. Note that Equation (4.9) requires a uniform coupon rate and yield rate for all redemption dates in the issue.

EXAMPLE 4.7   (*Serial bond*)

On August 15, 2000 a corporation issues a 10% serial bond with face amount 50,000,000. The redemption is scheduled to take place at 5,000,000 every August 15 from 2010 to 2014 and 25,000,000 on August 15, 2015. Find the price of the entire issue on the issue date at a yield of $i^{(2)} = .125$.

SOLUTION

The present value of all of the redemption payments is

$$K = 5,000,000\left[v_{.0625}^{20} + v_{.0625}^{22} + v_{.0625}^{24} + v_{.0625}^{26} + v_{.0625}^{28} \right]$$
$$+ 25,000,000 \cdot v_{.0625}^{30} = 9,976,960.$$

Then the price of the serial bond is

$$P = K + \frac{r}{j}(F - K)$$

$$= 9,976,960 + \frac{.05}{.0625}(50,000,000 - 9,976,960)$$

$$= 41,995,392.$$ □

4.4 NOTES AND REFERENCES

The reference book *Standard Securities Calculation Methods*, provides a comprehensive collection of calculation and quotation methods used in financial practice. *The Handbook of Fixed Income Securities*, by F. Fabozzi covers a wide range of topics on bonds and other fixed income investments. The text by Butcher and Nesbitt details several numerical procedures for approximating yield rates, and provides additional references on the subject.

4.5 EXERCISES

The exercises without asterisks are intended to comprehensively cover the material presented in the chapter. Exercises with an asterisk can be regarded as supplementary exercises which cover topics in more depth, either theoretically or computationally, than those without an asterisk.

Unless specified otherwise, it is assumed that all coupon rates are quoted as annual rates but payable semiannually, all yield rates are nominal annual rates convertible semiannually, and bonds are valued just after a coupon has been paid.

SECTION 4.1

4.1.1   Find the prices of the following bonds, all redeemable at par. Show how to compare their prices without actually calculating the numerical values.
(a) A 10-year 100, 5% bond yielding 7.2%
(b) A 10-year 100, 5½ % bond yielding 7.7%
(c) A 12-year 100, 5% bond yielding 7.2%
(d) A 12-year 100, 5½ % bond yielding 7.7%

4.1.2   A 6% bond maturing in 8 years with semiannual coupons to yield 5% convertible semiannually is to be replaced by a 5.5% bond yielding the same return. In how many years should the new bond mature? (Both bonds have the same price, yield rate and face amount).

4.1.3   In the table in Section 4.1 excerpted from the U.S. Bureau of Public Debt, a 10-year treasury bond is listed as having been issued on January 15, 2004 and maturing on January 15, 2014. The coupon rate is 2%, the yield rate at issue is listed as 2.019%, and the price at issue is listed as 99.829. Verify that this is the correct price for this bond.

4.1.4   The *National Post* ©, a Canadian daily newspaper, has listings after each trading day of the closing prices and yields of a number of bonds that traded the previous day. In the March 2, 2004 edition, there was the following listing for a Government of Canada bond:

Coupon	Maturity Date	Bid $	Yield %
4.25	Sep 01/09	102.76	3.69

(a) Verify that this is the correct price for the bond.

(b) In this listing, the price per $100 is rounded to the nearest $.01, and the yield rate is rounded to the nearest .01%. The quoted yield rate could be any number from 3.685% to 3.695% (and would be rounded to 3.69%, we can think of 3.695% as 3.6949999%). Find the resulting prices at the two ends of that range of yield rates.

(c) The bid price of 102.76 could have been rounded from an actual price between 102.755 and 102.765. Find the yield rates that correspond to those prices (this will require the unknown interest calculator function, or bond yield function, depending upon which calculator is used).

4.1.5   An n-year 4.75% bond is selling for 95.59. An n-year 6.25% bond at the same yield would sell for 108.82. The face and redemption amount of the bond is 100. Find the yield rate.

4.1.6   Bond A has n coupons remaining at rate r_1 each, and sells to yield rate i_1 effective per coupon period. Bond B has the same face value and number of coupons remaining as Bond A, but the coupons are at rate r_2 each and the yield rate is i_2 effective per period. If $i_2 \cdot r_1 = i_1 \cdot r_2$ and $i_2 > i_1 > r_1$, which of the following statements are true?

I.   The price of Bond B exceeds the price of Bond A.

II.   The present value of Bond B's coupons on the purchase date exceeds the present value of Bond A's coupons.

III. The present value of the redemption amount for Bond B exceeds the corresponding present value for Bond A.

4.1.7   Two bonds, each of face amount 100, are offered for sale at a combined price of 240. Both bonds have the same term to maturity but the coupon rate for one is twice that of the other. The difference in price of the two bonds is 24. Prices are based on a nominal annual yield rate of 3%. Find the coupon rates of the two bonds.

4.1.8   A 5% bond with face amount 1000 is redeemable in k years and is purchased for 1300. A 4% bond with the same face amount and the same redemption date as the first bond has a purchase price of 1100. The nominal annual yield rate is the same for both bonds Find that rate.

4.1.9   A 7% bond has a price of 79.30 and a 9% bond has a price of 93.10, both per 100 of face amount. Both are redeemable in n years and have the same yield rate. Find n.

4.1.10   When a certain type of bond matures, the bondholder is subject to a tax of 25% on the amount of discount at which he bought the bond. A 1000 bond of this type has 4% *annually* paid coupons and is redeemable at par in 10 years. No tax is paid on coupons. What price should a purchaser pay to realize an effective annual yield of 5% after taxes?

4.1.11   Smith purchases a 20-year, 8%, 1000 bond with semiannual coupons. The purchase price will give a nominal annual yield to maturity, convertible semiannually, of 10%. After the 20th coupon, Smith sells the bond. At what price did he sell the bond if his actual nominal annual yield is 10%?

4.1.12   Show that Equations (4.5a) and (4.5b) are algebraically equivalent.

4.1.13 The March 2, 2004 *Wall Street Journal* provides the following quotation for a U.S. Treasury Bond that traded the previous day.

Rate	Maturity (Mo/Yr)	Asked	Ask Yield
5.25	February 29	104:18	4.93

Treasury bonds mature on the 15th day of the maturity month. Verify the bond price.

4.1.14 In the bond quotations of a financial newspaper, a quote was given for the price on February 20, 2004 of an 11% bond with face amount 100 maturing on April 1, 2023. The yield was quoted as 11.267%. Find the quoted price to the nearest .001.

4.1.15 Suppose the redemption amount C is not necessarily equal to the face amount F on a bond. Using $g = \frac{Fr}{C}$ as the *modified coupon rate*, show that Equations (4.1), (4.2) and (4.3) become

$$P \quad = \quad C \cdot v_j^n + Cg \cdot a_{\overline{n}|j}, \qquad\qquad (4.1E)$$

$$P \quad = \quad C + C(g-j) \cdot a_{\overline{n}|j}, \qquad\qquad (4.2E)$$

and

$$P \quad = \quad K + \frac{g}{j}(C-K). \qquad\qquad (4.3E)$$

Describe the relationship linking the relative sizes of P and C to the relative sizes of g and j.

4.1.16 A 1000 bond bearing coupons at annual rate 6.5%, payable semiannually, and redeemable at 1050 is bought to yield a nominal rate of 8% convertible semiannually. If the present value of the redemption amount is 210, what is the price to the nearest 10?

4.1.17 A company issues 1,000,000 in bonds. The prevailing yield rate on the bonds is 12%. The company considers having coupons at 8% and a maturity of 15 years. On second thought, the company decides on a maturity date of 20 years. What coupon rate must the bond issue have in order for the company to raise the same amount of revenue as it would have on the 15-year issue? Suppose the company issued the bonds with a maturity date of 10 years. What coupon rate is required to raise the same amount as under the other two issues?

4.1.18 A bond has face amount 100 and coupon rate 10%.

(a) Suppose the bond is purchased for 110 just after a coupon has been paid. Find the yield rate on the bond to the nearest .001% for each of $n = 2, 5, 10, 20, 30$ (the number of coupons remaining).

(b) Repeat part (a) assuming the bond was purchased for 90.

*4.1.19 You have decided to invest in two bonds. Bond X is an n-year bond with semi-annual coupons, while bond Y is an accumulation bond (zero-coupon bond), which is a bond which has no coupon payments, discussed further in Chapter 6) redeemable in $\frac{n}{2}$ years.

The desired yield rate is the same for both bonds. You also have the following information:

Bond X
- Par value is 1000.
- The ratio of the semi-annual bond rate to the desired semi-annual yield rate, $\frac{r}{i}$ is 1.03125.
- The present value of the redemption value is 381.50.

Bond Y
- Redemption value is the same as the redemption value of bond X.
- Price to yield is 647.80.

What is the price of bond X?

*4.1.20 Consider two bonds, each with face amount 1. One bond matures 6 months from now and carries one coupon of amount r_1. The other bond matures 1 year from now and carries two semiannual coupons of amount r_2 each. Both bonds have the same selling price to yield nominal annual $i^{(2)}$. Find a formulation for $i^{(2)}$ in terms of r_1, r_2 and constants.

*4.1.21 Two bonds each carry the same number of coupons, one at coupon rate r_1 and one at coupon rate r_2 per coupon period. The first bond sells at a premium of p per unit of face amount and the second sells at a discount of q per unit of face amount. If both have the same yield rate j per coupon period, express j in terms of r_1, r_2, p and q.

*4.1.22 A bond issue carries quarterly coupons of 2% of the face amount outstanding. An investor uses Makeham's Formula to evaluate the whole outstanding issue to yield an effective annual rate of 13%. Find the value of H used in the formula $P = K + H(C-K)$.

*4.1.23 A bond with face and redemption amount of 3000 with *annual* coupons is selling at an effective annual yield rate equal to twice the annual coupon rate. The present value of the coupons is equal to the present value of the redemption amount. What is the selling price?

*4.1.24 On November 1, 1999 Smith paid 1000 for a government savings bond of face amount 1000 with annual coupons of 8%, with maturity to occur on November 1, 2011. On November 1, 2005 the government issues new savings bonds with the same maturity date of November 1, 2011, but with annual coupons of 9.5% (Smith's bond will still pay 8%). The government offers Smith a cash bonus of X to be paid on the maturity date if he holds his old bond until maturity. Smith can cash in his old bond on November 1, 2005 and buy a new bond for 1000. If both options yield 9.5% from November 1, 2005 to November 1, 2011, find X.

*4.1.25 Show that if $(1+j)^t$ is approximated by $1+jt$, then the quoted price of a bond at time t, $0 \le t \le 1$, since the last coupon is the linearly-interpolated value at t between P_0 and P_1. (This is the linearly interpolated price exclusive of the accrued coupon.)

*4.1.26 Show that $P_0(1+j) - Fr = P_1$. Then assuming that $r = j$ and $P_0 = F$, show that $P_1 = F$.

*4.1.27 Suppose that a bond has semiannual coupons of amount Fr each. At six-month effective yield rate j, a continuous payment for six months equivalent to a semiannual coupon is $\bar{r} \cdot F = \dfrac{Fr}{s_{\overline{1}|j}}$.

Suppose that the quoted price at time t (where $0 \le t \le 1$ is measured since the last coupon) is redefined to be the price-plus-accrued minus $\bar{r} \cdot F \cdot \bar{s}_{\overline{t}|j}$. Show that the quoted price in part (ii) of Example 4.2 would then become exactly 100 per 100 of face amount. Show that $\bar{r} \cdot F \cdot \bar{s}_{\overline{t}|j}$ is approximately equal to $t \cdot Fr$.

*4.1.28 During the time when compound interest calculations were done by hand and with reference to interest tables, bond tables were constructed listing prices at issue (per 100 of face amount) of bonds with varying maturity dates, coupon rates and yield rates. Thus the bond price $P(n,r,j)$ is written as a function of n, r and j. Show that $P(n,r,j)$ is a linear function of r but not of n or j. Thus linear interpolation with respect to the coupon rate gives exact results, but linear interpolation with respect to the yield rate gives approximate results.

*4.1.29 Using one of the bond price formulas given by Equation (4.1), (4.2) or (4.3), find formulations for each of the following derivatives.

(a) $\frac{\partial P}{\partial r}, \frac{\partial P}{\partial j}$, and $\frac{\partial P}{\partial n}$

(b) $\frac{\partial r}{\partial P}$ and $\frac{\partial n}{\partial P}$

(c) $\frac{\partial r}{\partial n}$ and $\frac{\partial n}{\partial r}$, assuming P, F and j are fixed values.

*4.1.30 On the issue date Smith buys a 20-year 12% bond with face amount 10,000. He pays a price which gives him a yield of 9%. Ten years later, just after a coupon payment, Smith sells the bond. He is given two opinions regarding the capital gain or loss incurred in the bond transaction. The first opinion states that the capital gain or loss is the price at which it is sold less the price originally paid for the bond and; the second opinion states that the gain or loss is the sale price less the book value of the bond. The book value is taken as the price of the bond based on the original yield rate. For each opinion on the calculation of capital gain or loss, find each of the following:

(a) Smith's capital gain or loss if, at the time he sells the bond, the yield from the time of sale to maturity is (i) 6%, (ii) 9%, (iii) 12% , or (iv) 15%.

(b) Smith's capital gain or loss if his yield for the 10 years he held the bond is (i) 6%, (ii) 9%, (iii) 12%, or (iv) 15%.

*4.1.31 Suppose $0 \le t \le 1$, and P_t, the price of a bond at time t coupon periods after the previous coupon, is based on the formulation described in Exercise 4.1.27. Show that $P_t \le F, P_t = F$, and $P_t \ge F$ according as $r \le j, r = j$, and $r \ge j$, respectively. Note that Example 4.2 shows that these equivalences might not all be valid if the price-plus-accrued is used instead of the price.

*4.1.32 Find the prices of the bond in Example 4.2 using each of the following approaches.

(a) $P_t = P_0(1+j)^t - \dfrac{Fr \cdot \bar{s}_{\overline{t}|j}}{\bar{s}_{\overline{1}|j}}$ (See Exercise 4.1.27)

(b) $P_t = P_0[1 + t \cdot j] - t \cdot Fr$

*4.1.33 (a) Suppose a bond has face (and redemption) amount F, coupon rate r per coupon period, and n coupons remaining until maturity. If the bond is purchased one period before the next coupon with a yield rate of j per coupon period, and if we define the quantity $G = \dfrac{Fr}{j}$, show that the purchase price can be written as $P = G + (F - G) \cdot v_j^n$.

(b) If the redemption amount for this bond is C, show that the purchase price is $P = G + (C - G) \cdot v_j^n$.

*4.1.34 Let $n \ge 1$, $0 \le t \le 1$, and $g(j) = [F \cdot v_j^n + Fr \cdot a_{\overline{n}|j}](1+j)^t$.

(a) Show that $g(j)$ is strictly decreasing and convex (i.e.,

$$g'(j) < 0 \text{ and } g''(j) > 0).$$

(b) Show that $\lim_{j \to -1} g(j) = +\infty$ and $\lim_{j \to \infty} g(j) = 0$.

(c) Use parts (a) and (b) to show that if $P > 0$ the equation

$$P = [F \cdot v_j^n + Fr \cdot a_{\overline{n}|j}](1+j)^t$$

has a unique solution for j.

*4.1.35 Bonds A and B have the same face value and the same number of coupons remaining. Bond A has a coupon rate of r_1 per coupon period and Bond B has a coupon rate of r_2 per coupon period. Their prices are P_1 and P_2, respectively, at the same yield rate. Bond C has the same face value, the same number of coupons, and the same yield rate as the first two bonds, but Bond C has a coupon rate of r_3 per coupon period. Express the exact price of Bond C in terms of P_1, P_2, r_1, r_2, and r_3.

*4.1.36 It was pointed out in Section 3.1.2 that when a loan is amortized with n equally spaced (but not necessarily level) payments, the interest rate per period on the loan is $i = \dfrac{I_T}{OB_0 + OB_1 + \cdots + OB_{n-1}}$.

The coupons and redemption payments of a bond can be regarded as payments on a loan amortized at the yield rate. The total interest paid over the lifetime of a loan is the total amount of the payments minus the amount of the original loan. Then, in the case of a bond with n coupons remaining and valued just after a coupon has been paid, the total interest paid over the lifetime of the bond is $n \cdot Fr + C - P$, where the coupons plus redemption represent loan payments, and the price represents the loan amount. The initial outstanding balance is $OB_0 = P$, and the outstanding balance decreases or increases to C at time n, when the redemption amount is paid.

(a) Assuming that the average OB_t is, approximately $\dfrac{P+C}{2}$, show that an approximation to the yield rate is

$$ j = \frac{r - \dfrac{P-C}{n \cdot C}}{1 + \dfrac{P-C}{2C}}. \qquad (4.15a) $$

This approximation is called the *bond salesman's formula*.

(b) Suppose OB_t changes linearly from $OB_0 = P$ to $OB_n = C$. Show that under this approximation $OB_t = P - t \cdot \dfrac{P-C}{n}$, and

$$j \approx \frac{r - \dfrac{P-C}{n \cdot C}}{1 + \dfrac{(n+1) \cdot (P-C)}{2 \cdot n \cdot C}}. \tag{4.15b}$$

(c) Apply the formulas in parts (a) and (b) to obtain approximations of the yield rate for the bond described in part (a) of Example 4.3.

*4.1.37 (a) Calculate the Taylor polynomial of degree 1 of $\frac{1}{a_{\overline{n}|j}}$, use it in the relationship $j = r - \frac{P-F}{F \cdot a_{\overline{n}|j}}$, and solve for j. This results in the same approximation found in part (b) of Exercise 4.1.36.

(b) Repeat part (a) with the Taylor polynomial of degree 2. Use this to find the approximate yield rate for the bonds in Exercise 4.1.18.

SECTION 4.2

4.2.1 Graph OB_k for each of the three cases in Example 4.4.

(a) Show that for a bond bought at a premium, the graph of OB_k is concave downward.

(b) Show that for a bond bought at a discount, the graph of OB_k is convex upward.

4.2.2 A 10% bond has face amount 10,000. For each combination of the following number of coupon periods and six-month yield rates, use a computer spreadsheet program to construct the amortization table and draw the graph of OB_k: $n = 1, 5, 10, 30$; $j = .025, .05, .075$.

4.2.3 Find the total amount paid, the total interest and the total principal repaid in the amortization of Table 4.3.

4.2.4   The amortization schedule for a 100, 5% bond with semi-annual coupons yielding a nominal annual rate of $i^{(2)} = 6.6\%$ gives a value of 90.00 for the bond at the beginning of a certain 6-month period just after a coupon has been paid. What is the book value at the start of the next 6-month period?

4.2.5   A bond of face amount 100 is purchased at a premium of 36 to yield 7%. The amount for amortization of premium in the 5th coupon is 1.00. What is the term of the bond?

4.2.6   A bondholder is subject to a tax of 50% on interest payments at the time interest is received, and a tax (or credit) of 25% on capital gains (or losses) when they are realized. Assume that the capital gain (or loss) on the bond is the difference between the purchase price and the sale price (or redemption amount if held to maturity), and the full amount of each coupon is regarded as interest. For each of the cases in Example 4.4, find the bond's purchase price so that the stated yield is the *after-tax* yield (based on the bond being held to maturity).

4.2.7   Among a company's assets and accounting records, an actuary finds a 15-year bond that was purchased at a premium. From the records, the actuary has determined the following:

(i) The bond pays semi-annual interest.

(ii) The amount for amortization of the premium in the 2nd coupon payment was 977.19 .

(iii) The amount for amortization of the premium in the 4th coupon payment was 1046.79.

What is the value of the premium?

*4.2.8 Using Table 4.3, show that the bond payments can be regarded as payments on two separate loans. The first loan is of amount F with interest only at rate j (per coupon period) for n periods, plus return of F at the end of n periods. The second loan is an amortization of $P - F$ over n periods at effective rate j (per coupon period), with payments of $F(r-j)$ per coupon period. This second loan is the amortization of premium if $P > F$.

*4.2.9 Suppose the redemption amount on a bond is C, not necessarily equal to the face amount F. Construct the bond's amortization table in the form of Table 4.3.

*4.2.10 A 30-year bond with face amount 10,000 is bought to yield $i^{(2)} = .08$. In each of the following cases find the purchase price of the bond and the bond's coupon rate.

(a) The final entry in the amortization schedule for accumulation of discount is 80.

(b) The final entry in the amortization schedule for amortization of premium is 80.

(c) The first entry in the amortization schedule for accumulation of discount is 80.

(d) The first entry in the amortization schedule for amortization of premium is 80.

(e) The final entry in the schedule for interest due is 500.

(f) The final entry in the schedule for interest due is 400.

(g) The final entry in the schedule for interest due is 300.

(h) The first entry in the schedule for interest due is 500.

(i) The first entry in the schedule for interest due is 400.

(j) The first entry in the schedule for interest due is 300.

SECTION 4.3

4.3.1 An 8% serial bond of face amount 2,000,000 issued June 15, 2000 is to be redeemed by 10 semiannual installments of 100,000 each starting June 15, 2005, followed by 5 semiannual installments of 200,000 each starting June 15, 2010. Find the price of the entire issue to yield $i^{(2)} = .10$.

4.3.2   A 100,000,000 serial bond issued June 1, 1986 carries a semiannual coupon rate of 8%. The redemption of the bond takes place over a 30-year period, with redemptions of 10,000,000 made every 3 years, starting on June 1, 1989. What is the price of this bond to yield $i^{(2)} = .10$?

4.3.3   An *annuity bond* has level payments (coupon plus redemption) every coupon period. Thus it is a serial bond, but the redemption amounts decrease every period. A 10-year 10% annuity bond with face amount 100,000 has semiannual payments of $\dfrac{100,000}{a_{\overline{20}|.05}}$, of which some would be coupon payment and some would be redemption payment. A purchaser wishes a yield of $i^{(2)} = .12$. Find the price of the bond and construct the amortization schedule for the first 2 years.

4.3.4   (a) Suppose that the redemption amounts are $C_1, C_2, \ldots, C_m$ (not necessarily equal to $F_1, F_2, \ldots, F_m$). Show that if $\dfrac{r \cdot F_t}{C_t} = g$ for all $t = 1, 2, \ldots, m$, then the price can be written as $P = K + \dfrac{g}{j}(C - K)$, where K is the present value of the redemption amounts at yield rate j.

(b) Suppose $\dfrac{r \cdot F_t}{C_t} \neq g$ for all t. Let each C_t be written as $C_t = C_t' + C_t''$, where $\dfrac{r \cdot F_t}{C_t'} = g$ for each t. Show that P can now be written as $P = K + \dfrac{g}{j}(C' - K')$, where K is, as before, the present value of the full redemption amounts, and $C' = \displaystyle\sum_{t=1}^{m} C_t'$ and $K' = \displaystyle\sum_{t=1}^{m} C_t' \cdot v_j^{n_t}$.

(c) Now suppose that each C_t' is taken so that $\dfrac{r \cdot F_t}{C_t'} = j$. Show that $P = C' + K - K'$ (see Exercise 4.1.33).

4.3.5   A 10% bond with face amount 100 is callable on any coupon date from 15½ years after issue up to the maturity date which is 20 years from issue.

(a)   Find the price of the bond to yield a minimum nominal annual rate of (i) 12%, (ii) 10%, and (iii) 8%.

(b)   Find the minimum annual yield to maturity if the bond is purchased for (i) 80, (ii) 100, and (iii) 120.

4.3.6   Repeat Exercise 4.3.5 assuming that the bond is callable at a redemption amount of 110, including the redemption at maturity.

4.3.7   On June 15, 2005 a corporation issues an 8% bond with a face value of 1,000,000. The bond can be redeemed, at the option of the corporation, on any coupon date in 2016 or 2017 at par, on any coupon date in 2018 through 2020 for amount 1,200,000, or on any coupon date in 2021 through June 15, 2023 at redemption amount 1,300,000.

(a)   Find the price to yield a minimum nominal annual rate of (i) 10% and (ii) 6½%.

(b)   Find the minimum nominal annual yield if the bond is bought for (i) 800,000, (ii) 1,000,000, or (iii) 1,200,000.

CHAPTER 5

MEASURING THE RATE OF RETURN
OF AN INVESTMENT

In the previous chapters we have looked at valuing various series of cashflows, such as general annuities in Chapter 2, loans in Chapter 3, and coupon bonds in Chapter 4. The inverse relationship between valuation interest rate and present value should be clear from the examples of previous chapters. From general reasoning, it seems that when calculating the present value of a series of cashflows, the interest rate used for valuation can be thought of as a "rate of return" by either party in the transaction (the purchaser and the seller of the series of cashflows).

In many circumstances, the valuation rate at which a present value is calculated can be a meaningful measure of the rate of return earned by the lender or paid by the borrower, and can be used to determine a preference for one transaction over another. For example, suppose that an investor has $100,000 available with which to purchase a 20-year annual payment annuity-immediate. Financial Institution A offers annual payments of $8,024.26, and Financial Institution B offers payments of $8,718.46. The investor would choose Financial Institution B, which offers a larger annual payment. We can find the effective annual interest rate for each of the two annuities by solving for i in the equation $100,000 = K a_{\overline{20}|i}$, where K is the payment amount. The interest rates are 5% for Institution A and 6% for Institution B, and we see that the investor has chosen the annuity that has the higher interest rate. This interest rate may be referred to as the "yield rate" on the transaction, but more likely it would be referred to as the **internal rate of return** on the transaction.

5.1   INTERNAL RATE OF RETURN AND NET PRESENT VALUE

5.1.1 THE INTERNAL RATE OF RETURN ON A TRANSACTION

A general financial transaction involves a number of amounts invested or paid out at various points in time as well as a number of payments received. The internal rate of return (**IRR**) for the transaction is the interest rate at which the value of all amounts invested is equal to the value of payments received. As will be seen below, any valuation point can be used in setting up an equation of value to solve for an internal rate of return on a transaction, although there will usually be some natural valuation point, such as the starting date or the ending date of the transaction. The yield-to-maturity for coupon bonds presented in Chapter 4 is the internal rate of return for the bond purchase transaction, because it is the rate at which the price paid for the bond is equal to the present value of the coupon and redemption payments to be received.

Example 2.24 of Section 2.3 presents some properties of the internal rate of return on a transaction. The following is a summary of the properties presented there.

Suppose that a transaction consists of a single amount invested, say $L > 0$, at time 0, and several future payments to be received, say $K_1, K_2, \ldots, K_n$ at times $1, 2, \ldots, n$, with each $K_j > 0$. Then for the equation of value

$$L = K_1 \cdot \frac{1}{1+i} + K_2 \cdot \frac{1}{(1+i)^2} + \cdots + K_n \cdot \frac{1}{(1+i)^n}, \text{ there is only one solution for } i$$

that satisfies $i > -100\%$. If $L < \sum_{j=1}^{n} K_j$, then this unique solution is positive, $i > 0$. For instance, with the annuity-immediate from Institution B described at the start of this chapter, the amount invested is $L = 100,000$, there are $n = 20$ payments received, and the total amount received is

$$\sum_{j=1}^{n} K_j = 20 \times 8,718.46 = 174,369.20 > 100,000 = L. \text{ It follows that}$$

there is a unique positive solution for i to the equation $100,000 = 8,718.46 a_{\overline{20}|i}$ (that solution is $i = .06$).

It is possible to extend this notion of IRR to more complex transactions. Let us consider the situation in which there are payments received of amounts

$A_0, A_1, A_2, \ldots, A_n$ at times $0 = t_0 < t_1 < t_2 < \cdots < t_n$, and disbursements (payments made out) of amounts $B_0, B_1, B_2, \ldots, B_n$ at the same points in time, where all $A_j \geq 0$ and all $B_j \geq 0$. The net amount received at time k is $C_k = A_k - B_k$, which can be positive or negative. If a payment of B_j is disbursed at time t_j but there is no payment received at that time, then $A_j = 0$. Conversely, if there is a payment received of A_k at time t_k but no payment disbursed at that time, then $B_k = 0$. In the context of the annuity example presented at the start of this chapter, from the point of view of Institution B selling the annuity, $A_0 = 100,000$ (the company receives the 100,000 from the purchaser of the annuity) and

$$A_1 = A_2 = \cdots = A_n = 0; \ B_0 = 0$$

and

$$B_1 = B_2 = \cdots = B_{20} = 8,718.46,$$

(these are the annuity payments made by the company); the net amounts received by the company are

$$C_0 = 100,000$$

and

$$C_1 = C_2 = \cdots = C_{20} = -8,718.46.$$

In general we wish to find the compound interest rate i for which the value of the series of disbursement cashflows is equal to the value of the series of receipt cashflows, at any point in time. The equation of value at time 0 for this general situation is

$$A_0 + A_1 \cdot v^{t_1} + A_2 \cdot v^{t_2} + \cdots + A_n \cdot v^{t_n}$$
$$= B_0 + B_1 \cdot v^{t_1} + B_2 \cdot v^{t_2} + \cdots + B_n \cdot v^{t_n}, \qquad (5.1a)$$

or, equivalently,

$$\sum_{k=0}^{n} C_k \cdot v^{t_k} = 0. \qquad (5.1b)$$

Recall that as long as compound interest is in effect, the equation of value can be set up at any time point t, and the value(s) of i for which the equation holds would be the same. For instance, the equation of value set up at time t_n is

$$C_0(1+i)^{t_n} + C_1(1+i)^{t_n-t_1} + \cdots + C_{n-1}(1+i)^{t_n-t_{n-1}} + C_n$$

$$= \sum_{k=0}^{n} C_k(1+i)^{t_n-t_k} = 0. \qquad (5.2)$$

The definition of an **internal rate of return** on a transaction is that it is a solution for i in Equation 5.2 (or equivalently, in Equation 5.1). The strict definition of the internal rate of return does not depend on any reinvestment options that might be available during the transaction. It can be seen, however, from Equation (5.2) that the interpretation of i as the periodic yield rate for the entire transaction is equivalent to an implicit assumption that all amounts are reinvested at rate i at all times during the transaction. (Section 2.4 of Chapter 2 considered situations in which amounts received were reinvested at interest rates other than the original yield or valuation rate.)

For instance, one interpretation that the yield rate (or rate of return) earned by the annuitant is 6% for the 20-year period of the annuity from Institution B described at the start of this chapter is that the invested amount of $100,000 should grow to $100,000(1.06)^{20} = 320,713.55$ at the end of 20 years. In order for this to occur, as each annuity payment is received it must be reinvested into an account earning 6% per year, so that at the end of 20 years the accumulated value of the reinvested deposits is $8,718.46 s_{\overline{20}|.06} = 320,714.$

| **EXAMPLE 5.1** | (*Internal rate of return*) |

Smith buys 1000 shares of stock at 5.00 per share and pays a commission of 2%. Six months later he receives a cash dividend of .20 per share, which he immediately reinvests commission-free in shares at a price of 4.00 per share. Six months after that he buys another 500 shares at a price of 4.50 per share, along with a commission of 2%. Six months after that he receives another cash dividend of .25 per share and sells his existing shares at 5.00 per share, again paying a 2% commission. Find Smith's internal rate of return for the entire transaction in the form $i^{(2)}$.

| **SOLUTION** |

Let time 0 represent the time of the original share purchase. Then $A_0 = 0$ and $B_0 = 5100,$ the initial outlay including commission. Measuring time in 6-

month intervals, we have $t=1$ at 6 months with $A_1 = 200$ and $B_1 = 200$, since he receives and immediately reinvests the dividend of 200, buying an additional 50 shares. Then $t=2$ is at 12 months with $A_2 = 0$ and $B_2 = 2295$ (buying an additional 500 shares for a total of 1550 shares), and $t=3$ is at 18 months with $A_3 = 387.50 + 7595 = 7982.50$ (the dividend on 1550 shares plus the proceeds from the sale of the shares after commission) and $B_3 = 0$. The net amounts received are $C_0 = -5100$, $C_1 = 0$, $C_2 = -2295$, and $C_3 = 7982.5$, so we wish to solve the equation, $-5100 - 2295 \cdot v^2 + 7982.5 \cdot v^3 = 0$, or, equivalently,

$$f(j) = 5100(1+j)^3 + 2295(1+j) - 7982.5 = 0,$$

where the v and j factors are based on 6-month interest rates so that $i^{(2)} = 2j$. Using a financial calculator with multiple cashflow capability such as the TI BA II PLUS or the HP-12C, the unknown interest rate is found to be $j = 3.246\%$, or equivalently, $i^{(2)} = 6.49\%$. □

Note that the transaction in Example 5.1 has a unique positive solution for j, the effective 6-month internal rate of return. This is true because the function $f(j)$ is a strictly increasing function of j and $f(0) < 0$ and $\lim_{j \to \infty} f(j) = \infty$, and therefore there is a unique $j > 0$ that solves the equation $f(j) = 0$. The internal rate of return on a transaction can be a meaningful measure when comparing the relative advantages of two or more financial transactions. The following section considers in more detail the complications that can arise when finding and interpreting an internal rate of return for a transaction.

5.1.2 UNIQUENESS OF THE INTERNAL RATE OF RETURN

The transaction in Example 5.1 has a unique positive solution for the internal rate of return. As mentioned above, we saw in Example 2.24 that for certain financial transactions there is a unique solution for internal rate of return that is greater than -100%. It is possible in a more general situation that there are no real solutions for the internal rate of return, or that there are several real solutions all of which are greater than -100%. The following example illustrates this.

EXAMPLE 5.2 (*Internal rate of return*)

Smith has a line of credit account that allows him to make withdrawals from or payments to the account at any time. The balance may be negative, indicating the amount that he owes to the account, or positive, indicating the amount the account owes him. Balances in the account, whether positive or negative, earn interest at rate i per period. Solve for i for each of the following sets of transactions on Smith's line of credit. Assume the line of credit was opened at time 0 and was closed with a balance of zero just after time 2, and that the A's are withdrawals from the line of credit, and the B's are payments to the line of credit. Thus the payment of B_2 made to the line of credit clears the outstanding balance on the account.

(a) $t_1 = 1, t_2 = 2, A_0 = 0, A_1 = 2.3, A_2 = 0, B_0 = 1, B_1 = 0, B_2 = 1.33$

(b) $t_1 = 1, t_2 = 2, A_0 = 0, A_1 = 2.3, A_2 = 0, B_0 = 1, B_1 = 0, B_2 = 1.32$

(c) $t_1 = 1, t_2 = 2, A_0 = 0, A_1 = 2.3, A_2 = 0, B_0 = 1, B_1 = 0, B_2 = 1.3125$

(d) $t_1 = 1, t_2 = 2, A_0 = 0, A_1 = 2.3, A_2 = 0, B_0 = 1, B_1 = 0, B_2 = 1.2825$

SOLUTION

(a) The C_k are $C_0 = -1, C_1 = 2.3$, and $C_2 = -1.33$, so that the equation of value at time 0 is $-1 + 2.3 \cdot v - 1.33 \cdot v^2 = 0$. Solving this quadratic equation produces only imaginary roots for v, and thus no real roots for i.

(b) The C_k are $C_0 = -1, C_1 = 2.3$, and $C_2 = -1.32$, The equation of value at time 2 (remember that it can be set up at any point of time) is $-(1+i)^2 + 2.3(1+i) - 1.32 = 0$, which is a quadratic equation in $1+i$. Solving the quadratic results in $i = .1$ or $.2$, so both interest rates of 10% and 20% are solutions.

(c) The C_k are $C_0 = -1, C_1 = 2.3, C_2 = -1.3125$. The equation of value at time 2 is $-(1+i)^2 + 2.3(1+i) - 1.3125 = 0$, producing $i = .05$ or $.25$.

(d) The C_k are $C_0 = -1, C_1 = 2.3, C_2 = -1.2825$. The equation of value at time 2 is $-(1+i)^2 + 2.3(1+i) - 1.2825 = 0$, so that $i = -.05$ or $.35$. ☐

For the simple annuity transaction discussed at the start of this section, it was possible to do a meaningful comparison of the two annuities by comparing their internal rates of return. The situations described in Example 5.2 illustrate the difficulties that can arise when solving for an internal rate of return on a transaction, and the limitations that occur when using only the IRR as a measure of the relative performance of an investment. Since C_0 and C_1 are the same for all four transactions, it is easy to compare the transactions by comparing the C_2 values. We see that transaction (a) has the largest payment to pay off the line of credit at time 2, with the final payment getting progressively smaller as we consider (b), (c), and (d). Therefore to minimize his cost in repaying the line of credit, Smith would prefer (d), although this is not readily apparent by comparing the internal rates of return. (Note that (a) does not even have an internal rate of return to use for comparison purposes.) Later in this section we will consider alternative methods for measuring the return on a financial transaction and for comparing financial transactions.

Financial transactions that have a unique internal rate of return greater than -100% can be compared in a meaningful way by comparing their internal rates of return. It is therefore useful to be able to identify conditions on a financial transaction that imply a unique internal rate of return greater than -100%. We continue to describe a financial transaction using the cashflow series $C_0, C_1, \ldots, C_n$, where C_t denotes the net amount received at time t (positive for cash inflow and negative for cash outflow). It is possible to formulate conditions on the C_k that guarantee a unique $i > -1$.

Example 2.24 illustrates one basic, but common situation in which there is a unique internal rate of return. If $C_0 > 0$ and $C_k < 0$ for $k = 1, 2, \ldots, n$, then there is a unique internal rate of return that is greater than -100%. Furthermore, if $\sum_{k=0}^{n} C_k < 0$ then the unique internal rate of return is strictly positive. The typical transactions that correspond to this situation are loans of a single amount repaid by one or more payments in the future, or annuity purchases in which the purchase is made with a single payment and is followed by annuity payments in the future. Additional conditions that result in a unique internal rate of return are considered in Exercise 5.1.7.

In practice, the terms of most financial transactions result in a unique internal rate of return. However, as pointed out with Example 5.2, problems can arise when solving for the internal rate(s) on a transaction. It is not possible to compare the relative merits of two transactions on the basis of internal rate alone if one of the transactions does not have a real-valued internal rate. Even if each of two transactions has a unique internal rate, it may not be the case that a comparison of those rates is sufficient to decide which transaction is preferable (see Exercise 5.1.5).

5.1.3 PROJECT EVALUATION USING NET PRESENT VALUE

An alternative way of comparing transactions is by means of **net present value** (NPV). Suppose that an individual is trying to choose between two possible cashflow series. Assume the two cashflow series being considered have the same level of risk associated with them. It can be postulated that at a particular point in time (labeled time 0), each individual has an interest rate i (sometimes called the individual's **interest preference rate**) that is the appropriate interest rate for valuing (discounting) the two series of cashflows. The net present value at a particular point in time (labeled time 0) of each cashflow series is simply the present value of the series of payments, both positive (cash inflow) and negative (cash outflow) using the interest rate i described above. To compare two transactions whose net cashflow vectors are $\mathbf{C} = (C_0, C_1, \ldots, C_n)$ and $\mathbf{C}' = (C_0', C_1', \ldots, C_n')$, we compare

$$P_i(\mathbf{C}) = \sum_{k=0}^{n} C_k \cdot v_i^{t_k} \text{ with } P_i(\mathbf{C}') = \sum_{k=0}^{n} C_k' \cdot v_i^{t_k}.$$ The cashflow vector whose present value is larger is preferable.

Note that in the transactions of Example 5.2, for any interest preference rate that exceeds -1, we have $P_i(C_a) < P_i(C_b) < P_i(C_c) < P_i(C_d)$ (see Exercise 5.1.2). The same is true for the two annuities considered at the start of this section. Exercise 5.1.5 provides an example of two transactions for which one is preferable at certain interest preference rates, and the other is preferable at other interest preference rates.

The approach described above is a commonly used method in capital budgeting; it is also called the **net present value method** and the interest rate used for discounting cash flows may be referred to as the *cost of capital*. A simple criterion that is used to determine whether or not an investment project is acceptable is based on the sign of the NPV. A positive NPV indicates that the investment will be profitable, while a negative NPV indicates that it will not be profitable. Note that the IRR is the interest rate for which the NPV is 0. Figure 5.1 shows the graphs of the NPV's of the four cases considered in Example 5.2.

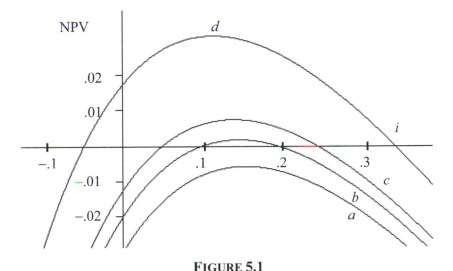

FIGURE 5.1

Example 5.2 was constructed to highlight some anomalous behavior that can occur when considering IRR and NPV. For instance, it may be difficult to interpret why 5.2(b) should be rejected due to negative NPV when the valuation rate i is either less than 10% or greater than 20%. IRR and NPV are the most commonly used methods for evaluating financial projects, but there are other methods than can be applied as well.

5.1.4 ALTERNATIVE METHODS OF VALUING INVESTMENT RETURNS

Capital budgeting refers to the process in financial management whereby criteria are set for evaluating alternative investment opportunities. Comparing investments via their internal rates of return or via their net present values are two of several standard capital budgeting methods. Example 5.2 and the comments following it point out the limitations of the internal rate of return to evaluate investments.

The internal rate of return and the net present value are two examples of *discounted cash-flow procedures.* There are a number of project appraisal methods that make use of the "cost of capital," which can be regarded as the cost of borrowing to fund a project. We now present a few more project appraisal methods.

Profitability Index:

At a specified rate of interest i (cost of capital), calculate the ratio

$$I = \frac{present\ value\ of\ cash\ inflows}{present\ value\ of\ outflows},$$

where each present value is calculated at the beginning of the project. This ratio is an index measuring the return per dollar of investment. This method is often used when the "outflow" is a single amount invested at time 0 and the "inflow" is a series of payments to be received in the future. As a simple illustration, suppose that an investment of 1,000 can be made into one of two projects. The first project will generate income of 250 per year for 5 years starting in one year, and the second project will generate income of 140 per year for 10 years. If the cost of capital is $i = 5\%$ then the profitability indexes for the two projects are:

Project 1: $I = \dfrac{250a_{\overline{5}|.05}}{1000} = 1.0824$ and Project 2: $I = \dfrac{140a_{\overline{10}|.05}}{1000} = 1.0810.$

Project 1 would be preferable to Project 2 since it has a higher profitability index. Note that the preference may reverse if the cost of capital is changed. For example, with a cost of capital of 4%, Project 2 will have a higher profitability index than Project 1.

Note that if the internal rate of return is used to find the present value, then $I = 1$, because then the present value of cash inflows is equal to the present value of cash outflows.

Payback Period

If the investment consists of a series of cash outflows followed by a series of cash inflows $(C_0, C_1, C_2, \ldots, C_t < 0$ and $C_{t+1}, C_{t+2}, \ldots, C_n > 0)$ the payback period is the number of years required to recover the original amounts invested. Thus the first k for which $-\sum_{s=0}^{t} C_s \le \sum_{r=t+1}^{k} C_r$ is the payback period.

In the two project example considered under the Profitability Index method, we see that for Project 1 we have $C_0 = -1000$ and $C_1 = \cdots = C_5 = 250$, and the payback period is 4 years (the 1000 is paid back after 4 payments of 250). For Project 2 the payback period is just over 7 years.

A variation on this method is the *discounted payback period* method, which incorporates a cost of capital i. In that case, the payback period is the first k for which

$$-\sum_{s=1}^{t} C_s \, v_i^s \;\leq\; \sum_{r=t+1}^{k} C_r \cdot v_i^r \,.$$

For Project 1, we have $t = 0$. If the cost of capital is $i = .05$ and $k = 4$ we have

$$-\sum_{s=0}^{t} C_s v^s \;=\; -C_0 \;=\; 1000$$

and

$$\sum_{r=t+1}^{k} C_r \cdot v^{k-r} \;=\; \sum_{r=1}^{4} C_r \cdot v^r \;=\; 250 a_{\overline{4}|.05} \;=\; 886.49,$$

but for $k = 5$ we have

$$\sum_{r=t+1}^{k} C_r \cdot v^r \;=\; \sum_{r=1}^{5} C_r \cdot v^r \;=\; 250 a_{\overline{5}|.05} \;=\; 1082.37,$$

Therefore, discounted payback occurs sometime during the 5th year.

Modified Internal Rate of Return (MIRR)

Calculation of the MIRR uses a cost of capital rate i. To find the MIRR, say j, we formulate two accumulated values at the time the project ends. The first is the accumulated value of all payments made, accumulated at the (unknown) MIRR j. The second is the accumulated value of all payments received, accumulated at the cost of capital i. We set the two accumulated values equal and solve for j. The rationale behind this method is that payments received will be reinvested and the return on these reinvested amounts should be at least the cost of capital (note that if we assume that the reinvestment is at rate j instead of rate i, the solution would give us the original IRR). For Project 1 with a single payment made of 1000 and 5 annual payments received of 250 starting one year from now, and with a cost of capital of $i = 5\%$, , the MIRR equation is

$$1000(1+j)^5 \;=\; 250 s_{\overline{5}|.05} \;=\; 1381.41,$$

from which we get $j = 6.68\%$

Project Return Rate and Project Financing Rate

During the course of a project with cash inflows and outflows, at some points in time the investor may be a "net borrower" with money being owed by the investor at that time, and at other times the investor may be a "net lender" with a positive balance invested at that time. Suppose that the cost of borrowing, the *project financing rate*, is i during the period of time that the investor is a net borrower. Suppose that the return on the investment, the *project return rate*, is j during the period of time the investor is a net lender. If the net value of the project is set to 0 at the time of completion of the project, it is possible to establish an algebraic relationship between i and j. Solving for j from i would give a minimum project return needed for the project to break even at the time of completion. This approach is only meaningful if there are both times at which the investor is in a net lending position and times at which the investor is in a net borrowing position. For projects in which the investor is always in the net lending position until the project completion, the IRR is unique and a meaningful measure of investment return.

Part (a) of Example 5.2 can be used as an illustration. Suppose that we assume a project financing rate of i. Let us suppose that at time 0 the investor is in a net lender position with an amount of 1 invested. At time 1 the value of the investment is $1 + j$, since the project return rate has been earned during the time the investor is in a lender position. At time 1, the investor receives 2.3 from his line of credit and is in a net borrower position with amount owing $1 + j - 2.3$. At time 2, this amount owing is $(j - 1.3)(1 + i)$. The investor returns to a breakeven position by investing 1.33 at time 2. The investor's net position at time 2 can be expressed as $(j-1.3)(1+i) + 1.33 = 0$. Solving for j results in $j = 1.3 - \frac{1.33}{1+i}$. We can see that as the project financing rate i increases, the project return rate needed for a breakeven position increases as well.

5.2 DOLLAR-WEIGHTED AND TIME-WEIGHTED RATE OF RETURN

Managers of investment funds often report the return or yield of a fund on an annual basis. There are two standard methods for measuring the annual return on a fund that are adaptations of concepts that have already been developed.

5.2.1 DOLLAR-WEIGHTED RATE OF RETURN

The **dollar-weighted rate of return** is the internal rate of return for the fund, but in practice the equation of value is based on simple interest applied from each transaction point (deposit/withdrawal) to the year-end for which the rate is being measured. In this section, when dollar-weighted return is referenced, it will be assumed that we are referring to the simple interest form just mentioned.

To find the dollar-weighted rate of return on a fund over the course of a year, the following information is needed:

(i)   the amount in the fund at the start of the year,

(ii) the amounts and times of all deposits to, and withdrawals from the fund during the year, and

(iii) the amount in the fund at the end of the year.

An equation of value is created in the following form:

Amount of initial fund balance plus all deposit amounts accumulated to the end of the year with simple interest

–   amount of all withdrawals from the fund accumulated to the end of the year with simple interest

=   fund balance at the end of the year (after all deposits/withdrawals have taken place).

If all times and amounts of deposits and withdrawals are known, along with the initial fund balance and the final fund balance, then it is a simple matter to solve for the interest rate that makes the equation valid. That interest rate is the dollar-weighted return for the year. Note that this equation of value is the same one we would use to solve for the internal rate of return, but for IRR we would use compound interest instead of simple interest. For periods of less than a year, the difference between compound and simple interest in the dollar-weighted equation will not usually be large.

The following example illustrates how to find the dollar weighted rate of return.

EXAMPLE 5.3   (*Dollar-weighted return*)

A pension fund receives contributions and pays benefits from time to time. The fund began the year 2005 with a balance of $1,000,000. There were contributions to the fund of $200,000 at the end of February and again at the end of August. There was a benefit of $500,000 paid out of the fund at the end of October. The balance remaining in the fund at the start of the year 2006 was $1,100,000.

Find the dollar-weighted return on the fund, assuming each month is $\frac{1}{12}$ of a year.

SOLUTION

We will denote by i the dollar-weighted return. The equation of value for the dollar-weighted return is

$$1,000,000(1+i) + 200,000\left(1+\frac{10}{12}i\right)$$

$$+200,000\left(1+\frac{4}{12}i\right) - 500,000\left(1+\frac{2}{12}i\right) = 1,100,000.$$

The initial balance of 1,000,000 earns interest for a full year. For the deposit of 200,000 at the end of February, we have applied simple interest for the 10 months remaining until the end of the year. Similar comments apply to the other deposit and the withdrawal. Solving for i results in

$$i = \frac{1,100,000 + 500,000 - 1,000,000 - 200,000 - 200,000}{1,000,000 + 200,000\left(\frac{10}{12}\right) + 200,000\left(\frac{4}{12}\right) - 500,000\left(\frac{2}{12}\right)}$$

$$= \frac{200,000}{1,150,000} = .1739.$$

Note that the amount 200,000 in the numerator is the net amount of interest earned during the year. It is the net amount by which the account increased after accounting for deposits and withdrawals. The account started at 1,000,000, there was a net withdrawal during the year of 100,000, but the balance at the end of the year had risen by 100,000 from the balance at the start of the year. Therefore, 200,000 must have been investment (or interest) income added to the account. The denominator is the "average amount on deposit during the year." The initial balance is "on deposit for the full year," the deposit of 200,000 at the end of February is on deposit for the remaining $\frac{10}{12}$ of the year (10 months), and the deposit of 200,000 at the end of August is on deposit for the remaining $\frac{4}{12}$ of the year (4 months). Withdrawals reduce the average balance on deposit during the year; so the 500,000 withdrawal made at the end of October reduces the average balance on deposit for the remaining $\frac{2}{12}$ of the year. □

We see from Example 5.3 that the dollar-weighted return can be described as

$$\frac{total\ amount\ of\ interest\ earned\ during\ the\ year}{average\ amount\ on\ deposit\ for\ the\ year}.$$

In general, suppose the following information is known:

(i) the balance in the fund at the start of the year is A,

(ii) for $0 < t_1 < t_2 < \cdots < t_n < 1$, the net deposit at time t_k is amount C_k (positive for a net deposit, negative for a net withdrawal), and

(iii) the balance in the fund at the end of the year is B.

Then the net amount of interest earned by the fund during the year is

$$I = B - \left[A + \sum_{k=1}^{n} C_k \right],$$ and the dollar-weighted rate of interest earned by

the fund for the year is $\dfrac{I}{A + \sum_{k=1}^{n} C_k (1 - t_k)}$.

An approximation to this dollar-weighted rate of return can be found by assuming that the total net deposits/withdrawals are uniformly spread throughout the year, and are approximated as occurring at mid-year. The total net deposit/withdrawal for the year is still $C = \sum_{k=1}^{n} C_k$, and the approximate dollar-weighted return is $\dfrac{I}{A + \frac{1}{2}C}$. Using this approximation, the dollar-weighted rate of return in Example 5.3 becomes

$$\frac{200,000}{1,000,000+\frac{1}{2}(-100,000)} = .2105.$$

In this case this is a poor approximation because the deposits and withdrawals are not approximately equally spread over the year (deposits are early, withdrawal is late).

If compound interest had been used in setting up the equation of value in Example 5.3, to find the IRR the resulting equation would be

$$1,000,000(1+i) + 200,000(1+i)^{10/12} + 200,000(1+i)^{4/12}$$
$$-500,000(1+i)^{2/12} = 1,100,000.$$

The solution to this equation is the internal rate of return $i = .1740$ (very close to the dollar-weighted return of $.1739$ found in Example 5.3).

5.2.2 TIME-WEIGHTED RATE OF RETURN

The **time-weighted rate of return** for a one year period is found by compounding the returns over successive parts of the year. Suppose that during the course of a year, the following interest rates occur: 6-month rate of 4%, followed by 3-month rate of 3%, followed by 3-month rate of 2%. If we assume reinvestment in successive periods, then an investment of 1 made at the start of the year will grow (with reinvestment at the corresponding rates) to $(1.04)(1.03)(1.02) = 1.0926$. The time-weighted rate of return for the year would be 9.26%, which is found by compounding the rates in successive fractions of the year. Notice that the fact that the first fraction of the year was 6 months, and the second and third were 3 months each, was not relevant. The important point in this example is that the year was broken into 3 successive pieces, with rates of 4%, 3% and 2% in the three successive pieces, which compounded to 1.0926.

In general, in order to find the time-weighted rate of return, we need the return for each piece of the year, for the pieces into which the year has been broken. The time length of each piece of the year is irrelevant. It is typical to break the year into the pieces defined by the points at which deposits or withdrawals occur. We adapt the situation presented in Example 5.3 to provide an example for the time-weighted return.

| **EXAMPLE 5.4** | (*Time-weighted rate of return*) |

A pension fund receives contributions and pays benefits from time to time. The fund value is reported after every transaction and at year end. The details during the year 2005 are as follows:

	Date	Amount
Fund values:	01/1/05	1,000,000
	03/1/05	1,240,000
	09/1/05	1,600,000
	11/1/05	1,080,000
	01/1/06	900,000

	Date	Amount
Contributions received:	02/28/05	200,000
	08/31/05	200,000
Benefits paid:	10/31/05	500,000
	12/31/05	200,000

Find both the time-weighted and dollar-weighted rates of return.

| **SOLUTION** |

The fund's earned rates for various parts of the year are as follows:

01/1/05 to 02/28/05: $\dfrac{1,240,000-200,000-1,000,000}{1,000,000}=.04$

03/1/05 to 08/31/05: $\dfrac{1,600,000-200,000-1,240,000}{1,240,000}=.1290$

09/1/05 to 10/31/05: $\dfrac{1,080,000+500,000-1,600,000}{1,600,000}=-.0125$

11/1/05 to 12/31/05: $\dfrac{900,000+200,000-1,080,000}{1,080,000}=.0185$

Then the time-weighted rate of return for 2005 is

$$i_T = (1.04)(1.1290)(.9875)(1.0185)-1 = .1809.$$

This can also be formulated as

$$i_T = \left(\frac{1,040,000}{1,000,000}\right)\left(\frac{1,400,000}{1,240,000}\right)\left(\frac{1,580,000}{1,600,000}\right)\left(\frac{1,100,000}{1,080,000}\right) - 1 = .1809$$

The dollar-weighted rate of return is found by solving for i in the equation

$$100,000\left[10(1+i) + 2\left(1+\tfrac{5}{6}i\right) + 2\left(1+\tfrac{1}{3}i\right) - 5\left(1+\tfrac{1}{6}i\right) - 2\right] = 900,000, \text{ so that}$$

$i_M = .1739$. Note that if the equation of value had been formulated using compound interest for fractions of a year, the equation would be

$$100,000\left[10(1+i) + 2(1+i)^{5/6} + 2(1+i)^{1/3} - 5(1+i)^{1/6} - 2\right] = 900,000,$$

which cannot be solved algebraically. Using numerical approximation methods, the solution to this equation is $i_M = .1740$ (the internal rate of return) to 4 decimal places, very close to the solution of the simple interest version of the equation. ☐

The information in Example 5.4 adds some detail to the information provided in Example 5.3. In Example 5.4 we are given the updated fund value after each transaction. This allows us to find the fund value just before each deposit and withdrawal, and therefore we can find the return earned by the fund for each transaction period. For instance, the fund balance on January 1 was 1,000,000. Just before the deposit on February 28, the fund balance was 1,040,000 (the March first balance of 1,240,000 minus the deposit of 200,000 made on February 28). Therefore, the growth factor in the fund from January 1 to February 28 is $\frac{1,040,000}{1,000,000} = 1.04$ (4%). We make similar calculations for each successive transaction period, and compound them over the full year.

It is possible to concoct transactions in which the time-weighted and dollar-weighted returns are quite far apart from one another.

An investment fund manager generally does not have control over the timing or amounts of cash inflows and outflows for the fund. The time-weighted return is often used to compare the relative performance of various investment fund managers since the method eliminates the impact of money flows in and out of the fund.

5.3 APPLICATIONS AND ILLUSTRATIONS

5.3.1 THE PORTFOLIO METHOD AND THE INVESTMENT YEAR METHOD

It is possible that when new funds are added to an existing investment account, the "new money" is kept segregated from the rest of the fund for some period of time. The existing fund may be earning interest at one rate in the coming year, and the new money might earn interest at a different rate. "New money" may be segregated every year for several years in terms of the interest rate earned before being integrated into a larger pooled fund. This may continue for several years. For instance, an existing investment fund may be scheduled to earn a 4% return in 2003, a 4.2% return in 2004 and a 4.5% return in 2005, but new contributions might be segregated from the main fund for 2 years and scheduled to earn 5% in 2003 and 4.8% in 2004. In 2005 and thereafter, the "new money" contributed in 2003 earns the same as the "main" fund. Under this situation, there may be a 2-year segregation period for all new contributions, so that new money that is contributed in 2004 might earn a different rate of return than the 4.8% return in 2004 earned by money that was new in 2003.

The "portfolio year rate" refers to the interest rate earned by the main or pooled fund, and would be classified by the year the interest is earned only. In the example above, the 4% return in 2003 would be the portfolio rate for 2003 and the 4.2% return in 2004 would be the portfolio rate for 2004. The "investment year rate" refers to the interest rate earned by "new money" before it has been incorporated into the pooled fund. The investment year rate on new money would be classified by (i) the year in which new money was received, and (ii) the current year interest is earned. The 5% rate is the investment year rate in 2003 for new money received in 2003, and 4.8% would be the investment year rate in 2004 for new money that had been received in 2003. The following example illustrates this idea.

EXAMPLE 5.5

(*Investment Year Method and Portfolio Year Method*)

You are given the following table of interest rates:

Calendar Year of Original Investment	Investment Year Rates (in %)					Portfolio Rates (in %)
y	i_1^y	i_2^y	i_3^y	i_4^y	i_5^y	i^{y+5}
1992	8.25	8.25	8.40	8.50	8.50	8.35
1993	8.50	8.70	8.75	8.90	9.00	8.60
1994	9.00	9.00	9.10	9.10	9.20	8.85
1995	9.00	9.10	9.20	9.30	9.40	9.10
1996	9.25	9.35	9.50	9.55	9.60	9.35
1997	9.50	9.50	9.60	9.70	9.70	
1998	10.00	10.00	9.90	9.80		
1999	10.00	9.80	9.70			
2000	9.50	9.50				
2001	9.00					

Suppose that the amount in a fund is 1000 on January 1, 1997. Let the following be the accumulated value of the fund on January 1, 2000:

P: under the investment year method
Q: under the portfolio yield method
R: if the balance is withdrawn at the end of every year and is reinvested at the new money rate.

Determine the ranking of P, Q, and R.

SOLUTION

For a new investment in 1997, under the investment year method, the rates earned in successive years are found in the row for 1997 in the table. The rate earned in 1997 is 9.50%, the rate earned in 1998 is 9.50%, and the rate earned in 1999 is 9.60%.

The portfolio rates are found in the final column of the table. For 1997 we use $i^{1992+5} = 8.35\%$, for 1998 we use $i^{1993+5} = 8.60\%$, etc.

The new money rates are from the first column of the investment year table for years 1997, 1998 and 1999 $\left(i_1^y.\right)$ A new investment made in 1997 earns 9.50% in 1997, a new investment made in 1998 earns 10.00% in 1998, and a new investment made in 1999 earns 10.00% in 1999.

Under the three methods, the deposit grows according to the following rates

	1997	1998	1999
P	9.50%	9.50%	9.60%
Q	8.35%	8.60%	8.85%
R	9.50%	10.00%	10.00%

$$P = 1000(1.095)(1.095)(1.096) = 1314,$$
$$Q = 1000(1.0835)(1.086)(1.0885) = 1281,$$
$$R = 1000(1.095)(1.10)(1.10) = 1325.$$

We see that $R > P > Q$. This relationship could be determined by comparing the interest rates in the table above without doing the actual calculations.

5.3.2 INTEREST PREFERENCE RATES FOR BORROWING AND LENDING

In Section 5.1 the concept of an individual's interest preference rate was introduced as the rate at which that individual would value future payments. It might also be the cost of capital at which the individual could borrow. In using such a rate (i_P) for valuation, when a transaction is regarded as taking place in an account with amounts credited and debited from that account (such as a line of credit), it is implicitly assumed that over the term of the transaction the individual would receive interest credited at rate i_P when the account is in a net surplus position and pay interest at rate i_P when the account is in a net deficit position. In the context of a transaction taking place in an account by means of deposits and withdrawals, it is reasonable to extend the notion of interest preference rates somewhat further by attributing a pair of rates to the individual, one rate at which the account would pay interest when in a surplus position (i_S), and another rate at which the account would charge interest when in a deficit position (i_D). In this framework it would be possible to compare two transactions by comparing the amount (net profit) in the account at the end of each transaction.

EXAMPLE 5.6 (*Interest preference rates*)

A line of credit loan of 10,000 is to be used for investment purposes. There are two investment alternatives. The first will provide payments of 3000 each year for 10 years starting one year from now. The second will provide payments of 8000 two years and five years from now, and 7000 seven years and ten years from now. The investor plans to deposit all proceeds from the investment into the line of credit account. When there is a balance owing in the account, interest is charged at 15% per year, and when there is surplus in the account interest is credited at 9% per year. Find the account balance after 10 years for each investment alternative.

SOLUTION

Investment 1 results in the following sequence of account balances:

$t = 0: -10,000$

$t = 1: -10,000(1.15) + 3000 = -8500$

$t = 2: -8,000(1.15) + 3000 = -6775$

$t = 3: -4791.25$

$t = 4: -2509.94$

$t = 5: 113.57$

$t = 6: 113.57(1.09) + 3000 = 3123.79$

$$\vdots$$

$t = 10: 3123.79(1.09)^4 + 3000 \cdot s_{\overline{4}|.09} = 18,129$

Investment 2 results in the following sequence:

$t = 2: -10,000(1.15)^2 + 8000 = -5225$

$t = 5: -5225(1.15)^3 + 8000 = 53.43$

$t = 7: 53.43(1.09)^2 + 7000 = 7063.48$

$t = 10: 7063.48(1.09)^3 + 7000 = 16,147$

The first investment would result in a larger gain at the end of the tenth year.

$\square$

5.3.3 ANOTHER MEASURE FOR THE YIELD ON A FUND

We now consider the case of a fund which may have deposits and with-drawals made continuously, and investment income earned continuously.

Suppose that a fund of money is observed over time, and the amount in the fund at time t is $F(t)$. The fund earns interest and also receives and/or makes payments from time to time. If we wish to find the average annualized yield earned by the fund from time t_1 to time t_2 measured in years, we can formulate the yield as the internal rate of return i (in the context of Section 5.1), where

$$F(t_2) \;=\; F(t_1)(1+i)^{t_2-t_1} + \sum_t c_t(1+i)^{t_2-t} + \int_{t_1}^{t_2} \overline{c}(t)(1+i)^{t_2-t}\, dt,$$

c_t represents the net amount received $(+)$ or paid out $(-)$ at time t, and $\overline{c}(t)$ is the net continuous rate of payment (received or paid out) at time t.

The relationship between $F(t_1)$ and $F(t_2)$ can be more simply stated as

$$F(t_2) \;=\; F(t_1) + I_{t_1 t_2} + N_{t_1 t_2}, \tag{5.3}$$

where I represents interest earned for the period on the initial $F(t_1)$ as well as on contributions (less interest lost on withdrawals), and N represents the net amount of new money received by the fund during the period where

$$N_{t_1 t_2} \;=\; \sum_t c_t + \int_{t_1}^{t_2} \overline{c}(t)\, dt. \tag{5.4}$$

Suppose that the time interval from t_1 to t_2 is one year, and let us make the simplifying assumption that N is uniformly received during the course of the year. Then $F(t_2)$ is a combination of the accumulated value of $F(t_1)$ after one year and the accumulated value of a continuous one-year level annuity paying N during the year, so that $F(t_2) = F(t_1)(1+i) + N \cdot \overline{s}_{\overline{1}|i}$ Using Equation (5.3) it follows that

$$F(t_2) \;=\; F(t_1)(1+i) + \left[F(t_2) - F(t_1) - I\right] \cdot \overline{s}_{\overline{1}|i}.$$

Since $\overline{s}_{\overline{1}|i} = \int_0^1 (1+i)^s\, ds = \frac{i}{\delta}$, it is not possible to solve exactly for i. A simple approximation often used in practice is based on the trapezoidal rule for approximate integration, which gives $\int_0^1 (1+i)^s\, ds \approx 1 + \frac{i}{2}$. With this approximation we see that

$$F(t_2) \approx F(t_1)(1+i) + \left[F(t_2) - F(t_1) - I\right]\left(1 + \frac{i}{2}\right), \qquad (5.5)$$

from which it follows that

$$i \approx \frac{2I}{F(t_1) + F(t_2) - I}. \qquad (5.6)$$

In Exercise 5.3.3 we derive the approximation

$$i \approx \frac{2I}{2 \cdot \int_{t_1}^{t_2} F(t)\, dt - I}. \qquad (5.7)$$

It may be the case that $F(t)$ is changing continuously for part of the period from t_1 to t_2 (say from t_1 to t'), and there is then a significant payment (or withdrawal) at time t', with $F(t)$ again changing continuously from t' to t_2. Then $F(t)$ is piecewise continuous from t_1 to t_2. In such a case the integral in Equation (5.7) can be approximated by approximating $\int_{t_1}^{t'}$ and $\int_{t'}^{t_2}$ separately.

EXAMPLE 5.7   (*Yield on a fund*)

A large pension fund was valued at 350,000,000 on January 1, 2010. During 2010 the contributions to the fund totaled 80,000,000, benefit payments totaled 20,000,000, and the fund recorded interest income of 40,000,000. Estimate the yield on the fund for 2010 in each of the following cases.

(a) Contributions, benefit payments, and interest income occur uniformly and continuously throughout the year.

(b) Benefit payments, interest income, and 20,000,000 of the contributions are uniformly spread throughout the year, but there is a lump sum contribution of 60,000,000 on September 1, 2010.

(c) Same as (b) except that the lump sum contributions are 50,000,000 on May 1 and 10,000,000 on September 1, 2010.

SOLUTION

(a) Let January 1, 2010 be $t = 0$ and January 1, 2011 be $t = 1$. Note that $F(1) = 350 + 80 - 20 + 40 = 450$ (million). Equation (5.6) can be directly applied, producing $i \approx \dfrac{2(40)}{350 + 450 - 40} = .1053$.

(b) The lump-sum contribution is made at $t = \frac{2}{3}$. Since the part of the contributions other than the lump sum, along with the benefits and interest income, are uniformly spread over the year, then just before this lump-sum contribution the approximate value of the fund is $F_{-}\left(\frac{2}{3}\right) = 350 + \frac{2}{3}(80-60) - \frac{2}{3}(20) + \frac{2}{3}(40) = 376.67$. Just after the lump-sum contribution the value of the fund is

$$F_{+}\left(\frac{2}{3}\right) = 376.67 + 60 = 436.67,$$

and the value of the fund at the end of the year is the same as in (a), $F(1) = 450$. We can assume that $F(t)$ is linear from $t = 0$ to $t = \frac{2}{3}$ (just before the lump sum payment) and from $t = \frac{2}{3}$ (just after the lump sum payment) to $t = 1$. Based on the method described in the comments following Equation (5.7), we approximate $\int_{0}^{1} F(t)\, dt$ by approximating each of the integrals $\int_{0}^{2/3} F(t)\, dt$ and $\int_{2/3}^{1} F(t)\, dt$. Using the trapezoidal rule the approximate values of the integrals are

$$\int_{0}^{2/3} F(t)\, dt = \frac{2/3}{2}[350 + 376.67] = 242.22$$

and

$$\int_{2/3}^{1} F(t)\, dt = \frac{1/3}{2}[436.67 + 450] = 147.78,$$

so that the approximation to $\int_{0}^{1} F(t)\, dt$ is 390. Then using Equation (5.7) we have $i \approx \dfrac{2(40)}{2(390) - 40} = .1081$.

(c) Just before the lump sum contribution at $t = \frac{1}{3}$ the fund value is $F_{-}\left(\frac{1}{3}\right) = 350 + \frac{1}{3}(80-60) - \frac{1}{3}(20) + \frac{1}{3}(40) = 363.33$, and it is

$$F_+\left(\tfrac{1}{3}\right) = 363.66 + 50 = 413.33$$

just after that contribution. Just before the lump sum contribution at $t = \tfrac{2}{3}$ the fund value is

$$F_-\left(\tfrac{2}{3}\right) \;=\; 413.33 + \tfrac{1}{3}(80-60) - \tfrac{1}{3}(20) + \tfrac{1}{3}(40) \;=\; 426.66,$$

and we have $F_+\left(\tfrac{2}{3}\right) = 426.66 + 10 = 436.66$ just after that contribution. As in parts (a) and (b) we have $F(1) = 450$. Then

$$\int_0^1 F(t)\,dt \;=\; \int_0^{1/3} F(t)\,dt + \int_{1/3}^{2/3} F(t)\,dt + \int_{2/3}^1 F(t)\,dt.$$

The trapezoidal rule for approximate integration is applied as follows:

$$\int_a^b g(x)\,dx \;\approx\; \frac{b-a}{2}[g(a)+g(b)] \;.$$

Applying the trapezoidal rule to each integral as in part (b), we find

$$\int_0^1 F(t)\,dt \;=\; 118.89 + 140 + 147.78 \;=\; 406.67,$$

so that

$$i \;\approx\; \frac{2(40)}{2(406.66)-40} \;=\; .1034.$$

5.4 NOTES AND REFERENCES

Several books contain a discussion of conditions relating to the existence and uniqueness of yield rates for financial transactions. Discussions can be found in Butcher and Nesbitt, in *The Theory of Interest*, by Kellison, and also in *An Introduction to the Mathematics of Finance*, by McCutcheon and Scott. The notion of interest preference rates introduced in the paper "A New Approach to the Theory of Interest" in *TSA*, Volume 32 (1980), by D. Promislow provides a fresh and useful alternative to yield rates as a way of comparing investments. An idea similar to that of interest preference rates is discussed in McCutcheon and Scott.

The internal rate of return and discounted cashflow methods of capital budgeting are analyzed in considerable detail in the papers "Mathematical Analysis of Rates of Return under Certainty" and "An Analysis of Criteria for Investment and Financing Decisions under Certainty," by Teicherow, Robichek, and Montalbano, which appeared in *Management Science*, Volumes 11 and 12 (1965). The notation $F_t(k,r)$ is introduced there to denote the future value at time t of a cashflow with k as the project financing rate of interest (the rate charged when the investment is in a deficit or loan outstanding position) and r as the project investment rate (the rate earned when the investment is in a surplus position). This is similar to the pair of interest preference rates discussed in Section 5.3.

The paper "Axiomatic Characterization of the Time-weighted Rate of Return," by K.B. Gray and R.B. Dewar in *Management Science*, Volume 18, No. 2 (1971) argues that the time-weighted rate of return is "the only measure appropriate for measuring the performance of fund managers."

5.5 EXERCISES

The exercises without asterisks are intended to comprehensively cover the material presented in the chapter. Exercises with a asterisk can be regarded as supplementary exercises which cover topics in more depth, either theoretically or computationally, than those without a asterisk.

SECTION 5.1

5.1.1   Repeat part (a) of Example 5.2 by setting up the equation of value at time $t_2 = 2$, and repeat part (b) by setting up the equation of value at time 0.

5.1.2   Show that for any $i > -1$, for the transactions in Example 5.2 we have $P_i(C_a) < P_i(C_b) < P_i(C_c) < P_i(C_d)$.

5.1.3   Repeat Example 5.1 removing all commission expenses on the purchase and sale of shares.

5.1.4   Transactions A and B are to be compared. Transaction A has net cashflows of $C_0^A = -5$, $C_1^A = 3.72$, $C_2^A = 0$, $C_3^A = 4$ and Transaction B has net cashflows

$$C_0^B = -5, \ C_1^B = 3, \ C_2^B = 1.7, \ C_3^B = 3.$$

Find the yield rate for each transaction to at least 6 decimal places. Show that Transaction A is preferable to B at interest preference rates less than 11.11% and at interest preference rates greater than 25%, and Transaction B is preferable at interest preference rates between 11.11% and 25%.

5.1.5   A project requires an initial capital outlay of 30,000 and will return the following amounts (paid at the ends of the next 5 years):

14,000,   12,000,   6,000,   4,000,   2,000.

Solve for each of the following.

(a) Internal rate of return.

(b) Modified internal rate of return assuming a cost of capital of 10% per year.

(c) Net present value based on a cost of capital of 10% per year.

(d) The payback period.

(e) The discounted payback period assuming a cost of capital of 10% per year.

(f) The profitability index.

*5.1.6   (a) Suppose there is a k between 0 and n such that either

(i) $C_0, C_1, \ldots, C_k \leq 0$ and $C_{k+1}, C_{k+2}, \ldots, C_n \geq 0$ (i.e., all the negative net cashflows precede the positive net cashflows), or

(ii) $C_0, C_1, \ldots, C_k \geq 0$ and $C_{k+1}, C_{k+2}, \ldots, C_n \leq 0$ (i.e., all the positive net cashflows precede the negative net cashflows).

Assuming that $C_0 \neq 0$, show that there is a unique $i > -1$ for which $\sum_{s=1}^{n} C_s \cdot v^{t_s} = 0$. (Hint: show that the function

$$\sum_{s=0}^{k} C_s \cdot (1+i)^{t_k - t_s} + \sum_{s=k+1}^{n} C_s \cdot (1+i)^{t_k - t_s}$$

is monotonic, either increasing for all i or decreasing for all i, and check the limits as $i \to \infty$ and $i \to -1$.)

(b) For each $t = 1, 2, \ldots, n$, define G_t to be $G_t = G_{t-1}(1+i) + C_t$, where $G_0 = C_0$. Show that $G_n = 0$ is the equation of value at time n for the sequence of net cashflows. Suppose that (i) there is at least one solution $i > -1$ for which $\sum_{s=1}^{n} C_s \cdot v^{t_s} = 0$, and (ii) at that interest rate $G_t > 0$ for all $t = 0, 1, \ldots, n-1$. Show that the solution for i is unique. (Hint: if $i' > i''$ are both solutions then $G_n' = 0 = G_n''$ for both i' and i'', but $G_t' > G_t''$ for $t = 1, 2, \ldots, n$, which is a contradiction.)

(c) Let $C_0, C_1, \ldots, C_n$ be an arbitrary sequence of net cashflows, and let $F_0 = C_0$, $F_1 = C_0 + C_1$, $F_2 = C_0 + C_1 + C_2$, $F_t = C_0 + C_1 + \cdots + C_t$, $F_n = C_0 + C_1 + \cdots + C_n$, so that F_t is the cumulative total net cashflow at the tth cash-flow point. Suppose that both F_0 and F_n are non-zero, and that the sequence $\{F_0, F_1, \ldots, F_n\}$ has exactly one change of sign. Show that there is a unique $i > 0$ for which $\sum_{s=0}^{n} C_s \cdot v^{t_s} = 0$, although there may be one or more negative roots.

(d) Show that the transaction in Example 5.1 satisfies both (a) and (c) above, but none of the transactions in Example 5.2 satisfy the conditions in parts (a) or (c) above.

(e) *Descartes' rule of signs* (discovered by 16th Century mathematician Rene Descartes) states that for a polynomial of the form $P(x) = C_n x^n + C_{n-1} x^{n-1} + \cdots + C_1 x + C_0$, the number of positive roots of $P(x)$ is less than or equal to the number of sign changes in the sequence $C_n, C_{n-1}, \ldots, C_1, C_0$, and the number of negative roots of $P(x)$ is less than or equal to the number of sign changes in the sequence

$$(-1)^n C_n, \quad (-1)^{n-1} C_{n-1}, \ldots, (-1)C_1, C_0.$$

Show that Descartes Rule of signs shows that the transaction in Example 5.1 has at most one positive root and no negative roots.

*5.1.7 Smith buys an investment property for 900,000 by making a down payment of 150,000 and taking a loan for 750,000. Starting one month after the loan is made Smith must make monthly loan payments, but he also receives monthly rental payments on the property such that his net outlay per month is 1200, which is set for 2 years. In addition there are taxes of 10,000 payable 6 months after the loan is made and annually thereafter as long as Smith owns the property. Two years after the original purchase date Smith sells the property for $Y \geq 741,200$, out of which he must pay the balance of 741,200 on the loan.

(a) Show that part (a) of Exercise 5.1.6 guarantees a unique yield rate on the 2-year transaction.

(b) Use part (c) of Exercise 5.1.6 to find the minimum value of Y that guarantees a unique positive rate of return over the two year period.

5.1.8 Suppose $Y = 1,000,000$ in Exercise 5.1.7. Apply various approximation methods to find the yield rate in the form $i^{(12)}$.

*5.1.9 An investment company offers a 15-year "double your money" savings plan, which requires a deposit of 10,000 at the start of each year for 15 years. At the end of 15 years each participant receives 300,000. If a participant opts out of the plan, he gets back his deposits accumulated at 4% up to the time he opts out. Opting out occurs at the start of a year when a new payment is due, from the start of the 2nd to the start of the 15th year.

Someone who opts out at the start of the second year will get back $10,000\ddot{s}_{\overline{1}|.04}$, someone opting out at the start of the third year will get back $10,000\ddot{s}_{\overline{2}|.04}$, etc.

The company's experience shows that out of 100 new participants, the numbers that opt out each year are 5 at the start of the 2nd year, 4 at the start of each of the 3rd and 4th years, 3 at the start of each of the 5th and 6th years, 2 at the start of each of the 7th through 9th years, and 1 at the start of each of the 10th through 15th years. The deposits received by the company can be reinvested at effective annual rate i.

(a) Assuming 100 initial participants, find the company's net profit at the end of 15 years, after all plans have been settled, as a function of i, and show that it is an increasing function of i.

(b) What value of i gives no net profit to the company?

*5.1.10 Apply part (a) of Exercise 5.1.6 to conclude that the company's net profit in Exercise 5.1.9 is positive if $i > i_0$ and negative if $i < i_0$.

*5.1.11 Part (a)(ii) of Exercise 5.1.6 is solved by showing that the function

$$g(i) = \sum_{s=0}^{k} C_s \cdot (1+i)^{t_k - t_s} + \sum_{k+1}^{n} C_s (1+i)^{t_k - t_s}$$ is monotonic. This does not

necessarily imply that the function $h(i) = v^{t_k} \cdot g(i)$ is also monotonic, where $h(i)$ is the left side of the equation of value for the transaction at time 0. Suppose that $C_0 = -1$, $C_1 = -1$, $C_2 = 2$ and $C_3 = 2$.

(a) Show that $g(i)$ is a decreasing function of i.

(b) Find the value of i_0 for which the function $h(i)$ decreases for $0 < i < i_0$ and increases for $i > i_0$.

*5.1.12 (a) A transaction has net cashflows of $C_0, C_1, C_2, ..., C_n$, and i_0

is a yield rate for this transaction (i.e., $\sum_{s=0}^{n} C_s \cdot v^{t_s} = 0$).

Suppose now that the cashflows are "indexed to inflation" at periodic rate r, so that the transaction is modified to $C'_0 = C_0$, $C'_1 = C_1(1+r)$, $C'_2 = C_2(1+r)^2, ..., C'_n = C_n(1+r)^n$. Show that $i'_0 = (1+r) \cdot i_0 + r$ is a yield rate for the new transaction.

(b) Smith can borrow 10,000 at $i = 12\%$ and repay the loan with 15 annual payments beginning one year after the loan is made. He will invest the 10,000 in equipment that will generate revenue at the end of each year for 15 years. He expects revenue of 1200 after one year, and he expects subsequent revenue to increase by an inflationary factor of $1 + r$ per year thereafter. He will apply the full amount of his annual revenue as an annual loan payment, until the loan is repaid. Find the smallest value of r that will allow repayment of the loan in 15 years.

*5.1.13 When net cashflow occurs continuously, say at rate $\overline{C}(t)$ at time t, then the equation of value for a yield rate (force of interest) for the transaction over the period from 0 to n is

$$\int_0^n \overline{C}(t) \cdot e^{-\delta t} \, dt \;=\; 0.$$

If the transaction also has discrete net cashflow of amounts $C_0, C_1, \ldots, C_n$ at times $0, 1, \ldots, n$ then the overall equation of value for yield rate is

$$\sum_{s=0}^{n} C_s \cdot e^{-\delta \cdot t_s} + \int_0^n \overline{C}(t) \cdot e^{\delta t} \, dt \;=\; 0.$$

(a) Suppose a company is marketing a new product. The production and marketing process involves a startup cost of 1,000,000 and continuing cost of 200,000 per year for 5 years, paid continuously. It is forecast that revenue from the product will begin one year after startup, and will continue until the end of the original 5-year production process. Revenue (which will be received continuously) is estimated to start at a rate of 500,000 per year and increase linearly (and continuously) over a two-year period to a rate of 1,000,000 per year at the end of the 3rd year, and then decrease to a rate of 200,000 per year at the end of the 5th year. Solve for the yield rate δ earned by the company over the 5-year period.

(b) Suppose that the revenue starts (after 1 year) at a rate of 400,000 per year, and increases continuously and exponentially at rate r per year, so that the rate of revenue at time t is $400,000 \cdot e^{r(t-1)}$, where t measures time in years since the start of the production process. Find the value of r necessary for this to be a "break-even" transaction, in which the yield rate is $\delta = 0$.

*5.1.14 A loan of 100,000 is to be repaid by the sinking fund method over a 25-year period. The lender receives annual interest payments at rate 10% per year, and the borrower accumulates the principal by means of annual deposits in a sinking fund earning annual interest at rate 6%. After the 10th deposit to the sinking fund, the rate is increased to 8%.

(a) At the time the loan is issued, the borrower is not aware of the future interest rate change in the fund, and decides to make level annual deposits (starting one year after the loan) under the assumption that the interest rate will stay at 6% for the full 25 years. When the rate change is announced after 10 years, the borrower changes the level of future deposits so that the accumulated value will be 100,000 at the time of the 25th deposit. Find the borrower's yield rate on this transaction.

(b) Suppose that the rate change after 10 years is known by the borrower on the issue date of the loan, and he calculates a level deposit which will accumulate to 100,000 based on the 25-year schedule of interest rates. Find the borrower's yield rate in this case.

(c) From the viewpoint of the lender, suppose that he accumulates his interest income in a fund earning interest at the same rates as the borrower's sinking fund. Find the lender's yield rate on the transaction.

SECTION 5.2

5.2.1   On January 1, 2005, an investment account is worth 100,000. On April 1, 2005, the value has increased to 103,000 and 8,000 is withdrawn. On January 1, 2007, the account is worth 103,992. Assuming a dollar-weighted method for 2005 and a time-weighted method for 2006, the effective annual interest rate was equal to x for both 2005 and 2006. Calculate x.

5.2.2   An investor deposits 50 in an investment account on January 1. The following summarizes the activity in the account during the year:

Date	Value Immediately Before Deposit	Deposit
March 15	40	20
June 1	80	80
October 1	175	75

In June 30, the value of the account is 157.50. On December 31, the value of the account is X. Using the time-weighted method, the equivalent effective annual yield during the first 6 months is equal to the (time-weighted) effective annual yield during the entire 1-year period. Calculate X.

5.2.3   Fund X has unit values which are 1.0 on January 1, 2005, .8 on July 1, 2005 and 1.0 on January 1, 2006. A fund manager receives contributions of 100,000 on January 1, 2005 and 100,000 on July 1, 2005 and immediately uses the entire contributions to purchase units in Fund X. Find the time-weighted and dollar-weighted rates of return for 2005.

5.2.4   The details regarding fund value, contributions and withdrawals from a fund are as follows:

	Date	Amount
Fund Values:	1/1/05	1,000,000
	7/1/05	1,310,000
	1/1/06	1,265,000
	7/1/06	1,540,000
	1/1/07	1,420,000
Contributions Received:	6/30/05	250,000
	6/30/06	250,000
Benefits Paid:	12/31/05	150,000
	12/31/06	150,000

Find the effective annual time-weighted rate of return for the two-year period of 2005 and 2006.

5.2.5   You are given the following information about an investment account:

Date	Value Immediately Before Deposit	Deposit
January 1	10	
July 1	12	X
December 31	X	

Over the year, the time-weighted return is 0%, and the dollar-weighted return is Y. Calculate Y.

5.2.6   You are given the following information about the activity in two different investment accounts:

Date	Account K Fund Value Before Activity	Deposit	Withdrawal
1/1/1999	100.0		
7/1/1999	125.0		X
10/1/1999	110.0	$2X$	
12/31/ 1999	125.0		

Date	Account L Fund Value Before Activity	Deposit	Withdrawal
1/1/1999	100.0		
7/1/1999	125.0		X
12/31/1999	105.8		

During 1999, the dollar weighted return for investment Account K equals the time weighted return for investment Account L, which equals i. Calculate i.

5.2.7   An association had a fund balance of 75 on January 1 and 60 on December 31. At the end of every month during the year, the association deposited 10 from membership fees.

Withdrawals	
February 28	5
June 30	25
October 15	80
October 31	35

Calculate the dollar-weighted rate of return for the year.

SECTION 5.3

5.3.1   A large pension fund has a value of 500,000,000 at the start of the year $(t = 0)$. During the year the fund receives contributions of 100,000,000, pays out benefits of 40,000,000 and has interest income of 60,000,000. Estimate the yield rate on the fund for each of the following circumstances:

(a) Contributions, benefits and interest are uniformly spread throughout the year.

(b) Benefits and interest are uniformly spread throughout the year, and the contributions are made in one lump-sum at time (i) $t = 0$, (ii) $t = \frac{1}{4}$, (iii) $t = \frac{1}{2}$, (iv) $t = \frac{3}{4}$, or (v) $t = 1$.

5.3.2   Suppose a fund receives new money of amount N in two equal installments, one at the beginning of the year and one at the end of the year. Show that Equation (5.6) is an exact measure of i for the year.

*5.3.3   Recall from Chapter 1 that at force of interest δ_t, the amount of interest earned from time t_1 to time t_2 on a fund whose amount is $F(t)$ at time t is $I = \int_{t_1}^{t_2} F(t) \cdot \delta_t \, dt$. Show that the average force of interest earned over that time period is then

$$\delta = \frac{\int_{t_1}^{t_2} F(t) \cdot \delta_t \, dt}{\int_{t_1}^{t_2} F(t) \, dt} = \frac{I}{\int_{t_1}^{t_2} F(t) \, dt}.$$

Suppose the time from t_1 to t_2 is one year. The equivalent effective annual i is $i = e^{\delta} - 1$. Show that for "small" values of δ, i is approximately equal to $\frac{\delta}{1 - \frac{\delta}{2}}$ and use this to get an approximation for i in terms of I and $\int_{t_1}^{t_2} F(t) \, dt$. Show that using the trapezoidal rule to approximate $\int_{t_1}^{t_2} F(t) \, dt$ results in Equation (5.6).

*5.3.4 Suppose the first investment in Example 5.6 pays X per year. Find the value of X for which the balance at the end of 10 years is the same as it is for the second investment.

CHAPTER 6

THE TERM STRUCTURE OF INTEREST RATES

When a borrower arranges with a lender to take a loan, there are a number of factors that the lender will consider in setting the interest rate on the loan. For instance, the lender would be concerned with the *credit rating* of the borrower, which is a measure of how likely the borrower is to be able to make the scheduled loan payments. The lender would also likely be concerned with the length of time over which the loan is to be repaid. An investor in a fixed-term deposit with some financial institution would have similar concerns. If the investment is in a government security such as a Treasury bill or coupon bond (U.S. or Canadian), then there would not likely be any concern with the credit rating of the government, and the main consideration in determining the desired return would be the length of time until maturity of the investment. The relationship between the time to maturity and the yield rate on fixed income securities such as Treasury bills and coupon bonds is referred to as the **term structure of interest rates,** and a graph representing that relationship is called a **yield curve.**

The term structure changes from day to day as a result of changing economic conditions, but it is usually the case that longer term investments tend to have higher associated rates of return than shorter term investments. This is referred to as a *normal term structure.* For example, the following excerpt and graph from the Bloomberg © website on March 12, 2004 illustrates a graph of yield-to-maturity versus time to maturity for US Treasury bills (less than one year maturity), notes (up to 10 year maturity) and bonds (over 10 year maturity). There is a clear increasing trend in the yield rate as the time to maturity increases.

U.S. TREASURIES					
Bills					
	COUPON	MATURITY DATE	CURRENT PRICE/YIELD	PRICE/YIELD CHANGE	TIME
3-Month	N.A.	06/10/2004	0.93/0.94	0.01/0.006	03/12
6-Month	N.A.	09/09/2004	0.97/0.99	0.01/0.01	03/12
Notes/Bonds					
	COUPON	MATURITY DATE	CURRENT PRICE/YIELD	PRICE/YIELD CHANGE	TIME
2-Year	1.625	02/28/2006	100-06/1.5	-0-03/0.048	03/12
3-Year	2.250	02/15/2007	100-29/1.9	-0-05/0.054	03/12
5-Year	2.625	03/15/2009	99-16/2.72	-0-11/0.074	03/12
10-Year	4.000	02/15/2014	101-26/3.76	-0-17/0.065	03/12
30-Year	5.375	02/15/2031	109-31/4.71	-0-25/0.048	03/12

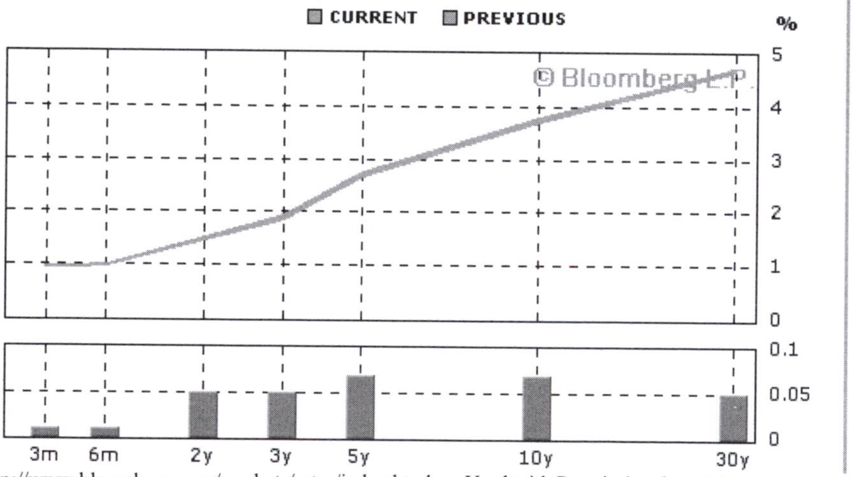

http://www.bloomberg.com/markets/rates/index.html   Used with Permission from Bloomberg L.P.

FIGURE 6.1

The nature of the term structure at a particular point in time is related to economic conditions at that point in time. The following yield curves were taken from the website of Stockcharts.com © and represent the term structure of U.S. Treasury securities at several points in time. We see that during the year from May, 2000 to April, 2001, the term structure changed from being *inverted* (in May and August, 2000), meaning that yield rates are lower for long term than for short term investments, to a *flat* term structure in September, to a more normal increasing term structure by April 2001. The one year period that has been chosen for this illustration is somewhat of an anomaly. Prior to early 2000, the term structure had a normal shape for several years, and from early 2001 to the time of publication of this book it has had a normal shape.

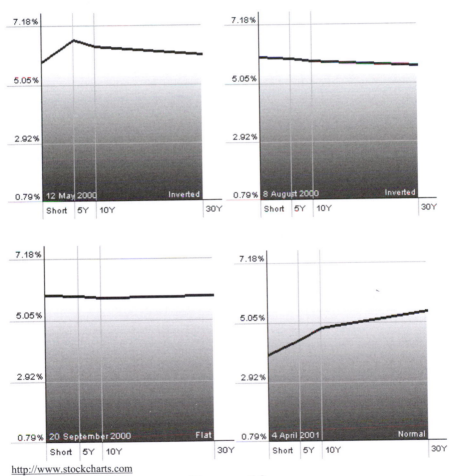

FIGURE 6.2

There are various theories that attempt to relate the shape of the yield curve to economic conditions and investor behavior. We will not look into such theories in this book, but we will be concerned with the relationship between the yield curve and pricing of fixed income securities.

In the Bloomberg website excerpt above, prices and yields of a few representative Treasury securities are given in the table. The actual yield curve would be based on a more complete collection of Treasury securities that traded on March 12, 2004.

Governments issue bonds of various terms to maturity on a regular basis, and over time there may be bonds issued at different times that mature on the same date. One of the bonds listed in the Bloomberg website excerpt is a 2.25% coupon Treasury note maturing on February 15, 2007. In a more complete listing of Treasury notes, there can be found another one also maturing on February 15, 2007 that has a 6.25% coupon. The following information was taken from the Yahoo © website based on the close of trading on March 12, 2004. We see the 2.25% bond listed along with the 6.25% bond. The 6.25% bond has a larger coupon and therefore will have a higher price than the 2.25% bond. The two bonds mature at the same time, and so we might anticipate that they should have the same yield rate. The yield rates on the two bonds differ very slightly, and we might attribute the difference to some roundoff error, or perhaps to slightly changed market conditions between the last trade of the 2.25% bond and the last trade of the 6.25% bond on March 12, 2004. Keep in mind the conventions describing coupon bonds that were discussed in Chapter 4. In particular, recall that coupon rate and yield rates are quoted as nominal annual rates compounded semi-annually

	Coupon	Maturity	Yield	Price
T-Note (3-yr)	2.25	02-15-2007	1.913	100.950
T-Note	6.25	02-15-2007	1.909	112.259

http://bond.finance.yahoo.com

FIGURE 6.3

There are many other examples of bonds that mature on the same date but have different coupon and yield rates. From the financial pages of the *Globe and Mail* © newspaper from Canada reporting on closing bond prices and yields for March 12, 2004, there are quotations for two Government of Canada bonds that both mature on June 1, 2010. There is a 5.50% bond priced at 109.50 with a yield of 3.77%, and there is a 9.50% bond priced at 131.80 with a yield of 3.72%. Again, the difference between the yield rates on the two bonds is small. A more careful look at each of these pairs of bonds that mature simultaneously reveals a consistency in the difference between the yield rates. For both pairs of bonds we see that the bond with the higher coupon rate has the lower yield to maturity. We might expect that bonds from the same issuer with the same maturity date should have the same yield rates, but we just have seen examples in which the yield rates are not exactly the same. We shall shortly see why this must (theoretically) be the case.

The payments on a coupon bond consist of the coupon payments and the redemption payment on the maturity date. From the point of view of the amortization of a bond, in a sense, a coupon bond "matures a little bit" every time a coupon is paid, so we are mixing maturity dates over the course of the series of bond payments.

If we were to consider a *zero-coupon bond* (also called a *discount bond*), then the only bond payment would be a single payment on the maturity date, and the yield to maturity would be a clear measure of yield rate for single payments made at that particular date. If we know the pricing of zero-coupon bonds for many maturity terms from very short term to very long term, we can always represent a given set of cashflows as an appropriate series of zero-coupon bonds, and the total present value of the set of cashflows is the sum of the present values of the component zero-coupon bonds.

When we speak of the term structure of interest rates, we can loosely mean the more vague relationship between the term of an investment and the rate of return, where we could have a different relationship for different risk-classes of investments. We can have a term structure for U.S. Treasury issues, or we can have a term structure for AA risk rated corporate bonds, etc. The generally accepted definition of the term structure is the relationship between the time to maturity and the yield to maturity of zero-coupon bonds of a particular risk class. The yield to maturity of a zero coupon bond is called the **spot rate of interest** for that maturity.

6.1 SPOT RATES OF INTEREST

As mentioned earlier, a zero-coupon bond or pure discount bond is a bond that pays a specified maturity amount on a specified date. Bond issuers do not usually issue zero-coupon bonds directly, but in the secondary market, investors are allowed to separate and resell individually each of the coupon and redemption payments that will be made by the issuer of the bond. The U.S. Treasury describes this procedure in the STRIPS program in the following excerpt from the U.S. Treasury website.

Treasury STRIPS

The Treasury STRIPS program was introduced in January 1985. STRIPS is the acronym for Separate Trading of Registered Interest and Principal of Securities. The STRIPS program lets investors hold and trade the individual interest and principal components of eligible Treasury notes and bonds as separate securities.

What is a stripped security?

When a Treasury fixed-principal or inflation-indexed note or bond is stripped, each interest payment and the principal payment becomes a separate zero-coupon security. Each component has its own identifying number and can be held or traded separately. For example, a Treasury note with 10 years remaining to maturity consists of a single principal payment at maturity and 20 interest payments, one every six months for 10 years. When this note is converted to STRIPS form, each of the 20 interest payments and the principal payment becomes a separate security. STRIPS are also called zero-coupon securities because the only time an investor receives a payment during the life of a STRIP is when it matures.

How do I buy STRIPS?

The Treasury does not issue or sell STRIPS directly to investors. STRIPS can be purchased and held only through financial institutions and government securities brokers and dealers.

Why do investors hold STRIPS?

STRIPS are popular with investors who want to receive a known payment at a specific future date. For example, some State lotteries invest the present value of large lottery prizes in STRIPS to be sure that funds are available when needed to meet annual payment obligations that result from the prizes. Pension funds invest in STRIPS to match the payment flows of their assets with those of their liabilities.

STRIPS are also referred to as "coupons and residuals" (the residuals being payments that come at maturity). Each day there are quotations of prices and yields of STRIPS for Treasury issues, with payments due from a few months to many years. These yields make up the term structure (for that day) for "risk-free" investments (risk-free in the sense that the U.S. government guarantees that the payments will be made) and are referred to as **spot rates of interest** for the various terms to maturity. The price of a STRIP is quoted in the financial press as the present value of $100 payable at that STRIPS's payment point. The price per dollar can be used as a present value factor for payments due at that time point.

TABLE 6.1

Globe and Mail ©				
Issuer	**Coupon**	**Maturity**	**Price**	**Yield**
CMHC	0.000	12/01/2004	98.67	1.90
Canada	0.000	03/01/2005	97.98	2.15
Canada	0.000	06/01/2005	97.45	2.15
Canada	0.000	10/01/2005	96.54	2.30
Canada	0.000	03/01/2006	95.38	2.43
Canada	0.000	04/01/2006	95.05	2.50
Canada	0.000	09/15/2006	93.62	2.66
Canada	0.000	10/01/2006	93.50	2.66
Canada	0.000	12/01/2006	92.64	2.84
Canada	0.000	06/01/2007	91.43	2.81
Canada	0.000	10/01/2007	89.90	3.03
Canada	0.000	03/15/2008	88.12	3.19
Canada	0.000	06/01/2008	86.86	3.38
Canada	0.000	10/01/2008	85.84	3.39
Canada	0.000	12/01/2008	85.05	3.47
Canada	0.000	03/01/2009	83.86	3.58
Canada	0.000	12/01/2009	80.48	3.84
Canada	0.000	12/01/2010	76.18	4.10
Canada	0.000	06/01/2011	73.91	4.24
Canada	0.000	12/01/2011	72.11	4.29
Canada	0.000	06/01/2012	69.76	4.44
Canada	0.000	12/01/2012	68.13	4.46
Canada	0.000	12/01/2013	64.58	4.56
Canada	0.000	12/01/2014	61.09	4.66
Canada	0.000	06/01/2015	59.37	4.71
Canada	0.000	12/01/2016	54.22	4.88
Canada	0.000	06/01/2017	52.28	4.97
Canada	0.000	12/01/2017	50.74	5.01
Canada	0.000	12/01/2018	47.88	5.07
Canada	0.000	06/01/2019	46.48	5.10
Canada	0.000	06/01/2020	43.99	5.13
Canada	0.000	06/01/2021	41.33	5.20
Canada	0.000	06/01/2022	38.84	5.26
Canada	0.000	06/01/2025	33.45	5.23

Recall that the convention regarding bond yield quotations is to use a nominal annual rate compounded semi-annually. This convention also applies to the quotation of yields on STRIPS. The figures below are excerpts from the the *Globe and Mail* © and *Wall Street Journal* © for closing prices March 12, 2004 for U.S. Treasury STRIPS and Canadian Treasury STRIPS.

TABLE 6.2

Wall St. Journal ©											
U.S. Treasury Strips											
Maturity	Type	Bid	Asked	Chg	Ask Yld	Maturity	Type	Bid	Asked	Chg	Ask Yld
May 04	ci	99.27	99.27	···	0.93	Aug 06	ci	96.00	96.02	−4	1.67
May 04	np	99.27	99.27	···	0.93	Oct 06	np	95.18	95.19	−1	1.75
Jul 04	ci	99.21	99.21	···	1.03	Nov 06	ci	95.10	95.12	···	1.79
Aug 04	ci	99.19	99.19	···	0.95	Nov 06	np	95.11	95.12	···	1.78
Aug 04	np	99.19	99.19	···	0.97	Feb 07	ci	94.14	94.16	−1	1.95
Nov 04	ci	99.09	99.10	···	1.05	Feb 07	np	94.19	94.20	−1	1.90
Nov 04	bp	99.10	99.10	···	1.04	May 07	ci	93.22	93.24	−1	2.05
Nov 04	np	99.10	99.10	···	1.04	May 07	np	93.23	93.25	−1	2.04
Jan 05	ci	99.14	99.14	−1	0.67	Aug 07	np	93.00	93.02	−1	2.12
Feb 05	ci	99.02	99.03	−1	1.01	Aug 07	ci	92.24	92.26	−1	2.19
Feb 05	np	99.00	99.00	−3	1.09	Aug 07	np	92.30	93.00	−1	2.13
May 05	ci	98.26	98.27	···	1.01	Nov 07	ci	92.02	92.05	−1	2.24
May 05	bp	98.23	98.24	···	1.09	Nov 07	np	92.09	92.11	−1	2.19
May 05	np	99.22	98.22	···	1.13	Feb 08	ci	91.03	91.01	−1	2.38
May 05	np	98.22	98.22	···	1.13	Feb 08	np	91.10	91.12	−1	2.32
Jul 05	ci	98.30	98.31	···	0.78	May 08	ci	90.01	90.04	−1	2.52
Aug 05	ci	98.13	98.14	···	1.12	May 08	np	90.09	90.12	−1	2.45
Aug 05	bp	98.07	98.08	−1	1.25	Aug 08	ci	89.09	89.11	−1	2.57
Aug 05	np	98.09	98.10	···	1.12	Nov 08	ci	88.07	88.10	−1	2.68
Nov 05	ci	97.25	97.26	···	1.34	Nov 08	np	88.14	88.16	−1	2.63
Nov 05	np	97.25	97.26	···	1.34	Feb 09	ci	87.05	87.08	−2	2.80
Nov 05	np	97.25	97.26	···	1.34	May 09	ci	86.07	86.10	−2	2.87
Jan 06	ci	98.01	98.02	···	1.07	May 09	np	86.23	86.26	−1	2.76
Feb 06	ci	97.10	97.11	···	1.40	Aug 09	ci	85.23	85.16	−1	2.91
Feb 06	bp	97.08	97.09	···	1.44	Aug 09	np	85.18	85.21	−1	2.88
Feb 06	np	97.08	97.10	···	1.43	Nov 09	ci	84.29	84.28	−1	2.92
May 06	np	98.20	96.21	···	1.57	Nov 09	bp	83.26	83.29	−2	3.12
Jul 06	ci	96.29	96.30	−4	1.33	Feb 10	ci	83.02	83.05	−2	3.14
Jul 06	np	96.03	96.09	···	1.63	May 10	np	82.04	82.07	···	3.20

Table 6.2 is a partial listing of the Treasury Strips quotations for March 12, 2004. A more complete listing would have maturities ranging up to

about 30 years. The term structure graph in Figure 6.1 presented earlier is a graph of time to maturity versus yield to maturity for the complete set of Treasury securities for all maturity dates. In the listing of US Treasury STRIPS, we see, for example, that the present value (the ask price) on March 12, 2004 of a payment of $100 to be made on May 15, 2010 is quoted as $82.07, which is $82\frac{7}{32} = $82.22 (treasury note payments and maturities usually take place on the 15th of a month, and remember that price quotations give fractions of a dollar in increments of $\frac{1}{32}$). This can be regarded as a zero-coupon bond maturing on May 15, 2010.

The quoted yield rate for that ask price is 3.20%. This will be a nominal annual rate compounded semi-annually. As of March 12, 2004, there are 6 years, 2 months and 3 days until the payment is made. This corresponds to 12 full half-year periods plus (approximately) 2.1 months for a total of $12 + \frac{2.1}{6} = 12.35$ interest (half-year) periods. The present value of $100 due in 12.35 interest periods at a rate of 1.60% per interest period is $100(1.016)^{-12.35} = 82.20. The quoted price of $82.22 is within the roundoff error range for interest rates quoted to the nearest .01%.

There seem to be some anomalies in the quoted values in Tables 6.1 and 6.2. For instance, in what appears to be a fairly steady increasing trend in the yield rates with increasing time to maturity, we see that the yield rate for the January, 2006 US Treasury STRIP is 1.07%, which is noticeably lower than the yield rate of 1.34% for the November, 2005 STRIP. Also, there are different STRIPS that mature at the same time but have different yields. These differences may be due to a number of factors. If a STRIP payment has a callable feature, it may end up being paid earlier than the maturity date stated, and the price and yield would be quoted on the basis of its earliest call date, but it would be listed in the table by its latest call date. Also, STRIPS are separated into coupon interest payments, treasury note payments and treasury bond payments. The size of the payment available may have some implications in the market as to the liquidity (demand and/or availability) for that amount of a STRIP.

The yield rates in the excerpts above are market versions of the term structure of interest rates (for government securities) in the U.S. and in Canada on March 12, 2004. Although the quotations listed are not a complete description of the term structure, we have enough information to calculate the present value of most risk-free sets of cashflows. For example, the Bloomberg website excerpt in Figure 6.1 lists a 2.25% bond maturing February 15, 2007 as having a price of $100.91 and a yield to maturity of 1.9%. This bond would make payments of $1.125 on August 15, 2004, February 15 and August 15 in both 2005 and 2006 and February 15, 2007, along with a payment of $100 on February 15, 2007. We can find the present value of each of these payments separately using the term structure represented in the STRIPS quotations.

Theoretically, the sum of the separate present values of these payments should be the same as the price of the full bond. This is sometimes referred to as the **Law of One Price**. The Law of One Price is an economic rule which states that in an *efficient market*, a security must have a single price, no matter how that security is created. A coupon bond is an obligation to make a certain series of payments, which can be constructed as a series of appropriately sized and timed STRIPS.

| **EXAMPLE 6.1** | (*Using the term structure to price a bond*)

Suppose that the current term structure has the following yields on zero-coupon bonds, where all yields are nominal annual rates of interest compounded semi-annually.

Term	½ Year	1 Year	1 ½ Year	2-Year
Zero Coupon Bond Rate	8%	9%	10%	11%

Find the price per $100 face amount and yield to maturity of each of the following 2-year bonds (with semi-annual coupons):

(i) zero-coupon bond , (ii) 5% annual coupon rate,

(iii) 10% annual coupon rate.

| **SOLUTION** |

(i) Price is $100\left(1+\frac{.11}{2}\right)^{-4} = 80.72$ and yield to maturity is (nominal) 11%.

(ii) Price is $2.5\left[(1.04)^{-1}+(1.045)^{-2}+(1.05)^{-3}\right]+102.5(1.055)^{-4} = 89.59$. Yield to maturity is (nominal) 10.9354%.

(iii) Price is $5\left[(1.04)^{-1} + (1.045)^{-2} + (1.05)^{-3}\right] + 105(1.055)^{-4} = 98.46$.

  Yield to maturity is (nominal) 10.8775%. □

In Example 6.1, if a 5%, two-year bond was available in the bond market, it would have to be priced at 89.59. If it had a market price over 89.59, then (theoretically) it would be possible to purchase $2.50 STRIPS maturing in ½-year, 1 year and 1½-years along with a $102.50 STRIP maturing in 2 years for a total cost of $89.59, and then resell the collection of STRIPS as a 2-year, 5% bond at a price higher than $89.59 resulting in a positive return on a net investment of 0. Reversing these actions would result in positive return for a net investment of 0 if the bond had a market price below $89.59. Later in this chapter we will discuss the concept of **arbitrage**, which involves making a riskless, positive profit with no net investment. In most theoretical models of financial markets it is assumed that no arbitrage opportunities exist.

For the 2.25% Treasury Note mentioned above, pricing the note using Treasury STRIPS does not quite replicate the quoted price because of distortions in the pricing of STRIPS that was mentioned above. Using the average price for simultaneous maturities in the US Treasury STRIP listing above, we have the following present value factors on March 12, 2004 for various payment dates.

TABLE 6.3

Payment Date	Present Value Factor
August 15, 2004	.9959
February 15, 2005	.9905
August 15, 2005	.9828
February 15, 2006	.9731
August 15, 2006	.9606
February 15, 2007	.9459

The entry in Table 6.3 for August 15, 2004 is based on the STRIP quote from Table 6.2 of a price of 99.19 for an August 2004 STRIP maturity. The value 99.19 refers to a price of $99\frac{19}{32} = 99.59$ for a STRIP of face amount 100. This corresponds to a present value factor of .9959. The other entries in Table 6.3 are found in a similar way.

Using these zero-coupon bond values, the present value of the bond payment would be

$$1.125(.9959+.9905+.9828+.9731+.9606) + 101.125(.9459) = 101.17.$$

To get the quoted price, we subtract the accrued coupon, which is $\frac{26}{182} \times 1.125 = .16$ (26 days from February 15, 2004 to March 12, 2004, out of a coupon period of 182 days from Feb. 15 to Aug. 15, 2004). According to this method of pricing the bond, the quoted price should be 101.01. This is somewhat different from the quoted price on the Bloomberg website of 100.91. The bond price for March 12, 2004 was quoted in the *Wall Street Journal* at a price of 100.97, still a little different from 101.01, but within roundoff error. The difference between the Bloomberg quote and the Wall Street Journal quote might be due to different times at which the quotes were taken.

The algebraic description of the term structure and spot rates is as follows. At the present moment, we consider a zero-coupon bond maturing t years from now, with a spot rate of s_t measured as an effective annual rate of interest. The present value of a payment of 1 due in t years is $(1+s_t)^{-t}$. The set of rates $\{s_t\}_{t>0}$ is the term structure of interest rates as of this moment. Any set of future cashflows can be valued now using the term structure. Suppose that payments of amounts $C_1, C_2, ..., C_n$ are due in $t_1, t_2, ..., t_n$ years from now. The total present value of the series of cashflows is $C_1(1+s_{t_1})^{-t_1} + C_2(1+s_{t_2})^{-t_2} + \cdots + C_n(1+s_{t_n})^{-t_n}$.

The payments on a coupon bond can be valued using spot rates as described in the previous paragraph. In Chapter 4 bond valuation was presented with prices calculated using the yield to maturity. The yield to maturity of a coupon bond is a single interest rate that is applied to find the present value of all payments to be made by the bond. The yield to maturity is actually an average of the spot rates for the payment periods represented by the bond.

6.2 THE RELATIONSHIP BETWEEN SPOT RATES OF INTEREST AND YIELD TO MATURITY ON COUPON BONDS

We have seen in the previous section that we can find the present value of a series of payments if the term structure is known. We can also find the price of a bond if the yield to maturity is known. These two alternative valuation methods for a coupon bond lead to a relationship between spot rates and yield to maturity. The following is an exaggerated example to illustrate the relationship.

EXAMPLE 6.2 (*Spot rates vs. yield to maturity*)

Suppose that the term structure of interest rates has the following schedule of spot rates for maturities of 1, 2, 3 and 4 years:

Maturity	1 Year	2 Year	3 Year	4 Year
Spot Rate	.05	.10	.15	.20

Use this term structure to find the price and yield to maturity for a 5% annual coupon bond maturing in (i) 1 year, (ii) 2 years, (iii) 3 years, and (iv) 4 years. Also use this term structure to find the price and yield to maturity for a 4 year 10% annual coupon bond.

SOLUTION

1-year bond: The bond pays 105 in 1 year, so the price is $(105)(1.05)^{-1} = 100$.

The bond is bought at par because the coupon rate and the yield rate are the same, 5%.

2-year bond: The bond pays 5 in 1 year, and 105 in 2 years. The price is $5(1.05)^{-1} + 105(1.10)^{-2} = 91.54$. The yield to maturity for this 2-year bond is .0987. Note that this yield to maturity for the 2-year bond is smaller than the spot rate of .10 for a zero coupon bond with a 2-year maturity. The yield rate is also larger than the 1-year spot rate of 5%.

3-year bond: The bond pays 5 in 1 year, 5 in 2 years, and 105 in 3 years. The price is $5[(1.05)^{-1} + (1.10)^{-2}] + 105(1.15)^{-3} = 77.93$. The yield to maturity for this 3-year bond is .1460. Again, note that this yield to maturity for the 3 year bond is smaller than the spot rate of .15 for a zero coupon bond with a 3-year maturity.

4-year bond: The bond pays 5 in 1, 2 and 3 years, and 105 in 4 years. The price is $5\left[(1.05)^{-1} + (1.10)^{-2} + (1.15)^{-3}\right] + 105(1.20)^{-4} = 62.82$. The yield to maturity for this 4-year bond is .1912. Again, this yield to maturity for the 4-year bond is smaller that the spot rate of .20 for a zero coupon bond with a 4-year maturity.

4 year, 10% bond: The bond pays 10 in 1, 2 and 3 years, and 110 in 4 years. The price is $10[(1.05)^{-1} + (1.10)^{-2} + (1.15)^{-3}] + 110(1.20)^{-4} = 77.41$. The yield to maturity for this 4-year bond is .1848. Again, this yield to maturity for the 4 year bond is smaller that the spot rate of .20 for a zero coupon bond with a 4-year maturity.   □

We can identify some patterns that occur in Example 6.2. Example 6.2 has an increasing term structure. We note that the yield to maturity for the 4-year 5% bond was 19.12% and for the 4-year 10% bond it was 18.48%. This is consistent with the behavior we have seen in some bonds quoted in the previous section. We saw quotes as of March 12, 2004 for U.S. Treasury notes maturing February 15, 2007. The 2.25% note had a yield to maturity of 1.913% and the 6.25% note had a yield to maturity of 1.909%. This phenomenon of the higher coupon bond with the same maturity date having a lower yield to maturity will always occur **when the term structure of spot interest rates is increasing** (in other words, for a normal yield curve). The general reasoning explanation for this phenomenon is that, in the minimum coupon case of a zero coupon bond maturing in n periods, the yield to maturity is the same as the spot rate, say s_n. If a bond has non-zero coupons, there will be payments occurring both before and at time n, and payments before time n will be valued at a lower spot rate than s_n (since the spot rates will be increasing up to s_n). The yield to maturity is the single interest rate such that the present value of all payments at that rate is equal to the bond price. The yield to maturity is a weighted average of the spot rates up to time n, where the weight is related to the size of the payments occurring before time n. A higher coupon bond makes larger payments earlier and puts more weight on early payments, and therefore puts more weight on earlier spot rates. Since we are assuming an increasing term structure, the smaller spot rates occur at the earlier payment times, and putting more weight on those smaller spot rates brings the average yield to maturity down. We can describe this algebraically in the following way. Suppose that the coupon is r per year in Example 6.2(iv). Then the price of the bond is

$$r\left[(1.05)^{-1} + (1.10)^{-2} + (1.15)^{-3}\right] + (100+r)(1.20)^{-4} \qquad (1)$$

Suppose that we denote the yield to maturity as y_r for this bond. The price can also be formulated as

$$r\left[(1+y_r)^{-1} + (1+y_r)^{-2} + (1+y_r)^{-3}\right] + (100+r)(1+y_r)^{-4}.$$

We can see that $.05 < y_r < .20$, since any yield larger than .20 must result in a present value smaller than (1), and any yield smaller than .05 must result in a present value greater than (1). y_r is an average rate of return for the 2-year period, but the average is weighted by how much emphasis is made on each payment. As mentioned above, if $r = 0$, then the yield is .20 since the price is made up of only a payment at time 4. As r gets larger, more weight is put on payments at earlier time points, and the average return y_r (the yield to maturity) is a weighted average in which more weight is put on the earlier spot rates, which are lower than .20. This suggests that as r increases from 0, the yield decreases from .20. That is why in Example 6.2, we see the yield to maturity for the 4-year bond dropping as the coupon rate rises. The reverse behavior would occur in the case of a decreasing term structure (an inverted yield curve). Exercise 6.1.6 at the end of this chapter provides a derivation of this behavior.

Economic conditions and the investment climate are constantly changing. Each day there will be changes in investor perceptions, and one of the ways that these changes can be observed is in yield rates in the bond market. The term structure will evolve from day to day. Earlier in this chapter graphs of the term structure were presented for various points in time. These graphs were excerpted from the internet site Stockcharts.com. On that website (www.stockcharts.com/charts/YieldCurve.html) there is a "Dynamic Yield Curve" graphic, which shows the term structure evolving through time, day by day, for a period of several years.

6.3 FORWARD RATES OF INTEREST

In the previous section of this chapter we saw that at any point in time there is a term structure of spot rates of interest, where the spot rate for a particular time to maturity represents the yield rate on a zero-coupon bond with that time to maturity. We will denote by s_t the spot rate (effective annual rate) for a zero-coupon bond maturing t years from now, so that the price now of a zero-coupon bond maturing for amount 1 in t years from now is $(1+s_t)^{-t}$.

Suppose that the current term structure has spot rates of $s_1 = .08$ for a one year maturity and $s_2 = .09$ for a two year maturity. An investment of amount 1 right now in a one year zero-coupon bond will grow to 1.08 in one year, while an investment of 1 right now in a two year zero-coupon bond will grow to $(1.09)^2 = 1.1881$ in two years. Let us suppose that we are able to borrow money at the same rate at which we can invest in zero-coupon bonds. Suppose that we borrow an amount of 1 today for one year so that we are committed to pay 1.08 back in one year. We invest that amount of 1 in a two year zero-coupon bond which will pay 1.1881 two years from now. The net effect of this transaction is that we invest 1.08 one year from now and receive 1.1881 two years from now. We have postponed, for one year, a one year investment, and our one year return on that postponed investment is $\frac{1.1881}{1.08} - 1 = .1001$. This rate of 10.01% is a **one year forward rate of interest**. It is the rate of interest that should be charged for a one year loan that begins one year from now. If it were possible to arrange to take a loan for one year starting one year from now at an interest rate of less than 10.01% then it would be possible to make an arbitrage gain (guaranteed positive return for net investment of 0). Arbitrage will be discussed in the next section of this chapter, where the assertion in the previous sentence will be verified.

One interpretation of a forward rate of interest is that it is the interest rate that we expect to be in effect in the future based on the current interest rate environment. We would make decisions about arranging now to borrow or invest at future points in time based on the forward rates that we currently see. Interest rates change from time to time, so the related forward rates would change over time as well. For instance, even though the current spot rates of 8% for one year and 9% for two years implies a one year forward rate of 10.01%, it is possible that one year from now interest rates may have changed and when this year elapses the one year rate at that time might not be 10.01%.

If we know the value of s_t for all times $t > 0$, then we can calculate forward rates of interest for any period of time in the future. An investment of 1 made now in an $(n-1)$-year zero coupon bond will grow to $(1+s_{n-1})^{n-1}$ in $n-1$ years. An investment of 1 now in an n-year zero coupon bond will grow to $(1+s_n)^n$ in n years. This implies that an investment of amount $(1+s_{n-1})^{n-1}$ made $n-1$ years from now should grow to $(1+s_n)^n$ one year later (n years from now,) and this in turn implies that the interest rate that should be used to arrange transactions that will take place between $n-1$ and n years from now is $\dfrac{(1+s_n)^n}{(1+s_{n-1})^{n-1}} - 1$. This is the $(n-1)$-year forward, one year interest rate, and we will denote it by the symbol $i_{n-1,n}$, so that $1 + i_{n-1,n} = \dfrac{(1+s_n)^n}{(1+s_{n-1})^{n-1}}$. The forward rate for the period from time 0 to time 1 is $i_{0,1} = s_1$ (not really a forward rate, since "forward rate" refers to a rate on a transaction that starts in the future, not now).

Rewriting the equation for $i_{n-1,n}$ above we have

$$(1+s_{n-1})^{n-1} \cdot (1+i_{n-1,n}) = (1+s_n)^n.$$

Then starting with $i_{0,1} = s_1$, we can express accumulated values into the future with forward rates of interest as an alternative to the term structure rates:

AV in 1 year $1 + s_1 = 1 + i_{0,1}$

AV in 2 years $(1+s_2)^2 = (1+s_1)(1+i_{1,2}) = (1+i_{0,1})(1+i_{1,2})$

AV in 3 years $(1+s_3)^3 = (1+s_2)^2(1+i_{2,3}) = (1+i_{0,1})(1+i_{1,2})(1+i_{2,3})$

The general expression that we get is

$$(1+s_n)^n = (1+i_{0,1})(1+i_{1,2})\cdots(1+i_{n-1,n})$$

for the accumulated value at time n of an investment of 1 made now.

| **EXAMPLE 6.3** | (*Spot rates vs. forward rates*) |

Suppose that the term structure of interest rates has the following schedule of spot rates for maturities of 1, 2, 3 and 4 years:

Maturity	1 year	2 year	3 year	4 year
Spot Rate	.05	.10	.15	.20

Find the one year forward rates of interest for years 1, 2, 3 and 4 that are implied by this term structure.

| **SOLUTION** |

$s_1 = .05,\ s_2 = .10,\ s_3 = .15,\ s_4 = .20$ are the term structure rates.

$$i_{0,1} = s_1 = .05,\ i_{1,2} = \frac{(1+s_2)^2}{1+s_1} - 1 = \frac{(1.1)^2}{1.05} - 1 = .1524,$$

$$i_{2,3} = \frac{(1+s_3)^3}{(1+s_2)^2} - 1 = \frac{(1.15)^3}{(1.1)^2} - 1 = .2596, \text{ and}$$

$$i_{3,4} = \frac{(1+s_4)^4}{(1+s_3)^3} - 1 = \frac{(1.20)^4}{(1.15)^3} - 1 = .3634.$$

are the forward rates for each of the four years. □

Example 6.3 is a rather extreme example, but we can identify some patterns from it. The term structure is increasing and the forward rate for each future year (after the first year) is greater than the zero-coupon yield for maturities at the end of that year; i.e.,

$$i_{1,2} = .1524 > .10 = s_2, \qquad i_{2,3} = .2596 > .15 = s_3,$$

and $i_{3,4} = .3634 > .20 = s_4$. It is not difficult to see why this is always the case when the term structure rates s_t are increasing as t increases. In fact, if $s_n > s_{n-1}$ then

$$i_{n-1,n} = \frac{(1+s_n)^n}{(1+s_{n-1})^{n-1}} - 1 = \frac{(1+s_n)^{n-1}}{(1+s_{n-1})^{n-1}} \times (1+s_n) - 1 > s_n, \text{ since } \frac{1+s_n}{1+s_{n-1}} > 1.$$

An increasing term structure will result in increasing forward rates for the first few years, but there is no guarantee that the forward rates themselves will continue to increase. Exercises 6.3.1 and 6.3.2 at the end of the chapter will show the variations that can occur in forward interest rate behavior, and how forward rates are related to spot rates.

6.4 APPLICATIONS AND ILLUSTRATIONS

6.4.1 ARBITRAGE

An arbitrage is a financial transaction which returns a positive amount on an investment of amount 0 with no risk. An alternative equivalent definition of an arbitrage is an investment with no risk which has a return greater than the risk-free rate. An arbitrage is a "free lunch," or something for nothing. For example, if the stock of XYZ corporation has a quoted market price of US $100 on the New York Stock Exchange, and at the same time has a quoted price that is equivalent to US $101 on the Toronto Stock Exchange, it would be possible to "buy low and sell high" at the same instant making a profit of $1 per share. Such an imbalance in markets is unlikely to occur, and if it does occur, it is unlikely to last long. In most models of financial market behavior, it is assumed that no arbitrage opportunities exist, since investors are rational and would immediately exploit any market imbalance. It is not unusual to see small price differences in financial instruments trading on different markets, but it would take a large amount invested to make any significant profit on the difference, and there is a risk that during the time it takes to make such investments the price differential may disappear.

The website of Wikipedia (en.wikipedia.org/wiki/Main_Page), an online encyclopedia, gives the following anecdote on arbitrage. Long-Term Capital Management (LTCM) lost over four billion dollars mismanaging this concept in September 1998. LTCM had attempted to make money on the difference between different bond instruments. For example, it would buy U.S treasury bonds and sell Italian bond futures. The concept was that because Italian bond futures had a less liquid market, in the short term Italian bond futures would have a higher return than U.S. bonds, but in the long term, the prices would converge. Because the difference was small, a large amount of money had to be borrowed to make the buying and selling profitable.

The downfall in this system began on August 17, 1998, when Russia defaulted on its ruble debt and domestic dollar debt. Since the markets were already nervous due to the Asian monetary crisis, investors began selling non-U.S. treasury debt and buying U.S. treasuries, which were considered a safe investment. As a result the return on U.S. treasuries began decreasing because there were many buyers, and the return on other bonds began to increase because there were many sellers. This caused the difference between the returns of U.S. treasuries and other bonds to increase, rather than to decrease as LTCM was expecting. Eventually this caused LTCM to fold, and a bailout had to be arranged to prevent a collapse in confidence in the economic system. An ironic footnote is that they *were* right long-term (the LT in LTCM), and a few months after they folded, their portfolio became very profitable. However the long-term does not matter if you cannot survive the short-term.

When the assumption is made that no arbitrage opportunities exist, it is usually also assumed that financial transactions can be arranged by any investor to buy or to sell, at the same price, any financial instrument. In considering the term structure of interest rates earlier in this chapter, we saw that the term structure of spot rates of interest for zero-coupon bonds implied the existence of forward rates of interest. For example, a one-year effective annual spot rate of interest of $s_1 = .08$ and a two-year spot rate of $s_2 = .09$ implies a one year forward, one-year effective annual rate of $i_{1,2} = \frac{(1.09)^2}{1.08} - 1 = .1001$. If we assume that there are no arbitrage opportunities, then right now, the only rate at which someone can arrange a one-year forward loan for a one year period is at 10.01%. If any other interest rate is offered for a one-year forward one year loan or investment, then an arbitrage opportunity will exist.

EXAMPLE 6.4   (*Arbitrage on forward interest rates*)

Suppose that the one year zero coupon bond yield rate is 8% and the two-year zero coupon bond yield rate is 9% (both effective annual rates). For each of the situations in (a) and (b), construct transactions that provide an arbitrage gain, i.e., a positive profit for a net investment of 0. Assume that it is possible to borrow or lend at the zero coupon rates for their maturity periods.

(a) A borrower offers to pay you an interest rate i above 10.01% for a one year investment starting one year from now.

(b) A lender offers to lend you money for one year at rate j starting one year from now at an interest rate less than 10.01%.

| SOLUTION |

(a) Borrow 1000 at the two year zero-coupon yield rate of 9%, so that you must repay $1000(1.09)^2 = 1,188.10$ two years from now. Invest the 1000 in a one-year zero coupon bond for one year at the one-year rate of 8%, so that you receive 1080 one year from now. Arrange to lend that amount to the borrower at rate i starting one year from now. You have made a net investment of 0, and at the end of two years the borrower pays you $1080(1+i)$. Since $i > .1001$ it follows that the amount you receive from the borrower at the end of two years is

$$1080(1+i) > 1080(1.1001) = 1188.10.$$

You have more than you need to repay your two year loan. You have made a guaranteed positive gain on an investment of 0.

(b) Borrow 1000 at the one year zero coupon yield rate of 8%. You must repay 1080 in one year. Invest the 1000 at the two-year zero coupon yield of 9%, so that you will receive 1881.10 in two years. Arrange to borrow 1080 from the lender one year from now at the one year rate of j. At the end of one year, when you receive 1080 from the lender, you pay the 1080 as repayment of your own one year loan. At the end of two years you receive 1881.10 from your two year investment, and you have to repay $1080(1+j)$ to the lender from whom you borrowed 1080. Since $j < .1001$, the amount you must repay at the end of two years is $1080(1+j) < 1080(1.1001) = 1881.10$. Therefore, the proceeds of your two year investment is more than enough to repay your loan and the difference is a guaranteed profit to you, having invested a net amount of 0.

In both cases (a) and (b) you have made an arbitrage profit. □

6.4.2 THE FORCE OF INTEREST AS A FORWARD RATE

When we considered the term structure earlier in this chapter we considered an example in which the zero-coupon yield rates were known for 1, 2, 3 and 4 years. We can imagine a situation in which we know the zero-coupon yield rate for any time to maturity t (including fractional times). For instance, if we have zero-coupon yields for maturities monthly into the future, then it is possible to find forward rates in effect for one-month starting any number of months from now.

Suppose that for any maturity time t in the future, we know the zero-coupon bond yield rate as a continuously compounded rate. For a zero-coupon bond that matures at time t, let us denote by α_t the continuously compounded yield rate, so that the present value of 1 due at time t is $(e^{-\alpha_t})^t = e^{-t \cdot \alpha_t}$. Alternatively, an investment of 1 can be made now to accumulate to $a(t) = e^{t \cdot \alpha_t}$ at time t.

In Chapter 1, the force of interest was defined as an instantaneous rate of interest (actually, it was defined as a nominal annual rate of interest that is compounded continuously). For an investment whose value at time t is $a(t)$ (and is continuously changing), the force of interest at time t was defined to be $\delta_t = \frac{a'(t)}{a(t)}$. It was seen in Chapter 1 that the value of the investment at time t can be expressed as $a(t) = e^{\int_0^t \delta_u \, du}$. The force of interest is describing how the investment will be growing (instantaneously) at time t in the future, so it is a continuously compounded version of a t-period forward rate of interest.

We can now relate α_t, the continuously compounded term structure yield on zero-coupon bonds, to δ_t the force of interest (continuously compounded forward rate) at time t. It is possible to formulate the term structure if the force of interest is known, and the reverse is true as well. From the two representations of $a(t)$ above we have

$$a(t) \;=\; e^{t \cdot \alpha_t} \;=\; e^{\int_0^t \delta_u \, du},$$

so that

$$t \cdot \alpha_t \;=\; \int_0^t \delta_u \, du$$

and

$$\alpha_t = \frac{1}{t} \cdot \int_0^t \delta_u \, du.$$

We see that the continuously compounded term structure rate for maturity at time t is an average of the force of interest over the period from time 0 to time t. This is similar to what occurs with effective annual rates for the relationship between the term structure and forward rates. We saw in Section 6.3 that

$$(1+s_n)^n = (1+i_{0,1})(1+i_{1,2})\cdots(1+i_{n-1,n}),$$

so that

$$1 + s_n = \left[(1+i_{0,1})(1+i_{1,2})\cdots(1+i_{n-1,n}) \right]^{1/n};$$

this is the geometric mean of the year-by-year forward growth factors $1+i_{0,1}, 1+i_{1,2}, \ldots, 1+i_{n-1,n}$ (s_n is the zero-coupon yield for an n-year maturity, and $i_{k-1,k}$ is the $k-1$ year forward rate for the one year period from time $k-1$ to time k).

If we differentiate both sides of the equation $t \cdot \alpha_t = \int_0^t \delta_u \, du$ with respect to t, we get $\alpha_t + t \cdot \frac{d\alpha_t}{dt} = \delta_t$. Note that if the term structure is "flat," i.e. $\alpha_t = \alpha$ (constant) for all t, then the force of interest is also constant, $\delta_t = \alpha_t + t \cdot \frac{d\alpha_t}{dt} = \alpha + 0 = \alpha$ for all t. Also, if the force of interest is constant at $\delta_t = \delta$ for all t, then $\alpha_t = \frac{1}{t} \cdot \int_0^t \delta_u \, du = \delta$ for all t.

Suppose that the continuous term structure rate α_t is increasing as t increases (meaning that $\frac{d\alpha_t}{dt} > 0$); then $\delta_t > \alpha_t$, and the reverse inequality is true if the term structure is falling for maturities at time t. This is similar to the behaviour that we saw for the effective annual versions of term structure and forward rates in Section 6.3, where forward rates of interest are larger than zero-coupon yields if the term structure of zero-coupon yields is increasing with time to maturity.

EXAMPLE 6.5 | (*Continuous Term Structure and Forward Rates*)

Suppose that the yield to maturity for a zero-coupon bond maturing at time t is $\alpha_t = .09 - (.08)(.94)^t$, a continuously compounded rate.

(a) Find the related forward rate δ_t.

(b) A borrower plans to borrow 1000 in one year and repay the loan with a single payment at the end of the second year. Determine the amount that will have to be paid back based on the stated term structure.

SOLUTION

(a) The forward rate at time t is

$$\delta_t = \alpha_t + t \cdot \frac{d\alpha_t}{dt} = .09 - (.08)(.94)^t - (.08)(.94)^t (\ln .94) \cdot t.$$

(b) The forward loan can be arranged by selling a one-year zero-coupon bond with face amount 1000. When the bond is sold, an amount of $1000e^{-\alpha_1} = 1000e^{-[.09-(.08)(.94)]} = 985.31$ is received. This amount is invested in a 2-year zero-coupon bond, which will mature at a value of

$$985.31e^{2\alpha_2} = 985.31e^{2[.09-(.08)(.94)^2]} = 1024.11.$$

We can also solve for the amount outstanding by using the continuously compounded forward rate (which is the force of interest). The amount outstanding at the end of the second year will be

$$1000e^{\int_1^2 \delta_t \, dt} = 1000e^{\int_1^2 [.09-(.08)(.94)^t-(.08)(.94)^t(\ln .94)\cdot t] \, dt} = 1024.11. \quad \square$$

6.4.3 AT-PAR YIELD

We have seen that if the term structure of zero-coupon yield rates is either rising or falling, then two bonds with the same maturity date but different coupon rates will have different yield to maturity values. There is another measure of bond yield that relates to the term structure, and that is the **at-par**

yield. Given a term structure of zero-coupon yield rates, the at-par yield rate for a coupon bond maturing at time t is defined to be the rate r_t such that a bond with coupon rate r_t that matures at time t has a yield to maturity that is also r_t, so that the bond will be priced at par (recall from Chapter 4 that a bond for which the coupon rate and yield rate are equal will be priced at par). For a given term structure it is not difficult to find the at par yield for any maturity time t. Suppose that the term structure spot rates are $\{s_t : t = 1, 2, ...\}$ for zero-coupon bonds maturing in $1, 2, ...$ years, and suppose that the at-par yield is r_n for an n-year coupon bond with annual coupons. Since this is the at-par yield, the coupon rate is also r_n and the bond price is 1 (for a bond with face amount 1) so that

$$(1+s_n)^{-n} + r_n \cdot \sum_{k=1}^{n} (1+s_k)^{-k} = 1, \text{ and then } r_n = \frac{1-(1+s_n)^{-n}}{\sum_{k=1}^{n} (1+s_k)^{-k}}.$$

EXAMPLE 6.6   (*Finding the at-par yield*)

Suppose that the term structure of interest rates has the following schedule of spot rates for maturities of 1, 2, 3 and 4 years:

Maturity	1-year	2-year	3-year	4-year
Spot Rate	.05	.10	.15	.20

Find the at-par yield for bonds with annual coupons that mature in 1, 2, 3 and 4 years.

SOLUTION

The key point in finding the at-par yield is that the price of the bond should be 100 for a face amount of 100.

1-Year Bond: $100 = 100(1+r_1)\left(\frac{1}{1.05}\right)$. Solving for r_1 results in $r_1 = .05$.

2-Year Bond: $100 = 100r_2\left(\frac{1}{1.05}\right) + 100(1+r_2)\left(\frac{1}{1.10}\right)^2$

Solving for r_2 results in $r_2 = .0976$.

3-Year Bond: $100 = 100r_3\left(\frac{1}{1.05}\right) + 100r_3\left(\frac{1}{1.10}\right)^2 + 100(1+r_3)\left(\frac{1}{1.15}\right)^3$

Solving for r_3 results in $r_3 = .1406$.

4-Year Bond:

$$100 = 100r_4\left(\frac{1}{1.05}\right) + 100r_4\left(\frac{1}{1.10}\right)^2 + 100r_4\left(\frac{1}{1.15}\right)^3 + 100(1+r_4)\left(\frac{1}{1.20}\right)^4$$

Solving for r_4 results in $r_4 = .1774$.   □

When a government issues a coupon bond, the coupon rate is usually chosen so that the bond is priced at, or close to par. This will depend on prevailing rates in the financial markets at the time the bond is issued. The at-par yield that prevails at the time a coupon bond is issued is the coupon rate that should be chosen in order for the bond to be priced at par when it is issued.

There is a close relationship between the yield curve of the term structure of zero-coupon bond yield rates, forward rates of interest, yield to maturity of coupon bonds and at-par yield rates. The following example illustrates some of the relationships that exist under the "normal" increasing term structure.

EXAMPLE 6.7   (*Forward rates and at-par yields*)

Suppose that the term structure of interest rates is increasing with the yield rate for a zero coupon bond maturing at time t-years being

$$s_t = .09 - (.08)(.94)^{t-1}.$$

The spot rates are $s_1 = .01$, $s_2 = .0148$, $s_3 = .0193,...$, etc. Find the implied forward rates of interest and the at-par yield rates for the 1st through the 60th year and draw a graph of the three series of rates.

SOLUTION

To find the n-year forward rate $i_{n,n+1}$ for the year starting n years from now, we use the relationship $i_{n,n+1} = \dfrac{(1+s_{n+1})^{n+1}}{(1+s_n)^n} - 1$. To find the n-year at-par yield rate r_n for an n-year coupon bond with annual coupons, we use the relationship $r_n = \dfrac{1-(1+s_n)^{-n}}{\sum\limits_{k=1}^{n}(1+s_k)^{-k}}$.

The table of rates is as follows.

Table 6.4

Year	Spot Rate	Forward Rate	At-Par Yield
1	0.0100	0.0100	0.0100
2	0.0148	0.0196	0.0148
3	0.0193	0.0284	0.0192
4	0.0236	0.0364	0.0233
5	0.0275	0.0436	0.0271
6	0.0313	0.0502	0.0306
7	0.0348	0.0562	0.0338
8	0.0381	0.0616	0.0367
9	0.0412	0.0665	0.0394
10	0.0442	0.0709	0.0418
11	0.0469	0.0748	0.0440
12	0.0495	0.0784	0.0460
13	0.0519	0.0815	0.0479
14	0.0542	0.0844	0.0495
15	0.0564	0.0869	0.0510
16	0.0584	0.0891	0.0524
17	0.0603	0.0911	0.0536
18	0.0621	0.0928	0.0547
19	0.0637	0.0944	0.0557
20	0.0653	0.0957	0.0565
21	0.0668	0.0969	0.0573
22	0.0682	0.0979	0.0581
23	0.0695	0.0987	0.0587
24	0.0707	0.0994	0.0593
25	0.0719	0.1000	0.0598

Table 6.4 (Continued)

Year	Spot Rate	Forward Rate	At-Par Yield
26	0.0730	0.1005	0.0603
27	0.0740	0.1009	0.0607
28	0.0749	0.1012	0.0611
29	0.0759	0.1014	0.0614
30	0.0767	0.1016	0.0617
31	0.0775	0.1017	0.0620
32	0.0782	0.1018	0.0622
33	0.0790	0.1018	0.0625
34	0.0796	0.1017	0.0627
35	0.0802	0.1016	0.0628
36	0.0808	0.1015	0.0630
37	0.0814	0.1014	0.0631
38	0.0819	0.1012	0.0633
39	0.0824	0.1010	0.0634
40	0.0828	0.1008	0.0635
41	0.0833	0.1006	0.0636
42	0.0837	0.1004	0.0636
43	0.0841	0.1001	0.0637
44	0.0844	0.0999	0.0638
45	0.0847	0.0996	0.0639
46	0.0851	0.0993	0.0639
47	0.0854	0.0991	0.0640
48	0.0856	0.0988	0.0640
49	0.0859	0.0985	0.0640
50	0.0861	0.0983	0.0641
51	0.0864	0.0980	0.0641
52	0.0866	0.0977	0.0641
53	0.0868	0.0975	0.0642
54	0.0870	0.0972	0.0642
55	0.0872	0.0970	0.0642
56	0.0873	0.0967	0.0642
57	0.0875	0.0965	0.0642
58	0.0876	0.0962	0.0643
59	0.0878	0.0960	0.0643
60	0.0879	0.0958	0.0643

The graph of this data is below.

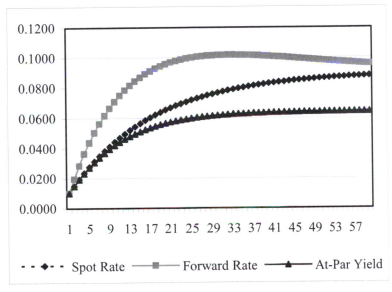

FIGURE 6.4

There are a few features in this example that we note. The term structure of spot rates is increasing in this example. When the term structure of spot rates is increasing as the maturity date increases, the forward rate for the one year period $t-1$ to t is greater than the spot rate for maturity at time t, i.e., $i_{t-1,t} > s_t$. As can also be seen from Example 6.7, the forward rates are not necessarily increasing even though the spot rates are increasing. An increasing term structure of spot rates also results in increasing at-par yield rates as time to maturity increases. If the term structure of spot rates is decreasing, the forward rates are smaller than spot rates and the at-par yield rates are decreasing. These characteristics are considered in the exercises.

The following graph of spot rates, forward rates and at-par yield rates around the time this book was being prepared (early 2004) was excerpted from the website of J. Huston McCulloch, Department of Economics of Ohio State University.

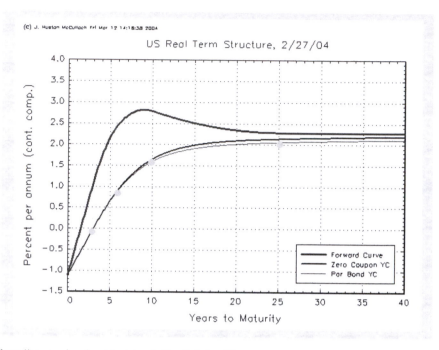

http://economics.sbs.ohiostate.edu/jhm/ts/ts.html#arc

FIGURE 6.5

6.4.4 INTEREST RATE SWAPS

An **interest rate swap** is a contractual agreement between two parties to
exchange a series of payments for a stated period of time. Interest rate
swaps may be implemented for a number of reasons. An interest rate swap
can be used to convert *floating-rate liability* into *fixed-rate liability* or
vice-versa. The **floating rate of interest** is a short-term interest rate that
changes periodically, depending on the transaction to which it is being
applied. The 1-month yield on a US T-Bill is an example of a floating rate
of interest. A loan that requires monthly interest at a floating rate will have
each month's new interest rate based on market conditions for the new
month. A floating rate mortgage usually has monthly interest charges
using an updated rate each month. A swap can also change the risk
characteristics of assets or liabilities that are associated with the swap.

As an example of an interest rate swap, consider two borrowers, A and B. In the following discussion, the prime rate of interest refers to the short-term interest rate that banks charge their most creditworthy borrowers. Borrower A has a high credit rating, and can borrow in the fixed-rate market (medium to long-term bond market) at a rate of 8%, or in the floating-rate market (short-term or spot market) at prime plus 1%. Borrower B has a medium credit rating and can borrow in the fixed-rate market at 9% or in the floating-rate market at prime plus 1.5%. Borrower A wishes to borrow an amount in the floating-rate market and B wishes to borrow the same amount in the fixed-rate market. It is possible to construct an arrangement between A and B that will allow both of them to borrow at lower rates than those described above. The two borrowers construct the following swap.

A borrows in the fixed-rate market at 8% and loans the funds to B at a rate of 8.5%. B borrows in the floating-rate market at prime plus 1.5% and loans the funds to A at prime plus 1.25%. The net effect for borrower A is that borrower A pays 8% on the fixed-rate loan, receives 8.5% from B and pays prime plus 1.25% to B, for a net payment rate of prime plus .75%. The net effect for borrower B is that B pays prime plus 1.5% on the floating-rate loan, B receives prime plus 1.25% from A and B pays 8.5% to A, for a net payment rate of 8.75%. A's net payment rate of prime plus .75% is .25% below the floating rate that A would pay directly, and B's net payment rate of 8.75% is .25% below the fixed-rate that B would pay directly.

What allows this arrangement to be made is that the differential between fixed and floating rates for A is not the same as that for B, and the two borrowers are able to take advantage of that by taking parallel loans (or back-to-back loans) and swapping them.

The situation described above is an arrangement between borrowers A and B without making use of a financial intermediary to make the swap arrangements. In practice, a financial intermediary would make the swap arrangements for them, and would receive as income a percentage of the principal involved. In the example above, the swap administered by the financial intermediary could be structured as follows:

(i) borrower A borrows at fixed rate 8% (not necessarily from the intermediary);

(ii) borrower B borrows at floating rate prime plus 1.5% (also not necessarily from the intermediary);

(iii) the intermediary agrees with A to accept from A floating rate interest payments at prime at the same time as paying A fixed interest at 7.2%;

(iv) the intermediary agrees with B to accept from B fixed interest payments at 7.3% at the same time as paying B floating rate interest payments at prime.

The net effect for borrower A is that A pays prime plus .8%;
The net effect for borrower B is that B pays a fixed rate of 8.8%;

The net effect for the intermediary is that the intermediary receives "spread income" that is equal to .1% of the principal amount. This is income earned by the intermediary as a result of the spread rates between borrowers A and B; it is not interest on an amount invested in the usual sense.

More generally, suppose that borrower A can borrow at fixed rate i_A and floating rate $j_A =$ prime rate $+ f_A$, and borrower B can borrow at fixed rate i_B and floating rate $j_B =$ prime rate $+ f_B$. If $i_B - i_A > f_B - f_A$ then an interest rate swap can be constructed between A and B that allows A to borrow at floating rate prime rate $+ r_A$ and allows B to borrow at fixed rate r_B, where $r_A < f_A$ and $r_B < i_B$. This is done as follows:

(i) let $c = (i_B - i_A) - (f_B - f_A)$;

(ii) A borrows at fixed rate i_A and lends the funds to B at fixed rate $i_B - c$;

(iii) B borrows at floating rate prime rate $+ f_B$ and lends the funds to A at a floating rate of prime rate $+ f_B - \frac{c}{2}$.

The net effect for A is that A pays

$$i_A - (i_B - c) + \text{prime} + f_B - \frac{c}{2} \;=\; \text{prime} + i_A - i_B + f_B + \frac{c}{2}\,.$$
$$=\; \text{prime} + f_A - \frac{c}{2}$$
$$=\; \text{prime} + r_A \;<\; \text{prime} + f_A$$

The net effect for B is that B pays

$$\text{prime} + f_B - \left(\text{prime} + f_B - \frac{c}{2}\right) + i_B - c \;=\; i_B - \frac{c}{2} \;=\; r_B \;<\; i_B.$$

If $d < c$, then it is possible for an intermediary to receive a fee at rate d under the following arrangement:

(i)   A borrows at fixed rate i_A;

(ii) B borrows at floating rate $\text{prime} + f_B$;

(iii) the intermediary agrees with A to accept from A floating rate interest payments at prime at the same time as paying A fixed interest at rate $i_A - \left(f_A - \frac{c}{2} + \frac{d}{2}\right)$;

(iv) the intermediary agrees with B to accept from B fixed interest payments at $i_B - f_B - \frac{c}{2} + \frac{d}{2}$ at the same time as paying B floating rate interest payments at prime.

The net effect for borrower A is that A pays

$$i_A + \text{prime} - \left[i_A - \left(f_A - \frac{c}{2} + \frac{d}{2}\right)\right] \;=\; \text{prime} + f_A - \frac{c}{2} + \frac{d}{2};$$

the net effect for borrower B is that B pays

$$\text{prime} + f_B + i_B - f_B - \frac{c}{2} + \frac{d}{2} - \text{prime} \;=\; i_B - \frac{c}{2} + \frac{d}{2};$$

the net effect for the intermediary is that the intermediary receives a fee of

$$\text{prime} - \left[i_A - \left(f_A - \frac{c}{2} + \frac{d}{2}\right)\right] + i_B - f_B - \frac{c}{2} + \frac{d}{2} - \text{prime}$$
$$= \; (i_B - i_A) - (f_B - f_A) - c + d \;=\; d.$$

The practice of interest rate swapping began in the late 1970's. It has grown incredibly quickly since that time. An estimate of 1992 activity in interest rate and currency swaps is 5 trillion dollars (US), and an estimate of the same activity in 2004 is over 30 trillion dollars.

6.5 NOTES AND REFERENCES

There are a number of theories that attempt to explain the nature of the term structure and its relationship to economic conditions. A review of several of these theories can be found in Chapter 6 of the 5th Edition of *The Handbook of Fixed Income Securities*, and in Chapter 20 of the 5th edition of "Modern Portfolio Theory and Investment Analysis", by E. Elton and M. Gruber. The Elton and Gruber book also provides an extensive bibliography for stochastic models of the term structure, a topic which is beyond the scope of this book.

A good introduction to interest rate and currency swaps can be found in *Interest Rate and Currency Swaps* by R. Dattatreya, S. Venkatesh and V. Venkatesh.

6.6 EXERCISES

The exercises without asterisks are intended to comprehensively cover the material presented in the chapter. Exercises with a asterisk can be regarded as supplementary exercises which cover topics in more depth, either theoretically or computationally, than those without a asterisk.

SECTIONS 6.1 AND 6.2

6.1.1   A 10% bond with face amount 100 matures in 7 years.

   (a) Find the value of the bond based on each of the following term structures for zero-coupon bond spot rates, where $i_{0,t}$ denotes the nominal annual spot rate convertible semiannually for a t-year term zero-coupon bond.

   (i) $i_{0,.5} = .075$ $i_{0,1} = .0775$ $i_{0,1.5} = .08$ $i_{0,2} = .08$

   $i_{0,2.5} = .0825$ $i_{0,3} = .085$ $i_{0,3.5} = .085$ $i_{0,4} = .09$

   $i_{0,4.5} = .0925$ $i_{0,5} = .095$ $i_{0,5.5} = .095$ $i_{0,6} = .0975$

   $i_{0,6.5} = .10$ $i_{0,7} = .1025$

(ii) $i_{0,.5} = .14$ $i_{0,1} = .1375$ $i_{0,1.5} = .135$ $i_{0,2} = .1325$

$i_{0,2.5} = .13$ $i_{0,3} = .1275$ $i_{0,3.5} = .125$ $i_{0,4} = .1225$

$i_{0,4.5} = .12$ $i_{0,5} = .1175$ $i_{0,5.5} = .115$ $i_{0,6} = .1125$

$i_{0,6.5} = .11$ $i_{0,7} = .1075$

(iii) $i_{0,.5} = .12$ $i_{0,1} = .12$ $i_{0,1.5} = .12$ $i_{0,2} = .12$

$i_{0,2.5} = .12$ $i_{0,3} = .12$ $i_{0,3.5} = .12$ $i_{0,4} = .12$

$i_{0,4.5} = .12$ $i_{0,5} = .12$ $i_{0,5.5} = .12$ $i_{0,6} = .12$

$i_{0,6.5} = .12$ $i_{0,7} = .12$

(b) For each of the bond prices found in (a), find the corresponding yield to maturity.

(c) Repeat part (a) for an 8% bond and for a 12% bond.

6.1.2 (a) You are given the following information about two 10 year bonds. Both bonds have face amount 100 and coupons payable semi-annually, with next coupon due in ½-year.

Bond 1: Coupon rate 4% per year, price 85.12
Bond 2: Coupon rate 10% per year, price 133.34.

Find the yield rate (annual rate compounded semi-annually) for a 10 year zero-coupon bond.

(b) You are given the following term structure (effective annual interest rates) for zero coupon bond maturities up to n years: $s_1 = s_2 = \cdots = s_{n-1} < s_n$ (flat term structure except for n-year maturity). An n-year bond has annual coupon rate $r > 0$ and annual coupons. Show that the yield to maturity for the bond j must satisfy $s_{n-1} < j < s_n$.

6.1.3   You are given the following term structure:

$$s_1 = .15, \qquad s_2 = .10, \qquad s_3 = .05.$$

These are *effective annual rates of interest* for zero-coupon bonds of 1, 2 and 3 years maturity, respectively. A newly issued 3-year bond with face amount 100 has annual coupon rate 10%, with coupons paid *once per year* starting one year from now. Find the price and effective annual yield to maturity of the bond.

6.1.4   The term structure of effective annual yield rates for zero-coupon bonds is given as follows: 1 and 2-year maturity, 10%; 3 and 4-year maturity, 12%. Find the price of a 4-year bond with face amount 100, and annual coupons at rate 5%. The first coupon will be paid in one year.

6.1.5   You are given the following information for 4 bonds. All coupon and yield-to-maturity rates are nominal annual convertible twice per year.

Bond	Time to Maturity	Coupon Rate	YTM
1	½-year	4%	.05
2	1-year	6%	.10
3	1½-year	4%	.15
4	2-year	8%	.15

Find the associated term structure for zero-coupon bonds with maturities of ½-year, 1 year, 1½-year, and 2 year (quotations should be nominal annual rates convertible twice per year).

*6.1.6   Assume that the pricing of a coupon bond is consistent with its pricing based on separate coupons and redemption using the term structure of spot rates as in Exercise 6.1.1. Let $H(r,t)$ denote the current term structure for the yield to maturity of a coupon bond with coupon rate r and time t to maturity. Then $s_t = H(0,t)$ is the current term structure for zero-coupons bonds. Let $r_1 \geq r_2$.

(a) Suppose $H(0,t)$ is a decreasing function of t for all t. Show that $H(r,t)$ is also a decreasing function of t, and

$$H(r_1,t) \geq H(r_2,t) \geq H(0,t)$$

for any t.

(b) Suppose $H(0,t)$ is an increasing function of t for all t. Show that $H(r,t)$ is also an increasing function of t, and

$$H(r_1,t) \leq H(r_2,t) \leq H(0,t)$$

for any t.

(c) Suppose $H(0,t)$ is constant for all t. Show that $H(r,t)$ is also constant and $H(r,t) = H(0,t)$ for any t.

SECTION 6.3

6.3.1   Let $i_{0,1}, i_{0,2}, i_{0,3}, \ldots, i_{0,n}$ be the effective annual rates of return for zero-coupon bonds with maturities of 1 year, 2 years, 3 years , ..., n years, respectively. Let $i_{1,2}, i_{2,3}, \ldots, i_{n-1,n}$ be the corresponding annual forward rates for year 2, year 3 , ..., year n, respectively.

(a) Find an expression for $i_{k-1,k}$ in terms of the $i_{0,t}$'s.

(b) Show that $(1+i_{0,1})(1+i_{1,2})\cdots(1+i_{k-1,k}) = (1+i_{0,k})^k$
for $k = 1,2,\ldots,n$.

(c) Show that $\frac{d}{di_{0,k}}i_{k-1,k} > 0$ and $\frac{d}{di_{0,k-1}}i_{k-1,k} < 0$.

(d) Show that if $i_{0,k} > i_{0,k-1}$, then $i_{k-1,k} > i_{0,k}$.

6.3.2   Consider the following two yield curves (representing perhaps annual yields on two different classes of zero-coupon bonds), based on the notation of Exercise 6.3.1:

(i) $i_{0,k} = .09 + .001k;$

(ii) $i_{0,k} = .09 + .002k - .0001k^2$, both for $k = 1, 2, \ldots, 10$.

For each of these yield curves, calculate the corresponding forward rates of interest for years 2 to 10, and plot the forward rates on a graph along with a plot of the yield curve. (Note that since both yield curves are increasing, part (d) of Exercise 6.3.1 guarantees that the graph of the forward rates will lie above the graph of the corresponding yield curve. Note also that for yield curve (ii), although the yield curve is increasing, the corresponding forward rates do not form an increasing sequence.)

6.3.3   A 6-month T-Bill of face amount 100 can be bought today for 97.800, and a 1-year T-Bill of face amount 100 can be bought today for 95.400. Find the forward rate of interest for the 6-month period beginning 6 months from today, quoted as a nominal annual rate of interest compounded semi-annually.

6.3.4   According to the current term structure of interest rates, the effective annual interest rates for 1, 2 and 3 year maturity zero-coupon bonds are

        1-year .08,   2-year .10,   3-year .11.

Find the one-year forward effective annual rate of interest and find the two year forward effective annual rate of interest.

6.3.5   The following term structure is given as effective annual rates of interest on zero-coupon bonds:

        1-year maturity: 6%   2-year maturity: 7%   3-year maturity: 9%

(a) Find (i) the 1-year forward effective annual interest rate for a 1-year period, $i_{1,2}$ and (ii) the 2-year forward effective annual interest rate for a 1-year period, $i_{2,3}$.

(b) The effective annual rate of interest for a 4-year zero-coupon bond is s_4. Find the minimum value of s_4 needed so that $i_{3,4} \geq i_{2,3}$, where $i_{3,4}$ is the 3-year forward effective annual interest rate for a 1-year period and $i_{2,3}$ is found in part (a).

6.3.6   The term structure of effective annual yield rates for zero-coupon bonds is given as follows:

> 1 and 2-year maturity, 10%;
> 3 and 4-year maturity, 12%.

You are given the price of a 5-year bond with face amount 100, and annual coupons at rate 5% is 73.68. Find the 4-year forward effective annual interest rate (in effect for the 5th year).

*6.3.7   Let s_t denote the term structure or yield curve of spot rates, so that s_t is the effective annual yield rate for a zero-coupon bond maturing in t years. Let $i_{t-1,t}$ denote the term structure of forward rates, so that $i_{t-1,t}$ is the forward rate in effect in the tth year from now.

(a) Prove each of the following relationships between s_t and $i_{t-1,t}$.

(i) If s_t is increasing, then $s_t \leq i_{t-1,t}$.

(ii) If s_t is decreasing, then $s_t \geq i_{t-1,t}$.

(b) (i) Construct an increasing yield curve s_t for which $i_{t-1,t}$ is decreasing for $t \geq 2$.

(ii) Construct a decreasing yield curve s_t for which $i_{t-1,t}$ is increasing for $t \geq 2$.

*6.3.8   Suppose that r_t denotes the continuously compounded yield rate on a zero-coupon bond maturing at time t (the term-structure). Suppose that δ_t is the continuously compounded t-year forward rate (force of interest at time t). Prove the following:

(i) If $\lim_{t \to \infty} r_t = r$ (where $0 \le r \le \infty$), then $\lim_{t \to \infty} \delta_t = r$; and

(ii) if $\lim_{t \to \infty} \delta_t = r$ (where $0 \le r < \infty$), then $\lim_{t \to \infty} r_t = r$.

SECTION 6.4

6.4.1   Yield rates for zero coupon bonds are as follows:
            1 year maturity, 10% (effective annual);
            2 year maturity, 8% (effective annual).

You take the following actions:

(i) Sell a one-year zero-coupon bond with maturity value 1000.

(ii) Invest the proceeds in a two-year zero-coupon bond.

Which of the following represents your overall net position?

(a) One year forward investment for one year at 6%

(b) One year forward investment for one year at 12%

(c) One year forward loan for one year at 6%

(d) One year forward loan for one year at 12%

(e) Two year loan for 9%

6.4.2   Suppose that yield rates on zero-coupon bonds are currently 6% for a one-year maturity and 7% for a two-year maturity (effective annual rates).

Suppose that someone is willing to lend money to you starting one year from now to be repaid two years from now at an effective annual interest rate of 7%. Construct a transaction in which an arbitrage gain can be obtained (positive net gain for net investment of 0).

6.4.3   Yield rates for zero coupon bonds are as follows:

         1 year maturity, 8% (effective annual);

         2 year maturity, 10% (effective annual).

You take the following actions.

(i) Sell a two year zero-coupon bond with maturity value 1000.

(ii) Invest the proceeds in a one year zero-coupon bond.

Which of the following represents your overall net position?

(a) One year forward investment for one year at 10%

(b) One year forward investment for one year at 12%

(c) One year forward loan for one year at 10%

(d) One year forward loan for one year at 12%

(e) Two year investment for 9%

6.4.4   The current term structure has the following nominal annual spot rates, $i^{(2)}$:

         6-month spot rate is 8%;
         1-year spot rate is 10%;

         1½-year spot rate is x%.

(a) Based on this term structure, a 1½-year bond with (nominal annual) coupon rate 10% has a YTM of 11%. Find x.

(b) Suppose that the forward rate (quoted as a nominal annual rate of interest) for the period from 1 to 1½ years is 11%. Find x in that case.

(c) You predict that 6 months from now, the 6-month spot rate will be 10%. Construct a strategy to implement now, involving sale and purchase of zero-coupon bonds that will make a profit for you if your prediction is correct.

6.4.5   The effective annual yield on a one-year zero coupon bond is 8% and the effective annual interest rate on a two-year zero coupon bond is 8.5%. You are able to arrange a one-year forward loan at rate i for a one-year period. Suppose that under these conditions it is possible to make a riskless profit with the following strategy:

(i)   borrow amount 1 for one year at 8% effective annual,

(ii)   invest amount 1 for 2 years at 8.5% per year effective annual

(iii) arrange a one-year forward one-year length loan of amount 1.08 at rate i (starting one year from now) and repay the loan in (i)

(iv) use the proceeds from (ii) to repay loan (iii) at the end of the second year.

For what full range of i will this strategy result in a positive amount left over after all 3 transactions are settled at the end of the second year?

*6.4.6 $i_{t-1,t}$ is the forward rate of interest for the one year period starting $t-1$ years from now, s_t is the spot rate (yield rate) of interest for zero-coupon bonds maturing in t years, and r_t is the at-par yield rate for bonds with annual coupons maturing in t years. All rates are effective annual rates. Show the following implications:

(a) s_t is an increasing function of t for all $t \Leftrightarrow i_{t-1,t} > s_t$ for all t.

(b) s_t is a decreasing function of t for all $t \Leftrightarrow i_{t-1,t} < s_t$ for all t.

(c) $i_{t-1,t}$ is an increasing function of t for all t
     $\Rightarrow s_t$ is an increasing function of t for all t
     $\Rightarrow r_t$ is an increasing function of t for all t.

(d) $i_{t-1,t}$ is a decreasing function of t for all t
     $\Rightarrow s_t$ is an decreasing function of t for all t
     $\Rightarrow r_t$ is an decreasing function of t for all t.

CHAPTER 7

CASHFLOW DURATION AND IMMUNIZATION

An investor who holds a fixed-income investment such as a bond will see the value of the bond change over time for a number of reasons. It was seen in the discussion of bond amortization in Chapter 4 that there is a natural progression of the amortized value of a bond toward the maturity value as the bond approaches its maturity date. Over the lifetime of the bond, the market value of the bond will also converge to the maturity amount as well. These longer term changes in bond values are somewhat predictable, although the market value will fluctuate to a large extent as a result of changing market conditions, such as interest rates and the perception of the chance of the bond defaulting on some of its scheduled payments. Default risk for bonds will be considered in Chapter 8.

The market value of a bond at a particular time is directly related to the yield to maturity that prevails in the bond market at that time. Yield rates fluctuate with economic conditions and changes in market yield rates can have a sudden and significant impact on the market value of a bond. There is no guarantee that when an investor buys a bond, the yield rate at which the bond was bought will continue to be the bond's yield rate for the entire term of the bond. In fact, the yield rate will almost surely not stay constant as time goes on. The next example illustrates one of the reasons why yield rates on a particular bond might change over time.

EXAMPLE 7.1 (*Yield curve slide*)

Suppose that the current term structure of interest rates has the following schedule of spot rates for maturities of 1, 2, 3 and 4 years:

Maturity	1-year	2-year	3-year	4-year
Spot Rate	.05	.10	.15	.20

Suppose a 4-year zero coupon bond with maturity amount 100 is purchased. Suppose further that as time goes on, the term structure does not change, so that at any time the spot rates are the same as they are now. Find the book value and market value of the bond in one, two and three years.

SOLUTION

The purchase price is $100(1.2)^{-4} = 48.23$. In one year the amortized (book) value will be $100(1.2)^{-3} = 57.87$. At that time the bond will be three years from maturity, so the market yield will be 15% (we are assuming that the term structure will be the same, so three year zero coupon bonds will always have a yield rate of 15%). In one year the market value of the bond will be $100(1.15)^{-3} = 65.75$. Note that after one year the holder of the bond will have had a one-year *holding period return* of $\frac{65.75}{48.23} - 1 = .3633 \,(36.33\%)$. At the end of the second year the book value will be $100(1.2)^{-2} = 69.44$ and the market value will be $100(1.1)^{-2} = 82.64$. At the end of the third year the book value will be $100(1.2)^{-1} = 83.33$ and the market value will be $100(1.05)^{-1} = 95.24$. At the end of the fourth year the bond matures and its value (book and market) is 100. These book and market values are summarized in the following table.

Time	Book Value	Market Value
0	48.23	48.23
1	57.87	65.75
2	69.44	82.64
3	83.33	95.24
4	100.00	100.00

The phrase "yield curve slide" in the title of this example refers to the move away from book value that the market value takes as time goes on. This occurs not because there is any change in the term structure, but because the term structure is not constant.

Economic conditions may change, and rates of return demanded by investors may change, so that the market value of the bond might not always be equal to the bondholder's book value. If the market yield rate for the bond is higher than the bondholder's original (book) yield, then the present value of the payments represented by the bond will be less at the higher market yield rate than at the original yield rate (with the reverse occurring if the market yield is below the book yield). There is no requirement that the bondholder must sell the bond before maturity, and if the bondholder keeps the bond until maturity he will realize the original book yield-to-maturity as the internal rate of return on his investment no matter what changes in interest rates occur during the term of the bond. If the bondholder sells the bond before maturity at a price other than the book value, the bondholder's return (internal rate of return) for the period that the bond was held will not be the original book yield, but will be related to the market yield at the time of sale.

Suppose that in Example 7.1 above, the investor purchases the 4-year zero coupon bond at the yield rate of 20% per year for a price of 48.23. Suppose that later that same day some significant event occurs that changes the economic and financial outlook of investors and the 4-year spot rate suddenly changes to 22%. The value of the 4-year zero coupon bond becomes $100(1.22)^{-4} = 45.14$, an almost immediate loss of 3.09 (about 6.4% of the original purchase price). Of course the numerical values used in this illustration are not likely values to occur in the world's major financial markets, and they exaggerate the possible consequences of short term changes in interest rates. The following section presents a systematic analysis of the sensitivity of a bond's price to changes in the yield rate.

7.1 DURATION OF A SET OF CASHFLOWS AND BOND DURATION

The present value of any fixed series of payments such as those paid out by a bond is sensitive to changes in the yield rate or term structure that is used to value the payments. The conventional measure of the risk, volatility, or sensitivity of a bond's price (or the present value of any fixed series of payments) to changes in the market yield rate is based on the derivative (instantaneous rate of change) of the bond's present value with respect to changes in the yield rate.

We will first consider the sensitivity of the value of a zero coupon bond to changes in the yield rate. Suppose that a zero-coupon bond matures for amount 1 in n years and is currently priced at an effective annual yield rate i for n-year maturities. The current price of the bond is $P = (1+i)^{-n}$.

If we regard the price as a function of the yield rate i, and we differentiate with respect to i, we get $\frac{d}{di}P = -n(1+i)^{-n-1}$. The derivative is negative because increasing the yield rate results in a decreasing present value.

In considering the sensitivity of the bond's price to changes in the yield rate we are mainly concerned with the magnitude of the relative rate of change in price per dollar invested. The magnitude of the relative rate of change in price per dollar invested is called the **modified duration** of the bond. The modified duration is

$$DM = -\frac{\frac{d}{di}P}{P} = \frac{n(1+i)^{-n-1}}{(1+i)^{-n}} = n(1+i)^{-1} = nv. \quad (7.1)$$

We multiply $\frac{d}{di}P$ by -1 to clear the negative sign on the derivative, and we divide by P (the amount invested) to get a quantity per dollar invested.

A related measure is D, the **Macaulay duration** of the bond (often just called the duration of the bond). The Macaulay duration is the modified duration multiplied by $1+i$, so that $D = DM \cdot (1+i)$. For the n-year zero coupon bond, the Macaulay duration is $D = DM \cdot (1+i) = nv(1+i) = n$. Duration is measured in units of years. We would say that the n-year zero coupon bond has a (Macaulay) duration of n years. The use of the word "duration" for this measure of sensitivity is based on the fact that for a zero coupon bond, this measure of sensitivity to changes in interest rate is equal (numerically) to the "duration" until maturity.

Since it is the derivative of price per dollar invested with respect to change in yield rate, the modified duration is a more direct measure than the Macaulay duration of the relative change in price that will occur when there is a change in the yield rate. The derivative $\frac{d}{di}P$ is the limit as $h \to 0$ of $\frac{P(i+h)-P(i)}{h}$, where h represents a small yield rate change. As an approximation, for small changes in the yield rate, the change in the value of the bond is $P(i+h) - P(i) \doteq h \cdot \frac{d}{di}P(i) = -h \cdot P(i) \cdot DM$.

| EXAMPLE 7.2 | (*Duration of a zero coupon bond*) |

Suppose that the effective annual yield rate is 10% for all maturities of zero coupon bonds. Find the modified duration and Macaulay duration for a 1-year, 10-year and 30-year zero coupon bond. For a bond maturity amount of 100, find the actual and the approximate change in price expected using the differential approximation for each bond when there is a 1 basis point decrease in the yield rate (a basis point is .01%).

| SOLUTION |

Using the expressions developed for modified duration and Macaulay duration, we have the following table. As a decimal, a 1 basis point increase or decrease in yield rate is a change of .0001.

Term to Maturity	1-Year	10-Year	30-Year
Bond Price $P(i)$	90.909091	38.55433	05.7309
Modified Duration	00.909091	9.090910	27.2727
Macaulay Duration	01.000000	10.00000	30.0000
Approximate Change in Price Using DM	00.008264	00.035049	00.015630
Approximate Relative Change in Price	00.000091	00.000909	00.002727
Actual Price at Yield Rate 9.99%	90.917356	38.589400	05.746507
Actual Change in Price	00.008265	00.035067	00.015652
Actual Relative Change in Price	00.000091	00.000910	00.002731

□

It could have been anticipated that the n-year present value factor $(1+i)^{-n}$ is more sensitive to changes in i when n is large than when n is small, although we see that the dollar change in value for the 10-year bond is greater than that for the 30-year bond. When we say that the longer term bond is more sensitive to changes in the yield rate, we mean that the relative change in value of the longer term bond is greater for the 30-year bond than for the 10-year bond. Using relative change in value as the measure of sensitivity, we see that the sensitivity increases with the time to maturity of the bond. Furthermore, the modified duration provides a good approximation to these relative price changes. The relative change in price of the 30-year bond is about 3 times that of the 10-year bond, which, in turn, is about 10 times that of the 1-year bond.

The differential approximation applied to the change in bond price related to a change in yield rate is not presented from the point of view of being of practical value in terms of approximating the bond price after the change in interest rate. It is easy to calculate the exact new value of the bond at the new yield rate without relying on approximation. The main point of Example 7.2 is to illustrate numerically how the sensitivity of the bond price to changes in yield relates to the time to maturity of the bond.

The duration measures presented above can be extended to measure the sensitivity of the present value of any series of cashflows to changes in the yield rate used to value the series. We will now suppose that a series of payments is being valued at a yield rate that is the same for each payment no matter when it occurs. This, for instance, is how a coupon bond is valued using the yield to maturity. Suppose that we consider a series of n annual payments starting one year from now at an effective annual valuation rate of i (the yield to maturity for valuing the series of payments). Suppose that the series of payments is $K_1, K_2, \ldots, K_n$. The present value of the series of payments is

$$
\begin{aligned}
P &= K_1(1+i)^{-1} + K_2(1+i)^{-2} + \cdots + K_t(1+i)^{-t} + \cdots + K_n(1+i)^{-n} \\
&= \sum_{t=1}^{n} K_t(1+i)^{-t}.
\end{aligned}
$$

We can formulate a measure of the sensitivity of P to changes in i. This would be

$$
\begin{aligned}
\frac{d}{di}P &= -K_1(1+i)^{-2} - 2K_2(1+i)^{-3} - \cdots - tK_t(1+i)^{-t-1} - \cdots - nK_n(1+i)^{-n-1} \\
&= -\sum_{t=1}^{n} tK_t(1+i)^{-t-1}.
\end{aligned}
$$

The modified duration (sometimes referred to as "volatility") of the set of cashflows is

$$
DM = -\frac{\frac{d}{di}P}{P} = \frac{\sum_{t=1}^{n} tK_t(1+i)^{-t-1}}{P} = \frac{\sum_{t=1}^{n} tK_t(1+i)^{-t-1}}{\sum_{t=1}^{n} K_t(1+i)^{-t}}, \quad (7.2)
$$

and the Macaulay duration is

$$D \;=\; (1+i)\cdot DM \;=\; \frac{\displaystyle\sum_{t=1}^{n} tK_t(1+i)^{-t}}{P} \;=\; \frac{\displaystyle\sum_{t=1}^{n} tK_t(1+i)^{-t}}{\displaystyle\sum_{t=1}^{n} K_t(1+i)^{-t}}. \qquad (7.3)$$

Suppose that in Equation 7.3 we define the factor w_t as $w_t = \dfrac{K_t(1+i)^{-t}}{P}$.

The Macaulay duration can then be written in the form $D = \sum_{t=1}^{n} w_t \cdot t$.

Note that since $P = \sum_{t=1}^{n} K_t(1+i)^{-t}$, it follows that $\sum_{t=1}^{n} w_t = 1$. The w_t factors can be thought of as "weights," and the Macaulay duration is a weighted average of the payment times from 1 to n.

In this interpretation, the Macaulay duration is a weighted average of the times at which the n payments are made. The weight applied to the payment at time t is $w_t = \dfrac{K_t(1+i)^{-t}}{P}$, which is the fraction of the overall present value of the series that is represented by that particular payment at time t. For an n-year zero coupon bond, there is only one payment, and it occurs at time n, so the weight for that payment is 1 since it accounts for the entire present value, and hence the Macaulay duration is $1 \times n = n$. In general, duration is measured in units of years. The duration of an n-year zero-coupon bond would be n years.

A coupon bond has relatively small coupon payments and then a large payment on the maturity date. Therefore, the weights applied to the coupons would be relatively small and the weight applied to the redemption payment would be relatively large. We would expect the Macaulay duration of a coupon bond to be close to n if the coupons are small. As the coupons get larger (relative to the redemption amount) the duration should get smaller. This is illustrated in the following example.

EXAMPLE 7.3   (*Duration of a coupon bond*)

A bond with annual coupons has face amount F, coupon rate r per year, n annual coupons until maturity, and is valued at yield rate j per year.

Calculate the duration of the bond for all possible combinations of parameters $r = .05, .10, .15$; $n = 2, 10, 30, 60$; and $j = .05, .10, .15$.

| SOLUTION |

The bond payments at times $1, 2, \ldots, n$ are $K_t = Fr$ for $t = 1, 2, \ldots, n-1$ and $K_n = F + Fr$. Thus the duration is

$$
D = \frac{\sum_{t=1}^{n} t \cdot Fr \cdot v_j^t + n \cdot F \cdot v_j^n}{\sum_{t=1}^{n} Fr \cdot v_j^t + F \cdot v_j^n}.
$$

At a yield rate of 5% per year, the duration values are as shown in Table 7.1a. Note that the first term in the numerator of D is an increasing annuity with arithmetically increasing payments.

TABLE 7.1a

Coupon Rate	Coupons Until Maturity			
	2	10	30	60
.05	1.952	8.108	16.141	19.876
.10	1.913	7.270	14.328	18.772
.15	1.880	6.797	13.613	18.391

At a yield rate of 10% per year, the durations are given in Table 7.1b.

TABLE 7.1b

Coupon Rate	Coupons Until Maturity			
	2	10	30	60
.05	1.950	7.661	11.434	11.124
.10	1.909	6.759	10.370	10.964
.15	1.875	6.281	9.987	10.910

At a yield rate of 15% per year, the durations are given in Table 7.1c.

TABLE 7.1c

Coupon Rate	Coupons Until Maturity			
	2	10	30	60
.05	1.948	7.170	8.209	7.689
.10	1.905	6.237	7.719	7.671
.15	1.870	5.772	7.551	7.665

☐

For an n-year bond with annual coupons at rate r per year and valued at an effective annual yield rate of i per year, the Macaulay duration of the bond can be shown to be $D = \dfrac{1+i}{i} - \dfrac{1+i+n(r-i)}{r[(1+i)^n - 1]+i}$. (See Exercise 7.1.3.)

7.1.1 DURATION OF A PORTFOLIO OF SERIES OF CASHFLOWS

Suppose that m separate series of annual cashflows are under consideration. Suppose that each cashflow series is an n-year series, with the payments for cashflow series k denoted $c_1^{(k)}, c_2^{(k)}, \ldots, c_n^{(k)}$. At effective annual interest rate i the present value of cashflow series k is $X_k = c_1^{(k)}(1+i)^{-1} + c_2^{(k)}(1+i)^{-2} + \cdots + c_n^{(k)}(1+i)^{-n}$, for $k = 1, 2, \ldots, m$. The Macaulay duration of the kth cashflow series is $D_k = -(1+i)\dfrac{\frac{d}{di} X_k}{X_k}$, so that $D_k \cdot X_k = -(1+i)\dfrac{d}{di} X_k$.

The aggregate present value of the collection of all series of cashflows is $X = \sum\limits_{k=1}^{m} X_k$, and $\dfrac{d}{di} X = \dfrac{d}{di} \sum\limits_{k=1}^{m} X_k$. The Macaulay duration of the combination of all the series of cashflows is

$$D = -(1+i)\frac{\frac{d}{di} X}{X} = \frac{\sum\limits_{k=1}^{m} -(1+i)\frac{d}{di} X_k}{X} = \frac{\sum\limits_{k=1}^{m} D_k \cdot X_k}{X}.$$

If we define the factor v_k to be $v_k = \dfrac{X_k}{X}$, then $D = \sum\limits_{k=1}^{m} v_k \cdot D_k$, and $\sum\limits_{k=1}^{m} v_k = 1$. We see that the Macaulay duration of the overall portfolio of series of cashflows can be represented as a weighted average of the durations of the individual series of cashflows, where the weight applied to duration D_k is $v_k = \frac{X_k}{X}$, which is the fraction of the present value of the overall portfolio represented by cashflow series k.

Two different cashflow series that have the same present value and the same duration at a common yield rate of i would have the same sensitivity to changes in the yield rate. We would describe the two series as being "matched" in the sense of present value and duration. This is a concept that will be explored further in the next section on cashflow matching and "immunization" of a series of cashflows.

Consider a bond portfolio consisting of two bonds, each of face amount 50:

(i) a 2-coupon bond with coupon rate 5% per coupon period, and

(ii) a 60-coupon bond with coupon rate 15% per coupon period.

Suppose the yield rate for short term (2-coupon) bonds is 5% per coupon period, and the yield on long (60-coupons) bonds is 15%. Since the yield rate is equal to the coupon rate for each bond, both bonds are currently valued at their par values of 50 each, so the total value of the portfolio is 100. These bonds are found in Tables 7.1a and 7.1c, with durations of 1.952 and 7.665, respectively. It follows from the comments in the previous paragraph that the duration of the portfolio is $(.5)(1.952+7.665) = 4.81$.

Now consider a second portfolio consisting of a single bond of face amount 100, with 6 coupons and a coupon rate of 10%, valued at a yield rate of 10% per coupon period. This bond will be priced at its par value of 100. The duration of this bond is 4.79. Thus, the portfolios have the same value and almost the same duration at the current yield rates.

The yield rates can be summarized in a yield curve (Figure 7.1a). Let us consider the effect on the portfolios that results from a change in the yield curve. Suppose that there is a +1% *parallel shift* in the yield curve (Figure 7.1b), so that the yield rates for all bond maturities increase by 1%. The value of the first portfolio becomes 95.96, and the value of the second portfolio becomes 95.77. Thus, as expected, both portfolios decrease in value by nearly the same amount as a result of a uniform (parallel) shift in the yield rate, since they have nearly the same duration. Suppose, instead, that the yield curve flattens slightly (Figure 7.1c), so that the yield on the 2-coupon bond increases to 6%, the yield on the 6-coupon bond stays at 10%, and the yield on the 60-coupon bond decreases to 14%. The value of the first portfolio becomes 102.65, but the second stays at 100. The purpose of this discussion is to point out that although two portfolios may currently have *matched* value and duration, the effects of non-parallel shifts in the yield curve may differ from one portfolio to another.

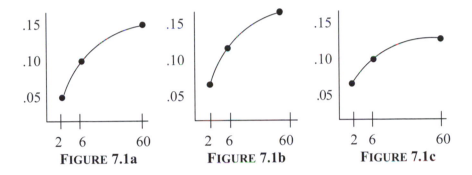

FIGURE 7.1a   FIGURE 7.1b   FIGURE 7.1c

Note that the yield curves represented here are not term structure curves (of zero coupon bonds), but rather they are graphs of yield to maturity versus time to maturity for the specific coupon bonds described above. In Section 6.2 we saw the relationship between yield curve for coupon bonds and the term structure curve, and how the yield to maturity for a coupon bond can be found if the term structure is known.

One of the important interpretations of duration is that two separate cashflow series that have the same duration will be affected in the same way by small changes in yield to maturity. In particular, if the Macaulay duration of a series of cashflows is D, then a zero coupon bond maturing in D years will have the same Macaulay duration. If the zero coupon bond has the same present value as the series of cashflows, then for small changes in the yield to maturity, the change in present value of the cashflow series will be about the same as the change in value of the zero coupon bond.

When there are future liabilities to be paid as a series of future cash outflows and we are holding investments (assets) that will provide future cash inflows that will be used to pay for the liabilities, we would like to try to match the present value of the two cashflow series to ensure that assets will be sufficient to cover liabilities. It may be beneficial to try to match the durations of the liability and asset cashflow series, so that (at least) small changes in interest rates will not adversely affect the balance between the present values of the two series. This notion of asset-liability matching is considered in the next section of this chapter.

It is clear that if an investor perceives that interest rates will increase, then the investor's risk of a loss in value of bond holdings is more limited with bonds of small duration, whereas if the perception is that rates will decrease, the investor's potential for gain in value of bond holdings is greater with bonds of larger duration. Duration is used to compare volatility of bond price with respect to yield rate, but would not be used in practice to actually calculate approximate changes in price as done in Example 7.2. Duration is more likely to be used to compare relative volatilities of two or more sets of cashflows.

7.2 ASSET-LIABILITY MATCHING AND IMMUNIZATION

In the course of conducting business, an enterprise will make commitments involving future income and outgo of capital. To maintain a viable (and profitable) position, the company will make investments so that funds will be available to provide for outgoing payments as they come due. Projected at time 0, the net outgoing payment at time $t > 0$ represents the company's *liability due* (or *outgo*) L_t at time t. The funds available from investment income and investments maturing at time t to cover that liability represent the company's *asset income* (or *proceeds*) A_t at time t. If the company can arrange its investments so that asset income exactly covers the liability due at each point in time, so that $A_t = L_t$ for all t, then the projected asset income and liabilities due are said to be *exactly matched*. Asset-liability matching is generally considered from the point of view of asset income and liability due cash flows occurring at discrete (usually equally spaced) points of time, $t = 0, 1, 2, \ldots, n$. It is also possible to consider continuous models of asset-liability matching, where A_t is the *rate* of asset income and L_t is the *rate* of liability due at time t.

EXAMPLE 7.4   (*Exact matching of assets and liabilities*)

A small company terminating its operations has decided to provide each of its three employees with a severance package that pays 10,000 per year (at the end of each year) up to and including at age 65, plus a lump sum payment of 100,000 at age 65. In case of death of an employee before age 65, the payments continue until that employee would have been 65. The three employees are now exact ages 50, 53 and 55. The company determines that the payments due under this package can be met by the income and maturities generated by three bonds, each with a face amount of 100,000 and an annual coupon rate of 10% and with maturities of 10, 12, and 15 years. Determine the cost to the company to fund the severance package if the bonds have (effective annual) yield rates of 10% for the 10-year bond, 11% for the 12-year bond and 12% for the 15-year bond.

SOLUTION

Applying any of the bond price formulas from Chapter 4 gives prices of 100,000 for the 10-year bond, 93,507.64 for the 12-year bond and 86,378.27 for the 15-year bond, for a total cost of 279,885.91. With the purchase of these bonds, the company's liabilities to the three employees are exactly matched.   □

As a variation on Example 7.4, suppose there are bonds available with a variety of coupon rates and maturity dates (including, perhaps, zero-coupon bonds). The company might have several alternative combinations of investments whose asset income flows match the liabilities. Linear programming can be used to find the minimum cost combination of investments which matches asset flow to liability flow (see Exercise 7.2.1).

In Example 7.4, once the company purchases the bonds, the payments to the employees are guaranteed at the exact amounts on the exact dates needed. It may not always be possible to obtain an exact match between projected asset income and liabilities due. Example 7.6 below considers alternative ways of setting up asset cashflows in an attempt to match the liabilities (payments to employees) that do not involve exact matching. A simpler illustration of the risk involved in asset-liability matching is illustrated in the following example.

EXAMPLE 7.5 *(Asset-Liability Matching)*

Suppose that there will be liability cashflows of amounts 1 each at time 1 and time 2, so that $L_0 = 0, L_1 = L_2 = 1$. Suppose also that at time 0, the term structure is flat with yield rates of 10% for all zero coupon bond maturities. The present value at time 0 of the liabilities is

$$v_{.1} + v_{.1}^2 = 1.735537.$$

There are various ways of trying to structure asset cashflows to pay for the liabilities. Each of the following asset cashflows has the same present value at time 0 at an interest rate of 10% as the series of liability cashflows.

(i) $A_0 = 0, A_1 = A_2 = 1$. This series of asset cashflows provides exact matching with the liability cashflows.

(ii) $A_0 = 1.735537, A_1 = A_2 = 0$. Not exact matching, but present values at 10% of assets and liabilities are matched at time 0.

(iii) $A_0 = A_1 = 0, A_2 = 2.1$. Not exact matching, but present values at 10% of assets and liabilities are matched at time 0.

We can interpret each of these three cases in the following way.

(i) A one year zero-coupon bond with face amount 1 and a two-year zero-coupon bond with face amount 1 are purchased to provide the asset cashflow. The cost of the two bonds is 1.735537 at time 0, and they will provide the exact asset cashflow to pay for the liabilities as they come due.

(ii) We assume that cash deposits can be made into an account earning interest at a rate of 10%. The initial asset cashflow at time 0 is a payment of 1.735537 which is deposited into the account. At time 1, the deposit account has grown to $1.735537(1.1) = 1.909091$. The liability of amount 1 due at time 1 is paid by making a withdrawal from the account, leaving a balance of .909091 in the account. At time 2 the account has grown to $.909091(1.1) = 1.000000.$. The liability of amount 1 due at time 2 is paid by making a withdrawal from the account, leaving a balance of 0 in the account.

(iii) A line of credit account is set up which charges interest at a rate of 10% when money is owing to the account. The liability of amount 1 due at time 1 is paid by taking a withdrawal of amount 1 from the line of credit at that time. The amount owed to the line of credit account at time 2 is 1.1 (one year of interest is added to the balance that was owing at time 1). At time 2 when the asset cashflow of 2.1

is received, it pays for the liability of amount 1 due at time 2 and it pays off the balance owing of 1.1 in the line of credit account. This leaves a net asset-liability position of 0 at time 2.   □

The three asset cashflow series that are presented in Example 7.5 each have the same present value at 10% at time 0 of 1.735537. This matching of the present values is generally the first step in the matching of liabilities and assets. In each of these examples, we see that if the interest rate environment that was in effect at time 0 continues to be in effect during the term of the cashflows, there will be a net surplus-deficit position of 0 at the time the cashflows end. An interest rate of 10% for any zero-coupon maturity was in effect at time 0, and it was assumed to continue for the two year period. We have really just restated a basic principle of compound interest which states that if the present values of two cashflow streams are equal at a particular point in time, then their values will be equal at any other point in time, providing the interest rate used for valuation stays constant.

In this elementary presentation of asset-liability matching concepts, we are assuming that the term structure at time 0 is flat with a yield to maturity of i_0 for all times to maturity. In attempting to match assets with liabilities we start out by ensuring that the present values of the two cashflow streams are equal at time 0 using the interest rate in effect at time 0, say i_0. This can be represented algebraically as follows:

$$PV_A(i_0) \;=\; \sum_0^n A_t v_{i_0}^t \;=\; \sum_0^n L_t v_{i_0}^t \;=\; PV_L(i_0). \qquad (7.4)$$

Equation (7.4) can be written in the form $\sum_0^n (A_t - L_t) v_{i_0}^t = 0,$ or equivalently

in the form $\sum_0^n (A_t - L_t)(1+i_0)^{n-t} = 0.$

We can interpret this last equation in the following way. At each cashflow time point t there is a net cashflow received of amount $A_t - L_t,$ which can be positive or negative. In Example 7.5(iii), we imagined that a line of credit account is in place in which interest is charged to the account at rate i_0 when the balance is negative and interest is credited to the account at the same rate i_0 when the balance in the account is positive. As the net cashflow amount is received at time t, we regard it as being deposited into or withdrawn from the line of credit account, depending upon whether $A_t - L_t > 0$ or $A_t - L_t < 0$. At each intermediate point in time there would be a net balance in the account that could be positive or negative. Equation (7.4) can be interpreted as saying that the balance in the account is 0 at the time of the final net cashflow. In other words, the net surplus-deficit position is 0 at the time the series of asset and liability cashflows ends.

The complication that arises in asset-liability matching is that although asset and liability cashflow present values may be matched at time 0 using valuation interest rate i_0, if there is a change in the interest rate, the present values might no longer match, and the surplus-deficit position at the time the cashflows end may no longer be 0. The imbalance that occurs depends on the relationship between asset and liability cashflow amounts.

In Example 7.5(i) it can be seen that once the 1 and 2 year zero coupon bonds are purchased to provide the asset cashflows, changes in interest rate are irrelevant in that as the zero-coupon bonds mature, they exactly pay the liability amounts required.

In Example 7.5(ii), the asset cashflow of amount 1.735537 was deposited into an account earning interest at rate 10%, and if the deposit account continued to earn 10% per year for the two year period, the assets would be exactly enough to pay for the liabilities. Suppose that for the first year the interest is 10% on the account, but at time 1, the interest rate on the deposit account changes to 9% for the 2nd year (from time 1 to time 2). The balance in the account just after the liability payment at time 1 is still .909091, but the balance in the account at the end of the second year just before the liability payment is $(.909091)(1.09) = .990909$. After the liability payment of amount 1 at time 2, the balance in the account is $-.009091$, so there is a deficit position in the assets as compared to the liabilities.

It is difficult or impossible to anticipate the future behavior of interest rates, so even though asset and liability cashflow present values are matched at time 0 based on the interest rate environment at time 0, future interest rate changes can put the asset and liability valuations out of balance. What we may attempt to do is structure the asset cashflows so that small changes in the interest rate do not put the asset-liability relationship into a deficit position. One way we have seen to do that is have assets exactly matched with liabilities, so that $A_t = L_t$ for all $t = 0,1,2,...,n$. In that case Equation (7.4) holds for any rate i_0, and there will never be a surplus or deficit position in the asset-liability relationship no matter how interest rates change.

Without exact matching, there is the risk that if the valuation rate of interest deviates from its original value of i_0 to some other value, say i, then $PV_A(i) < PV_L(i)$ and the asset income flow will not be sufficient to balance the liabilities due.

F.M. Redington developed a theory of **immunization** for an asset/liability flow. According to this theory, with a careful structuring of asset income in relation to liabilities due, small deviations in the interest rate from i_0 to i result in $PV_A(i) > PV_L(i)$, for both $i > i_0$ and $i < i_0$. Therefore, whether the interest rate increases or decreases (by a small amount), the present value of the assets at the new rate of interest will be larger than the present value of the liabilities, and the asset-liability relationship will not change from a matched to a deficit position.

The basic theory of immunization is as follows. Suppose asset income has been allocated so as to balance liabilities due at interest rate i_0 according to Equation (7.4). Suppose this allocation of asset income also satisfies the conditions

$$\frac{d}{di}PV_A(i)\Big|_{i_0} = \frac{d}{di}PV_L(i)\Big|_{i_0} \tag{7.5}$$

and

$$\frac{d^2}{di^2}PV_A(i)\Big|_{i_0} > \frac{d^2}{di^2}PV_L(i)\Big|_{i_0}. \tag{7.6}$$

If we define the function $h(i)$ to be

$$h(i) = PV_A(i) - PV_L(i), \tag{7.7}$$

then $h(i_0) = h'(i_0) = 0$ (from Equations (7.4) and (7.5)), and $h''(i_0) > 0$ (from Equation (7.6)). It follows that $h(i)$ has a *relative minimum* at i_0. In other words, for some interval around i_0, say (i_L, i_U), if $i_L < i < i_U$ then $h(i) > h(i_0) = 0$, or, equivalently, $PV_A(i) > PV_L(i)$.

With the asset/liability flow immunized in this way, a *small change* in the interest rate from i_0 to i where i is in an appropriate interval around i_0 as described in the previous paragraph, results in a *surplus* position in the sense that there is an excess of the present value of asset income over liabilities due when valued at the new rate i. The change in the interest rate must be small enough so that i stays within the interval. This immunization of the portfolio against small changes in i is called **Redington immunization**.

The second derivative of a function at a point is sometimes referred to as the convexity of the function at that point. Equation 7.6 can be interpreted as saying that the convexity of the present value function of the assets as a function of the rate of interest is greater than the convexity of the present value of the liabilities.

In Exercise 7.2.3 it is shown that Equation (7.5) is equivalent to

$$\sum t \cdot A_t \cdot v_{i_0}^t \ = \ \sum t \cdot L_t \cdot v_{i_0}^t, \tag{7.8}$$

and if Equation (7.5) is true then Equation (7.6) is equivalent to

$$\sum t^2 \cdot A_t \cdot v_{i_0}^t \ > \ \sum t^2 \cdot L_t \cdot v_{i_0}^t. \tag{7.9}$$

It follows from Equation (7.5) that $PV_A(i)$ and $PV_L(i)$ have the same volatility (modified duration) with respect to interest rates. It is not surprising, then, that a consequence of the conditions for immunization given by Equations (7.4) and (7.5) is that at interest rate i_0, the assets and liabilities have the same modified duration. This says that for small changes in the interest rate away from i_0, the changes in the present value of the assets and the present value of the liabilities are approximately the same.

Let us denote by $DM(i_0)$ the common modified duration of assets and liabilities at rate i_0.

If the conditions in Equations (7.4) and (7.5) are satisfied, and since $DM(i_0)$ is a time constant (the weighted average time to maturity or discounted mean term of the A_t's or L_t's), it follows that Equation (7.9) is equivalent to

$$\sum [t - DM(i_0)]^2 \cdot A_t \cdot v_{i_0}^t \quad > \quad \sum [t - DM(i_0)]^2 \cdot L_t \cdot v_{i_0}^t. \quad (7.10)$$

Therefore if Equations (7.4) and (7.5) are satisfied, the asset/liability match is immunized if the asset income flow is more dispersed or widely spread (in time) about $DM(i_0)$ than the liabilities due. The liability cashflow series in Example 7.4 is used in the following example to illustrate how the conditions for immunization might be met by ensuring a greater dispersion of asset cashflows than liability cashflows.

EXAMPLE 7.6   (Redington immunization)

To immunize the liabilities due in the severance package described in Example 7.4, the company purchases an investment portfolio consisting of two zero-coupon bonds, due at times t_1 and t_2 (measured from the starting date of the severance package). Suppose that the term structure is flat at an effective annual rate of 10%, so that all assets and liabilities are valued at 10%. For each of the following pairs t_1 and t_2, determine the amounts of each zero-coupon bond that must be purchased and whether or not the overall asset/liability portfolio is in an immunized position:

(a) $t_1 = 0$, $t_2 = 15$;   (b) $t_1 = 6$, $t_2 = 12$;   (c) $t_1 = 2$, $t_2 = 14$.

SOLUTION

Let X be the amount of zero-coupon bond purchased with maturity at t_1 and Y the amount with maturity at t_2. In order to satisfy Equation (7.4) we must have $X \cdot v_{.10}^{t_1} + Y \cdot v_{.10}^{t_2} = \sum L_t \cdot v_{.10}^t = 300,000$ (this is the present value of the liabilities).

In order to satisfy Equation (7.5) we must have

$$
\begin{aligned}
t_1 \cdot X \cdot v_{.10}^{t_1} + t_2 \cdot Y \cdot v_{.10}^{t_2} &= \sum t \cdot L_t \cdot v_{.10}^t \\
&= 30,000v + 2(30,000)v^2 + 3(30,000)v^3 \\
&\quad + \cdots + 9(30,000)v^9 + 10(130,000)v^{10} \\
&\quad + 11(20,000)v^{11} + 12(120,000)v^{12} \\
&\quad + 13(10,000)v^{13} + 14(10,000)v^{14} \\
&\quad + 15(110,000)v^{15} \\
&= 2,262,077.228.
\end{aligned}
$$

Solving these two equations for X and Y in each of the three cases, we obtain the values

(a) $X = 149,194.85,\ Y = 629,950.53$;

(b) $X = 395,035.30,\ Y = 241,699.38$; and

(c) $X = 195,407.21,\ Y = 525,977.96$

The third immunization condition, Equation (7.6), requires that

$$
t_1^2 \cdot X \cdot v_{.10}^{t_1} + t_2^2 \cdot Y \cdot v_{.10}^{t_2} > \sum t^2 \cdot L_t \cdot v_{.10}^t
$$

The right-hand side of the inequality is equal to

$$
\begin{aligned}
30,000v &+ 2^2(30,000)v^2 + 3^2(30,000v^3 \\
&\quad + \cdots + 9^2(30,000)v^9 + 10^2(130,000)v^{10} \\
&\quad + 11^2(20,000)v^{11} + 12^2(120,000)v^{12} + 13^2(10,000)v^{13} \\
&\quad + 14^2(10,000)v^{14} + 15^2(110,000)v^{15} \\
&= 22,709,878.
\end{aligned}
$$

In case (a) $t_1^2 \cdot X \cdot v_{.10}^{t_1} + t_2^2 \cdot Y \cdot v_{.10}^{t_2}$ (the left hand side of equation (7.6)) is 33,931,158, so this portfolio is immunized. In case (b) the left hand side is 19,117,390, so for small changes in the interest rate away from 10% (positive or negative), the present value of assets will be less than the present value of liabilities. In case (c) the left side is 27,793,236, so the portfolio is again immunized.   □

In Exercise 7.2.8 you are asked to show that in case (a) of Example 7.6 the portfolio is actually *fully immunized.* The portfolio is **fully immunized** if $\sum A_t \cdot v^t \geq \sum L_t \cdot v^t$ for *any* $i > 0$. In case (c) $h(i)$ has a relative minimum at $i_0 = .10$, but $\sum A_t \cdot v^t < \sum L_t \cdot v^t$ for sufficiently large values of i. That is, in case (c), a deficit may occur if the change in interest is large enough so that i is far enough from 10%. Thus, in case (c), the portfolio satisfies the conditions of Redington immunization at $i_0 = .10$, but the portfolio is not fully immunized. The graphs of $h(i)$ for cases (a) and (c) of Example 7.4 are shown in Figure 7.2 (not to scale).

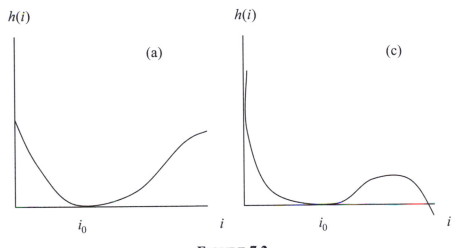

FIGURE 7.2

As time goes on, changes in interest rates may occur. This consideration, along with changing times until liabilities are due and asset income is received, may require that the asset portfolio be updated to maintain an immunized position.

We now investigate further the concept of *full immunization* defined above. Suppose liabilities due consist of a single liability of amount L_s at time $s \geq 0$. Suppose also that Equations (7.4) and (7.5) are satisfied with the current values of $i_0, s, L_s, t_1, t_2, A_{t_1}$, and A_{t_2}, where $t_1 \leq s$ and $t_2 \geq s$ at interest rate i_0 per unit time. Then Equations (7.4) and (7.5) become

$$A_{t_1} \cdot v_{i_0}^{t_1} + A_{t_2} \cdot v_{i_0}^{t_2} = L_s \cdot v_{i_0}^s \tag{7.11}$$

and

$$t_1 \cdot A_{t_1} \cdot v_{i_0}^{t_1} + t_2 \cdot A_{t_2} \cdot v_{i_0}^{t_2} = s \cdot L_s \cdot v_{i_0}^s. \tag{7.12}$$

To simplify notation we define $a = s - t_1$ and $b = t_2 - s$. As before, the function $h(i) = PV_A(i) - PV_L(i) = A_{t_1} \cdot v_i^{t_1} + A_{t_2} \cdot v_i^{t_2} - L_s \cdot v_i^s$ will be the present value of asset minus liability flow, valued at interest rate i. With some algebraic manipulation (see Exercise 7.2.9) $h(i)$ can be formulated as

$$h(i) = v_i^s \cdot A_{t_1} (1+i_0)^a \left[\left(\frac{1+i}{1+i_0} \right)^a + \frac{a}{b} \left(\frac{1+i}{1+i_0} \right)^{-b} - \left(1 + \frac{a}{b} \right) \right]$$

$$= v_i^s \cdot A_{t_1} \cdot g(i) \tag{7.13}$$

We see that $h(i_0) = 0$ and $g(i_0) = 0$ and

$$g'(i) = a(1+i)^{-1} \left[\left(\frac{1+i}{1+i_0} \right)^a - \left(\frac{1+i}{1+i_0} \right)^{-b} \right].$$

Since $a \geq 0$ and $b \geq 0$, it follows that $g'(i) \geq 0$ if $i \geq i_0$, and $g'(i) \leq 0$ if $i \leq i_0$. Therefore, $g(i)$ is increasing for $i \geq i_0$ and $g(i)$ is decreasing for $i \leq i_0$. The function $g(i)$ has an absolute minimum at $i = i_0$, and since $g(i_0) = 0$, it follows that $g(i) \geq 0$ for any interest rate i. Therefore $h(i) \geq 0$ for all i, and the asset/liability flow is fully immunized against changes in interest rates of any size.

This full immunization of a single liability due can be seen from another point of view. Earlier in this chapter we saw that the duration of a single amount payable at time t in the future is simply equal to t. It then follows from Equation (7.10) that any allocation of asset income involving two or more non-zero A_t's that satisfies Equations (7.11) and (7.12) will result in full immunization, since the right hand side of (7.10) is zero for a single liability due but the left hand side will exceed zero.

| **EXAMPLE 7.7** | *(Full immunization)* |

Use the method of full immunization outlined in Equations (7.11), (7.12) and (7.13) to find the values of A_0 and A_{15} that immunize $L_{12} = 120,000$, assuming $i_0 = .10, t_1 = 0, t_2 = 15$ and $s = 12$.

SOLUTION

We wish to solve the two equations

$$A_0 \cdot v_{.10}^0 + A_{15} \cdot v_{.10}^{15} \;=\; 120,000 \cdot v_{.10}^{12} \;=\; 38,235.70$$

and

$$0 \cdot A_0 \cdot v_{.10}^0 + 15 \cdot A_{15} \cdot v_{.10}^{15} \;=\; 12\big(120,000 \cdot v_{.10}^{12}\big) \;=\; 458,828.38.$$

The solution is $A_0 = 7647.14$ and $A_{15} = 127,776.00$. Note that $h(0) = 15,423.14$, $h(.10) = 0$, $\lim_{i \to \infty} h(i) = A_0 = 7647.14$, and $h(i)$ is decreasing for $0 \le i < .10$ and increasing for $i > .10$. If the interest valuation rate were to drop to 0 from $i_0 = .10$, a profit of 15,423.14 could be made, since some of the assets could be sold while still maintaining sufficient assets to cover liabilities at the new interest rate of 0.   □

Assuming s, L_s, and i_0 are known, Equations (7.11) and (7.12) involve the unknown quantities A_{t_1}, A_{t_2}, t_1 and t_2. In general, given any two of these four quantities, there will be a unique solution for the other two so as to fully immunize the portfolio. (Cases may arise in which one of the A's or t's is negative, or there may be infinitely many or no solutions; see Exercise 7.2.11) In Exercise 7.2.4, it is shown that if each of the liabilities due in Example 7.4 is fully immunized (at $i = .10$) according to the method above, using $t_1 = 0$ and $t_2 = 15$, then the total asset income allocated for all liabilities combined is the same as in part (a) of Example 7.6.

The methods developed in this section can be applied to continuous asset/liability flows, with integration of payments replacing summation. When formulating immunization relationships, it is sometimes more convenient to represent present and accumulated values in terms of force of interest rather than effective annual rate of interest. This is considered in Section 7.3.4 later in this chapter.

In discussing Redington immunization and full immunization, there have been the following two implicit assumptions.

(1) The *term structure* of interest rates is constant or *flat* for all maturities.

(2) When interest rate changes occur, the change is the same throughout the term structure. In other words, there is a *parallel shift* in the term structure.

These implicit assumptions have been reflected in the examples. In practice it is not common to find a flat yield curve, and shifts in the term structure are usually not parallel, so that it may not be possible to fully immunize a portfolio (arbitrage opportunities do not survive long in the marketplace). Suppose in Example 7.7 the 10% interest rate becomes 11% for the 12-year term and 11.1% for the 15 year term. Then the present value of the asset flow is

$$7647.14 + 127,776.00 \cdot v_{.111}^{15} \quad = \quad 33,994.58$$

while the present value of the liabilities is $120,000 \cdot v_{.11}^{12} = 34,300.90$. The portfolio is not immunized against this almost parallel shift in the yield curve. The theory of immunization can be extended to situations involving term structures that are not flat and shifts in the term structure that are not parallel, and even stochastic models of the term structure.

7.3   APPLICATIONS AND ILLUSTRATIONS

7.3.1   DURATION BASED ON CHANGES IN A NOMINAL ANNUAL YIELD RATE COMPOUNDED SEMIANNUALLY

The presentation of duration in Section 7.1 assumed that the series of cashflows had annual payments and the yield rate was an effective annual rate of interest. The presentation could have been based on any equally spaced period for the payments with a yield rate that was compounded with the same frequency as the payments are made. The units in which duration is measured would be based on the payment period, so a duration of 10 would mean 10 payment periods. In practice, the conventional units for duration are years. It is a simple matter to convert from describing duration in terms of the payment period to describing duration in terms of years.

In practice, bond coupons are paid semiannually and bond yields are quoted as nominal annual rates of interest compounded semiannually. Consider an n-year zero coupon bond with a yield rate quoted as a nominal annual rate of interest convertible semiannually, $i^{(2)}$. If we define $j = \frac{i^{(2)}}{2}$ then the present value of the bond is $P = (1+j)^{-2n}$, and the Macaulay duration would be $-(1+j)\frac{\frac{d}{dj}(1+j)^{-2n}}{(1+j)^{-2n}} = 2n$ half-years (the interest rate j is a half-year rate), which we could describe as n years. If the derivative in the numerator is taken with respect to the nominal annual rate $i^{(2)}$, then the Macaulay duration becomes

$$-(1+j)\frac{\frac{d}{di^{(2)}}\left(1+\frac{i^{(2)}}{2}\right)^{-2n}}{(1+j)^{-2n}} \;=\; -(1+j)\frac{-2n\left(1+\frac{i^{(2)}}{2}\frac{i^{(2)}}{2}\right)^{-2n-1}\cdot\frac{1}{2}}{(1+j)^{-2n}}$$

$$= \; -(1+j)\frac{-n(1+j)^{-2n-1}}{(1+j)^{-2n}} \;=\; n\text{-years}.$$

What has happened is that since $j = \frac{i^{(2)}}{2}$, derivatives with respect to $i^{(2)}$ are half as big as derivatives with respect to j.

EXAMPLE 7.8 (*Macaulay duration*)

A 10-year 5% bond has semiannual coupons and is currently valued at a yield to maturity of 5%, where the yield is a nominal annual rate convertible semiannually. Find the Macaulay duration of the bond (in years).

SOLUTION

The semiannual coupons are 2.5 each and the semiannual yield rate is 2.5%.

The Macaulay duration as measured in half-years is

$$D \; = \; \frac{\displaystyle\sum_{t=1}^{20} 2.5t(1.025)^{-t} + 100(20)(1.025)^{-20}}{\displaystyle\sum_{t=1}^{20} 2.5(1.025)^{-t} + 100(1.025)^{-20}} \; = \; 15.979.$$

Note that the first term in the numerator is the increasing annuity $2.5(Ia)_{\overline{20}|.025}$.

The Macaulay duration is $\frac{1}{2} \times 15.979 = 7.989$ years. ☐

Theoretical analysis of financial mathematics often is based on continuous compounding (force of interest) for valuations. If the yield to maturity on a cashflow series is δ, then the present value is $P = \sum_{t=1}^{n} K_t e^{-\delta t}$. If sensitivity is based on changes in δ, then $\frac{d}{d\delta} P = -\sum_{t=1}^{n} t K_t e^{-\delta t}$, and the rate of

change of the present value per dollar invested is $\dfrac{\frac{d}{d\delta} P}{P} = \dfrac{-\displaystyle\sum_{t=1}^{n} t K_t e^{-\delta t}}{\displaystyle\sum_{t=1}^{n} K_t e^{-\delta t}}.$

The duration would be the negative of this factor. The duration of a zero coupon bond maturing in n years is n. In Section 7.1 there was a distinction between modified duration and Macaulay duration when duration is based on sensitivity to changes in the interest rate i. Note that there is no distinction between modified and Macaulay duration when we are basing sensitivity on changes in the force of interest.

7.3.2 DURATION BASED ON SHIFTS IN THE TERM STRUCTURE

The duration measure that was developed in Section 7.1 is based on the change in the yield to maturity for the cashflow series. We have seen in Chapter 6 that valuation of a cashflow series can be done using the term structure of spot rates of interest (yields on zero-coupon bonds). In the duration measure considered in Section 7.1, there is an implicit assumption that the term structure is flat, with the same yield to maturity, say s, for payments at any time in the future. In that case, as pointed out in Section 6.1, the yield to maturity for any coupon bond will also be s for any term to maturity and any coupon rate.

In practice, it is not usually the case that the term structure is flat. It is most often the case that the term structure is an increasing function of time to maturity for zero coupon bonds.

For a series of annual payments of amounts $K_1, K_2, ..., K_n$, the present value of the series using a yield to maturity i for all payments is

$$P = \sum_{t=1}^{n} K_t (1+i)^{-t}, \text{ and the modified duration is } -\frac{\frac{d}{di} P}{P} = \frac{-\frac{d}{di} \sum_{t=1}^{n} K_t (1+i)^{-t}}{\sum_{t=1}^{n} K_t (1+i)^{-t}}.$$

The derivative in the numerator can be expressed in an alternative, but equivalent way, $\frac{d}{di} \sum_{t=1}^{n} K_t (1+i)^{-t} = \frac{d}{d\alpha} \sum_{t=1}^{n} K_t (1+i+\alpha)^{-t} \Big|\alpha = 0$ (evaluated at $\alpha = 0$).

We will continue to use the notation introduced in Section 6.1 for the spot rates of interest (yields on zero coupon bonds), so that s_t denotes the yield on a zero coupon bond maturing in t years. The present value of a series of n annual payments starting one year from now with payment amounts of $K_1, K_2, ..., K_n$ can be expressed as $P_{TS} = \sum_{t=1}^{n} K_t (1+s_t)^{-t}$. Suppose that a change in the term structure occurs in which each zero coupon yield in the term structure is "shifted" by amount α, so that the yield on a t-year zero coupon bond becomes $s_t + \alpha$. The present value of the series of payments can be formulated as a function of α, $P_{TS}(\alpha) = \sum_{t=1}^{n} K_t(1+s_t+\alpha)^{-t}$, and note that $P_{TS}(0) = P$.

The derivative of $P_{TS}(\alpha)$ with respect to α is

$$\frac{d}{d\alpha}P_{TS}(\alpha) = \frac{d}{d\alpha}\sum_{t=1}^{n}K_t(1+s_t+\alpha)^{-t} = -\sum_{t=1}^{n}tK_t(1+s_t+\alpha)^{-t-1}.$$

This derivative evaluated at $\alpha = 0$ is $P'_{TS}(0) = -\sum_{t=1}^{n}tK_t(1+s_t)^{-t-1}$. The modified duration of the series of payments based on the change in α is

$$-\frac{P'_{TS}(0)}{P_{TS}(0)} = \frac{\sum_{t=1}^{n}tK_t(1+s_t)^{-t-1}}{\sum_{t=1}^{n}K_t(1+s_t)^{-t}}.$$ Since we are assuming that the spot rates are all changing by amount α simultaneously, this situation is referred to as a "parallel shift in the term structure."

| EXAMPLE 7.9 | (*Duration based on change in term structure*)

Suppose that the current term structure of interest rates has the following schedule of spot rates for maturities of 1, 2, 3 and 4 years:

Maturity	1-year	2-year	3-year	4-year
Spot Rate	.05	.10	.15	.20

A four year bond has annual coupons at 10%. Find the modified duration for the bond based on a parallel shift in the term structure. Find the yield to maturity for the bond. Find the modified duration for the bond based on a change in the yield to maturity.

| SOLUTION |

The bond price for a bond with face amount 100 is

$$P_{TS} = 10\left[(1.05)^{-1}+(1.10)^{-2}+(1.15)^{-3}+(1.20)^{-4}\right]+100(1.20)^{-4} = 77.41.$$

The modified duration of the bond based on a parallel shift in the term structure is

$$-\frac{P'_{TS}(0)}{P_{TS}(0)} = \frac{\sum_{t=1}^{n} t K_t (1+s_t)^{-t-1}}{\sum_{t=1}^{n} K_t (1+s_t)^{-t}}$$

$$= \frac{10[(1.05)^{-2}+2(1.10)^{-3}+3(1.15)^{-4}+4(1.20)^{-5}]+100(4)(1.20)^{-5}}{10[(1.05)^{-1}+(1.10)^{-2}(1.15)^{-3}(1.20)^{-4}]+100(1.20)^{-4}}$$

$$= 2.82 \text{ years.}$$

The yield to maturity for the bond is i, where

$$77.41 = 10\left[(1+i)^{-1}+(1+i)^{-2}+(1+i)^{-3}+(1+i)^{-4}\right]+100(1+i)^{-4}.$$

Solving for i results in $i=.1847$. The modified duration of the bond based on changes in the yield to maturity is

$$\frac{10[(1.1847)^{-2}+2(1.1847)^{-3}+3(1.1847)^{-4}+4(1.1847)^{-5}]+100(4)(1.1847)^{-5}}{10[(1.1847)^{-1}+(1.1847)^{-2}+(1.1847)^{-3}+(1.1847)^{-4}]+100(1.1847)^{-4}} = 2.88.$$

Even with this extreme case of an increasing term structure, the difference between the modified duration based on term structure and that based on yield to maturity is not large.   ☐

When changes occur in the term structure, the change is generally not a parallel shift. Short term rates tend to be more volatile than longer term rates. Suppose we consider the following model for the price of the bond based on the term structure in Example 7.9,

$$P_{TS}(\alpha) = 10\left[(1.05+\alpha)^{-1}\right.$$
$$\left.+(1.1+.75\alpha)^{-2}+(1.15+.5\alpha)^{-3}+(1.2+.25\alpha)^{-4}\right]+100(1.2+.25\alpha)^{-4}$$

Under this model, the 1 year rate is most sensitive to a change in α, and the longer term maturities are less and less sensitive. The modified duration with respect to change in α is

$$-\frac{P'_{TS}(0)}{P_{TS}(0)}$$

$$= \frac{10[(1.05)^{-2}+2(.75)(1.10)^{-3}+3(.5)(1.15)^{-4}+4(.25)(1.20)^{-5}]+100(4)(.25)(1.20)^{-5}}{10[(1.05)^{-1}+(1.10)^{-2}+(1.15)^{-3}+(1.20)^{-4}]+100(1.20)^{-4}}$$

$$= .94.$$

It is not surprising that the duration is smaller than in Example 7.9, since most of the variability is in the shortest term rates.

Although shifts in the term structure are usually not parallel, the measure of duration based on yield to maturity can be useful when comparing the interest rate risk of various bonds. If two sets of series of payments have the same duration, they have approximately the same sensitivity to a small change in yield to maturity or to a small change in the term structure.

7.3.3 SHORTCOMINGS OF DURATION AS A MEASURE OF INTEREST RATE RISK

We have already discussed one of the shortcomings of duration as a measure of the sensitivity of the present value of a series of payments to changes in interest rates. The conventional measures of duration that we considered in Section 7.1 are based on yield to maturity and parallel shifts in the term structure. In reality, this is not the way interest rates change.

A second shortcoming is that the duration of a series of payments will change as time goes on, even if there is no change in the yield rate. For a zero coupon bond, the modified duration is the time to maturity, which decreases as time goes on since we are getting closer to the maturity date. If two series of payments valued at the same yield to maturity i have the same present value and the same modified duration at time 0, then at any later time, if they continue to be valued at the same yield to maturity i as they were earlier, they will continue to have matching present values and modified durations at that later time. If, however, at the later time they are valued at a yield to maturity other than i, their present values and durations may no longer be matched. This is illustrated in the following example.

EXAMPLE 7.10 (*Duration drift*)

We consider the following two portfolios of bonds

Portfolio 1: A 10-year zero coupon bond with face amount 100.

Portfolio 2: A 5-year zero coupon bond with face amount 41.39 combined with a 20-year zero coupon bond with face amount 86.46.

We assume that the yield to maturity for all bonds is $i = 10\%$.

Show that the present value and duration of the two portfolios are matched at any time before 5 years if the yield to maturity stays at 10%. Suppose that after one year the yield to maturity for all bonds is 11%. Find the present values and Macaulay durations of the two portfolios.

| SOLUTION |

The present values and durations at time 0 of the two portfolios are:

Portfolio 1: $P^{(1)} = 100(1.1)^{-10} = 38.55$ and $D^{(1)} = 10$
(for a zero coupon bond).

Portfolio 2: $P^{(2)} = 41.39(1.1)^{-5} + 86.46(1.1)^{-20} = 38.55$ and

$$D^{(2)} = \frac{41.39(5)(1.1)^{-5} + 86.46(20)(1.1)^{-20}}{38.55} = 10.$$

At time t the present value of Portfolio 1 is

$$P_t^{(1)} = 100(1.1)^{-10}(1.1)^t = 100(1.1)^{-(10-t)} = 38.55(1.1)^t,$$

and the present value of Portfolio 2 is also

$$P_t^{(2)} = \left[41.39(1.1)^{-5} + 86.46(1.1)^{-20}\right](1.1)^t$$
$$= 41.39(1.1)^{-(5-t)} + 86.46(1.1)^{-(20-t)} = 38.55(1.1)^t.$$

At time t the numerator of the Macaulay duration for Portfolio 1 is

$$100(10-t)(1.1)^{-(10-t)} = 100(10)(1.1)^{-(10-t)} - 100t(1.1)^{-(10-t)}.$$

At time t the numerator of the Macaulay duration for Portfolio 2 is

$$41.39(5-t)(1.1)^{-(5-t)} + 86.46(20-t)(1.1)^{-(20-t)}$$
$$= 41.39(5)(1.1)^{-(5-t)}$$
$$+ 86.46(20)(1.1)^{-(20-t)} - t\left[41.39(1.1)^{-(5-t)} + 86.46(1.1)^{-(20-t)}\right].$$

Since the durations were matched at time 0, it must be true that

$$100(10)(1.1)^{-10} = 41.39(5)(1.1)^{-5} + 86.46(20)(1.1)^{-20},$$

and therefore

$$100(10)(1.1)^{-10}(1.1)^t \;=\; \left[41.39(5)(1.1)^{-5}+86.46(20)(1.1)^{-20}\right](1.1)^t.$$

Also, since at time 0 the present values are matched, we have

$$100(1.1)^{-10} \;=\; 41.39(1.1)^{-5}+86.46(1.1)^{-20},$$

and therefore

$$100(1.1)^{-10}(1.1)^t \;=\; \left[41.39(1.1)^{-5}+86.46(1.1)^{-20}\right](1.1)^t.$$

It follows that the numerators of the Macaulay durations of Portfolios 1 and 2 are equal at any time t before 5 years, so that the durations are matched at any time t before 5 years.

With a yield to maturity of 11% at time 1, the present values at time 1 of the two Portfolios are:

Portfolio 1: $P^{(1)} = 100(1.11)^{-9} = 39.09$ and $D^{(1)} = 9$
                 (for a 9-year zero coupon bond).

Portfolio 2: $P^{(2)} = 41.39(1.11)^{-4}+86.46(1.11)^{-19} = 39.17$ and

$$D^{(2)} \;=\; \frac{41.39(4)(1.11)^{-4}+86.46(19)(1.11)^{-19}}{39.17} \;=\; 8.56. \quad \square$$

In Example 7.10, it was seen that if the yield to maturity was still 10% at time 1, the two Portfolios would be matched in both present value and duration (duration is 9 at time 1). It was also seen for Portfolio 2 that if the yield rate rose to 11% at time 1, the Macaulay duration was reduced to 8.56. Exercise 7.1.1 shows more generally that for a series of more than one payment, as the yield to maturity increases the duration will decrease.

A third shortcoming of duration as a measure of the sensitivity of the present value of a series of payments to changes in the yield to maturity is related to the "convexity" of the graph of the present value as a function of yield to maturity. Convexity is based on the second derivative of the present value with respect to changes in the yield to maturity. A more convex present value graph results in a present value that reacts more dramatically to a change in the yield to maturity. Suppose we consider a 10 year zero coupon bond valued at an effective annual yield to maturity of 10%. The present value of the bond is $100(1.1)^{-10} = 38.5543$, and the modified duration is 9.0909. With a 1 basis point drop (.01%) in the yield to maturity, the price will be $100(1.0999)^{-10} = 38.5894$, which is a relative change in value of $\frac{.0351}{38.5543} = .000910$. Since the duration is 9.090909, we would expect a relative change of about $9.090909 \times .0001 = .000909$. Suppose instead that there is a 100 basis point drop in the yield to maturity. The price of the bond becomes $100(1.09)^{-10} = 42.2411$, which is a relative change in value of $\frac{3.6868}{38.5543} = .095626$. Since the duration is 9.090909, we would expect a relative change of about $9.090909 \times .01 = .090909$. The actual relative change in price is further from the change suggested by the duration measure for a 100 basis point change than for the 1 basis point change because of the convexity of the present value curve. This is illustrated in the following graph. The curved line is a graph of the actual value of $(1+i)^{-10}$, and the straight line is the approximation based on the duration of the bond at $i = .10$. It can be seen from the graph that as a result of the convexity of the curve, as i gets further from 10%, the actual value of the bond is further from that predicted by the linear differential approximation using the duration of the bond.

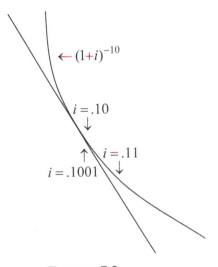

FIGURE 7.3

7.3.4 A GENERALIZATION OF REDINGTON IMMUNIZATION

Suppose that the annual asset cashflow series is $A_1, A_2, \ldots, A_n$ and the annual liability cashflow series is $L_1, L_2, \ldots, L_n$, and suppose that the current continuously compounded term structure is $\delta_{0,t}$ (for a zero coupon bond maturing in t years), but after an instantaneous interest rate shock the term structure changes to $\delta_{0,t}^*$. We define the function $g(t)$ to be $g(t) = \dfrac{e^{-t\delta_{0,t}^*}}{e^{-t\delta_{0,t}}} - 1$. Then the change in the present value of the surplus (present value of asset minus liability cashflows) is

$$S^* - S = \sum_{t>0}(A_t - L_t)(e^{-t\delta_{0,t}^*} - e^{-t\delta_{0,t}}) = \sum_{t>0}(A_t - L_t)e^{-t\delta_{0,t}}g(t).$$

Using Taylor's expansion about 0 to the 2nd derivative term and the weighted theorem of the mean for integrals applied to the function $g(t)$ it can be shown that

$$S^* - S = g(0)\sum_{t>0}(A_t - L_t)e^{-t\delta_{0,t}} + g'(0)\sum_{t>0}t(A_t - L_t)e^{-t\delta_{0,t}}$$
$$+ \frac{1}{2}g''(c)\sum_{t>0}t^2(A_t - L_t)e^{-t\delta_{0,t}}$$

for some value of c between 0 and n. The value of c depends on the nature of the interest rate shock. If the present value of asset and liability cashflows are matched, and the first "moment" of their present values is matched under the current term structure (before the interest rate shock), then $\sum_{t>0}(A_t - L_t)e^{-\delta_{0,t}^*} = \sum_{t>0}t(A_t - L_t)e^{-\delta_{0,t}^*} = 0$. Note that since $g(0) = 0$, the first condition is not needed, and also, in general, first moments being matched is similar to, but not exactly the same as parallel shift duration matching for effective annual interest rates. Then,

$$S^* - S = \frac{1}{2}g''(c)\sum_{t>0}t^2(A_t - L_t)e^{-t\delta_{0,t}}.$$

If the interest rate shock is a parallel shift in the term structure, say

$$\delta_{0,t}^* = \delta_{0,t} + \varepsilon,$$

we have

$$g(t) = \frac{e^{-t\delta_{0,t}^*}}{e^{-t\delta_{0,t}}} - 1 = e^{-t\varepsilon} - 1,$$

and

$$g''(c) = \varepsilon^2 e^{-c\varepsilon},$$

so that

$$S^* - S = \frac{1}{2}\varepsilon^2 e^{-c\varepsilon} \sum_{t>0} t^2 (A_t - L_t) e^{-t\delta_{0,t}}.$$

If the usual Redington immunization requirement for immunization is satisfied (2nd moment of present value of asset minus liability is positive, $\sum_{t>0} t^2 (A_t - L_t) e^{-t\delta_{0,t}} \geq 0$), then $S^* - S \geq 0$ and the assets immunize the liabilities. This analysis is valid even if the term structure is not flat.

7.4   NOTES AND REFERENCES

The concept of duration was introduced by Frederick Macaulay in the book titled *Some Theoretical Problems Suggested by the Movements of Interest Rates, Bond Yields and Stock Prices in the United States since 1856*, published by the National Bureau of Economic Research in 1938. The concept of duration was not widely used in practice until the 1970's.

The early development of immunization theory can be found in the paper *Review of the Principles of Life Office Valuations*, by F.M. Redington, published in the Journal of the Institute of Actuaries in 1952. A discussion of full immunization can be found in Chapter 10 of *An Introduction to the Mathematics of Finance*, by J.J. McCutcheon and W.F. Scott, published in 1986 by Oxford: Heinemann Professional Publishing.

7.5 EXERCISES

The exercises without asterisks are intended to comprehensively cover the material presented in the chapter. Exercises with a asterisk can be regarded as supplementary exercises which cover topics in more depth, either theoretically or computationally, than those without a asterisk.

SECTION 7.1

7.1.1   Use a computer spreadsheet program to repeat Example 7.3 for parameter values

$$r = .04, .06, .08; \quad n = 2, \ 10, 20, 40; \quad \text{and} \quad j = .03, .05, .07.$$

Holding 2 of the three parameters r, n, j fixed, identify the behavior of D as a function of the other parameter.

7.1.2   Suppose that the yield rate and coupon rate on an n-coupon bond are the same. Show that the duration is $\ddot{a}_{\overline{n}|}$ valued at the yield rate. Find the duration of a 6-coupon bond with coupon rate 10% per coupon period and yield rate 10% per coupon period.

7.1.3   Show that the (annualized) Macaulay duration for a coupon bond redeemable at par with annual coupon rate $r^{(2)}$ per year (payable semiannually), and yield to maturity of $i^{(2)}$ per year (payable semiannually) with n full coupon periods remaining, is

$$\frac{1+j}{2j} - \frac{1+j+n(r-j)}{2r\left[(1+j)^n - 1\right] + 2j}, \quad \text{where } r = \frac{1}{2}r^{(2)} \text{ and } j = \frac{1}{2}i^{(2)}.$$

7.1.4   Develop an expression for the duration of a level n-payment annuity-immediate of 1 per period with interest rate i per period, and show that it is equal to $\frac{1}{d} - \frac{n}{is_{\overline{n}|i}}$.

7.1.5   Under the current market conditions Bond 1 has a price (per 100 of face amount) of 88.35 and a Macaulay duration of 12.7, and Bond 2 has a price (per 100 of face amount) of 130.49 and Macaulay duration of 14.6 . A portfolio is created with a combination of face amount F_1 of Bond 1 and face amount F_2 of Bond 2. The combined face amount of the portfolio is $F_1 + F_2 = 100$, and the Macaulay duration of the portfolio is 13.5. Find the portfolio value.

7.1.6   A 3-year annual coupon bond has coupons of 10 per year starting one year from now and matures in 3 years for amount 100. The YTM for the bond is 11.8% (effective annual). Find the Macaulay duration for the bond.

*7.1.7 $D(r,n,j)$ denotes the duration of a bond of face amount F, with n coupons at rate r per coupon period, and with yield rate j. Find

(a) $\lim\limits_{n\to\infty} D(r,n,j),$ (d) $\lim\limits_{r\to 0} D(r,n,j),$

(b) $\lim\limits_{n\to 1} D(r,n,j),$ (e) $\lim\limits_{j\to\infty} D(r,n,j),$ and

(c) $\lim\limits_{r\to\infty} D(r,n,j),$ (f) $\lim\limits_{j\to 0} D(r,n,j),$

*7.1.8   For the cashflow series with payments $K_1, K_2, \ldots, K_n$, made at times $1, 2, \ldots, n$, suppose that $L = \sum\limits_{t=1}^{n} K_t \cdot v^t$ at rate i_0 per payment period. Show that $\frac{d}{di}\left[L(1+i)^D\right]\Big|_{i=i_0} = 0$, where D is the Macaulay duration.

*7.1.9   Consider a bond with continuous coupons at rate r per period and redemption amount 1 in n periods, valued at yield rate δ.

(a) Express $\frac{dL}{d\delta}$ in terms of continuous annuity symbols and the factors r, n and δ. The duration is $D = -\frac{1}{L} \cdot \frac{dL}{d\delta}$.

(b) Find an expression for $\frac{dD}{dn}$. Show that it has the same sign as

$\delta + (r-\delta)\left[r(n-\bar{a}_{\overline{n}})+\delta\bar{a}_{\overline{n}}\right]$, so that if $r \geq \delta$, then D increases with n, but if $r < \delta$, then D is increasing for $n = 0$ to $n = n_0$, and then is decreasing for $n > n_0$. This accounts for the smaller durations for the 60-coupon bonds than the 30-coupon bonds in line 1 of Table 7.1b and lines 1 and 2 of Table 7.1c.

*7.1.10 Verify algebraically that the duration of a coupon bond is a decreasing function of the coupon rate.

*7.1.11 Using a 7 year 10% bond with a face amount of 100 and term structure (i) of Exercise 6.1.1, find $\frac{d}{d\alpha} \sum\limits_{t=1}^{14} K_t \left[1+\frac{1}{2}(i_{0,.5t}+\alpha)\right]^{-t}$ and

find $\frac{d}{d\alpha} \sum\limits_{t=1}^{14} K_t \left[1+\frac{1}{2}(.0990+\alpha)\right]^{-t}$ at $\alpha = 0$.

*7.1.12 It is assumed that the term structure of interest rates is flat, so that the yield on a zero coupon bond with any time to maturity is $j > 0$ per year (effective annual). An investor owns a portfolio of two bonds, one of which has present value 50,000 and Macaulay duration 8 years, and the other has present value 30,000 and Macaulay duration 6 years.

The investor would like to rebalance the portfolio so that the Macaulay duration of the portfolio after rebalancing is 7 years. The rebalancing will be done by selling some of one of the bonds to decrease the holding of that bond and using the proceeds to buy more of the other bond to increase the holding of the other bond. The total value of the portfolio will still be 80,000 after rebalancing. Which of the following is the correct action to rebalance the portfolio?

(a) No action is needed since the portfolio already has a duration of 7 years.

(b) Sell 20,000 of the 6-year duration bond and buy 20,000 of the 8-year duration bond.

   (c) Sell 10,000 of the 6-year duration bond and buy 10,000 of the
       8-year duration bond.

   (d) Sell 20,000 of the 8-year duration bond and buy 20,000 of the
       6-year duration bond.

   (e) Sell 10,000 of the 8-year duration bond and buy 10,000 of the
       6-year duration bond.

*7.1.13 It is assumed that the term structure of interest rates is flat, so that
   the yield on a zero coupon bond with any time to maturity is i per
   year (effective annual). Two bonds with the same face amount and
   the same number $(n \geq 2)$ of annual coupons to maturity are being
   compared. Bond 1 has coupon rate r_1 (per year) and Bond 2 has
   coupon rate r_2 per year. If $r_2 > r_1 \geq 0$, which of the following
   statements is true about the bond prices P_1 and P_2 and the bond
   Macaulay durations D_1 and D_2.

   (a) $P_1 > P_2$ and $D_1 > D_2$

   (b) $P_1 < P_2$ and $D_1 > D_2$

   (c) $P_1 > P_2$ and $D_1 < D_2$

   (d) $P_1 < P_2$ and $D_1 < D_2$

   (e) None of A, B, C, or D is true in general.

*7.1.14 Suppose that $K_t \geq 0$ for $t = 1, \ldots, n$ and that $K_t > 0$ for at least
   two values of t. Show that $\frac{d}{dj} D < 0$.

*7.1.15 Show that for an annual cashflow series with the first payment at
   time 1, $\lim_{j \to \infty} D = 1$.

SECTION 7.2

7.2.1 Liabilities of 1 each are due at the ends of periods 1 and 2. There are three securities available to produce asset income to cover these liabilities, as follows:

(i) A bond due at the end of period 1 with coupon at rate .01 per period, valued at a periodic yield of 14%;

(ii) A bond due at the end of period 2 with coupon rate .02 per period, valued at a periodic yield of 15%;

(iii) A bond due at the end of period 2 with coupon rate .20 per period, valued at a periodic yield of 14.95%.

Determine the cost of the portfolio that exactly-matches asset income to liabilities due using

(a) bonds (i) and (ii) only.

(b) bonds (i) and (iii) only

(c) Show that the combination of securities in (b) minimizes the cost of all exact-matching portfolios made up of a combination of the three securities. Note that the minimum cost exact-matching portfolio does not use the highest yielding security in this case.

7.2.2 In order to match asset income to the liabilities in Example 7.4 so that $PV_A(.10) = PV_L(.10)$, a level annual payment annuity-immediate with n payments is purchased to provide the asset income flow. For each of $n = 5, 15, 50, 100$, find the required annual payment and calculate both $\sum t \cdot A_t \cdot v'_{.10}$ and $\sum t^2 \cdot A_t \cdot v'_{.10}$. Which value of n provides the nearest match to the relation $\sum t \cdot A_t \cdot v'_{.10} = \sum t \cdot L_t \cdot v'_{.10}$? Solve for the exact value of n for which $\sum t \cdot A_t \cdot v'_{.10} = \sum t \cdot L_t \cdot v'_{.10}$. Determine whether this provides Redington immunization for the portfolio.

7.2.3 (a) Show that Equation (7.5) is equivalent to Equation (7.8)

(b) Show that if Equation (7.5) is true, then Equation (7.6) is equivalent to Equation (7.9).

7.2.4   For each of the liabilities due in Example 7.4 find the values of A_0 and A_{15} at $i = .10$, according to the method of full immunization described in Section 7.2. Find the total of all A_0's and the total of all A_{15}'s separately, and show that this gives the same asset income as that found in part (a) of Example 7.6.

7.2.5   A liability of 1 is due at time 10. An attempt is made to fully immunize this liability at $i_0 = .10$ by means of two zero-coupon bonds of amounts A_{t_1} and A_{t_2} due at times t_1 and t_2, respectively. In each of the following cases, solve for the two missing quantities out of $A_{t_1}, A_{t_2}, t_1, t_2,$ given the other two.

(a) $t_1 = 5, t_2 = 15$

(b) (i) $t_1 = 5, A_{t_1} = .40$

   (ii) $t_1 = 5, A_{t_1} = .70$ (no solution for $t_2 \geq 10$)

(c) (i) $t_1 = 5, A_{t_2} = .90$ (two solutions for $t_2 \geq 10$)

   (ii) $t_1 = 5, A_{t_2} = 1.5$ (one solution for $t_2 \geq 10$)

   (iii) $t_1 = 5, A_{t_2} = .75$ (no solutions for $t_2 \geq 10$)

(d) (i) $t_2 = 15, A_{t_1} = .80$

   (ii) $t_2 = 15, A_{t_1} = 1.1$ (no solution for $A_{t_2} \geq 0, 0 \leq t_1 \leq 10$)

   (iii) $t_2 = 15, A_{t_1} = .01$ (no solution for $0 \leq t_1 \leq 10$)

(e) (i) $t_2 = 15, A_{t_2} = .80$

   (ii) $t_2 = 15, A_{t_2} = 1.5$ (no solution for $t_1 \geq 0$)

(f) $A_{t_1} = .40, A_{t_2} = .90$

7.2.6   A financial institution has taken over the business of another company. One of the acquired liabilities is a capital redemption policy that obligates the payment of 1,000,000 by the institution to the policyholder in exactly 12 years, and requires the policyholder to make annual premium payments (at the start of each of the remaining 12 years) of 15,000. Out of the assets of the acquired company, the financial institution wants to allocate a single asset income payment A_{t_0} to be made at time t_0 so that, along with the asset income represented by the premiums payable by the policyholder, the capital redemption policy will be fully immunized at the current interest rate of 10%. Find t_0 and the asset income amount A_{t_0} that must be allocated, and show that this fully immunizes the policy.

7.2.7   Liability payments of 100 each are due to be paid in 2, 4 and 6 years from now. Asset cashflow consists of A_1 in 1 year and A_5 in 5 years. The YTM for all payments is effective annual interest at 10%. An attempt is made to have the asset cash flow immunize the liability cashflow by matching present value and duration.

(a) Find A_1 and A_5.

(b) Determine whether or not the conditions for Redington immunization are satisfied at the effective annual rate of 10%.

*7.2.8 (a) Consider the function $h'(i)$ for the portfolio of assets and liabilities in part (a) of Example 7.6. Use one of the methods of Section 5.1 (such as the *rule of signs* of Exercise 5.1.7) to show that $h'(i) = 0$ has only one solution for $i \geq 0$. (This unique solution is $i = .10$.) Note that $h(0) > 0, h(.10) = 0$, $h'(.10) = 0$ and $\lim_{i \to \infty} h(i) = 149,195$. Use these facts to conclude that $h(i)$ has its overall minimum at $i = .10$.

(b) Show that for (very) large values of i, $h(i) < 0$ for the portfolio of assets and liabilities in part (c) of Example 7.6. (Try increasing values of i, such as 200%, 400%, and so on.)

*7.2.9 (a) Multiply Equation (7.11) by s and subtract Equation (7.12) to show that $a \cdot A_{t_1} \cdot v_{i_0}^{t_1} = b \cdot A_{t_2} \cdot v_{i_0}^{t_2}$.

(b) Use part (a) to solve for L_s in terms of A_{t_1}, a, b and v_{i_0}.

(c) Use parts (a) and (b) to write $h(i)$ as given in Equation (7.13).

*7.2.10 For each of parts (a), (b), and (c) of Example 7.6, determine $h(i)$ for $i = .03, .08, .12$ and $.20$.

*7.2.11 Let $i_0 > 0$, $L_s > 0$ and s be given. Show that in each of the following cases there is a unique solution for the unknown quantities in Equations (7.11) and (7.12), with the solution consisting of positive numbers.

(a) $t_1 \le s$ and $t_2 \ge s$, with t_1 and t_2 given

(b) $t_2 \ge s$ and A_{t_2} satisfying $A_{t_2} \cdot v_{i_0}^{t_2 - s} \le \frac{s}{t_2} \cdot L_s$, with t_2 and A_{t_2} given

(c) $t_1 \le s$ and A_{t_1} satisfying $A_{t_1} (1 + i_0)^{t_2 - s} \le L_s$, with t_1 and A_{t_1} given

(d) $t_2 \ge s$ and $A_{t_1} \le L_s$, with t_2 and A_{t_1} given

*7.2.12 It is assumed that the term structure of interest rates is flat, so that the yield on a zero coupon bond with any time to maturity is $j = .08$ per year (effective annual). Suppose that a company has liabilities consisting of 10 annual payments of 1000 each starting in one year. You are given:

$$\sum_{k=1}^{10} v_{.08}^k = 6.7101, \qquad \sum_{k=1}^{10} k v_{.08}^k = 32.6869,$$

$$\sum_{k=1}^{10} k^2 v_{.08}^k = 212.9687$$

(i) The company wishes to invest in assets in order to immunize the liabilities against small changes in j. The assets will consist of some cash now (at time 0) and a zero coupon bond maturing at time 10. The present value and duration of the assets must match the present value and duration of the liabilities. Find how much of the asset portfolio should be in cash (nearest $1).

(ii) Suppose that a liability payment of 5000 payable in 11 years is added to the existing liability payments. An attempt to immunize is made using the same two assets as in question (a) (cash and a zero coupon bond maturing at time 10). Which of the following statements is correct regarding the additional asset amount C needed at time 10?

(a) $C \leq 5000$ and the assets immunize the liabilities (for small changes in j)

(b) $C \leq 5000$ and the assets do not immunize the liabilities (for small changes in j)

(c) $C > 5000$ and the assets immunize the liabilities (for small changes in j)

(d) $C > 5000$ and the assets do not immunize the liabilities (for small changes in j)

(e) $C = 0$ and the assets do not immunize the liabilities (for small changes in j)

*7.2.13 Cash flow 1 consists of three non-zero payments: A in 5 periods, B in 10 periods and C in 15 periods. Cash flow 2 consists of 2 non-zero payments: X is 6 periods and Y in 12 periods. As of now, at YTM j per period for all maturities, the two sets of cashflows have the same present value and the same Macaulay duration. Suppose that one period from now the YTM is still j for all maturities. Show that

(a) the two sets of cash flows will have the same present value;

(b) the two sets of cash flows have the same Macaulay duration at that time; and

(c) the Macaulay duration one period from now is exactly 1 less than it is now.

CHAPTER 8

ADDITIONAL TOPICS IN FINANCE AND INVESTMENT

In this chapter we provide an introduction to several types of investments that are of considerable importance in modern financial markets. In Chapter 6 we introduced the concept of a forward rate of interest. In this chapter we consider the more general concept of a forward contract and the related concept of a futures contract. Some concepts related to equity investments are introduced, particularly short sale of a stock and a simple model for pricing an option on a stock. Some of the concepts introduced in this chapter require an elementary background in probability.

In modeling the behavior of financial markets, it is generally assumed that there is always available a "risk-free" rate of return that can be obtained by any investor. The interpretation of the risk-free rate of return would be the return available on government treasury bills or bonds. It is assumed that there is no risk of default in treasury securities (the government can print the money needed to repay its obligations). The risk-free rate of return will be referred to from time to time throughout this chapter.

8.1 FORWARD AND FUTURES CONTRACTS

8.1.1 FORWARD CONTRACTS

A **forward contract** is an agreement to buy or sell a certain asset at a certain future time (the delivery date, time T) for a certain price (the "delivery price"), all agreed to at the time the contract is made (time 0), and with the contract being settled on the delivery date. The buyer, say investor A (who is agreeing to buy the asset at the delivery date), has a *long position* and the seller (investor B) has a *short position*.

An investor may enter a forward contract to lock in the future price of an asset that will have to be bought or sold so as to avoid the risk of paying a higher price (or selling for a lower price) for the asset at the delivery date. An investor may use a forward contract to speculate on the future price of the asset. For instance, suppose that a speculator enters into a forward contract to purchase 1000 ounces of gold in one year at 300 per ounce. If the price of gold is more than 300 per ounce one year from now then the speculator will have made a profit. He will buy the gold at 300 an ounce and immediately sell it at a higher price. If the price of gold is below 300 per ounce a year from now, the speculator will incur a loss at that time, since he is obligated to buy at 300 per ounce but the gold is actually worth less than that. Suppose that the long position in the gold contract is taken by a jewelry company that wishes to secure the purchase of 1000 ounces of gold in one year for production purposes. The jewelry company wants to take possession of the gold in one year rather than attempt to make a gain on the change in the gold price. The jewelry company is creating a **hedge position** to secure the price for the gold that it will buy, and the company is referred to as a **hedger** in this situation. The company would not actually realize a gain or loss in a year if the price of gold is above or below 300 per ounce in one year because the company is going to use the gold in its jewelry production and will not resell the gold directly (but an "opportunity" gain or loss would occur).

At the time the contract is made no money changes hands, and the contract is constructed so that it has value 0 for both the buyer and seller. To see why the value is 0 to both parties when they first enter into the forward contract we consider the following. We assume that the forward contract held by each party to the agreement is negotiable (can be bought by others). Suppose at the same time as investors A and B sign their contract, investor C wishes to enter into a long forward contract on the same asset with the same delivery date. In a "rational" market, at that same instant, investor C should be able to find an investor D who will take the same short position as investor B (the same delivery price as the contract between investors A and B). Therefore, if investor C instead wanted to buy investor A's contract, investor C wouldn't be willing to pay anything because he could arrange for a contract with investor D at no current cost (when a forward contract is first created, no money changes hands). Since investor C would not be willing to pay anything for investor A's contract, it follows that investor A's contract has value 0.

As time goes on, the value of the forward contracts might not continue to be 0. If K is the delivery price, and if delivery is at time T, and if S_T is the spot price of the asset at the time of delivery, then the value of the long position at delivery time T is $S_T - K$ (and the short position value at time T is $K - S_T$). This is because when time T arrives, the holder of the long position is obligated to purchase the asset for amount K, but since the asset value at that time is actually S_T, the holder of the long position will have a net value of $S_T - K$ (which can be positive or negative).

EXAMPLE 8.1   (*Forward contract in gold*)

At time $T = 0$, a corporation enters into a forward contract with a gold refiner to purchase 1000 ounces of gold in one year (at time $T = 1$) at the delivery price of $K = 300$ per ounce. Suppose that at the time of delivery ($T = 1$) the spot price of gold is 280 (the spot price is the price at that moment). The value of the long position held by the corporation is $1000 \times (280 - 300) = -20,000$ (this is $1000(S_T - K)$). The reason that this is the value of the long position at time 1 is that the corporation is "locked in" by the forward contract to buying gold for 300 per ounce at that time, whereas it is available at the price of 280 per ounce at time 1 ("current price" of 280 on the delivery date). If the corporation were to try to sell the long position of the forward contract at time 1, a buyer of that long position would be obligated to buy 1000 ounces of gold at 300 per ounce.

Why would someone buy an obligation that required them to spend 300,000 for 1000 ounces of gold when they could buy that gold on the market for 280,000? The answer is that no one would do that. In fact, in order to buy into that obligation someone would want 20,000 in compensation to cover the extra cost of buying the gold at 300,000 instead of 280,000; the corporation would have to give an individual 20,000 in order for the individual to take over the corporation's obligation to buy the gold.

The point is that the corporation is forced by its contract to pay 300,000 for the gold, whereas the gold is available on the market for 280,000. That is why the value of the long position on the forward contract is $-20,000$ under these circumstances.

By similar reasoning, the short position has a value of 20,000, since the gold refiner will sell gold to the corporation at 300 per ounce that is only (at time 1) worth 280 per ounce. If the gold price at time 1 happened to be 300 per ounce, then both the long and short positions in the forward contract would have value 0. The values of the long and short positions will always cancel each other out.   ☐

Two parties can enter into a forward contract to buy and sell gold at any time with any delivery date and delivery price they choose. In a rational market, according to financial theory, all investors would behave the same way at any given time. At any time and for each later delivery date there will be a "forward price" for gold set by market forces. When a forward contract is created at time 0 with delivery at time T for delivery price K, this delivery price might also be referred to as "the forward price at time 0 for delivery at time T." At the time t between time 0 and time T, it would be possible to create a new forward contract with delivery at time T (which is $T - t$ time periods in the future from time t). The delivery price for delivery at time T for this new contract can also be called the "forward price at time t for delivery at time T", and might not be the same as K, which was the delivery price for delivery at time T on the contract that was set up at time 0.

We consider further the forward contract described in Example 8.1. Suppose that the original contract is made on February 1, 2005 (time 0), with a delivery date of Feb 1, 2006 (time 1). Suppose also that on August 1, 2005 (time ½) the forward price for gold for delivery on February 1, 2006 (time 1) is 310 per ounce. This would be the ½ -year forward price for gold on August 1, 2005. Note that the corporation and the gold refiner who entered into the forward contract on Feb. 1, 2005 are still locked in to their delivery price of 300 (which was the forward price at time 0 when their contract was made). The value of the corporation's long position in the forward contract that was made on Feb. 1, 2005 (time 0) is no longer equal to 0 on August 1, 2005 (at time ½). The long contract will be worth more than 0 at time ½ . The reason for this is that investor C, who wishes, on August 1, 2005, to enter into a long position forward contract to buy gold on Feb. 1, 2006 will have to agree to pay a delivery price of 310 on Feb. 1, 2006. The corporation holds a contract to buy gold for 300 per ounce on Feb. 1, 2006. It will be worth something to investor C to buy the corporation's contract and only have to pay 300 instead of 310 per ounce for the gold on Feb. 1, 2006.

As we have just seen, the forward price for gold to be delivered at time 1 can change as time goes on, and the value of the original forward contract (both the long position and the short position) can change also (but any new forward contract always has value 0 when it is first made).

Suppose that the risk free rate of interest (continuously compounded) is r. In most elementary models of financial behavior it is assumed that investors can both invest and borrow at the risk free rate of interest (a somewhat unrealistic assumption). It is also assumed that no arbitrage opportunities exist, which means that it is impossible to arrange an investment which has a net amount invested of 0 but has a guaranteed positive return. Another equivalent definition of the no-arbitrage assumption is that it is not possible for a risk-free investment to earn a return greater than the risk-free rate.

If the spot price of gold at time 0 is S_0 then the delivery price for a forward contract with delivery time T must be $S_0 e^{rT}$ (the delivery price must be the accumulated value to time T of the initial spot price at time 0). That this is true can be seen in the following way.

Suppose that investor A is willing to enter into a long forward contract in which he will pay a delivery price of $C > S_0 e^{rT}$. You can construct the following strategy. You enter into a short position on the forward contract with investor A taking the long position. No money changes hands. You are obligated to sell to investor A an ounce of gold at time T for amount C (and he is obligated to buy). At the same time you enter into this contract (time 0) you borrow S_0 at the risk free rate and buy one ounce of gold at today's spot price of S_0. You hold on to the ounce of gold until time T, at which time you sell the gold to investor A and he pays you C. Since $C > S_0 e^{rT}$, you have more than enough to repay your loan at the risk free rate. The excess is a guaranteed profit to you for a net investment of 0. The assumption that no such arbitrage opportunities exist in a market implies that such a transaction would not be possible and there would not be such an investor A. A similar argument shows that if someone was willing to sell (deliver) gold at time T at a price less than $S_0 e^{rT}$, then an arbitrage gain would be available.

It is possible to formulate the value of a forward contract (long or short position) at any point in time between the initial contract date and the delivery date.

Suppose that at time 0 a forward contract is arranged with the following characteristics: spot price at time 0 is S_0, delivery is at time T, delivery price is K, and risk free rate (continuously compounded) is r. From what we have seen above, it must be the case that $S_0 = Ke^{-rT}$. Suppose that at a later time, say $t < T$, the spot price is S_t. The value of the long position in the original forward contract at time t is $S_t - S_0 e^{rt}$. The reason this is true can be seen as follows. Assuming that the risk free rate is still r, a new investor at time t who wants to enter into a long position forward contract that has delivery at time T would agree to a delivery price of $S_t e^{r(T-t)}$ (since the time is $T - t$ until delivery, assuming the risk free rate is still r). If the new investor were to take over the long forward position on the original contract, he would have to agree to a delivery price of K at time T. The amount that the new investor would be willing to pay to take over the original long position in the forward contract would be the present value of the reduction in what he would have to pay at delivery; that present value is $\left[S_t e^{r(T-t)} - K \right] e^{-r(T-t)} = S_t - Ke^{-r(T-t)} = S_t - S_0 e^{rt}$. This is the present value (at time t) of the delivery price he would have to pay if he entered a new contract minus the delivery price he would have to pay if he took over the original contract, and it is also the current spot price (at time t) minus the accumulated value to time t of the spot price when the original forward contract was entered at time 0.

The value of the short position of the original forward contract at time t is $-(S_t - S_0 e^{rt}) = S_0 e^{rt} - S_t$ (the combined value at any time of the long and short positions is always 0).

EXAMPLE 8.1 (*Continued*)

Suppose that the spot price of gold is 305 one-quarter year after the original forward contract is made. Find the value of the long position in the forward contract at that time assuming a continuously compounded risk free rate of interest of 5%.

SOLUTION

When the contract was first made at time 0, the delivery price was 300. This implies that the spot price at time 0 must have been S_0, where $S_0 e^{.05} = 300$. Thus, $S_0 = 285.37$. Since the spot price at time $t = .25$ is $S_{.25} = 305$, it follows that the value of the long position in the forward contract is $S_{.25} - S_0 e^{(.05)(.25)} = 305 - 285.37 e^{.0125} = 16.04$. The value of the short position at that time would be -16.04.   □

In the discussion above, gold can be replaced by any asset which does not produce any income from the time the forward contract is entered to the time the contract matures. We now consider a forward contract on an income producing asset such as a risk free (government treasury) bond. The asset to be delivered on the delivery date is a bond.

Let I_0 be the present value at time 0, at the risk free rate, of income to be received from time 0 until the maturity of the forward contract. With a delivery price of K, the following Portfolios A and B have the same value.

Portfolio A: one long forward contract on the security plus cash amount equal to Ke^{-rT},

Portfolio B: one unit of the security, combined with borrowing of amount I_0 at the risk free rate.

The income from the security in portfolio B will repay the loan, and result in only the security being held at time T, therefore the two portfolios result in the same financial position at time T. Then the no-arbitrage assumption leads to $K = (S_0 - I_0)e^{rT}$. For a forward contract created at time $t < T$ with delivery at time T for the security, the delivery price would be $(S_t - I_t)e^{r(T-t)}$, where I_t is the present value at time t of the cash income to be paid from time t to T. The value at time t of the long position on the original forward contract is $S_t - I_t - Ke^{-r(T-t)}$. (This is the present value of the difference between what would have to be paid as delivery price on a new forward contract arranged at time t and the original forward contract). Note that the spot price, S_t, includes the income to be received between now and the delivery time, but that income will not be paid to the long position holder of the forward contract, since the long position holder takes delivery after that income is paid. Thus, the delivery price should not include the income paid by the security between now and the time of delivery.

An alternative way of looking at this situation is to see that the forward price should be the amortized value of the security at time T. This is the initial price (spot price at time 0) accumulated to time t minus the accumulated income (coupons) to time t.

EXAMPLE 8.2   *(Forward contract on a bond)*

A coupon bond has a spot price of 860. The bond will pay coupons of 40 in 6 months and in one year.

(a) Suppose that the risk free rate is 10% (per year continuously compounded) for a 6 month zero-coupon bond maturity and 10% for a one year zero-coupon bond maturity. The delivery price for a one year forward contract on the bond, with delivery immediately after the coupon payment, is

$$K = \left(860 - 40e^{-.1(.5)} - 40e^{-.1(1)}\right)e^{.1(1)}$$
$$= \left[860e^{.1(.5)} - 40\right]e^{.1(.5)} - 40 = 868.40.$$

Suppose that immediately after the first coupon is paid (time .5), the continuously compounded risk free rate of interest is still 10% for 6 month maturities. If the spot price of the bond has risen to 870, then at time .5 the delivery price for a forward contract maturing at time 1 (just after the coupon is paid) is $(870 - 40e^{-.1(.5)})e^{.1(.5)} = 874.61$, and the value of the original forward contract entered at time 0 will be

$$S_{.5} - I_{.5} - Ke^{-r(.5)} = 870 - 40e^{-.1(.5)} - 868.40e^{-.1(.5)} = 5.90.$$

(b) Suppose that the risk free rates are 8% (per year continuously compounded) for a 6-month maturity and 10% for a one year maturity. The delivery price for a one year forward contract on the bond, with delivery immediately after the coupon payment, is

$$K = \left(860-40e^{-.08(.5)}-40e^{-.1(1)}\right)e^{.1(1)}$$
$$= \left[860e^{.08(.5)}-40\right]e^{.12(.5)}-40 = 867.97$$

(the continuously compounded ½ year forward rate of interest at time 0 is $.12 = \frac{.1-.08(.5)}{.5}$).

Suppose that immediately after the first coupon is paid (time .5), the continuously compounded risk free rate of interest is still 8% for 6 month maturities. If the spot price of the bond has risen to 870 at time .5, then at time .5 the delivery price for a forward contract maturing at time 1 (just after the coupon is paid) for delivery at time 1 is

$$(870-40e^{-.08.(.5)})e^{.08(.5)} = 865.51,$$

and the value of the original forward contract entered at time 0 will be

$$S_{.5}-I_{.5}-Ke^{-r(.5)} = 870-40e^{-.08(.5)}-867.97e^{-.08(.5)} = -2.37. \qquad \Box$$

8.1.2 FUTURES CONTRACTS

It is usually the intention of the original parties to a forward contract to actually take part in the transaction specified for the future date, although it is possible for one of the parties to sell his side of the contract to a third party. For both hedging and speculation on future changes in value of a particular financial instrument or commodity, futures contracts are much more widely used than forward contracts. A **futures contract** is similar in many respects to a forward contract. One of the differences is that in setting up a forward contract, there is no restriction regarding the goods to be exchanged or the future date on which the transaction will take place, whereas futures contracts are restricted to a (reasonably broad) group of financial instruments and commodities, and they expire on specific days (such as the second Friday of the expiry month) in various months. The existence of centralized facilities, such as the Chicago Board of Trade and International Monetary Market, for the trading of futures contracts and standardization of the contracts has led to a highly liquid and efficient market in futures contracts. A few examples of goods on which futures contracts are traded are the following:

(1) Japanese yen, with a standard contract size of 12.5 million yen.

(2) 8% U.S. Treasury Bonds, maturing in 15 years, with a standard contract size of 100,000.

(3) 30-day Interest Rate Future, with a standard contract size of 5,000,000. Interest rate futures are based on an underlying government Treasury bill or corporate investment certificate with an appropriate term to maturity.

(4) Pork Bellies, with a standard contract size of 40,000 pounds.

Another distinction between a futures contract and a forward contract is that with a forward contract there is generally no exchange of goods and money until the delivery date of the forward contract, whereas with a futures contract the purchaser of either a long (buyer) or short (seller) position must place a fraction of the cost of the goods with an intermediary (usually a futures broker) and give assurances that the remainder of the purchase price will be paid and the item delivered when required. Usually 2-10% of the contract value (depending on the type of commodity) is paid to a futures broker to be held in an account, with the rest of the contract amount owed *on margin*. As will be seen shortly, futures investments tend to be highly leveraged and very risky.

Suppose a 6-month <u>forward</u> contract to purchase 100,000 Canadian dollars is bought on January 15 with a price of .85 US per Canadian dollar to be paid on July 15. The exchange of funds relating to this contract will not take place until July 15. On January 15, a 6-month <u>futures</u> contract for 100,000 Canadian dollars that expires July 15 may also have a future delivery price .85 US per Canadian dollar, but the purchaser of this futures contract will have to pay a *margin* of $1,350 US (about 1.6% of the contract value) plus a broker commission on the purchase date. If the purchaser holds the futures contract until the expiration or delivery date, then he must pay the remaining $83,650 US ($85,000 minus the original margin paid). A futures contract provides considerable leverage and risk, since changes in the contract value are reflected directly in the equity that the contract holder has with the broker or investment dealer. Suppose that a short time after the contract is issued, the Canadian dollar has risen in value relative to the US dollar, and the effect on the July 15 futures price is that it has risen to .88 US. The futures contract value becomes $88,000 US and the contract holder's equity rises $3000 above the original margin amount (actually, the present value of 3000 due in 6 months). This is true because the holder of the long position has a contract that will allow him to buy for $85,000 US something (the $100,000 CDN) that is worth $88,000 US.

Thus a relatively small change in the value of the underlying commodity can have effects which are proportionally much larger on the equity of the contract holder. If the future price of the Canadian dollar drops any significant amount, the equity of the holder of the long position may drop enough so that the futures broker may require an additional margin payment to maintain a minimum level of equity for the futures contract holder. Suppose that a minimum 2% margin is required for the Canadian dollar futures contract just mentioned. The purchaser of a long position on a futures contract would pay $1,700 US to open the contract. If the Canadian dollar drops in value to 84 cents US, then the value of the contract has fallen by $1000 US, and the investor's equity has dropped to $700 US. When margin falls below its required level, the broker will require the futures contract holder to add an amount to the account to bring the account balance above the minimum margin level. Amounts are added in increments called the "maintenance margin." For Canadian dollar futures contracts the maintenance margin is $1,000 US. In the situation just described, the broker would require the contract holder to add $1,000 to his account.

To maintain order in the futures market, there is a limit on the amount by which the value of a contract can change in a given day.

As mentioned above, the purchaser of a forward contract will usually proceed with the purchase of the goods at the specified date in the future. The holder of a futures contract usually does not intend to hold the contract until maturity, but rather hopes to gain from a hedged or speculative position by selling the contract before expiration.

The purchaser of a futures contract may be attempting to hedge a position. For example, a company may have a substantial investment in bonds or other interest-sensitive securities. The risk of adverse interest rate changes affecting the value of these securities may be reduced by the purchase (or sale) of an appropriately related futures contract. This is illustrated in the following example.

| **EXAMPLE 8.3** | (*Futures contract*) |

The holder of a 1,000,000 12% bond with a maturity of 25 years wishes to create a short-term hedge in potential changes in the bond's value by selling an appropriate number of 100,000 15-year 8% Treasury bond futures contracts which expire in a short period of time. The bondholder's objective is to neutralize the effect of a small change in interest (yield) rate on the current value of his bond. Suppose the current yield on the 25-year bond is 10% and the current yield on 15-year Treasury bonds is 9.5%, and that small changes in yield on the two bonds are numerically equal. Find the number of 100,000 T-bond futures contracts that must be sold by the bondholder to create the hedge.

| **SOLUTION** |

Let $P(i^{(2)})$ denote the price of the 25-year bond at yield rate $i^{(2)}$, and let $j = \frac{i^{(2)}}{2}$. Then

$$\frac{d}{di^{(2)}} P(i^{(2)}) = 1,000,000 \cdot \frac{1}{2} \cdot \frac{d}{dj} \left[v_j^{50} + .06 \cdot a_{\overline{50}|j} \right]$$

$$= 500,000 \left[-50 v_j^{51} + .06(-v_j)(Ia)_{\overline{50}|j} \right].$$

With $i^{(2)} = .10$, we have $j = .05$ and $\frac{d}{di^{(2)}} P(i^{(2)}) = -10,538,299$, or an

approximate decrease in value of 105,383 for an increase of 1% in $i^{(2)}$. Since the futures contract expires in a short time, we will value the 15-year bonds as of now. Let $Q(i^{(2)})$ denote the price of a 15-year 8% 100,000 Treasury bond at yield rate $i^{(2)}$, and let $j = \frac{i^{(2)}}{2}$. Then

$$\frac{d}{di^{(2)}} Q(i^{(2)}) = 100,000 \cdot \frac{1}{2} \cdot \frac{d}{dj} \left[v_j^{30} + .04 \cdot a_{\overline{30}|j} \right]$$

$$= 50,000 \left[-30 v_j^{31} + .04(-v_j)(Ia)_{\overline{30}|j} \right].$$

With $i^{(2)} = .095$ we have $j = .0475$ and $\frac{d}{di^{(2)}} Q(i^{(2)}) = -722,316$. In

order to hedge the bond position, the required number of T-bond contracts to sell is $\frac{10,538,299}{722,316} = 14.6$.

If interest rates increase, the reduction in the value of the 25-year bond is offset by the increase in value of the futures contracts. For instance, suppose that the yield on the 25-year bond changes from 10% to 10.1% and the yield on the 15-year bonds goes to 9.6%. The price of the 25-year bond will change from 1,182,559 to 1,172,100, a drop of 10,459. The price of one 15-year bond will change from 88,135 to 87,417, a drop of 718. The drop in value of 14.6 15-year bonds is 10,483. The change in value of a short position on the futures contract in the 15-year bonds is an increase of 10,483, which approximately matches the drop in value of the 25-year bond actually being held.   □

As another example of a hedge consider a bondholder, whose bonds will mature in six months, who plans to reinvest the proceeds in a new bond issue at that time. The price of the new purchase can be locked in now by purchasing a six-month futures contract on a bond similar to that which will be purchased. The locked-in price is the one reflected in the value of the futures contract when it is purchased. Any changes in yield over the six months will change the ultimate cost of the bonds to be purchased in six months, but if the futures contract is equivalent to the bonds to be bought, then the changes in the value of the futures contract will cancel those in the actual bond price.

It is often the case that the futures contract purchaser has no intention of taking delivery (or the contract seller has no intention of making delivery) at the termination of the contract. The purchaser of the contract may be interested in it as an investment, hoping that the value of the underlying commodity or security will increase, so that the contract can be sold to another purchaser at a higher price before the delivery date.

Financial practice is always evolving, and new types of financial instruments appear from time to time (with some types occasionally disappearing). A futures contract is an example of a **derivative investment**. A derivative investment is one whose value is related to (or derived from) some underlying asset. In the case of a futures contract, the value of the contract is related to the value of the underlying commodity. By the mid 1990's investment derivatives, particularly sophisticated types of options, had attained a certain glamour and notoriety. As a result of highly risky investing in derivatives, a few companies (centuries old Baring's Investment Bank of England for example) and at least one local government (Orange County in California) have faced serious losses or even bankruptcy.

8.2   STOCKS, SHORT SALE AND OPTIONS

8.2.1 STOCK VALUATION

Shares of common stock represent ownership in a corporation, entitling the stockholder to certain privileges including the right to vote on matters regarding the management of the corporation. In addition the common stock owner, from time to time, receives **dividends** that reflect a share of the profit earned by the corporation.

Among the many factors affecting the price of a stock are the nature of the company's business, the quality of the company's management, current economic conditions, and forecasts of future conditions as they relate to the company's current and prospective profitability. An investor in stock would be looking for a return on that investment in the form of future dividends and share price increases. For an investor with a long-term outlook, intending to hold the stock indefinitely, the price (or value) of the stock might be regarded as the present value of future dividends expected to be paid on the stock. If d_t denotes the expected dividend payable at the end of the tth year (with time measured from the purchase date of the stock), and i is the (long-term) annual rate of valuation for this investment, then according to the **dividend discount model for valuing stocks**, the price of the stock can be valued as

$$P = \sum_{t=1}^{\infty} \frac{d_t}{(1+i)^t}. \tag{8.1a}$$

Another formulation would use separate forward rates each year for valuation, so that

$$P = \frac{d_1}{(1+i_1)} + \frac{d_2}{(1+i_1)(1+i_2)} + \cdots. \tag{8.1b}$$

Yet another formulation is based on spot rates, $i_{0,t}$, for discounting payments (recall that the spot rate $i_{0,t}$, for a zero-coupon bond maturing in t years, is the rate at which a payment due at time t will be discounted):

$$P = \frac{d_1}{(1+i_{0,1})} + \frac{d_2}{(1+i_{0,2})^2} + \cdots. \tag{8.1c}$$

A stock is a more risky security than a government bond, so the term structure of spot rates that relate to risk-free zero-coupon bonds would not be appropriate for valuation of dividends on a stock. The spot rate $i_{0,t}$ would not be the same as the risk-free zero-coupon spot rate s_t.

8.2.2 SHORT SALE OF STOCK

Stocks are bought by investors who anticipate gains from dividends and increases in share prices. The typical way in which to invest in a stock is to buy the stock now, wait (and hope) for a price increase, and sell the stock later; buy low and sell high. An alternative way to buy low and sell high is to reverse the order of buying and selling, The stock investor can try to sell high (first) and buy low (later). Arranging the stock investment in this way is done by means of a **short sale** of the stock.

An investor who believes the share price of a stock will fall over a period of time can **sell short** the stock (sell something he does not own) at the current price and cover or close the short sale (buy the stock) at a later date when (he hopes) the stock can be purchased at a lower price. In theory, the short seller is "borrowing" the stock from someone who owns it and then selling it (at whatever the market price is at that time). The loan is repaid by giving the lender back the stock at some later date. This requires the short seller to buy the stock at that later date (at whatever is the market price at that later date) in order to be able to repay the lender of the stock. The lender of the stock never relinquishes ownership in the stock, and is entitled to any benefits that result from stock ownership, specifically dividends. Therefore, when the loan of the stock is repaid, the borrower (short seller) must provide the lender (the actual owner of the stock) with the stock that was borrowed plus any dividends that the stock had paid during the time of the loan. If the dividends were payable before the short sale is closed, there may be interest due on the dividends from the time of dividend payment to the time of the close of the short sale.

Suppose that the value of the stock is S_0 at the time the short sale is opened, and the value of the stock is S_1 at the time the short sale is closed (the stock is bought back). When the short sale is closed, the net gain made by the short seller is $S_0 - S_1$ (the price when the stock was sold minus the price when the stock was bought). This net gain will be positive if $S_1 < S_0$, so that the stock is bought for less than the price at which it was sold. In other words, the short seller has a positive net gain if the stock price drops from the time the short sale was initiated to the time the short sale is terminated. The short seller will experience a net loss on the transaction if $S_1 > S_0$. If the stock pays a dividend of amount D at the time the short sale is terminated, then the short seller must pay that amount to the original owner of the stock, and the net gain made by the short seller becomes $S_0 - S_1 - D$ (and interest will be payable on the dividend if it was payable before the short sale was terminated).

In practice, this transaction is arranged through an investment dealer. The investment dealer will take the position of the lender of the stock in the short sale, meaning that the investment dealer is owed the shares borrowed and sold by the short seller, with the understanding that the short seller will eventually purchase the stock and give it to the dealer. When an investor is a short seller of stock, the investment dealer who executes the transaction will usually require a certain amount of **margin** to be paid by the short seller at the time the short sale is made. This margin may be up to 50% of the value of the stock at the time the short sale is made, and it is held in an account administered by the investment dealer (the margin account). If the stock pays a dividend before the short position is closed, the short seller must pay the dividend amount to the investment dealer, or the amount is deducted from the margin account. The money in the margin account is owned by the investor, and the investment dealer may pay interest on the margin account. A simplified view of a short sale transaction that is initiated at time 0 and completed at time 1 can be summarized as follows.

(i)   Stock price at time 0 is S_0.

(ii) Margin required at time 0 is M.

(iii) Margin account pays interest at rate i per period.

(iv) Stock pays dividend of amount D at time 1.

(v) Stock price at time 1 is S_1.

The short seller opens the margin account at time 0 with a deposit of amount M. The short sale is initiated at time 0. The short seller has a "short sale credit" of amount S_0 as a result of selling the stock for that amount. This amount S_0 does not appear in the margin account, since it represents money that was obtained by selling the borrowed stock, so it is not really the property of the short seller. At time 1, the original margin deposit of M into the margin account will have grown with interest to $M(1+i)$. Also at time 1, when the short sale is terminated, the investor must "pay" S_1 to buy the stock. The net gain on the short sale transaction is $S_0 - S_1$, and this actual dollar amount is added to the margin account, increasing the balance in the market if $S_0 - S_1 > 0$ and decreasing the balance if $S_0 - S_1 < 0$. At time 1 the dividend is payable, and that amount is deducted from the margin account. The net amount in the margin account at time 1, after interest is added to the margin account, and after the short sale is closed and the dividend is paid is $M(1+i) + S_0 - S_1 - D$. Therefore, an initial investment of amount M (the original margin deposit required) has grown to $M(1+i) + S_0 - S_1 - D$ over the course of the period. The actual return or yield j earned by the short sale investor over the period is found from the relationship

$$M(1+j) = M(1+i) + S_0 - S_1 - D.$$

When a dividend is payable, it is deducted from the margin account.

EXAMPLE 8.4   (*Short Sale of Stock*)

The margin requirement on a short sale of stock is 50% of the value of the stock, and the margin account pays 10% per year. The value of the stock being sold short is 100 at the start of the year. The stock pays a dividend of amount 5 at the end of the year. The stock is sold short at the start of the year, and the short sale is closed at the end of the year at the time the dividend is paid. Find the net return earned by a short seller over the one year period if the stock price at the end of the year is

(a) 90   (b) 100   (c) 110

SOLUTION

The amount of margin required is 50 at the start of the year. The balance in the margin account at the end of the year is

$$50(1.1) + 100 - S_1 - 5 \;=\; 150 - S_1.$$

For the three cases considered, this amount will be

(a) 60   (b) 50   (c) 40

The net return earned by the short seller in these cases will be

(a) $\frac{60}{50} - 1 = .20,$ (b) $\frac{50}{50} - 1 = 0,$ (c) $\frac{40}{50} - 1 = -.20$ □

In practice, the equity in the short seller's margin account is regularly updated when there are movements in the stock price. If the stock price increases, the short seller may be required to add to the margin account to maintain a minimum margin level (this is a *margin call*). This is illustrated in the following example.

EXAMPLE 8.5   (*Short sale of stock*)

The current price of a share of stock in Corporation XYZ is 50. Smith sells short 1000 shares of XYZ stock. Smith's investment dealer charges a commission of 2% of the value of stock purchased or sold short and also requires that Smith open a margin account for the short sale. While Smith is "short the stock," the margin account must maintain a balance of at least 40% of the value of the stock. Thus, when the short sale is initiated, Smith must deposit 20,000 into the margin account, and pay the investment dealer a commission of 1000. It is assumed that the margin account earns no interest.

(a) Suppose that the stock price drops to 40, at which time Smith "covers the short sale." If the commission on the stock purchase is deducted from the margin account, find the equity in the account after the short sale is covered.

(b) Repeat part (a) if the price rises to 60. Suppose that the price rises to 60 but Smith does not wish to cover the short sale yet. Find the amount Smith must add to the margin account to maintain the required balance of 40% of the stock value.

(c) Suppose that the stock pays a dividend of 2 per share while the short sale is in effect. Find the least amount by which the share price must drop in order that Smith not get a "margin call" to add to the margin account to maintain the 40% minimum balance.

SOLUTION

(a) When Smith sells the stock short, Smith has a credit of 70,000 (the 50,000 sale price of the stock and the 20,000 in the margin account) and owes 1000 shares of stock. At a price of 40, the cost of purchasing the stock is 40,000 plus 800 in commission. Smith's equity after the transaction is then $70,000 - 40,800 = 29,200$. Smith's overall gain is 9,200 minus the initial 1000 commission on the short sale, for a net gain, after commissions, of 8200. Smith's gain could also have been found as $1000 \times (50-40) - commission = 10,000 - 1800 = 8200$. Smith has made a gain of 8200 on an investment of 20,000, resulting in a return of 41% on the transaction.

(b) Smith must now have a margin account balance of

$$.40 \times 60,000 = 24,000,$$

and so must add 4000 to the margin account.

(c) Smith's account has 2000 deducted to pay for dividends, leaving a balance of 18,000. In order for the account to be at least 40% of the stock value, it must be the case that $18,000 \geq .40 \times 1000 \times P$. Thus, $P \leq 45$, so that the stock must drop in value by at least 5 in order to avoid a margin call. □

8.2.3 OPTIONS

An option, in the financial sense, is a contract conveying a right to buy or sell designated securities or commodities at a specified price during a stipulated period. The specified price mentioned in this definition is called the option's **strike price** or **exercise price**. A **call option** gives the holder the right to buy (or call away) a specified amount of the underlying security from the option issuer (writer), and a **put option** gives the holder the right to sell (or put) a specified amount of the underlying security to the option issuer. An *American option* allows the right to buy or sell to be exercised any time up to the expiration date, and a *European option* allows the option to be exercised only on the expiration date.

As time goes on, new option contracts on a particular security are introduced on a regular basis; when this occurs there are generally several contract types set up with strike prices varying from somewhat below to somewhat above the market price of the underlying security at the time the option is introduced. The contracts are set up with strike prices at increments appropriately related to the value of the underlying security. For example, if the underlying stock price is 30, options may be issued with strike prices of 25, 30 or 35. New options also will be introduced so that exercise dates of up to one year in the future are always available. When option values are quoted in a financial publication, the expiration date is given as a particular month, but it is understood that there is a specific day in that month when the option expires (usually the 2nd or 3rd Saturday).

There will always be two parties to an options contract, the purchaser of the option and the writer (or issuer) of the option. For a call option, as indicated above, the purchaser has the right to buy stock at the strike price by a certain date. In exchange for receiving a payment for writing the option, the writer of the call option has the obligation to provide to the option purchaser the stock at the strike price, if the option purchaser exercises the option. Similar comments apply to put options.

Suppose that on January 15 an investor obtains a call option to purchase a share of XYZ Corporation before July 20 at a price of 50 per share. An investor holding such an option would exercise it only if the share price goes above 50, since the investor could then exercise the option and buy the stock at 50 and immediately sell the stock at the higher current price. If XYZ Corporation has a share price of 55 on January 15, the value on that date of the call option with a strike price of 50 is at least its *intrinsic value* of 5. The **intrinsic value** of a call option is the excess, if any, of the share price over the strike price (for a call option). The intrinsic value can also be regarded as the immediate return that the option holder could realize by exercising the option and buying a share at 50 and selling it at 55 (transaction costs such as commissions are being excluded). There is also a possibility that the stock price will increase above 55 before July 20. This suggests that the value of the option is more than the intrinsic value of 5. The value of the option above the intrinsic value is the *time value* or *time premium*, which takes into account the possible increase in the price of the underlying security before the expiration date.

A call option whose strike price is less than the market price of the underlying security is said to be *in-the-money*, so if the strike price is 50 and the share price is 55, the call option is in-the-money. On the other hand, if XYZ Corporation has a price of 45 per share on January 15, then the option is *out-of-the-money*, and has no intrinsic value. An out-of-the-money option will still have a time value, since it is still possible for the share price to rise sufficiently before the expiration date to put it in-the-money. It is possible that the option will stay out-of-the-money until the expiration date, in which case it will expire without having been exercised, and the original cost of the option to the option purchaser is lost, whereas the writer of the option made a gain. A similar analysis can be applied to put options.

The actual price paid for an option depends on the perceptions of investors regarding the behavior of the underlying stock's price prior to the option's expiration date. For an option that expires at time 1, as time moves closer to the expiration date, the value of a call option approaches the limit $\max[0, S_1 - K]$, where S_1 is the price of the stock at time 1, and K is the strike price of the option. Note also that there is a lower limit to the potential loss on the transaction, from the call option holder's point of view, namely the amount paid for the option. This loss occurs if the option expires unexercised. The potential profit does not have an upper limit since it depends on the level to which the stock's price can rise. For the writer of the call there is a limit to the profit, namely the price received for the sale of the call. If the holder exercises the option, the call writer is obliged to buy the stock on the market (or use existing inventory of that stock) and sell to the holder of the call. There is no limit to the call writer's potential liability, since there is no limit on the potential price of the stock that the call writer will have to buy in order to cover the call. There is a wide variety of investment strategies such as *spreads and straddles* that involve the purchase or writing of options in combination with purchase or (short) sale of the underlying stock.

Since the introduction of *"exchange-traded options"* in 1973, a considerable amount of research has been done into the valuation of options. In order to determine the value of an option on an underlying security, a combination of selling (or buying) the option and buying (or selling) an appropriate amount of the security is made that forms *a riskless hedge* that provides the same return as would be realized over the same period when investing at the *risk-free rate of return*, the rate of return available on essentially risk-free government securities. The way in which such a riskless hedge is constructed can best be seen in an elementary illustration in which, on the expiration date, the price of the underlying security will be one of two possible values. This is called the **binomial model**.

Suppose that a stock has a current price of 100, and at the end of the current period the stock's price will be either 110 or 90. Suppose that the stock has a call option on it to purchase at a strike price of 105 at the end of the period. Suppose investor A writes the call option on one share and investor B purchases the call option. If the stock price is 110 at the time the option expires, the value of the option at that time will be $110 - 105 = 5$. In that case, at time 1 investor B (the holder of the option) can buy the stock from investor A for 105 when he exercises the option, and sell the stock at the market price for 110. On the other hand, investor B will allow the option to expire unexercised if the stock's price is 90, so the value of the option in this case is 0 on the expiration date.

Suppose that at the same time investor A sells the option on one share, he also purchases ¼ share of the stock for $¼(100) = 25$. Let us denote by C_0 the value of the option to purchase one share at the start of the period. The net amount invested by investor A is $25 - C_0$, the amount paid for the ¼-share of stock minus the amount received from the sale of the option. At the time of expiration, one of two events will occur; the stock price will be either 110 or 90. If the stock price is 110 at the time of expiration, then at that time the net value of investor A's combined investment is $27.50 - 5 = 22.50$ (the value of the stock investor A holds minus the cost of fulfilling the obligation to the option holder). If the stock price is 90 at the time of expiration, then the net value of investor A's combined investment is $22.50 - 0 = 22.50$. Thus, the net value of the investment at the end of the period is 22.50 no matter what the stock price is. This is a riskless hedge for investor A, in the sense that the value of the investment at the end of the period will be 22.50 with certainty.

According the financial principle that no arbitrage opportunities exist, any riskless investment must earn the same return as the risk-free rate of interest. In order to determine the price of the option at the start of the period, investor B's riskless investment should be equivalent to a riskless investment in a government security over the same period. Suppose that the risk-free rate of return for the period is 1%. In order for the investment to be equivalent to a risk-free investment in the government security, we must have $(25-C_0)(1.01) = 22.50$, so that $C_0 = 2.7228$.

In the general binomial model for stock price movement, suppose the current stock price is S_0, and suppose that at the end of the current period the stock price will be either S_1^+ or S_1^-, where $S_1^+ > S_1^-$. Suppose there is a call option on the stock with a strike price of K. The value of the option at the end of the period is either C_1^+ or C_1^-, depending on whether the stock price is S_1^+ or S_1^-. It is possible to create a riskless hedge by selling a call option on one share of stock at the same time as purchasing h shares of stock, where $h = \frac{C_1^+ - C_1^-}{S_1^+ - S_1^-}$ is called the *hedge ratio*.

The net amount invested by the writer (seller) of the call option at the start of the period is $h \cdot S_0 - C_0$, and the value of the investment at the end of the period is $h \cdot S_1^+ - C_1^+ = h \cdot S_1^- - C_1^-$, whether the stock price goes to S_1^+ or S_1^-. If the risk-free rate of return is r for the period, then

$$(h \cdot S_0 - C_0)(1+r) \ = \ h \cdot S_1^+ - P_1^+ \ = \ h \cdot S_1^- - C_1^-.$$

Since $h, S_0, S_1^+, S_1^-, C_1^+, C_1^-$ and r are known, it is possible to solve for C_0.

This binomial model for stock prices and option valuation can be extended to a two-period scenario in which the stock price S_0 moves to one of two prices S_1^+ or S_1^- at the end of the first period. For each price at the end of period 1 there are two possible prices to which the stock can move at the end of period 2, which may be different for S_1^+ and S_1^-. This generalization can be continued to more than two consecutive periods. The period can be shortened and the number of periods, n, can be increased, allowing a limiting case in which, as $n \to \infty$, the stock price becomes a continuous stochastic process.

The limiting case described in the previous paragraph is the *Black-Scholes option pricing formula*. The formula assumes that the stock pays no dividends prior to expiry of the option, and that $\{\ln[S_t] \mid 0 \le t \le n\}$ forms a Brownian motion stochastic process with variance σ^2 per unit time period, where S_t is the stock price at time t. (It is possible to adjust the formulation to account for dividends). This assumption regarding the behavior of the stock's price can be more simply described by saying that the continuously compounded annual rate of return on the stock has a normal distribution with variance σ^2; in practice, σ^2 is estimated as a sample variance based on historical data for the stock. The following parameters are also required for the valuation formula:

δ - the risk-free force of interest
S_0 - the current price of the stock
K - the exercise (strike) price of the option
n - the time (in years) until expiry of the option

The Black-Scholes formula gives the price of the call option at the current time as

$$C \;=\; S_0 \cdot \Phi(d_1) - K \cdot e^{-n\delta} \cdot \Phi(d_2), \qquad (8.2)$$

where

$$d_1 \;=\; \frac{\ln\!\left(\frac{S_0}{K}\right) + \left(\delta + \frac{1}{2}\sigma^2\right) \cdot n}{\sigma \sqrt{n}}, \qquad (8.3)$$

$$d_2 \;=\; \frac{\ln\!\left(\frac{S_0}{K}\right) + \left(\delta - \frac{1}{2}\sigma^2\right) \cdot n}{\sigma \sqrt{n}}, \qquad (8.4)$$

and $\Phi(x)$ is the cumulative distribution function of the standard normal distribution.

| **EXAMPLE 8.6** | (*Black-Scholes option pricing formula*) |

The price on January 15 of a share of XYZ stock is 50. Use the Black-Scholes option pricing formula to find the value on January 15 of an option to buy 1 share of XYZ, with an expiration date of July 20, and with an exercise price of (a) 45, (b) 50, and (c) 55. Assume the risk-free force of interest is .08, and the continuously compounded rate of return on the stock has a standard deviation of $\sigma = .03$.

| **SOLUTION** |

$S_0 = 50$, $n = \frac{186}{365} = .5096$, $\delta = .08$, $\sigma^2 = .0009$, $e^{-n\delta} = .9601$.

(a) $K = 45$ so $d_1 = 6.8341$ and $d_2 = 6.8127$, implying
$\Phi(d_1) = \Phi(d_2) = 1.0000$, implying an option price of
$50(1) - 45(.960053)(1) = 6.7976$;

(b) $K = 50$ so $d_1 = 1.9143$ and $d_2 = 1.8929$, implying $\Phi(d_1) = .9722$
and $\Phi(d_2) = .9708$, implying an option price of
$50(.9722) - 50(.960053)(.9708) = 2.0090$;

(c) $K = 55$ so $d_1 = -2.5362$ and $d_2 = -2.5576$, implying
$\Phi(d_1) = .0056$ and $\Phi(d_2) = .00527$, implying an option price of
$50(.0056) - 55(.9601)(.00527) = .0017$.   □

Options are available on a variety of financial instruments, including government Treasury Bonds (both long and short term) and foreign currency contracts. Options provide the investor with a certain amount of *leverage* in the investment. On a call option, the option price (or *premium*) on an in-the-money option will fluctuate in tandem, more or less, with the price of the underlying security. Thus the option investor can make the same numerical gain as the holder of the underlying security, but the premium paid by the option investor is, typically, considerably less than the price of the underlying security. The call option buyer's potential loss is limited to the original cost of the option (but it could be a 100% loss if the option expires out of the money).

As mentioned earlier in this chapter, options are one example of the class of investments known as derivative investments or derivatives. The value of a derivative investment is derived from or tied to the value of some underlying investment; the option value is completely dependent upon the value of the underlying stock. The previous paragraph indicated that the value of an option is generally a fraction of the value of the underlying stock but may be subject to similar price changes. From Example 8.6 we see that the Black-Scholes price of the call option with strike price 50 is 2.01. If the stock price rises to 55 by the expiration date, the option value rises to 5, which is 150% increase, while the stock itself has risen from 50 to 55, which is a 10% increase. On the other hand, if the stock price drops to 45 at the expiration date, the call option has a value of 0, which is a 100% loss of the investment in the option, while the stock has had a 10% decrease in value. The call option is generally considerably more risky than the underlying stock, and this is a feature of most derivative investments. A **leveraged investment** is one for which small percentage changes in the underlying investment can result in large percentage changes in the related derivative investment. A call option is an example of a leverage investment.

8.2.4 MUTUAL FUNDS

An investment company can pool the money of many individual investors and purchase various types of financial instruments such as stocks, and/or bonds. Each individual would own a portion of the fund. The portion of the fund owned is determined by the amount invested as a fraction of the total value of the fund. The individual's ownership in a mutual fund is represented by the number of fund units owned by the individual. The price per unit would be found as the total value of the fund divided by the number of units held by individual investors. As new investors purchase units the fund managers continue to buy investments. If an investor wishes to sell units, the fund company can buy back the units and may have to sell some investments to raise money needed to pay the investor.

The fund would be managed by investment professionals who make the decisions as to what instruments in which to invest. Some funds are designed to invest in specialized sectors of the financial markets. For instance, a fund can invest mainly in energy stocks, such as those of oil and gas exploration companies, or electrical utility companies. The investment managers would generally charge an annual fee, typically anywhere from 1% to 3% of the fund's value. There are thousands of mutual funds available, ranging in size from a few million to many billions of dollars.

An individual investing in a mutual fund has the advantage of diversifying the investment over the range of instruments owned by the fund. Another (possible) advantage is the benefit of the expertise of the investment fund manager. Mutual funds are generally quite liquid investments, with valuations updated each day.

8.2.5 EXCHANGE TRADED FUNDS

One of the motivations for investing in a mutual fund is to obtain a diversified market return that has less risk than an individual stock might have. An alternative to mutual funds that has become popular in recent years is exchange traded funds. An exchange traded fund tracks a particular market index, such as the Dow Jones Industrial, or the Standard and Poor's 500 (index of 500 major stocks). The fund trades like a stock and is listed on a major market, and can be bought or sold at any time during a trading day. A mutual fund has its value updated at the end of each trading day, whereas the value of an exchange traded fund fluctuates constantly throughout the day as the price of an individual stock would. Exchange traded funds tend to have smaller management fees than mutual funds, but there is no "investment expertise" in the management of the exchange traded fund since its value always runs parallel to the index that it is tracking.

8.2.6 CAPITAL ASSET PRICING MODEL

A stock will have a certain amount of risk associated with it. The stock's price will be related to the level of prices in the stock market as a whole, so that part of the risk, called the *market risk* (or *systematic risk*), for an individual stock will be related to general factors that affect the overall economy. In addition, because of the specific nature of the stock's industry group and the position of the issuing corporation in that industry, there will be *non-market risk* or *diversifiable risk*. Diversifiable risk can be managed by carefully choosing the mix of stocks in the overall portfolio. If an investor's portfolio exactly matches the portfolio used to measure overall market performance, such as the portfolio used for the Dow Jones index or the Standard & Poor's index, then the risk of the portfolio will be entirely market risk as measured by the standard portfolio. The market and non-market risks are generally assumed to be independent.

The valuation rate (or sequence of rates) used in price formulas (8.1) for a specific stock, may be related to the risk classification of that stock.

The relationship between the rate of return on a stock over a period of time and the average return on the entire stock market (represented by a broad market portfolio such as Standard and Poor's 500 index) during the same period is represented by the stock's *characteristic line*, given by

$$R_s = \alpha_s + \beta_s \cdot R_m + e_s, \tag{8.5}$$

where R_s is the (random) return on the stock for the period under consideration, α_s is the part of the stock's return not related to the market, β_s is the expected change in R_s, given a change of 1 unit in the market return R_m, R_m is the (random) return on the entire market for the period, and e_s is a random variable (with mean 0) measuring the non-market risk (usually assumed to be independent of R_m).

The factor β_s is called the *beta* of the stock, and measures the volatility of the stock's return in relation to the return on the entire market (see Exercise 8.2.13). The larger the beta for a stock, the larger the expected return and the larger the risk (standard deviation of return). These parameters change over time; estimates of α_s and β_s can be obtained using statistical regression based on historical data.

Taking the expected value of both sides of Equation (8.5) results in

$$\overline{R}_s = \alpha_s + \beta_s \cdot \overline{R}_m. \tag{8.6}$$

Under reasonable assumptions regarding investor behavior, this relationship can be written as the **capital asset pricing model**

$$\overline{R}_s = R_f + \beta_s(\overline{R}_m - R_f). \tag{8.7}$$

In Equation (8.7) R_f denotes the risk-free rate of return available, as measured by an appropriate government security. We do not derive this model in this text.

8.3 FIXED INCOME INVESTMENTS

Chapter 4 considered many aspects of bond valuation. Coupon bonds and zero coupon bonds are examples of "fixed income investments." Bonds issued by the federal government provide a safe and predictable income stream. Investors who are willing to tolerate some risk of default in exchange for a (potentially) higher return can invest in bonds issued by a less secure borrower such as a municipal government or a corporation.

Some states and municipalities issue bonds that have coupons which are totally or partially tax exempt. Depending on the tax situation of an investor, this might be a desirable feature of the income received.

Bond rating agencies such as Standard and Poor's and Dominion Bond Rating Service provide credit ratings of many kinds of fixed income investments. These credit ratings are a measure of the risk that an investor faces that some of the scheduled fixed income payments might not be made due to default on the part of the bond issuer. Example 8.8 later in this chapter considers the tradeoff between higher risk and higher return on a bond. There are a number of fixed income investments besides bonds that are available to investors. In this section we will briefly describe several of these types of investments.

8.3.1 CERTIFICATES OF DEPOSIT

A Certificate of Deposit (CD) is a deposit that an investor makes to a bank, savings and loan, or credit union. In Canada CD's are referred to as Guaranteed Investment Certificates (GIC). The interest rate and maturity date on a CD is usually fixed at the time the deposit is made. CD's are generally insured by the federal government through the US Federal Deposit Insurance Corporation or the Canadian Deposit Insurance Corporation for principal amounts up to $100,000. For CD's that are arranged for maturities less than a year, principal and interest are returned together at the time of maturity. For a CD that has a maturity of longer than one year, interest payments are usually arranged to be paid semi-annually or annually, with the principal amount returned at the time of maturity.

8.3.2 MONEY MARKET FUNDS

A money market fund is a mutual fund that invests in mostly very short term, highly secure instruments such as government treasury bills and CD's. Technically, a money market fund is a mutual fund. But practically, it is close to being a savings account without the guarantees provided with bank accounts. The fund tends to earn a higher rate of interest than is available in typical bank savings accounts, and usually pays interest every month, but it may require an initial investment that is several thousand dollars. Some money market funds allow the account holder to write checks. Money in the fund is generally available to the account holder at short notice.

8.3.3 MORTGAGE-BACKED SECURITIES

Lending institutions can pool together a number of mortgage loans and sell shares of the loans to individual investors. When an individual takes a mortgage loan on a property, it is not unusual for the individual to have the loan insured. The Federal Housing Authority (FHA) is a US government agency that provides insurance for mortgage loans.

The Government National Mortgage Association (GNMA) provides federal government backing guaranteeing the loan payments on these federally insured mortgages. This federal government guarantee makes Mortgage Backed Securities (MBS) very secure investments. The investor in an MBS becomes, in a sense, the lender who then receives mortgage payments from the borrowers. An investor receives monthly payments which reflect a share of the monthly payments being made by the borrowers on the underlying mortgages.

Mortgage loans often have a provision that allows the borrower to repay principal before the scheduled end of the mortgage loan; these are referred to as prepayments. When prepayments take place on a mortgage held in an MBS, the prepayment is spread among the various investors. There is a risk to the MBS investor that prepayments will result in the investment maturing earlier than was originally scheduled in the pool of mortgages.

MBS investments provide a secure monthly income with annual returns that tend to be up to 2% higher than yields on medium term (5 to 10 year) treasury bonds. There is also a very liquid secondary market in MBS securities.

8.3.4 TREASURY INFLATION PROTECTED SECURITIES (TIPS) AND REAL RETURN BONDS

The US federal treasury and the Bank of Canada issue inflation protected bonds. The structure of a TIPS is similar to that of a standard coupon bond in that there is a coupon rate and maturity amount. The difference is that the maturity amount is regularly adjusted based on the rate of inflation that has occurred since the TIPS was issued. When it is time for a coupon payment, the coupon rate is multiplied by the inflation-adjusted maturity amount. Also, at the time of maturity, the amount paid is the inflation-adjusted maturity amount based on the accumulated inflation rate since the TIPS was issued.

| EXAMPLE 8.7 | (*TIPS*) |

Suppose that the coupon rate on a TIPS is 5% every six months and the maturity amount of the bond is 10,000 at the time the bond is issued, with the bond to mature 2 years after it is issued. Furthermore, suppose that we set the Consumer Price Index (CPI) to 1 at the time the bond is issued. Suppose that the CPI over the next 2 years has the following values:

Time	6-month	12-month	18-month	24-month
CPI	1.02	1.03	1.06	1.08

Determine the final maturity amount and the coupon amounts on each payment date.

| SOLUTION |

The maturity amount will be updated on each coupon payment date, and on the maturity date, and the coupon amount will be 5% of the inflation-adjusted maturity value.

Time	6-month	12-month	18-month	24-month
Adj. Mat. Value	10,200	10,300	10,600	10,800
Coupon	510	515	530	540

On the maturity date the maturity amount paid to the bondholder will be 10,800. □

8.3.5 BOND DEFAULT AND RISK PREMIUM

One issuer of a bond may not be as financially stable or secure as another. Based on various analyses of the bond issuer, such as historical performance as to default, the performance of the industry group with which the issuing company is associated, and so on, it may be possible to estimate probabilities of default. There are a number of bond-rating services which classify borrowers as to their creditworthiness, with ranks from AAA (highest) to C (lowest).

| EXAMPLE 8.8 | (*Default risk*)

Analysis of a bond with 3 years remaining until maturity indicates an estimated probability of default of .05 in any given coupon period until maturity, given that default has not yet occurred. The bond has a nominal annual coupon rate of 14%, payable semiannually, and a face amount of 100,000. If default occurs, the bond will pay no coupon for the coupon period in which it occurred, but will pay 50% of the redemption amount at the time of default and no further coupons. Using expected present value, what price should an investor pay for the bond based on an annual yield of 12%, payable semiannually?

| SOLUTION |

With a reference point of $t = 0$ (where $t = 6$ represents the maturity date), the probabilities of default each period are as follows:

Period	Default Probability	Probability of Full Payment
1	.05	.95
2	$(.95)(.05)$	$(.95)^2$
3	$(.95)^2(.05)$	$(.95)^3$
4	$(.95)^3(.05)$	$(.95)^4$
5	$(.95)^4(.05)$	$(.95)^5$
6	$(.95)^5(.05)$	$(.95)^6$

We can find the total expected present value in two ways. The first approach is to find the expected payment at each of times 1 to 6 and sum them.

The possible payments at time 1 are 7000 (the coupon if default doesn't take place during the first coupon period, this has probability .95) and 50,000 (reduced redemption if default occurred, this has probability .05). The expected present value is $[7000(.95) + 50,000(.05)]v$.

The possible payments at time 2 are 7000 (if default hasn't occurred during the first 2 periods, this has probability $.95^2$), 50,000 (if default occurs in the 2nd period, this has probability $(.95)(.05)$) and 0 (if default occurred in the first period, this has probability .05), with expected present value $[7000(.95)^2 + 50,000(.95)(.05)]v^2$.

Continuing in this way to time 6, we get that the total expected present value of the coupons, default payment, and redemption amount is

$$\begin{aligned}
&[7000(.95) + 50,000(.05)v] \\
&\quad + [7000(.95)^2 + 50,000(.95)(.05)]v^2 \\
&\qquad + [7000(.95)^3 + 50,000(.95)^2(.05)]v^3 \\
&\qquad\quad + [7000(.95)^4 + 50,000(.95)^3(.05)]v^4 \\
&\qquad\qquad + [7000(.95)^5 + 50,000(.95)^4(.05)]v^5 \\
&\qquad\qquad\quad + [107,000(.95)^6 + 50,000(.95)^5(.05)]v^6 \\
&\qquad\qquad\qquad = \quad 91,897.18.
\end{aligned}$$

As an alternative approach, we can find the total present value received for each of 7 possible events:

(1) default in period 1, (2) default in period 2,..., (6) default in period 6, (7) no default. In event (1), the total present value received is $50,000v$, with probability .05. In event (2), the total present value received is $7000v + 50,000v^2$, with probability $(.95)(.05)$. Continuing in this way leads to the same expected present value as the first approach.

At the price of 91,897.18, if all coupon payments are met and the redemption amount is paid, the yield on the bond would be $i^{(2)} = .1759$. ☐

The difference between the *promised yield to maturity* of 17.59% and the *expected yield to maturity* of 12% in Example 8.8 is the *default premium* on the bond, which is 5.59%. The expected yield rate on a bond which has a risk of default will be larger than the yield on a government (risk-free) bond with the same coupon rate and time to maturity. The difference between this expected yield (12% in Example 8.8) and the yield on the corresponding risk-free bond (say 8%) is called the *risk premium*. The total of the *risk premium* and the default premium on a bond is the *yield spread* for that bond (4% + 5.59% = 9.59% in Example 8.8).   □

8.4 FOREIGN CURRENCY EXCHANGE RATES

Corporations involved in international trade that are scheduled to receive delayed payment in various foreign currencies, but whose expenditures are mainly in their own country's currency, are concerned with the fluctuation of exchange rates among the currencies. There are a number of ways to protect against adverse fluctuations in exchange rates, including the use of *foreign currency futures* and forward markets for currency exchange as discussed in Section 8.1. Forward rate contracts can be established for periods as short as one month or as long as 10 years into the future.

The economic factors that determine the relationships among foreign currencies are very complex. One important factor is the relationship between interest rates in the various countries. The following example gives a simple illustration of the effect of interest on the exchange rate between currencies of different countries.

EXAMPLE 8.9   (*Exchange and interest rates*)

According to today's spot exchange rate between the Canadian and U.S. currencies, $1 CDN is equivalent to $.85 US. Suppose interest rates for the coming year are 6% in Canada and 3% in the U.S. What should be the one-year forward exchange rate between the values of the two currencies in order that the relationship between the currencies remains unchanged with regard to borrowing and lending for one year?

SOLUTION

One year from now $1.06 CDN will be required to repay a loan of $1 CDN now. Similarly, one year from now $.85 × 1.03 = $.8755 US will be required to repay a loan of $.85 US now. In order to maintain a market balance between the currencies, one year from now $1.06 CDN should be equivalent to $.8755 US, or $1 CDN should be equivalent to $\frac{\$.8755}{1.06} = \$.8259$ U.S. dollars.   ☐

The situation in Example 8.9 can be generalized as follows. Suppose the spot exchange rate today between currencies A and B is that 1 unit of currency A is equivalent to C_s units of currency B. Let the annual interest rate on currency A (in the country with that currency) be i_A and the annual interest rate on currency B be i_B. In order to balance two one-year loans in the respective currencies, the relationship between the currencies one year from now should be $1 + i_A$ units of currency A equivalent to $C_s(1+i_B)$ units of currency B, or one unit of currency A equivalent to

$$C_f = \frac{C_s(1+i_B)}{1+i_A}, \tag{8.8}$$

where C_f is the one-year forward rate of exchange.

The relationship between the spot and forward rates of exchange can also be explained in terms of the inflation rates in the respective currencies. If the real (inflation-adjusted) rates of interest over the following year are the same in the two currencies, then $i_A^{real} = \frac{i_A - r_A}{1 + r_A} = i_B^{real} = \frac{i_B - r_B}{1 + r_B}$, where r_A and r_B are the annual inflation rates in currencies A and B. Then

$$1 + i_A^{real} = \frac{1+i_A}{1+r_A} = 1 + i_B^{real} = \frac{1+i_B}{1+r_B},$$

so $\frac{1+i_B}{1+i_A} = \frac{1+r_B}{1+r_A}$, and therefore

$$C_f = \frac{C_s(1+i_B)}{1+i_A} = \frac{C_s(1+r_B)}{1+r_A}. \tag{8.9}$$

This relationship can be explained as follows: if one unit of currency A is now worth C_s units of currency B, then to maintain the same balance of purchasing power between the currencies one year from now, $1+r_A$ units of currency A should have the same value as $C_s(1+r_B)$ units of currency B, which is the relationship of Equation (8.9).

Using the approximation $\frac{1+x}{1+y} \approx 1+x-y$, Equation (8.8) becomes $C_s(1+i_B-i_A) \approx C_f$, or

$$\frac{C_f - C_s}{C_s} \approx i_B - i_A. \tag{8.10}$$

The relationship in Equation (8.10) is called the *interest rate parity theorem*, which states that the percentage difference between the spot and forward exchange rates is approximately equal to the difference between the interest rates on the two currencies.

The relationships in Equations (8.8), (8.9), and (8.10) are quite simplistic, and do not account for all of the dynamics affecting exchange rates. For instance, a typical way in which a country supports its currency is by increasing the rate of interest on government securities. The reasoning behind this is that as the rate of return increases in the country's currency, there will be more foreign demand for that currency in order to invest at the higher rate, and the demand for the currency will increase its value in terms of other currencies. However if we increase i_A in Equation (8.8) while keeping i_B unchanged, the ratio $\frac{C_f}{C_s}$ must decrease. It is not clear whether this occurs because of a decrease in C_f or because of an increase in C_s. The most likely scenario is that both C_f and C_s increase, but C_s increases proportionally more than C_f since the increased rate i_A may change (decrease) before the forward exchange could take place.

8.5. NOTES AND REFERENCES

Practical information on the nature of forward contracts, options and futures is available from trading exchanges such as the Chicago Board Options Exchange and the Chicago Board of Trade.

There are many good references for topics in finance and portfolio analysis. A very readable introduction to the binomial pricing model for options can be found in *Financial Calculus: An Introduction to Derivative Pricing*, by M. Baxter and A. Rennie, published by Cambridge Publishing. Discussions of the Black-Scholes option pricing model can be found in *Modern Portfolio Theory and Investment Analysis*, by E Elton and M. Gruber, published by John Wiley. The Black-Scholes formula was developed in the research paper *The Pricing of Options and Corporate Liabilities*, by F. Black and M. Scholes in the Journal of Political Economy in 1973. Groundwork for the Black-Scholes formula was also done by R. Merton. Merton and Scholes were awarded the 1997 Nobel prize in economics for their work on investment derivatives (Black had died prior to the award being given).

A discussion of default premium and risk premium can be found in *Investments* by W. Sharpe, published by Prentice-Hall.

8.6 EXERCISES

The exercises without asterisks are intended to comprehensively cover the material presented in the chapter. Exercises with a asterisk can be regarded as supplementary exercises which cover topics in more depth, either theoretically or computationally, than those without a asterisk.

SECTION 8.1

8.1.1 *Forward contract on a security with no income*. The current spot price of platinum is $420 per ounce. The one year continuously compounded risk free rate of interest is 5%.

    (a) Find the one year forward price of platinum per ounce, assuming the price is consistent with the existence of no arbitrage opportunities.

    (b) Suppose that the one year forward price for platinum is $450 per ounce. Construct a strategy from which an investor can obtain a riskless profit.

(c) Suppose that an investor takes a long one year forward position in one ounce of platinum in which the forward (delivery) price is based on no arbitrage. Six months later the price of platinum is still $420. Find the value of the long position of the contract at that time (6 months after the contract was entered), assuming that the risk free rate of interest is still 5% (as a continuously compounded annual rate).

8.1.2   *Forward contract on a security which provides known income.* An investor takes a short position in a one year forward contract on a 30-year Treasury Bond. The Treasury Bond to be delivered in one year is assumed to have an 8% coupon rate (payable semiannually) and a face (and maturity) amount of 100.

(a) Assuming a flat term structure, with continuously compounded annual return of 6% for all terms to maturity, find the one year forward price, assuming no arbitrage.

(b) Assume a flat term structure, with continuously compounded annual return of 6% for all terms to maturity. Suppose that the one year forward price on the bond is $125. Construct a strategy from which an investor can earn a riskless profit.

(c) Suppose that the annual yield to maturity on 31 year bonds is 6% compounded semiannually at the time the one year forward contract is entered. Suppose also that, the 6-month and 1 year risk free rates of interest are 5% compounded continuously at the time the forward contract is entered. What one year forward yield to maturity for 30 year bonds is implied by these conditions under the assumption of no arbitrage?

8.1.3   *Futures contract on soybeans.* In November 2005 an investor opens a long position on one June 2006 contract in soybeans. The contract size is for 5000 bushels of soybeans. The futures price is $4.95 per bushel on the day the contract is purchased. Initial margin required on a soybean contract is 1200, with maintenance margin of 1000. The day after opening the contract, the futures price for the June 2005 contract in soybeans has dropped to $4.90 per bushel. Find the amount that the investor must add to the margin account to keep the contract open, and find the investor's one day percentage loss.

8.1.4   *Futures contract on a banker's acceptance.* In November 2005, a corporate treasurer expects that the company will be receiving a payment of 1,000,000 in two months (January), and plans to invest in a 3-month (¼-year) investment at that time. The treasurer wishes to hedge the investment rate that can be obtained when the investment will be made in two months, and takes a long position in one 3-month banker's acceptance futures contract (1,000,000 contract amount) with maturity in March 2006. When the futures contract is entered (say today), the futures price is quoted at 94.00. In two months (January), when the 1,000,000 is received, the treasurer sells the futures contract. For each of the following scenarios, find the 3-month net return obtained for the 3 months following the receipt of the 1,000,000 that will be invested in January.

(i)   2 months from now, the 3-month investment rate is 6.5% (convertible quarterly) and the March futures contract price is 93.60.

(ii) 2 months from now, the 3-month investment rate is 5.5% (convertible quarterly) and the March futures contract price is 94.40.

(iii) 2 months from now, the 3-month investment rate is i% (convertible quarterly) and the March futures contract price is $100 - k$.

8.1.5   The current spot price for one ounce of gold is 280. The continuously compounded risk-free interest rate is .08 for all maturities.

(a) Find the delivery price on a forward contract for one ounce of gold with delivery date (i) in 1 year, and (ii) in 2 years.

(b) At time $t = 0$ Smith enters a 2-year forward contract to buy an ounce of gold (long) and at the same time enters a 3-year forward contract to sell an ounce of gold (short). Find the combined value of Smith's forward contracts at time $t = 1$ as a function of S_1 (the spot price of an ounce of gold at time $t = 1$).

(c) Suppose that at time $t = 1$ the continuously compounded risk-free rate of interest for all maturities is .10. Repeat part (b).

8.1.6   In November 2005, a corporate treasurer expects that the company will be receiving a payment of 1,000,000 in two months (January, 2006), and plans to invest in a 3-month (¼-year) investment at that time. The treasurer wishes to hedge the investment rate that can be obtained when the investment will be made in two months, and takes a long position in one 3-month banker's acceptance futures contract (1,000,000 contract amount) with maturity in March 2006. When the futures contract is entered (say today), the futures price is quoted at 96.00. In two months (January), when the 1,000,000 is received, the treasurer sells the futures contract, and the futures price at that time is 95.00. Find the 3-month net return obtained for the 3 month period following the receipt of the 1,000,000 that will be invested in January if the 3-month investment rate in January is 5.0% (convertible quarterly). Note that an increase of .01 in the price of a 1,000,000 3-month banker's acceptance long futures contract results in a gain of 25 in the value of the contract.

8.1.7   An investor opens a short position in a futures contract in a 3-month banker's acceptance. At the time that the position is opened, the quoted price for a contract is 98.00 (one contract is for 1,000,000 banker's acceptance). The margin required to open the account is $500. One week later the quoted price on the futures contract is 98.10. The speculator closes the account. Find the speculator's one-week rate of return on the initial investment of 500.

8.1.8   A coupon bond has a spot price of $860. The bond will pay coupons of $40 in 6 months and in one year. The risk free rates are 8% (per year continuously compounded) for 6 month maturity and 10% for one year maturity. Find the delivery price for a one year forward contract on the bond, with delivery immediately after the coupon payment.

8.1.9   The term structure is currently flat, with zero-coupon bonds having nominal annual yield rates of 10% compounded semi-annually for all maturities. A long term bond has an 8% coupon rate (payable semi-annually) with next coupon six months from now. The price of the bond today is 76.00 (per 100 face amount).

   (a) Find the no-arbitrage delivery price (per 100 face amount) for a forward contract on the bond with delivery to take place one year from today.

(b) An individual takes a long position in a forward contract on the bond today, with delivery to take place in one year, based on the delivery price in (a). Six months from the time the forward contract in (a) was made, the term structure is still flat with zero-coupon bonds having nominal annual yield rates of 10% compounded semi-annually for all maturities, and (after the first coupon has been paid) the bond price is 76.50. Find the value of the long position on the forward contract six months after the contract was made.

8.1.10 The spot price of gold today is S_0 per ounce and the risk free rate of interest for a two year maturity is r compounded continuously. Smith takes a long position in a 2-year forward contract to purchase gold. At the end of one year the spot price of gold is G and the risk free rate of interest for a one year maturity is δ compounded continuously. Assume that all delivery prices are determined assuming no arbitrage opportunities are available.

Find the value of Smith's contract at the end of one year.

8.1.11 The risk free rate of interest is 8% with continuous compounding and the dividend yield on a stock index is 3% per year compounded continuously. The current value of the index is 1000. Find the 3-month futures price of the stock index.

8.1.12 At the close of trading today, the nominal annual rate of interest on a 6-month (assume ½-year) banker's acceptance is 6%, and the nominal annual rate of interest on a 3-month (assume ¼-year) banker's acceptance is 5.7%. Find the implied quoted price at the close of trading today (under the no arbitrage assumption) for a futures contract expiring in 3 months on a 3-month banker's acceptance.

8.1.13 The price today of a futures contract expiring in one year on a 10-year Government of Canada bond with 6% coupons payable semi-annually is 92.00. The price today of an 11-year Government of Canada bond with 6% coupons payable semiannually is P, and the risk-free rate of interest for 6-month and 1 year maturities is r compounded continuously. Which of the following combinations of P and r result in an arbitrage opportunity?

(i) $P = 93.00, r = .06$ (ii) $P = 92.38, r = .06$

8.1.14   The continuously compounded risk free rate of interest for the coming year is 10%. An ounce of gold can be purchased today for 300 per ounce. A one-year forward contract in gold entered into today has a delivery price of 350 per ounce. Construct a strategy consisting of buying or selling gold in combination with going long or short on the one year forward contract, for which the strategy requires a net investment of 0 right now, but which will result in a risk free profit one year from now. Find the amount of the risk free profit that results from the strategy.

8.1.15   Just at the close of trading on November 16, 2005 a farmer takes a short position on a May 2006 futures contract in cotton. The contract size is 50,000 pounds. The futures price at the time the contract is opened is 0.55 per pound. The contract requires maintaining a margin account with a minimum balance of 5% of the futures price. Suppose that on Nov. 17, 2005, the closing price of May 2006 futures in cotton rises to 0.56 per pound. Find the effect on the margin account of the change in the futures price, and whether and how much the farmer must add to the account to maintain the 5% margin.

SECTION 8.2

8.2.1   Stock of the XYZ Corporation is expected to pay annual dividends in the years to come. The next dividend will be of amount 1.00 and is due one year from now. Dividends are expected to grow at the rate of 5% per year. A prospective purchaser plans to hold the stock for 10 years. The purchaser uses an effective annual interest rate of 15% for valuation purposes.

   (a) If the purchaser anticipates a stock price of 50.00 (excluding dividend) when he sells 10 years from now, what value will he put on the stock now?

   (b) Suppose the purchaser is willing to pay 20.00 now for the stock. What stock price is implied 10 years from now?

8.2.2   The stock of XYZ Corporation is currently valued at 25 per share. An annual dividend has just been paid and the next dividend is expected to be 2 with each subsequent dividend $1+r$ times the previous one. The valuation is based on an annual interest rate of 12%. What value of r is implied? Suppose the dividends are payable quarterly with the next one due in exactly one quarter. For the next four quarters the dividend will be .50 each quarter. Every year (after every 4 quarters) the dividend is increased by a factor of $1+s$. If the stock is now valued at 25 based on a nominal annual interest rate of $i^{(4)} = .12$, what value of s is implied?

Short Sales

8.2.3   An investor sells short 500 shares of ABC Corporation on June 1, at a time when the price per share is $120. The position is closed out 3 months later, August 31, when the price per share is $100. A dividend of $4 per share was paid July 31, one month before the short position is closed out.

(a) Find the net gain on the transaction, ignoring any effect of interest over the 3 months.

(b) Suppose that the investor must open a margin account at the time the short position is taken. The margin required is 50% of the value of the stock sold short. The investor also earns 1% per month, compounded monthly, on the margin account. Find the investor's 3-month rate of return on the investment.

8.2.4   Today Smith sells short 1000 shares of stock in ABC Corp. Today's price per share of ABC Corp stock is 10. Smith is required to open a margin account with the investment dealer and deposit 50% of the value of the stock sold short. Smith must also pay a commission to the investment dealer, the commission being 1% of the value of the stock sold short. The margin account pays interest at effective annual rate 5%. One year after the initial short sale, Smith covers the short sale by buying 1000 shares of the stock. The stock price at the end of the year is X. Smith again must pay commission of 1% of the value of the stock purchased. After all transactions are complete, Smith's net gain for the year is 100. Find X.

8.2.5   Bill and Jane each sell a different stock short for a price of 1000. For both investors, the margin requirement is 50%, and interest on the margin is credited at an effective annual rate of 6%. Bill buys back his stock one year later at a price of P. At the end of the year, the stock paid a dividend of X. Jane also buys back her stock after one year, at a price of $(P-25)$. At the end of the year, her stock paid a dividend of $2X$. Both investors earned an effective annual yield of 21% on their short sales. Calculate P.

8.2.6   Jose and Chris each sell a different stock short for the same price. For each investor, the margin requirement is 50% and interest on the margin debt is paid at an effective annual rate of 6%. Each investor buys back his stock one year later at a price of 760. Jose's stock paid a dividend of 32 at the end of the year while Chris's stock paid no dividends. During the 1-year period, Chris's return on the short sale is i, which is twice the return earned by Jose. Calculate i.

Options

8.2.7   On January 15 the share price of XYZ Corporation stock is 100, the value of a July 20 call at 110 is 1, the value of a July 20 call at 90 is 15, the value of a July 20 put at 110 is 14, and the value of a July 20 put at 90 is 1.50. For each of the following strategies, determine the profit on the transaction, after exercising the option or letting it expire on July 20, whichever is more profitable, as a function of the share price (excluding commissions and interest).

(a) On January 15 buy a call at 110 and sell the stock after exercising the option.

(b) On January 15 buy the stock and sell a call at 110.

(c) On January 15 buy a call at 110 and sell a call at 90.

(d) On January 15 buy a call at 90 and sell a call at 110.

(e) On January 15 buy a put at 90 and buy a call at 110.

(f) On January 15 buy a put at 110 and buy a call at 90.

(g) On January 15 sell a put at 90 and sell a call at 90.

8.2.8   Repeat Example 8.6:

(a) if the stock price on January 15 is 45, and

(b) if the stock price on January 15 is 55.

8.2.9   Smith enters into a 1 year forward contract to sell an ounce of platinum one year from now. Today's price of platinum is 400 per ounce and the delivery price is 415.

(a) Find the continuously compounded annual risk free rate of interest for a one year maturity, assuming the contract is set up with no arbitrage opportunities.

(b) Suppose that Smith does not own an ounce of platinum right now, but plans to purchase it in one year, and then in order to complete the forward contract, Smith will immediately sell it at that time for 415. Smith decides to buy a call option today with an expiry date of 1 year and a strike price of 410. The price of the call option today is 10. Smith borrows 10 at the risk free rate (found in part (a)) to buy the option. Suppose that the price of platinum at the end of the year is P. At the end of the year, after the forward contract and options contract expire, find Smith's gain for the year as a function of P.

8.2.10 A stock currently sells for X per share. You buy one share of stock, and you *sell* a one-year European call option with strike price X; the call option price is $C > 0$. If the call option is not exercised at the end of the year then you will sell the stock at the end of the year. Under what circumstances will you realize a positive gain at the end of the year (S_1 denotes the stock price at the end of one year)? (Assume that no margin is necessary on the original short sale of stock, and no interest is earned on the proceeds of the sale of the call option).

8.2.11 The stock price at time 0 is 120. At time 1, the stock price will be either 144 or 100. The risk free effective annual rate of interest from time 0 to time 1 is $r = .10$.

(i) A put option on the stock with exercise price 110 expires at time 1. Find the number of units of risk-free bond in the replicating portfolio at time 0.

(ii) Someone is willing to sell you a call option with expiry at time 1, strike price 120. The price they will sell for is 15. Which of the following strategies at time 0 will result in risk-free arbitrage gain at time 1?

(a) Borrow 15 at the risk free rate and buy the call option.

(b) Sell short .5455 shares of stock, and invest the amount at the risk free rate.

(c) Sell short .5455 shares of stock, buy the call for 15 and invest the remaining amount at the risk free rate.

(d) Borrow 80.46, buy the call and buy .5455 shares of stock.

(e) Borrow 65.46 and buy .5455 shares of stock.

8.2.12 A long position is taken at time 0 in a forward contract for delivery of a stock at time T with delivery price X (delivery price is based on the assumption of no arbitrage). Which of the following combinations of European options expiring at time T has the same value as the forward contract at time T?

(a) Sell a put option with strike price X, buy a call option with strike price X.

(b) buy a put option with strike price X, sell a call option with strike price X.

(c) sell a put option with strike price X, sell a call option with strike price X.

(d) buy a put option with strike price X, buy a call option with strike price X.

(e) None of (a), (b), (c) or (d) has the same value at time T as the forward contract.

*8.2.13 Use Equation (8.5) to show that under the assumption that R_m and e_s are independent, the covariance between R_s and R_m is $\beta_s \cdot Var(R_m)$.

*8.2.14 Keeping all other parameters fixed, sketch the graph of the call option price according to the Black-Scholes formula as a function of

(a) S_0,   (b) K,   (c) n,   (d) δ, and   (e) σ.

SECTION 8.3

8.3.1   A government is issuing a 5-year 15% bond with face amount 1,000,000,000. The perception in the investment community is that the government is somewhat unstable, and it is forecast that there is a 10% chance that the government will default on interest payments by the first or second years, a 20% chance of default by the third or fourth years, and a 25% chance of default (on interest and principal) by the fifth year. All probabilities are *unconditional* (measured from time 0, so that, for instance, the probability that the 7th coupon will be paid is .8).

(a) Find the price to be paid for this issue for an investor to earn yield $i^{(2)} = .18$ on the expected payments.

(b) Based on the price found in part (a), find the yield to maturity if all payments are actually made.

(c) Suppose that the risk of default on the redemption amount is only 10%, but the other default risks are as stated. Repeat parts (a) and (b).

SECTION 8.4

8.4.1 (a) Smith has 10,000 U.S. dollars. He can buy Canadian dollars today at the exchange rate of 1 US = 1.38 CDN., or he can sign a forward contract guaranteeing him an exchange rate of 1 US = 1.42 CDN one year from now. If he exchanges his U.S. dollars for Canadian dollars today, he can earn interest at effective annual rate 9% on his Canadian dollars. Alternatively, he can sign the forward exchange rate contract and invest his 10,000 US at effective annual rate i, exchanging his US dollars for Canadian dollars next year. If he ends up with the same amount of Canadian funds in one year either way, what is i?

(b) Suppose Smith has just signed the forward contract. Later in the day the Canadian interest rate increases from 9% to 10%, but the US interest rate remains at i. What spot rate of exchange would Smith now regard as fair, assuming again that he would end up in one year with same amount of Canadian funds?

8.4.2 The Canadian dollar today is worth $.625 US. For one-year maturity, the continuously compounded risk-free rate of return in Canada is .03 and in the US it is .02. A currency speculator believes that the Canadian dollar will increase in value to $.65 US one year from now. Formulate a strategy in which the speculator can receive a gain for a net investment of 0 if the speculator's belief turns out to be correct.

8.4.3 A recent quotation of spot and forward currency rates listed the following rates of Canadian (CDN $), United States (US $) and British (UK £) currencies.

Spot rate of exchange:
   US $1 = CDN $1.5997,   US $1 = UK £0.7090

1 year forward rate of exchange:
   US $1 = CDN $1.6100,   US $1 = UK £0.7200

The effective annual risk-free rate of interest in Canada at the time of these quotations was 2.00%. According to the no-arbitrage assumption, find the corresponding effective annual risk-free interest rate in Britain.

8.4.4 The exchange rate between the Canadian and US dollar today is US $1 = CDN $1.545. Canadian continuously compounded risk free interest rate is .0600, 1 year maturity. As of today, the no-arbitrage one year forward contract on US dollars has a delivery price of CDN $1.540.

(a) Show that the implied continuously compounded one-year risk free rate in the US is .0632.

(b) Suppose that a foreign currency dealer offers to buy or sell (long or short) a one year forward contract on US dollars with a delivery price of CDN $1.55. Construct a transaction that results in a riskless profit; you may buy or sell the forward contract, and you may borrow or invest at the risk free rates in Canadian (.0600 continuously compounded) and US (.0632 continuously compounded) dollars.

8.4.5 A recent quotation of spot and forward currency rates listed the following rates of Canadian (CDN), United States (US) and Japanese (JP) currencies.

Spot rate of exchange:
   US $1 = CDN $1.5589,   JP ¥1 = CDN $0.014200

1 year forward rate of exchange:
   US $1 = CDN $1.5495,   JP ¥1 = CDN $0.014997

The effective annual risk-free rate of interest in the US at the time of these quotations was 6.13%. According to the no-arbitrage assumption, find the corresponding effective annual risk-free interest rate in Japan.

APPENDIX

CALCULATOR NOTES

This Appendix presents a review of calculator financial functions related to the topics covered in this book for some of the financial calculators allowed on the examinations of the Society of Actuaries, Casualty Actuarial Society, and the Joint Board for the Enrollment of Actuaries. The calculator functions are reviewed with the objective of indicating efficient ways in which these functions can be implemented. Also, for the Texas Instruments BA II PLUS$^{©}$, several examples from Society of Actuaries exams will be presented illustrating the use of the calculator.

The SOA and CAS allow the use of the Texas Instruments BA II PLUS calculator and the Texas Instruments BA-35 Solar calculator. The Joint Board allows those calculators as well as a number of other calculators, including the Hewlett-Packard HP-12C calculator. Detailed guidebooks for the operation of and functions available on the Texas Instruments calculators can be found at the following internet site:

http://education.ti.com/us/global/guides.html#finance.

Guidebooks for the Hewlett-Packard calculator can be found at

http://www.hp.com/calculators/.

It is my opinion the BA II PLUS has more advanced functions as compared with the BA-35 calculator, and for the professional exam involving mathematics of finance and compound interest, the BA II PLUS is the recommended calculator.

For each of the BA II PLUS and the HP-12C calculators listed above, financial functions will be reviewed in the order that the related concepts are covered in Chapters 1 to 8 of this book. It will be assumed that you have available and have reviewed the appropriate guide book for the calculator that you are using.

The BA II PLUS will be reviewed first and the HP-12C second.

Some of the numerical values in this appendix will be rounded off to fewer decimals than are actually displayed in the calculator display. It will be assumed, however, unless otherwise indicated, that individual calculations will not be rounded before they are used in subsequent calculations.

TEXAS INSTRUMENTS BA II PLUS

It will be assumed that unless indicated otherwise, each new keystroke sequence starts with clear registers. Calculator registers are cleared with the keystroke sequences

$\boxed{\text{2nd}}$ $\boxed{\text{CLR WORK}}$ $\boxed{\text{CE/C}}$ and

$\boxed{\text{2nd}}$ $\boxed{\text{CLR TVM}}$ $\boxed{\text{CE/C}}$.

It will also be assumed that the calculator is operating in US date format and US commas and decimals format, with the display showing 9 decimals. These are the default settings for the calculator, but they can be changed in the "FORMAT" work sheet, which is accessed with the keystroke sequence $\boxed{\text{2nd}}$ $\boxed{\text{FORMAT}}$. Although the number of decimals to display is set to 9, in the examples below it will often be the case that dollar amounts are written as rounded to the nearest .01.

CHAIN (CHN) AND ALGEBRAIC OPERATING (AOS) SYSTEM MODES

When the calculator is operating in chain calculation mode, the usual algebraic order of operations is not respected. For instance, the keystroke sequence $1 + 2 \times 3$ $\boxed{=}$ results in an answer of 9. This is true because the calculation of $1 + 2$ is performed first, resulting in 3, which is then multiplied by 3, resulting in 9. When the calculator is in AOS mode, the result of the keystroke sequence above will be 7. This is true because in the hierarchy of algebraic operations, multiplication is done before addition, so 2×3 is calculated first, resulting in 6, and then the addition operation is applied resulting in $1 + 6$, which is 7. The order of operations mode can be selected in the "FORMAT" worksheet.

ACCUMULATED AND PRESENT VALUES OF A SINGLE PAYMENT USING A COMPOUND INTEREST RATE

Accumulated values and present values of single payments using annual (or more general periodic) effective interest rates can be determined using the calculator functions as described below.

ACCUMULATED VALUE:

We use Example 1.1 to illustrate this function.
A deposit of 1000 made at time 0 grows at effective annual interest rate 9%.
The accumulated value at the end of 3 years is $1000(1.09)^3 = 1,295.03$.
This can be found using the calculator in two ways.

1. We use standard arithmetic operators in standard calculator mode
    with the following keystrokes.

    1.09 $\boxed{y^x}$ 3 $\boxed{=}$ $\boxed{\times}$ 1000 $\boxed{=}$

    The screen should display 1,295.029. In this function, $y=1.09$ and $x=3$.

2. We use time value of money functions (TVM).

    $\boxed{2nd}$ $\boxed{P/Y}$ $\boxed{\downarrow}$ 1 then enter (this sets 1 compounding period per year).

    $\boxed{2nd}$ $\boxed{QUIT}$ (this returns calculator to standard-calculator mode)

    1000 $\boxed{PV}$ (this sets PV to 1000),

    9 $\boxed{I/Y}$ (this sets the annual interest rate at 9%)

    3 $\boxed{N}$ (this sets the number of years to 3),

    $\boxed{CPT}$ $\boxed{FV}$ (this computes the accumulated value, also called future
    value).
The screen should display $-1,295.029$.

The calculator interprets the PV of 1000 as an amount received (a cash inflow) and the FV as the amount that must be paid back (a cash outflow), so the FV is a "negative" cashflow. If the PV had been entered as -1000, then FV would have been positive. This is part of the "sign convention" used by the BA II PLUS.

PRESENT VALUE:

We use Example 1.5(a) to illustrate this function.
The present value of 1,000,000 due in 25 years at effective annual rate .195 is $1,000,000v^{25} = 1,000,000(1.195)^{-25} = 11,635.96$.
This can be found using the calculator in two ways:

1. 1.195 $\boxed{y^x}$ 25 $\boxed{+/-}$ $\boxed{=}$ $\boxed{\times}$ 1000000 $\boxed{=}$

The screen should display 11,635.96. This keystroke sequence can be replaced by:

1.195 $\boxed{1/x}$ $\boxed{y^x}$ .25 $\boxed{=}$ $\boxed{\times}$ 1000000 $\boxed{=}$

2. Using time value of money functions, we have

$\boxed{\text{2nd}}$ $\boxed{\text{P/Y}}$ $\boxed{\downarrow}$ 1 $\boxed{\text{ENTER}}$ $\boxed{\text{2nd}}$ $\boxed{\text{QUIT}}$

1000000 $\boxed{\text{FV}}$ 19.5 $\boxed{\text{I/Y}}$

25 $\boxed{\text{N}}$ $\boxed{\text{CPT}}$ $\boxed{\text{PV}}$.

The screen should display $-11,635.96$. (the earlier comment about the negative value applies here).

As a more general procedure, in the equation $(PV)(1+i)^N = FV$, if any 3 of the 4 variables PV, i, N, FV are entered, then the 4th can be found using the $\boxed{\text{CPT}}$ function.

UNKNOWN INTEREST RATE:

As an example of solving for the interest rate, we consider Example 1.5(c).

An initial investment of 25,000 at effective annual rate of interest i grows to 1,000,000 in 25 years. Then $25,000(1+i)^{25} = 1,000,000,$ from which we get $i = (40)^{1/25} - 1 = .1590$ (15.90%). This can be found using the calculator power function with the following keystrokes:

40 $\boxed{y^x}$ .04 $\boxed{=}$ $\boxed{-}$ 1 $\boxed{=}$, the screen should display 0.158997234.

Using financial functions, the keystroke sequence solving for i is

$\boxed{\text{2nd}}$ $\boxed{\text{P/Y}}$ $\boxed{\downarrow}$ 1 $\boxed{\text{2nd}}$ $\boxed{\text{QUIT}}$

25000 $\boxed{\text{PV}}$ 1000000 $\boxed{+/-}$ $\boxed{\text{FV}}$

25 $\boxed{\text{N}}$ $\boxed{\text{CPT}}$ $\boxed{\text{I/Y}}$

The screen should display 15.89972344 (this is the % measure).

UNKNOWN TIME PERIOD:

As an example of solving for an unknown time period, suppose that an initial investment of 100 at monthly compound rate of interest i grows to 300 in n months at monthly interest rate $i=.75\%$. Then $100(1.0075)^n = 300$, from which we get $n = \frac{\ln 3}{\ln 1.0075} - = 147.03$ months. This can be found using the calculator $\boxed{\text{LN}}$ function.

Using financial functions, the keystroke sequence solving for n is

$\boxed{\text{2nd}}$ $\boxed{\text{P/Y}}$ $\boxed{\downarrow}$ 1 $\boxed{\text{2nd}}$ $\boxed{\text{QUIT}}$
100 $\boxed{\text{PV}}$ 300 $\boxed{+/-}$ $\boxed{\text{FV}}$
.75 $\boxed{\text{I/Y}}$ $\boxed{\text{CPT}}$ $\boxed{\text{N}}$.

The screen should display 147.03026. Slightly more than 147 months of compounding will be required. The calculator returns a value of n based on compounding including fractional periods, so that the value of 147.03026 means that $100(1.0075)^{147.03026} = 300$.

ACCUMULATED AND PRESENT VALUES OF A SINGLE PAYMENT USING A COMPOUND DISCOUNT RATE

Present and accumulated values of single payments using an effective rate of discount can be made in the following way. Clear calculator registers before starting the keystroke sequence.

Present Value Using a Compound Discount Rate:

The present value of 500 due in 8 years at effective annual rate of discount 8% is $500(1-.08)^8 = 500(.92)^8 = 256.61$.
This can be found using the calculator in a few ways:

1. We use standard arithmetic operators in standard calculator mode with the following keystrokes.

    .92 $\boxed{y^x}$ 8 $\boxed{=}$ $\boxed{\times}$ 500 $\boxed{=}$

    The screen should display 256.61.

2. 500 $\boxed{\text{FV}}$ 8 $\boxed{+/-}$ $\boxed{\text{I/Y}}$

    8 $\boxed{+/-}$ $\boxed{\text{N}}$ $\boxed{\text{ENTER}}$ $\boxed{\text{CPT}}$ $\boxed{\text{PV}}$

The screen should display −256.61. The calculator has calculated

$$PV = -FV(1+I)^{-N} = -500(1-.08)^{-(-8)} = -500(.92)^8 = -256.61.$$

(Remember the sign convention for payments in and payments out.)

The following keystroke sequence could also be used.

3. 500 $\boxed{\text{PV}}$ 8 $\boxed{+/-}$ $\boxed{\text{I/Y}}$

    8 $\boxed{\text{N}}$ $\boxed{\text{CPT}}$ $\boxed{\text{FV}}$

We have calculated $-500(1-.08)^8 = -256.61$.

Accumulated Value Using a Compound Discount Rate:

A deposit of 25 made at time 0 grows at effective annual discount rate 6%. The accumulated value at the end of 5 years is

$$25(1-.06)^{-5} = 25(.94)^{-5} = 34.06 \text{ (nearest .01)}.$$

This can be found using the calculator in two ways.

1. We use standard arithmetic operators in standard calculator mode with the following keystrokes.

    .94 $\boxed{y^x}$ 5 $\boxed{+/-}$ $\boxed{=}$ $\boxed{\times}$ 25 $\boxed{=}$

    The screen should display 34.06 (rounded to nearest .01).

2. 25 $\boxed{\text{PV}}$ 6 $\boxed{+/-}$ $\boxed{\text{I/Y}}$

    5 $\boxed{+/-}$ $\boxed{\text{N}}$ $\boxed{\text{CPT}}$ $\boxed{\text{FV}}$

The screen should display −34.06 (negative sign indicating outflow). As a third approach, we could also find the effective annual interest rate and accumulate.

CONVERSION BETWEEN EFFECTIVE ANNUAL AND NOMINAL RATES

The nominal annual interest rate compounded m times per year can be found from the effective annual rate of interest and vice-versa using calculator functions as illustrated below.

Nominal Interest Rates

A nominal annual interest rate of .24 (24%) compounded monthly is equivalent to an effective annual rate of interest of $i = .2682$ (26.82%).

The relationship $i = \left(1 + \frac{i^{(12)}}{12}\right)^{12} - 1$ can be used, or the equivalent rates can be found in the following way using the $\boxed{\text{ICONV}}$ function.

Conversion from nominal annual to effective annual interest rate:

We apply the following sequence of keystrokes.

$\boxed{\text{2nd}}$ $\boxed{\text{ICONV}}$ (NOM= appears),

24 $\boxed{\text{ENTER}}$ (the nominal rate) $\boxed{\downarrow}$ $\boxed{\downarrow}$ (C/Y= appears)

12 $\boxed{\text{ENTER}}$ (number of compounding periods),

$\boxed{\downarrow}$ $\boxed{\downarrow}$ (EFF= appears) $\boxed{\text{CPT}}$.

The screen should display 26.82. We have converted the nominal annual interest rate of 24% (keyed in as 24) compounded monthly (keyed in as 12) to the equivalent effective annual interest rate of 26.82%.

Conversion from effective annual to nominal annual interest rate:

$\boxed{\text{2nd}}$ $\boxed{\text{ICONV}}$ $\boxed{\downarrow}$ (EFF= appears)

26.82 $\boxed{\text{ENTER}}$ $\boxed{\downarrow}$ (C/Y= appears)

12 $\boxed{\text{ENTER}}$ $\boxed{\downarrow}$ (NOM= appears)

$\boxed{\text{CPT}}$

The screen should display 23.9966 (round to 24). We have converted the effective annual interest rate of 26.82% (key in 26.82) to the equivalent nominal annual interest rate compounded monthly (key in 12) of 24%.

Nominal Discount Rates

The nominal annual discount rate compounded m times per year can be found from the effective annual rate of interest and vice-versa using calculator functions as illustrated below.

A nominal annual discount rate of .09 (9%) compounded quarterly is equivalent to an effective annual rate of interest of $i = .0953\,(9.53\%)$. The relationship $i = \left(1 - \frac{d^{(4)}}{4}\right)^{-4} - 1$ can be used, or the equivalent rate can be found in the following ways.

Use the keystroke sequence $\boxed{\text{2nd}}$ $\boxed{\text{P/Y}}$ 4 $\boxed{\text{ENTER}}$ $\boxed{\text{2nd}}$ $\boxed{\text{QUIT}}$. This sets the number of compounding periods per year to 4 and returns to standard calculation functions. It is important to do this step first, entering the number of compounding periods in the year.

1. We first find the equivalent effective annual rate of interest from the given nominal annual rate of discount.

    4 $\boxed{+/-}$ $\boxed{\text{N}}$ 9 $\boxed{+/-}$ $\boxed{\text{I/Y}}$ 1 $\boxed{\text{PV}}$ $\boxed{\text{CPT}}$ $\boxed{\text{FV}}$

The display should read -1.0953; we interpret this as indicating that the effective annual rate of interest is 9.53%. We have calculated

$$\left(1 + \frac{I}{-N}\right)^{P} = \left(1 + \frac{-.09}{4}\right)^{-4} = FV = -1.0953,$$

where $P = 4$ was entered with the P/Y function, $N = -4$ was entered with 4 $\boxed{+/-}$ $\boxed{\text{N}}$, and $I = -.09$ (or $d = 9\%$) was entered with 9 $\boxed{+/-}$ $\boxed{\text{I/Y}}$.

2. We now find the equivalent nominal annual rate of discount from the given effective annual rate of interest.

    4 $\boxed{+/-}$ $\boxed{\text{N}}$, Key in 1.09531 $\boxed{+/-}$ $\boxed{\text{FV}}$,
    Key in 1 $\boxed{\text{PV}}$, Key in $\boxed{\text{CPT}}$ $\boxed{\text{I/Y}}$.

The display should read -9.00; this is the negative of the equivalent nominal annual rate of discount compounded 4 times per year.

Note that when we enter FV, we enter $-(1+\text{EFF})$.

LEVEL PAYMENT ANNUITY VALUATION

The accumulated value and present value of a level payment annuity-immediate can be found using calculator functions. Clear calculator registers before starting the keystroke sequence. The calculator should be in standard calculator mode.

Accumulated Value of Annuity-Immediate:

A deposit of 1000 is made at the end of each year for 20 years. The deposits earn interest at an effective annual rate of interest of 4%. The accumulated value of the deposits at the time of (and including) the 20th deposit is $1000s_{\overline{20}|.04} = 1000\left[\frac{(1.04)^{20}-1}{.04}\right] = 29,778$. This can be found using the calculator.

Use the keystroke sequence $\boxed{\text{2nd}}$ $\boxed{\text{P/Y}}$ 1 $\boxed{\text{ENTER}}$ $\boxed{\text{2nd}}$ $\boxed{\text{QUIT}}$ (this sets the number of compounding periods per year to 1 and returns to standard calculation functions). It is important to do this step first, so that the compounding period corresponds to the payment period.

20 $\boxed{\text{N}}$ 4 $\boxed{\text{I/Y}}$ 0 $\boxed{\text{PV}}$ 1000 $\boxed{\text{PMT}}$ $\boxed{\text{CPT}}$ $\boxed{\text{FV}}$

The display should read $-29,778.08$, the negative of the accumulated annuity value.

Present Value of Annuity-Immediate:

Payments of 50 will be made at the end of each month for 10 years. The monthly compound interest rate is ¾ %. The present value of the annuity one month before the first payment is made is

$$50a_{\overline{120}|.0075} = 50\left[\frac{1-v_{.0075}^{120}}{.0075}\right] = 3,947.08$$

(10 years, 12 months per year).

The calculator should still have $\boxed{\text{2nd}}$ $\boxed{\text{P/Y}}$ set to 1 (if not, use the keystroke sequence outlined above to set P/Y to 1). This means that the rate entered as I/Y will be a rate per period. In this example the period is one month. We use the following sequence of keystrokes.

120 $\boxed{\text{N}}$ .75 $\boxed{\text{I/Y}}$ $\boxed{\text{ENTER}}$ 50 $\boxed{\text{PMT}}$ $\boxed{\text{ENTER}}$
0 $\boxed{\text{FV}}$ $\boxed{\text{CPT}}$ $\boxed{\text{PV}}$

The display should read $-3,947.08$, the negative of the present value of the annuity.

In the general equation for an annuity-immediate $PV = PMT \cdot a_{\overline{N}|i}$ if any 3 of the 4 variables PV, PMT, N, i (in %) are given, then the calculator functions can be used to solve for the 4th variable. The same is true for the equation $PMT \cdot s_{\overline{N}|i} = FV$ (keep in mind that when PMT is entered as positive, FV or PV are returned as negative, and vice-versa).

Finding the Payment Amount:

A loan of 1000 is to be repaid with monthly payments for 3 years at a compound monthly interest rate of .5%. The monthly payment is K where $1000 = Ka_{\overline{36}|.005}$, so that $K = \dfrac{1000}{a_{\overline{36}|.005}} = 30.42$.

This can be found using the following sequence of keystrokes:

36 $\boxed{\text{N}}$ .5 $\boxed{\text{I/Y}}$ $\boxed{\text{ENTER}}$ 1000 $\boxed{\text{PV}}$ 0 $\boxed{\text{FV}}$ $\boxed{\text{CPT}}$ $\boxed{\text{PMT}}$

The display should read -30.42.

Finding the Interest Rate:

Suppose that the loan payment is 35 for a 36 payment loan of amount 1000 and the interest rate is to be found. Then $1000 = 35a_{\overline{36}|i}$. There is no algebraic solution for i. The following keystrokes give us i.

36 $\boxed{\text{N}}$ 1000 $\boxed{\text{+/-}}$ $\boxed{\text{PV}}$ 35 $\boxed{\text{PMT}}$ 0 $\boxed{\text{FV}}$ $\boxed{\text{CPT}}$ $\boxed{\text{I/Y}}$

The display should read 1.31(%). That is the effective rate of interest per month.

Finding the Number of Payments:

We will use Example 2.13 to illustrate the calculator function for finding the unknown number of payments. In Example 2.13, Smith wishes to accumulate 1000 by means of semiannual deposits earning interest at nominal annual rate $i^{(2)} = .08$, with interest credited semiannually.

In part (a) of Example 2.13, Smith makes deposits of 50 every six months. We wish to solve for n in the equation $1000 = 50 \cdot s_{\overline{n}|.04}$.

The following keystrokes give us n.

1000 $\boxed{\text{FV}}$ 50 $\boxed{+/-}$ $\boxed{\text{PMT}}$ 4 $\boxed{\text{I/Y}}$ 0 $\boxed{\text{PV}}$ $\boxed{\text{CPT}}$ $\boxed{\text{N}}$

The display should read 14.9866. 14 deposits are not sufficient and 15 full deposits are more than sufficient. The accumulated value of the deposits just after the 14th deposit is $50 \cdot s_{\overline{14}|.04} = 914.60$, so an additional deposit of 85.40 is needed at the time of the 14th deposit to bring the total accumulated value to 1000. The accumulated value 6 months after the 14th deposit is

$$50 \cdot \ddot{s}_{\overline{14}|.04} = 50(1.04) \cdot s_{\overline{14}|.04} = 951.18 \, ,$$

so a deposit of 48.18 is needed at time 15 to bring the accumulated value to 1000.

The next functions reviewed relate to finding the value of an annuity-due.

Annuity-Due:

The accumulated value and present value of a level payment annuity-due can be found using calculator functions. The same methods apply that were used for annuities-immediate, with the additional requirement that keystrokes $\boxed{\text{2nd}}$ $\boxed{\text{BGN}}$ $\boxed{\text{2nd}}$ $\boxed{\text{SET}}$ $\boxed{\text{2nd}}$ $\boxed{\text{QUIT}}$ must be entered to make the calculator view payments as being made at the beginning of each period (there is a screen indication of the BGN mode when it is invoked; when in BGN mode, in order to return to END mode, use the keystrokes $\boxed{\text{2nd}}$ $\boxed{\text{BGN}}$ $\boxed{\text{2nd}}$ $\boxed{\text{SET}}$ $\boxed{\text{2nd}}$ $\boxed{\text{QUIT}}$, and BGN should disappear from the screen display, and the calculator is in END mode). In the equation $PV = PMT \cdot \ddot{a}_{\overline{N}|i}$, if any 3 of PV, PMT, N, i are entered, we can find the

4th. In the equation $FV = PMT \cdot \ddot{s}_{\overline{N}|i}$ any 3 of FV, PMT, N, i are entered, we can find the 4th (as before, PMT and PV or FV are opposite signs).

Finding the Time and Amount of a Balloon Payment:

We can use the calculator functions to find the balloon payment required to repay a loan which has level payments for as long as necessary with a final balloon payment. In Example 2.15(a) of Chapter 2, a loan of 5000 is being repaid by monthly payments of 100 each, starting one month after the loan is made, for as long as necessary plus an additional fractional payment at the time of the final regular payment. At interest rate $i^{(12)} = .09$, we are to find the number of full payments that are required to repay the loan, and the amount of the additional fractional payment required if the additional fractional payment is made at the time of the final regular payment. We find the number of payments needed with the following keystrokes (the calculator should be in END mode).

5000 $\boxed{\text{PV}}$ 100 $\boxed{+/-}$ $\boxed{\text{PMT}}$ .75 $\boxed{\text{I/Y}}$ $\boxed{\text{CPT}}$ $\boxed{\text{N}}$

The display should read 62.9. This indicates that the 62nd payment is not quite enough to repay the loan. The additional payment needed, say X, at the time of the 62nd regular payment of 100 is found from the relationship $X = 5000(1.0075)^{62} - 100 \cdot s_{\overline{62}|.0075} = 89.55$. The keystrokes that will produce the value of X are

5000 $\boxed{\text{PV}}$ 100 $\boxed{+/-}$ $\boxed{\text{PMT}}$ .75 $\boxed{\text{I/Y}}$ 62 $\boxed{\text{N}}$ $\boxed{\text{CPT}}$ $\boxed{\text{FV}}$

The display should read −89.55.

ANNUITIES WHOSE INTEREST AND PAYMENT PERIODS DIFFER

A function is available to calculate annuity values when the interest period and payment period do not coincide. The following examples illustrate the use of this calculator function.

1. Annuity-immediate of 10 annual payments of 1 each, with interest at a nominal annual rate of 8% compounded quarterly. The present value one year before the first payment is $a_{\overline{10}|j}$, where

$$j = (1.02)^4 - 1 = .082432$$

is the effective annual rate of interest that is equivalent to the nominal annual. The present value will be $a_{\overline{10}|.082432} = 6.6367$. The annuity value can be found using financial functions with the following sequence of keystrokes:

$\boxed{\text{2nd}}$ $\boxed{\text{P/Y}}$ 1 $\boxed{\text{ENTER}}$ (this sets 1 payment per year),

$\boxed{\downarrow}$ 4 $\boxed{\text{ENTER}}$ (this sets C/Y=4 interest conversion periods per year), $\boxed{\text{2nd}}$ $\boxed{\text{QUIT}}$.

10 $\boxed{\text{N}}$ (10 annual payments),

8 $\boxed{\text{I/Y}}$ (nominal annual interest rate of 8%),

1 $\boxed{+/-}$ $\boxed{\text{PMT}}$ $\boxed{\text{CPT}}$ $\boxed{\text{PV}}$.

The display should read 6.637, the present value of the annuity. To find the accumulated value of the annuity, we continue with the following keystrokes.

0 $\boxed{\text{PV}}$ $\boxed{\text{CPT}}$ $\boxed{\text{FV}}$

The display should read 14.655, the accumulated value of the annuity.

Note that if we find the equivalent effective annual rate of interest first, $i = .082432$, we could have found the annuity value as follows without setting C/Y to 4. This is done in the following way (C/Y and P/Y are both set to 1).

10 $\boxed{\text{N}}$ (10 annual payments),

8.2432 $\boxed{\text{I/Y}}$ (effective annual interest rate),

1 $\boxed{+/-}$ $\boxed{\text{PMT}}$ $\boxed{\text{CPT}}$ $\boxed{\text{PV}}$

The display should read 6.637, the present value of the annuity.

2. Annuity-immediate of 1 per month for 5 years at effective annual rate of interest 6%. The equivalent one-month interest rate is $j = (1.06)^{1/12} - 1 = .004868$ and the present value of the annuity one month before the first payment is $a_{\overline{60}|j} = 51.924$. The annuity value can be found using financial functions with the following sequence of keystrokes.

2nd P/Y 12 ENTER (this sets 12 payments per year),

↓ 1 ENTER (this sets C/Y=1 interest conversion period per year),

then 2nd QUIT .

5 2nd xP/Y N (5 × 12 = 60 monthly payments),

6 I/Y (effective annual interest rate),

1 +/− PMT CPT PV

The display should read 51.924, the present value of the annuity.

As with Case 1 above, we could have used an alternative approach based on the one-month effective interest rate of .004868. P/Y and C/Y should be set to 1 before the following keystrokes.

60 N .4868 I/Y (monthly effective interest rate),

1 +/− PMT CPT PV

The display should read 51.923, the present value of the annuity.

VALUATION OF INCREASING AND DECREASING ANNUITIES

The values of $(Ia)_{\overline{n}|i}$ (present value) and $(Ds)_{\overline{n}|i}$ (accumulated value) can be found using calculator financial functions. From those values we can then find $(Is)_{\overline{n}|i} = (Ia)_{\overline{n}|i} \cdot (1+i)^n$, and $(Da)_{\overline{n}|i} = (Ds)_{\overline{n}|i} \cdot v^n$.

The following two examples illustrate the method.

Finding $(Ia)_{\overline{n}|i}$:

Suppose that we wish to find $(Ia)_{\overline{20}|.08} = \dfrac{\ddot{a}_{\overline{20}|.08} - 20v^{20}}{.08}$. We first find the numerator with the following keystrokes.

2nd BGN 2nd SET 2nd QUIT

20 N 8 I/Y 1 +/− PMT 20 FV CPT PV

The display should read 6.3126, which is $\ddot{a}_{\overline{20}|.08} - 20v^{20}$.

In this sequence of keystrokes, we have created a series of 20 payments <u>received</u> of 1 each at the start of each year ($\boxed{\text{BGN}}$), combined with a payment of 20 <u>paid out</u> at the end of 20 years ($\boxed{\text{FV}}$). The net present value is $\ddot{a}_{\overline{20}|.08} - 20v^{20} = 6.3126$. Then, $(Ia)_{\overline{20}|.08} = \dfrac{6.3126}{.08} = 78.908$.

Note that instead of entering 1 $\boxed{+/-}$ $\boxed{\text{PMT}}$ we could enter 1 $\boxed{\div}$ .08 $\boxed{=}$ $\boxed{+/-}$ $\boxed{\text{PMT}}$, and instead of entering 20 $\boxed{\text{FV}}$ we could enter 20 $\boxed{\div}$ .08 $\boxed{=}$ $\boxed{\text{FV}}$. Then $\boxed{\text{CPT}}$ $\boxed{\text{PV}}$ includes division by .08. Note that we cannot use these calculator functions to find $(Is)_{\overline{n}|i}$, but since the numerator of $(Is)_{\overline{n}|i}$ is $\ddot{s}_{\overline{n}|i} - n$, we can find $\ddot{s}_{\overline{n}|i}$ first, then subtract n , and then divide by i .

Finding $(Ds)_{\overline{n}|i}$:

Suppose that we to find $(Ds)_{\overline{35}|.04} = \dfrac{35(1.04)^{35} - s_{\overline{35}|.04}}{.04}$. We first find the numerator with the following keystrokes. The calculator payment mode should be set to END.

35 $\boxed{\text{N}}$ 4 $\boxed{\text{I/Y}}$ $\boxed{\text{ENTER}}$ 35 $\boxed{+/-}$ $\boxed{\text{PV}}$
1 $\boxed{\text{PMT}}$ $\boxed{\text{CPT}}$ $\boxed{\text{FV}}$

The display should read 64.4609, which is $35(1.04)^{35} - s_{\overline{35}|.04}$.

In this sequence of keystrokes we have created an initial payment <u>received</u> of 35 at time 0 ($\boxed{\text{PV}}$), and a series of 35 payments of 1 each <u>paid out</u> at the <u>end</u> of each year. The net accumulated value at the end of 35 years is

$$35(1.04)^{35} - s_{\overline{35}|.04} = 64.4609 \ (\boxed{\text{FV}}).$$

Then,

$$(Ds)_{\overline{35}|.04} = \frac{64.4609}{.04} = 1,611.52.$$

Note that we could have incorporated division by .04 into the keystroke sequence by keying in 35 $\boxed{\div}$ .04 $\boxed{=}$ $\boxed{+/-}$ $\boxed{PV}$ instead of 35 $\boxed{+/-}$ $\boxed{PV}$, and by keying in 1 $\boxed{\div}$ .04 $\boxed{=}$ $\boxed{PMT}$ instead of 1 $\boxed{PMT}$.

It is also possible to use the cashflow worksheet to find present and accumulated values of a series of non-level payments. There is a limitation that allows an initial payment, CF_0, and up to 24 more payment amounts.

This would be a less efficient way of finding $(Ia)_{\overline{20}|.08}$, for instance.

DEPRECIATION

An asset has a purchase price of 1200 and a salvage value of 100. According to the sum-of-years-digits method with a 10-year depreciation period, the depreciation amounts and book values will be

$$D_1 = \tfrac{10}{55} \cdot (1200 - 100) = 200,$$

$$D_2 = \tfrac{9}{55} \cdot (1200 - 100) = 180, \ldots, D_{10} = 20,$$

$$B_1 = 1000, \ B_2 = 820, \ldots, B_9 = 120, \ B_{10} = 100.$$

These values can be found using the calculator depreciation worksheet with the following sequence of keystrokes.

1 $\boxed{2nd}$ $\boxed{DEPR}$, then $\boxed{2nd}$ $\boxed{SET}$ until SYD shows in the display.

Then, $\boxed{\downarrow}$ gets us to LIF=, and we key in 10 $\boxed{ENTER}$ (depreciation over 10 years).

Then $\boxed{\downarrow}$ gets us to MOl =, which we skip, and $\boxed{\downarrow}$ again gets us to CST=, and we enter 1200 $\boxed{ENTER}$ (initial cost).

Then $\boxed{\downarrow}$ gets us to SAL=, and we enter 100 $\boxed{ENTER}$ (salvage value).

Then $\boxed{\downarrow}$ gets us to YR=, and we can enter any year, say 5 $\boxed{\text{ENTER}}$.

Then $\boxed{\downarrow}$ gets us DEP=120, which is D_5;

Then $\boxed{\downarrow}$ gets us RBV=400, which is B_5 .

We can use the same functions for declining balance (a discount rate must be entered), and straight line depreciation.

LOAN AMORTIZATION

For a loan with level payments, there are calculator functions for finding outstanding balances, interest or principal paid in a single payment, and interest or principal paid in a range of payments. Parameters are entered for P/Y, N, I/Y, PV as with the usual annuity valuation. The calculator will give us the payment using the PMT key. The following example illustrates how we get the amortization quantities.

We use Example 3.3 to illustrate these functions. A homebuyer borrows $250,000 to be repaid over a 30-year period with level monthly payments beginning one month after the loan is made. The interest rate on the loan is a nominal annual rate of 9% compounded monthly. The loan payment is $K = \dfrac{250,000}{a_{\overline{360}|.0075}} = 2,011.56$.

The outstanding balance at the end of the first year (after the 12th monthly payment) $OB_{12} = 2,011.56a_{\overline{348}|.0075} = 248,292.01$. The principal repaid in the 12th payment is $PR_{12} = Kv^{360-12+1} = 2,011.56v^{349} = 148.25$, and the interest paid in the 12th payment is $I_{12} = K(1-v^{360-12+1}) = 1,863.30$. The principal repaid in the 2nd year (the 13th through 24th payments inclusive) is

$$PR_{13} + PR_{14} + \cdots + PR_{23} + PR_{24} = K(v^{348}+v^{347}+\cdots+v^{338}+v^{337})$$
$$= 1,868.21,$$

the interest paid in the 2nd year is

$$I_{13} + I_{14} + \cdots + I_{23} + I_{24} = K(1-v^{348} + 1-v^{347} + \cdots + 1-v^{338} + 1-v^{337})$$

$$= 12K - (PR_{13}+PR_{14}+\cdots+PR_{23}+PR_{24}) = 22,270.46.$$

These calculations can be completed using calculator functions. We first clear the calculator registers.

[2nd] [P/Y] 1 [ENTER] [2nd] [QUIT] (sets payment period to 1)
360 [N] .75 [I/Y] 250000 [PV] [CPT] [PMT]

The value $-2,011.56$ is returned (we must key in [CPT] [PMT] in order to use the amortization functions).

To find OB_{12} use the following keystrokes.

[2nd] [AMORT] (this opens the amortization worksheet).
The display reads P1 =. Key in 12 [ENTER] [↓] .
The display reads P2 =. Key in 12 [ENTER] .
Then using [↓] again, the display should read BAL $= 248,292.01$.
This is OB_{12}.
Using [↓] again gives the display PRN= -148.25; this is $-PR_{12}$.
Using [↓] again gives the display INT= $-1,863.30$; this is $-I_{12}$.

To find $I_{13} + I_{14} + \cdots + I_{23} + I_{24}$ and $P_{13} + P_{14} + \cdots + P_{23} + P_{24}$ use the following keystrokes while still in the amortization worksheet (we leave a worksheet using the [2nd] [QUIT] sequence of keystrokes).

Use [↓] until Pl= appears again and enter 13 (key in 13 [ENTER]).

Then use [↓] and P2= appears and we enter 24 (key in 24 [ENTER]).

The next use of [↓] given us BAL $= 246,473.79$, the outstanding balance at the end of the period to time 24 months).

[↓] again gives us PRN $=-1,868,21$; this is $P_{13} + P_{14} + \cdots + P_{23} + P_{24}$, the total amount of principal paid in payments 13 to 24 (the second year).

$\boxed{\downarrow}$ again gives us INT $= -22,270.46$; this is $I_{13} + I_{14} + \cdots + I_{23} + I_{24}$, the total amount of interest paid in payments 13 to 24.

Note that $P_{13} + P_{14} + \cdots + P_{23} + P_{24} = OB_{12} - OB_{24}$ could be found from OB_{12} and OB_{24}, and

$$I_{13} + I_{14} + \cdots + I_{23} + I_{24}$$
$$= 12K - (PR_{13} + PR_{14} + \cdots + PR_{23} + PR_{24})$$
$$= 12K - (OB_{12} - OB_{24}).$$

BOND VALUATION AND AMORTIZATION

It is possible to calculate the price or yield to maturity of a bond using the calculator's bond worksheet. We use Example 4.1(a) to illustrate the bond worksheet functions.

Finding The Bond Price on a Coupon Date:

A 10% bond with semiannual coupons has a face amount (par value) of 100 and is issued on June 18, 1990. The bond has a maturity date of June 18, 2010. We wish to find the price of the bond on its issue date using a nominal annual yield rate of 5% convertible semi-annually.

The bond price is $100v_{.025}^{40} + 100(.05) \cdot a_{\overline{40}|.025} = 162.76$ (nearest .01). If the bond has maturity value 110. then the price is

$$110v_{.025}^{40} + 100(.05) \cdot a_{\overline{40}|.025} = 166.48.$$

These prices can be found using the following sequence of keystrokes.

$\boxed{2nd}$ $\boxed{BOND}$ (this opens the bond worksheet).
The display shows SDT = (there may be a date here).
Key in 6.1890 $\boxed{ENTER}$ (valuation date, June 18, 1990)
Using $\boxed{\downarrow}$ gives us CPN=, and we key in 10 $\boxed{ENTER}$ (coupon amount of 10 per year).

Using ↓ gives us RDT=, and we key in 6.1810 ENTER (redemption date 20 years later, June 18, 2010).

Using ↓ gives us RV=, and we key in 100 ENTER . (redemption amount of 100)

Using ↓ gives us ACT, which we leave (refers to actual day count for bond valuation).

Using ↓ gives us 2/Y (we leave this setting since the coupons are paid twice per year; for coupons once per year we would use 2nd SET to change the display to 1/Y, which means we want "1 coupon per year").

Using ↓ gives us YLD=, and we key in 5 ENTER (nominal yield rate per year, compounded 2/Y).

Using ↓ gives us PRI=, and using CPT results in 162.76 (nearest .01) on the display. This is the bond price based on a face amount of 100. Multiplying by 1,000,000 gives the price for a 100,000,000 face amount bond.

To change the maturity value to 110, we use ↓ until we reach RV=, and we enter 110. Then use ↓ until we get to PRI= again, and use CPT . The resulting display should be 166.48.

Finding The Bond Yield on a Coupon Date:

We can use the worksheet to find the yield rate from the price. Suppose that the bond above with face amount 100 has a price of 150. There is no algebraic solution for the yield-to-maturity $i^{(2)} = 2j$, where j, the 6-month yield rate is the solution of the equation $150 = 100v_j^{40} + 5a_{\overline{40}|j}$.

The yield-to-maturity can be found using the calculator in the bond worksheet as follows.
SDT=6-18-1990 (enter 6.1890),
CPN=10, RDT=6-18-2010 (enter 6.1810),
RV=100, ACT, 2/Y, bypass YLD=, PRI=150.

Use ↓ to get to YLD= and then use CPT to calculate the yield rate.

The display should read 5.76 (YTM is $i^{(2)} = .0576$, which is $j = 2.88\%$ every 6-months).

The previous calculations can also done using the calculator annuity functions as follows.

2nd | P/Y | 2 | ENTER | 2nd | QUIT

(ensures yield period and coupon period are the same).

40 | N | (40 6-month periods),

5 | I/Y | (nominal annual yield rate),

5 | +/− | PMT | (coupon payment every 6 months),

100 | +/− | FV | (maturity value),

CPT | PV | should result in 162.76.

For the bond with maturity amount 110 we do the following.

40 | N | 5 | I/Y | 5 | +/− | PMT | 110 | +/− | FV | CPT | PV

This should result in 166.48.

To find the yield rate for a price of 150 we do the following.

40 | N | 150 | PV | 5 | +/− | PMT | 100 | +/− | FV | CPT | I/Y

This should result in 5.76 (the nominal annual yield).

Bond Amortization:

The bond amortization components can be found using the calculator's amortization worksheet in much the same way they are found for loan amortization.

A bond has face amount 1000, coupon rate 5% per coupon period, maturity value 1000, 20 coupon periods until maturity and yield-to-maturity 6% (per coupon period). The bond's amortized value just after the 5th coupon is

$$BV_5 = 1000v_{.06}^{15} + 1000(.05) \cdot a_{\overline{15}|.06} = 902.88.$$

This can be found using the following keystrokes.

2nd | P/Y | 1 | ENTER | 2nd | QUIT

20 $\boxed{\text{N}}$ 6 $\boxed{\text{I/Y}}$ 50 $\boxed{+/-}$ $\boxed{\text{PMT}}$ 1000 $\boxed{+/-}$ $\boxed{\text{FV}}$ $\boxed{\text{CPT}}$ $\boxed{\text{PV}}$

The 20-year bond price of 885.30 should appear.

Then $\boxed{\text{2nd}}$ $\boxed{\text{AMORT}}$ should result in P1 =. Key in 5 $\boxed{\text{ENTER}}$ $\boxed{\downarrow}$.
This should result in P2 =, and again enter 5 $\boxed{\text{ENTER}}$.

Then $\boxed{\downarrow}$ should result in 902.88, the balance just after the 5th coupon.

Using the $\boxed{\downarrow}$ key again gives PRN=3.94, which is the negative of the principal repaid in the 5th payment (the amount of write-up is 3.94, since the bond was purchased at a discount). Using the $\boxed{\downarrow}$ key again gives INT=-53.94, which is the negative of the amount of interest due in the 5th payment.

Bond Price and Yield Between Coupon Dates:

The bond examples considered here have had valuation take place on a coupon date. It is also possible to use the bond worksheet functions to find the price (given the yield) or the yield (given the price) of a bond at any time, on or between coupon dates.

We use Example 4.2 to illustrate the valuation of a bond between coupon dates. A bond has face amount 100, with an annual coupon rate of 10% and coupons payable semi-annually. The bond matures on June 18, 2010 and is purchased on August 1, 2000 at a yield rate of 5% (nominal annual yield compounded semi-annually). The quoted purchase price from Example 4.2 is 138.60. This can be found using the following keystrokes in the bond worksheet.

SDT=8-01-2000 (enter 8.0100),
CPN=10, RDT=6-18-2010 (enter 6.1810),
RV=100, ACT, 2/Y, YLD=5 ($\boxed{\text{ENTER}}$ must be used after each entry).

At PRI=, use $\boxed{\text{CPT}}$ to calculate the price.
The display should read 138.60. Note that this is the quoted price which excludes the accrued coupon. The accrued coupon amount is found at AI= .

If a price had been entered instead of a yield rate, we could have computed the yield.

INTERNAL RATE OF RETURN AND NET PRESENT VALUE

The internal rate of return for a series of payments received and payments made can be found in a couple of different ways, depending upon the nature of the series of payments. When we consider a level payment annuity with or without a balloon payment at the time of the last annuity payment, we can enter values into the variables

$\boxed{N}$, $\boxed{PV}$, $\boxed{PMT}$ and $\boxed{FV}$, and then use $\boxed{CPT}$ $\boxed{I/Y}$ to find the interest rate which satisfies the relationship $PV = PMT \cdot a_{\overline{n}|j} + FV \cdot v_j^n$. The internal rate of return is j.

We can use the cashflow worksheet ($\boxed{CF}$) to enter a cashflow at time 0, CF_0, along with up to 24 additional cashflows at the end of 24 successive periods, $C01, C02, \ldots, C24$. Once these cashflow amounts are entered, we can use the $\boxed{IRR}$ function (internal rate of return) to calculate an internal rate of return. It is a solution j to the relationship

$$CF_0 + C01 \cdot v_j + C02 \cdot v_j^2 + \cdots + C24 \cdot v_j^{24} = 0.$$

The cashflow amounts can each be positive (an amount received) or negative (an amount paid out).

Calculating Internal Rate of Return

We illustrate how the internal rate of return in Example 5.1 can be found in this way. Example 5.1 has the following series of cashflows, where time is measured in 6-month intervals:

$$C_0 = -5100, C_1 = 0, \ C_2 = -2295, \text{ and } C_3 = 7982.5.$$

The cashflow worksheet is cleared using $\boxed{CF}$ $\boxed{2nd}$ $\boxed{CLR\ WORK}$

The following series of keystrokes solves for the internal rate of return j, where j will be the 6-month internal rate of return:

Key in $\boxed{CF}$, the display should read CFo= ,

Key in 5100 $\boxed{+/-}$ $\boxed{ENTER}$ $\boxed{\downarrow}$, the display should read C01=,

Key in 0 $\boxed{ENTER}$ $\boxed{\downarrow}$ $\boxed{\downarrow}$, the display should read C02=,

Key in 2295 $\boxed{+/-}$ $\boxed{\text{ENTER}}$ $\boxed{\downarrow}$ $\boxed{\downarrow}$, the display should read C03=,
Key in 7982.5 $\boxed{\text{ENTER}}$,
Key in $\boxed{\text{IRR}}$ $\boxed{\text{CPT}}$. The display should read 3.246 .
This is the 6-month internal rate of return.

As seen in Example 5.2, a series of cashflows may have a unique internal rate of return, it may have more than one internal rate of return, or it may have no internal rate of return. If we attempt to solve for the internal rate of return with the calculator function for Example 5.2, we get the following results:

5.2(a) $C_0 = -1, C_1 = 2.3$, and $C_2 = -1.33$, and the calculator returns an "Error 7" message when $\boxed{\text{IRR}}$ $\boxed{\text{CPT}}$ is keyed in, which generally occurs when there is no solution for the internal rate of return.

5.2(b) $C_0 = -1, C_1 = 2.3$, and $C_2 = -1.32$, and the calculator returns an IRR of 10%. This is the smaller of the two solutions, 10% and 20%.

5.2(c) $C_0 = -1, C_1 = 2.3, C_2 = -1.3125$, and the calculator returns an IRR of 5%, again the smaller of the two solutions, 5% and 25%.

5.2(d) $C_0 = -1, C_1 = 2.3, C_2 = -1.2825$, and the calculator returns an IRR of -5%, again the smaller of the two solutions, -5% and 35%.

Calculating Net Present Value:

The calculator $\boxed{\text{NPV}}$ function can be used to calculate the present value of a series of cashflows that have been entered into the cashflow worksheet. We use Example 5.2(a) as an illustration. Suppose that we wish to find the present value at time 0 of the three cashflows

$$C_0 = -1, C_1 = 2.3, \text{ and } C_2 = -1.33,$$

using an interest rate of 10%.

This would be $-1 + 2.3v_1 - 1.33v_1^2$. We can find this present value as follows. We enter the cashflows $C_0 = -1, C_1 = 2.3$, and $C_2 = -1.33$, into the $\boxed{\text{CF}}$ worksheet as shown above. Immediately after C_2 has been entered, and while still in the cashflow worksheet, press $\boxed{\text{NPV}}$. The display will read I=0. We key in 10 $\boxed{\text{ENTER}}$ $\boxed{\downarrow}$ $\boxed{\text{CPT}}$.

The display should read NPV = -0.008264. This is the present value of the cashflows valued at an interest rate of 10% per period.

In the cashflow worksheet it is possible to specify an initial cashflow amount CF0, and 24 additional amounts C1 to C24. Each cashflow amount may be made multiple times ("grouped" cashflows of the same amount made at successive points in time).

We use Example 2.5 to illustrate this application. Suppose that 10 monthly payments of 50 each are followed by 14 monthly payments of 75 each. If interest is at a monthly effective rate of 1%, what is the accumulated value of the series at the time of the final payment? The following keystrokes give us the accumulated value.

$\boxed{\text{CF}}$ 0 $\boxed{\text{ENTER}}$ $\boxed{\downarrow}$

Key in 50 $\boxed{\text{ENTER}}$ $\boxed{\downarrow}$ 10 $\boxed{\text{ENTER}}$ $\boxed{\downarrow}$ (this sets a payment amount of C01=50 to be made for F01=10 successive periods),

Key in 75 $\boxed{\text{ENTER}}$ $\boxed{\downarrow}$ 14 $\boxed{\text{ENTER}}$ $\boxed{\downarrow}$ (this sets a payment amount of C02=75 to be made for F02=14 successive periods after the first 10 periods).

Key in $\boxed{\text{NPV}}$ 1 $\boxed{\text{ENTER}}$ $\boxed{\downarrow}$ $\boxed{\text{CPT}}$

The screen should display 1,356.47. This is the present value of the 24 payments one month before the first payment.

With NPV = 1,356.47 still displayed, Key in $\boxed{\text{PV}}$.
Key in $\boxed{\text{2nd}}$ $\boxed{\text{QUIT}}$ 24 $\boxed{\text{N}}$ 1 $\boxed{\text{I/Y}}$ $\boxed{\text{CPT}}$ $\boxed{\text{FV}}$

This should result in the display FV $= -1,722.36$. This is the accumulated value of the series of 24 payments at time of the final payment.

As a variation on Example 2.5, suppose that 10 deposits of 50 per month are made into an account earning monthly interest rate i. Suppose further that one month after the 10th deposit, monthly withdrawals are made from the account of amount 75 per month. The account balance is 0 just after the 14th withdrawal. We wish to find the monthly interest rate on the account. We wish to solve for i in the equation $50s_{\overline{10}|\,i} = 75a_{\overline{14}|\,i}$.

This equation is equivalent to $50a_{\overline{10}|\,i} = 75v^{10}a_{\overline{14}|\,i}$. We can place this in the context of internal rate of return, where we wish to find the internal rate of return for a sequence of cashflows of 10 payments <u>paid</u> of 50 each (C01=50, F01=10) followed by 14 payments received of 75 each (C02= − 75, F02=14), and whose total initial present value is CF0=0. We use the following keystrokes:

$\boxed{\text{CF}}$ 0 $\boxed{\text{ENTER}}$ $\boxed{\downarrow}$ 50 $\boxed{\text{ENTER}}$ $\boxed{\downarrow}$ 10 $\boxed{\text{ENTER}}$ $\boxed{\downarrow}$
75 $\boxed{+/-}$ $\boxed{\text{ENTER}}$ $\boxed{\downarrow}$ 14 $\boxed{\text{ENTER}}$ $\boxed{\text{IRR}}$ $\boxed{\text{CPT}}$.

The display should read IRR = 6.518.

EXAMPLES FROM SOA/CAS EXAM FM/2
(FORMERLY COURSE 2 COMPOUND INTEREST)

May 2003, #33 (Annuity Valuation)

At an effective annual interest rate of i, $i > 0$,, both of the following annuities have a present value of X:

(i)   A 20-year annuity-immediate with annual payments of 55
(ii) A 30-year annuity-immediate with annual payments that pays 30 per year for the first 10 years, 60 per year for the second 10 years, and 90 per year for the final 10 years.

Calculate X.

(A) 575   (B) 585   (C) 595   (D) 605   (E) 615

SOLUTION

The series of cashflows representing the difference between (i) and (ii) is a series of 10 payments of $55 - 30 = 25$ each, followed by a series of 10 payments of $55 - 60 = -5$ each, followed by a series of 10 payments of -90 each. The interest rate that makes the present value of this series equal to 0 is found using the IRR function as follows.

Key in $\boxed{\text{CF}}$ 0 $\boxed{\text{ENTER}}$ $\boxed{\downarrow}$ 25 $\boxed{\text{ENTER}}$ $\boxed{\downarrow}$ 10 $\boxed{\text{ENTER}}$,
$\boxed{\downarrow}$ 5 $\boxed{+/-}$ $\boxed{\text{ENTER}}$ $\boxed{\downarrow}$ 10 $\boxed{\text{ENTER}}$,
$\boxed{\downarrow}$ 90 $\boxed{+/-}$ $\boxed{\text{ENTER}}$ $\boxed{\downarrow}$ 10 $\boxed{\text{ENTER}}$,
$\boxed{\text{IRR}}$ $\boxed{\text{CPT}}$. The display should read IRR = 7.177.

This is the interest rate per year. Set P/Y and C/Y to 1. The following keystrokes give us the value of X.

$\boxed{\text{2nd}}$ $\boxed{\text{QUIT}}$ $\boxed{\text{2nd}}$ $\boxed{\text{CLR TVM}}$
20 $\boxed{\text{N}}$ 7.177 $\boxed{\text{I/Y}}$ 55 $\boxed{+/-}$ $\boxed{\text{PMT}}$ $\boxed{\text{CPT}}$ $\boxed{\text{PV}}$.

The display should read 574.74. Answer: A

May 2003, #8 (Annuity Valuation) *(This is also Exercise 2.2.2)*

Kathryn deposits 100 into an account at the beginning of each 4-year period for 40 years. The account credits interest at an effective annual interest rate of i. The accumulated amount in the account at the end of 40 years is X, which is 5 times the accumulated amount in the account at the end of 20 years. Calculate X.

(A) 4695   (B) 5070   (C) 5445   (D) 5820   (E) 6195

SOLUTION

We denote the 4-year rate of interest by j. Then the accumulated value at the end of 40 years is $X = 100\ddot{s}_{\overline{10}|j}$. (10 4-year periods, with valuation one full 4-year period after the 10th deposit). The accumulated value at the end of 20 years is $100\ddot{s}_{\overline{5}|j}$.

We are given that $100\ddot{s}_{\overline{10}|j} = 5 \times 100\ddot{s}_{\overline{5}|j}$, which is the same as

$$100 s_{\overline{10}|j} - 5 \times 100 s_{\overline{5}|j} = 0$$

(after we multiply both sides of the equations by v_j). This can be interpreted as saying that 5 payments of 100 per period, followed by 5 payments of -400 per period has an accumulated value (and present value) of 0. We can use the IRR function to find j as follows.

Key in $\boxed{CF}$ 0 $\boxed{ENTER}$ $\boxed{\downarrow}$ 100 $\boxed{ENTER}$ $\boxed{\downarrow}$ 5 $\boxed{ENTER}$,

$\boxed{\downarrow}$ 400 $\boxed{+/-}$ $\boxed{ENTER}$ $\boxed{\downarrow}$ 5 $\boxed{ENTER}$ $\boxed{IRR}$ $\boxed{CPT}$.

The display should read IRR = 31.95.
The 4-year interest rate is $j = .3195$.
Then we apply the following keystrokes.

$\boxed{2nd}$ $\boxed{QUIT}$ $\boxed{2nd}$ $\boxed{CLR\ TVM}$

$\boxed{2nd}$ $\boxed{BGN}$ $\boxed{2nd}$ $\boxed{SET}$ $\boxed{2nd}$ $\boxed{QUIT}$

10 $\boxed{N}$ 31.95 $\boxed{I/Y}$

100 $\boxed{PMT}$ $\boxed{CPT}$ $\boxed{FV}$.

The display should read $-6,194.44$.   Answer: E

May 2003, #26 (Decreasing Annuity) (*Exercise 2.3.13*)

1000 is deposited into Fund X, which earns an effective annual rate of 6%. At the end of each year, the interest earned plus an additional 100 is withdrawn from the fund. At the end of the tenth year, the fund is depleted. The annual withdrawals of interest and principal are deposited into Fund Y, which earns an effective annual rate of 9%. Determine the accumulated value of Fund Y at the end of year 10.

(A) 1519   (B) 1819   (C) 2085   (D) 2273   (E) 2431

SOLUTION

The 10 deposits to Fund Y are $160, 154, 148, \ldots, 112, 106$.

These can be entered as 10 separate cashflows in the $\boxed{CF}$ worksheet. The NPV function at 9% will give a present value (one year before the deposit of 160) of 880.59. Then the FV at the end of 10 years will be 2,085. Answer: C

November 2001, #16 (Increasing Annuity) (*Exercise 2.3.12*)

Olga buys a 5-year increasing annuity for X. Olga will receive 2 at the end of the first month, 4 at the end of the second month, and for each month thereafter the payment increases by 2. The nominal interest rate is 9% convertible quarterly. Calculate X.

(A) 2680   (B) 2730   (C) 2780   (D) 2830   (E) 2880

SOLUTION

With monthly rate j, $X = 2(Ia)_{\overline{60}|j}$.

We are given 3-month rate .0225, so that $(1+j)^3 = 1.0225$, and therefore, $j = .007444$. The numerator of $(Ia)_{\overline{60}|j}$ can be found by the following keystrokes.

$\boxed{2nd}$ $\boxed{BGN}$ $\boxed{2nd}$ $\boxed{SET}$ $\boxed{2nd}$ $\boxed{QUIT}$

$\boxed{2nd}$ $\boxed{P/Y}$ 12 $\boxed{ENTER}$ $\boxed{\downarrow}$ $\boxed{C/Y}$ 4 $\boxed{ENTER}$ $\boxed{2nd}$ $\boxed{QUIT}$,

60 $\boxed{N}$ 1 $\boxed{+/-}$ $\boxed{PMT}$ 9 $\boxed{I/Y}$ 60 $\boxed{FV}$ $\boxed{CPT}$ $\boxed{PV}$

This results in the display reading PV = 10.1587.

Then $\boxed{\div}$ .007444 $\boxed{\times}$ 2 results in 2,729 on the display. Answer: B

May 2003, #25 (Loan Repayment)

John borrows 1000 for 10 years at an effective annual interest rate of 10%. He can repay this loan using the amortization method with payments of P at the end of each year. Instead, John repays the 1000 using a sinking fund that pays an effective annual rate of 14%. The deposits to the sinking fund are equal to P minus the interest on the loan and are made at the end of each year for 10 years.

Determine the balance in the sinking fund immediately after repayment of the loan.

(A) 213   (B) 218   (C) 223   (D) 230   (E) 237

SOLUTION

P is found as follows. Clear all registers and be sure that I/Y and P/Y are both set to 1 and payment mode is END. Apply the following keystrokes.

10 $\boxed{\text{N}}$ 10 $\boxed{\text{I/Y}}$ 1000 $\boxed{\text{PV}}$ $\boxed{\text{CPT}}$ $\boxed{\text{PMT}}$

The screen displays −162.75. The deposits to the sinking fund are 62.75 each. The accumulated value of the sinking fund deposits at 14% is found as follows.

10 $\boxed{\text{N}}$ 14 $\boxed{\text{I/Y}}$ 62.75 $\boxed{\text{PMT}}$ 0 $\boxed{\text{PV}}$ $\boxed{\text{CPT}}$ $\boxed{\text{FV}}$

The display reads −1,213.42.

After the principal loan amount of 1,000 is paid, 213 is left in the sinking fund. Answer: A

May 2003, #42 (Bond Amortization)

A 10,000 par value 10-year bond with 8% annual coupons is bought at a premium to yield an effective annual rate of 6%.

Calculate the interest portion of the 7th coupon.

(A) 632   (B) 642   (C) 651   (D) 660   (E) 667

SOLUTION

The AMORT functions can be used as follows.

10 $\boxed{\text{N}}$ 6 $\boxed{\text{I/Y}}$ 800 $\boxed{+/-}$ $\boxed{\text{PMT}}$ 10000 $\boxed{+/-}$ $\boxed{\text{FV}}$ $\boxed{\text{CPT}}$ $\boxed{\text{PV}}$

The display reads 11,472.02 (the bond price). Then

$\boxed{\text{2nd}}$ $\boxed{\text{AMORT}}$ 7 $\boxed{\text{ENTER}}$ $\boxed{\downarrow}$ 7 $\boxed{\text{ENTER}}$ $\boxed{\downarrow}$

shows BAL = 10,534.60 (the book value after the 7th coupon).

Then $\boxed{\downarrow}$ shows PRN = −158.42 (the negative of the principal repaid),

and $\boxed{\downarrow}$ shows INT = −641.58 is the negative of the interest paid.

Answer: B

HEWLETT PACKARD HP-12C CALCULATOR

ACCUMULATED AND PRESENT VALUES USING COMPOUND INTEREST

Accumulated values and present values of single payments using effective annual interest rates can be made in the following way. Clear calculator registers before starting the keystroke sequence with $\boxed{f}$ REG and $\boxed{f}$ FIN.

Accumulated Value:

We use Example 1.1 to illustrate this function.
A deposit of 1000 made at time 0 grows at effective annual interest rate 9%. The accumulated value at the end of 3 years is $1000(1.09)^3 = 1,295.03$. This can be found using the calculator in two ways.

This can be found using the calculator in two ways:

1.	Keystrokes	Display	Comments
	1.09 $\boxed{\text{ENTER}}$	1.09	$1.09 = 1 + i$ is entered
	3 $\boxed{y^x}$	1,295.029	$(1.09)^3$
	1000 $\boxed{\times}$	1,295.029	$1000(1.09)^3$

2.	3 $\boxed{n}$	3.0	3 compounding periods
	9 $\boxed{i}$	9.0	Interest rate is $i = .09$ (9%)
	1000 $\boxed{\text{PV}}$	1000.0	1000 invested at time 0
	0 $\boxed{\text{PMT}}$	0.0	No other payments made (this is redundant if registers are clear)
	$\boxed{\text{FV}}$	−1,295.029	$−1000(1.09)^3$

The screen should display −1,295.029 (the negative sign is part of the HP-12C "cashflow convention" in which amounts received are positive and amounts paid are negative; the interpretation is that 1000 is borrowed (received) at time 0 and 1,295.03 is paid back at time 3). If the PV had been entered as −1000 then FV would have been positive.

Present Value:

We use Example 1.5(a) to illustrate this function.
The present value of 1,000,000 due in 25 years at effective annual rate
.195 is This can be found using the calculator in following ways:

1. | Keystrokes | Display | Comments |
    |---|---|---|
    | 1.195 $\boxed{\text{ENTER}}$ | 1.195 | $1.195 = 1 + i$ is entered |
    | 25 $\boxed{\text{CHS}}$ $\boxed{y^x}$ | .011636 | $(1.195)^{-25} = v^{25}$ |
    | 1000000 $\boxed{\times}$ | 11,635.96 | $1,000,000v^{25} = 1,000,000(1.08)^{-25}$ |

    Note that the first two keystrokes can be replaced by:

1.195 $\boxed{1/x}$	.83682	$(1.195)^{-1} = v_{.195}$ is entered
25 $\boxed{y^x}$	.011636	$(1.195)^{-25} = v^{25}$

2. | 25 $\boxed{\text{n}}$ | 25.00 | Number of periods |
    |---|---|---|
    | 19.5 $\boxed{\text{i}}$ | 19.50 | Interest rate period |
    | 1000000 $\boxed{\text{FV}}$ | 1000000 | Accumulated (future) value at time 25 |
    | $\boxed{\text{PV}}$ | $-11,635.96$ | $1,000,000v^{25} = FV \cdot v_i^n$ |

As a more general procedure, in the equation $(PV)(1+i)^n = FV$, if any 3
of the 4 variables PV, i, n, FV are entered, then the 4th can be found using
the key functions.

Unknown Interest Rate:

As an example of solving for the interest rate, we consider Example 1.5(c).

An initial investment of 25,000 at effective annual rate of interest i grows to
1,000,000 in 25 years. Then $25,000(1+i)^{25} = 1,000,000$, from which we
get $i = (40)^{1/25} - 1 = .1590$ (15.90%). This is found using the calculator
power function.

The keystroke sequence of financial functions for solving for i is
25 $\boxed{\text{n}}$, 25000 $\boxed{\text{CHS}}$ $\boxed{\text{PV}}$, 0 $\boxed{\text{PMT}}$, 1000000 $\boxed{\text{FV}}$. Then press $\boxed{\text{i}}$.

The screen should display 15.90 (this is the % measure).

Unknown Time Period:

As an example of solving for an unknown time period, suppose that an initial investment of 100 at monthly compound rate of interest i grows to 300 in n months at monthly interest rate $i = .75\%$. Then $100(1.0075)^n = 300$, from which we get $n = \frac{\ln 3}{\ln 1.0075} = 147.03$ months.

This can be found using the calculator $\boxed{\text{LN}}$ function.

Using financial functions, the keystroke sequence solving for n is

$100\,\boxed{\text{CHS}}\,\boxed{\text{PV}}$, $0\,\boxed{\text{PMT}}$, $1000000\,\boxed{\text{FV}}$, $.75\,\boxed{\text{i}}$. Then press $\boxed{\text{n}}$.

The screen should display 148.0 (this is the number of months rounded to the next integer, so that 147 months are not sufficient, and 148 are more than sufficient).

ACCUMULATED AND PRESENT VALUES USING COMPOUND DISCOUNT

Accumulated values and present values of single payments using an effective annual rate of discount can be made in the following way.

Present Value:

The present value of 500 due in 8 years at effective annual rate of discount 8% is $500(1-08)^8 = 500(.92)^8 = 256.61$.

This can be found using the calculator in two ways:

1. Key in .92 $\boxed{\text{ENTER}}$, Key in 8 $\boxed{y^x}$, Key in 500 $\boxed{\times}$.
    The screen should display 256.61.

2. Key in 8 $\boxed{\text{CHS}}$ $\boxed{\text{n}}$, Key in 8 $\boxed{\text{CHS}}$ $\boxed{\text{i}}$, Key in 500 $\boxed{\text{FV}}$
    Key in 0 $\boxed{\text{PMT}}$. Then press the $\boxed{\text{FV}}$ key.

The screen should display −256.61.

Accumulated Value:

A deposit of 25 made at time 0 grows at effective annual discount rate 6%. The accumulated value at the end of 5 years is

$$25(1-.06)^{-5} = 25(.94)^{-5} = 34.06.$$

This can be found using the calculator in two ways:

1. Key in .94 $\boxed{\text{ENTER}}$, Key in 5 $\boxed{\text{CHS}}$ $\boxed{y^x}$, Key in 25 $\boxed{\times}$.
    The screen should display 34.06 (rounded to nearest .01).

2. Key in 5 $\boxed{\text{CHS}}$ $\boxed{\text{n}}$, Key in 6 $\boxed{\text{CHS}}$ $\boxed{\text{i}}$, Key in 25 $\boxed{\text{PV}}$,
    Key in 0 $\boxed{\text{PMT}}$. Then press the $\boxed{\text{PV}}$ key.

The screen should display -34.06 (the negative sign is part of the HP-12C "cashflow convention" in which amounts received are positive and amounts paid are negative; the interpretation is that 25 is borrowed (received) at time 0 and 34.06 is paid back at time 5). If the PV had been entered as -25, then FV would have been positive.

EQUIVALENT NOMINAL AND EFFECTIVE INTEREST RATES

The nominal annual interest rate compounded 12 times per year can be found from the effective annual rate of interest and vice-versa.

A nominal annual interest rate of .24 (24%) compounded monthly is equivalent to an effective annual rate of interest of $i = .2682$ (26.82%). The relationship linking equivalent nominal and effective interest rates is

$i = \left(1 + \frac{i^{(12)}}{12}\right)^{12} - 1$ or equivalently, $i^{(12)} = 12\left[(1+i)^{1/12} - 1\right]$.

Given $i^{(12)} = .24$, we have $i = \left(1 + \frac{.24}{12}\right)^{12} - 1 = (1.02)^{12} - 1 = .2682$.

Conversely, if we are given $i = .2682$ and we wish to find $i^{(12)}$, we use

$$i^{(12)} = 12\left[(1.2682)^{1/12} - 1\right] = .24.$$

The usual calculator functions $\boxed{+}, \boxed{\times}, \boxed{y^x}$, etc., are used. This approach applies for any number of compounding periods.

When the nominal annual rate of interest is compounded monthly ($m = 12$), we can use the following calculator approach.

1. Finding i from $i^{(12)}$: Suppose we are given $i^{(12)} = .24$.

    Key in 1 $\boxed{g}$ $\boxed{12\times}$, Key in 24 $\boxed{g}$ $\boxed{12\div}$, Key in 1 $\boxed{PV}$.

    Then press the $\boxed{FV}$. The display should read -1.2682.

    This will be $-(1+i)$, so that $i = .2682$ is the equivalent effective annual rate of interest.

2. Finding $i^{(12)}$ from i. Suppose we are given $i = .2682$.

    Key in 1 $\boxed{g}$ $\boxed{12\times}$, Key in 1 $\boxed{PV}$, Key in 1.2682 $\boxed{CHS}$ $\boxed{FV}$.

    Then press the $\boxed{i}$. The display should read 2.00.

    This will be $\frac{i^{(12)}}{12}$, so that $i^{(12)} = .24$ is the nominal annual rate of interest.

VALUATION OF LEVEL PAYMENT ANNUITIES

The accumulated value and present value of a level payment annuity-immediate can be found using calculator functions.

Accumulated Value:

A deposit of 1000 is made at the end of each year for 20 years. The deposits earn interest at an effective annual rate of interest of 4%. The accumulated value of the deposits at the time of (and including) the 20th deposit is $1000s_{\overline{20}|.04} = 1000\left[\frac{(1.04)^{20}-1}{.04}\right] = 29,778$. This can be found using the calculator in the following way:

Key in 20 $\boxed{n}$, Key in 4 $\boxed{i}$, Key in 0 $\boxed{PV}$,

Key in 1000 $\boxed{PMT}$, Key in $\boxed{FV}$. The display should read $-29,778$, the negative of the accumulated annuity value.

Present value:

Payments of 50 will be made at the end of each month for 10 years. The monthly compound interest rate is $\frac{3}{4}$ %. The present value of the annuity one month before the first payment is made is

$$50a_{\overline{120}|.0075} = 50\left[\frac{1-v_{.0075}^{120}}{.0075}\right] = 3,947$$

(10 years, 12 months per year). This can be found using the calculator in the following way:

Key in 120 $\boxed{n}$, Key in .75 $\boxed{i}$, Key in 50 $\boxed{PMT}$,

Key in 0 $\boxed{FV}$, Key in $\boxed{PV}$. The display should read $-3,947$, the negative of the accumulated annuity value.

In the general equation $PV = PMT \cdot a_{\overline{n}|i}$, if any 3 of the 4 variables PV, PMT, n, i (in%) are given, then the calculator functions can be used to solve for the 4th variable. The same is true for the equation $PMT \cdot s_{\overline{n}|i} = FV$ (keep in mind that when PMT is entered as positive, FV or PV are returned as negative, and vice-versa).

Finding the Payment Amount:

A loan of 1000 is to be repaid with monthly payments for 3 years at a compound monthly interest rate of .5%. The monthly payment is K where $1000 = Ka_{\overline{36}|.005}$, so that $K = \dfrac{1000}{a_{\overline{36}|.005}} = 30.42$.

This can be found using as follows:

Key in 36 $\boxed{n}$, Key in .5 $\boxed{i}$, Key in 1000 $\boxed{PV}$,

Key in 0 $\boxed{FV}$, Key in $\boxed{PMT}$.
The display should read -30.42.

Finding the Interest Rate:

Suppose that the loan payment is 35 and the interest rate is to be found. Then $1000 = 35a_{\overline{36}|i}$. There is no algebraic solution for i.

The following keystrokes give us i:

Key in 36 $\boxed{n}$, Key in 1000 $\boxed{PV}$, Key in 35 $\boxed{CHS}$ $\boxed{PMT}$,

Key in 0 $\boxed{FV}$, Key in $\boxed{i}$.

The display should read 1.307 (this is i per month measured in %).

Finding the Number of Payments:

A loan of 1000 is to be repaid with level payments of 20 at the end of each month for as long as necessary. Interest is at a rate of 1 % per month. Determine the number for full payments of 20 needed and the amount of a smaller final payment one month after the last payment of 20.

We must first find n in the equation $1000 = 20a_{\overline{n}|.01}$.

We can do this as follows:

Key in 1 $\boxed{i}$, Key in 1000 $\boxed{PV}$, Key in 20 $\boxed{CHS}$ $\boxed{PMT}$,
Key in 0 $\boxed{FV}$, Key in $\boxed{n}$.
The display should read 70.

This indicates that the 70th payment of amount 20 will be at least enough to repay the loan; there should be 69 payments of 20 followed by a smaller 70th payment of amount X. This is the way the HP-12C solves for the number of payments in this situation, it rounds n up to the next integer.

We solve for X from the equation $1000 = 20a_{\overline{69}|.01} + Xv^{70}$. This can be done on the calculator in two alternative ways:

Key in 69 $\boxed{n}$, Key in 1 $\boxed{i}$, Key in 1000 $\boxed{PV}$, Key in 20 $\boxed{CHS}$ $\boxed{PMT}$,
Key in $\boxed{FV}$. The display should read -13.11. This is the (negative of the) additional amount needed to repay the loan at time 69 along with the 69th regular payment. The additional amount needed at time 70 to repay the loan is $13.11 \times 1.01 = 13.24$.

Key in 70 $\boxed{n}$, Key in $\boxed{i}$, Key in 1000 $\boxed{PV}$, Key in 20 $\boxed{CHS}$ $\boxed{PMT}$,
Key in $\boxed{FV}$. The display should read 6.76. This is the amount of the overpayment at time 70 if 70 payments of the full amount of 20 had been made. The smaller amount needed at time 70 is $20 - 6.76 = 13.24$.

Annuity-due:

Annuity due calculations are similar to annuity-immediate calculations. We must first set the payment mode to "BEGIN" by using the blue function key $\boxed{g}$ followed by $\boxed{BEG}$. The calculator will then view payments as being made at the beginning of each period. In the equation $PV = PMT \cdot \ddot{a}_{\overline{Nn}|\,i}$, if any 3 of PV, PMT, n, i are entered, we can find the 4th. In the equation $FV = PMT \cdot \ddot{s}_{\overline{n}|\,i}$ if any 3 of FV, PMT, n, i are entered, we can find the 4th (as before, PMT and PV or FV are opposite signs).

The following is an example of the calculation of an annuity-due. Deposits of 100 each are made to an account at the start of each year for 25 years. The accumulated value at the end of the 25th year is 3000. To find the effective annual rate of interest, we are solving for i in the equation $3000 = 100 \cdot \ddot{s}_{\overline{25}|\,i}$. We can use the following approach:

Key in $\boxed{g}$ $\boxed{BEG}$, Key in 25 $\boxed{n}$, Key in 0 $\boxed{PV}$,

Key in 100 $\boxed{CHS}$ $\boxed{PMT}$, Key in 3000 $\boxed{FV}$, key in $\boxed{i}$.

The display should read 1.375 (this is i in %).

VALUATION OF INCREASING AND DECREASING ANNUITIES

$(Ia)_{\overline{n}|\,i}$ can be found using the formula $\frac{\ddot{a}_{\overline{n}|}-nv^n}{i}$.

For instance, $(Ia)_{\overline{20}|.01} = \frac{\ddot{a}_{\overline{20}|.01}-20v^{20}}{.01} = \frac{18.2260-20(16.3909)}{.01} = 183.51$.

The following series of keystrokes will also find $(Ia)_{\overline{20}|.01}$. The calculator should be in $\boxed{BEG}$ mode. Key in 20 $\boxed{n}$, Key in $\boxed{i}$, Key in 1 $\boxed{CHS}$ $\boxed{PMT}$, Key in 20 $\boxed{FV}$, Key in $\boxed{PV}$. The display should read 1.8351 (this is $\ddot{a}_{\overline{20}|.01} - 20v^{20}$, the numerator in the algebraic form for $(Ia)_{\overline{20}|.01}$.) Then key in $\boxed{\div}$ $\boxed{.01}$ (divide by .01), and the result should be 183.51.

By having the calculator in $\boxed{\text{BEG}}$ mode and entering -1 for $\boxed{\text{PMT}}$ and entering 20 for $\boxed{\text{FV}}$, the calculator finds the PV of the 20 payments of 1 at the beginning of each year minus the present value of 20 at the end of the 20th year. This will be $\ddot{a}_{\overline{20}|.01} - 20v^{20}$, the numerator needed for $(Ia)_{\overline{20}|.01}$.

$(Ds)_{\overline{n}|i}$ can be found using the formula $\dfrac{n(1+i)^n - s_{\overline{n}|}}{i}$. For instance,

$$(Ds)_{\overline{15}|.005} = \frac{15(1.005)^{15} - s_{\overline{15}|.005}}{.005} = \frac{16.1652 - 15.5364}{.005} = 125.74.$$

The following series of keystrokes will also find $(Ds)_{\overline{15}|.005}$. The calculator should be in $\boxed{\text{END}}$ mode.

Key in 15 $\boxed{\text{n}}$, Key in .5 $\boxed{\text{i}}$, Key in 15 $\boxed{\text{CHS}}$ $\boxed{\text{PV}}$,

Key in 1 $\boxed{\text{PMT}}$, Key in $\boxed{\text{FV}}$.

The display should read .62869 (this is $15(1.005)^{15} - s_{\overline{15}|.005}$, the numerator in the algebraic form for $(Ds)_{\overline{15}|.005}$).

These calculator methods may be marginally faster than calculating the numerator of $(Ia)_{\overline{20}|.01}$ directly and then dividing by .01 (and the same for $(Ds)_{\overline{15}|.005}$).

AMORTIZATION OF A LEVEL PAYMENT LOAN

For a loan with level payments, there are calculator functions for finding outstanding balances, interest or principal paid in a single payment, and interest or principal paid in a range of payments. Parameters are entered for n, i, PV as with the usual annuity valuation. The calculator will give us the payment using the PMT key. The following example illustrates how we get the amortization quantities.

We use Example 3.3 to illustrate these functions. A homebuyer borrows

$250,000 to be repaid over a 30-year period with level monthly payments beginning one month after the loan is made. The interest rate on the loan is a nominal annual rate of 9% compounded monthly. The loan payment is $K = \dfrac{250,000}{a_{\overline{360}|.0075}} = 2,011.56$.

The outstanding balance at the end of the first year (after the 12th monthly payment) $OB_{12} = 2,011.56 a_{\overline{348}|.0075} = 248,292.01$. The principal repaid in the 12th payment is $PR_{12} = Kv^{360-12+1} = 2,011.56 v^{349} = 148.25$, and the interest paid in the 12th payment is $I_{12} = K(1-v^{360-12+1}) = 1,863.30$. The principal repaid in the 2nd year (the 13th through 24th payments inclusive) is

$$PR_{13} + PR_{14} + \cdots + PR_{23} + PR_{24} = K(v^{348} + v^{347} + \cdots + v^{338} + v^{337})$$
$$= 1,868.21,$$

the interest paid in the 2nd year is

$I_{13} + I_{14} + \cdots + I_{23} + I_{24} = K(1-v^{348} + 1-v^{347} + \cdots + 1-v^{338} + 1-v^{337})$
$12K - (PR_{13}+PR_{14}+\cdots+PR_{23}+PR_{24}) = 22,270.46$.

These calculations can be completed using the calculator functions. Clear all registers.

Key in 360 $\boxed{n}$, Key in .75 $\boxed{i}$, Key in 250,000 $\boxed{PV}$ (sets 360 payments, .75% interest and loan amount 250,000). Key in $\boxed{PMT}$. The display should read $-2,011.56$ (the negative of the payment amount).

Key in 12 $\boxed{f}$ $\boxed{AMORT}$. The display should read $-22,430.69$. This is the (negative) total amount of interest paid in the first 12 payments. Key in $\boxed{x \gtrless y}$. The display should read $-1,707.99$. This is the (negative) total amount of principal repaid in the first 12 payments.

Key in $\boxed{RCL}$ $\boxed{PV}$. The display should read 248,292.01. This is OB_{12}, the outstanding balance after the 12th payment.

At this point, the time origin in the calculator's amortization register is set at time 12, just after the 12th payment.

Key in 12 $\boxed{f}$ $\boxed{\text{AMORT}}$. The display should read $-22,270.46$.

This is the (negative of the) interest in payments 13 through 24 (the 2nd year of the loan). In other words, this is the interest in the 6th payment, $I_{13} + \cdots + I_{24} = 22,270.46$. Key in $\boxed{x \gtrless y}$. The display should read $-1,868.21$. This is the (negative) amount of principal paid in payments 13 through 24, $PR_{13} + \cdots + PR_{24}$.

Key in $\boxed{\text{RCL}}$ $\boxed{\text{PV}}$. The display should read $246,423.79$.
This is OB_{24}, the outstanding balance after the 24th monthly payment.

BOND VALUATION AND AMORTIZATION

It is possible to calculate the price or yield to maturity of a bond using the calculator's financial functions. We consider the case of a bond valued on a coupon date just after the coupon has been paid. We use Example 4.1(a) to illustrate these functions.

A 10% bond with semiannual coupons has a face amount of 100 and is issued on June 18, 1990. The bond has a maturity date of June 18, 2010. We wish to find the price of the bond on its issue date using a nominal annual yield rate of 5% convertible semi-annually.

The bond price is $100v_{.025}^{40} + 100(.05) \cdot a_{\overline{40}|.025} = 162.76$ (nearest .01). If the bond has maturity value 110. then the price is $110v_{.025}^{40} + 110(.05) \cdot a_{\overline{40}|.025} = 166.48$.

These prices can be found using the calculator in the following way which is quite similar to a loan amortization.

Key in 40 $\boxed{n}$, Key in 2.5 $\boxed{i}$, Key in 5 $\boxed{\text{CHS}}$ $\boxed{\text{PMT}}$

Key in 100 $\boxed{\text{CHS}}$ $\boxed{\text{FV}}$ (sets n as 40 coupon payments, i as 2.5% 6-month yield rate, $5 = 100 \times .05$ as the coupon payment, and 100 as the redemption value).

Key in $\boxed{PV}$. The display should read 162.76, the price of the bond (one period before the first coupon).

Key in 110 $\boxed{CHS}$ $\boxed{FV}$ (resets the redemption amount to 110).

Key in $\boxed{PV}$. The display should read 166.48, the price of the bond.

The book value of the bond with face amount 1000 just after the 5th coupon is

$$BV_5 = 100v_{.025}^{35} + 100(.05) \cdot a_{\overline{35}|.025} = 157.86.$$

This can be found using the following keystrokes.

Key in 40 $\boxed{n}$, Key in 2.5 $\boxed{i}$, Key in 5 $\boxed{CHS}$ $\boxed{PMT}$, Key in 100 $\boxed{CHS}$ $\boxed{FV}$. Key in $\boxed{PV}$. The display should read 162.76.

Key in 5 $\boxed{f}$ $\boxed{AMORT}$. The display should read -20.11. This is the negative of the amount of interest paid in the first 5 coupons.

Key in $\boxed{x \gtrless y}$. The display should read -4.89. This is the negative of the amount by which the bond has been written down in the first 5 coupons. The book value should be $162.76 - 4.89 = 157.87$.

Key in $\boxed{RCL}$ $\boxed{PV}$. The display should read 157.87. This is the book value just after the 5th coupon.

Finding the Bond Yield on a Coupon Date:

We can use the worksheet to find the yield rate from the price. Suppose that the bond above with face amount 100 has a price of 150. There is no algebraic solution for the yield-to-maturity $i^{(2)} = 2j$, where j, the 6-month yield rate is the solution of the equation $150 = 100v_j^{40} + 5a_{\overline{40}|j}$.

The yield-to-maturity can be found using the calculator as follows:

Key in 40$\boxed{n}$, Key in 150 $\boxed{PV}$, Key in 5 $\boxed{CHS}$ $\boxed{PMT}$, Key in 100 $\boxed{CHS}$ $\boxed{FV}$. Then key in $\boxed{i}$. The display should read 2.879. This indicates that the yield rate is $j = .02879$ (2.879%) per coupon period (6 months).

The bond examples considered here have had valuation take place on a coupon date. The HP-12C has bond functions to find the price (given the yield) or the yield (given the price) of a bond at any time, on or between coupon dates.

We use Example 4.2 to illustrate the valuation of a bond between coupon dates. A bond has face amount 100, with an annual coupon rate of 10% and coupons payable semi-annually. The bond matures on June 18, 2010 and is purchased on August 1, 2000 at a yield rate of 5% (nominal annual yield compounded semi-annually). The quoted purchase price from Example 4.2 is 138.60 (this quoted price does not include the accrued coupon). This can be found using the following keystrokes.

Key in 10 $\boxed{\text{PMT}}$, Key in 5 $\boxed{\text{i}}$,
Key in 8.012000 $\boxed{\text{ENTER}}$, Key in 6.182010 $\boxed{\text{f}}$ $\boxed{\text{PRICE}}$.
The display should read 138.598 .

Suppose that we were given a price of 125.50 and we are to find the yield rate. The follow keystroke sequence results in the yield rate.

Key in 10 $\boxed{\text{PMT}}$, Key in 125.50 $\boxed{\text{PV}}$,
Key in 8.012000 $\boxed{\text{ENTER}}$, Key in 6.182010 $\boxed{\text{f}}$ $\boxed{\text{YTM}}$.
The display should read 6.465. This is the yield rate expressed as a nominal annual rate compounded semi-annually.

The conventions used by the HP-12C for the bond function calculations are that coupon rates and yield rates are nominal annual rates convertible two times per year, and bond prices are "quoted" prices which do not include the accrued coupon.

INTERNAL RATE OF RETURN AND NET PRESENT VALUE

The internal rate of return for a series of payments received and payments made can be found in a couple of different ways, depending upon the nature of the series of payments. When we consider a level payment annuity with or without a balloon payment at the time of the last annuity payment, we can enter values into the variables

$\boxed{n}$, $\boxed{PV}$, $\boxed{PMT}$ and $\boxed{FV}$, and then use $\boxed{i}$ to find the interest rate which satisfies the relationship

$$PV = PMT \cdot a_{\overline{n}|j} + FV \cdot v_j^n.$$

The internal rate of return is j.

We can use the cashflow functions to enter a cashflow at time 0, CF_0, along with up to 24 additional cashflows at the end of up to 20 successive periods, $CF_1, CF_2,\ldots, CF_{20}$. Once these cashflow amounts are entered, we can use the $\boxed{IRR}$ function (internal rate of return) to calculate an internal rate of return. It is a solution j to the relationship

$$CF_0 + CF_1 \cdot v_j + CF_2 \cdot v_j^2 + \cdots + CF_{20} \cdot v_j^{20} = 0.$$

The cashflow amounts can each be positive (an amount received) or negative (an amount paid out).

We illustrate how the internal rate of return in Example 5.1 can be found in this way. Example 5.1 has the following series of cashflows, where time is measured in 6-month intervals:

$$C_0 = -5100, C_1 = 0, \ \ C_2 = -2295, \text{ and } C_3 = 7982.5.$$

The following series of keystrokes solves for the internal rate of return j, where j will be the 6-month internal rate or return:

Key in 5100 $\boxed{CHS}$ $\boxed{g}$ $\boxed{CF_0}$ (this enters $C_0 = -5100$),

Key in 0 $\boxed{g}$ $\boxed{CF_j}$ (this enters $C_1 = 0$),

Key in 2295 $\boxed{CHS}$ $\boxed{g}$ $\boxed{CF_j}$ (this enters $C_2 = -2295$),

Key in 7982.5 $\boxed{g}$ $\boxed{CF_j}$ (this enters $C_3 = 7982.5$),

Key in $\boxed{f}$ $\boxed{IRR}$. The display should read 3.246.
This is the 6-month internal rate of return.

Calculating Net Present Value:

The calculator $\boxed{\text{NPV}}$ function can be used to calculate the present value of a series of cashflows that have been entered into the cashflow worksheet. We use Example 5.2(a) as an illustration. Suppose that we wish to find the present value at time 0 of the three cashflows

$$C_0 = -1, C_1 = 2.3, \text{ and } C_2 = -1.33,$$

using an interest rate of 10%.

This would be $-1 + 2.3v_1 - 1.33v_1^2$. We can find this present value as follows. We enter the cashflows $C_0 = -1, C_1 = 2.3, \text{ and } C_2 = -1.33$, as shown above. Immediately after C_2 has been entered, we apply the following keystrokes:

Key in 10 $\boxed{\text{i}}$, key in $\boxed{\text{f}}$ $\boxed{\text{NPV}}$.
The display should read -0.008264.
This is the present value of the cashflows at the 10% interest rate.

ANSWERS TO TEXT EXERCISES

CHAPTER 1

SECTION 1.1

1.1.1 $K = 979.93$

1.1.2   (a) 10.25%;   (b) .091, .084

1.1.3   (a) 3500;   (b) 3700.61;   (c) 3714.87;   (d) 3722.16

1.1.4 $n = 2.3$

1.1.5 $i = 107.35\%$; $i = 67.59\%$;   913.32;   451 days

1.1.6   (a) $i \leq .4069$ (b) $i \leq \left(\frac{j}{1-j}\right)\left(\frac{365}{n-m}\right)$

1.1.7   (a) 278.93

1.1.8   (a) 9.694 years;   (b) 9.682 years;   (c) 110.41 months;
        (d) 11.61%;   (e) .9197%

1.1.9   (a) $(1.0075)^{67/17} = 1.0299 < 1.03$
        (b) $(1.015)^{67/17} = 1.0604 > 1.06$

1.1.10 12.04%;   −21.57%

1.1.14   (a) $X = 1 + j_1 t_1$ (b) $X = \dfrac{1+it}{1+j_2(t-t_1)}$

(e)

j_1	X	j_2
.03	1. 0073	. 1807
.08	1. 0195	. 1530
.13	1. 0317	. 1260
.18	1. 0439	. 0996
.23	1. 0561	. 0738

1.1.18   (a) $\dfrac{3a+b}{2} < c$ (b) 720   (c) $a+b-c$

1.1.20   224.5 days, or August 12 or 13 (depending upon whether or not the year is a leap year).

SECTION 1.2

1.2.1 $X = 379.48$

1.2.2   1-month rate of .01, $X = 67.98$
3-month rate of .03, $X = 67.57$

1.2.3 $i = 26.92\%$

1.2.4   494.62

1.2.5   (a) 1,607,391   (b) 1,747,114   (c) 1,795,551

1.2.6 $j = .0389$

1.2.7   75,686

1.2.8 $X = 4997$

1.2.9 $j < k$

1.2.10   No real roots for solution for i

1.2.11 (a) $n(1+i)^{n-1}$ (c) $(1+i)^n \ln(1+i)$

       (b) $-nv^{n+1}$ (d) $-v^n \ln(1+i)$

1.2.12 (a) $B_1 = B_0(1+i) + \sum\limits_{k=1}^{n} a_k[1 + i(1-t_k)]$

       (b) $\overline{B} = B_0 + \sum\limits_{k=1}^{n} a_k(1-t_k)$

1.2.14 (a) $P = 95,250.52$

       (b) $\frac{dP}{di} = -45,239.03$ if $i = .10$, $\Delta P \approx -45.24$

       (c) $\frac{dP}{di} = -23,733.34$ if $i = .10$, as T-Bill approaches
       maturity, volatility goes to 0

1.2.15 12.68

1.2.16 903.98

1.2.17 (a) 13,150   (b) 13,160.27   (c) 13,150.76   (d) 13,161.12

1.2.18 $i = .0351$

SECTION 1.3

1.3.1 $m = 2, i = .1236$;
       $m = 12, i = .126825$;
       $m = 365, i = .127475$;
       $m = \infty, i = .127497$

1.3.2   (a) 414.64   (b) 409.30   (c) 407.94

1.3.3 $i^{(365)} \geq .144670$

1.3.4 $i = .0946$

1.3.5 $-.78\%$

1.3.6 (a), $i^{(.5)} = .105, i^{(.25)} = .116025, i^{(.1)} = .159374, i^{(.01)} = 137.796$

(b) $i = .0954, .0878, .0718, .0243$

1.3.7 .1365

1.3.8 (b) .1080

1.3.10 $m = 4$; nominal annual rate of 16% cannot accumulate to an effective rate of more that 17.35%

1.3.11 $\lim\limits_{m \to 0} f(m) = 1, \ \lim\limits_{m \to 0} g(m) = \infty$

1.3.12 $m = 8.111, i = .104495$

SECTION 1.4

1.4.2 .1154

1.4.3 (a) 5187.84   (b) 5191.68   (c) 5204.52   (d) 5200

1.4.4 $X = 38.9$

1.4.6 (a) $i = \dfrac{365}{n} \left[\dfrac{1}{1 - d \cdot \frac{n}{365}} - 1 \right] = \dfrac{d}{1 - d \cdot \frac{n}{365}}$; as n increases, i increases

(b) $t = 1, d = .099099$; $t = .50, d = .104265$; $t = \frac{1}{12}, d = .109001$

1.4.8 .0266

1.4.9 1-month effective interest = .009902, discount = .009805
2-month effective interest = .019901, discount = .019513
3-month effective interest = .03, discount = .029126
4-month effective interest = .040199, discount = .038645
6-month effective interest = .0609, discount = .057404
1-year effective interest = .125509, discount = .111513

1.4.11 $d = .0453$ (this is the nominal discount rate
                                                 compounded 4 times per year)

1.4.12 $i = .0909$

1.4.13 $j = .0436$

1.4.14   (a) Discount from $t = 1$ to $t = \frac{1}{2}$ is .5, discount from $t = \frac{1}{2}$ to
                   $t = 0$ is .25
             (b) $d^{(m)} \leq m$

SECTION 1.5

1.5.1 $k = 102$

1.5.2 $Z = 1953$

1.5.3 $X = 784.6$

1.5.4 $i - \delta = .23\%$

1.5.5   .045

1.5.6   (a) $i = .1008$

             (b) $i_1 = .091629,$ $i_2 = .099509,$
                    $i_3 = .102751,$ $i_4 = .104532,$ $i_5 = .105659$

             (c) 821.00

1.5.7   1215

1.5.8 $i' > 2i,\ d' < 2d$

1.5.9 $i^{(4)} = .0339$

1.5.10 $A(t) = A_1(t) \cdot A_2(t)$

1.5.11 $m = 1.6$

1.5.12   (a) 1044.73

       (b) For $0 < t \leq \frac{1}{4}$, $A(t) = 1000[1 + .08t]$,

           for $\frac{1}{4} < t \leq \frac{1}{2}$, $A(t) = 1000(1.02)\left[1 + .08\left(t - \frac{1}{4}\right)\right]$,

           for $\frac{1}{2} < t \leq \frac{3}{4}$, $A(t) = 1000(1.02)^2 1\left[+ .08\left(t - \frac{1}{2}\right)\right]$,

           for $\frac{3}{4} < t \leq 1$, $A(t) = 1000(1.02)^3\left[1 + .08\left(t - \frac{3}{4}\right)\right]$.

1.5.13   (a) $\dfrac{A\left(t + \frac{1}{m}\right) - A(t)}{A\left(t + \frac{1}{m}\right)}$

       (b) $d^{(m)} = m \cdot \dfrac{A\left(t + \frac{1}{m}\right) - A(t)}{A\left(t + \frac{1}{m}\right)}$ (c) $\lim\limits_{m \to \infty} d^{(m)} = \dfrac{A'(t)}{A(t)}$

1.5.14 $\dfrac{d}{d\delta} i = e^{\delta}$, $\dfrac{d}{d\delta} d = e^{-\delta}$, $\dfrac{d}{d\delta} i^{(m)} = e^{\delta/m}$, $\dfrac{d}{d\delta} d^{(m)} = e^{-\delta/m}$

1.5.15 $\dfrac{d}{dt} \delta_t = \dfrac{d}{dt} \dfrac{A'(t)}{A(t)} = \dfrac{A(t)A''(t) - [A'(t)]^2}{[A(t)]^2}$

SECTION 1.6

1.6.1   (a) $i_{real} = -.043478$

       (b) Net gain is 5000 (in year-end dollars)

1.6.2 $-.0309$

1.6.3   (b) The real growth in taxes paid will be 1.015873 (1.59%) and the real growth in ATI is $.990476 = 1 - .009524$

1.6.5 $i = 1.070175$

1.6.6 One year from now, 1000 US $\equiv$ 1382.4306 CDN, or equivalently.
        .723364 US $\equiv$ 1 CDN

1.6.8 (a) Real after-tax rate of return on standard term deposit is
        $\frac{i(1-t_x)-r}{1+r}$, and on inflation-adjusted term deposit is

        $\frac{r+i'(1+r)(1-t_x)-r}{1+r} \;=\; i'(1-t_x).$

        (b) If $i' = .02$ and $r = .12$, then i is equal to

            (i) .1424   (ii) .1824   (iii) .2224   (iv) .3224

CHAPTER 2

SECTION 1.2

Section 2.1

2.1.2 3665.12, 36.65

2.1.3 $i = .1225$

2.1.4 (a) 2328.82

2.1.5 $11S - 100$

2.1.6 $I_t = (1+i)^{t-1} - 1$

2.1.7 $n = 15,\ P = 14.53;\quad n = 20,\ P = 17.19;\quad n = 25,\ P = 20.75$

2.1.8 (a) $(1+i)^n = 2,\ i = .014286,\ s_{\overline{3n}|i} = 490$

       (b) $\rightarrow\ v^n = \dfrac{2}{-1+\sqrt{1-\frac{4(Y-X)}{Y}}}$

       (c) .1355

2.1.9   640.72

2.1.10 $X = 8.92$

2.1.11   An investment of amount 1 is equal to the present value of the return of principal in n years plus the present value of the interest generated over the n years.

2.1.12   2825.49

2.1.13 $Y = 19,788.47$

2.1.14   109,926

2.1.15 $X = 575$

2.1.16 $i = .0689$

2.1.17 $v^n = .858$

2.1.18   294.84, ratio is 1.045

2.1.19 $K = 1079.68$

2.1.22   (a) $AV = R(1+\frac{i}{n})^n - k \cdot s_{\overline{n}|i} = R(1+j)$, where j is the effective annual earned rate

        (b) (i) $n = 12$ (ii) $n = 3$ (iii) $n = 1$

2.1.25   330.80

2.1.28 $v^n = .6180$

2.1.30 $i = .1539$

2.1.31   (a) $v_j [1+v_i] \cdot \frac{1}{1-v_j \cdot v_i}$ (b) (i) $\frac{v + 2v^2}{1-v^2}$ (ii) $\frac{1+2v}{1-v^2}$

2.1.33 $X = 573.76$, $Y = 449.54$

2.1.34 17th month

2.1.37 $a_{\overline{10}|} = 7.7748, \dfrac{s_{\overline{10}|}}{a_{\overline{10}|}} = A(t) = (1.12)^{\sqrt{10}} = 1.4310$

2.1.38 7.3729

2.1.39 (a) For $t > n$, $v^t \cdot s_{\overline{n}|} = v^{t-n} \cdot v^n \cdot s_{\overline{n}|} = v^{t-n} \cdot a_{\overline{n}|}$

(b) For $t > n$, $(1+i)^t \cdot a_{\overline{n}|} = (1+i)^{t-n} \cdot (1+i)^n \cdot a_{\overline{n}|} = (1+i)^{t-n} \cdot s_{\overline{n}|}$

SECTION 2.2

2.2.1 $Y = 9872$

2.2.2 $X = 6195$

2.2.3 $X = 3.71$

2.2.4 .088

2.2.6 (a) $X = 447.24$ (b) December 31, 2013, 290.30

2.2.7 1161.36

2.2.8 April 30, 2013

2.2.9 26 deposits

2.2.10 January 1, 2016

2.2.11 2.208%

2.2.12 (a) $i = \dfrac{1}{A} - \dfrac{1}{B}$

(b) $i = \dfrac{1}{A} - \dfrac{B-A}{A^2}$

(c) Solve quadratic in v^n in terms of B and A and then $i = \dfrac{1-v^n}{A}$

2.2.13 $i = .076$

2.2.14 $i^{(12)} = .1680, \ K = 345.02$

2.2.15 $X = 490.85$ on April 1, 2018

2.2.16 $X = 39.84$

2.2.17   The 2-month effective rate is j

(a) $25a_{\overline{36}|j} = 150a^{(6)}_{\overline{6}|.06} = 755.83$ where $j = (1.06)^{1/6} - 1$

(b) $25v_j^4 \, a_{\overline{36}|j} = 50v_{.02}^2 a^{(2)}_{\overline{18}|.02} = 724.08$ where $j = (1.02)^{1/2} - 1$

(c) $25v_j^3 \, a_{\overline{36}|j} = 730.92$ where $j = (1.015)^{2/3} - 1$

(d) $25(1+j)s_{\overline{36}|j} = 1092.02$ where $j = (.97)^{-1/3} - 1$

(e) $25(1+j)^6 s_{\overline{36}|j} = 1144.57$ where $j = e^{.01} - 1$

2.2.18   In all cases j represents the 2-year effective rate of interest

(a) 10,123.81
(b) 6235.03
(c) 67,895.89
(d) 75,168.66
(e) 11,743.76

2.2.20 $\bar{a}_{\overline{n}|} = \dfrac{r(1 - e^{-pn})}{(1+r)p} + \dfrac{(1 - e^{-(p+s)n})}{(1+r)(p+s)}$

2.2.21   (a) $K' \le 2K$

2.2.22   (a) (i) July 1, 2006   (ii) February 28, 2007

(b) (i) January 10, 2007   (ii) January 1, 2008

2.2.23   (a) 23   (b) 22

2.2.24   2 terms , $n = 24.8$;

3 terms, $n = 29.7$ or 150.3 (150.3 is an unrealistic answer)

2.2.25 $\quad i = \frac{B - A - 1}{A}$

2.2.28 (a) $i = (1+j)^m - 1$

2.2.29 (a) $\frac{1}{m} \cdot s_{\overline{n \cdot m}|j} = \frac{1}{m} \cdot \frac{(1+j)^{n \cdot m} - 1}{j} = \frac{1}{m} \cdot \frac{(1+i)^n - 1}{(1+i)^{1/m} - 1}$

2.2.30 (c) $a_{\overline{n}|i} < a_{\overline{n}|i}^{(m)} < \overline{a}_{\overline{n}|i} < \ddot{a}_{\overline{n}|i}^{(m)} < \ddot{a}_{\overline{n}|i}$

2.2.31 (a) $\dfrac{dn}{di} = \dfrac{\frac{\delta L}{K - LiK} + v \ln(1 - \frac{Li}{K})}{\delta^2}, \quad \dfrac{dn}{dK} = \dfrac{-Li}{\delta K(K - Li)}, \quad \dfrac{dn}{dL} = \dfrac{i}{\delta(K - Li)}$

  (b) $\dfrac{dn}{di} = \dfrac{\frac{\delta M}{J + Mi} - v \ln(1 + \frac{Mi}{J})}{\delta^2}, \quad \dfrac{dn}{dJ} = \dfrac{-Mi}{\delta J(J + Mi)}, \quad \dfrac{dn}{dM} = \dfrac{i}{\delta(J + Mi)}$

SECTION 2.3

2.3.1   419,242

2.3.2 $k = 6\%$

2.3.3 $K = 4$

2.3.4 $R = 548$

2.3.6 $r = .0784$

2.3.7   (a) 27,823   (b) 36,766   (c) 57,639   (d) $X = 19,974$

2.3.8   (i) 30,407   (ii) 59,704   (iii) 151,906

2.3.9 $i = .0640$

2.3.10 $\frac{Y}{X} = 2.03$

2.3.11 $i = .102$

2.3.12 $X = 2729$

2.3.13   2,085

2.3.14 $n = 19$

2.3.15 $X = 44.98$

2.3.16 $25a_{\overline{25}|} + 3(Da)_{\overline{25}|}$

2.3.17 $i = .10$

2.3.18   (i) $PV = 3875.57,\ AV = 33,247.03$
         (ii) $PV = 3992.96,\ AV = 20,055.21$
         (iii) $PV = 4091.73,\ AV = 12,016.45$
         (iv) $PV = 4168.59,\ AV = 7148.51$

2.3.19   (i)   PV before deindexing is 168,620, after deindexing it is 84,310
         (ii) PV before deindexing is 84,310, after deindexing it is 56,207
         (iii) PV before deindexing is 56,207, after deindexing it is 42,155
         (iv) PV before deindexing is 166,497, after deindexing it is 83,249
         (v)   PV before deindexing is 83,249, after deindexing it is 55,499
         (vi) PV before deindexing is 164,354, after deindexing it is 82,177

2.3.20   (a) $n = 505$ (b) 5,569,741

2.3.21   (a) $i = .1014$ (b) $i = .1266$

2.3.22   24.03

2.3.23   39.4

2.3.29 $i^{(2)} = .21,\ \dfrac{d}{di^{(2)}}\,K = 7459.13$ (or 74.59 per 1% increase in $i^{(2)}$)

$i^{(2)} = .13,\ \dfrac{d}{di^{(2)}}\,K = 7101.66$ (or 71.02 per 1% increase in $i^{(2)}$)

2.3.30 $\dfrac{500,000(1+i)^t}{19}$

2.3.31 $n = 19$, $X = 404.93$

2.3.32 (a) $n = 185$, $X = 532.46$
(b) $n = 99$, $X = 761.19$
(c) $n = 90$, $X = 93.85$
(d) Total withdrawn: (a) 185,532 (b) 148,271 (c) 144,957.

2.3.33 $i = .0820$

2.3.35 (b) $\dfrac{\ddot{a}_{\overline{k}}}{(i \cdot a_{\overline{k}})^2}$

2.3.41 (b) 1508

2.3.46 $PV = (A-B)a_{\overline{n}} + B(Ia)_{\overline{n}}$ $AV = As_{\overline{n}} + B(Is)_{\overline{n-1}}$

SECTION 2.4

2.4.2 (a) (i) 7469.44 (ii) 6794.19 (iii) 3813.44
(b) (i) 8.30% (ii) 13.68% (iii) 8.85%

2.4.4 (a) 7527.17 (b) 6590.70 (c) 7326.47

2.4.5 2.4.2 (a)(i) 5554 (ii) 5832 (iii) 3273
2.4.2 (b)(i) 9.08% (ii) 11.43% (iii) 8.81%
2.4.4 (a) 6461 (b) 5806 (c) 6454

2.4.6 (a) 80,898 (b) 18,311

2.4.9 11.69% after 12 months

2.4.11 22,250

2.4.12   (a) 63,920   (b) 67,659   (c) $t = 8$, $P_8 = 86,712$

2.4.13   .986

2.4.14   5000

2.4.15   36,329

2.4.16   286.3

CHAPTER 3

SECTION 3.1

3.1.3 $L = 58,490.89$, $PR_1 = 15.09$,
         $OB_{60} = 46,424$, $I_{61} = 464.24$, $PR_{61} = 435.76$

3.1.5   10,857.28

3.1.6 $OB_{40} = 6889$

3.1.7   97.44

3.1.9   (i) Monthly payment is 445.72, $OB_{1yr} = 14,651$
         (ii) Monthly payment is 452.61, $OB_{1yr} = 15,102$

3.1.11   (a) $K = 9.888857$, $OB_{1mo} = 1000.11$,
              $OB_{2mo} = 1000.22,\ldots$, $OB_{12mo} = 1001.41$

         (d) $OB_{3yr} = 1004.79$, $OB_{6yr} = 1011.64$, $OB_{9yr} = 595.46$

         (e) $I_T = K(72+144) - 1000 = 1135.99$, Interest in 1st year is
             120.08, Principal repaid in 1st year is -1.41

SECTION 3.2

3.2.2 Quarterly payment is 283.68, total interest paid is 404.15

3.2.3

Year (t)	OB_t	I_t	PR_t
0	862.00	—	—
1	706.00	43.10	156.00
2	542.20	35.30	163.80
3	370.21	27.11	171.99
4	189.62	18.51	180.59
5	0	9.48	189.62

3.2.4 $t = 35$ is June 1, 2007

3.2.5 (a) $i^{(12)} = .0495$ (b) $i^{(12)} = .15$

3.2.6 (a) 67.50

(b) Final smaller payment is on February 1, 2016 of amount 109.54

3.2.7 $X = 825$

3.2.8 $i = .09$

3.2.9 $k \le .1326$

3.2.10 (a) Example 3.1: pv of interest is 39.33, pv of principal is 960.67
Example 3.2: pv of interest is 356.16, pv of principal is 2643.84

(b) pv of interest is $L\left[1 - \frac{nv^{n+1}}{a_{\overline{n}|}}\right]$,   pv of principal is $L \cdot \frac{nv^{n+1}}{a_{\overline{n}|}}$

3.2.11 $K = 349.81$

3.2.12 192,858

3.2.13 (i) Total interest paid is $\frac{nL}{a_{\overline{n}|i}} - L$

(ii) Total interest paid is $Li \cdot \frac{n+1}{2}$

3.2.14 A: 541,184.58, B: 324,710.75, C: 134,104.67

3.2.15 (a) $OB_{10} = 58.40,$ smaller payment at time 11 is 58.98

3.2.16 $t = 11$

3.2.18 $\frac{2}{3}$

3.2.19 Principal paid in the first year is 478.74

3.2.20 (i) total interest is 161,976

(ii) final smaller payment is 734.49 on October 1, 2019, total interest is 82,139

(iii) 112,875

3.2.21 (a) February 28, 2019,   22,418.47   (b) 3,050,520

(c) 2,050,520

(i) 61,130   (ii) 130,523   (iii) 172,367

3.2.22 $n = 27$

3.2.25 Difference in interest is $K\left[\dfrac{12s_{\overline{3}|}}{a_{\overline{12}|}} - 3\right]$

3.2.26 (a) $i^{(12)} = .06,$ monthly payment is 644.30, total interest is 93,290

(i) reduced term is 1087.5 weeks, total interest is 75,170

(b) $i^{(12)} = .06,$ OB after exactly 52 weeks is 97,524.15, one day interest adjustment is 15.99

3.2.27 (a) $i^{(12)} = .06$

(i) reduced term is 1090.4 weeks total interest paid is 75,649

3.2.30 479.74

3.2.32 (a) $OB_t = ta_{\overline{n-t}|} + (Ia)_{\overline{n-t}|},$ $I_t = t - 1 - nv^{n-t+1} + \ddot{a}_{\overline{n-t+1}|},$ $PR_t = t - I_t$

(b) $OB_t = (Da)_{\overline{n-t}|},$ $I_t = n - t + 1 - a_{\overline{n-t+1}|}$ $PR_t = a_{\overline{n-t+1}|}$

3.2.37 (a) 15 yrs: $I_T = 51,894.23,$ 30 yrs: $I_T = 115,838.19$

       (b) 15 yrs: $I_T = 116,030.25,$ 30 yrs: $I_T = 270,300.53$

3.2.39 (a) 6902.98   (b) 6699   (c) 6600

3.2.41 (a)

t	OB	PR	I
0	10,000.00	—	—
1	9400.00	600.00	900.00
2	8740.00	660.00	840.00
3	8014.00	726.00	774.00
4	7215.40	798.60	701.40
5	6336.94	878.46	621.54
6	5370.63	966.31	533.69
7	4307.69	1062.94	437.06
8	3152.31	1155.38	341.62
9	1904.49	1247.82	252.18
10	556.85	1347.64	152.36
11	0	556.85	44.55

SECTION 3.3

3.3.1 (a) 100,000

3.3.2 $X = 13,454.36$

3.3.3 (b) $L = \dfrac{K s_{\overline{n}|j}}{1 + i \cdot s_{\overline{n}|j}}$

3.3.4 (a) 74,325   (b) 75,560

3.3.5 16,856.67

3.3.6 $j = .021322$

3.3.7 $X = 72.00$

3.3.8 (a)

T	AV	OB	I	PR
1	6902.85	93,097.95	10,000.00	6902.95
2	14,358.13	85,641.87	9447.76	7455.18

3.3.10 $L = \dfrac{\Sigma K_t v_j^t}{v_j^n + i a_{\overline{n}|j}}$, $Y = v_j^n + i \cdot a_{\overline{n}|j}$

3.3.11 (a) Total annual outlay is 16,244.17, $i' = .099566$

(b) Total annual outlay is 17,904.47, $i' = .122837$

3.3.13 (a) 14,185.22

(b) Amount in sinking fund at time loan is sold is 31,656.34

(i) 87,162.04   (ii) 75,042.37

(c) (i) $i_\alpha = .130206$, $i_\beta = .135051$

(ii) $i_\alpha = .123749$, $i_\beta = .128183$

3.3.14 $j = .08, i = .113821$; $j = .12, i = .12$; $j = .16, i = .123487$

SECTION 3.4

3.4.2   (a) 17,795   (b) 16,723   (c) 16,165

3.4.4 $P = \dfrac{Y}{v_h^n + j a_{\overline{n}|h}}$

3.4.5   330,117

3.4.7   (a) .1169   (b) .10   (c) .0858

3.4.9   (i) tax rate 25%:   (a) 15,000   (b) 15,000   (c) 15,000

(ii) tax rate 40%:   (a) 13,323   (b) 13,967   (c) 14,301
(iii) tax rate 60%:   (a) 11,087   (b) 12,589   (c) 13,369

3.4.10 (a) 75,942.28   (b) 46,188.00

3.4.11 Merchant's Rule: $X = 211.54$,   U.S. Rule: $X = 212.16$

3.4.13 Straight-Line: 41,078.46 each year
Actuarial: 16,058.78 in 1st year, 82,568.81 in 20th year

3.4.14 August 15th U.S. Rule payment is 328,
Merchant's Rule payment is 324

CHAPTER 4

SECTION 4.1

4.1.1   (a) 84.5069 (b) 84.8501 (c) 82.5199 (d) 82.9678

4.1.2 $21\frac{1}{2}$ years

4.1.4   (b) 102.79 and 102.74   (c) 3.692% and 3.690%

4.1.5 $i^{(2)} = .0525$

4.1.6   I. False   II. True   III. False

4.1.7   Coupon rates are .0225 and .045

4.1.8 $i^{(2)} = .035$

4.1.9   12 years

4.1.10 908.78

4.1.11 875.38

4.1.14 97.896

4.1.16 860

4.1.17 20 year issue requires (annual) coupon rate of .0834

4.1.18 (a) $n = 2,\ i^{(2)} = 0;$ $n = 5,\ i^{(2)} = .056544;$

  $n = 10,\ i^{(2)} = .075610;$ $n = 20,\ i^{(2)} = .084959;$

  $n = 30,\ i^{(2)} = .087875$

  (b) $n = 2,\ i^{(2)} = .216517;$ $n = 5,\ i^{(2)} = .149393;$

  $n = 10,\ i^{(2)} = .127669;$ $n = 20,\ i^{(2)} = .117242;$

  $n = 30,\ i^{(2)} = .114072$

4.1.19 1055

4.1.20 $i^{(2)} = \dfrac{4r_2 - 2r_1}{1 + r_1 - r_2}$

4.1.21 $\dfrac{qr_1 + pr_2}{q + p}$

4.1.22 $H = .6446$

4.1.23 2000

4.1.24 $X = 114.28$

4.1.29 (a) $\dfrac{\partial P}{\partial r} = Fa_{\overline{n}|j},\ \dfrac{\partial P}{\partial j} = F\left[-nv_j^{n+1} - rv(Ia)_{\overline{n}|j}\right],\ \dfrac{\partial P}{\partial n} = \dfrac{F(r-j)\delta v_j^n}{j}$

4.1.30 (a)

	1st Opinion	**2nd Opinion**
(i)	1,703 gain	2,512 gain
(ii)	809 loss	no gain or loss
(iii)	2,760 loss	1,951 loss
(iv)	4,289 loss	3,480 loss

  (b)

(i)	5,836 loss	5,027 loss
(ii)	809 loss	no gain or loss
(iii)	6,092 gain	6,901 gain
(iv)	15,461 gain	16,270 gain

4.1.32 (a) (i) 138,609,509 (b) (i) 138,606,077

4.1.35 $P_C = P_1 + \frac{r_3 - r_1}{r_2 - r_1} \cdot (P_2 - P_1)$

4.1.36 (c) from (a) $i^{(2)} = .111268$ from (b) $i^{(2)} = .111753$

SECTION 4.2

4.2.2 $n = 5, \ j = .025$

T	K_t	I_t	PR_t	OB_t
1	500	279.04	220.96	10,940.49
2	500	273.51	226.49	10,714.01
3	500	267.85	232.15	10,481.86
4	500	262.05	237.95	10,243.90
5	10,500	256.10	10,243.90	0

$n = 5, \ j = .075$

T	K_t	I_t	PR_t	OB_t
1	500	674.14	−174.14	9,162.67
2	500	687.20	−187.20	9,349.89
3	500	701.24	−201.24	9,551.10
4	500	716.33	−216.33	9,767.44
5	10,500	732.56	9,767.44	0

4.2.3 Total paid is $F + nFr$, total principal repaid is

$$P = F + F(r - j)a_{\overline{n}|j},$$

total interest paid is $nFr - F(r - j)a_{\overline{n}|j}$

4.2.4 90.47

4.2.5 13 years or 26 coupon periods

4.2.6 (a) 8764

4.2.7   48,739

4.2.10   (a) 8117.73, .06336   (b) 11,882.27, .09664

         (c) cannot occur   (d) 29,039.25, .2483

         (e) $r = .30$, $P = 68,821.07$ (f) $r = .04$, $P = 10,000$

         (g) cannot occur   (h) $r = .0515$, $P = 12,500$

SECTION 4.3

4.3.1   1,768,083

4.3.2   85,565,872

4.3.3   92,037.62

4.3.5   (a) (i) 84.95   (ii) 100.00   (iii) 117.59
         (b) (i) 12.8%   (ii) 10.0%   (iii) 7.76%

4.3.6   (a) (i) 85.93   (ii) 101.42   (iii) 120.55
         (b) (i) 12.9%   (ii) 10.16%   (iii) 8.05%

4.3.7   (a) (i) 859,061   (ii) 1,116,588
         (b) (i) 10.98%

CHAPTER 5

SECTION 5.1

5.1.1   (a) no real solution

         (b) i is .10 or .20

5.1.3 $j = .049301$

5.1.4 $i_A = .253304$, $i_B = .253280$

5.1.5   (a) .1203   (b) .1081   (c) 1126

(d) break even in 3rd year

(e) break even in 5th year

(f) 1.0375

5.1.7   (b) $Y \geq 938,800$

5.1.8 $i^{(12)} = .1528$

5.1.9   (b) 7.92%

5.1.11 (b) $i_0 = 416\%$

5.1.12 (b) $r > .0388$

5.1.13 (b) $r = .1077$

5.1.14 (a) .10601

(b) .10508

(c) lender's yield is .08617

SECTION 5.2

5.2.1   .0625

5.2.2   236.25

5.2.3   Time weighted return is 0, dollar-weighted return is .1667

5.2.4   .0910

5.2.5   −.25

5.2.6   .15

5.2.7   .110

SECTION 5.3

5.3.1　(a) .1132　(b) (i) .1034　(ii) .1081　(iii) .1132　(iv) .1188　(v) .125

5.3.4　2882

CHAPTER 6

Section 6.1 and 6.2

6.1.1　(a)　　　　(i)　100.5097　　(ii) 94.5315　　(iii)　90.7050

　　　　(b)　　　　(i)　9.90%　　　(ii) 11.15%　　(iii)　12.00%

　　　　(c) 8%:　(i)　90.34222　(ii) 85.23475　(iii)　81.41003

　　　　　12%:　(i)　110.6771　(ii) 103.8282　(iii)　100

6.1.2　(a) .0646

6.1.3　.0556,　$P=111.98$

6.1.4　78.97

6.1.5　.05, .10078, .15151, .15234

SECTION 6.3

6.3.1　(a) $i_{k-1,k} = \dfrac{(1+i_{0,k})^k}{(1+i_{0,k-1})^{k-1}} - 1$

6.3.2

K	(i)	(ii)
1	. 0910	. 0919
2	. 0930	. 0953
3	. 0950	. 0981
4	. 0970	. 1003
5	. 0990	. 1019
6	. 1010	. 1029
7	. 1030	. 1033
8	. 1050	. 1031
9	. 1070	. 1023
10	. 1090	. 1009

6.3.3   .0503

6.3.4   .1204 , .1303

6.3.5   (a) (i) .0801 (ii) .1311   (b) .1001

6.3.6   .1452

6.3.7   (b) (i) $i_{0,1} = .2$, $i_{0,2} = .201$, $i_{0,3} = .2011$

(ii) $i_{0,1} = .2$, $i_{0,2} = .199$, $i_{0,3} = .1989$

Other examples can be constructed

SECTION 6.4

6.4.1   (a)

6.4.3   (d)

6.4.4   (a) 11.09   (b) 10.33

6.4.5 $i < .09002$

CHAPTER 7

SECTION 7.1

7.1.1 $j = .03$

r	$n = 2$	$n = 10$	$n = 20$	$n = 40$
.04	1.96189	8.50869	14.5725	22.4642
.06	1.94491	8.06690	13.5336	20.8770
.08	1.9211	7.73079	12.8493	19.9706

7.1.2   4.79

7.1.4 $\dfrac{(Ia)_{\overline{n}|}}{a_{\overline{n}|}}$

7.1.5   102.26

7.1.6   2.73

7.1.7   (a) $\dfrac{1}{d}$ (d) n

       (b) 1 (if $n=1$)   (e) 1

       (c) $\dfrac{(Ia)_{\overline{n}|}}{a_{\overline{n}|}}$ (f) $\dfrac{n \cdot \frac{(n+1)}{2} \cdot r + n}{nr+1}$

7.1.9   (a) $L = r\bar{a}_{\overline{n}|} + e^{-n\delta}$, $\dfrac{dL}{d\delta} = -r(\overline{Ia})_{\overline{n}|} - ne^{-n\delta}$

7.1.11 -493 and -498

7.1.12   (e)

7.1.13   (b)

SECTION 7.2

7.2.1   (a) 1.6332   (b) 1.6328

7.2.2

N	PMT	$\sum t\, A_t v^t$	$\sum t^2\, A_t v^t$
5	79,139	843,038	2,962,020
15	39,442	1,883,680	16,896,161
50	30,257	3,171,124	60,020,920
100	30,002	3,297,823	69,034,390

Best match occurs at $n=15$; no immunization

7.2.4 $A_0 = 7,595.00$, $A_{15} = 25,454.55$ for the liability at $t=1$

7.2.5   (a) $A_{15} = .8053$, $A_5 = .3105$

(b) (i) $t_2 = 19.0530$, $A_{t_2} = .8432$

(ii) $A_{t_2} < 0$

(c) (i) $t_2 = 21.28$, $A_5 = .4302$ or $t_2 = 11.27$, $A_5 = .1258$

(ii) $t_2 = 31.92$, $A_5 = .5056$

(iii) no solution

(d) (i) $t_1 = 9.21$, $A_{t_2} = .2213$

(ii) no solution if $t_1 \leq 10$

(iii) no solution

(e) (i) $t_1 = 5.065$, $A_{t_1} = .3144$

(ii) no solution

(f) $t_1 = 4.74$, $t_2 = 18.30$

7.2.6 $t_0 = 16.15$, $A_{t_0} = 961,145$

7.2.7   (a) $A_1 = 71.44$, $A_5 = 229.41$

(b) conditions for Redington immunization are satisfied

7.2.9   (a) $(s - t_1) A_{t_1} v_{i_0}^{t_1} = (t_2 - s) A_{t_2} v_{i_0}^{t_2}$

(b) $L_s = A_{t_1} \cdot v^{t_1 - s} \left(1 + \dfrac{s - t_1}{t_2 - s} \right)$

7.2.10   (a) $h(.03) = 40,581$, $h(.08) = 2170$, $h(.12) = 1595$, $h(.2) = 23,154$

(b) $h(.03) = -12,596$,

$h(.08) = -690$,

$h(.12) = -514$,

$h(.2) = -7524$

(c) $h(.03) = 18,968$, $h(.08) = 994$, $h(.12) = 714$, $h(.2) = 9738$

7.2.12   (i) 3441   (ii) (c)

CHAPTER 8

SECTION 8.1

8.1.1   (a) 441.53

       (c) -10.63

8.1.2   (a) 126.15

       (c) .0607

8.1.3   Additional margin required is 250, one-day loss is 20.83%

8.1.4   (i) 1.523%

       (ii) 1.476%

8.1.5   (a) (i) 303.32   (ii) 328.83

       (b) 0

       (c) -5.89

8.16   .996875%

8.1.7 -50%

8.1.8   867.97

8.1.9   (a) 75.59

       (b) .70

8.1.10 $G - Ke^{-\delta} \;=\; G - S_0 e^{2r-\delta}$

8.1.11   1012.58

8.1.12   .9388

8.1.13   (i)   arbitrage opportunity exists

        (ii) no arbitrage opportunity exists

8.1.14   18.45

8.1.15   Add 525 to margin account

SECTION 8.2

8.2.1   (a) 18.33   (b) 56.74

8.2.2 $r = .04$, $s = .0418$

8.2.3   (a) 8000
          (b) 29.63%

8.2.4   9.95

8.2.5   900

8.2.6   16%

8.2.7   (a) P is the stock price on July 20.

          Profit is $P - 111$ if $P \geq 110$ (option is exercised on July 20)
          Profit is -1 if $P \leq 110$ (option is not exercised)

8.2.8   (a) $E = 45$, $P = 1.806$; $E = 50$, $P = .00034$; $E = 55$, $P = 0$

8.2.9   (a) .0368
          (b) $404.625 - Min(410, P)$

8.2.10   Positive gain if $S_1 > X - C$

8.2.11   (i) Sell short .2273 shares of stock, own 29.75 units of bond
          (ii) (c)

8.2.12   (a)

SECTION 8.3

8.3.1   (a) 722,854,822

(b) 25.0%

(c) 786,216,443 and 22.3%

SECTION 8.4

8.4.1   (a) .0593
(b) 1.3675

8.4.3   .0292

8.4.5   − .0012

BIBLIOGRAPHY

Baxter, M. and Rennie, A., *Financial Calculus: An Introduction to Derivative Pricing.* Cambridge Publishing, 1996

Black, F. and Scholes, M., "The Pricing of Options and Corporate Liabilities," The Journal of Political Economy, 1973.

Butcher, M.V. and C.J. Nesbitt, *Mathematics of Compound Interest.* Ann Arbor: Edwards Brothers, 1971.

"Canadian Criminal Code, Part IX, Section 347, Bill C-46," 1985, Government of Canada

"Canada Interest Act," R.S.C. 1985, C 1-15

"Consumer Credit Protection Act (Truth in Lending), Regulation Z," 1968, Congress of The United States of America

Elton, E.J. and M.J. Gruber, *Modern Portfolio Theory and Investment Analysis.* New York: John Wiley and Sons, 1984.

Fabozzi, F.J., *The Handbook of Fixed Income Securities*, McGraw-Hill 2000

Gray, *Axiomatic Characterization of the Time-weighted Rate of Return*

Kellison, S.G., *The Theory of Interest* (Second Edition). Homewood: Richard D. Irwin, Inc., 1991.

Macaulay, F, "Some Theoretical Problems Suggested by the Movements of Interest Rates, Bond Yields and Stock Prices in the United States since 1856," The National Bureau of Economic Research, 1938.

McCutcheon, J.J. and W.F. Scott, *An Introduction to the Mathematics of Finance*. Oxford: Heinemann Professional Publishing, 1986.

Promislow, D., "A New Approach to the Theory of Interest" in *TSA*, Volume 32 (1980)

Redington, F.M., "Review of the Principles of Life Office Valuations," The Journal of the Institute of Actuaries, 1952

Sharpe, W., *Investments*. Prentice-Hall, 1978

"Standard Securities Calculation Methods," Securities Industry Association, 1973

Teicherow, D., A. Robichek, and M. Montalbano, "Mathematical Analysis of Rates of Return under Certainty, Management Science," Volumes 11 (1965)

Teicherow, D., A. Robichek, and M. Montalbano, "An Analysis of Criteria for Investment and Financing Decisions under Certainty," Management Science, Volumes 12 (1965)

Volume 48 (1947) of the Transactions of the Actuarial Society of America

Venkatesh, R., Venkatesh, V., Dattatreya, R., *Interest Rate and Currency Swaps,* Chicago, IL : Probus Publishing Company, 1995

Websites

Altamira Investment Services:
www.altamira.com

Bank of Canada:
www.bankofcanada.ca

Bank of Montreal:
http://www4.bmo.com

Bloomberg LP:
http://www.bloomberg.com/markets/rates/index.html

Financial Calculators from KJE Computer Solutions:
www.dinkytown.net/java/SimpleLoan.html

The Hartford Insurance Company:
http://institutional.hartfordlife.com/

J. Huston McCulloch, Department of Economics of Ohio State University:
http://economics.sbs.ohio-state.edu/jhm/ts/ts.html

US Treasury, Bureau of the Public Debt:
http://www.treasurydirect.gov/RI/OFBills

Western and Southern Financial Corp: www.westernsouthernlife.com/

Wikipedia, online encyclopedia: en.wikipedia.org/wiki/Main_Page

Yahoo: http://finance.yahoo.com/bonds

INDEX